PLATE 1

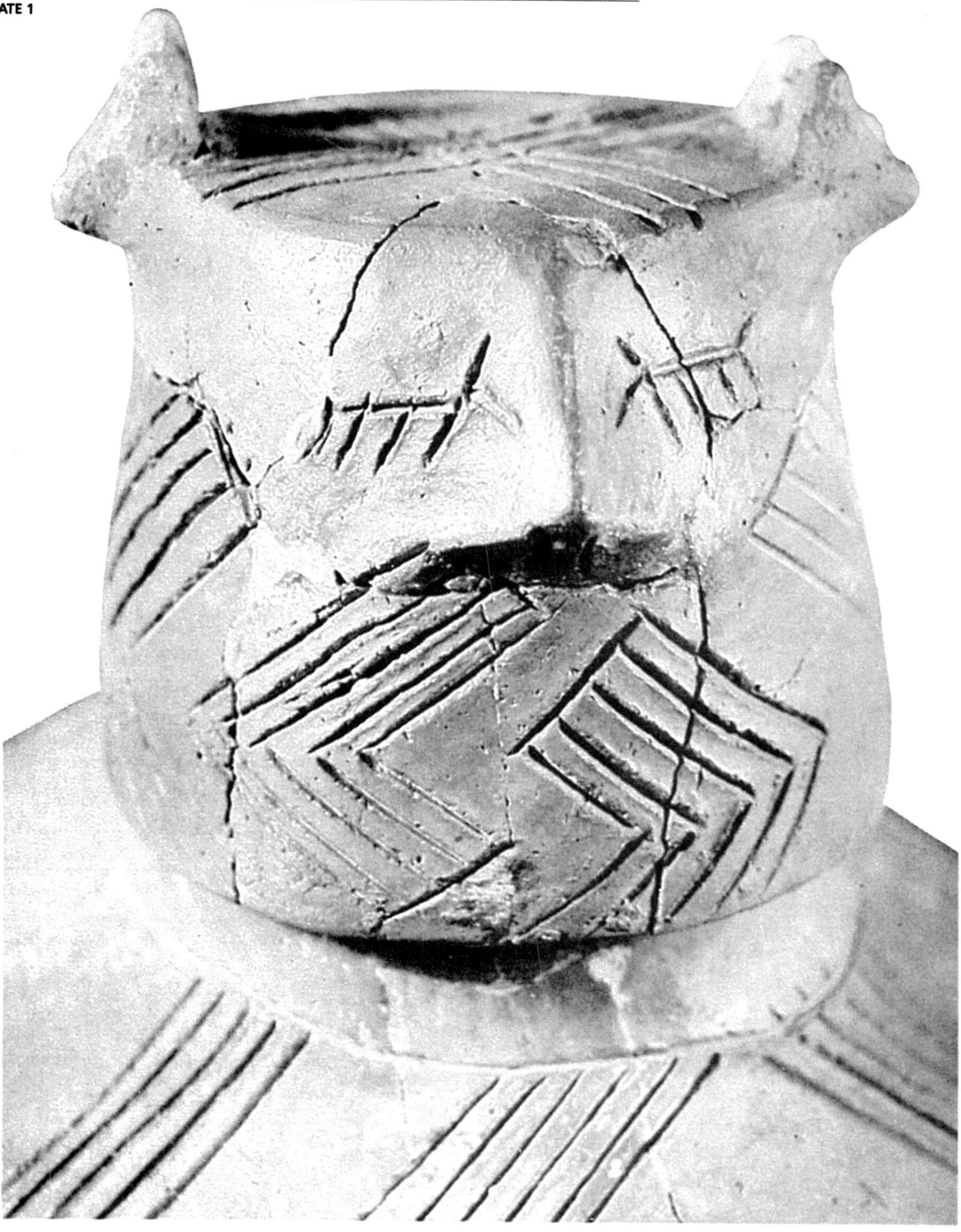

PLATE 2

PLATE 3

PLATE 2 The chevron marks the front and spirals the shoulders of this seated goddess wearing an oversized mask with supernatural eyes. Her status is indicated by a medallion attached to a V necklace. The mask is marked with tri-lines below the eyes and striations above. She has no mouth. Incisions are white-filled. H. 25 cm. The throne and legs broken. Vinča culture (Bariljevo near Priština, Kosovo Metohije, southern Yugoslavia; c. 4500 B.C.

PLATE 3 Temple model of clay with wide inverted T-shaped entrances on all sides and Bird Goddess mask on a cylinder in the roof. Her necklace is shown in relief around the cylinder. H. 17.1 cm, L 25.6 cm. Neolithic of Macedonia (Early Starčevo); c. 6000–5800 B.C. (Porodin near Bitolj, S Yugoslavia).

PLATE 1 (overleaf) Lid of a large pear-shaped vase with a representation of the Bird Goddess face (an owl with ears, large nose for beak, no mouth). Her eyes are symbols or script signs: tri-lines attached to horizontal dashes, vertical lines, and a V. The lid and the whole vase are incised with white-filled meanders and parallel lines. Early Vinča; end 6th mill. B.C. (Parţa, Banat, W Romania).

PLATE 4

PLATE 4 Vase fragment with a Bird Goddess face. The round eyes like sunlets are attached to double chevrons below, her special sign. H. of the fragment just over 5 cm. Stentinello culture, eastern Sicily (Trefontane, R. Simeto valley, west of Catania; c. 6000 B.C.).

PLATE 5

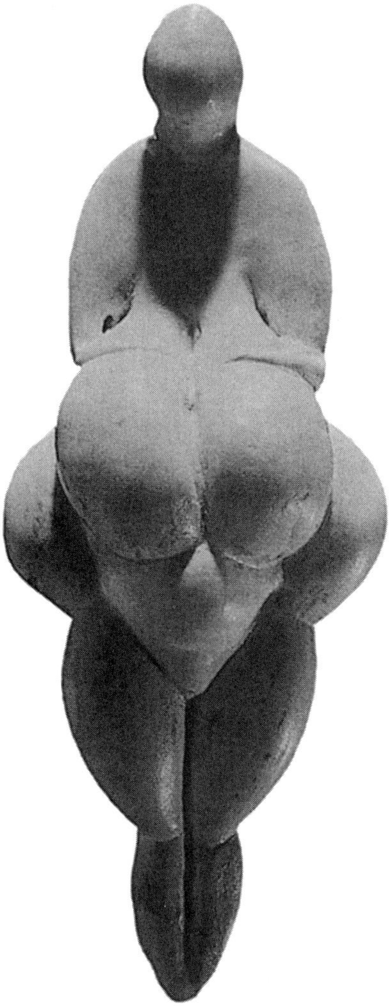

PLATE 6

PLATE 8

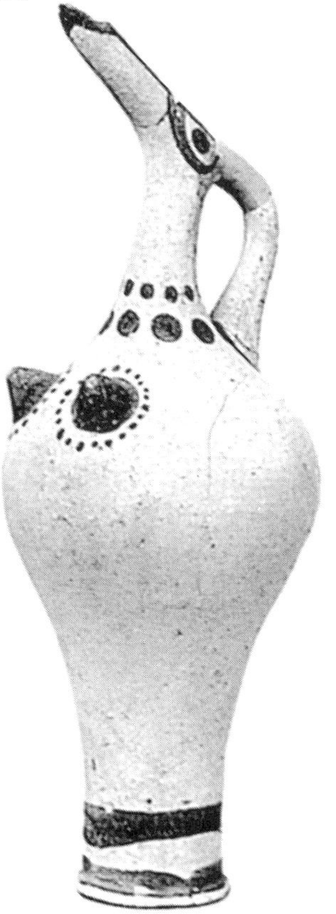

PLATE 7

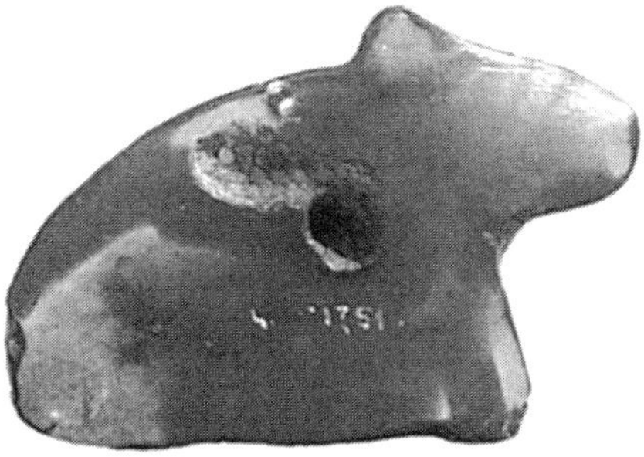

PLATE 5 This extraordinary mammoth-ivory sculpture conflates breasts and buttocks into a zone of eggs circling the figure's middle. H. 14.7 cm. Gravettian-Upper Périgordian. (Des Rideaux, at Lespugue, Haute Garonne, France; c. 23,000 B.C. Breasts in front were found damaged; here they are shown in reconstruction.)

PLATE 6 Figurine in a squatting posture. The focus is the female triangle in the center of the sculpture; tightly closed and pointed breasts and perpendicular lines across the arms. Limestone. H. 39.5 cm. Chalcolithic Cyprus (provenance unknown; c. 3000 B.C.).

PLATE 7 Amber bear with a schematized body. Length c. 8 cm. Narva culture; c. mid-3rd mill. B.C. (Tamula, N Estonia).

PLATE 8 The Goddess as nourishing vessel is portrayed into the Late Bronze Age and beyond. There are hundreds of graceful "nippled ewers," whose spouts are birds' beaks, from Thera in the Cyclades. Late Cycladic Bronze Age (Thera; 16th cent. B.C.).

PLATE 9

PLATE 9 The "assembly" of Snake Goddesses found in a vase probably ready to be placed on an altar (see fig. 215) and used for the reenactment of rites. Statuettes are of different proportions with antithetic snakes coiling over the abdomen, dotted triangles and lozenges over the ample thighs and legs, and cartouches with chevrons over the buttocks. The medium-sized figurines have a striated band across the abdomen and strips over the thighs. The little ones are not painted with symbols. The upper part of all the figurines is rendered very schematically. Only one (shown in the center) has arms with left hand touching the face (a ritual gesture). Early Cucuteni (Poduri-Dealul Ghindaru, Moldavia, NE Romania; c. 4800–4600 B.C.).

PLATE 10

PLATE 11

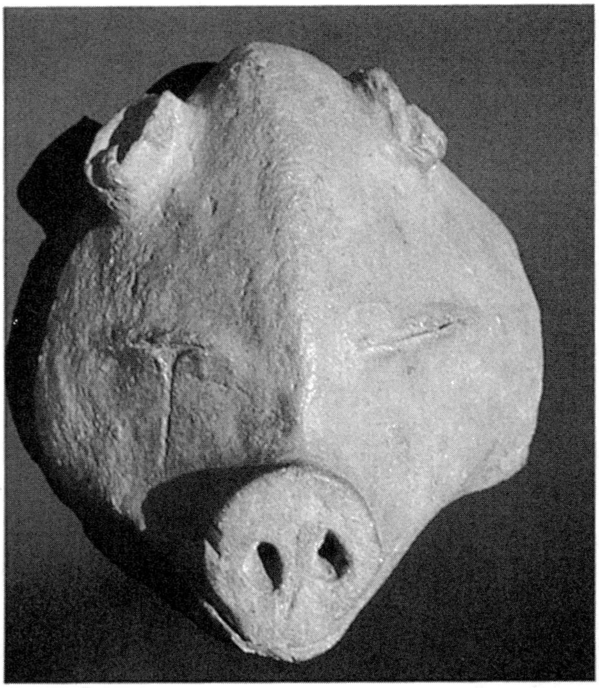

PLATE 10 Pregnant Goddess holding right hand on belly. Found leaning on her buttocks on the platform of a bread oven. H. 4 cm (head broken). Sesklo culture; 5900–5800 B.C. (Achilleion IVa, near Farsala, Thessaly, N Greece.).

PLATE 11 Clay mask of a sow probably used for ritual dances in worship of Pregnant Goddess (Earth Mother). H. 19 cm. Vinča culture, c. 4500 B.C. (Leskavica near Štip, SE Yugoslavia).

PLATE 12

PLATE 13

PLATE 12 This seated masked god holds a hook, symbol of renewal, over his shoulder; arm rings are indicated in relief. He may well be a forerunner of Master of Forests and Wild Animals. H. 25.6 cm. Tisza culture; c. 5000–4700 B.C. (Szegvár-Tüzköves, SE Hungary).

PLATE 13 The Owl Goddess from S France with breasts and schematic arms. She is associated with the hook, symbol of energy and renewal. H. 175 cm (see fig. 301, 2). The stela probably originates from a hypogeum of the Fontbuxian culture, early 3rd mill. B.C. (Mas de l'Aveugle, Collorgues, Gard.)

PLATE 14

PLATE 14 This marble figurine is typical of the Neolithic Stiff White Lady often found in graves and always associated with death. She stands rigidly with schematized folded arms, has an enormous pubic triangle. The only detail of the head is the nose. H. 7.2 cm. Neolithic of S Greece (environs of Sparta, Peloponnese; beginning of the 6th mill. B.C.).

PLATE 15

PLATE 15 The Sardinian Neolithic Stiff White Lady is rotund, not obese. In the center is the pubic triangle fused with the belly. Arms are pressed to her sides, legs fused with thighs and buttocks. Eyes are two horizontal dashes. Her massive head is topped with a polos. The figurine made of soft rock is from an oven-shaped tomb (see fig. 316.). H. c. 14 cm. Bonu Ighinu (Cuccuru s'Arriu, Oristano, central W Sardinia; mid-5th mill. B.C.).

PLATE 16

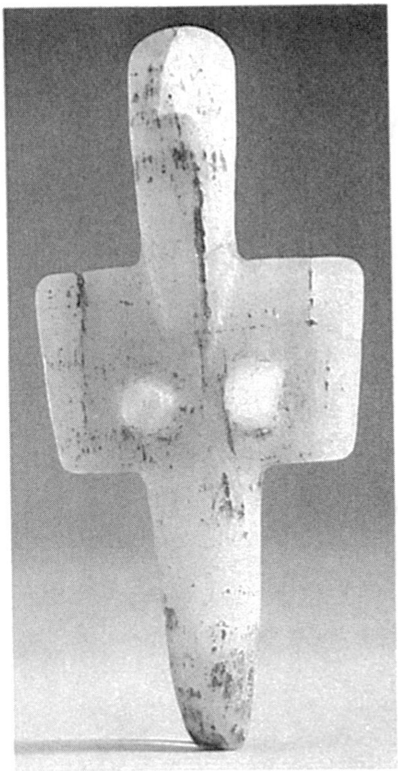

PLATE 16 "T-shaped" Stiff Nude. This alabaster statuette has folded arms which, together with upper body, form a solid rectangle. H. 9 cm. Ozieri culture (exact provenance unknown, Sardinia; end-5th mill. B.C.).

PLATE 17

PLATE 17 Life-size mask molded of clay found placed on woman's head, decorated with a gold crown, eyes, mouth, teeth, earrings, and two ring-shaped pendants with eyes attached to the chin. This grave also included additional earrings and plates, a mass of Aegean shell beads, a copper needle, a bone spindle whorl, a fragment of a bone figurine of a Stiff Nude, a lidded vase, and a large dish with graphite painting of a fourfold whorl design. Varna cemetery, E Bulgaria (Grave No. 2); mid-5th mill. B.C.

PLATE 18

PLATE 18 The hedgehog, symbol of life-generating uterus, occurs throughout Old European art. This hedgehog-shaped vase is of a fine light brown fabric. Karanovo VI (Nova Zagora, central Bulgaria; mid-5th mill. B.C.). The lid had an anthropomorphic Goddess's face (see figs. 399–400).

PLATE 19

PLATE 20

PLATE 21

PLATE 19 The Fish Goddess is the presiding deity at Lepenski Vir, a Neolithic sacred site. Such figures, carved from river boulders, were found at the head of altars (see fig. 242) of triangular shrines. The sculpture has breasts and is marked with a vulva in front. Ochre-painted on the back. Lepenski Vir II (Iron Gates region, N Yugoslavia; c. 6000 B.C.). The front view of this sculpture is illustrated in figure 407.

PLATE 20 Bulls and crescent (or horn) shapes (upper band) and sacred horns with butterflies or "double axes" (lower band) painted on sarcophagus from Crete. Note that bulls have heads of birds of prey (i.e., the bull, symbol of life-generating uterus, is hybridized with the Goddess of Death and Regeneration in the guise of a bird of prey). Late Minoan culture; 14th cent. B.C. (Khania Museum; W Crete.).

PLATE 21 The torsion of antithetic spirals stimulates the process of becoming on this footed vase. Cucuteni A_2 (Frumuşica, NE Romania; 46th–45th cents. B.C.). H. 13.5 cm.

PLATE 22

PLATE 23

PLATE 22 Antithetic spirals whirl around this lidded vase, stimulating the life power of the central egg, which is marked with a net design. Cucuteni (Drăguşeni, district of Botoşani, NE Romania; Cucuteni A_4 period, c. 42nd–41st cents. B.C.).

PLATE 23 Stone ring of Brogar, Orkney Islands, Scotland. Originally of 60 stones, diameter 103.7 m, surrounded by a ditch with two entrances; c. 3100 B.C. Regeneration rituals probably took place here through energetic ring dances, drawing on the Goddess's powers in stones.

PLATE 24

PLATE 24 Cucuteni dish painted with the circle in the center of the interior divided with an X sign, a crescent in each compartment. Huge spirals envelop the circle creating a dynamic composition of becoming. Cucuteni A_4 (Drăguşeni, Moldavia, NE Romania; c. 42nd–41st cens. B.C.).

THE LANGUAGE OF THE GODDESS

UNEARTHING THE HIDDEN SYMBOLS OF WESTERN CIVILIZATION

MARIJA GIMBUTAS

THE LANGUAGE OF THE GODDESS

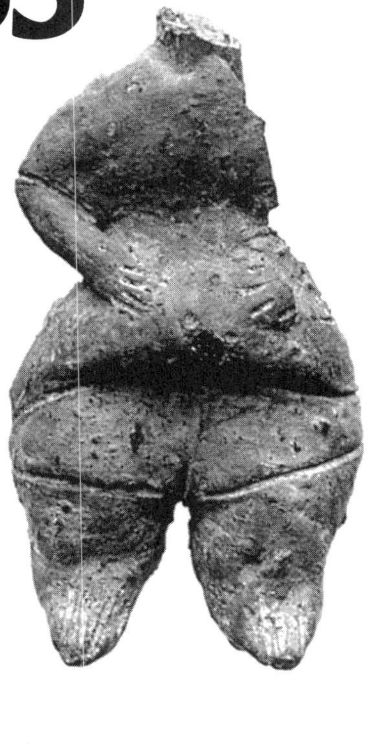

HarperSanFrancisco
A Division of HarperCollins*Publishers*

Acknowledgments

The preparation of this heavily illustrated volume during 1975–85 was made possible through the support of the Samuel H. Kress Foundation, the Ahmanson Foundation, and Lapis Press. I owe an enormous gratitude to all of them.

The manuscript in its early stages was edited by Joan Iten Sutherland. For her dedication, her editing skills, and patience in coordinating the text with illustrations, my heartiest thanks. To my colleagues and friends for reading the completed manuscript or its portions—to the late Joseph Campbell, the late Mircea Eliade, Dorothy Cameron, Ian Ferguson, Algirdas Julius Greimas, James Harrod, Patricia Reis, and Martha Walford—I am particularly indebted. Their support and encouragement have been invaluable.

Design and Production: Design Office, San Francisco, Bruce Kortebein, Leigh McLellan

FIRST HARPERCOLLINS PAPERBACK EDITION
PUBLISHED IN 1991

An Earlier Edition of This Book Was Cataloged as Follows:

Gimbutas, Marija Alseikaitė.
The language of the goddess / Marija Gimbutas. — 1st HarperCollins pbk. ed.
p. cm.
Includes bibliographical references and index.
ISBN 0-06-250418-5 (orig. pbk.)
ISBN 0-06-251243-9 (new pbk. : alk. paper)
1. Goddesses. 2. Symbolism. 3. Man, Prehistoric—Europe. 4. Religion, Prehistoric—Europe. I. Title.
[BL473.5.G55 1991]
291'.042'0936—dc20 91-10591
CIP

95 96 97 98 99 RRD(C) 10 9 8 7 6 5 4 3 2 1

This edition is printed on acid-free paper that meets the American National Standards Institute Z39.48 Standard.

Contents

II The Renewing and Eternal Earth

III Death and Regeneration

Conclusions

Foreword

As Jean-François Champollion, a century and a half ago, through his decipherment of the Rosetta Stone was able to establish a glossary of hieroglyphic signs to serve as keys to the whole great treasury of Egyptian religious thought from c. 3200 B.C. to the period of the Ptolemies, so in her assemblage, classification, and descriptive interpretation of some two thousand symbolic artifacts from the earliest Neolithic village sites of Europe, c. 7000 to 3500 B.C., Marija Gimbutas has been able, not only to prepare a fundamental glossary of pictorial motifs as keys to the mythology of that otherwise undocumented era, but also to establish on the basis of these interpreted signs the main lines and themes of a religion in veneration, both of the universe as the living body of a Goddess-Mother Creator, and of all the living things within it as partaking of her divinity—a religion, one immediately perceives, which is in contrast to that of Genesis 3:19, where Adam is told by his Father-Creator: "In the sweat of your face you shall eat bread till you return to the ground, for out of it you were taken; you are dust, and to dust you shall return." In this earlier mythology, the earth out of which all these creatures have been born is not dust but alive, as the Goddess-Creator herself.

In the library of European scholarship the first recognition of such a matristic order of thought and life antecedent to and underlying the historical forms of both Europe and the Near East appeared in 1861 in Johann Jakob Bachofen's *Das Mutterrecht*, where it was shown that in the codes of Roman Law vestigial features can be recognized of a matrilineal order of inheritance. Ten years earlier, in America, Lewis H. Morgan had published in *The League of the Ho-dé-no-sau-nee, or Iroquois*, a two-volume report of a society in which such a principle of "Mother Right" was still recognized; and in a systematic review, subsequently, of kinship systems throughout America and Asia, he had demonstrated an all but worldwide distribution of such a prepatriarchal order of communal life. Bachofen's recognition, around 1871, of the relevance of Morgan's work to his own marked a breakthrough from an exclusively European to a planetary understanding of this sociological phenomenon. There is to be recognized in Marija Gimbutas's reconstruction of the "Language of the Goddess" a far broader range of historical significance, therefore, than that merely of Old Europe, from the Atlantic to the Dnieper, c. 7000–3500 B.C.

Moreover, in contrast to the mythologies of the cattle-herding Indo-European tribes that, wave upon wave, from the fourth millennium B.C. overran the territories of Old Europe and whose male-dominated pantheons reflected the social ideals, laws, and political aims of the ethnic units to which they appertained, the iconography of the Great Goddess arose in reflection and veneration of the laws of Nature. Gimbutas's lexicon of the pictorial script of that primordial attempt on humanity's part to understand and live in harmony with the beauty and wonder of Creation adumbrates in archetypal symbolic terms a philosophy of human life that is in every aspect contrary to the manipulated systems that in the West have prevailed in historic times.

One cannot but feel that in the appearance of this volume at just this turn of the century there is an evident relevance to the universally recognized need in our time for a general transformation of consciousness. The message here is of an actual age of harmony and peace in accord with the creative energies of nature which for a spell of some four thousand prehistoric years anteceded the five thousand of what James Joyce has termed the "nightmare" (of contending tribal and national interests) from which it is now certainly time for this planet to wake.

Joseph Campbell

Introduction

The purpose of this book is to present the pictorial "script" for the religion of the Old European Great Goddess, consisting of signs, symbols, and images of divinities. These are our primary sources for reconstructing this prehistoric scene and are vital to any true understanding of Western religion and mythology.

Some twenty years ago when I first started to question the meaning of the signs and design patterns that appeared repeatedly on the cult objects and painted pottery of Neolithic Europe, they struck me as being pieces of a gigantic jigsaw puzzle—two-thirds of which was missing. As I worked at its completion, the main themes of the Old European ideology emerged, primarily through analysis of the symbols and images and discovery of their intrinsic order. They represent the grammar and syntax of a kind of meta-language by which an entire constellation of meanings is transmitted. They reveal the basic world-view of Old European (pre-Indo-European) culture.

Symbols are seldom abstract in any genuine sense; their ties with nature persist, to be discovered through the study of context and association. In this way we can hope to decipher the mythical thought which is the *raison d'être* of this art and basis of its form.

This present work grows out of the vast body of symbols preserved in the actual artifacts themselves. My primary presupposition is that they can best be understood on their own planes of reference, grouped according to their inner coherence. They constitute a complex system in which every unit is interlocked with every other in what appear to be specific categories. No symbol can be treated in isolation; understanding the parts leads to understanding the whole, which in turn leads to identifying more of the parts. This book explicitly seeks to identify the Old European patterns that cross the boundaries of time and space. These systematic associations in the Near East, southeastern Europe, the Mediterranean area, and in central, western, and northern Europe indicate the extension of the same Goddess religion to all of these regions as a cohesive and persistent ideological system.

I do not believe, as many archeologists of this generation seem to, that we shall never know the meaning of prehistoric art and religion. Yes, the scarcity of sources makes reconstruction difficult in most instances, but the religion of the early agricultural period of Europe and Anatolia is very richly documented. Tombs, temples, frescoes, reliefs, sculptures, figurines, pictorial painting, and other sources need to be analyzed from the point of view of ideology. For this reason it is necessary to widen the scope of descriptive archeology into interdisciplinary research. For this work I lean heavily on comparative mythology, early historical sources, and linguistics as well as on folklore and historical ethnography.

The world of the Goddess implies the whole realm in which she manifested herself. What were her major functions? What were the relations between her and her animals, plants, and the rest of nature? Her place in prehistory and in early history as a cosmogonic figure, the universal fruitful source, is no longer a novelty to many readers. In a number of books by religious historians, mythologists, and psychologists, she has been described as the Great Mother who gives birth to all things from her womb. She is usually represented as well-known Paleolithic "Venuses" and figurines from Neolithic Europe and Anatolia or from Bronze Age Crete. Analogies for her were sought from around the world: pre-Vedic Asia, Egypt, Mesopotamia, American Indian cultures, and elsewhere. These were simplistic and presented without the benefit of background studies. In order not to base my interpretation of symbols and functions of the divinities on such accidental analogies from all the continents of the world, I have focused my research strictly on European evidence, but including all the Neolithic and subsequent cultures, phase by phase. Then I follow the continuity of symbols and images forward to later prehistoric and historic times and also backwards, tracing their origin to the Paleolithic.

The materials available for the study of Old European symbols are as vast as the neglect that has been accorded that study. Of this rich body of material, the assemblage of ritual ceramics and other objects marked with symbols is most complete. The miniature sculptures, called figurines, found in quantity in almost every Neolithic settlement and cemetery are invaluable for reconstructing not only the symbolism but the religion itself. Because rituals were reenacted using these stone, ivory, bone, and clay figurines, much of the content of this prehistoric religion has been preserved. The tradition of marking figurines and other cult objects with symbols allows us to decipher their functions.

The richest sites where temples and paintings have been preserved are of paramount importance recreating these divinities, their functions, and their associated rituals. Findings at Çatal Hüyük in central Anatolia, dating from about 6400 to 5600 B.C.,* were made by James Mellaart in the 1960s. My own excavations at Achilleion, Thessaly, in 1973–74 uncovered some of the earliest European temples of c. 6000 B.C. The discovery of Mesolithic and Early Neolithic sacred burial areas at Lepenski Vir and Vlasac on the Danube in northern Yugoslavia, excavated by D. Srejović and Z. Letica in the 1960s, contributed precious information on funerary rituals and sculptures of divinities associated with regeneration. A remarkable surge of discoveries in Bulgaria,

*In uncalibrated chronology. The suggested actual age is from the end of the 8th to the end of the 7th millennium B.C.

Romania, Moldavia, and the western Ukraine after World War II revealed treasures of sculptures and painted pottery, as well as temples and temple models. Most of these date from the 6th and 5th millennia B.C. In the Mediterranean area, in addition to the great temples and tombs of Malta known from the early decades of the 20th century, excavations in Sardinia have revealed rock-cut and subterranean tombs, another rich source of information on funerary rituals and associated symbolism. The art and engravings of the megalithic tombs along the Atlantic coast of western and northwestern Europe and the British Isles provide valuable insights into the beliefs linked with death and regeneration.

Most of the illustrations reproduced here date from 6500 to 3500 B.C. in southeastern Europe and from about 4500 to 2500 in western Europe (the Neolithic began considerably later in the west). Examples from the Upper Paleolithic are also included to demonstrate the amazing longevity of certain images and designs. However, their persistence into the Bronze Age is not to be ignored. In fact, being more evolved than their predecessors and full of life-affirming grace, the motifs of Bronze Age Cyprus, Crete, Thera, Sardinia, Sicily, and Malta are magnificent sources for our purpose. Theran and other Minoan shrines, frescoes, and ceramic and stone carvings and sculptures are of the highest quality the Old World ever created. Historic records, myths, and rituals show that much of this great artistic culture pervaded ancient Greece, Etruria, and other parts of Europe.

Agricultural peoples' beliefs concerning sterility and fertility, the fragility of life and the constant threat of destruction, and the periodic need to renew the generative processes of nature are among the most enduring. They live on in the present, as do very archaic aspects of the prehistoric Goddess, in spite of the continuous process of erosion in the historic era. Passed on by the grandmothers and mothers of the European family, the ancient beliefs survived the superimposition of the Indo-European and finally the Christian myths. The Goddess-centered religion existed for a very long time, much longer than the Indo-European and the Christian (which represent a relatively short period of human history), leaving an indelible imprint on the Western psyche.

The ancient beliefs that were recorded in historical times or those that are still extant in rural and peripheral areas of Europe removed from the turbulences of European history—particularly in Basque, Breton, Welsh, Irish, Scottish, and Scandinavian countries or where Christianity was introduced very late, as in Lithuania (officially in 1387 but in reality not before the end of the 16th century)—are essential to the understanding of prehistoric symbols, since these later versions are known to us in their ritual and mythic contexts.

This volume is a study in archeomythology, a field that includes archeology, comparative mythology, and folklore, and one that archeologists have yet to explore. The mythologists on their part have ignored the rich archeological sources in spite of enormous possibilities they provide. It is hoped that this work will open avenues to folklore treasures as another source for reconstructing prehistoric ideology. Further research should yield a rich harvest. Recognizing two different symbolic systems—one reflecting a matristic-gylanic culture, the other an androcratic—within European prehistoric and historic mythology will enlighten the studies of origins of myths and symbols.

Dumézil (1898–1986) devoted his life work to establishing mythology as an independent branch of the social sciences. His studies have shown that mythic beings are the means for explaining the order of mankind and the origins of the universe, and that mythic thinking is not accidental but occurs within an organized system of divine activities and functions. Thus mythology reflects an ideological structure. Comparative studies show Indo-European mythology and society as consisting of three classes: sovereign, warrior, and pastoral-agricultural; these relate to divine functions in the three realms of the sacred, of physical force, and of prosperity. Thus first light was shone on the nature of Indo-European life and ideology. Unfortunately, Dumézil, mainly because he did not use archeological sources, dissociated his system of three functions from the preceding matristic system that reflected an entirely different pantheon of goddesses and a different social structure. This is where his model failed. Typically, Old European goddesses were relegated to the third function, prosperity or fertility, and thus became grouped as "lowest gods," "*dieux derniers*." In some contexts, however, for instance in dealing with the Greek Athena or Irish Machas, Dumézil admitted that the goddesses are multifunctional, performing in all three realms. In one of his works he even states that they form "the thorn in his system" (Dumézil 1947: 1352).

It is clear that Indo-European mythologies are mixed with the pre-Indo-European, and that a reliable system cannot be reconstructed without first distinguishing and then weeding out these earlier elements. Dumézil's model does not work if applied to these hybrid mythologies. The goddesses inherited from Old Europe, such as Greek Athena, Hera, Artemis, Hekate; Roman Minerva and Diana; Irish Morrígan and Brigit; Baltic Laima and Ragana; Russian Baba Yaga, Basque Mari, and others, are not "Venuses" bringing fertility and prosperity; as we shall see, they are much more. These life-givers and death-wielders are "queens" or "ladies" and as such they remained in individual creeds for a very long time in spite of their official dethronement, militarization, and hybridization with the Indo-European heavenly brides and wives. The Old European goddesses never became *"déesses dernières,"* even in Christian times. All this calls for a vertical expansion of the Dumézilian method.

Archeological materials are not mute. They speak their own language. And they need to be used for the great source they are to help unravel the spirituality of those of our ancestors who predate the Indo-Europeans by many thousands of years.

My focus is on the period beginning with early agriculture in Europe, some nine to eight thousand years ago. The Neolithic farmers evolved their own cultural patterns in the course of several millennia. Food gathering gave way to food producing and hunting to a settled way of life, but there was no corresponding major change in the structure of symbolism, only a gradual incorporation of new forms and the elaboration or transformation of the old. Indeed, what is striking is not the metamorphosis of the symbols over the millennia but rather the continuity from Paleolithic times on. The major aspects of the Goddess of the Neolithic—the birth-giver, portrayed in a naturalisitic birth-giving pose; the fertility-giver influencing growth and multiplication, portrayed as a pregnant nude; the life or nourishment-giver and protectress, portrayed as a bird-woman with breasts and protruding buttocks; and the death-wielder as a stiff nude ("bone")—can all be traced back to the period when the first sculptures of bone, ivory, or stone appeared, around 25,000 B.C. and their symbols—vulvas, triangles, breasts, chevrons, zig-zags, meanders, cupmarks—to an even earlier time.

The main theme of Goddess symbolism is the mystery of birth and death and the renewal of life, not only human but all life on earth and indeed in the whole cosmos. Symbols and images cluster around the parthenogenetic (self-generating) Goddess and her basic functions as Giver of Life, Wielder of Death, and, not less importantly, as Regeneratrix, and around the Earth Mother, the Fertility Goddess young and old, rising and dying with plant life. She was the single source of all life who took her energy from the springs and wells, from the sun, moon, and moist earth. This symbolic system represents cyclical, not linear, mythical time. In art this is manifested by the signs of dynamic motion: whirling and twisting spirals, winding and coiling snakes, circles, crescents, horns, sprouting seeds and shoots. The snake was a symbol of life energy and regeneration, a most benevolent, not an evil, creature. Even the colors had a different meaning than in the Indo-European symbolic system. Black did not mean death or the underworld; it was the color of fertility, the color of damp caves and rich soil, of the womb of the Goddess where life begins. White, on the other hand, was the color of death, of bones—the opposite of the Indo-European system in which both white and yellow are the colors of the shining sky and the sun. In no way could the philosophy that produced these images be mistaken for the pastoral Indo-European world with its horse-riding warrior gods of thundering and shining sky or of the swampy underworld, the ideology in which female goddesses are not creatrixes but beauties—"Venuses," brides of the sky-gods.

The Goddess-centered art with its striking absence of images of warfare and male domination, reflects a social order in which women as heads of clans or queen-priestesses played a central part. Old Europe and Anatolia, as well as Minoan Crete, were a gylany.* A balanced, nonpatriarchal and non-matriarchal social system is reflected by religion, mythologies, and folklore, by studies of the social structure of Old European and Minoan cultures, and is supported by the continuity of the elements of a matrilineal system in ancient Greece, Etruria, Rome, the Basque, and other countries of Europe.

While European cultures continued a peaceful existence and reached a true florescence and sophistication of art and architecture in the 5th millennium B.C., a very different Neolithic culture with the domesticated horse and lethal weapons emerged in the Volga basin of South Russia and after the middle of the 5th millennium even west of the Black Sea. This new force inevitably changed the course of European prehistory. I call it the "Kurgan" culture (*kurgan* meaning "barrow" in Russian) since the dead were buried in round barrows that covered the mortuary houses of important males.

The basic features of the Kurgan culture go back to the 7th and 6th millennia B.C. in the middle and lower Volga basin—patriarchy; patrilineality; small-scale agriculture and animal husbandry, including the domestication of the horse not later than the 6th millennium; the eminent place of the horse in cult; and, of great importance, armaments—bow and arrow, spear, and dagger. These characteristics match what has been reconstructed as Proto-Indo-European by means of linguistic studies and by comparative mythology. They stand in opposition to the Old European gylanic, peaceful, sedentary culture with highly developed agriculture and with great architectural, sculptural, and ceramic traditions.

So the repeated disturbances and incursions by Kurgan people (whom I view as Proto-Indo-European) put an end to the Old European culture roughly between 4300 and 2800 B.C., changing it from gylanic to androcratic and from matrilineal to patrilineal. The Aegean and Mediterranean regions and western Europe escaped the process the longest; there, especially in the islands such as Thera, Crete, Malta, and Sardinia, Old European culture

*Riana Eisler in her book *The Chalice and the Blade* (1987) proposes the term gylany (*gy-* from "woman," *an-* from *andros*, "man," and the letter l between the two standing for the linking of both halves of humanity) for the social structure where both sexes were equal.

flourished in an enviably peaceful and creative civilization until 1500 B.C., a thousand to 1500 years after central Europe had been thoroughly transformed. Nevertheless, the Goddess religion and its symbols survived as an undercurrent in many areas. Actually, many of these symbols are still present as images in our art and literature, powerful motifs in our myths and archetypes in our dreams.

We are still living under the sway of that aggressive male invasion and only beginning to discover our long alienation from our authentic European Heritage—gylanic, nonviolent, earth-centered culture. This book presents for the first time the concrete evidence of this long-standing culture and its symbolic language, whose vestiges remain enmeshed in our own system of symbols.

Categories of Symbols

A close look at symbolic associations greatly reduces the number of symbolic meanings. The classification of the symbols into interrelated groups is reflected in the division of the book into four parts with distinct themes: Part I, Life-Giving; Part II, The Renewing and Eternal Earth; Part III, Death and Regeneration; and Part IV, Energy and Unfolding.

The first category of symbols embraces the aquatic sphere since the prevalent belief was that all life comes from water. The symbols of water expanses, streams, and rain—zig-zags, wavy or serpentine bands, net, checkerboard—and of waterfowl belong here and are associated with the Goddess in the form of a woman/waterbird hybrid. In schematic versions, this image may have only breasts or exaggerated posteriors. This rich group of symbols is undoubtedly Paleolithic in origin.

The beginning of the portrayal of parts of the female body—breasts, buttocks, belly, vulva—goes back to the times when people who did not yet understand the biological process of reproduction (copulation as the cause of pregnancy) created a deity who was a macrocosmic extension of a woman's body. She is a cosmic Creatrix, Life and Birth Giver. These essential parts of the female body were endowed with the miraculous power of procreation. The mysterious moisture in the uterus and labyrinthine internal organs of the Goddess were the magical source of life.

The Birth-giving Goddess who is represented in a natural birth-giving posture or by her vulva as *pars pro toto* is present in the Upper Paleolithic. These symbols continued into the Neolithic and even later. She is linked with primeval mothers in animal form such as the bear, deer/doe, elk/doe, and in the Upper Paleolithic with the she-bison and mare. The preservation of such images into the late prehistoric and even historic era can be explained not only by the indestructibility of deeply ingrained life-giving and maternity symbols, but also as a strong memory of a matrilineal system when paternity was difficult to establish. It does not mean, however, that the paternal role in the process of reproduction was not understood in the Neolithic or at the latest in the Copper Age by people who were such keen observers of nature.

Innovations occurred with the advent of the Neolithic economy. The ram (the earliest domesticated animal) became sacred to the Bird Goddess, followed by the fleece symbol and the association of the Goddess with weaving and spinning. The beginning of the concept of the Life- and Birth-giving Goddess as a Fate—apportioner and determiner of the length of life, happiness, and wealth—and as a spinner and weaver of human life may go back to this Early Neolithic period.

At the same time, the discovery of pottery opened avenues for the creation of new sculptural forms as well as new ways of expressing symbols through pottery painting. Askoi (bird-shaped vases) and anthropomorphic or bird-woman vases appeared. Streams, chevrons, triangles, net-patterned bands, spirals, winding snakes, and snake coils became dominating motifs in pottery painting. Ceramic vessels as the Life-giving Goddess, marked with M's, zig-zags (water streams or amniotic fluid), nets, spiralling water waves, and other aquatic signs made their debut in the 6th millennium B.C.

The fertility and pregnancy symbols also have roots in the Upper Paleolithic. The Pregnant Goddess is already there. The bi-line (two dashes) is recorded in the Upper Paleolithic as a symbol of pregnancy, or the strength of two. As a consequence of the new farming economy, the Paleolithic Pregnant Goddess was transformed into an Earth Fertility deity. The fecundity of humans and animals, the fertility of crops, the thriving of plant cover, and the processes of growing and fattening were now of enormous concern. The sow, as a fast-growing and fast-fattening animal, became sacred to this Goddess. Originally probably a lunar goddess, fattening like the waxing moon, the Pregnant Goddess of the agricultural era became a chthonic (earth) deity, symbolic of rising, flourishing, and dying vegetation. The drama of seasonal changes intensified, which is manifested in summer/winter or spring/harvest rituals and in the emergence of a mother/daughter image and of a male God as a spirit of rising and dying vegetation.

As this book documents, throughout prehistory images of death do not overshadow those of life: they are combined with symbols of regeneration. The Death Messenger and the Death-wielder are also concerned with regeneration. Innumerable examples testify to the existence of this motif: vulture heads are placed within breasts, jaws, and tusks of ferocious boars are covered with breasts (as in the 7th millennium B.C. Çatal Hüyük shrines of central Turkey); images of the western European Owl Goddess on the tomb walls of megalithic graves and on stelae have breasts, or their inner body is a life-creating labyrinth with a vulva in the center.

As a symbol of regeneration, the uterus as such, or the similarly shaped bucranium (the form of the skull of an ox), or analagous animal forms—fish, frog, toad, hedgehog, turtle—played a role throughout most of post-Paleolithic prehistory as well as in later history. During the Neolithic, graves and temples assumed the shape of the egg, vagina, and uterus of the Goddess or of her complete body. The megalithic passage graves of western Europe quite probably symbolized the vagina (passage) and pregnant belly (*tholos*, round chamber) of the Goddess. The shape of a grave is an analogue of the natural hill with an omphalos (stone symbolizing the navel) on top, a universal symbol of the Earth Mother's pregnant belly with umbilical cord, as recorded in European folk beliefs.

The interplay of life- and death-giving functions in a divinity is particularly characteristic of dominant goddesses. The Life and Birth Giver can turn into a frightening image of death. She is a stiff nude or a mere bone with a supernatural pubic triangle where the transformation from death to life begins. The occasional ornithomorphic features of her mask and her vulture's feet betray her connection with the bird of prey and the ophidian features—long mouth, fangs, and small round eyes—link her with the poisonous snake. The stiff nude of the Upper Paleolithic, carved in bone without the protuberances of a life-producing body, is the ancestress of the Old European stiff nude, which was made of marble, alabaster, light-colored stone, or bone—materials having the color of death.

The masks of the Goddess of death (mid-5th millennium B.C., with large mouth and fangs and sometimes a hanging tongue may have generated the gorgoneion, the fearsome monster head, of ancient Greece. The earliest Greek gorgons, however, are not terrifying symbols that turn humans into stones. They are portrayed as having the wings of a bee and snakes as antennae and are decorated with a honeycomb design—all clearly symbols of regeneration.

One of the largest of these categories can be classified as symbols of energy and unfolding. Spirals, horns, crescents, half-circles (U-shapes), hooks, axes, hounds, he-goats, and excited (ithyphallic) men, which flank a rising, watery life column, serpent, tree of life, and anthropomorphic Goddess or her pregnant belly, are all energy symbols.

Antithetic snake or spiral heads fill Old European vase painting with motion and twisting. Whirls, crosses, and a variety of four-corner designs are symbols of the dynamism in nature which secures the birth of life and turns the wheel of cyclic time from death to life, so that life is perpetuated. In this series of transformations, the most dramatic is the change from one life form into countless others: from a bucranium to bees, butterflies, and plants, epiphanies of the Goddess of Regeneration.

The iconography of the Goddess in her various aspects always contains several types of symbols—abstract or hieroglyphic such as V, X, M, triangle, diamond, etc.; "representational" such as eyes, breasts, bird's feet; and animal, which are attributes of the various aspects of the Goddess (snake, bird, sow, bull, frog, bee, etc.). These three categories are tightly interwoven and stem from a holistic perception of the world, when nature was not classified as in modern universities, when humans were not isolated from the surrounding world, and when it was normal to feel the Goddess's power in bird or stone, or in her eyes or breasts alone, or even in her hieroglyphs. In each part of this book I shall deal with all of these categories.

I

LIFE-GIVING

The amazing repetition of symbolic associations through time and in all of Europe on pottery, figurines, and other cult objects has convinced me that they are more than "geometric motifs"; they must belong to an alphabet of the metaphysical. Further search for the links between these symbols and the image of a deity revealed that the V and chevron (double or triple V) are the Bird Goddess's insignia, and that other symbols of this family are associated with her mysterious source of life, the life waters, and with her functions as Life Giver.

The Bird Goddess as a whole had many functions, and some of her symbols—such as tri-line, net, triangle, and snake—are therefore transfunctional. They are associated with life creation and regeneration.

Figurine marked with chevrons and zig-zags; from SW Anatolia. See figure 15, page 11.

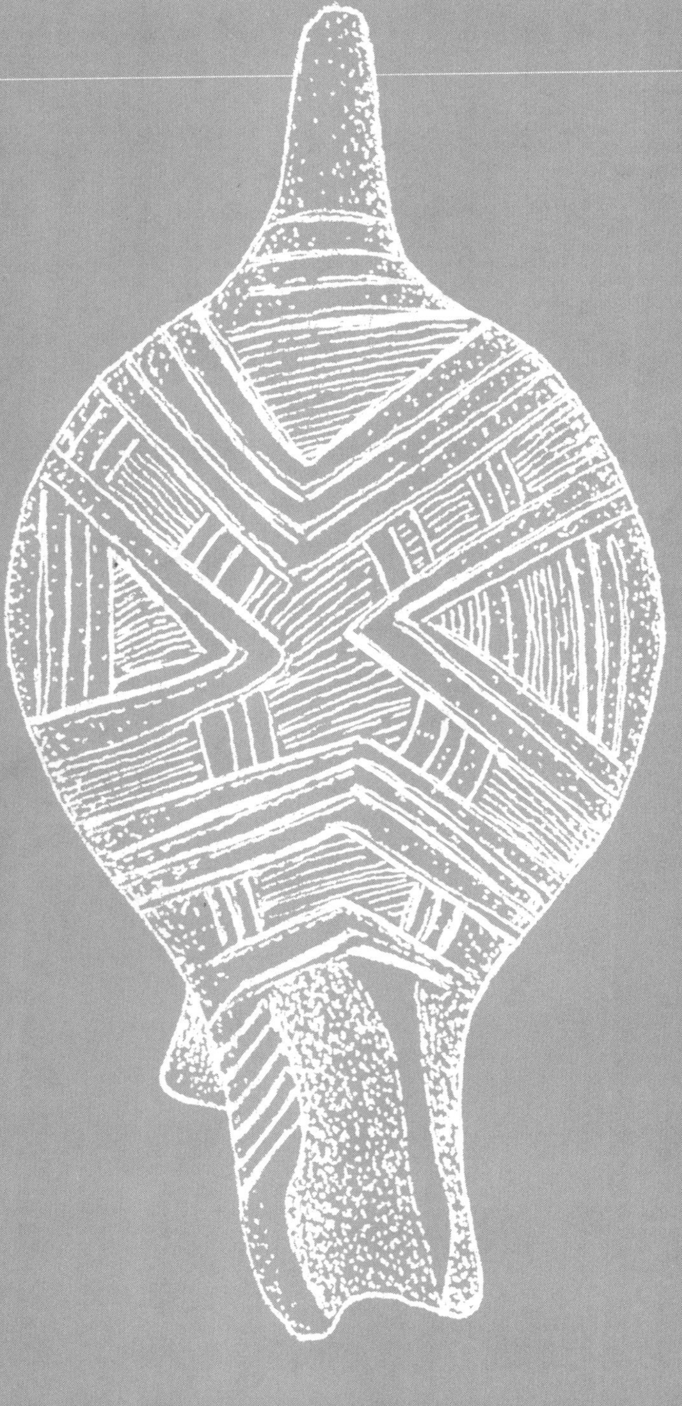

Third millennium schematic clay bird from Malta decorated with chevrons and triangles. See figure 11, page 9.

1/ *Chevron and V as Bird Goddess Symbols*

Chevrons, V's, zig-zags, M's, meanders, streams, nets, and tri-lines are frequent and repetitious Old European symbols. However, in all the literature on Neolithic and later ceramics they are considered to be just "geometric motifs"; the relation between design and symbol was not suspected. It took me years of detective work to discover how they were all related. In this chapter we shall deal with the symbols associated with the primary aspect of this Goddess, that of life-giving moisture of the Goddess's body—her breasts, eyes, mouth, and vulva.

In these life-creating and protecting functions, her animal forms are ram, deer, bear, and snake. The latter also appears in an anthropomorphic shape and seems to be an alter ego of the Bird Goddess.

We shall begin our journey with the Goddess's hieroglyphs, the V and chevron, and their links to waterbirds and aquatic symbols.

1.1 *On Upper Paleolithic and Mesolithic bird figurines and bird-woman hybrids*

Graphically, a pubic triangle is most directly rendered as a V. This expression and its recognition are universal and immediate. It is, nevertheless, amazing how early this bit of "shorthand" crystallized to become for countless ages the designating mark of the Bird Goddess.

Geese, cranes, and swans are encountered painted or engraved in Upper Paleolithic caves, engraved on bone objects marked with chevrons and parallel lines, or as ivory figurines. (FIGURE 1) Some representations of waterbirds are clearly anthropomorphized.

In eastern Europe and Siberia, the V, as a single sign or repeated as a chevron, was connected with the bird or with anthropomorphic bird sculptures from the time of the Upper Paleolithic. For example, waterbird figurines from Mal'ta in Siberia are marked with rows of incised V's, and faceless anthropomorphic waterbirds carved of mammoth ivory, from Mezin near Chernigov in the Ukraine, are marked with dashes or V's. (FIGURE 2) Their bodies and necks are incised with such symbols as chevrons, meanders, nets, bi-lines, tri-lines, and multiple parallel lines (see also fig. 37). The little figurines have a bird's posterior, but their divine generative function is emphasized by a large pubic triangle. Some of them are decorated by a series of panels, each with a somewhat different chevron design—chevrons in columns, opposed, or inverted. These figurines, tentatively dated to c. 18,000–15,000 B.C., are of inestimable value for the insight they afford into the antiquity of the V in connection with an ornithomorphic Goddess.

V's, chevrons, and multiple chevrons, inverted or opposed, appear during the latest Paleolithic and the Mesolithic engraved on bone and antler, as in the examples from the Magdalenian culture in France and the Romanello–Azilian culture of southwestern Romania. (FIGURE 3)

The association of the V or chevron, interconnected V's, juxtaposed V's, or a V joined to a meander, with images of the ornithomorphic Goddess and objects used in her cult remains constant for millennia, as we shall see.

FIGURE 1

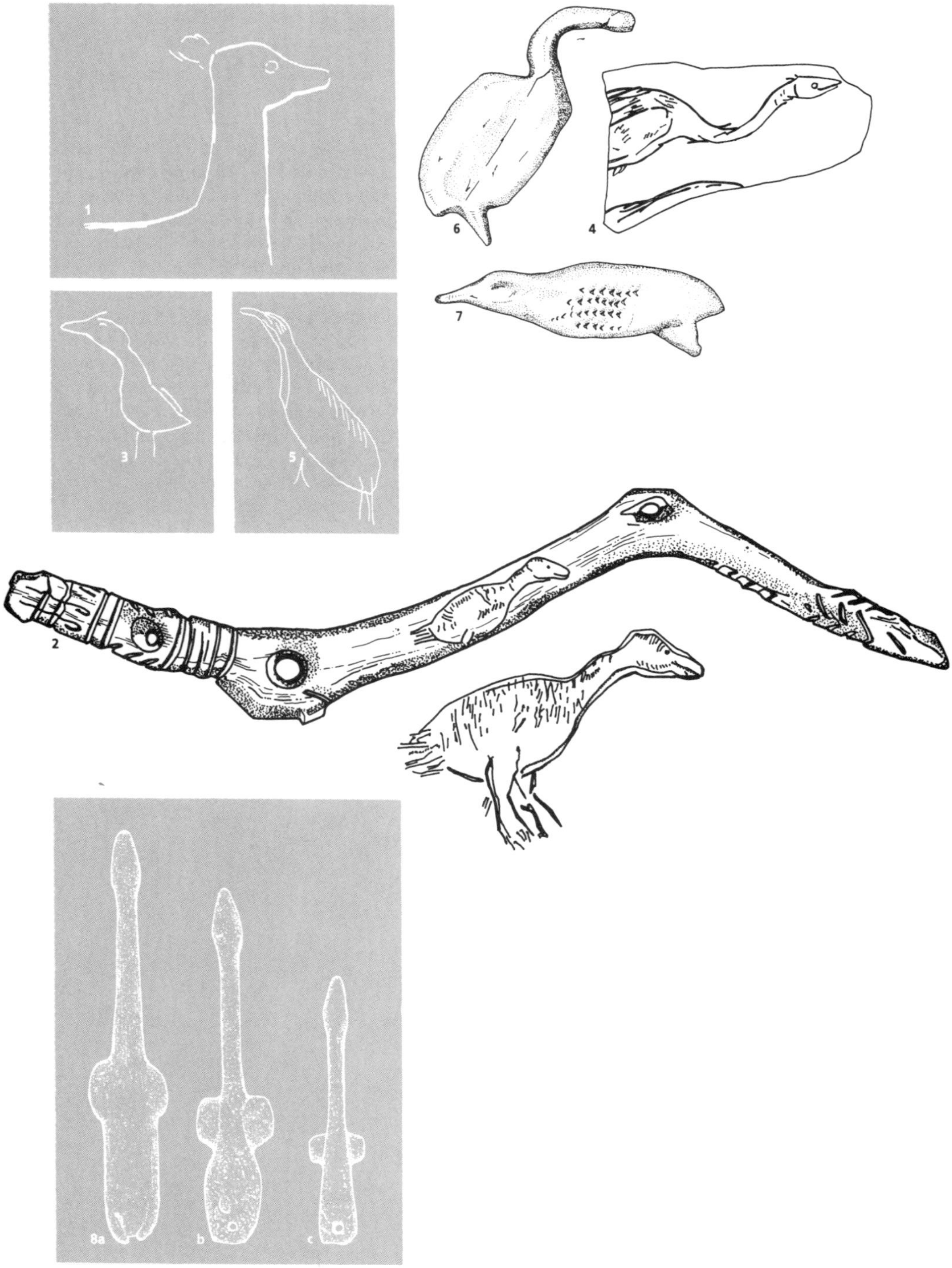

FIGURE 1 (1) A goose engraved in a niche of a cave (Labastide, Hautes Pyrénées, France; Middle Magdalenian, c. 13,000–11,000 B.C. (2) and (4) A goose and a swan engraved on bone. In (2) note that the perforated bone stick is marked with chevrons on both ends (Gourdan-Polignan, Haute Garonne; Magdalenian). (3) A goose (Gabillou at Mussidan, Dordogne; Magdalenian). (5) Crane or heron engraved in the cave of El Pendo (Escobedo, Santander, N. Spain; probably Magdalenian). (6–8) Bird sculptures in bone (Mal'ta, NW of Lake Baikal, Siberia; dated tentatively to 24,000 B.C. In (8) note that birds are anthropomorphized and that figurines are perforated. (1) H. 5.1 cm. (2) H. 33 cm. (3) H. 13.7 cm. (4) H. 10.8 cm. (5) H. 21.2 cm. (6) H. 6 cm. (7) H. 2.4 cm. (8) H. (a) 15.3 cm, (b) 13.2 cm, (c) 10 cm.

FIGURE 2

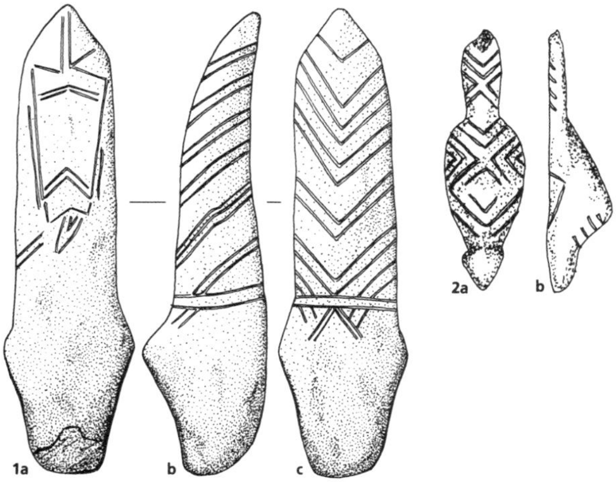

FIGURE 2 Abstract form and symbolic decoration combine in these Upper Paleolithic ivory figurines of anthropomorphized waterbirds incised with V's and chevrons (multiple V's). The decorations of the figure on the right serve to emphasize her pubic triangle, and thus her divine generative function (Mezin, upper Desna basin, Ukraine; c. 18,000–15,000 B.C.). (1) H. 29.3 cm. (2) H. 7.2 cm.

FIGURE 3

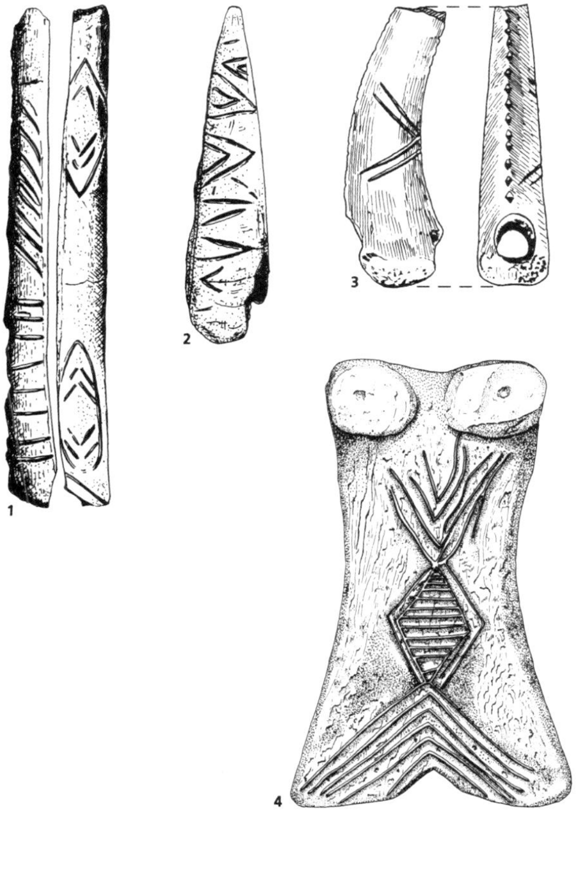

FIGURE 3 (1) Fragment of a reindeer-antler tool decorated with opposed chevrons on one side and straight and oblique incisions on the other (La Madeleine, Dordogne, S France; Late Magdalenian, c. 10,000 B.C.); (2) antler tool engraved with V's and chevrons (Gourdan, Haute-Garonne, Late Magdalenian); (3) antler tool and (4) abstract rendering of a female image in bone of the Epigravettian culture (Cuina Turcului, Iron Gate region of SW Romania; c. 8000 B.C.). (1) H. 13 cm. (2) H. 13 cm. (3) H. 24 cm. (4) H. 17 cm.

1.2 *As earliest decorative motifs on Neolithic pottery*

During the Neolithic, the V and the chevron frequently appear on vases, votive vessels, lamps, altars, plaques, and other objects. They stand alone or are framed by columns and panels in association with meanders, nets, and parallel lines.

The chevron and triangle are prevalent motifs on the earliest painted pottery of the Thessalian Sesklo culture, during the second half of the 7th millenium B.C. (FIGURE 4) The motif is given special placement, usually on the flat handle or below it, or at the center of the vessel. The chevron—single, double, or as a design element— also occurs on the earliest Neolithic ceramics of the Starčevo and Karanovo cultures in the central and eastern Balkans, during the first half of the 6th millenium B.C.

Richly decorated vases of the Late Neolithic, Copper Age, and Bronze Age share the tradition of the chevron motif framed in a panel, band, circle, or ellipse. The convention of borders serves to distinguish the chevron as symbol from the chevron as decorative motif. The isolated symbol has a denotative function, while the decorative elaboration developed from the single motif has a rather generalized significance and serves as a connotative context. It is not simply a random decoration but rather a configuration with symbolic reference. The device of enclosing the denotative symbol within clearly defined boundaries—much as a cartouche in Egyptian hieroglyphics defines a royal name—was soon widespread.

1.3 *Chevrons, V's, beaks, and birds*

The intimate connection in thought and meaning between the V sign, the chevron, and the bird is manifested by the presence of a single V or chevron on bird-shaped vases called askoi, on bird figurines, and on anthropomorphic birds and ornithomorphic female figures. (FIGURES 5–7) The askos form emerged at the earliest stage of the Pottery Neolithic in southeastern Europe (the middle of the 7th millenium B.C.), and continued throughout the whole of the Neolithic and the Bronze Age. It was one of the most characteristic Early Bronze Age vase forms of the Aegean and west Anatolia. The askos was consistently decorated with chevrons and parallel lines. A variant typical of Troy II–III was an askoid jug with a spout shaped like a bird's beak.

This Goddess, or the idea of a connection between the feminine and birds, is portrayed in bird-woman hybrids best recognized by their beaked or beak-masked faces. They usually have a neat hairdo or crown and a V-shaped necklace.

FIGURE 4

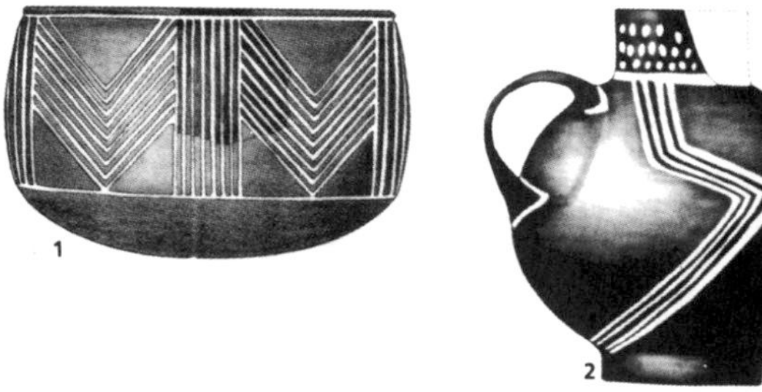

FIGURE 4 (1) Multiple chevrons are framed by vertical lines, thus emphasizing their symbolic rather than decorative character (Nea Makri, Attica, Greece; c. 6000–5800 B.C.). (2) Globular red-burnished vessel with white painted decoration. Small lateral V's accent juncture of handle to body, large lateral chevron sweeps vertically from neck to base (Tsangli mound, central Thessaly, Greece; c. 6100–5900 B.C.). (1) H. 11.7 cm. (2) H. 22.6 cm.

FIGURE 5

FIGURE 5 This example of a duck-shaped askos is decorated with soaring red chevrons painted on a white-slipped surface (Nemea, Peloponnese, Greece; approx. 6000 B.C.). H. 16.8 cm.

FIGURE 6

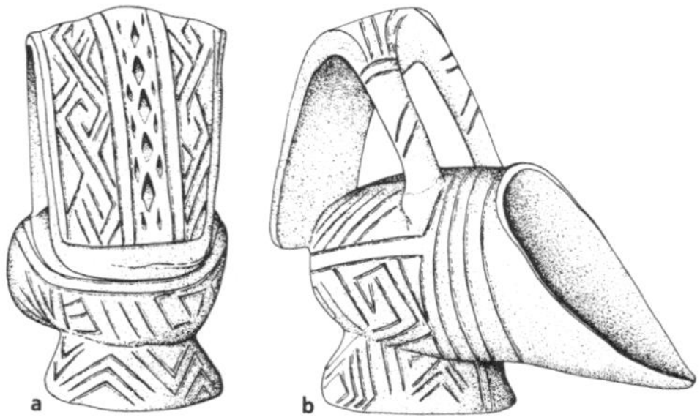

FIGURE 6 An askos of extraordinary form (its mouth is in the shape of an open beak) is decorated with chevrons, meanders, and parallel lines—the latter two symbols emphasizing the Bird Goddess's connection with the watery sphere and life-giving moisture (Dimini, near Volos, N Greece; c. 5000–4500 B.C.). H. 15.5 cm.

FIGURE 7

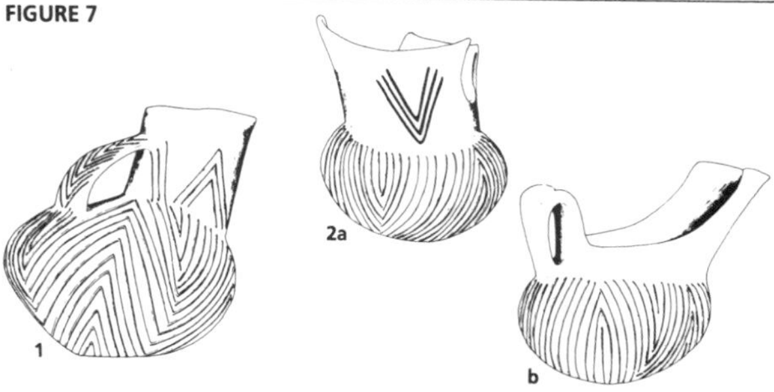

FIGURE 7 More than a thousand years later (see fig. 6) askoi from the Coţofeni culture are still being decorated with incised chevrons. The spout of (2) is marked, like a label, with a painted triple chevron (Basarabi, W Romania; 2nd half of the 4th mill. B.C.). (1) H. 19.6 cm. (2) H. 16 cm.

FIGURE 8

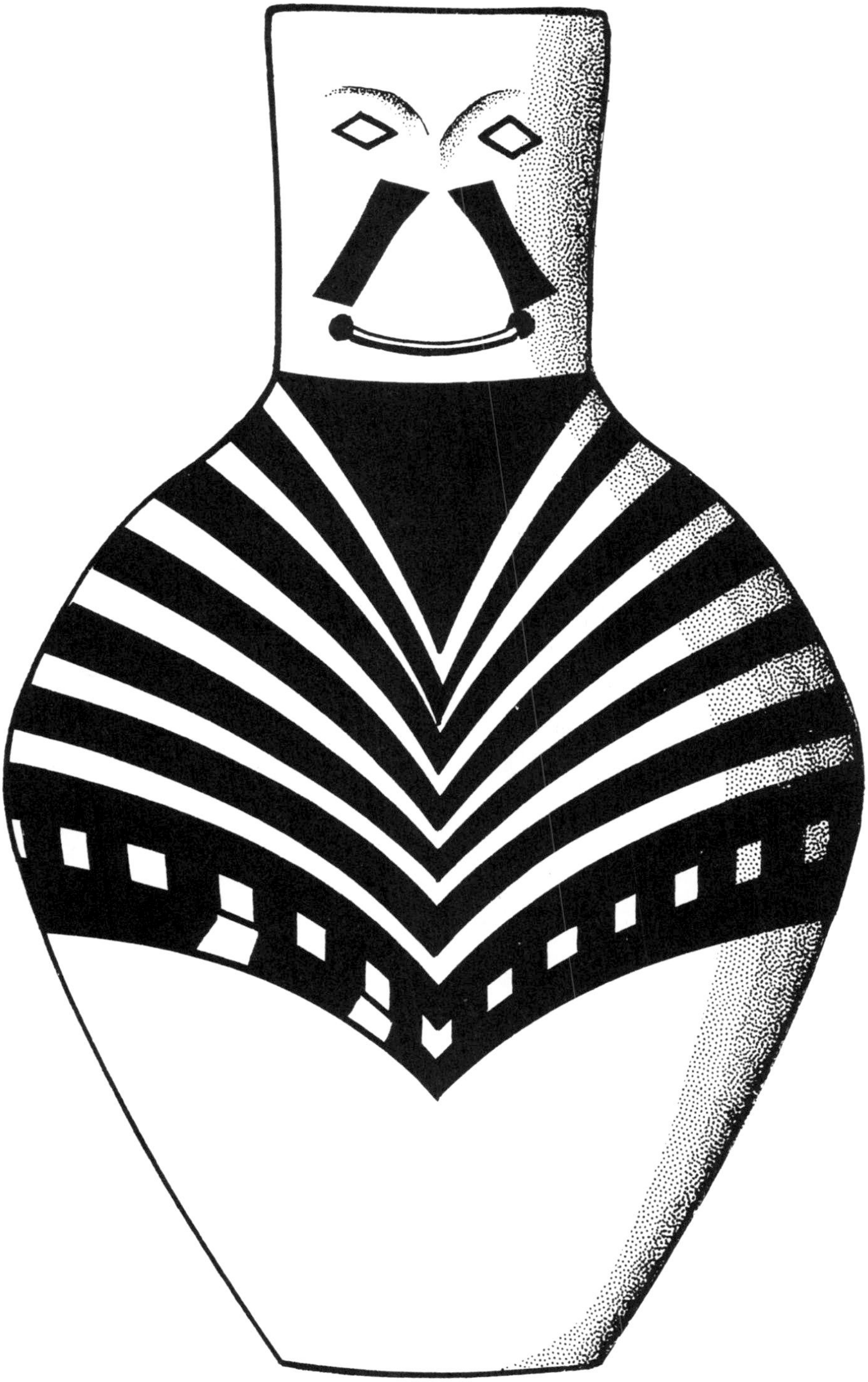

FIGURE 8 The connection between chevron and Bird Goddess is clear on this charming early Vinča vase (pithos), painted red on a cream background (Anza, Macedonia, Yugoslavia; 5200–5000 B.C.). H. 92 cm.

FIGURE 9

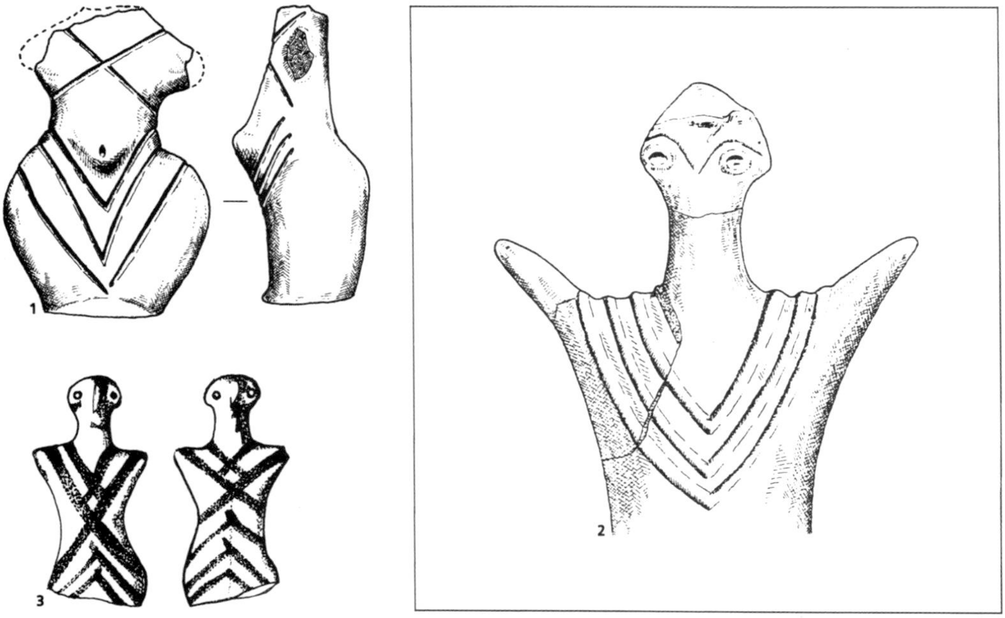

FIGURE 9 Terracotta figurines marked with V's and X's. (1) A figurine (probably Bird Goddess) incised with a triple V below the abdomen and an X over the chest. Red burnished. Neolithic Anatolia (Hacilar I C–D; mid-6th mill. B.C.). (2) This beaked and winged Goddess wears a triple-chevron collar to identify her. Lengyel culture of central Europe (Těšetice-Kyjovice, Moravia, Czechoslovakia; early 5th mill. B.C.). (3) These two figurines from the Cucuteni culture are painted in black with V's and X's (Cucuteni site, Moldavia, NE Romania; Cucuteni B period, 1st half of the 4th mill. B.C.). (1) H. 5 cm. (2) H. of detail 9.1 cm. (3) H. 5.8 cm.

FIGURE 10

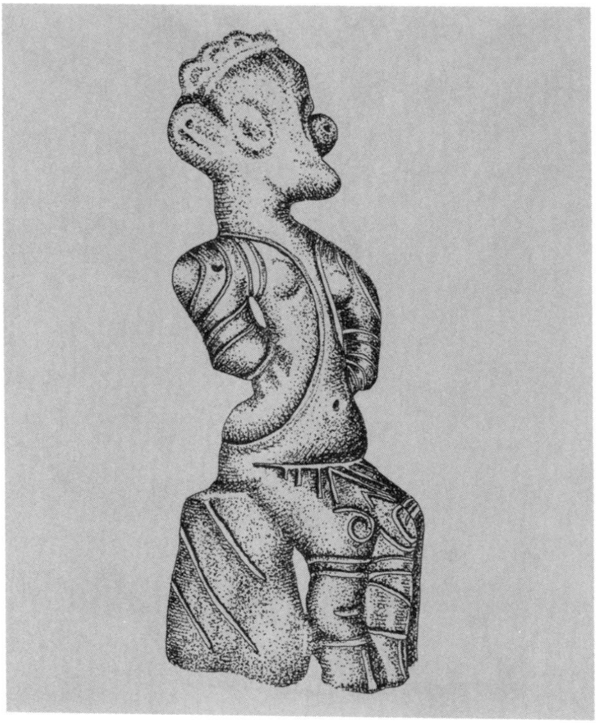

FIGURE 10 Another Bird Goddess, this one Late Vinča, is elaborately appointed. She sits on a throne incised with three lines and wears a crown, duck mask and bolero jacket; her apron is marked with chevrons, her knees with spirals, and her limbs with coiling lines (Svetozarevo, Central Yugoslavia; c. 4500 B.C.). H. 16 cm.

The chevron/bird/Bird Goddess association is well exemplified by figurines and vases with ornithomorphic features. Observe this intimate association on an Early Vinča vase from Anza in Macedonia: on the neck of the vessel are the beak and eyes of the Goddess; her cheeks are painted with the diagonal bands which seem to be her particular marking; the red-painted arms of a multiple chevron converge in the center of her "body" as symbolic adornment. (FIGURE 8) Another example is an ornithomorphic female figurine from the Lengyel culture, with beaked head, arm stumps (for wings), and a triple chevron as necklace. (FIGURE 9) Again, the seated duck-masked Late Vinča figurine from Svetozarevo, central Yugoslavia, wears an apron decorated with a triple chevron. (FIGURE 10)

This association-complex is common throughout the Bronze Age in the Mediterranean and Aegean areas. Graves of the Tarxien cremation cemetery (mid-3rd millennium B.C.) on the island of Malta yielded schematic figurines of birds with human legs, their flat, disc-shaped bodies incised on either side with a chevron or checkerboard motif, in striated and net-patterned bands; bi-lines, tri-lines, and multiple lines connect the chevrons or are incised over the legs and tail. (FIGURE 11) The large circular headdress of the beaked Lady from the Early Minoan period in Crete is painted with a triple chevron. A late Minoan beaked and winged Goddess or her dancing worshipper wears a flaring skirt which tapers to a V-shape in front. (FIGURE 12) Bronze Age vases from east-central Europe still occasionally feature the image of a beaked Goddess and her chevron. (FIGURE 13) And the Greek Geometric style is replete with birds in association with vertical or horizontal panels of chevrons. The chevron can also be seen on tiny bird figurines perched on the handles of other vases of the same period. (FIGURE 14)

FIGURE 11

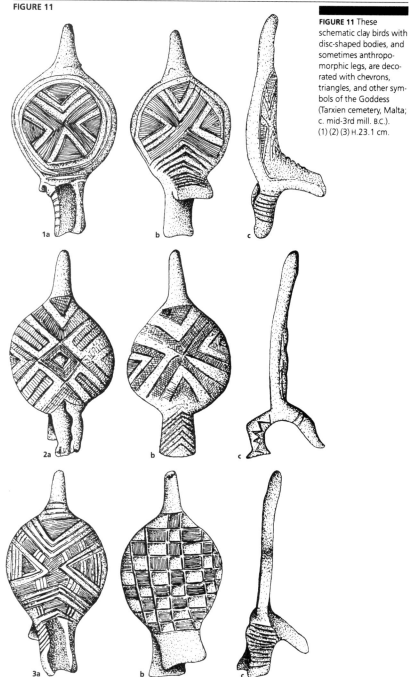

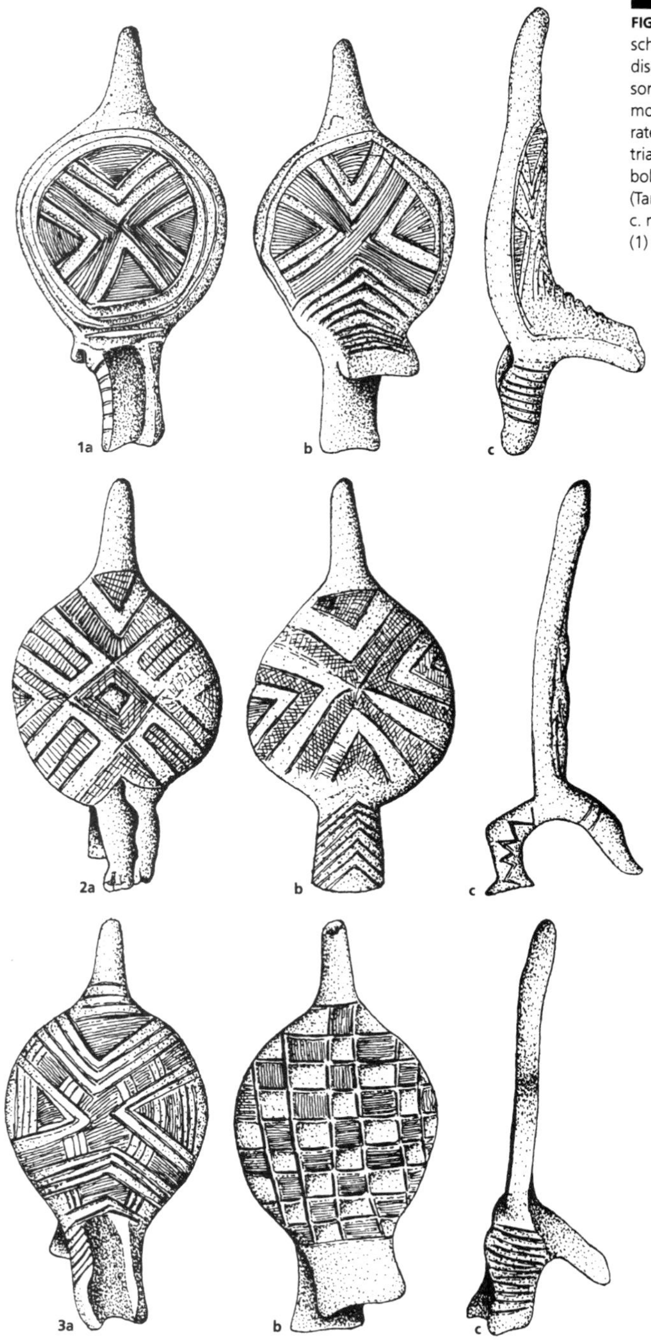

FIGURE 11 These schematic clay birds with disc-shaped bodies, and sometimes anthropomorphic legs, are decorated with chevrons, triangles, and other symbols of the Goddess (Tarxien cemetery, Malta; c. mid-3rd mill. B.C.). (1) (2) (3) H.23.1 cm.

FIGURE 12

FIGURE 12 Bronze Age Bird Goddess images from Crete. (1) Her crown bears a triple chevron; she is marked with a triangle on her forehead and a tri-line on her arm. She has the beak and large eyes typical of this Goddess (Gournes, Crete; Early Minoan). (2) On a lentoid seal of black marble, this dancing winged and beaked Goddess or her worshipper wears a skirt that tapers to a V-shape at the hem (Late Minoan III). (1) H. 8.2 cm. (2) H. 1.7 cm.

FIGURE 13

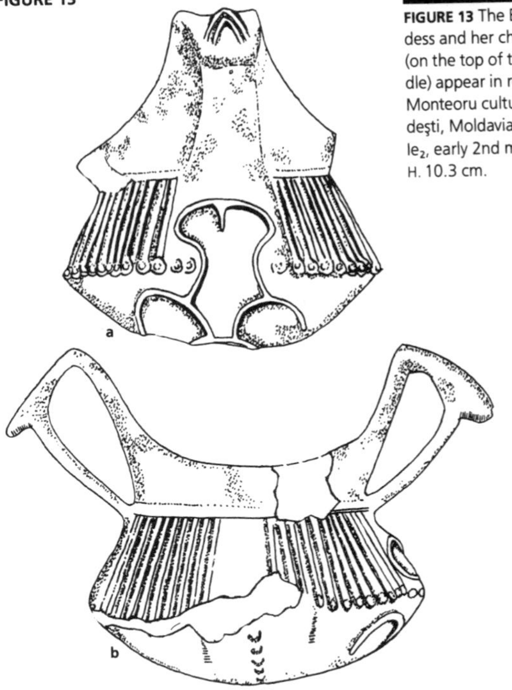

FIGURE 13 The Bird Goddess and her chevron (on the top of the handle) appear in relief. Monteoru culture (Cindeşti, Moldavia; Phase Ie$_2$, early 2nd mill. B.C.). H. 10.3 cm.

FIGURE 14

FIGURE 14 Still later, in the Iron Age, a common motif of the Greek geometric style remains the combination of birds and chevrons. Examples: (1) skyphos (Kameiros, Rhodes; 8th century B.C.) and (2) panel from an amphora (Attica, 8th century B.C.). (1) H. 10.5 cm. (2) H. 2.5 cm.

FIGURE 15

FIGURE 15 The body of this black and white encrusted violin-shaped terracotta is marked with chevrons on both sides, a zig-zag around the waist, an inverted V with a dash on the chest, and a double V at the tip of the head. Eyes are marked with two lines. Early Bronze Age II Anatolia (Çaykenar type, SW Anatolia; early 3rd mill. B.C.). H. 9.1 cm.

1.4 *The chevron on schematic figurines, seals, and cult vessels*

The symbolic character of these signs is best discerned on cult objects lacking other decorative treatment to distract the eye. Such objects include highly schematized figurines, seals, miniature vessels or lamps, and spindle whorls. The motifs most frequently applied to figurines are the chevron and the "cross-band" or X, formed by two V's touching at the apex. They commonly appear in association with the meander and two or three dashes, bands, or groups of parallel lines. (FIGURES 15, 16)

FIGURE 16

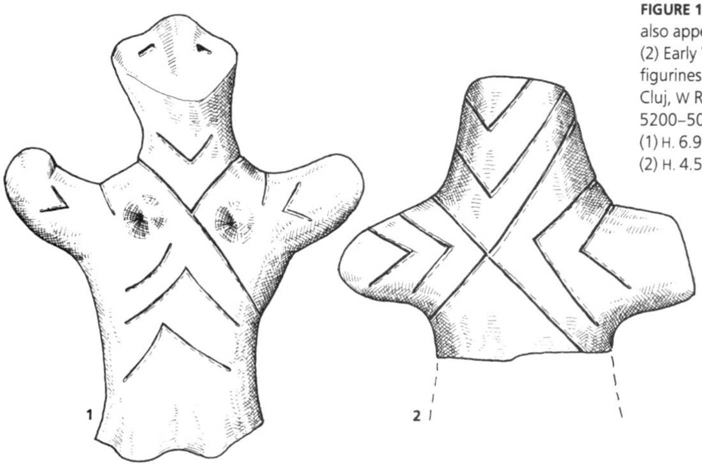

FIGURE 16 V's and X's also appear on (1) and (2) Early Vinča masked figurines (Turdaş, near Cluj, W Romania; 5200–5000 B.C.).
(1) H. 6.9 cm.
(2) H. 4.5 cm.

FIGURE 17

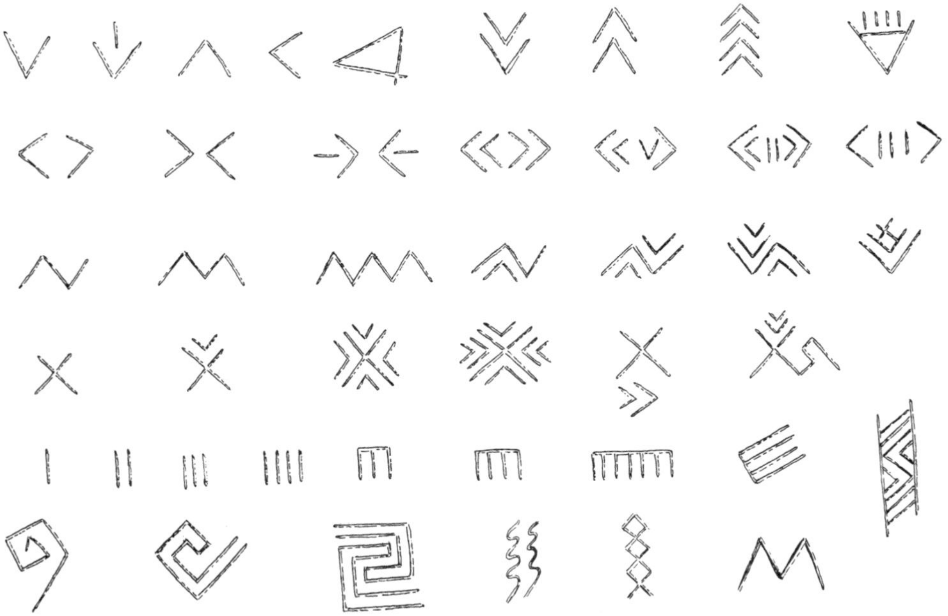

FIGURE 17 This is a set of symbols compiled from the markings on hundreds of Bird Goddess figurines and related cult objects from the Vinča culture (5200–4000 B.C.).

The catalog of signs identified on hundreds of figurines with ornithomorphic features from the Cucuteni, Karanovo, Tisza, Bükk, and Vinča cultures is as follows: simple V or chevron; juxtaposed V's; continuous V's; cross-band; dashes within the V; tri-lines; three or four lines connected by a dash, above the V or in isolation; meander; and M. Investigation of the full repertory of the "chevron family" of symbols leads to the following observations. (FIGURE 17)

1. The V or chevron and the X can appear alone or in combination (e.g., chevron between the arms of the cross-band). In isolation, the chevron and the cross-band seem to serve a closely related purpose, marking the object as belonging to the Deity. Their use in combination (chevrons above cross-bands or between the bands) may have the force of a customary blessing or invocational epithet.

2. The intimate relation of the V and X with the meander can be seen on many figurines and ritual vases. (FIGURE 18) Frequently, the meander is an extension of a

FIGURE 18

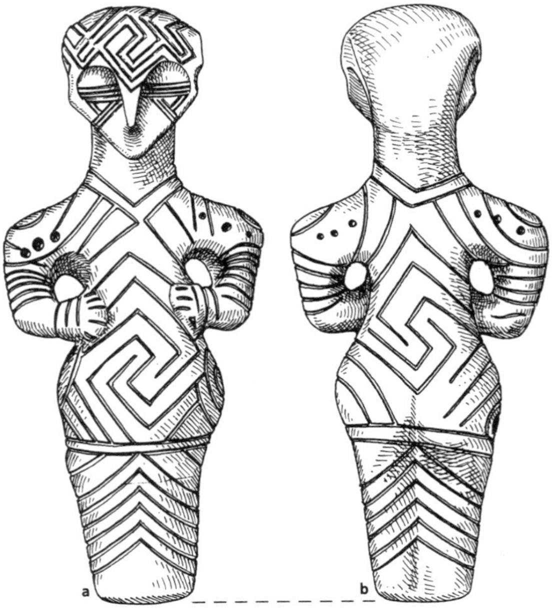

FIGURE 18 On this Vinča figurine, the meander is on the front and back while chevrons appear over the shoulders and legs. The masked head is reconstructed on the basis of related figurines and designs (see fig. 90). (Potporanj near Vršac, N Yugoslavia; c. 4500 B.C.)

FIGURE 19

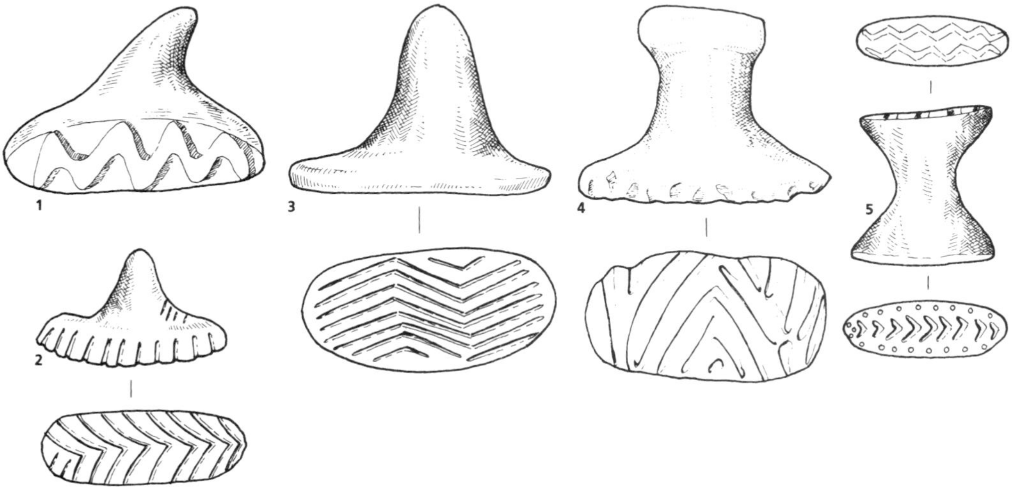

FIGURE 19 Neolithic stamp seals. (1) and (4) Early Sesklo (Nea Nikomedeia, Macedonia; 6300–6200 B.C.); (2) Starčevo (Anza; 5600–5400 B.C.); (3) Karanovo (Čevdar, Bulgaria; early 6th mill. B.C.); (5) Körös group of the Starčevo culture (Kopancs, SE Hungary; 5400–5300 B.C.); (6) Starčevo (Slatina, W Bulgaria; mid-6th mill. B.C.). (1) H. 3 cm. (2) H. 1.9 cm. (3) H. 3 cm. (4) H. 3.1 cm. (5) H. 2.6 cm.

V or cross-band. When not so attached, it seems to alternate as a symbol with the chevron.

3. Other frequent combinations are a single or double dash and three or four parallel lines within or above a V flanked by chevrons. The combination of several signs probably expresses a more complex meaning than the V alone.

The earliest known use of V's, chevrons, and the chevron and cross-band in a purely conceptual manner occurs on seals dating from the Early Neolithic (7th millennium B.C.); it continues throughout the duration of Old Europe and beyond. Neolithic seals—round, oval, or rectangular—were of the stamp type with opposed handle. (FIGURE 19) (Cylindrical seals came into use during the 5th millennium B.C.) One common motif is an X sign with multiple chevrons between the cross-arms. (FIGURE 20) Other popular designs are connected V's (zig-zags), parallel lines of zig-zags, and V's alternating with X's. The continued use of these signs into the Bronze Age is evidenced by Minoan seals from Knossos

FIGURE 20

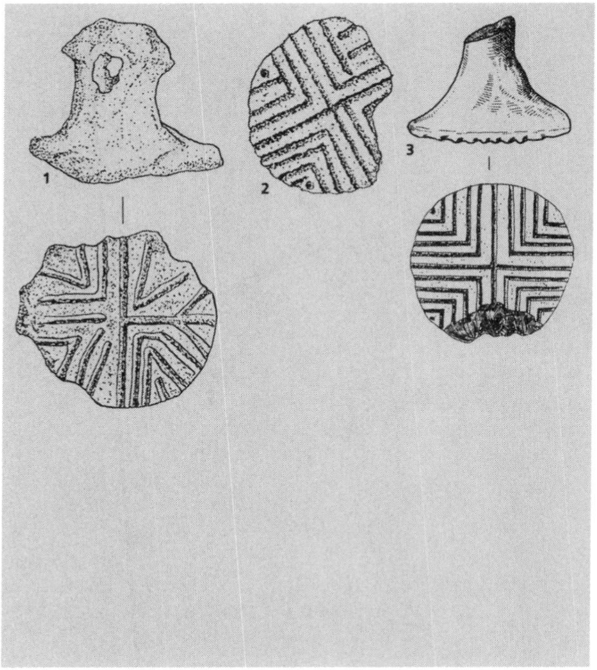

FIGURE 20 Such combinations of signs as an X with multiple chevrons undoubtedly conveyed a more complex meaning than did a single sign. Examples: (1) Sesklo (Sesklo; c. 6000 B.C.). (2) Cucuteni (Cucuteni, Moldavia, Romania; 44th and 43rd cents. B.C.). (3) Coţofeni (Coţofeni, S Romania; 3400–3200 B.C.). (1) DIA. 4 cm. (2) DIA. 3.5 cm. (3) DIA. 3.3 cm.

FIGURE 21

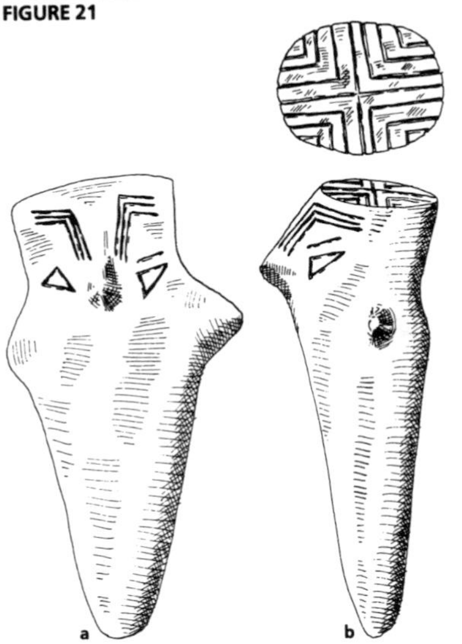

FIGURE 23

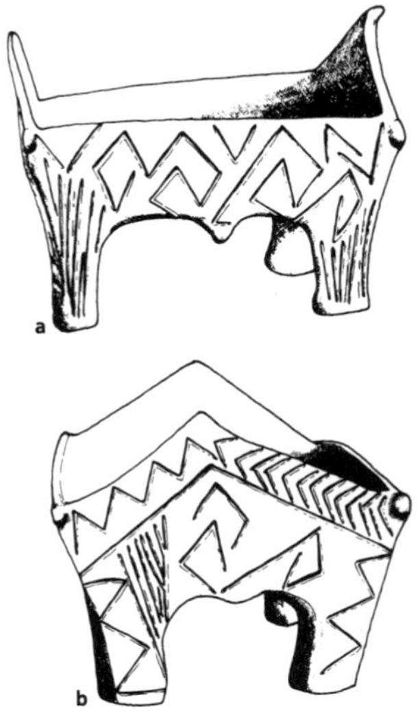

FIGURE 21 The X with chevrons between the arms is also found in the crowns of schematic ornithomorphic figurines. This classical Vinča example was found in a clay silo filled with wheat (Medvednjak, at Smederevska Palanka, central Yugoslavia; 5000–early 5th mill. B.C.). H. 6.2 cm.

FIGURE 23 Another religious object is this four-legged terracotta vessel of fine reddish-brown fabric incised with V's, interconnected V's, and parallel lines. Neolithic Macedonia (Vršnik, near Štip; c. 5500 B.C.). H. 15 cm.

FIGURE 22

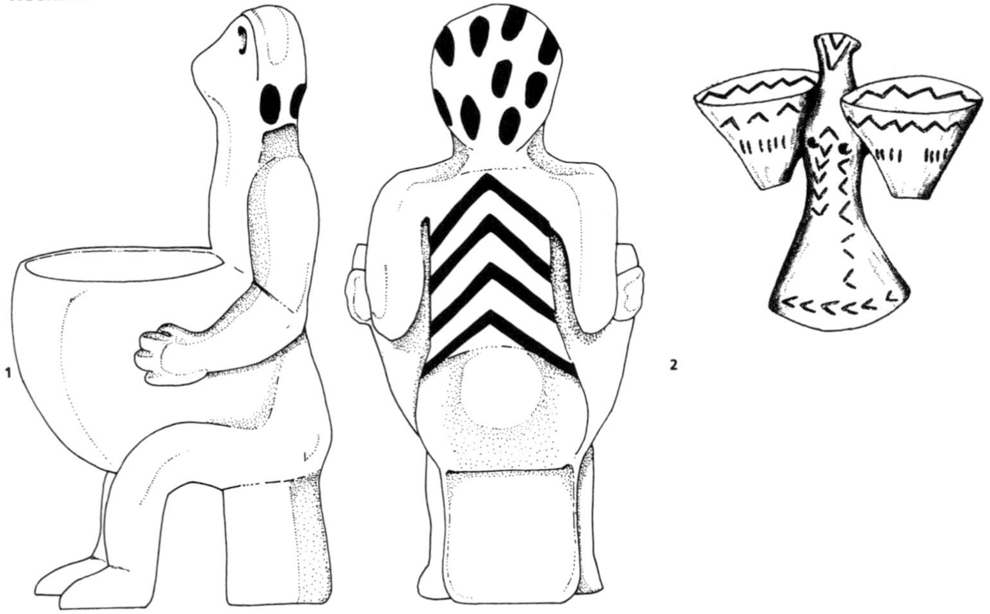

FIGURE 22 (1) This Neolithic seated figure holding a vessel (shown in reconstruction) is marked with chevrons on the back. Early Linear Pottery culture (Gaukönigshofen, R. Main Valley, Würzburg, Germany; 5500–5200 B.C.). (2) This probable Goddess worshipper marked with V's over the body and a chevron over the forehead carries two vessels which are also marked with V's, zigzags, and groups of parallel lines (Pyrgos, early Pre-Palatial Crete; early 3rd mill. B.C.).
(1) H. 13 cm.
(2) H. 6 cm.

and elsewhere. The X with chevrons between the cross-arms is also encountered on the caps and crowns of figurines. (FIGURE 21)

Symbols of the V and chevron family appear on a wide variety of cult vessels: basinlike containers supported by four legs, ladles, zoomorphic and anthropomorphic lamps or vases, and miniature pots. (FIGURES 22, 23) Their presence supports the theory that these objects were ritual vessels of the Bird Goddess.

1.5 *Chevrons and V's composing the arms and legs of the Goddess*

This peculiar representation of the Divinity as composed of her signs began in the Upper Paleolithic, and it continued through the millennia. Triangular signs and the so-called "barbed signs" engraved on Upper Paleolithic objects, considered by Leroi-Gourhan to be "male signs" (see Leroi-Gourhan 1967: Chart XXXIII, B), may have no male connotation at all, but rather constitute early manifestations of this configuration, i.e., an abstract rendering of the Divinity by her sacred signs.

I believe the same to be true of the so-called "tectiform" signs: one, two, or three vertical lines roofed by a chevron or an inverted V, often bearing V-shaped arms, and flanked by tri-lines or X's; they are known from the Magdalenian Font de Gaume, Les Combarelles, and Bernifal caves in association with female bison, mare, and mammoth figures. These tectiform signs are also probably abstract renderings of the Goddess. (FIGURE 24)

So-called "darts" (Y signs) engraved across bird-shaped figures (see Les Eyzies bone engravings in Marshack 1972: 202–206) also probably have nothing to do with darts but are a particular modification of the V, sacred sign of the Goddess.

Mesolithic Maglemosian engravings on bone objects from northern Germany and Zealand, Denmark, of stick figures

FIGURE 24

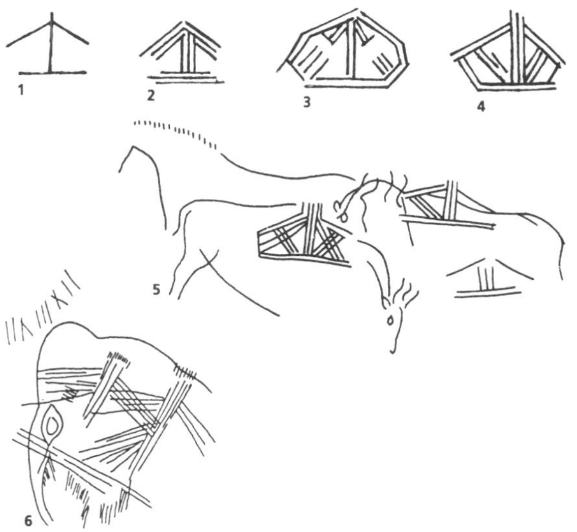

FIGURE 24 Portrayal of the Goddess as composed of her signs, or the substitution of symbols for her life- or birth-giving body parts, probably dates back to the Upper Paleolithic. The examples are painted in Magdalenian caves of Southern France ((1) and (3) through (5) Font-de-Gaume; (2) and (6) Bernifal; 15,000–13,000 B.C.).

FIGURE 25

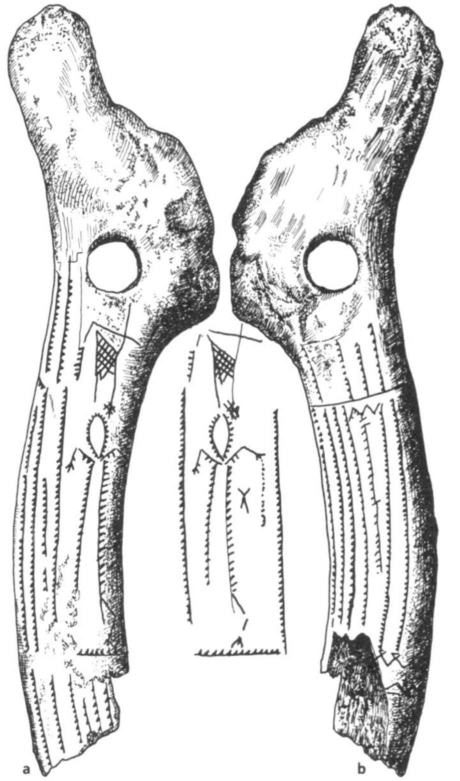

FIGURE 25 This convention continues in the Mesolithic, as in the figure engraved on this perforated elk's antler (shaft straightener). The figure's body is composed of barbed lines; it has V-shaped arms and the hands are bird's feet. It is surrounded by barbed parallel lines with zigzag top and bottom. Note that a net-patterned triangle is engraved above the figure and an X at the side (Podejuch, Szczecin area, N Poland; Mesolithic). H. 33.8 cm.

FIGURE 26

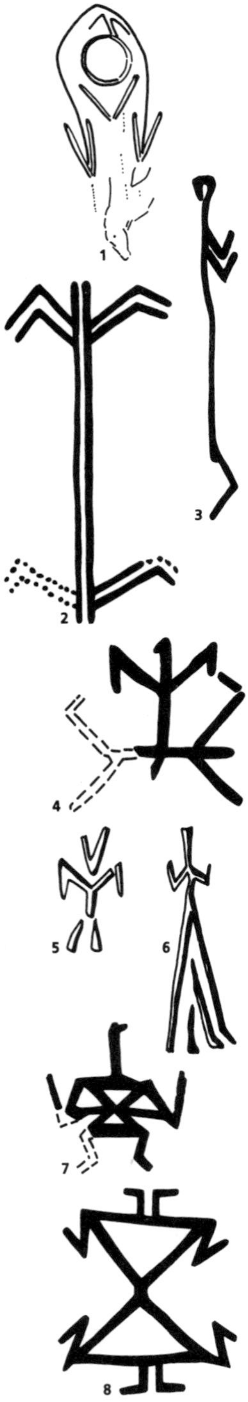

FIGURE 27

FIGURE 26 From the Upper Paleolithic into the Neolithic, Bronze Age, and Iron Age, stick figures with V-shaped limbs appear on bone, stone, and ceramics. Examples: (1) Upper Paleolithic engraving on bone (Schweizersbild, Kanton Schaffhausen, Switzerland; probably Magdalenian). (2) and (3) Engravings on bone from the Maglemose culture in Denmark (Koge Sonakke and Stensby, Zealand; Mesolithic). (4) Figure engraved on the interior of a vase from the Linear Pottery culture (Prohlis at Dresden, E Germany; c. 5000 B.C.). (5) and (6) Two figures engraved on earliest Cucuteni ("Pre-Cucuteni") vases in NE Romania (Traian-Dealul-Viei Moldavia; early 5th mill. B.C.). (7) Figure painted on the interior of an Early Minoan dish; note it has a bird head (Crete). (8) Figure painted on a Daunian dish (Siponto, SE Italy; 6th to 5th cents. B.C.). (1) H. 3.95 cm. (2) H. 5.3 cm. (3) H. 5.3 cm. (4) H. 2.7 cm. (5) H. 4 cm. (6) 7.2 cm. (7) H. 4.8 cm. (8) H. 6.6 cm.

FIGURE 27 The Goddess with one arm raised and one pointing down; the hands and legs are V's. This large vase is decorated with applied symbols: two such figures, zig-zags of various kinds, and bumps. The vase was found in the wall of a house. Starčevo, Körös group (Szajol-Felsőföld, SE Hungary; 5500–5400 B.C.). H. 71.6 cm.

FIGURE 28

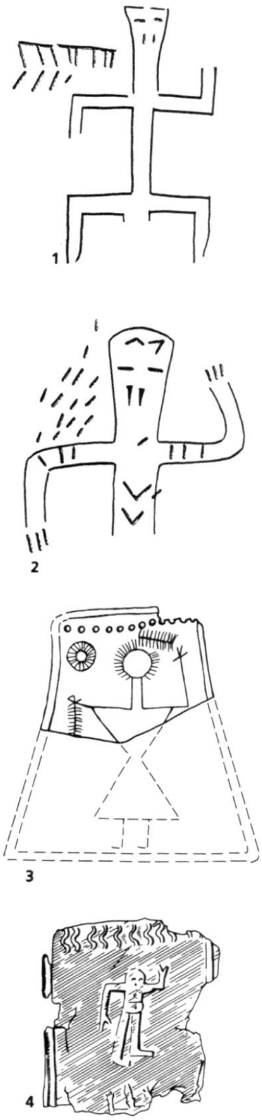

FIGURE 28 Schematic representations of figures with one arm raised and one pointing down appear in many areas of Europe on Neolithic and later pottery and plaques. Such figures emerge also as late as last centuries B.C. (1) Engraved on Karanovo I vases. They have two vertical lines for mouths; (2) is marked with V's and tri-lines and has three fingers. Karanovo culture (Azmak, near Stara Zagora, central Bulgaria; c. 5800 B.C.). (3) This figure with bird's claws for hands, with branches attached to the head and to the arm, and head radiating like the sun suggests that the gesture symbolizes regeneration and the Goddess who promotes or imparts it is Bird Goddess. In addition, the sun or eye symbol is shown next to the head. Ozieri culture, Sardinia (Conca Illònis; c. 4000–3800 B.C. (4) Similar figure with V-shaped hands engraved on a bronze plaque. Note there is a row of snakes above it and a frog-shaped figure below. Venedian culture (Cracow-Plaszow, S Poland; Late La Tène, last cents. B.C. Height of the figure 3 cm).
(1) H. 7.7 cm. (2) H. 7 cm. (3) H. 11.3 cm. (4) H. 6 cm.

with V-shaped limbs, and anthropomorphic stick figures with V or chevron arms and legs in Neolithic and later vase decoration, are also probably part of this tradition. (FIGURES 25, 26) Representations closely related to the Mesolithic figures are encountered on Central European Linear Pottery vases of c. 5000 B.C.

And in the Mediterranean region such peculiarly geometricized figures are known from the Minoan, Mycenaean, Cycladic, and Yortan (western Anatolia) cultures of the 3rd and 2nd millennia. During the Iron Age, they occur frequently in southern Italy on Daunian vases and inside flat dishes whose handles are winged figures.

In addition to the bisymmetric stick figure, another posture portrays the Divinity with one arm up and the other down; hands and legs are again depicted as V's. (FIGURE 27) Such representations in relief, centrally placed on large vases, are known from the earliest Neolithic levels of southeastern Hungary and central Bulgaria. On the Körös vase from the Tisza valley, Hungary, the figure is flanked by zig-zag bands. The Karanovo figures have two vertical lines for mouths and are marked with V's and tri-lines. Engraved or in relief on large vases, such figures reappear in various phases of the Karanovo, Starčevo-Körös, Vinča, and Tisza cultures. (FIGURE 28) The peculiar posture and associated symbols obviously indicate some function of the vessel, perhaps associated with regeneration ritual. In the later Neolithic of Sardinia such figures engraved on clay plaques appear in connection with eyes, suns, and branches. (FIGURE 28, 3) This grouping of symbols suggests that the gesture is very likely a sign of regeneration. Further, please note, the hands of the figure are not human; they are bird feet. Hence the divinity portrayed is the Bird Goddess in the Bird of Prey aspect among whose functions was the regeneration of life. Figures with one arm up and the other down continued to appear on vases and bronze plaques throughout the Bronze and Iron ages (see the engraving on a bronze plaque from the Iron Age in Poland). (FIGURE 28, 4)

Triangles and M signs below the breasts on masked figurine; from S Italy. See figure 36, page 23.

2/ *Zig-zag and M Sign*

2.1 *Zig-zag, the image of water*

In the iconography of all prehistoric periods of Europe as well as of the whole world, the image of water is zig-zag or serpentine. The zig-zag is the earliest symbolic motif recorded: Neanderthals used this sign around 40,000 B.C., or earlier. In the early 1970s, J. Kozlowski found at the Mousterian site of Bacho Kiro in Bulgaria a nonutilitarian fragment of bone that had been engraved with a zig-zag motif. Examining it under a microscope, Marshack found that when the marker came to the end of the engraved line in the zig-zag, he or she did not lift the tool to make a joining line in the other direction, but left it on the bone and turned and twisted that instead. It is clear that the engraving is an intentional zig-zag image (Marshack 1976: 139).

In the Upper Paleolithic, the zig-zag is a common motif and appears in association with anthropomorphic, bird, fish, and phallic images. At the site of Cro-Magnon in Les Eyzies, southern France, a reindeer rib dated to c. 30,000 B.C. (Aurignacian period) was excavated. Engraved on the rib was a crude anthropomorph with birdlike head overmarked with an M and a zig-zag motif. (FIGURE 29) If the head of the figure is of a waterbird, it represents the earliest human/waterbird hybrid marked with a symbol of water, a generative force.

The zig-zag alternates with the M sign, an abbreviated zig-zag. In Magdalenian times and later in Old Europe, zig-zags and M's are found engraved or painted within uterine and lens (vulva) shapes, suggesting the symbolic affinity between the zig-zag, M, female moisture, and amniotic fluid. (FIGURE 30)

2.2 *Single and multiple M's on vases*

The M alone, or in duplicate or triplicate, is frequently the central ornament on vases during the 6th and later millennia in Old Europe. The illustrated examples are from the end of the 6th and 5th millennium: the Linear Pottery culture of Central Europe, the Szakálhát group of Hungary, the Cortaillod culture of Switzerland and Late Neolithic Greece. (FIGURE 31) The sign also appears on Neolithic ceramics of the Near East; in Egypt, dishes of the Naquade I period are decorated with the M sign in association with chevrons.

Placement of the M varies. Sometimes it is the sole decoration of a vessel, sometimes engraved above or below the handles, and sometimes confined within a triangular, square, or lens-shaped panel. Dotted or discontinuous lines occasionally decorate the sign, as on the M engraved on the zoomorphic vessel from Battonya, lower Tisza basin.

The aquatic significance of the M sign seems to have survived in the Egyptian hieroglyph 𓈖, *mu*, meaning water, and in the ancient Greek letter M, *mu*.

FIGURE 29 Engraved reindeer rib. Aurignacian (site of Cro-Magnon at Les Eyzies, S France; rib dated to c. 30,000 B.C.). L. 5.8 cm.

FIGURE 30

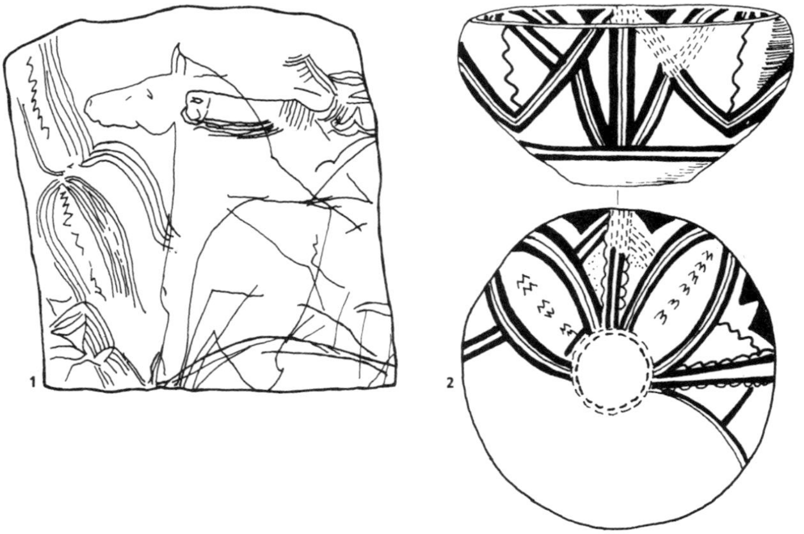

1

2

FIGURE 30 From Upper Paleolithic engravings to the vase painting for the first phases of the Cucuteni culture, the M or extended M sign appear within uterine or vulvar shapes. (1) Early Magdalenian (El Parpalló, Valencia, Spain; 15,000–13,000 B.C.). (2) Final Cucuteni (Vykhvatintsi, Soviet Moldavia; c. 3500 B.C.). (1) H. 7.5 cm. (2) DIA. 16.4 cm.

FIGURE 31

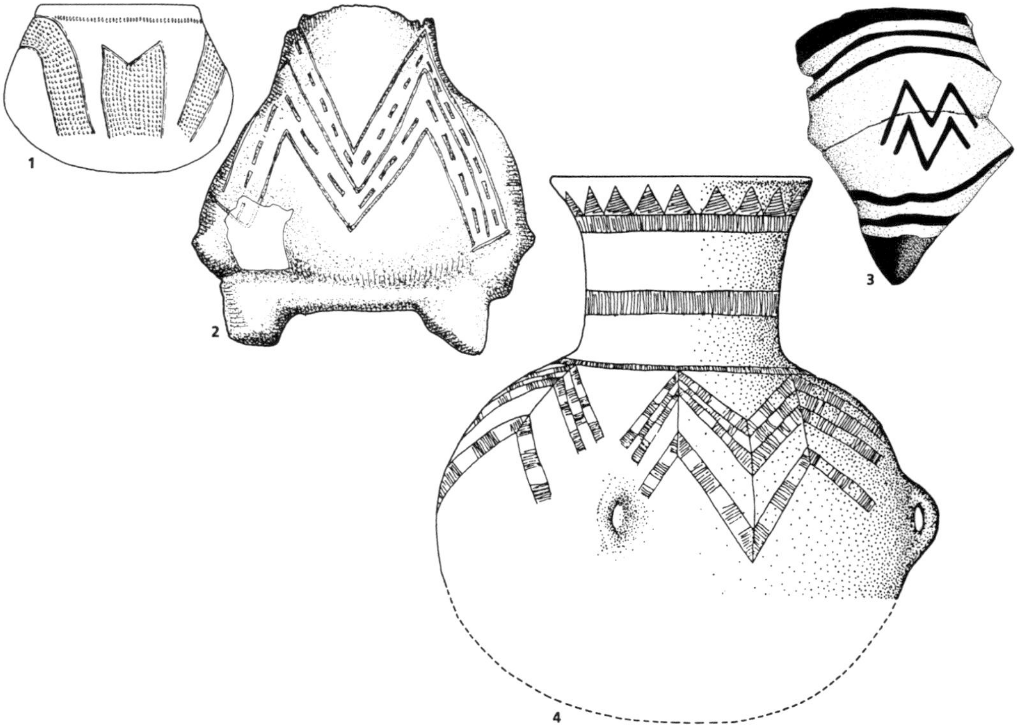

1

2

3

4

FIGURE 31 The M symbol is related to water and the Goddess in her life-giving function. It is often incised or painted as the primary decoration on vases. Examples: (1) M filled with dots and flanked by dotted water streams from the Linear Pottery culture (Elsloo, SE Holland; 5300–5100 B.C.). (2) Double M engraved in front of an askos. Tisza (Battonya, SE Hungary; 5200–5000 B.C.). (3) Painted pottery fragment with a double M from late Neolithic Greece (Corinth, Peloponnese; approx. end 5th mill. B.C.). (4) Triple M incised on a Linear Pottery vase (Charmoy, NE France). (1) H. 8 cm. (2) H. 19.5 cm. (3) H. 9 cm. (4) H. 18 cm.

2.3 *M attached to a chevron or V*

A long-enduring sign in the Neolithic, Copper, and Early Bronze ages which decorates terracottas of the Danubian region and Balkans is the "gabled chevron" consisting of an M on top of an inverted chevron or V. (FIGURE 32) It is frequently found inside dishes or on pots, lids, pendants, loom weights, and plaques. Often the sign alternates with meanders, multiple chevrons, and three parallel lines. The configuration was used over a span of two millennia in all phases of every cultural group. The combination of the chevron and M suggests the intimate relation between these symbols.

FIGURE 32

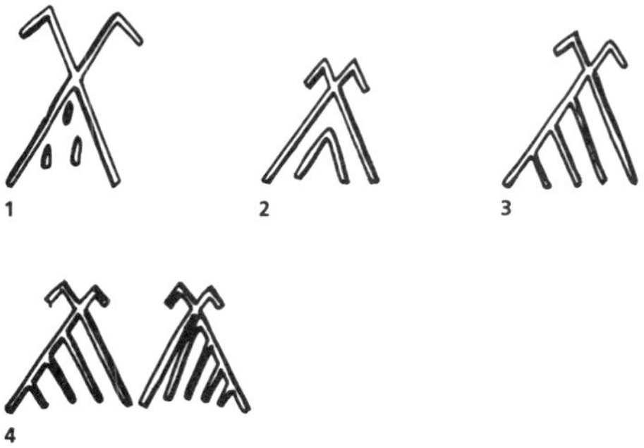

FIGURE 32 The "gabled chevron." Examples are from ceramics dated 5200–4000 B.C.. (1) Early Vinča (Vinča); (2) Tisza (Hódmesővásárhely, SE Hungary); (3) Linear Pottery culture (Prohlis, Germany); and (4) Tiszapolgár phase of the Polgár culture (Tiszarig, NE Hungary).

2.4 *Under the face of a deity*

The Starčevo and Tisza groups of southeastern Hungary and western Bulgaria, the Bükk culture in northeastern Hungary and Slovakia, and the early Vinča culture produced large vases—pithoi—on which a face above an M sign appears. The symbolic function of the M is indicated by its consistent position under the visage of the Deity. (FIGURES 33, 34) The Goddess's relationship to water is further emphasized by running spirals, meanders, framed nets and checkerboards, and stabbed designs with which the bodies of these vessels are covered. A Linear Pottery vase of the Želiezovce (Zseliz) complex at Budapest-Békasmegyer also bears the same motif. (FIGURE 35)

FIGURE 33

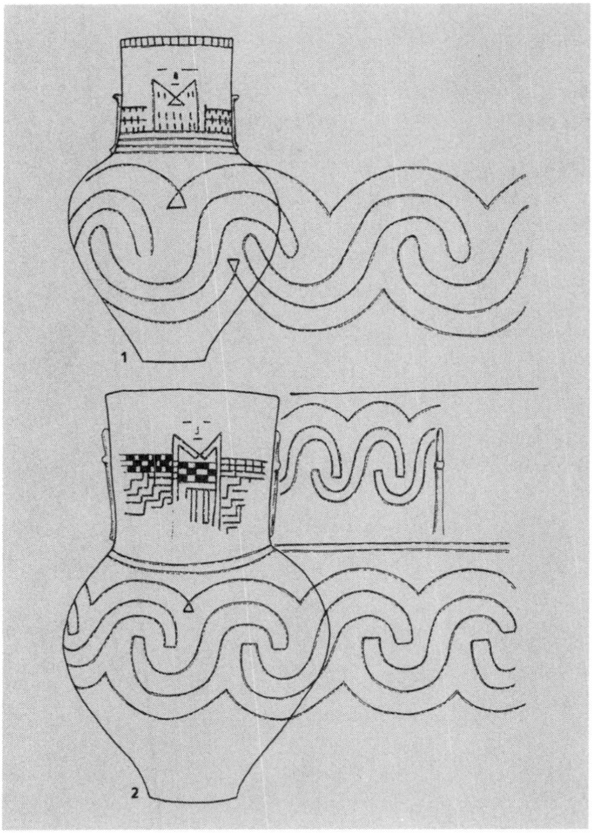

FIGURE 33 Several Old European cultures produced large vases, or pithoi, upon which the face of the Goddess floats above an M sign. The implication that these water containers are sacred to the Goddess who is the Source of moisture (and life) is reinforced by the presence of additional aquatic symbolism: meanders, large bands of running spirals, parallel and stabbed lines, and checkerboard patterns. (1) Tisza, Szakálhát group (Ilonapart, Szentes; SE Hungary, 5200–5000 B.C.). (2) Early Vinča (Vinča, 5200–5000 B.C.). (1) H. 41.7 cm. (2) H. 53 cm.

FIGURE 34

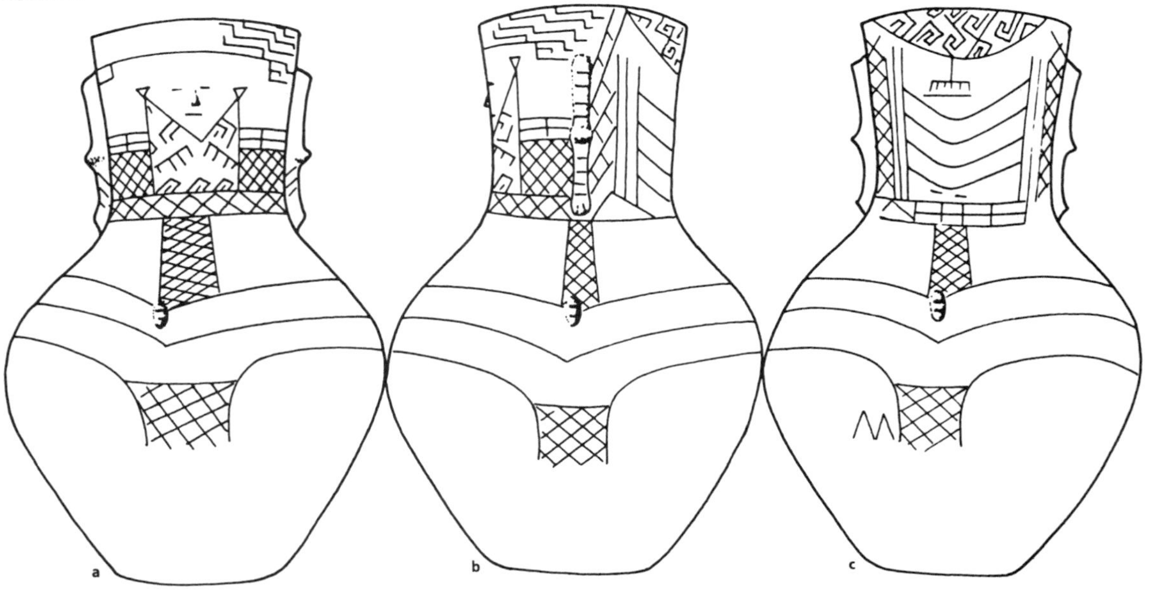

The conjunction of the M sign with the face of a divinity on large water containers is significant. Moreover, this divinity is associated with the design motifs which comprise Old European aquatic symbolism. This strengthens the implication that water containers were sacred to the Goddess, in whose power was the source of the water of life. The meaning of these symbolic associations is deepened when we consider that the M sign is also encountered below the Goddess's breast, the source of milk and universal nurture, as in the illustrated example from Passo di Corvo, a Neolithic settlement of southeastern Italy. (FIGURE 36)

FIGURE 35

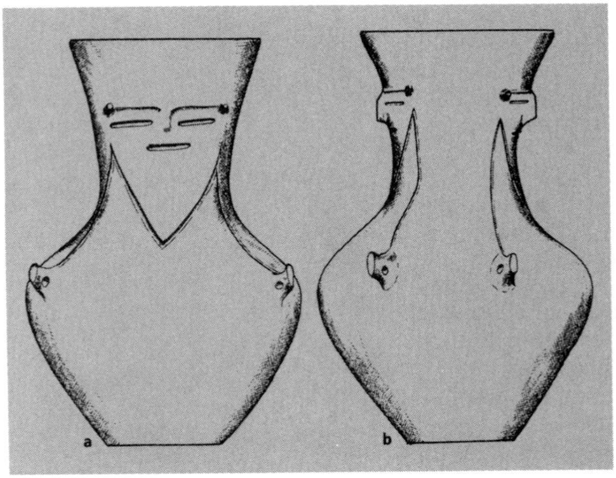

FIGURE 34 On this anthropomorphic pithos, the M is associated with "brush" signs, nets, and meanders. On a brick-red surface, the arms are painted in red and yellow and the belt around the body in white. Tisza, Szakálhát group (Battonya, SE Hungary; 5200–5000 B.C.). H. 40.1 cm.

FIGURE 35 This Linear Pottery vase represents a paired-down version of the Goddess face above an M motif. Želiezovce (Zseliz) complex (Békasmegyer, at Budapest, Hungary; c. 5000–4900 B.C.). H. 37.4 cm.

FIGURE 36

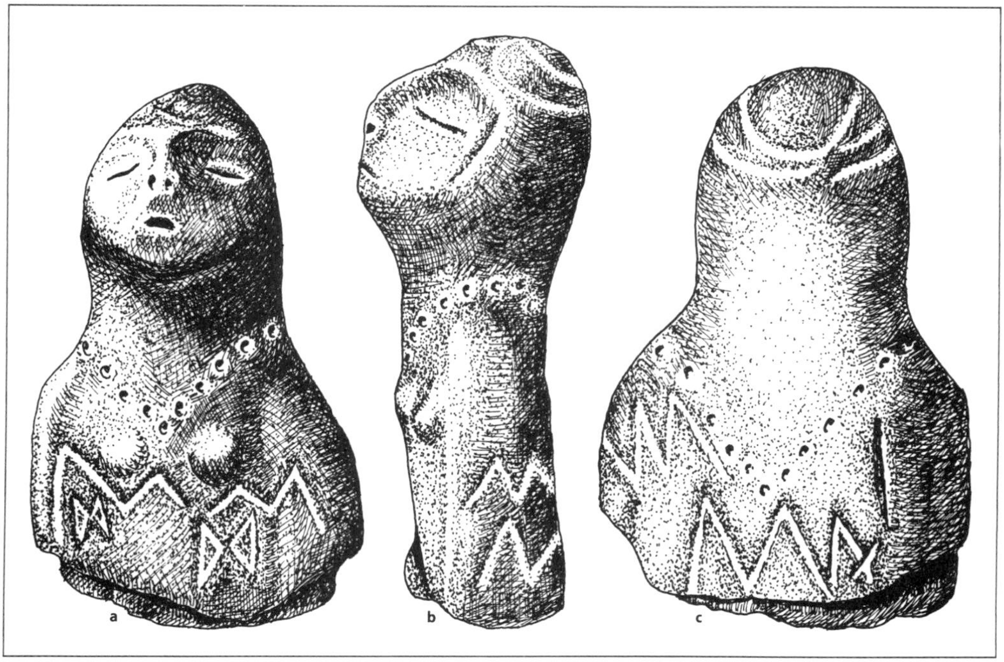

FIGURE 36 M signs also appear on figurines, particularly below the breasts, source of milk and nurture. This masked figurine also has M's on her back, and she wears a V-shaped necklace. Notice the butterflies, symbols of regeneration, beneath the M's. S Italian Neolithic (Passo di Corvo, near Foggia; c. 5300 B.C.). H. 6.5 cm.

Upper Paleolithic ivory figurine carved with meanders, the front marked with M's and a large pubic triangle (extended design). See figure 37, page 26.

3/ *Meander and Waterbirds*

3.1 *Its origin in the Upper Paleolithic and association with the waterbird*

The meandering snake and continuous meander first appeared in the art of the Upper Paleolithic. From the very beginning the meander was not used merely decoratively; it was a symbol, a metaphor for water. It is meaningfully associated with the chevron on ornithomorphic female figurines whose posteriors are engraved with meanders, while their fronts are marked with chevrons, M's, and a central triangle. (FIGURE 37) The ivory plaque from Mezin also includes both meander and chevron. (FIGURE 38) The symbolic connection between the two reflects the natural affinity between fowl and water, creature and habitat.

3.2 *On ducks and Bird Goddess sculptures*

The aqueous symbolic import of the meander is obvious when it occurs on figurines representing ducks or other birds, on an image of the Goddess wearing a bird mask, and on her temples. The meander design usually appears in association with the V or chevron (as in the Upper Paleolithic), on anthropomorphic bird sculptures, or on elaborate effigy vases of the Goddess. (FIGURE 39) Innumerable beaked and winged figurines are marked with meanders. (FIGURE 40) Significantly, temples and altar pieces of the Goddess are solidly covered with them, as on the clay temple model from Vădăstra, western Romania, c. 5200–5000 B.C. (FIGURE 41) Clearly, the realm of the Goddess is the mythic watery sphere.

The theme recurs in various culture groups and phases. An elaborate example is from the Tisza valley. The enthroned Goddess of Szegvár–Tüzköves is dressed in a "meander costume" decorated with panels of meandroid design, including several sets of ingeniously executed meander bands and squares complemented with bands of zig-zags. Her sign—a large V in relief—marks her throne. (FIGURE 42) Other finds at this very rich settlement included anthropomorphic vases with the face of the Divinity flanked by meanders on the neck; meandroid and zig-zag designs in a number of panels separated by tri-lines are engraved on the globular bodies.

The association of female images with meanders continued into the Iron Age, as at Siponto near Manfredonia, southeastern Italy, where Daunian stelae are usually decorated with panels of various meandroid designs (Nava 1980). A number of figurines with beaked faces from the Proto-Geometric and Geometric periods in Greece were decorated with panels of a meander design.

3.3 *On seals, spindle whorls, plaques, and ritual objects*

The meander, sometimes with a distinct snake head in the center, is known from the Neolithic and Copper Age excised on seals, spindle whorls, plaques, and cult objects; (FIGURE 43) it was also painted on vases as an individual sign amidst an all-over meander design. Cult vessels were frequently decorated with meanders over a striated or net-design background. Snake heads protruding from the corners were also marked with a meander, as on the illustrated example from Farcaşu de Sus in Romania. (FIGURE 44)

FIGURE 37

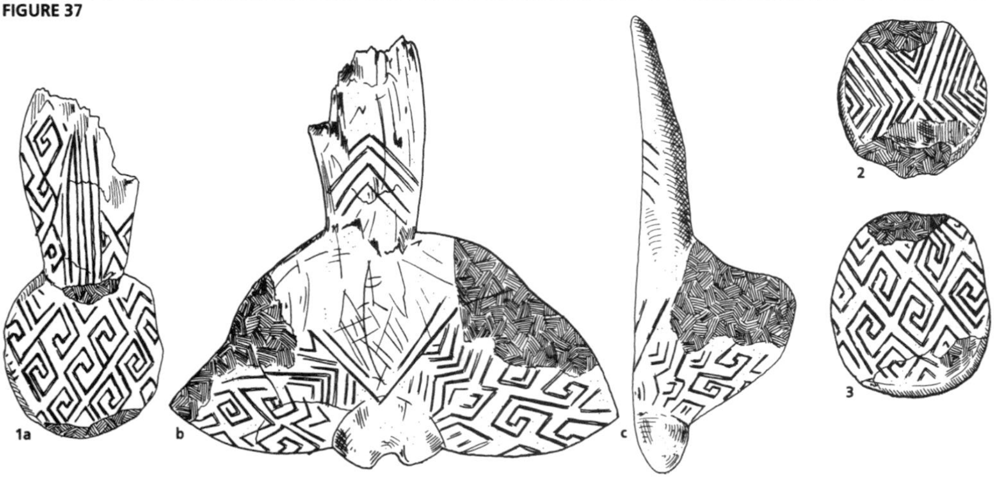

FIGURE 37 Like its sister symbol the V sign, the meander emerges in the Upper Paleolithic. From the first, it is associated with the Bird Goddess. (1) The posterior of this ornithomorphic ivory figurine is carved with meanders, while the front is marked with chevrons, M's, and a large pubic triangle. (2) and (3) Posteriors (back view) of two other figures (Mezin, on River Desna, W Ukraine; c. 18,000–15,000 B.C.). (1) H. 9.5 cm. (2) H. 10.5 cm. (3) H. 3.8 cm.

FIGURE 38

FIGURE 38 Chevron and meander are combined on this Upper Paleolithic ivory plaque. There are three perforations at the ends (Mezin; c. 18,000–15,000 B.C.). (2) L. 18 cm.

FIGURE 39

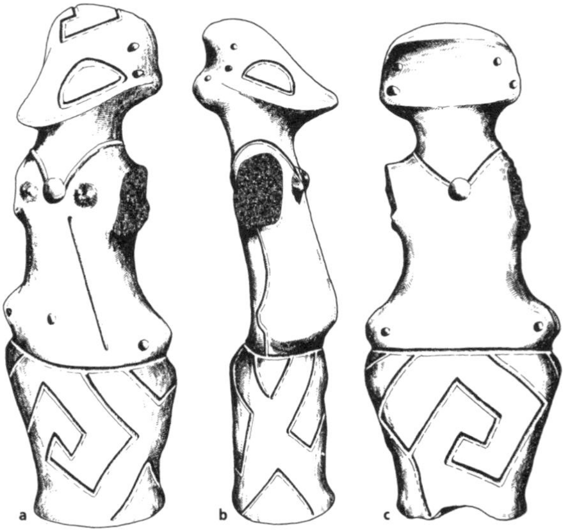

FIGURE 39 In the Neolithic and Copper Age, meanders mark Bird Goddess figurines like this terracotta duck-masked deity. Her skirt and the crown of her head bear white-encrusted meanders and V's; she is identified by her medallion on a V-shaped necklace. Late Vinča (Vinča; 4500 B.C.). H. 15.6 cm.

3.4 *As a decorative design motif on ceramics*

The meander design reached a peak of popularity during the Copper Age; meanders were incised or painted in rhythmic patterns on large vases and on the interior surface of dishes. The motif is particularly elaborate on Vinča, Lengyel, Petreşti, and Cucuteni ceramics. Symbolic use was distinguished by the customary framing, while variations of the basic design proliferated in bands over the neck and body of the vessel.

FIGURE 40

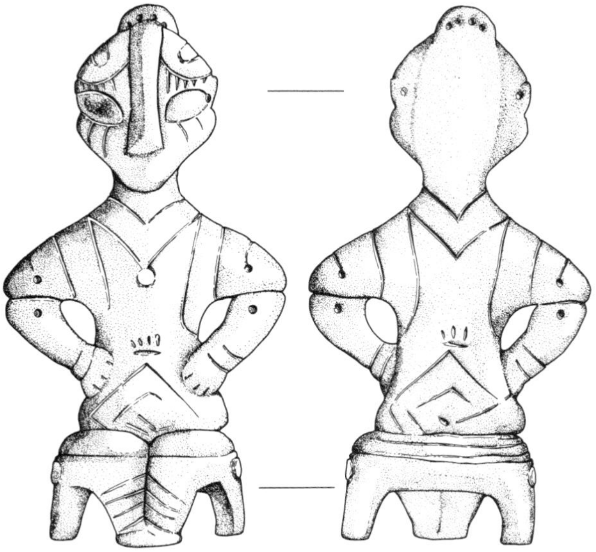

FIGURE 40 This Vinča figurine majestically sitting on a throne is marked with a meander, chevron, and brush in front and back. The medallion in front bespeaks her importance. Typically her mask has no mouth, but the nose is massive. Parallel lines above and below large almond-shaped eyes. Perforations are for attachments (not preserved). (Predionica near Priština, S Yugoslavia; Late Vinča, 4500 B.C.). H. 18.5 cm.

FIGURE 41

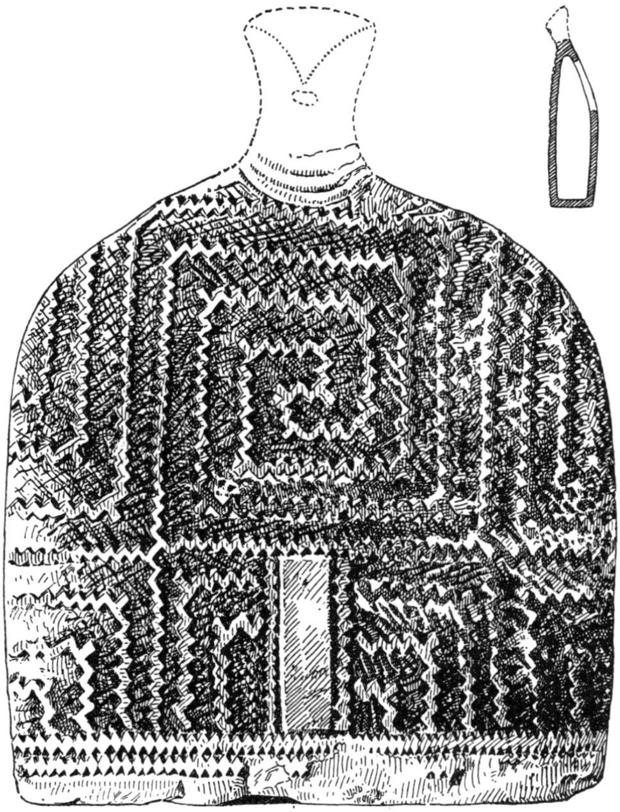

FIGURE 41 Temple models and altar pieces belonging to shrines of the Goddess are often solidly covered with meanders. This thought-provoking example depicts the Goddess's sphere as the watery realm, to which an entrance (at the bottom) has been provided. Vădăstra group of the Vinča culture (Vădăstra, SW Romania; c. 5200–5000 B.C.). H. 40 cm.

FIGURE 42

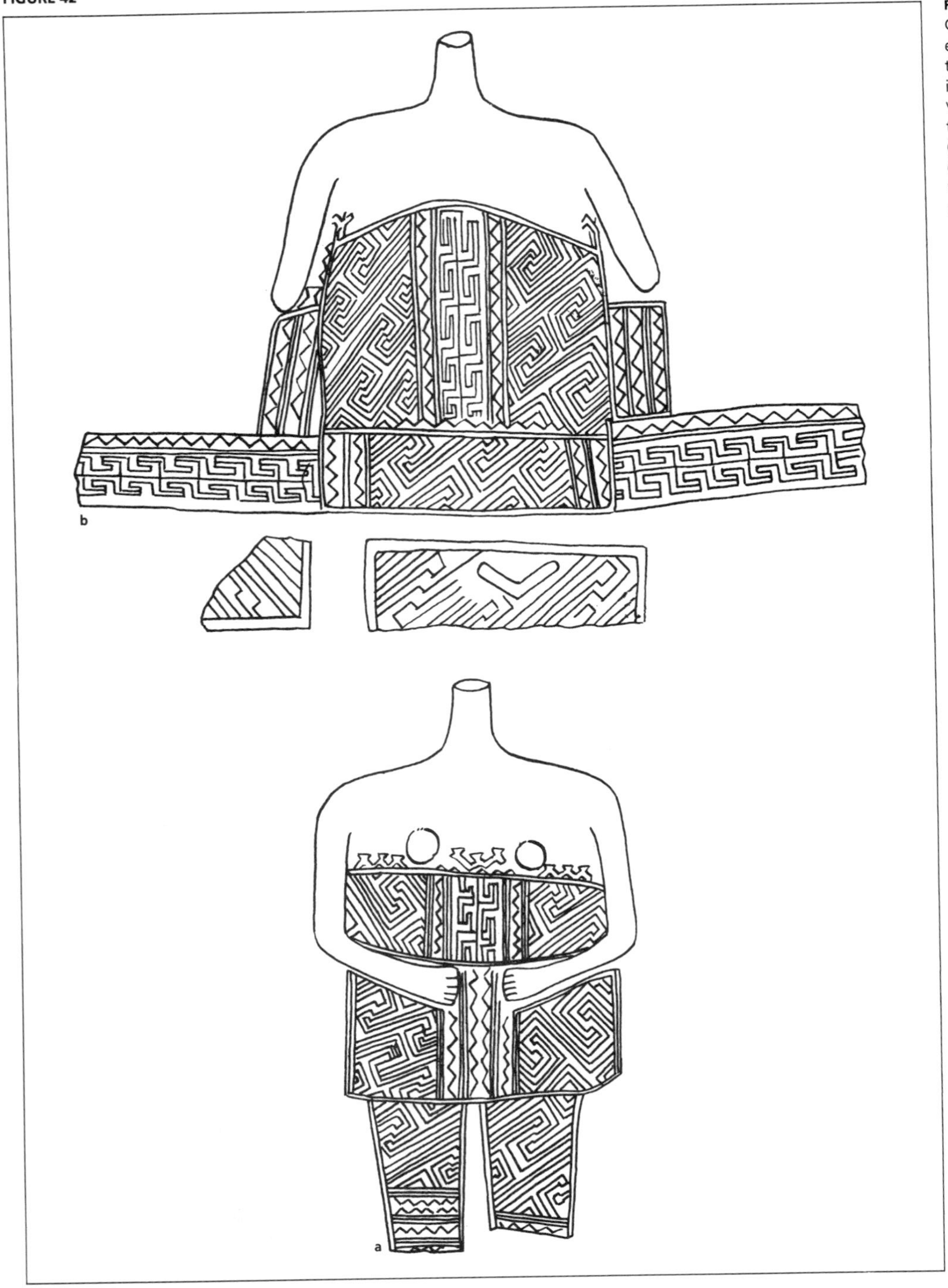

FIGURE 42 This enthroned Goddess wears an elaborate "meander costume" which is bordered in zig-zags (connected V's). Her identifying sign, the V, marks her throne (bottom panel). Tisza (Szegvár-Tüzköves at Szentes, SE Hungary; c. 5000 B.C. or earlier).

From the evidence examined above we deduce that the V, chevron, X, zig-zag, net, and meander, which appear on a large repertory of artifacts—seals, sacrificial containers, anthropomorphic vases, plaques, spindle whorls, loom-weights, altars, temple models, schematic figurines, articulated statuettes, etc.—are associated with the Bird Goddess or with the bird as her epiphany. Many objects on which these signs and symbols were engraved or painted served in her cult. V and X are her signs. Nets, meanders, and running snake/spiral bands (especially on water containers) link her with the cosmic waters which are her element. Greek Athena's name itself refers to a containing receptacle, a vessel (Kerényi 1978: 29).

The Bird Goddess was the Source and Dispenser of life-giving moisture, an early and enduring human preoccupation. As a waterbird, she united heaven and earth, and her terrestrial home was probably believed to be mirrored by a celestial watery realm. This cosmology also had a temporal component related to her annual migration. The new beginnings of life in the spring were heralded by her reappearance in Europe, and the long quiescent season by her departure.

Further discussion will deal with the significance of specific parts of the Goddess's body in her capacity as Source: the breasts, mouth, and eyes.

FIGURE 43

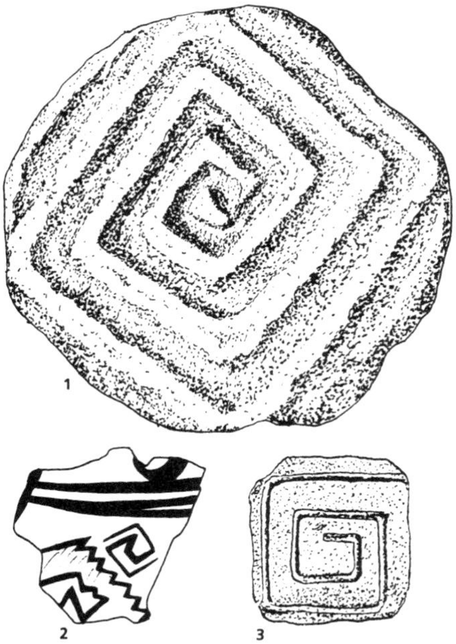

FIGURE 43 Like the symbols of the chevron family, meanders also appear on seals and as individual signs on ceramics. In this context, they probably function as conceptual markers or designators, part of the Old European symbolic language. Examples: (1) Körös seal (Kotacpart-Vatatanya, at Hódmesővásárhely; c. 5500 B.C.). (2) Red-painted meander on a Dimini vase (Gonia, Greece; c. 5000 B.C.). (3) Cucuteni seal (Frumuşica, Moldavia, Romania; 4500–4300 B.C.). (1) DIA. 7 cm. (2) H. 3 cm. (3) DIA. 3 cm.

FIGURE 44 Triangular ritual vessel decorated with a white-encrusted meander pattern over a net-design background and over snake protomes at the corners. Dudeşti variant of the Vinča culture (Farcaşu de Sus, SW Romania; early 5th mill. B.C.). H. 13.1 cm.

FIGURE 44

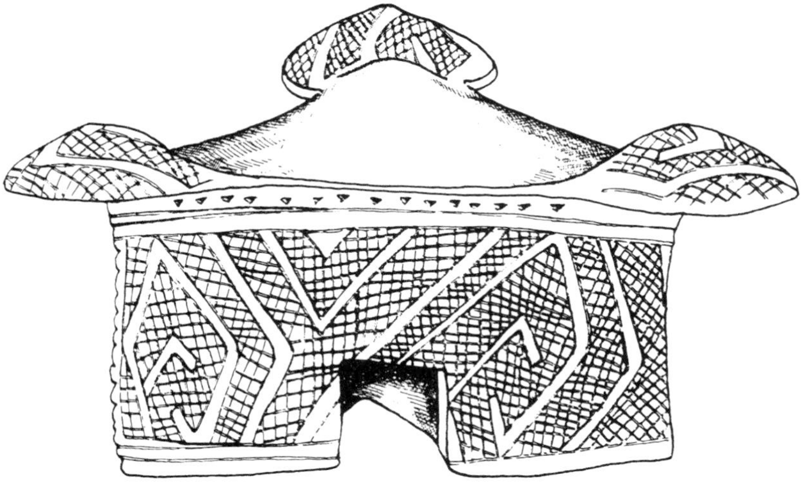

''Lady of Sé'' from the Lengyel culture, with elegant torso and well-molded breasts. See figure 54, page 34.

4/ *Breasts of the Bird Goddess*

4.1 *Upper Paleolithic figurines with breasts and breast-shaped pendants*

The image of a bird-masked female with large hanging breasts emerges in the Upper Paleolithic. Famous examples are the beaked "Venuses" of the Magdalenian culture. (FIGURE 45) These finger-painted figures have artfully delineated female bodies with pendulous breasts and wings instead of arms; some figures have a bird-like head or mask.

The use of chevrons and parallel lines as symbols when applied to the breasts of figurines can also be traced to the Upper Paleolithic. One of the earliest examples is an East Gravettian (Pavlovian) mammoth-ivory carving from Dolní Věstonice in Moravia. (FIGURE 46) Only the breasts are naturalistically rendered on the otherwise rod-shaped, abstract human figure. The neck merges with a featureless head in a single column; neither belly nor legs are indicated. Groups of parallel lines are incised at the upper end of the rod and below the notched breasts. A row of short lines is engraved from shoulder to shoulder across the back of the figurine, and beneath this are two groups of tri-line signs; two short lines are incised beneath eight parallel lines in the center of the back.

The Dolní Věstonice site yielded an even more abstract rendering of the female principle, signified solely by the breasts: an ivory pendant-bead of two breasts at the base of a conical neck. A double chevron incised beneath the throat is like the ornamentation already observed on the neck of beaked Neolithic and later figurines.

Pendant-beads in the shape of a single breast have been recovered from sites of the Aurignacian (La Ferrassie, Grotte de Fossellone, Polesini, and Castanet), Gravettian (Périgordian), and French Magdalenian (Saint-Germain-la-Rivière, Pape du Brassempouy, and Saint-Michel-d'Arudy), Italian Gravettian, and Epigravettian (Grotta di Paglicci, Barma Grande, and Arene Candide) periods. (FIGURE 47) Their presence in more than fifty Upper Paleolithic sites documents the enormous spatial and temporal spread of this stereotype. Castiglioni and Calegari (1975) have typologically and chronologically classified these carvings of ivory, antler, bone, and deer or reindeer canine teeth. The majority are incised with parallel lines in groups of three, four, or five; occasionally, a V or X appears beside the rows of parallel lines.

A totally geometric female image found at Předmosti, the East Gravettian site in Moravia, has a V-shaped head with narrow serrated bands within the V, breasts composed of large ovals of concentric lines marked with four vertical parallel lines, and egg-shaped buttocks of six concentric lines. (FIGURE 48) The belly region is not exaggerated. In this unusual composition, the artist clearly emphasizes the body parts of highest importance—breasts and buttocks—and greatly abstracts the rest. The V-shaped head would be enigmatic, except that we now know the V to be a sign of the Bird Goddess; it tells us that she is represented here. Strange arched and striated upper limbs are not human arms; rather they stand for wings.

The chevron appears on more naturalistic large-breasted Paleolithic figurines, as is shown by the ivory figurine from Kostienki I, dated to c. 20,000–17,000 B.C. (FIGURE 49) As we shall see from the discussion to follow, the association of breasts with V's and chevrons continues for many millennia after the Paleolithic, and over a vast area between the Near East and western Europe.

There is little doubt that the portrayal of exaggeratedly large breasts and breast-shaped pendants marked with notches, V's, X's, and parallel lines symbolizes the Bird Goddess as the divine Source of Nourishment—milk/rain—or as the Giver of Life in general. Perhaps she was invoked by incising her signs (V's and X's) or waterdrops and streams (parallel lines) on the breasts which represent her.

FIGURE 45

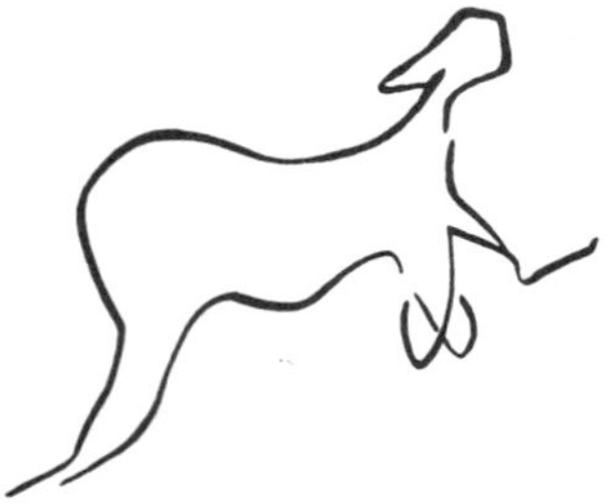

FIGURE 45 Finger-painted nude from the ceiling of a cave sanctuary has a bird head or mask, wing-like arms, and pendulous breasts. This figure was overdrawn by bands of lines, the "macaroni" motifs, suggesting her ties with streams or springs. Early Magdalenian (Pech Merle, Lot, S France; 15,000–13,000 B.C.).

FIGURE 46

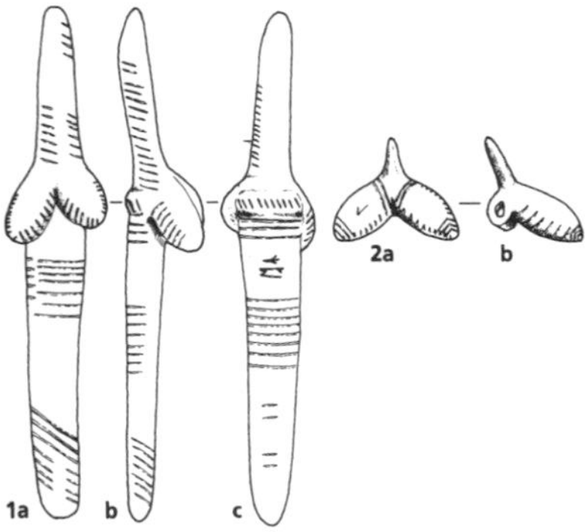

FIGURE 46 Upper Paleolithic carvings carefully marked with chevrons and parallel lines. (1) Mammoth tusk carving of a schematized female figure, full breasts on a columnar body. (2) Ivory pendant bead in the form of two breasts attached to a conical neck. East Gravettian (Dolní Věstonice, Moravia, Czechoslovakia; c. 25,000 B.C.). See also figure 73. (1) H. 8.5 cm. (2) H. 2.7 cm.

FIGURE 47

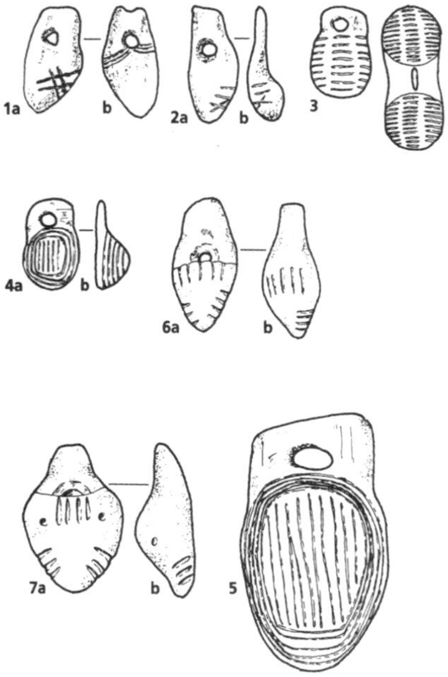

FIGURE 47 Breast-shaped pendant beads, usually perforated for hanging and marked with parallel lines, X's, and three or four lines. (1) Aurignacian (La Ferrassie, Dordogne, S France; c. 30,000 B.C.). (2) Late Magdalenian (Saint-Germain-la-Rivière, Dordogne, S France). (3) and (4) Epigravettian (Barma Grande, between Menton and Vintimille, Liguria). (5) Epigravettian (Arene Candide, Liguria, N Italy). (6) and (7) Epigravettian (Grotta di Fadets, N Italy). (1) H. 1.5 cm. (2) H. 1.6 cm. (3) H. (a) 1.3 cm, (b) 2 cm. (4) H. 1.3 cm. (5) H. 3.7 cm. (6) H. 1.9 cm. (7) H. 2.1 cm.

FIGURE 48

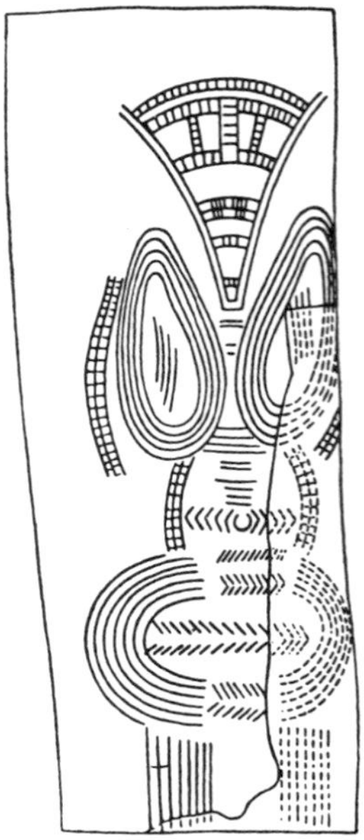

FIGURE 48 Upper Paleolithic Goddess with large breasts engraved on a mammoth-ivory in an intriguing geometrical style. She has an identifying V-shaped head, breasts marked with four parallel lines, and an egg-shaped vulva. East Gravettian (Předmosti, Moravia, Czechoslovakia; c. 20,000 B.C.). H. 15 cm.

FIGURE 49

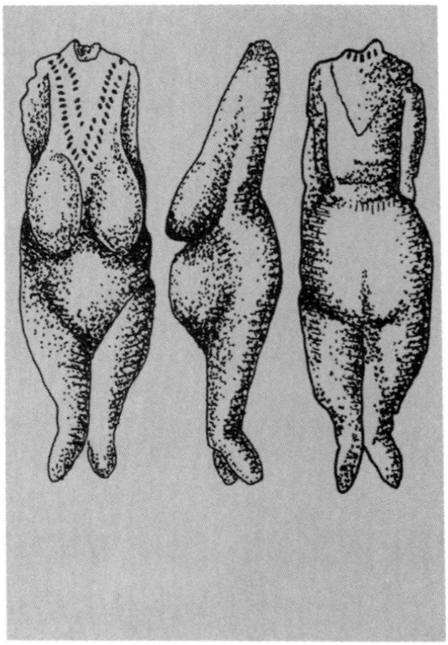

FIGURE 49 Upper Paleolithic ivory figurine incised with a chevron above her large breasts, found inside a house. (Kostienki I, Horizon I, River Desna, Ukraine; c. 20,000 B.C.). H. 15.5 cm.

4.2 *Neolithic figurines with breasts marked with Bird Goddess symbols*

The importance of the Goddess's breasts did not diminish in the agricultural era. Breasts were carefully modeled on clay figurines or stone sculptures, as with an impressive stone statue from Capdenac-le-Haut in southern France, which belongs to the classical Chassée culture of the 5th millennium B.C. (FIGURE 50) Above her breasts is the familiar V sign; her tri-fingered hands probably are bird's feet, and her mouth is a round hole, another characteristic feature of the Giver or Source.

The idea of breasts as the divine source of life-giving moisture is clearly demonstrated by a tiny winged and beaked figurine with enormous breasts that emerges from a dish—that is, from the water—of the Karanovo VI/Gumelniţa period, c. 4500 B.C. (FIGURE 51)

On a number of Neolithic figurines with beaked faces of the 6th millennium B.C., the sculpting of breasts seems to have been of primary interest. (FIGURES 52, 53) Prominent breasts, frequently with no other features, continue to be sculpted throughout the 5th and later millennia. (FIGURE 54)

FIGURE 50

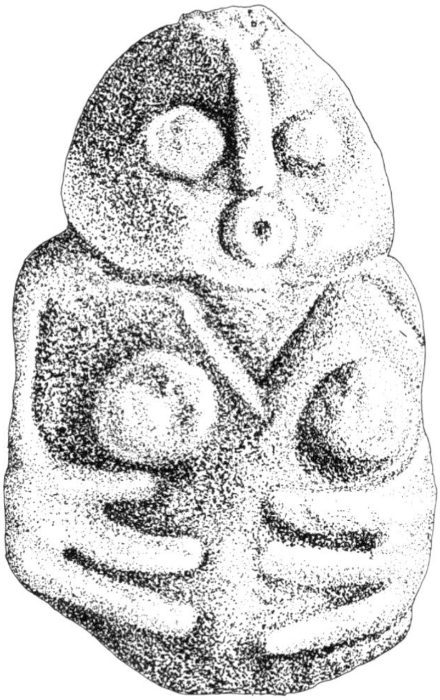

FIGURE 50 Large stone sculpture of a Bird Goddess from France. The figure has a deep V sign above her breasts and enormous three-fingered hands. Her round mouth, like her breasts, is a Divine Source. Chassée (Capdenac-le-Bout, Lot, S France; c. 4000 B.C.). H. 50 cm.

FIGURE 51

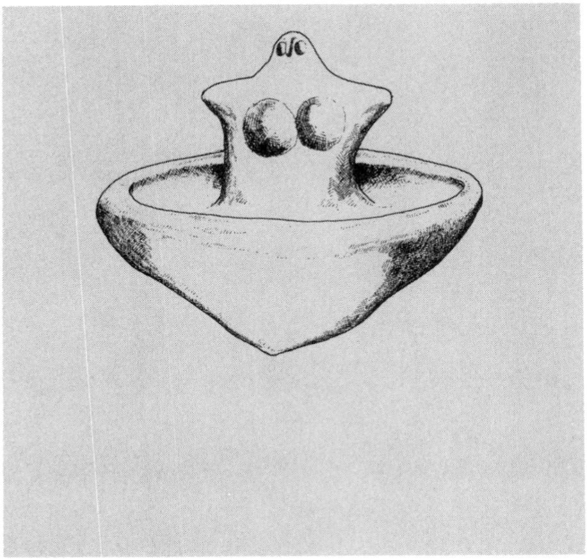

FIGURE 51 The Bird Goddess's breasts as the Source of life-giving moisture are portrayed in this winged and beaked figurine who rises full-breasted from the center of a dish. Karanovo VI/Gumelniţa (Ciolaneşti, S Romania; 4500–4300 B.C.). H. 9.1 cm.

FIGURE 52

FIGURE 54

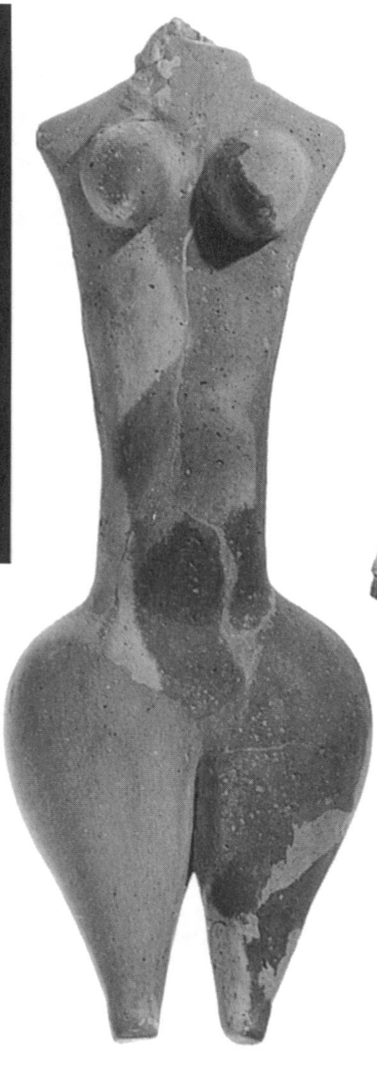

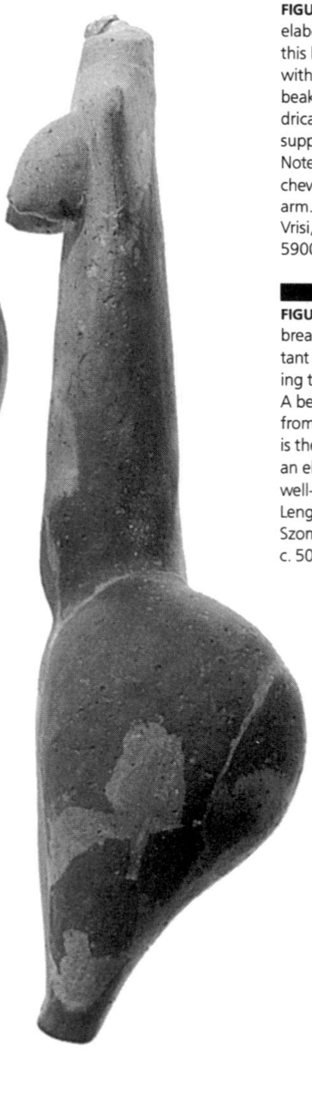

FIGURE 52 During the Neolithic, there was an Old European convention of figurines with beaked faces and prominent breasts. This highly schematized terracotta has few anatomical details other than her pinched beak, breasts, and the large thighs on which she rests. Starčevo (Porodin, near Bitolj, W Macedonia; early 6th mill. B.C.) H. 5 cm.

FIGURE 53 A more fully elaborated example is this bird-woman hybrid with neat coiffure, beaked face, high cylindrical neck, and arms supporting her breasts. Note the row of chevrons on her lower arm. Sesklo (Megali Vrisi, Tirnavos, Thessaly; 5900–5700 B.C.)

FIGURE 54 Prominent breasts remain an important sculptural motif during the next millennium. A beautiful example from the Lengyel culture is the "Lady of Sé" with an elegant torso and well-modeled breasts. Lengyel (Sé near Vas, Szombately, Hungary; c. 5000 B.C.) H. 21.3 cm.

FIGURE 53

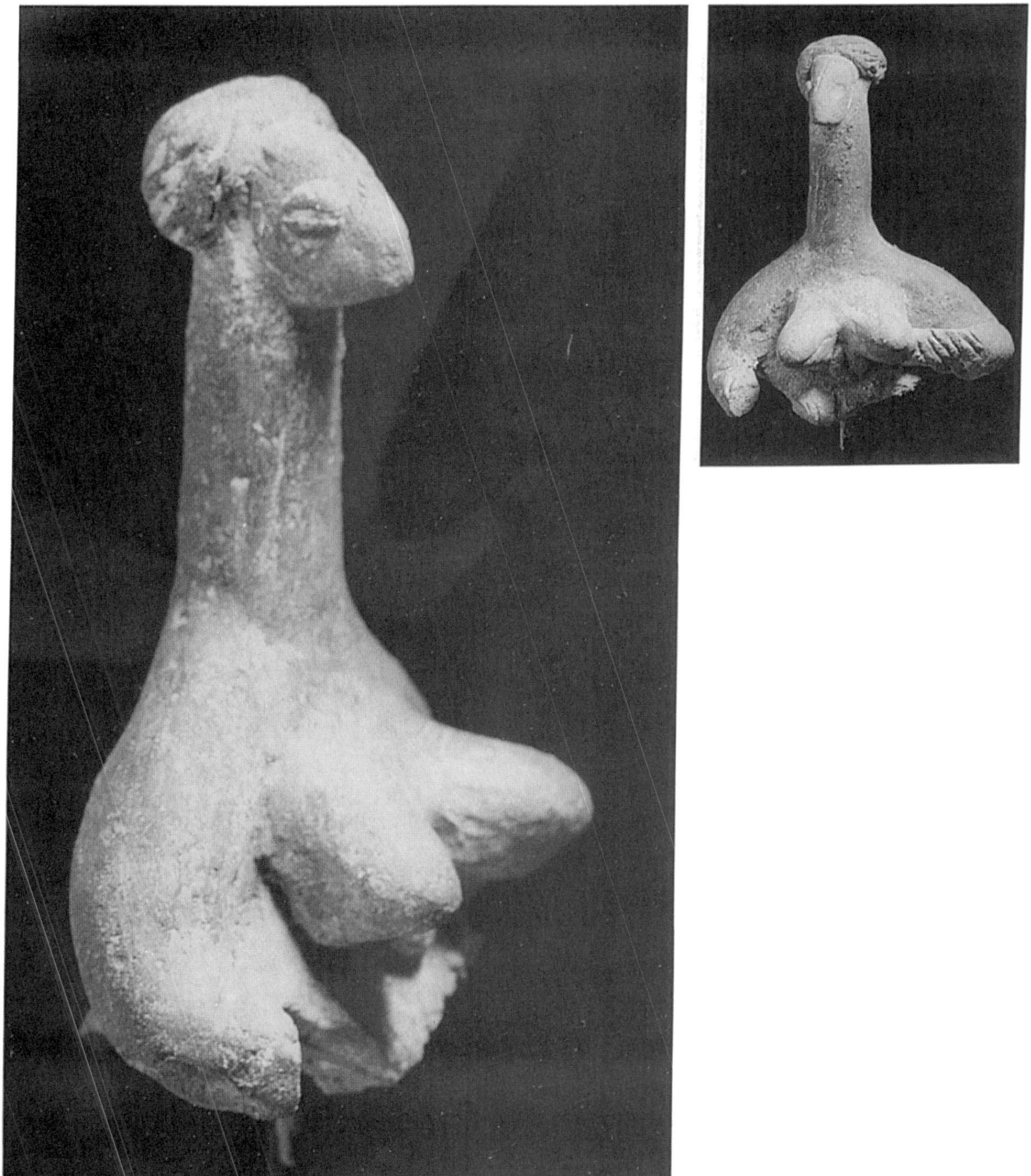

If the head of a figurine is broken, or if it is too schematic to allow recognition of the facial features, the Goddess's identity is revealed by breasts marked with chevrons, X's, three lines, parallel lines, meanders—symbols that regularly accompany the Bird Goddess. (FIGURES 55, 56) Random incisions on the breasts and torsos of terracotta figurines were perhaps symbolic of raindrops, or such marking was itself an act of invocation of milk or metaphorically of rain or nourishment. (FIGURE 57)

The theme of nourishment is more realistically conveyed in mother-and-child sculptures, as in the Vinča "Madonna from Gradac" (unfortunately with a broken head) who firmly holds a beaked anthropomorphic baby to her breast. (FIGURE 58) Vertical lines are incised above and across her breasts and shoulders; a chevron design marks her upper back and a net design her hips. A rather primitive Bükk figurine from northeastern Hungary, whose body is incised with zig-zag lines or "rain streams," conveys a similar idea. (FIGURE 59)

In the Aegean and Mediterranean area, breasts continue to be emphasized on Goddess effigies throughout the 3rd and 2nd millennia B.C. Perfect images of a bird-headed and human-breasted Goddess are preserved on Minoan seals. (FIGURE 60)

4.3 *The Goddess as a vase with breasts, nippled vase, and jug*

The metaphor of the Goddess as nourishing vessel is as early as pottery itself. Anthropomorphic vases recur throughout the various phases of the Neolithic and Copper and Bronze ages. Occasionally the top of the vase takes the place of the head. (FIGURE 61) We shall be concerned here with those with breasts and chevrons, zig-zags, parallel lines, or streams—vessels in the image of the Goddess as source of life-giving moisture.

FIGURE 55 The nourishing breasts of these schematic figurines are marked with V's, spirals, and parallel lines (including a joined group of four). There is a meander between the breasts, and two or three lines cross the shoulders. (1) and (2) Early Vinča (Vinča; 5200–5000 B.C.); (3) Classical Vinča (Rast, SW Romania; c. 5000 B.C.). (1) H. 7 cm. (2) H. 7.5 cm. (3) H. 5.3 cm.

FIGURE 56 This terracotta from Sardinia suggests a metaphor of breasts as divine eyes. Note that eyes are engraved over the breasts. Ozieri (Sa Ucca de Su Tintiriolu, Mara, N Sardinia; early 4th mill. B.C.) H. 6.9 cm.

FIGURE 57 Incised terracotta figurines (1) and (3) and painted figurine from a shrine (2). (1) Sesklo (Chaeroneia, central Greece; c. 5800–5600 B.C.). (2) Anatolian Neolithic (Shrine E IV 4, Çatal Hüyük, central Anatolia; mid-7th mill. B.C.). (3) Butmir (Butmir, near Sarajevo, Yugoslavia; early 5th mill. B.C.). (1) H. 7.4 cm. (2) H. 3 cm. (3) H. 6 cm.

FIGURE 55

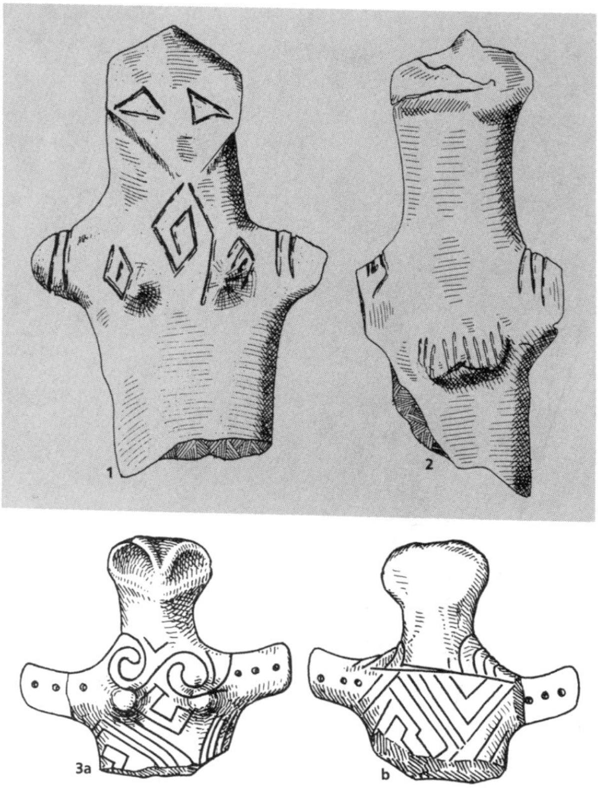

FIGURE 56

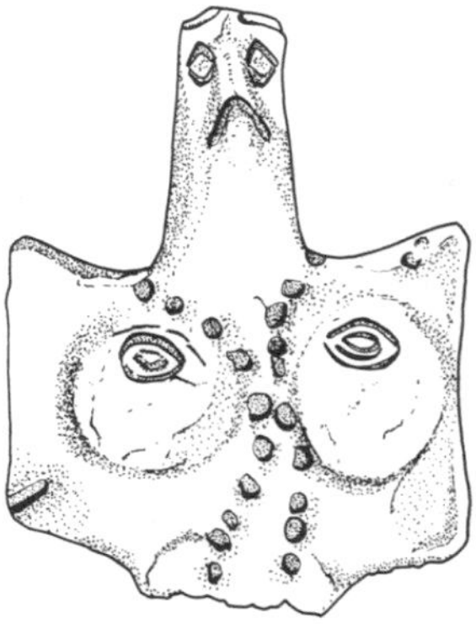

FIGURE 57

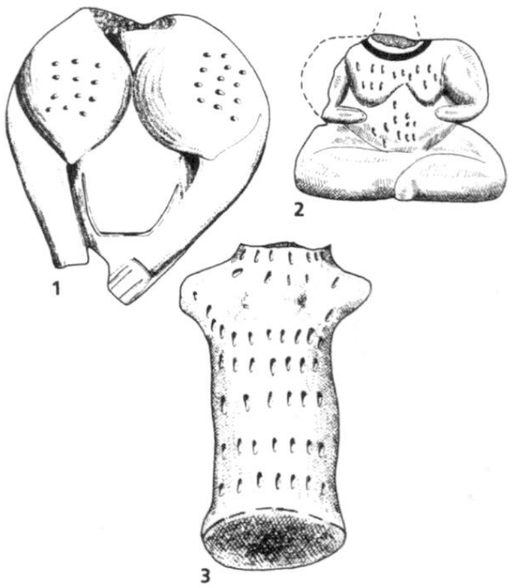

FIGURE 58

FIGURE 58 "Madonna from Gradac." The presence of life-giving milk is symbolized by groups of parallel lines incised across the breasts and shoulders. Note the beaked face on the baby. Vinča (Gradac, Morava valley, S Yugoslavia; c. 5000 B.C.; surface find)

FIGURE 59 This figurine is completely covered, front and back, in excisions encrusted with white paste. There are chevrons on her head and throat; zig-zags representing rain streams flow down her body. Her torso is an unmodulated block except for the breasts. Bükk (Tiszadada, at Kalvinháza, NE Hungary; c. 5000 B.C.) H. 10 cm.

FIGURE 61

FIGURE 59

FIGURE 60

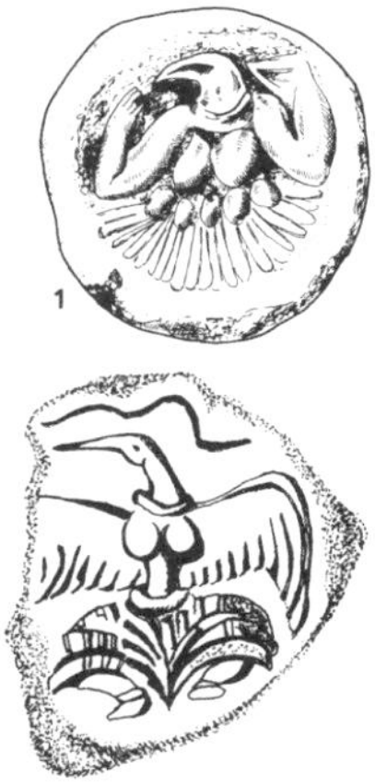

1

2

FIGURE 60 Bird-headed and winged figures with large breasts are from Minoan seal impressions (Zakros, E Crete; 1500–1450 B.C.). (1) H. 3.9 cm. (2) H. 4.7 cm.

FIGURE 61 The Goddess as nourishing vessel, her head replaced by the vase. Only the arms and breasts are modeled on her torso. Early Lengyel (Sé, Szombately, W Hungary; c. 5000 B.C.) Reconstructed; H. about 25 cm.

FIGURE 62

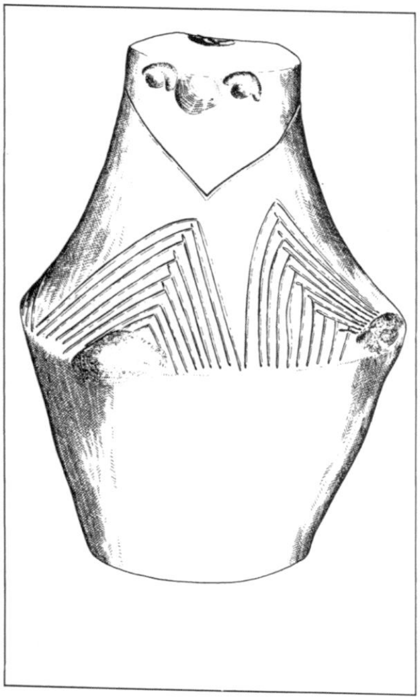

FIGURE 63

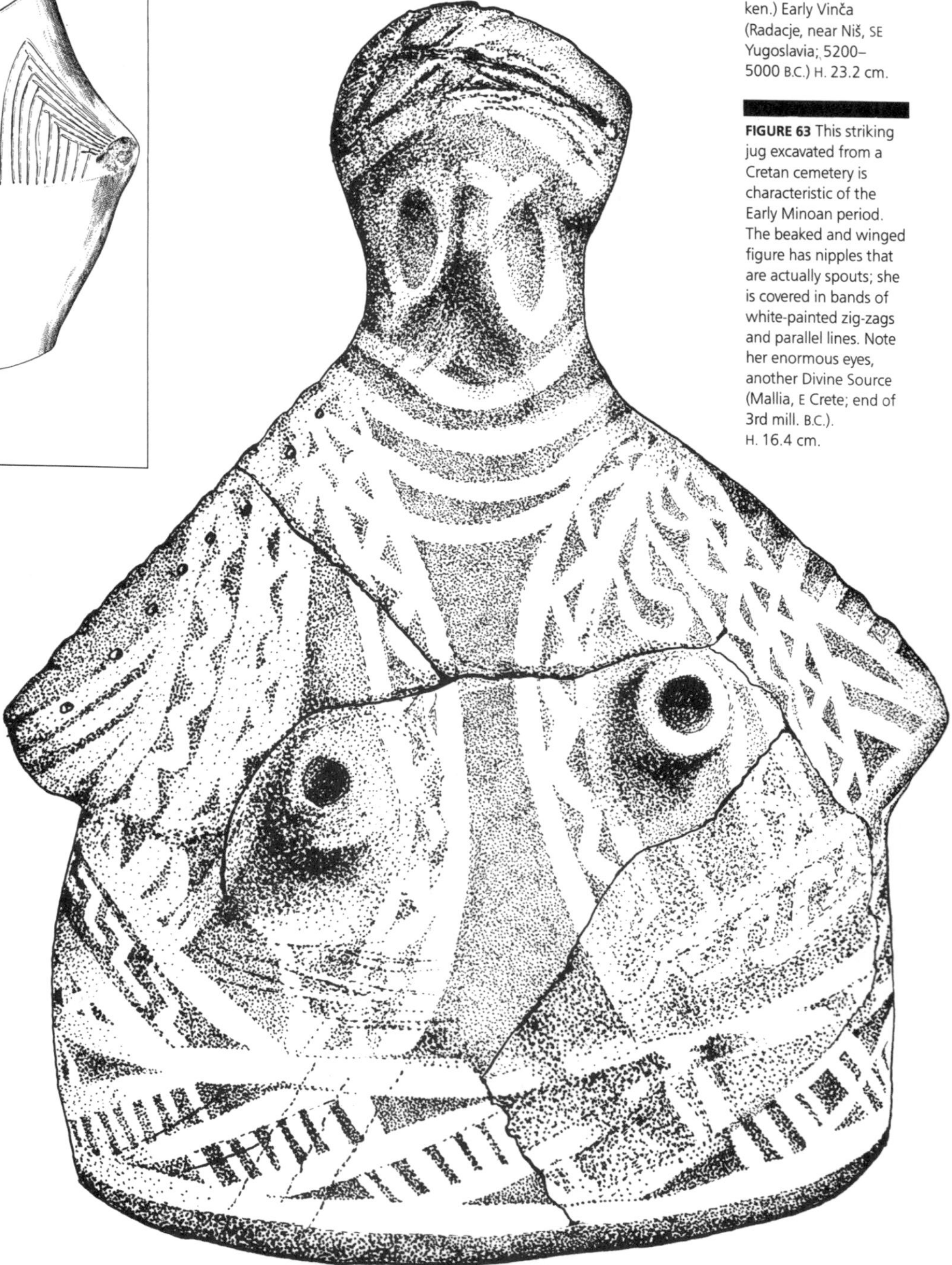

FIGURE 62 "Nippled vase," brown-colored with multiple chevrons above the nipples and a beaked mask on the neck. (The beak is broken.) Early Vinča (Radacje, near Niš, SE Yugoslavia; 5200–5000 B.C.) H. 23.2 cm.

FIGURE 63 This striking jug excavated from a Cretan cemetery is characteristic of the Early Minoan period. The beaked and winged figure has nipples that are actually spouts; she is covered in bands of white-painted zig-zags and parallel lines. Note her enormous eyes, another Divine Source (Mallia, E Crete; end of 3rd mill. B.C.). H. 16.4 cm.

The Early Vinča vessel with a triangular mask on the neck from Malča at Niš in southeastern Yugoslavia has nipples on four sides; above each is a multiple chevron. (FIGURE 62) Anthropomorphic vases with perforated breasts as spouts, large-eyed beaked faces, and special headgear are characteristic of the Early Minoan period. Bands of zig-zags, meanders, and parallel lines dominate the rich decoration on one such specimen from the cemetery of Mallia. (FIGURE 63) Another vessel, with breast-shaped spouts and painted panels of vertical and horizontal lines, is from a grave at Mochlos in eastern Crete (see Zervos 1956: 187).

Breast-decorated or nippled vases emerge in the 6th millennium B.C., and for five thousand years the motif does not diminish in importance. Occasionally breasts constitute the sole decoration of a vase. (FIGURE 64) Chevrons, parallel lines, and zig-zags or wavy parallel lines are the usual accompaniments, indicative of streams of milk flowing from the breasts. On Bükk vases, breasts are shown in the midst of snake heads, and wavy lines emanate from them. (FIGURE 65) The convention of chevrons on parallel lines on vases with breasts continues throughout the succeeding Bronze Age in east-central Europe (Baden and Coţofeni cultures), western Anatolia, the Aegean islands, and Crete. (FIGURES 66, 67) At Thera hundreds of "nippled ewers," dating from c. 1500 B.C., have been discovered. (FIGURE 67, 2)

FIGURE 64

FIGURE 64 Breasts are the sole decoration on a type of vase whose manufacture spans 5000 years of Old European history. The breasts on this nippled black vase are executed in concentric channelling. Vinča (Gradešnica, NW Bulgaria; c. 5000 B.C.) H. 20 cm.

FIGURE 65

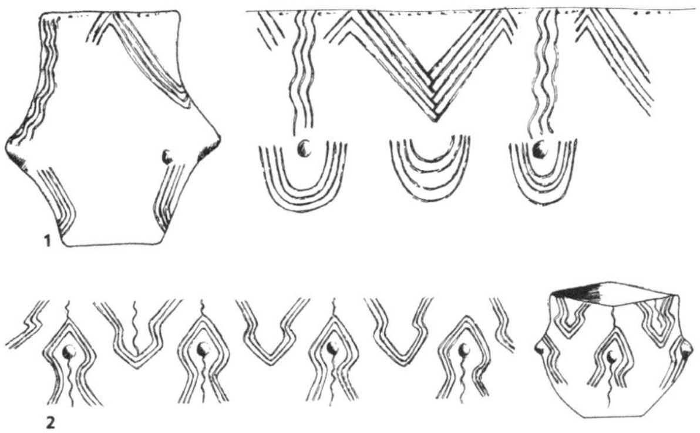

FIGURE 65 As on figurines, streams of milk flowing from the breasts on nippled vases are indicated by wavy lines and chevrons. On these Bükk vases, breasts, tri-lines, chevrons, M's, and, perhaps most interestingly, snake heads are associated. Tiszadob phase of Bükk culture ((1) Tiszavasvari-Jozsefháza and (2) Sarazsadany-Templomdom, NE Hungary; end of 6th mill. B.C.) (1) H. 12.6 cm. (2) H. 11.3 cm.

FIGURE 66

FIGURE 66 These Baden vases with breasts are tied to the Bird Goddess by the presence of (1) wings and intersecting chevrons and (2) a chevron necklace. ((1) Ráckeve and (2) Fonyód, Hungary; c. 3000 B.C.) (1) H. 20.3 cm. (2) H. 22.5 cm.

FIGURE 67

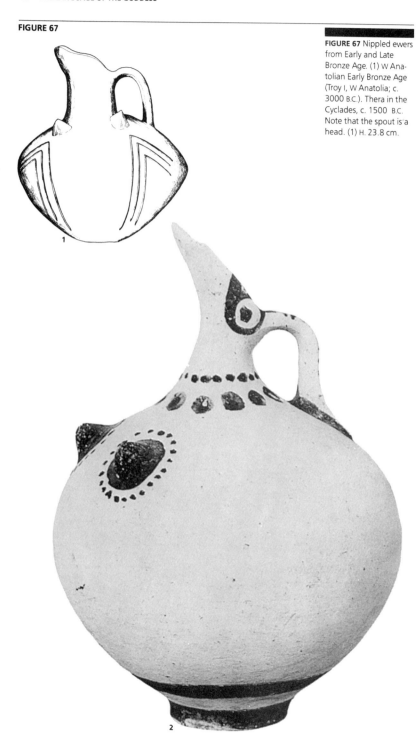

FIGURE 67 Nippled ewers from Early and Late Bronze Age. (1) W Anatolian Early Bronze Age (Troy I, W Anatolia; c. 3000 B.C.). Thera in the Cyclades, c. 1500 B.C. Note that the spout is a head. (1) H. 23.8 cm.

4.4 *The Bird Goddess's breasts on stone stelae and megalithic graves*

In southeastern Italy, stone stelae ("statue-menhirs") with sculpted breasts and incised chevrons above and below—their peaks between the breasts—have been discovered at Castellucio dei Sauri and tentatively dated to the Copper Age, c. 3000 B.C. (FIGURE 68) In France, Spain, Portugal, and England, statue-menhirs and stone slabs in gallery graves frequently display breasts and a necklace as the sole attributes of the Goddess portrayed. (FIGURES 69, 70) Occasionally her beak, eyes, and vulva are indicated. The breasts and necklace as *pars pro toto* appear on slabs in the gallery graves of Brittany between the end of the 4th and middle of the 3rd millennium B.C. As the most important attributes of the Goddess, they symbolize her presence and her regenerative potential in the grave.

From the breasts on the walls of funerary monuments as well as from their association with vultures and owls (see section 18.1) it can be perceived that the breast symbolism is more complex than it appears. The breasts are not nourishing the living alone; more importantly, they are regenerating the dead. The name of the goddess with breasts is preserved in Irish legend. The breasts of the goddess were thought to form the pair of hills in County Kerry called "Dá Chích Anann," The Paps of Ana (Doan 1980). Ana is identified with the Breton Ankou and the Irish Morrígan, Goddesses of Death and Guardians of the Dead.

4.5 *Breast-shaped amulets*

The Upper Paleolithic tradition of carving pendants in the form of breasts continues in the Neolithic, Copper, and Bronze ages. Neolithic pendants are carved of colored stone—green, black, or maroon. When gold comes into use in the Copper Age around 4500 B.C., disc-shaped pendants with embossed breasts appear. As symbols of the Goddess, pendants were probably valued for their protective qualities.

Round breast-shaped stone pendants with a nipple in the middle and two perforations for attachment to a string are well known from the Sesklo culture in Thessaly, c. 6000 B.C., (FIGURE 71) and also from Neolithic Lerna in the eastern Peloponnese. They are made from a variety of colored stones and are beautifully polished. In Greece, the tradition of carving breast-shaped amulets can be traced as late as the Middle Helladic.

Disc-shaped pendants of gold are known from the Danube region between the Alps and the Black Sea. Some of them have a circular cutout in the middle and embossed breasts on either side; others have three embossed breasts with chevron signs between. The latter were found in the Bodrogkeresztúr complex of Hungary, dated to the early part of the 4th millennium B.C. Much later, in the Iron Age, three-breasted anthropomorphic figurines reappear in Denmark (see Glob 1969).

FIGURE 68

FIGURE 69

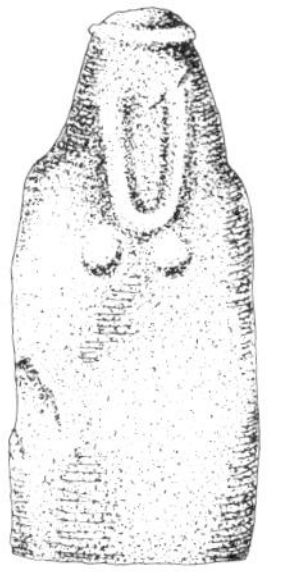

FIGURE 68 The statue-menhirs of southeast Italy have prominent breasts with triple chevrons above and below. Note the navel and band of parallel lines across the pelvic area. Italian Copper Age (Castellucio dei Sauri, Foggia, SE Italy; c. 3000 B.C.) H. approx. 160 cm.

FIGURE 69 In Western Europe, the Goddess's presence in megalithic graves is often symbolized by representations of her breasts and identifying necklace. This granite statue-menhir was found in 1878 under a church; it probably belongs to a megalithic gallery grave (Câtel, Guernsey, Great Britain; 3000–2500 B.C.). H. 159 cm.

FIGURE 70

FIGURE 71

FIGURE 70 The gallery graves of Brittany contain reliefs of the Goddess's breasts on the interior walls. On this stone are two pairs of breasts within an egg-shaped oval cartouche, one pair slightly larger than the other. Final Neolithic (Tresse, Brittany, France; c. 3000–2500 B.C.) L. of cartouche 50 cm.

FIGURE 71 Pendant amulet in the form of breasts carved of greenstone. Sesklo (Kyparisos tell, Thessaly, Greece; c. 6000 B.C.) H. 1.6 cm.

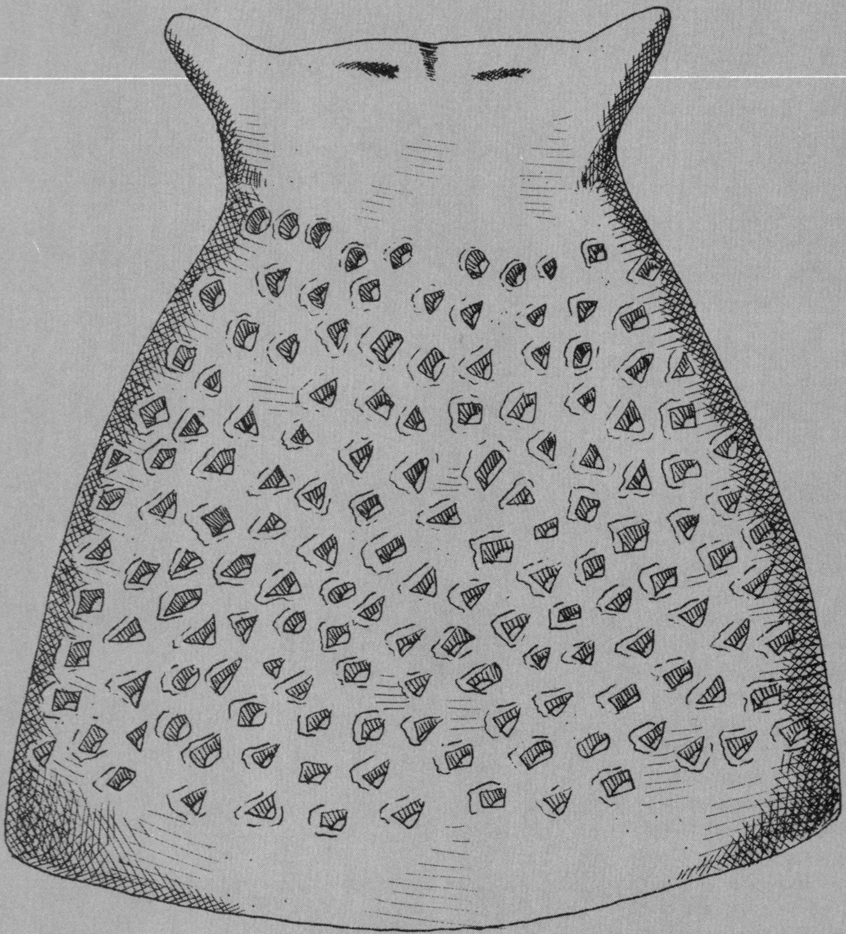

Owl-shaped vessel from Early Vinča, with holes. See figure 85, page 49.

5/ *Streams*

The belief in the sacredness of life-giving water at the sources of rivers, springs, and wells extends from prehistory to this century. We still hear of Living Water which imparts strength, heals the sick, rejuvenates the old, restores sight, and reassembles dismembered bodies and brings them back to life. The cult of wells and thermal springs, especially those at the source of larger streams and rivers, cannot be separated from the cult of the life-dispensing Goddess, single or triple. Historical sources—Greek, Roman, Celtic, and Baltic—speak again and again of goddesses and nymphs connected with certain rivers, springs, and wells. Rivers often have goddess names or local goddesses have river names, as, for example, the Boyne and the Shannon in Ireland (which allegedly owe their names to the Goddesses Bóand and Sinann). Sequana of the Gauls, the healing goddess after whom the river Seine is named, was worshipped at the source of the river where, in the 1960s, hundreds of wooden sculptures were found in the ruins of the Gallo-Roman sanctuary. They testify to the belief in the curative powers of the mineral waters emanating from the source. Not far from the source of the river a bronze statue of the goddess was discovered wearing a Greek chiton and mantle with a diadem on her head, riding on a barque with a swan's head for a prow (Doan 1987: 37, fig. 20). Life-giving goddesses known from folk memories, such as Irish Brigit and Baltic Laima, are owners of wells, the source of life. I assume this association existed as early as the Paleolithic, when sanctuaries were located at springs and mineral waters. At the Magdalenian sites of Montespan (Haute-Garonne) and Tuc d'Audoubert (Ariège), southern France, a stream flows from the mouth of the cave. Many cave sanctuaries, Paleolithic and Neolithic, contain lakes and subterranean rivers, and there is a marked correspondence between decorated Upper Paleolithic cave sanctuaries and mineral and thermal springs (Bahn 1978).

We cannot expect to perceive the sacredness of water in prehistoric art as well as we can in oral tradition and history, but there is much in these early designs and images that witnesses a long-lasting belief in the magical potency of streams and wells.

5.1 *On Upper Paleolithic and Mesolithic objects and figurines*

Streams in the form of "comets," or parallel lines in diagonal, vertical, or meander bands, are frequent motifs of Upper Paleolithic and Mesolithic mobiliary and parietal art. Long considered meaningless marks, they did not attract close scrutiny in spite of their frequency. Recently, however, Marshack has drawn our attention to the intentional character of the comet, diagonal band, and "macaroni" motifs (as they were called in earlier literature) engraved on various bone and stone objects dating from the final Paleolithic and Mesolithic (Marshack 1979). His examination of incised lines has shown that, in most cases, bands of lines are overcrossed by other bands or single lines, and that the markings are cumulative.

He believes that the comet form on the Magdalenian images at Altamira and on those in the Romanellian tradition of Italy represent the presence or source of a water flow (Marshack 1978). Often the comet is the initial element of compositions including subsequent continuing bands or serpentines. In illustration, (FIGURE 72) he describes a limestone plaquette from Roc de Marcamps (Gironde), France, on which a comet was incised first; afterwards a number of "streams" were added; still later, a serpentine band was superimposed. Marshack thinks the sequence of engraved markings—comet first, bands later—had some relation to their meaning and use (Marshack 1980). He also notes accumulations of essentially identical motifs on Mesolithic objects, for instance on a knife made from a rib found at the Maglemosian site of Ogaarde, Denmark. Streams and groups of parallel lines quite frequently occur on Mesolithic pebbles and Neolithic stamps.

Upper Paleolithic female images with pendulous breasts, probably portrayals of a divinity who appears as a waterbird hybrid (cf. fig. 45) often are associated with the "macaroni" motifs or are intentionally striated. (FIGURE 73) This may symbolize divine moisture within the body of the Goddess.

The continuity of the stream motif, from the Paleolithic into the Neolithic and later, suggests that this symbol was of primary potency. As we shall see, the association of streams with the eyes, breasts, and mouth of the Goddess emphasizes her role as benevolent dispenser. To ensure life, health, and abundance from the Divine Life Source, the stream symbol was indispensable—and ubiquitous.

FIGURE 72

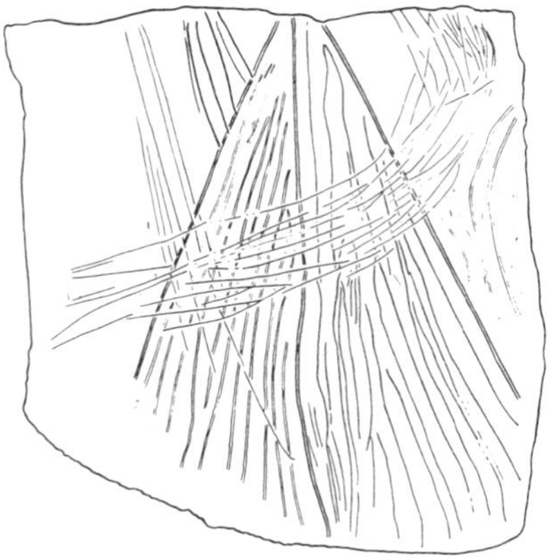

FIGURE 72 The "comet" motif is a common one in the Upper Paleolithic and Mesolithic. On this limestone plaque, three layers of successive incisions can be differentiated: the original comet, streams, and a serpentine band. It is believed that such markings symbolize the flow of (life, healing) water. Terminal Magdalenian or early Azilian (Roc de Marcamps, Gironde, France)

5.2 *As symbolic designs on vases*

A considerable number of vases from all phases of the Neolithic and Copper Age are decorated with painted or incised parallel lines in vertical or diagonal bands; with vertical zig-zags or wavy lines; and with other rain-simulating motifs indicated by garlands or vertical lines descending from clouds. (FIGURE 74) The stream motif may cover the shoulder of a vase or its entire surface. Often it is compartmentalized (enclosed and framed by bands), a customary treatment to indicate that the sign is being used as a symbol. (FIGURE 75) Such are the panels of zig-zagging streams with auxiliary V and X signs on the funnel-shaped vase from Vinča.

FIGURE 73

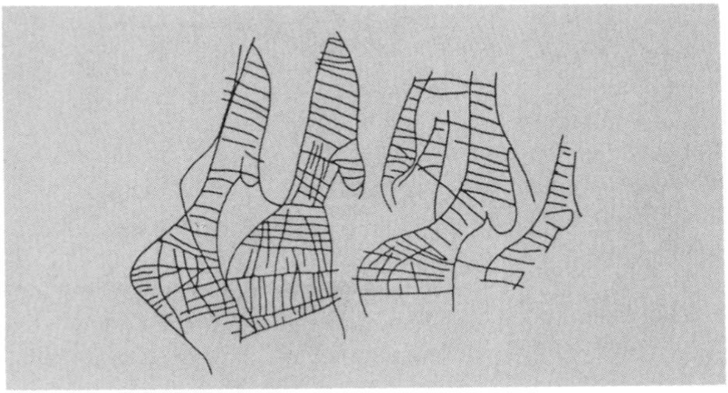

FIGURE 73 Figures whose large breasts and protruding posteriors give them the profiles of waterbirds are often intentionally striated and net-patterned, "filled with divine moisture," as on this Upper Paleolithic plaquette. Scale 2/3. (Gönnersdorf, upper Rhine, north of Koblenz, W Germany; Magdalenian V, c. 10,000 B.C.) H. 6.4 cm.

FIGURE 74

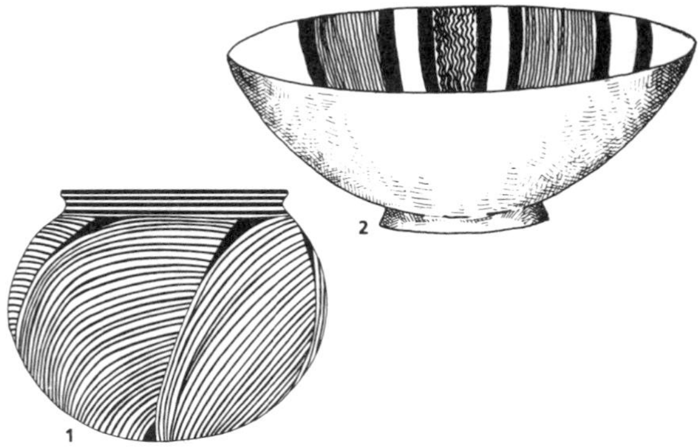

FIGURE 74 Examples of stream or rain-torrent motif from the Neolithic. (1) Vase painted in red on white with broad bands of curving lines suggestive of rain torrents. (2) Stream motif framed by dark bands, painted on the inside of a dish. Sesklo ((1) Lianokladi I, Thessaly; c. 5800 B.C. (2) Asea, central Peloponnese; mid-6th mill. B.C.) (1) H. 10 cm. (2) H. 12.2 cm.

On Late Cucuteni vases from the western Ukraine, the rain/water theme is associated with the beak and eyes of the Goddess by broad bands of parallel lines painted over the neck and shoulders. (FIGURE 76) An owl-shaped vessel (Bird Goddess effigy) from Troy has horizontal parallel lines front and back, and vertical ones over the funnel head. (FIGURE 77)

The association of the stream/parallel-line motif with the features and signs of the Bird Goddess is firmly established. The consistent presence of the motif on nippled vases is further evidence of the symbolic implications of the breasts of the Goddess. (FIGURE 78) A breast or nipple on four sides of a vase is accented by a stream above or below it, or a breast on the base or side of a vessel is enhanced by a whirl design formed by bands of streams. (FIGURE 79) The binocular-shaped bottomless funnels of the Cucuteni culture were usually decorated with the parallel-line/breast motif. They probably served as ritual vases in rain/milk invocation ceremonies.

The body of the Goddess is the Source incarnate. Streams or parallel lines, therefore, are associated not only with the breasts but also with other body parts—eyes, mouth, wings. For example, on the Vinča lid from Malča streams flow from the mouth. (FIGURE 80)

FIGURE 75

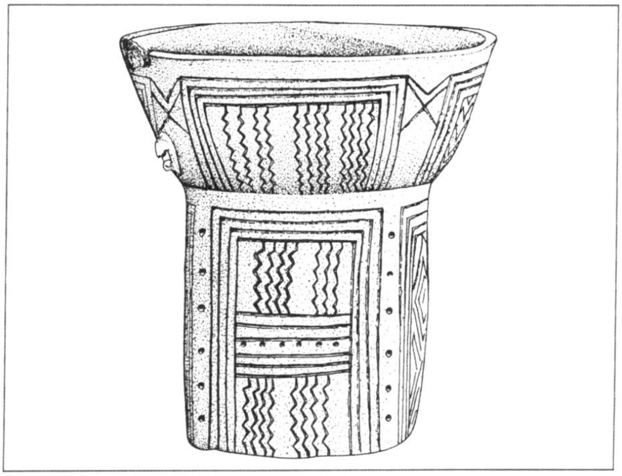

FIGURE 75 Funnel-shaped vase with zig-zagging torrents in the lower panel divided by two bands of tri-lines and six dots (2 x 3). The six dots are repeated on either side of the panel. Above X and V combinations join the panels with those on the other side, which are filled with meanders and chevrons. Early Vinča (Vinča; 5200–5000 B.C.) H. 23 cm.

FIGURE 76

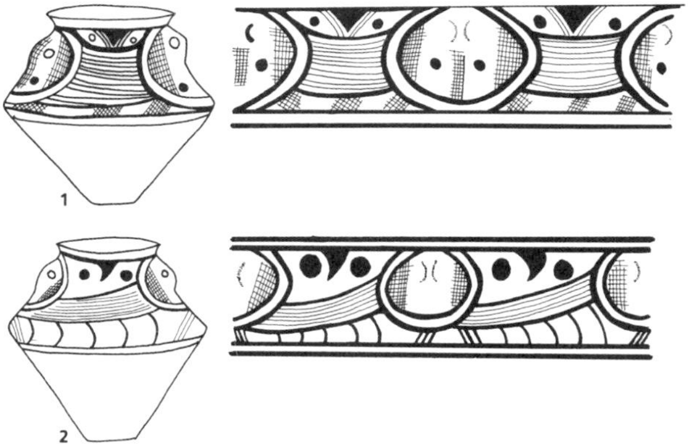

FIGURE 76 This watery motif is connected with the Bird Goddess on these vases painted black on red. Broad bands of parallel lines run over the neck and shoulders of the beaked Goddess portrayed. Late Cucuteni ((1) Petreni and (2) Staraja Buda, W Ukraine; 4000–3500 B.C.) (1) H. 22 cm. (2) H. 22.2 cm.

FIGURE 77

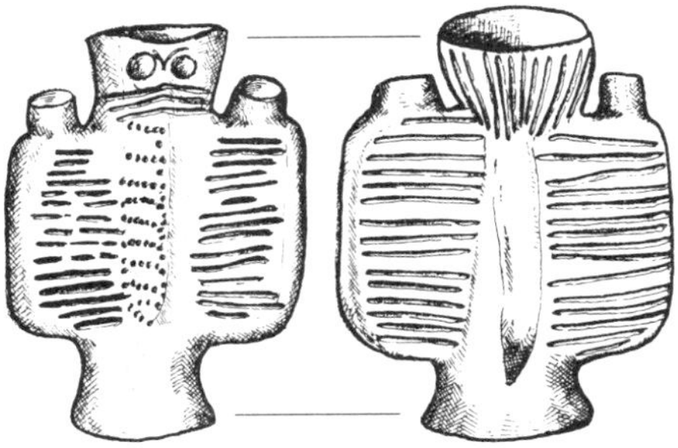

FIGURE 77 Parallel lines are associated with both a funnel shape and a beaked visage on this owlish vessel from Anatolia. W Anatolian Early Bronze Age (Troy II; early 3rd mill. B.C.) H. 8.5 cm.

FIGURE 79

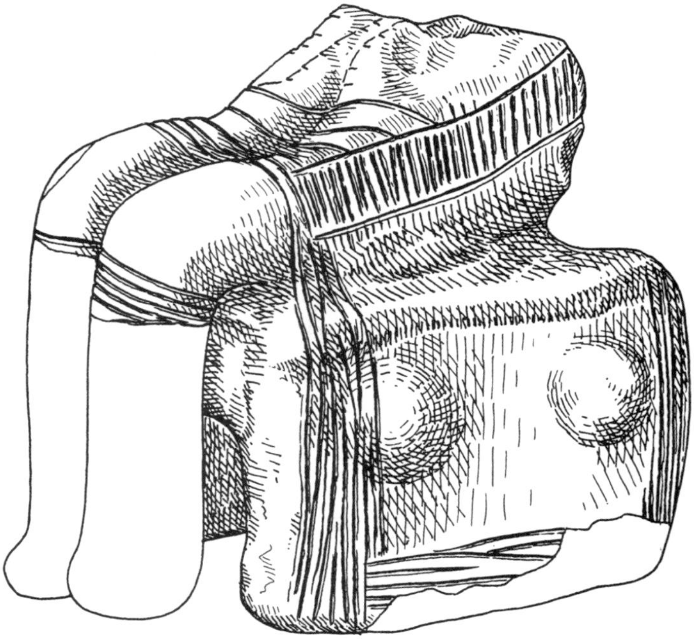

FIGURE 78 The stream motif is often associated with breasts, as on these nippled vases and sculpture. Here the torrents symbolize the nourishment which flows from the human divine breast. (1) Vinča (Rast, SW Romania; 5200–5000 B.C.). (2) Lengyel (Aszód, N of Budapest; c. 5000 B.C.). (1) H. of detail 11.9 cm. (2) H. 10.9 cm.

FIGURE 79 This Vinča figurine is seated on a throne decorated with a pair of breasts in relief; the stream motif runs from the Deity's body across the throne and over one of its symbolic breasts. Vinča (Crnokalačka Bara south of Niš, SE Yugoslavia; 5000–4500 B.C.) H. 11 cm.

FIGURE 78

FIGURE 80

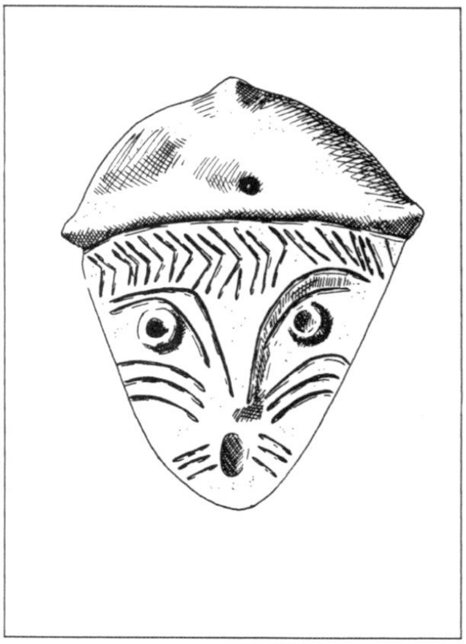

FIGURE 80 Pottery lid with streams in the form of tri-lines flowing from the Goddess's open mouth. Note the multiple chevrons across the forehead. Early Vinča (Malča, near Niš, S Yugoslavia; 5200–5000 B.C.) H. 11.6 cm.

Schematic Vinča figurines with arm stumps (wings) and bird-headed protomes on cult vases are sometimes "wrapped" by parallel lines; or parallel lines, like ribs, decorate the whole front. (FIGURE 81) Probably these markings are analogous to the stream motif as a symbol of propitiousness, abundance, and benevolence in general.

5.3 *Parallel-line squares on cult vessels and figurines*

A conventionalized treatment of the stream symbol evolved into framed squares of parallel lines. These were perhaps first conceived of as abbreviated versions of long streams, tiny extracts from an infinite continuum. Such squares most often decorate spouted vases and askoi. (FIGURE 82) They are combined with V's, brush signs, and winged figures on Early Vinča pottery; they appear as isolated signs on Yortan askoi (3000–2500 B.C.) and on Early Cypriot schematic planklike figurines (2300–2000 B.C.). (FIGURE 83, 1) Groups of four parallel lines mark stout anthropomorphic vases, probably ritual water containers. (FIGURE 83, 2)

FIGURE 81

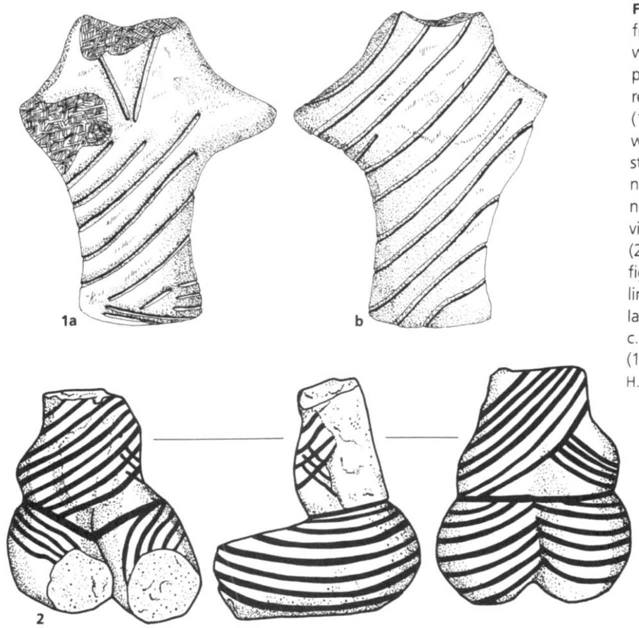

FIGURE 81 Terracotta figurines are sometimes wrapped in incised or painted parallel lines representing streams. (1) Vinča figurine torso with winglike arm stumps and a V-shaped necklace (Kormadin, near Belgrade, Yugoslavia; c. 4500 B.C.). (2) Seated Cucuteni B figurine painted in black lines (Trifeşti, district of Iaşi, NE Romania; c. 3800–3600 B.C.). (1) H. 6.35 cm. (2) H. 4.8 cm.

FIGURE 82

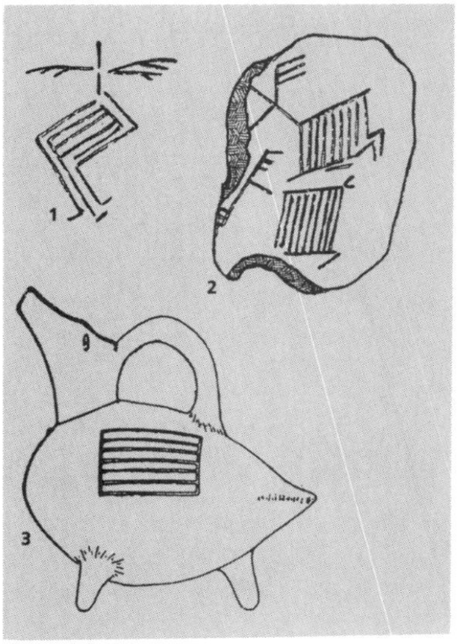

FIGURE 82 Examples of squares of parallel lines with winged figures decorating vases and an askos, widely separated by time and space. (1) and (2) Early Vinča (Vinča; 5200–5000 B.C.). (3) W Anatolian Early Bronze Age (Yortan, W Turkey; 3000–2500 B.C.). (1) H. 2.4 cm. (2) H. 3.5 cm. (3) H. 12.9 cm.

From the above we see that the parallel-line square is a symbol of the Bird Goddess and a metaphor for her propitiousness. The symbol was in use for thousands of years. It is present even on the Late Bronze Age and Iron Age ceramics of central Europe—for example on this Lusatian urn, on which mythical beings (the Goddess?) composed of parallel lines are incised. (FIGURE 84, 1) This symbol was inherited from Neolithic times, since such parallel-line-square figures are known from the Sardinian Ozieri culture, preceding the Lusatian by some 3000 years. (FIGURE 84, 2)

FIGURE 83

FIGURE 83 This anthropomorphic vase in the shape of a stout female figure is marked over the back with groups of four vertical lines in three rows and a tri-line around the neck. Two views: (a) back; (b) profile. Vinča (Orlavat, Vojvodina, R. Tamiš basin, N Yugoslavia; c. 5000 B.C.) H. 18.6 cm.

5.4 *Holed vessels*

Holed vessels, well evidenced in Neolithic, Copper, and Bronze Age sites, most probably belong to the ritual equipment of rain or fertility and abundance invocation rites. As a clue to their use, Karanovo sites (mid-6th to mid-5th millennium B.C.) have yielded funnel-shaped holed vessels which are attached to large vases. The magical liquid was apparently collected in the funnel; from there it dripped into the vase and was kept as sacred water. In addition, the water was probably sprinkled around from the vessel, perhaps in a rite of purification or blessing as is still common in the religious practices of today. Sprinkling water as an act of sympathetic magic to secure the fertility and abundance of fields, animals, and married couples is still practiced in European villages.

It is interesting to note that holed vessels are associated with bird and snake figures. (FIGURE 85) These creatures appear as protomes on the vessels, or snakes crawl up and around them, as seen on Minoan examples from the Palace of Knossos.

FIGURE 84

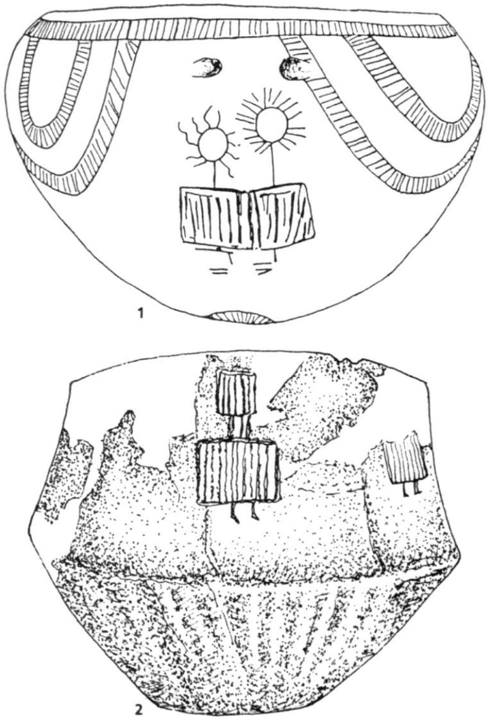

FIGURE 84 Parallel line squares appear as the bodies of divine figures through time and in various regions of Europe. (1) Two such figures were found engraved on a vase from a rock-cut tomb. Their heads are like radiating suns; their feet seem to be bird's claws. Ozieri culture (Serra Is Araus, San Vera Milis, Tomb III, Sardinia; 4th mill. B.C.). (2) This Late Bronze Age urn is incised with anthropomorphic figures composed of two parallel line squares. Lusatian (Lausitz) culture (Tresta Rządowa, woj. Piotrków, Poland; early 1st mill. B.C.) (1) H. 15.5 cm. (2) H. 23.2 cm.

FIGURE 85

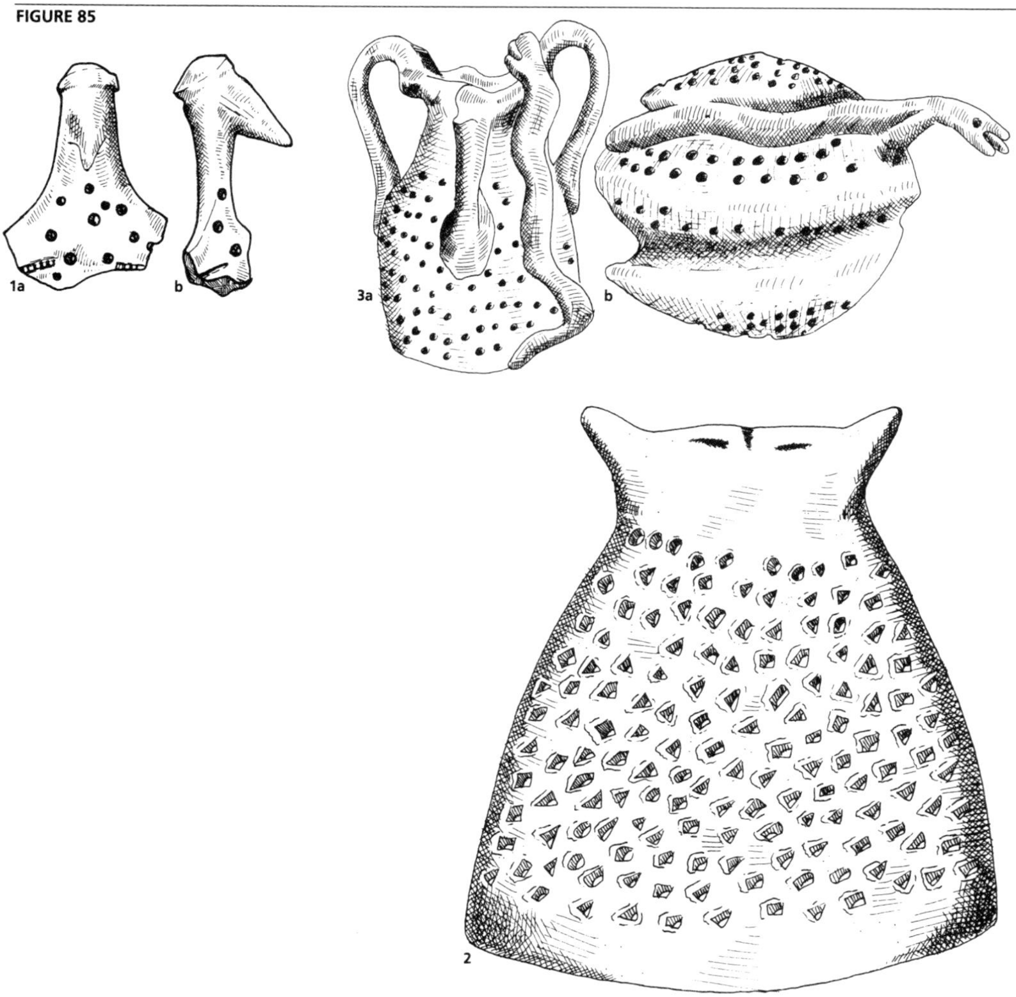

FIGURE 85 Holed vessels are sometimes shaped like birds and are associated with snakes. (1) Crowned bird's head, a handle from a vessel. Early Cucuteni (Vladeni, Moldavia; 5000–4500 B.C.). (2) Lidded owl-shaped vessel, on whose top is a hole surrounded by three sets of tri-lines. Early Vinča (Turdaş, near Cluj, W Romania; 5200–5000 B.C.). (3) Snakes crawl up and around holed vessels from the Palace of Knossos. Late Minoan I–II (Knossos, Crete; c. 1500–1450 B.C.) (1) H. 7.4 cm. (2) H. 15.7 cm. (3) H. (a) 16.8 cm, (b) 13.8 cm.

Vessel lid from Earliest Vinča; supernatural character of eyes made clear with enormous surrounding triangles. See figure 89, page 53.

6/ *Eyes of the Goddess*

6.1 *As a source of divine liquids*

The large eyes with which the Goddess is portrayed strongly suggest the epithet "All-seeing" for her. However, the symbolism which surrounds the eyes speaks for an even more fundamental attribute, namely that the eyes, like the Goddess's breasts or mouth, are a Divine Source. The concept of the eyes as source must have existed in the Upper Paleolithic; on the figurine from Dolní Věstonice, a stream flowing down the body of the deity begins at the eyes. (FIGURE 86) The idea of divine moisture from the eyes is present in the markings on artifacts of the Mesolithic and Pre-Pottery Neolithic periods.

The incised concentric semicircles on pebbles of the Natufian culture from the 10th millennium B.C. perhaps carry the same idea. The pebble effigies found in Jordan Valley Yarmukian sites of the Pottery Neolithic A are also marked with streams beginning at the slanted eyes and running down the pebble. (FIGURE 87) They speak for the continuity of the idea into the Neolithic. The eyes are the Bird Goddess's. Her identity is clear when the eyes are shown joined with V's and chevrons.

During the Copper Age and later, as we shall see from the description of Vinča lids that follows, the eyes are quite regularly encircled or accompanied by parallel lines, rainstreams, meanders, nets, and other symbols of the aquatic family.

FIGURE 86

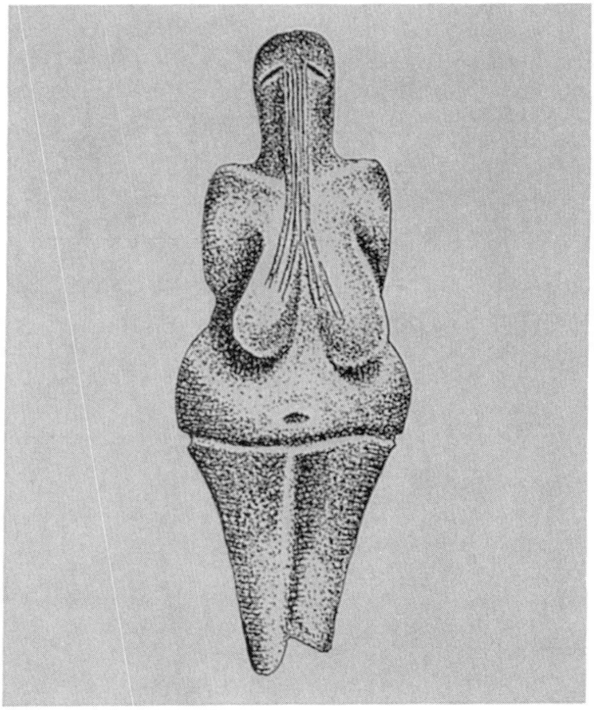

FIGURE 86 Upper Paleolithic figurine modeled from a paste of clay and ground bone with slit eyes from which streams flow down over full breasts. East Gravettian/Pavlovian (Dolní Věstonice, Moravia; c. 24,000 B.C.). H. 11 cm.

FIGURE 87

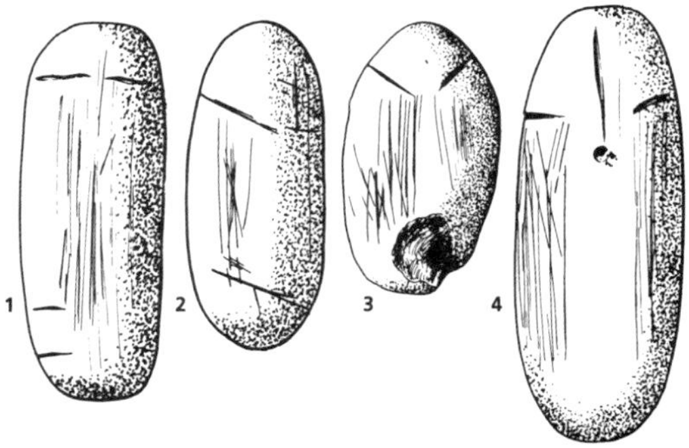

FIGURE 87 This theme of divine moisture flowing from the eyes continues in the Mesolithic and Neolithic, as these incised pebble effigies of the Pottery Neolithic A attest. Yarmukian (Sha'ar Hagolan, Jordan Valley, Lebanon; end 7th mill. B.C.) (1) H. 4.5 cm. (2) H. 3.9 cm. (3) H. 3.2 cm. (4) H. 5.1 cm.

6.2 *Vinča lids and masks*

These richly decorated lidded jars with owl eyes are a ceramic form uniquely characteristic of the Vinča people. The marks on the lids derive from the symbol system connoting the Bird Goddess: the meander, bands of parallel lines, the dotted meander, single or multiple V's, rows of striated triangles, groups of two or three diagonal lines, and framed columns of banded V's. (FIGURE 88) The presence of just these symbols would seem to designate the vessels as exclusively the property of the Goddess, consecrated to use in her rites.

FIGURE 88

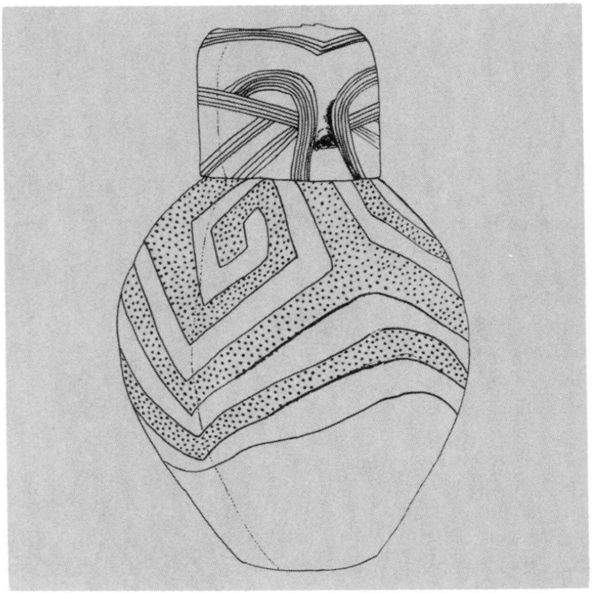

1

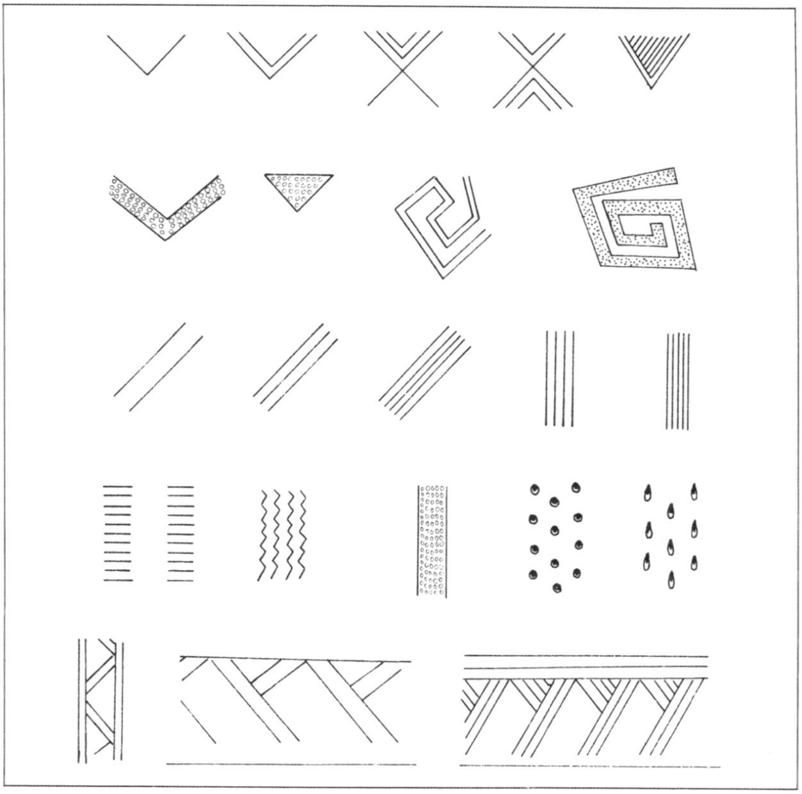

2

FIGURE 88 (1) The Vinča people produced a unique ceramic, the lidded jar with owl eyes. (2) This motif catalog of the lid decorations is an assemblage of Bird Goddess symbolism: V, X, meander, parallel lines, zig-zags, streams, etc., all associated with enormous and compelling eyes. (1) H. 58.3 cm.

In the past, Vinča lids have been interpreted as stylized representations of the head of a bear or cat. This they certainly are not; the fact is that there were no cats in Neolithic and Copper Age Europe. Since they have a beak but no mouth, the eyes and often the ear tufts of an owl, and symbolic markings indicative of the Bird Goddess, they are most probably what they seem—images of that deity. (FIGURE 89)

Motifs on lids have been categorized as follows:

1. Chevron (single or multiple): combined with cross-bands, amplified or "soaring," and combined with meanders
2. Meander: alone or combined with chevrons
3. Streams: diagonal and vertical bands of parallel lines, zig-zags, striated lines, or dots
4. Streams beneath the eyes in panels

The enormous eyes with their expression of supernatural perspicacity are the major design element. Bands of parallel lines or vertical striations above, below, or encircling the eyes constitute a metaphor for divine tears; the eyes of the Goddess are the source of life-sustaining water.

FIGURE 89

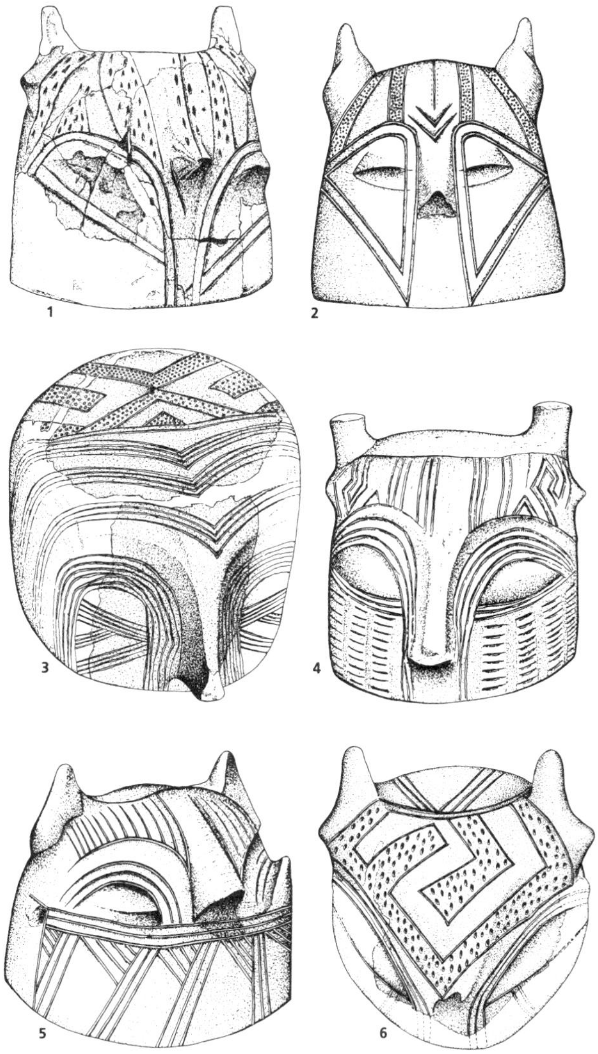

FIGURE 89 Some examples of the exquisite Vinča lids. (1) Double lines surround and emphasize the eyes; raindrop-incised bands flow over the forehead. Earliest Vinča (Vinča; c. 5200 B.C.). (2) The eyes' supernatural character is made clear with enormous surrounding triangles; note the double V's on the forehead. Early Vinča (Vinča; 5200–5000 B.C.). (3) Arched streams define the eyes; multiple chevrons stretch over the forehead and down the sides of the face; bands of dotted meanders cover the top and back. Mid-Vinča (Potporanj, at Vršac, E Yugoslavia; 5000–4500 B.C.). (4) Streams flow around the eyes and down beside the beak; bands of horizontal striations cover the area below the eyes; streams, V's, and meanders mark the forehead. Mid-Vinča (Fafos II, Kosovska Mitrovica, S Yugoslavia; 5000–4500 B.C.). (5) Tri-lines arch over the eyes and brush signs sweep back over the forehead; a panel of perpendicular diagonals fills the mask's lower half. Mid-Vinča (Vinča; 5000–4500 B.C.). (6) Streams flow around the eyes; the forehead is covered with a meander and the back of the head with a chevron. Mid-Vinča (Vinča; c. 5000–4500 B.C.).
(1) H. 21.1 cm.
(2) H. 14 cm.
(3) W. 13.7 cm.
(4) H. 12.6 cm.
(5) H. 11.1 cm.
(6) H. 12.4 cm.

FIGURE 90

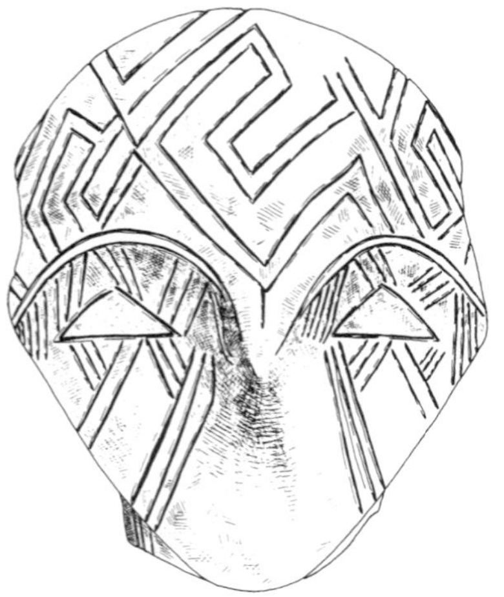

FIGURE 90 Beaked mask of a figure with triangular eyes surrounded by groups of parallel lines; meanders cover the forehead. Vinča (Potporanj, at Vršac, E Yugoslavia; 5000–4500 B.C.) H. 10 cm.

FIGURE 91

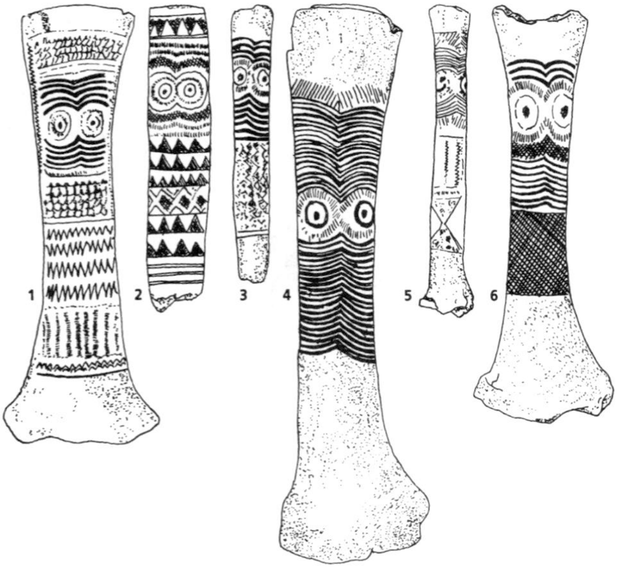

FIGURE 91 West European Eye Goddess is known from sepulchral artifacts and settlements. The eyes on these bone phalanges are surrounded by multiple eyebrows, triangles, hourglass shapes, and nets. Almeria-Los Millares culture (Almizaraque settlement, Almeria, Spain; 1st half of 3rd mill. B.C.) (1) H. 14.1 cm. (2) H. 9.9 cm. (3) H. 9.1 cm. (4) H. 17.9 cm. (5) H. 10 cm. (6) H. 13.5 cm.

The masks on elaborate Vinča figurines also feature enormous semicircular eyes, modeled in relief or incised and white-encrusted. (FIGURE 90) The treatment of the eyes is very similar to that of the lids, as is the aggregation of symbols that accompanies them.

6.3 *The "Eye Goddess" of western Europe*

The term Eye Goddess came into use after the publication in 1957 of *The Eye Goddess* by O. G. S. Crawford. The Goddess of the title was held to have originated in the Near East, her cult then diffusing across the Mediterranean to western Europe. Indeed, the resemblance of figurines from the temple of Tel Brak, eastern Syria (c. 3500 B.C.)—with their staring eyes and brows joined over the beak—to the stone idols of Spain and Portugal with the oculi-motif, is quite astonishing. The similarity however, most probably resulted from a universally held symbolic concept of Divine Eyes, from which western variants developed.

The west European Eye Goddess of France, Spain, Portugal, and Great Britain is manifested in the stelae, figurines, and amulets of megalithic cultures dating from the 5th to the 3rd (in Crawford's day considered to be the 3rd and 2nd) millennia B.C. Unquestionably, the eyes of the Goddess are the dominant feature on some of these monuments, justifying Crawford's appellation. But the powerful indication that the Eye Goddess is related to the southeast European Bird Goddess and is not a completely different divinity of indigenous origin is the symbolic markings on the monuments: chevrons, zig-zags, and parallel lines. This is virtually the same assemblage found on southeast European figurines, masks, and lids. The sole distinction of the west European Goddess is her characteristically owlish appearance. The round eyes

FIGURE 92

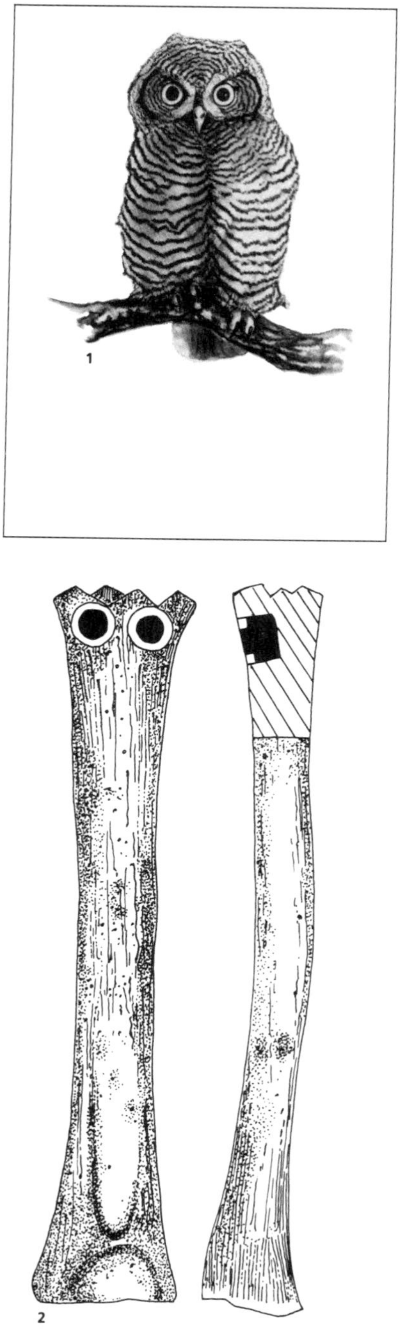

FIGURE 92 The similarity between the round eyes of an owl and on a Neolithic bone, symbol of death, is astonishing. The owl (1) has extraordinary visual powers; no wonder its eyes became "divine," a symbol of regeneration akin to the life-giving water, sun, and snake coil. (2) A simple bone (the polished epiphysis of a young animal) is used to represent the death aspect of the Goddess. Her numinous round eyes are of shell carefully inlaid and glued to the end of the bone. Linear Pottery culture (Ensisheim, upper Rhine, NE France; c. 5000 B.C.) (2) H. 11.5 cm.

so definitively establish her identity that often no auxiliary anthropomorphic features were deemed necessary.

The west European Eye Goddess is known almost exclusively from sepulchral artifacts—either as a large stone stela standing at the entrance to megalithic tombs, or as a figurine, bone phalange, stone cylinder, or schist plaque deposited within. We shall return to the necrotic personality of the Eye Goddess when we talk of her association with tombs and caves (see section 18); here we are interested only in the design context of the eye motif.

Phalange amulets from megalithic tombs in Spain and Portugal are incised with round eyes in the center or upper half of the bone, with additional designs above and below the eyes and on the back; the brows join to form a beak, the outer ends continuing around the eyes. (FIGURES 91–93). The central motif is often surrounded by many parallel lines; on some amulets the multiple eyebrow motif alternates with bands of zig-zags or nets. The eyes of stone cylinder figurines are flanked by double or triple chevrons and underlined by a semicircular line; the zig-zag design at the back of the head and over the crown is apparently a hair/water metaphor.

The third type of amulet, schist plaques perforated for suspension, has an indication of arms along the sides, the typical owl eyes and beak, and horizontal tri-lines over the cheeks. Chevrons, zig-zags, and striated triangle designs cover the rest of the plaque on both sides (see fig. 371).

FIGURE 93

1

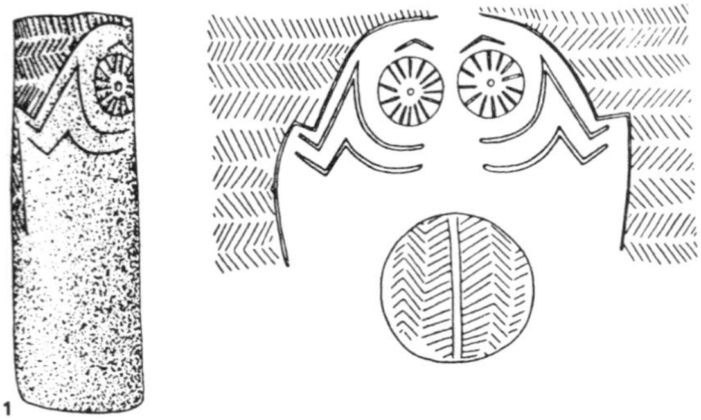

2

3

4

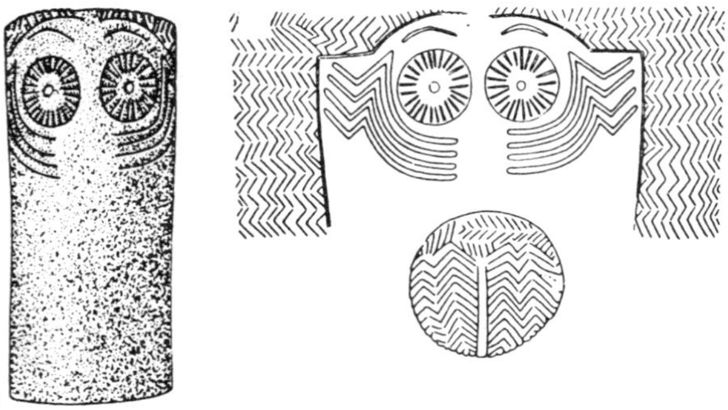

FIGURE 93 These stone "eye idols" from megalithic graves all share two or four lines curving under the eyes and ending as chevrons on the temples. The zigzag pattern over the top and back may represent hair, and the blank columns a part. Los Millares (Moron de la Frontera, Sevilla, Spain; probably early 3rd mill. B.C.) (1) H. 7.4 cm. (2) H. 7.4 cm. (3) H. 7.6 cm. (4) H. 7.6 cm.

The eye motif is also part of the design on bowls, dishes, and megaliths recovered from the Los Millares and other tholos tombs in Almeria. Their so-called "radiating sun" motif is a compound eye/sun symbol; it is more logically seen as a "radiant divine eye." The first example is composed of eyes and vulva, an abstract rendering of the Goddess. (FIGURE 94, 1) Often the eyes are associated with a single or multiple eyebrow motif and with multiple parallel lines and chevrons. On one richly decorated bowl, two units of the oculi motif and one unit of a stag with does are separated by panels of curved lines, horizontal striated bands, and three vertical dotted columns. (FIGURE 94, 2)

This compound symbolism is very likely associated with seasonal spring or summer rites. Antlers mysteriously appear in April and grow quickly through May and June; in July the tines are fully grown. They are an unmistakable metaphor for plant growth, in which seeds are sown in the spring and maturity is reached in summer. The associated multiple lines and garlands may be connected with spring rains, or they may represent a calendrical notation (note the twelve horizontal lines).

Suns as radiant divine eyes are also encountered on the megaliths of the tomb-shrines in Ireland, usually associated with dot-in-circles, concentric circles, and brushes. (FIGURE 94, 3) A magical affinity of owl eyes with a cupmark and cupmark in concentric circle, symbols of center and source, is represented in an engraving on a stone from Sess Kilgreen megalithic tomb. (FIGURE 94, 4) The act of fusion of the two symbols, eyes and cupmarks, itself was a ritual ensuring life forces. This stone is illuminated by the sun at the summer solstice (Brennan 1983: 89). Across the North Sea, the radiant eyes of the Owl Goddess appear on funerary vases of the Funnel-necked Beaker culture. (FIGURE 94, 5)

FIGURE 94

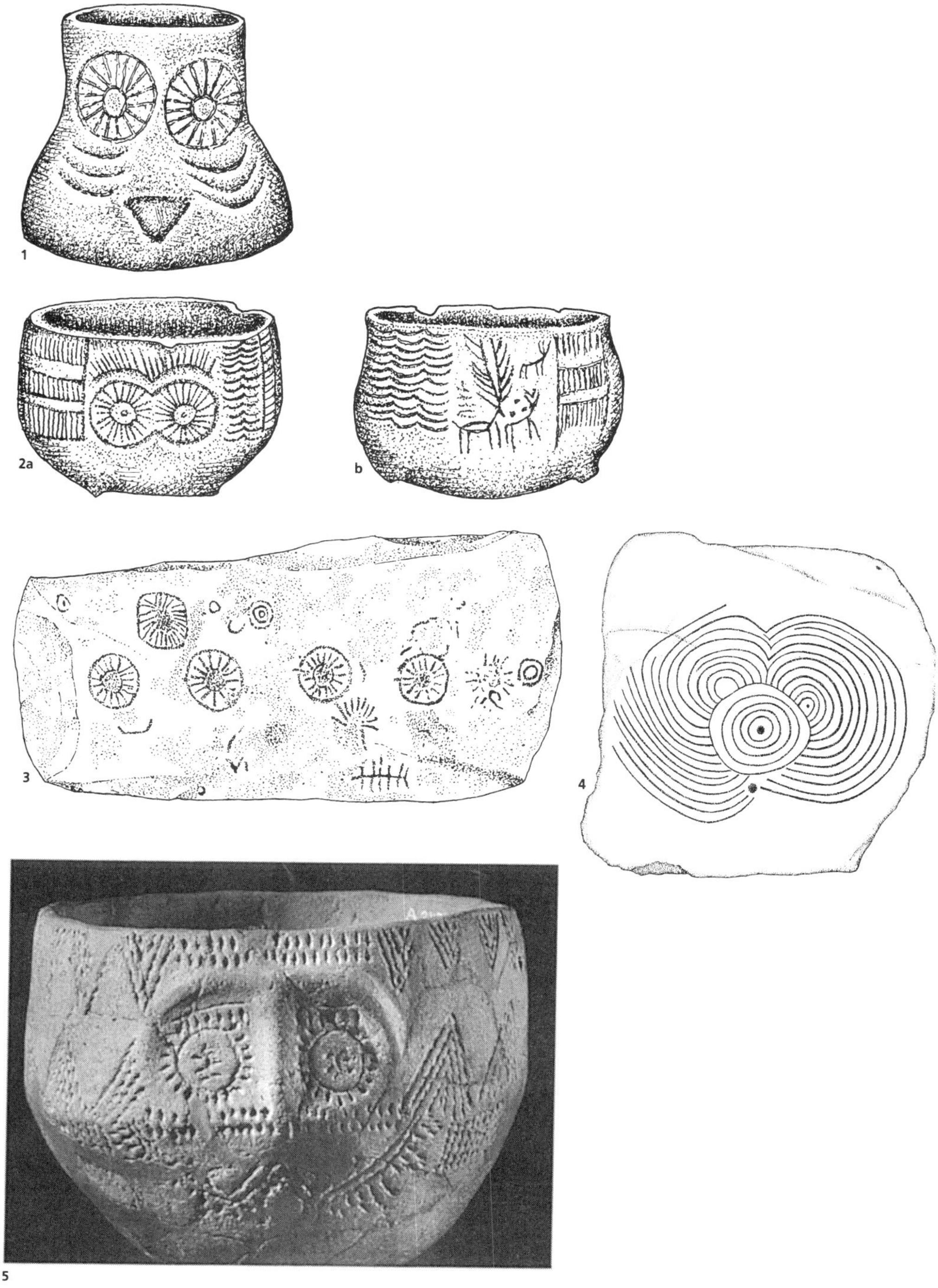

FIGURE 94 "Radiant divine eyes" appear on the tholos tomb artifacts that may be related to spring/summer growth rites. (1) Abstract rendering of the Goddess: eyes underlined by a curving tri-line with a vulva sign below. (2) Divine eyes with brush eyebrows and columns of curved lines, three horizontal bands of parallel lines, and three vertical dotted bands separating them from a stag and two deer. Los Millares (Almeria, Spain; c. 3000 B.C.). (3) These "radiant divine eyes" engraved on Irish stones are almost identical to those found on Spanish ceramics (see (1) and (2a)). Irish Neolithic (Dowth, County Mead, Ireland; c. 3200 B.C.). (4) Another example of the magical affinity between owl eyes and water-of-life (cupmarks) is from the small Sess Kilgreen megalithic tombstone at inner end of chamber. This compound symbol is illuminated by the sun on the summer solstice (County Tyrone, Ireland; c. 3000 B.C.). (5) In Neolithic Denmark, radiant eyes flanked with chevrons appear on vases of the Funnel-necked Beaker (TRB) culture. On this jar the design is incised and stabbed, but the eyebrows and beak of the Owl Goddess are in relief. (Suino, Kjong, Hammer herred. Copenhagen Nat. Museum. Approx. 3000 B.C.) (1) H. 10.9 cm. (2) H. 8 cm. (3) H. 90 cm. (4) H. 90 cm.

6.4 *As snake coils, ram horns, and eyes of the sun*

The pictorial association of eyes with snakes and the representation of eyes by snake coils was a widespread phenomenon in both southeastern and western Europe. The fusion of the two disparate elements into a single symbolic expression held for Old European artists a special fascination, to which they responded with particular ability. The dynamism of the serpent is a very ancient and recurrent human preoccupation. The snake's energy, it was believed, was drawn from water and the sun. The archaic metaphor that pairs the magical power of the serpent with the creative force in nature must have crystalized very early from a natural intuition. This imaginative metaphor is thoroughly integrated in the art of Old Europe: snake coils as Divine Eyes appear singly or joined (a double spiral) as a design motif on ceramics, temples, and tombs.

The magical affinity of snake and eye is pictorially expressed on Cucuteni vases of the early 4th millennium B.C. by their juxtaposition in painted bands, and by a double spiral with a broad undulant snake band above and below it. (FIGURE 95, 1, 2)

This motif continued in the Aegean area throughout the 3rd millennium B.C. A particularly interesting example is preserved on a sherd dating from the first half or middle of the 3rd millennium (Early Helladic II) from Aghios Kosmas in Attica. (FIGURE 95, 3) To the graphic metaphor of eyes and mouth as snake coils is added that of the brows as ram horns, symbol of the fecund energy of the ram, sacred animal of the Goddess (see section 9, below).

FIGURE 95

FIGURE 95 The dynamic energy of the snake is often coupled with the Divine Eye Source in southeast and west Europe. (1) On this Cucuteni lid, the eyes are snake spirals bordered by snakelike bands. Negative design in black on orange-red. Cucuteni B (Cucuteni, NE Romania; 3800–3600 B.C.). (2) On vase necks of the Cucuteni B culture, large eyes appear interspersed with two snakes and crescents (Valea Lupului, NE Romania; 3800–3600 B.C.). (3) The ram, sacred animal of the Goddess, is also associated with snakes and eyes. On this potsherd of the early 3rd millenium B.C., the eyes are snake coils and the eyebrows ram horns. The eyebrows are in relief, while the eyes are excised and white-encrusted. Early Helladic II Aghios Kosmas, Attica; mid-3rd mill. B.C.). (1) DIA. 10.8 cm.

FIGURE 96

FIGURE 96 Oculi motifs as snake coils or ram horns are engraved on the entrances to tombs, as on these rock-cut tombs in Sicily. Early Bronze Age (Castellucio, SE Sicily; 3000–2500 B.C.)

The oculi/snake-coil/ram-horn metaphor is engraved on entrance doors to the Early Bronze Age rock-cut tombs of southeastern Sicily. (FIGURE 96)

Magnificent snake coil oculi are abundant in the early great stone temples of Malta at Ġgantija, Haġar Qim, Bugibba, and Tarxien. (FIGURE 97) The V sign between the snake-coil eyes may represent a beak, or it may simply serve as a designation of the Goddess. The limestone blocks with oculi in relief serve to partition corridors and chambers in the temples, accentuating the presence of the Goddess. The most elaborately decorated blocks still extant can be seen in the temple of Tarxien (early 3rd millennium B.C.); its large slabs show various ways in which the motif developed as a decorative device—among them long blocks with a running spiral motif sprouting buds or branches. Collectively, the temples are witness to the outstanding talent and craftsmanship devoted at Malta to worship of the Goddess.

The megalithic art of western Europe is replete with snake coil and double-snake-coil-motifs, as independent units or as part of an anthropomorphic figure. In some cases the "double-snake-coil eye" and single-snake-coil motif occur together on a single stone surface (Herity 1974: 81, 92, 104; see also our fig. 370).

Linguistic evidence also reflects the peculiar interchangeability of the eyes and the sun. In Old Irish *súil* is "eye," while in other languages it means "sun" (cf. Lithuanian and Latvian *saule*, "sun": see Hamp 1975). Furthermore, there was a goddess named *Sulis* (quite likely the same noun as *súil*) equated with Minerva in Roman Britain. She was a patronness of the art of healing honored at thermal springs at Bath, *Aquae Sulis* (Jackson 1970: 68). Her epithet was *Suleviae* (in plural form), "twin-sunned." A semantic transfer, "eye"→"sun" in this divine epithet is quite clear. The magic regenerating eyes of this Goddess were seen as suns.

FIGURE 97

1

2

3

FIGURE 97 The dynamic snake and the Divine Eye Source combine in these snake oculi carved in relief on blocks from the magnificent temples of Malta and Ireland. ((1) Tarxien and (2) Haġar Qim, Malta; end 4th–early 3rd mill. B.C. (3) Newgrange tomb-sanctuary, curbstone 67, NE side of the mound, Boyne Valley, county Meath; c. 3200 B.C.)

FIGURE 98 Like Divine Eyes, cupmarks symbolize the source of life-giving moisture. British Neolithic (Baildon Moor, Yorkshire, England)

FIGURE 98

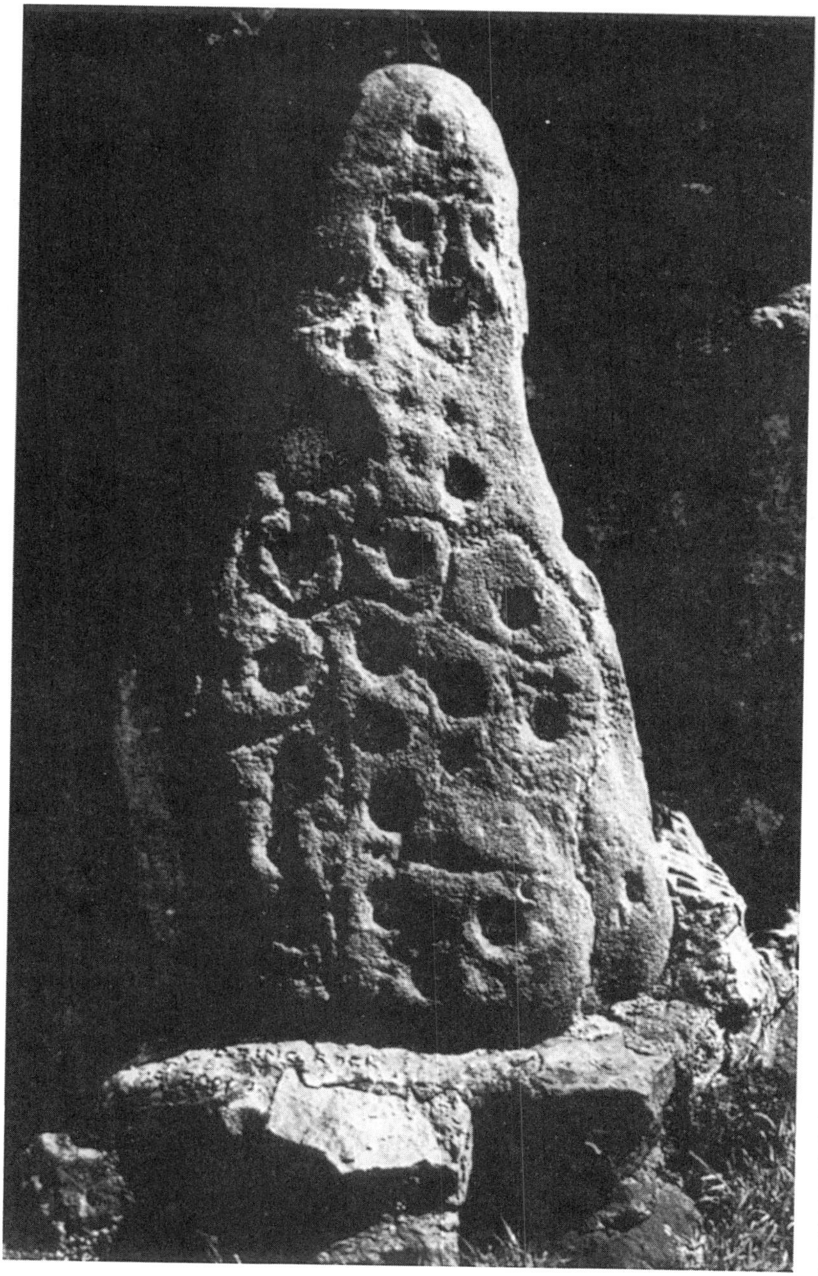

6.5 *As cupmarks and wells*

Predominant features of deliberately modified large rocks and human-shaped stones throughout Europe, particularly in the west and north, are small round hollows, the so-called cupmarks. They appear by the hundreds, alone or in association with eyes and snakes. Occasionally an anthropomorphic stone — the Goddess — is solidly covered with them. (FIGURE 98) Not infrequently they are surrounded by single, double, or multiple circles and are clearly metaphor — i.e., eyes that are simultaneously the source of divine liquid, the water of life itself, and its receptacles when it falls.

Their meaning is suggested by the fact that such cupmarks have to this day retained some of their symbolic significance in the European peasant subculture, which attributes healing powers to the rainwater which collects in them. Paralytics and those with other disabilities seek relief by drinking the holy water, washing in it, or rubbing it on the afflicted parts. In Greece, the July 26 feast of Saint Paraskevi (which means "Friday"), the heir of the prehistoric Goddess, is an especially good time for curing eye diseases. Hundreds of silver ex-votos representing human eyes can be seen adorning her icons (Megas 1963: 144). In the summer of 1986, I saw such votive offerings attached to the painting of the Saint in the chapels on the island of Paros, in the middle of the Aegean Sea.

A cupmark is a miniature well. Holy wells under large stones are sacrosanct and considered to be mysterious sources of the Goddess's life-giving moisture, a belief found in all Europe up to the 20th century. In prehistory and in folk memories, well and cupmark were symbolically interchangeable. Both were symbols of the centrally concentrated Goddess life force.

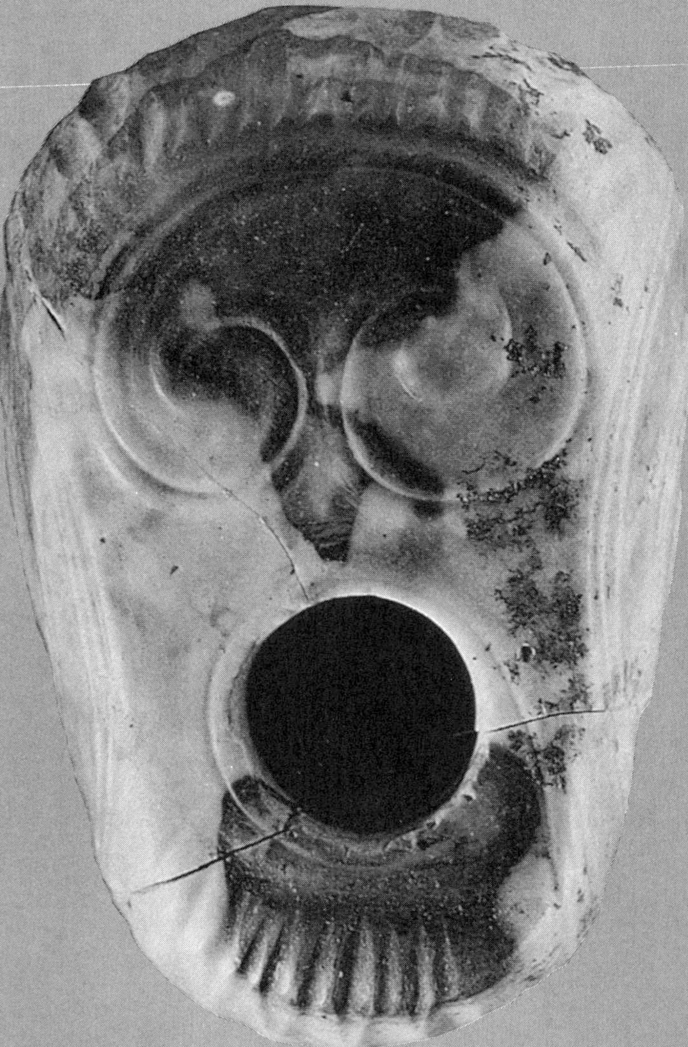

Masterfully carved anthropomorphic head with wide-open mouth and spiral eyes, snake spirals on both sides; from Knowth, Ireland. See figure 102, page 65.

7/ Open Mouth/Beak of the Goddess

The open mouth or beak is another expression of the Divine Source. This is manifested in Bird Goddess images, in shrine models shaped like a bird's nest and topped by a bird head with widely open beak, in the spouts of cult vases marked by the insignia of the Bird Goddess, and in vessels shaped like a fish mouth.

7.1 *On figurines and shrine models*

The open mouth is a very old and enduring symbolic feature of the stone or clay figurine; rendered as a round hole or a cupmark, it is encountered in the east Mediterranean and southeastern Europe from the 7th millennium B.C. on. The stone figurines with cupmarked mouths from the Yarmukian culture in Lebanon focus on that feature as the principal identifying element. (FIGURE 99) Other facial features are absent, except for engraved lines as eyes and perhaps two or three other lines.

The mouth as a round hole on a series of Sesklo and Starčevo figurine masks of the 7th and early 6th millennia apparently had the same symbolic significance as the cupmark. Wide open beaks are prominent on Butmir terracotta figurines wearing masks marked with inverted V signs. (FIGURE 100) The face of some Karanovo figurines of the mid-5th millennium have no features other than the open mouth; on others a beak is indicated, and there are three holes under the mouth. (FIGURE 101) Clay shrine models are occasionally topped by a bird head with a wide-open beak, which unmistakably establishes their tie with the Bird Goddess.

FIGURE 99

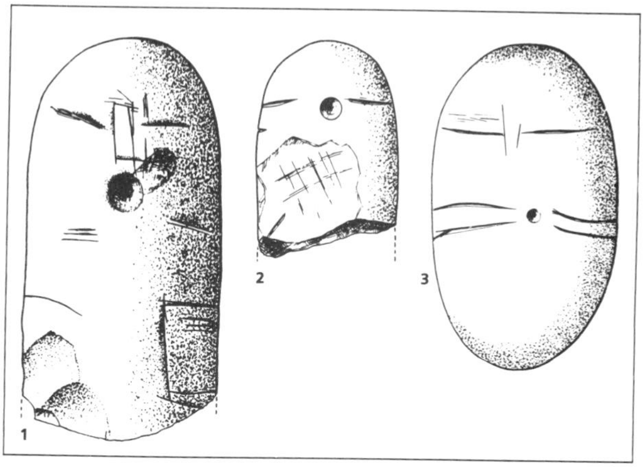

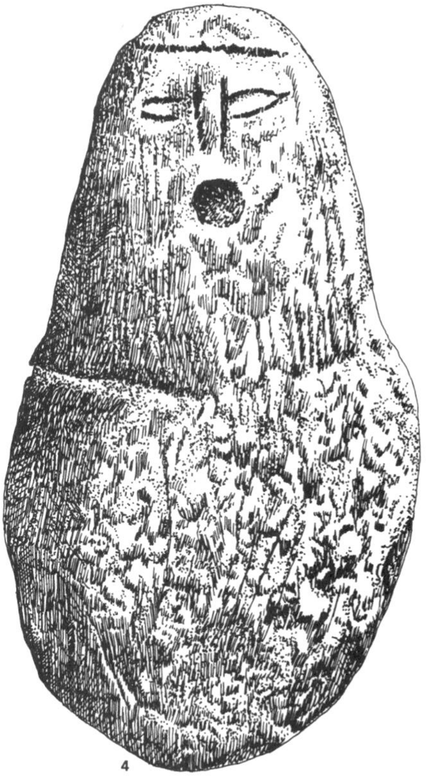

FIGURE 99 The open mouth is expressed on these stone Neolithic examples by cupmarks on otherwise almost featureless faces. (1–3) Yarmukian (Sha'ar Hagolan, Jordan Valley, Lebanon; end 7th mill. B.C.); (4) A similar type is this stone figurine also of the Pottery Neolithic A (Byblos, Lebanon; end 7th mill. B.C.).
(1) H. 7.3 cm. (2) H. 4.9 cm. (3) H. 5.8 cm. (4) H. 6.9 cm.

A numinous wide-open mouth can be seen on a masterfully carved anthropomorphic object of stone found in the tomb-sanctuary of Knowth, Ireland. (FIGURE 102) Above the round mouth are spiral-shaped eyes and a snake coil is carved on the side. Its symbolism harmonizes very well with that of Knowth and Newgrange where spiral oculi, snake coils, and cupmarks are very frequent motifs. They symbolize the generative Divine Source and are interchangeable symbols. This rare work of art proves that the loose geometric symbols engraved or hollowed on tomb walls and curbstones are not disassociated from the anthropomorphic divinity in whose power lies the regeneration of life. In the scholarly literature to date this outstanding piece of art and craftsmanship is described as the "macehead" of a priest/king or leader who built the grand tomb of Knowth (Eogan and Richardson 1982: 131). But clearly it speaks the language of the Goddess and should not be taken out of the context of Old European symbolism.

7.2 *The Goddess as a container with open mouth/spout*

The Goddess as an anthropomorphic container with the spout as mouth was a concept which took form shortly after the introduction of pottery and found frequent expression for several thousand years.

A good example is an early Vinča vase from Parţa, western Romania (c. 5200–5000 B.C.). (FIGURE 103) Its spout is in the shape of a human head supported by arms and incised with a multiple chevron on top; below the head/spout are a double M and a zig-zag sign, symbols of the Goddess and liquid respectively. When such vessels were used and liquid poured from the mouth of the Goddess, her function as Divine Source of sacred moisture was graphically reenacted.

FIGURE 100

1

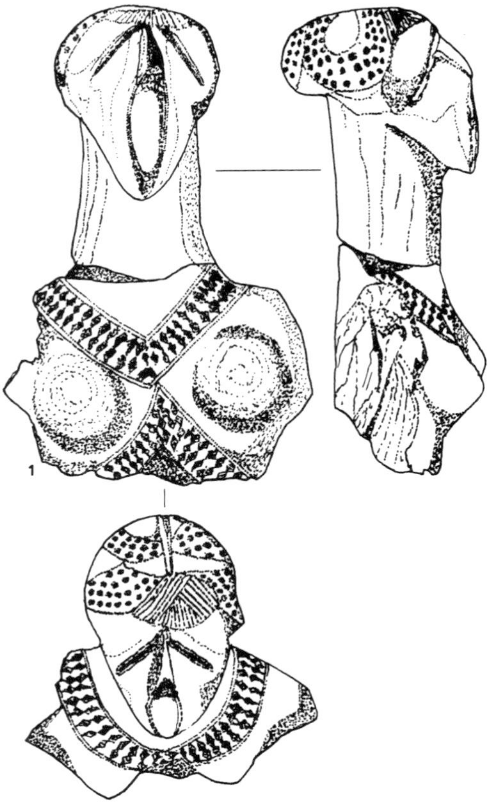

2

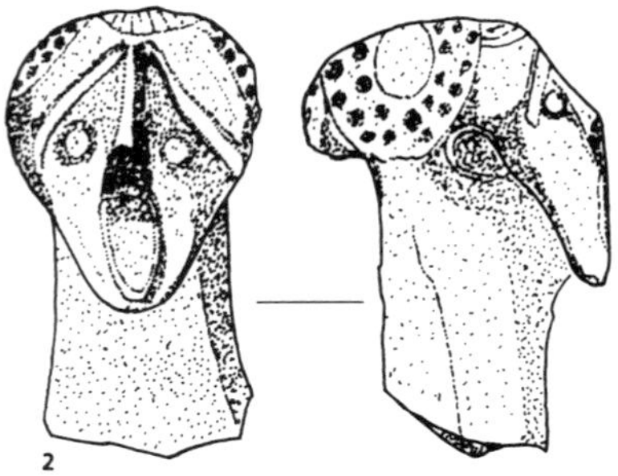

FIGURE 100 The style may be more sophisticated than in the 7th millenium, but the concept expressed is the same on these Butmir figurines wearing masks with wide-open beaks. The upper one has eyes formed by an inverted V, and the V motif is repeated between her breasts. The figurine below has brow-ridges formed by an inverted V. (Butmir, at Sarajevo; early 5th mill. B.C.) (1) H. 7.7 cm. (2) H. 4.4 cm.

FIGURE 101

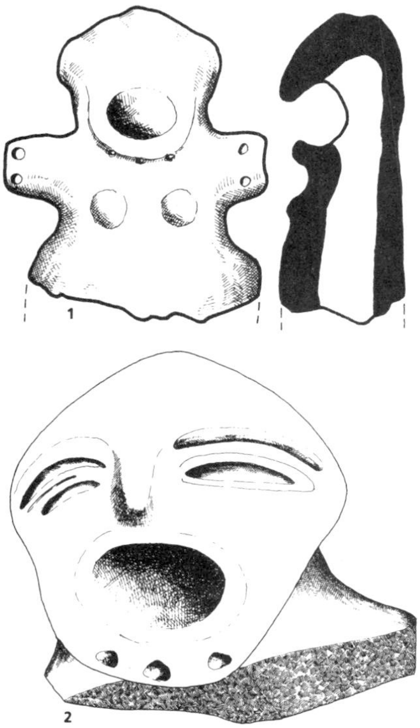

FIGURE 101 There are two distinct types of Karanovo VI figurines in this tradition. (1) Only the mouth is indicated on the face of this figurine, and it is enormous. (2) Eyes and a beaked nose fill out this mask with a gaping mouth. Note that on both types of figurines there are three holes below the mouth ((1) Ruse and (2) Hassan-Faka, C Bulgaria; mid-5th mill. B.C.). (1) H. 10 cm. (2) H. 7.5 cm.

FIGURE 102

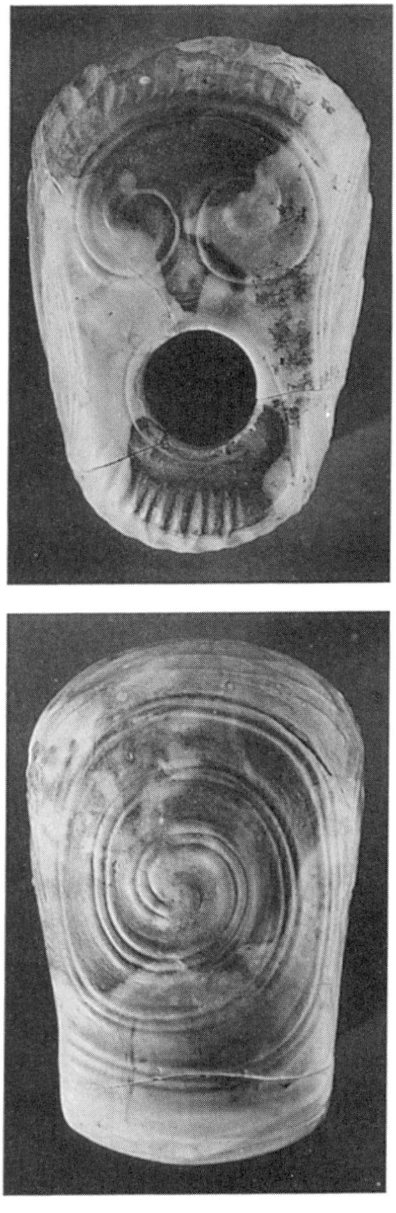

FIGURE 102 This masterfully carved stylized anthropomorphic head has a wide-open mouth, spiral eyes, snake spirals on both sides, and a fluted design along the forehead and chin. The object was manufactured from a block of flint, and the decoration is in relief. The surface was finished off by polishing. Found in the east tomb of Knowth on the ground floor, surrounded by a layer of shale, it lay at the entrance to the northern recess and possibly is contemporary with the early burial deposit in this tomb. Neolithic Ireland (Knowth, Boyne Valley, County Meath; c. 3500–3200 B.C.) H. 7.9 cm.

FIGURE 103

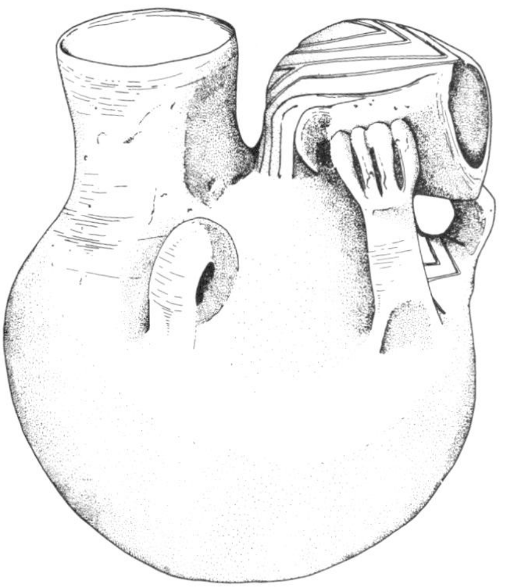

FIGURE 103 The spout on this intriguing vessel is the front of a head marked with chevrons supported by upraised arms. Between the arms are M and zig-zag signs identifying the figure as the Goddess, from whose mouth flows nourishing liquid. Early Vinča (Parţa, Timişoara, W Romania; 5200–5000 B.C.) H. 16.4 cm.

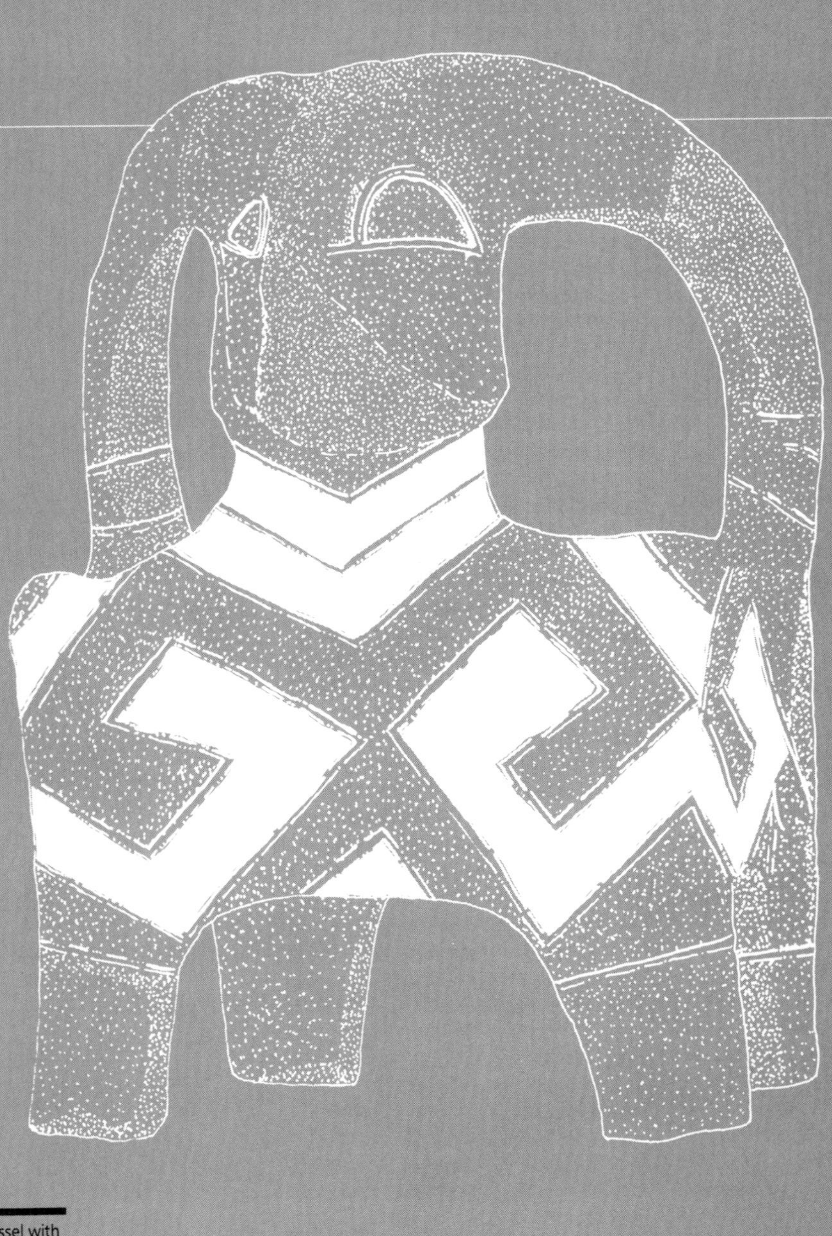

Ram-headed vessel with beaked face and chevron and meander; probably served as a lamp or sacrificial container in a Vinča copper mine. See figure 110, page 70.

8/ *Giver of Crafts: Associations with Spinning, Weaving, Metallurgy, and Musical Instruments*

We know from Greek myth that Athena invented earthenware, spinning and weaving, the flute, trumpet, plough, rake, ox yoke, horse bridle, chariot, and even the ship. In other words, she was the inventor not only of the womanly arts but of *all* arts. Was her predecessor—the prehistoric Bird Goddess, the Giver of All—also the Giver of Crafts?

Her associations with spinning, weaving, metallurgy, and music can be traced through her signs, incised on spindle whorls, loom-weights, crucibles, and musical instruments.

8.1 *Spinning and weaving*

The relation between the Bird Goddess and the art of spinning is evidenced by the chevron and the chevron combined with meander found on Neolithic and Copper Age spindle whorls. (FIGURE 104) The chevron long continues to be incised on spinning figures or on the chairs upon which they sit, even as late as in Ancient Greece. On an Attic Red-figure vase of c. 470–450 B.C., a chevron and parallel lines are painted over the chair of a spinning, seated woman (Stanford University Collection, No. 17410). Another clear connection between spinning and the Bird Goddess is a series of ancient Greek terracotta plaques showing an owl with human arms spinning wool (Nilsson 1950: 493–94).

Also appearing on spindle whorls is the M sign and zig-zag. (FIGURE 105) Numbers of spindle whorls produced c. 5500–4200 B.C. were inscribed with linear signs including V's and M's. The inscriptions are probably dedications or vows to the patroness of the craft of spinning.

FIGURE 104

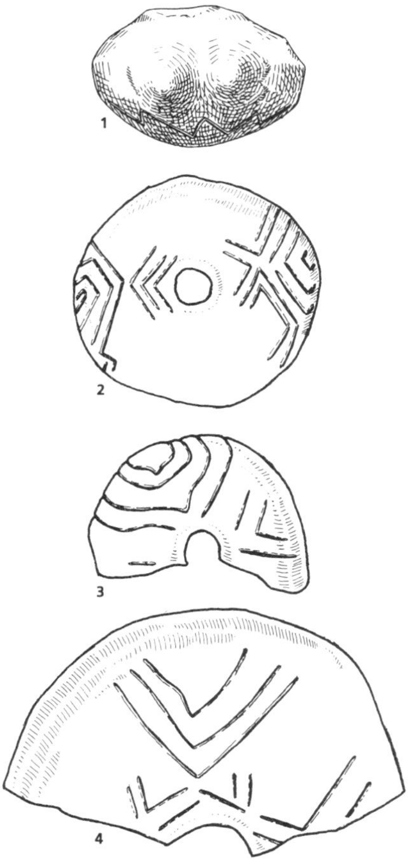

FIGURE 105

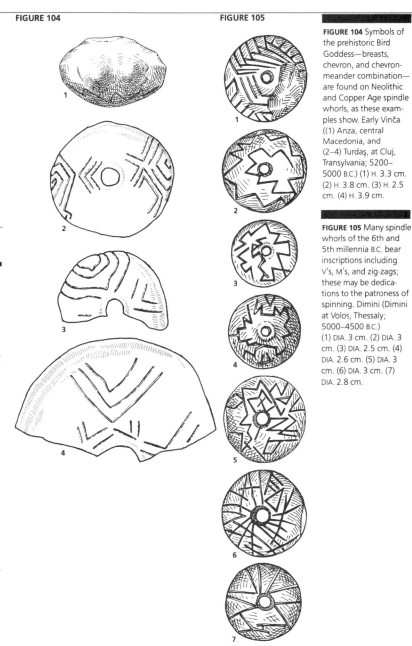

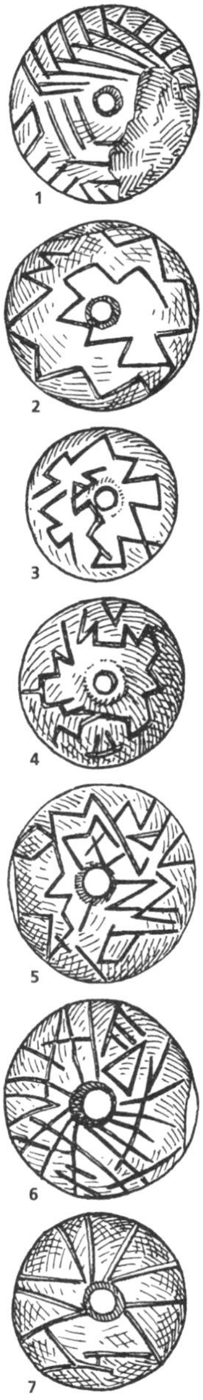

FIGURE 104 Symbols of the prehistoric Bird Goddess—breasts, chevron, and chevron-meander combination—are found on Neolithic and Copper Age spindle whorls, as these examples show. Early Vinča ((1) Anza, central Macedonia, and (2–4) Turdaş, at Cluj, Transylvania; 5200–5000 B.C.) (1) H. 3.3 cm. (2) H. 3.8 cm. (3) H. 2.5 cm. (4) H. 3.9 cm.

FIGURE 105 Many spindle whorls of the 6th and 5th millennia B.C. bear inscriptions including V's, M's, and zig-zags; these may be dedications to the patroness of spinning. Dimini (Dimini at Volos, Thessaly; 5000–4500 B.C.) (1) DIA. 3 cm. (2) DIA. 3 cm. (3) DIA. 2.5 cm. (4) DIA. 2.6 cm. (5) DIA. 3 cm. (6) DIA. 3 cm. (7) DIA. 2.8 cm.

FIGURE 106

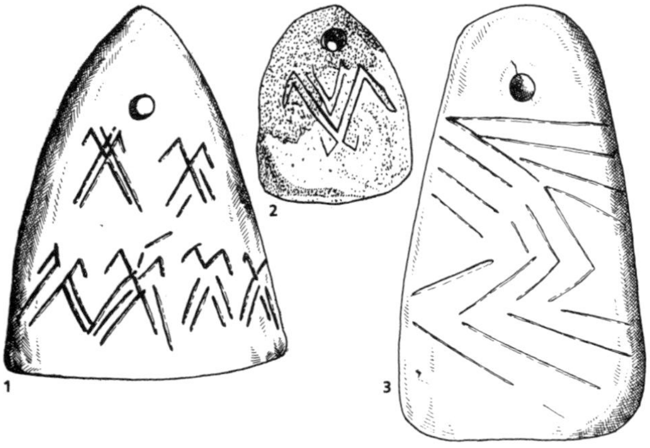

FIGURE 106 The Bird Goddess is also associated with weaving by the appearance of chevrons and M's on loom-weights. (1) Tisza (Varşand, SW Romania); (2) Szakálhát (Battonya, SE Hungary); (3) Karanovo VI (Gumelniţa, south of Bucharest, 5000–4500 B.C.) (1) H. 7.6 cm. (2) H. 6.5 cm. (3) H. 9 cm.

FIGURE 107

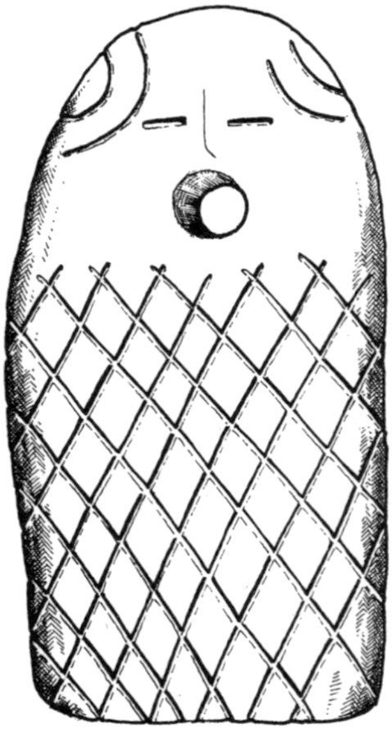

FIGURE 107 An early loom-weight in the form of the Goddess; her face comprises slit eyes, a pinched nose, and a perforation for a mouth; the lower part is covered with a net design. Starčevo (Pernik, Struma Valley; W Bulgaria; 5800–5600 B.C.) H. 8.8 cm.

FIGURE 108

FIGURE 108 This cylindrical four-sided figurine is marked with a fleece sign under each face and linear inscriptions below. Karanovo VI (Bereketskaja Mogila, Stara Zagora, C Bulgaria; 4600–4300 B.C.) H. 6 cm.

FIGURE 109 Evidence for the Bird Goddess's role as patroness of metallurgy includes (1) this lidded Cucuteni vase decorated with breasts and chevrons which contained more than 400 copper artifacts, mostly schematic anthropomorphic figurines (shown separately), ornaments, and two axes (Karbuna hoard, Soviet Moldavia; c. 4700–4500 B.C.); and (2) this Karanovo VI crucible whose interior is graced by two pairs of breasts (Goljamo Delčevo, NE Bulgaria; 4500–4300 B.C.). (2) DIA. 16.2 cm.

The link between weaving and the Goddess is evidenced by the appearance of her signs and features on loom-weights. (FIGURE 106) These include chevrons, M's, a beaked face, and a schematic figure of several triangles. One of the earliest specimens, dated to 5800–5600 B.C., is from Bulgaria. The Bird Goddess's pinched nose (beak) and incised eyes are at the tip of the loom-weight, and a round perforation symbolizes her open mouth. The remainder of the loom-weight is covered with a net pattern. (FIGURE 107)

In addition to the above, a fleece sign associated with a triangle (vulva) appears on loom-weights of the 5th millennium B.C.) Karanovo culture. (FIGURE 108) The fleece sign is a schematic rendering of the stretched-out hide of a sheep. This sign reminds us that the Bird Goddess is connected with the source of hides; the ram is an animal sacred to her (see section 9).

Further linking the Neolithic Goddess with weaving are numerous wall paintings of textiles at Çatal Hüyük, in the second shrine of Level III. Mellaart, the site's excavator, believes that this Goddess, like Athena afterwards, was already regarded as the patroness of weaving (Mellaart 1963: 82).

Twisting, spinning, weaving, and sewing are common to the Greek Athena, Roman Minerva, and the goddesses still alive in European folk beliefs: the Basque Andrea Mari, Irish St. Brigit, Baltic Laima, East Slavic Mokosh/Paraskeva-Pyatnitsa ("Friday"), and Romanian Sfînta Vineri ("St. Friday"). People would perform no work which involved turning, twisting, or spinning on Friday, the special day of the Goddess. Any twisting was tabu on that day in honor of St. Brigit in Ireland. A similar injunction against specific kinds of work honors St. Paraskeva-Pyatnitsa, who originated as the goddess Mokosh (known from the Old Kievan pantheon of A.D. 980 as the only female goddess among the male gods of Indo-European origin). "Women's work"– sewing, spinning, weaving—was prohibited on Friday, and on her annual feast day, October 28, women might not work to obviate blindness, sickness, or transformation into frogs. A sacrifice to Pyatnitsa consisted of flax, woven materials, lamb's wool, or thread put into a well surmounted by a wooden idol of her.

FIGURE 109

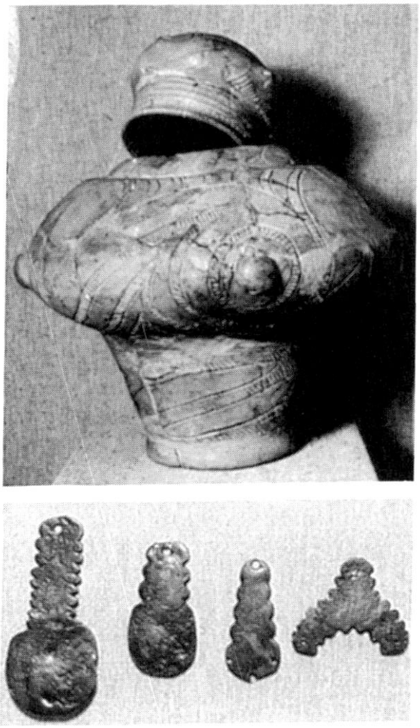

1

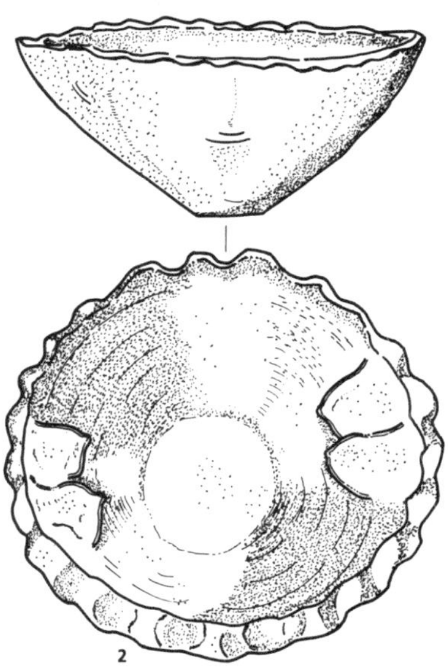

2

8.2 *Metallurgy and flint mining*

Decorative motifs on crucibles and metal artifacts evoke the Bird Goddess's role as patroness of metallurgy. In an early Cucuteni vase decorated with breasts and chevrons more than 400 copper objects including schematic anthropomorphic pendants have been kept stored, probably in association with the worship of the Goddess. (FIGURE 109, 1) A crucible from Goljamo Delčevo, northeastern Bulgaria, c. 4500–4300 B.C., has two pairs of breasts in the interior. (FIGURE 109, 2) Further, the same parallel line and chevron motifs appearing on Bird Goddess figurines decorate copper axes manufactured c. 4500–4000 B.C. (see Bognár-Kutzián 1972: figs. 5, 7).

From the copper mines of Rudna Glava, northern Yugoslavia, a four-footed cult vessel with ram's head is decorated with chevrons and meanders. (FIGURE 110, 1) It was discovered with exceptionally beautiful burnished Vinča vases of c. 5000 B.C. This is mute testimony to the occurrence of cult activities in mines, probably honoring the patroness of metallurgic crafts. Why else would fine pottery, and a cult vessel as well, be found there?

The ram-headed vessel must have served as a lamp or sacrificial container. It is marked with the same signs as are the majority of Vinča figurines portraying the Bird Goddess, namely a chevron under the throat and meanders over the lower body. Furthermore, the profile of the horned head's mask is peculiarly pointed—that is, beaked. The artist's notion very probably was to portray a ram with Bird Goddess features, the divinity and her sacred animal in one.

The decoration of the black burnished vases found in several caches at the Rudna Glava mines consists of a ram-horn/snake-spiral motif, concentric semicircles, and parallel lines, executed in incision and in a channelling technique. (FIGURE 110, 2, 3) The motifs harmonize well with those encountered on figurines portraying the Bird Goddess and on ram figurines as well, as will be seen from the next section.

The intimate relation of the Goddess with metallurgy is also evidenced in later times. In Cyprus, in the Late Bronze Age site at Kition, she is portrayed standing on a copper ingot (Karageorghis 1976: 170).

A memory of the Goddess's association with metalworking is even reflected in certain Latvian mythological songs preserved to our times. In their 63 variants, it is Laima (Fate), not the Indo-European Heavenly Smith (Latvian Kalējs), who forges spurs for the Heavenly Twins or warriors as in this song: "Where do you rush, Laima, with handful of hammers? To the smithy, to forge the spurs for young warriors" (Biezais 1955: 175). Irish Brigit had two sisters of the same name: Brigit, the woman of healing, and Brigit, the woman of smithcraft (Doan 1981: 107). In Roman reliefs, Vulcan, the divine smith, is frequently shown with Minerva, the Roman version of Athena.

The Goddess's connection with flint mines is suggested by the recovery of a gross female figurine carved of white chalk from Grimes's Grave in Norfolk, England. She was at the bottom of the mine set on a ledge in the wall, a triangular heap of blocks of mined flint lay in front of her, and there were seven red-deer antlers on top of the pile. Among the antlers were several balls of chalk. The Grimes's Grave mines are dated to around 2850 B.C. (Clarke 1963: 21, 22; Burl 1981: 44–65).

The placement of Goddess figurines, sculptures of her sacred animal and cult vases deep in shafts, her association with crucibles and ingots, and the recurrence of this association in various places and periods suggest that the link between the Goddess and metallurgical craft and flint mining was not accidental.

FIGURE 110

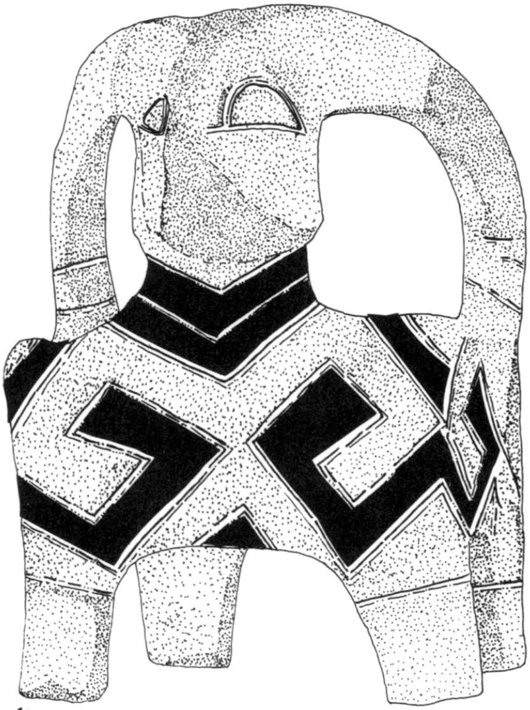

1a

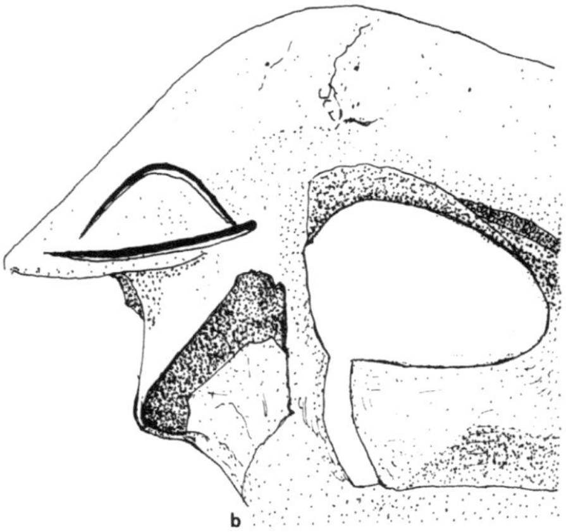

b

2

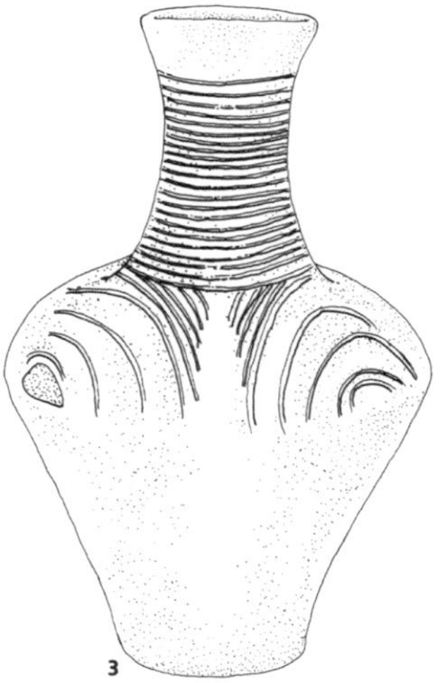

3

FIGURE 111

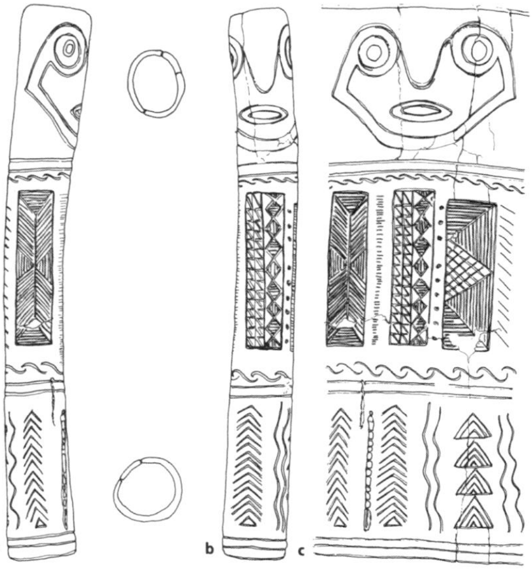

FIGURE 110 A cache of ritual artifacts was found in a copper mine, connecting the Goddess with metallurgy. (1) This ram-headed vessel with beaked face and chevron and meander decorations must have served as a lamp or sacrificial container. (2), (3) These black-burnished amphorae are incised and channeled in ram-horn/snake spiral, concentric semicircle, and parallel line motifs. Vinča (Rudna Glava, south of the Danube, Yugoslavia; c. 5000 B.C.)
(1) H. 18.6 cm. (2) H. 35.4 cm. (3) H. 41.1 cm.

FIGURE 111 This probable wind instrument is made of the diaphysis of a right human femur and provides evidence for the Bird Goddess association with music. An Owl Goddess mask with large round eyes is represented in the upper section; the eyes are two holes. The middle and lower sections are covered with panels of chevron, triangle, zigzag, lozenge, and snake designs; *a*, side; *b*, front view; *c*, extended design (Gaban shelter, near Trento, N Italy; Neolithic stratum). H. 22.9 cm.

8.3 *Music*

Was the Bird Goddess patroness of music from the beginning of agriculture, or even earlier? This is difficult to say. Examples of prehistoric musical instruments rarely are preserved unless they are themselves of bone, shell, or stone, or they are terracotta or chalk replicas of wood and skin instruments. However, some finds clearly indicate a relation with the Goddess as early as the Upper Paleolithic. The Magdalenian whistles made of hollow eagle bone with blow holes cut into them which if blown can give a high flute sound were curiously decorated with multiple chevrons and rows of tiny angles. These motifs link the instrument with the Bird Goddess (see Marshack 1972: figs. 43–56). The same can be said about the Upper Paleolithic musical instruments from eastern Europe. Red chevrons decorate a set of percussion instruments found inside the house at Mezin near Chernigov, W Ukraine, dated to c. 18,000–15,000 B.C. The house was built of mammoth bones and is thought to have served for festive occasions. The set included a shoulder blade, a thigh bone, two jaw bones, a fragment of pelvis, and a portion of a skull, all of mammoth. In addition, there were two ivory rattles and a "castanet bracelet" made of three bands and decorated with rows of chevrons engraved. This set is considered to be the earliest Stone Age "orchestra" (Bibikov 1975).

A wind instrument made of a human femur from the Neolithic stratum of the Gaban Shelter near Trento, northern Italy, has a Goddess's mask incised on the upper part. (FIGURE 111) The middle and lower sections are decorated in panels of multiple chevrons, striated triangles, bands of zig-zags and diamonds, and winding lines. The face portrayed on the mask has a long beak-shaped nose.

At Ovčarovo, an early Karanovo VI settlement (c. 4500 B.C.), a group of miniature ritual objects including three long cylindrical drums was found. (FIGURE 112) The associated clay miniatures consist of three altar stands, three tables, eight backed chairs, three lidded bowls, two large dishes, and four figurines with upraised arms (or wings) decorated with a meander design. The altar stands are decorated with chevrons, tri-lines, spirals, concentric circles, and several compound signs (V and spiral). The presence of these symbols, particularly of the meanders on the figurines, suggests that this miniature tableau might have replicated an actual ritual for the Bird Goddess in which drums were used. The Ovčarovo drums are not decorated, but cylindrical clay models of drums from other Karanovo sites are decorated with meanders and chevrons; one such was discovered at Bereketskaja tell near Stara Zagora, central Bulgaria (Stara Zagora Museum).

Evidence of the intimate relation between the drum and the Goddess also comes from the northwestern European Funnel-necked Beaker (TRB) culture. In central and northwestern Germany alone, more than 60 clay drums have been discovered; 33 were deposited in graves, some in collective megalithic tombs, others in subsequent stone cist or flat graves of the Walternienburg, Bernburg, and Salzmünde groups (Fischer 1955). The decoration on some of the drums is chevrons, zig-zags, triangles, checkerboards, pairs of hooks, and whirls—symbols common on funerary equipment and on the stones of megalithic tombs as well as on Bird Goddess figurines. The most explicit decoration consists of breasts, a pair on each side of the drum; they must have served as handles and to fasten the skin striking surface. (FIGURE 113) The breasts obviously are those of the Bird Goddess; they also appear in relief on orthostats of the gallery graves of Brittany (see figs. 69, 70).

Further evidence for this relation between the drum and the Goddess comes from the Bronze Age. At Folkton Wold, England, three chalk drums were recovered from a child's grave in a tumulus (barrow). (FIGURE 114) The main panel in the center of two of the drums is dominated by the face of the Goddess in owl form.

To this day European peasants produce musical instruments in the shape of waterbirds. (FIGURE 115) Some instruments have handles or ends shaped like a duck, goose, swan, or snake, as was the case in the Minoan culture of Crete. A lyre with alabaster handles in the shape of swans or geese has been discovered in the palace of Mallia (Herakleion Museum, case 44). There is no logical reason for these instruments to be in the form of waterbirds and snakes, but we may conjecture that traditions from prehistory have kept these shapes alive. From the earliest historical times the swan has been associated with music. Among the Egyptians the swan was the hieroglyphic for "music"; in Greece it was often represented as singing to the lyre.

Although the association through time of musical instruments with Bird Goddess symbols and with birds and snakes is not a direct proof that the Goddess was considered the inventor of music, it bespeaks at a minimum her very special relationship to it. A survival of the music theme is found in Plato's *Republic*. In the tale of Er, the concentric spheres of the heavens turn around a spindle, like a vast spindle whorl. Each sphere is associated with a siren (Bird Goddess) who sings its particular note, creating the Music of the Spheres.

FIGURE 112

FIGURE 113

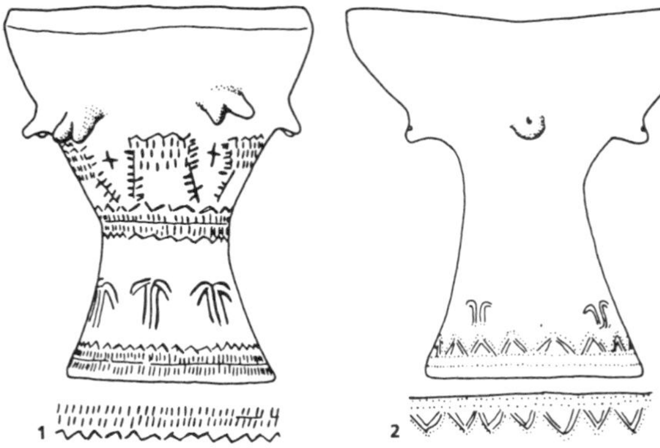

FIGURE 112 A very interesting assemblage of miniature ritual objects attests to the Goddess's association with music. Three drums (front) were found together with four winged figurines marked with V's, meanders, streams, and parallel lines; miniature tables with lidded vessels on top; eight chairs; and three altar screens painted on both sides with symbols—chevrons, serpents, parallel lines, a concentric circle. Karanovo VI (Ovčarovo, NE Bulgaria; mid-5th mill. B.C.)

FIGURE 113 More evidence for the connection between the Goddess and music is provided by these clay drums decorated with breasts, chevrons, zig-zags, pairs of hooks, and other signs. Salzmünde group ((1) Rössen and (2) Harth, central Germany; 3700–3500 B.C.)

FIGURE 114 Chalk replica of a Bronze Age drum has the face of an owl set off in a panel. Other decorative motifs include net-patterned triangles, lozenges, and tri-lines. (Folkton Wold, East Riding, Yorkshire; c. 2000 B.C.) H. 13.2 cm.

FIGURE 115 One clue as to whether the Bird Goddess served as the patroness of music comes from the historic period; European peasants still make musical instruments in the shape of waterbirds and snakes. These instrument handles are from modern Serbia. H. of details (1) 16.3 cm, (2) 15.8 cm, (3) 23.8 cm, (4) 23.3 cm, (5) 16 cm.

FIGURE 115

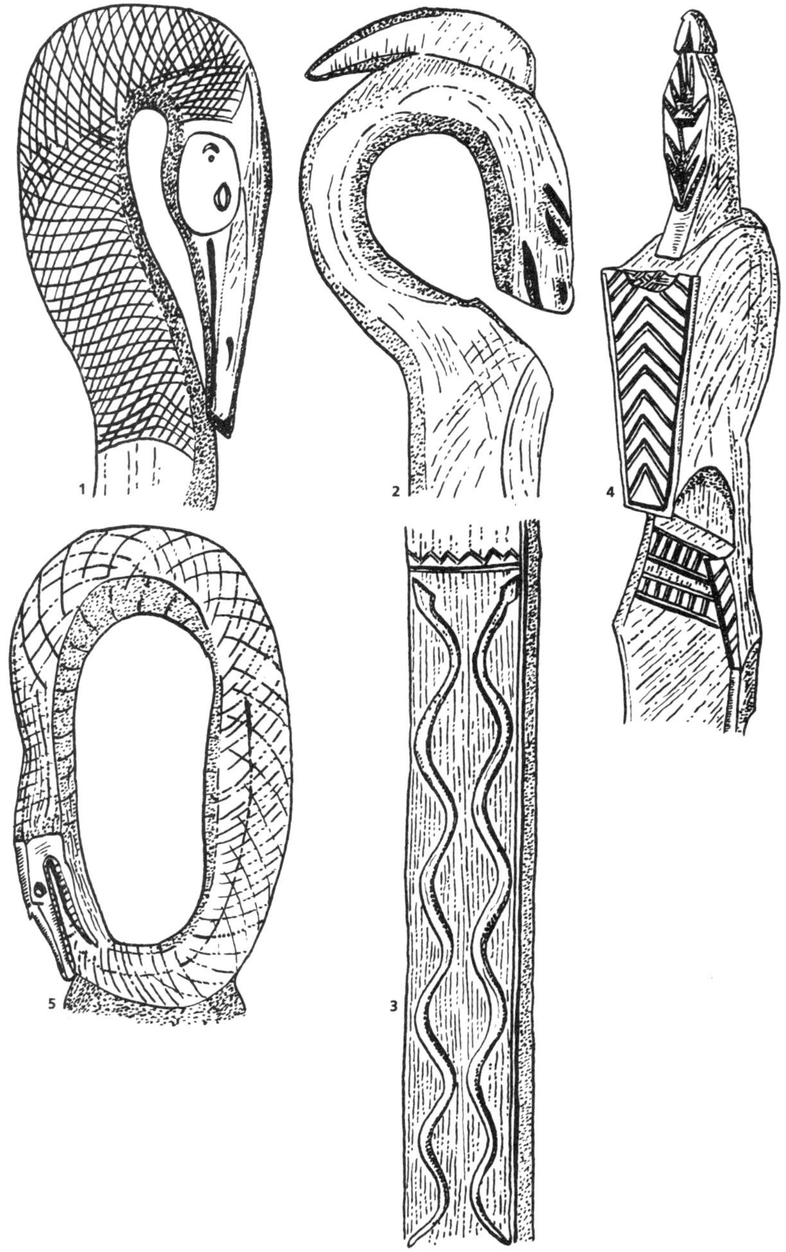

Terracotta ram figurine marked with groups of parallel lines; late Lengyel, Silesia. See figure 123, page 78.

9/ *The Ram, Animal of the Bird Goddess*

With the advent of animal domestication, it is not surprising that the ram emerges as a cult animal if one considers its importance to subsistence; sheep and goats account for 90% of animal bones found in Neolithic settlements. Its fleece provided warmth and its flesh nourishment.

From the 7th millennium B.C. onward, ram figurines are marked with chevrons, parallel lines, snake coils, tri-lines, and nets. The ram continues to be identified as an animal sacred to the Bird and Snake Goddess throughout the Copper and Bronze ages of Anatolia, the Aegean, the southern Balkans, Italy, and central, western, and northwestern Europe. Once the ram entered the conservative domain of religion, its veneration continued long after its importance to the economy declined during the Copper Age.

9.1 *Ram horns as stair motif on Neolithic vases and seals*

The ram-horn motif is found almost as frequently as the Goddess's insignia on Anatolian and Greek Neolithic pottery; it dominates design elements of Hacilar (central Anatolia) and Sesklo (Thessaly) ceramics. (FIGURE 116) Stylized ram horns on pottery from Hacilar II-V range from semi-naturalistic to completely abstract treatments.

If not for its association with the chevron and the beak, the "stair" design which developed from abstracted ram horns would have remained an undeciphered geometric motif. This design on painted wares of the Sesklo culture is nothing more than bands of interconnected ram heads. On the illustrated examples, stairlike ram horns cover the bodies of cups; a beak motif appears above the handles with chevrons beneath them.

Approximately a thousand years later, analogous treatments of stylized ram horns appear on the Dimini vases of Thessaly. On Serra d'Alto vessels of southeastern Italy (5th millennium B.C.), the ram's presence is indicated not only by the stair motif but also by fantastically stylized ram heads forming handles or appearing above them.

The ram-horn motif cannot be dismissed as a regional "style" of Hacilar, Sesklo, and Serra d'Alto pottery design, inasmuch as it is faithfully reproduced on seals for more than four millennia. The consistency of the motif equals that of other symbols—chevron, snake coil, meander, tri-line, streams, and net—with which it alternates or is associated.

FIGURE 116

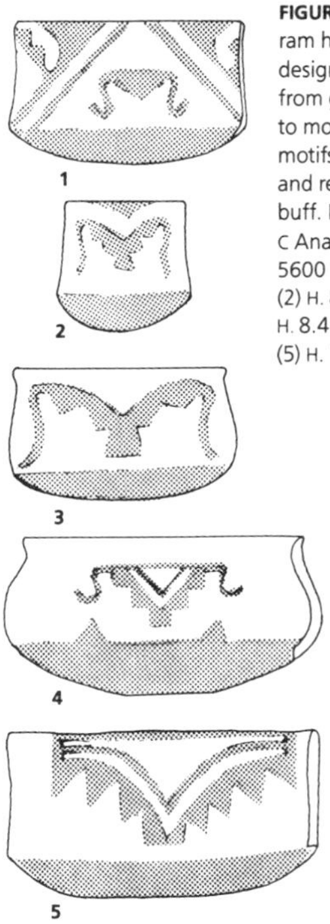

FIGURE 116 Portrayals of ram horns in ceramic design run the gamut from geometric "stair" to more naturalistic motifs. Painted brown and red on deep or pale buff. Hacilar II-V (Hacilar, C Anatolia; 6000–5600 B.C.) (1) H. 9.2 cm. (2) H. 8.4 cm. (3) H. 8.4 cm. (4) H. 10 cm. (5) H. 10.4 cm.

FIGURE 117

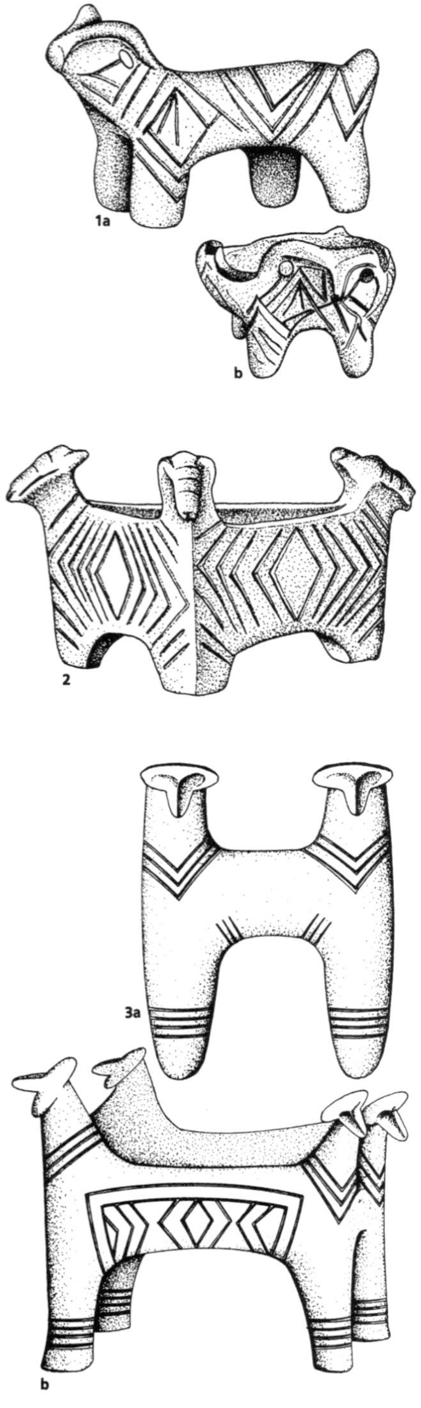

FIGURE 117 The association between the ram and Bird Goddess is clear on ram figurines and vessels incised with her insignia—chevrons, tri-lines, and parallel lines. Early Vinča ((1) and (2) Vinča; (3) Priština, S Yugoslavia; 5200–5000 B.C.) (1) H. 5.8 cm. (2) H. 7.3 cm. (3) H. 6.7 cm.

FIGURE 118

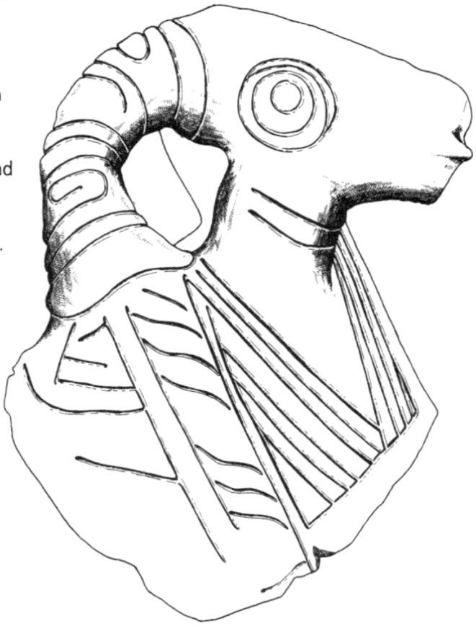

FIGURE 118 This soulful ram, a fragment of a shrine model, is elaborately decorated by incisions: a modified chevron over the chest, a bi-line on the neck, and snake spirals around the horns. Note the concentric circles for eyes. Vinča (Gradešnica, NW Bulgaria; 5000–4500 B.C.) H. 16.8 cm.

FIGURE 119

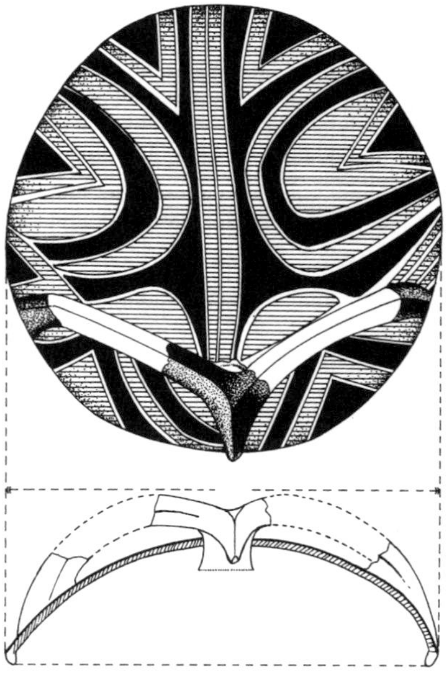

FIGURE 119 Some beautiful Gumelniţa and Cucuteni lids painted in various symbolic designs are opened by ram's head handles. White-bordered burgundy on brown. Karanovo VI (Gumelniţa, S Romania; mid-5th mill. B.C.) DIA. 25.5 cm.

9.2 *The Goddess's symbols on ram figurines*

The symbolic association of the ram and Bird Goddess is richly evidenced by zoomorphic figurines bearing the Goddess's insignia—V's, chevrons, inverted or opposed chevrons, and multiple parallel lines. (FIGURES 117–121)

The symbolic nature of stripes painted on ram figurines is clear, since stripes obviously have no natural connection with the animal's fleece. This tradition is represented by a striped terracotta ram from Neolithic Corinth. (FIGURE 122) A deep ridge on the belly may indicate that it represents a sacrificial animal.

Another design painted on ram figurines consists of clusters of three or four parallel lines. One of the largest and best preserved ram sculptures of the Lengyel culture so decorated was recovered from Jordanów (Jordansmühl) in Silesia. (FIGURE 123) Groups of parallel lines may here indicate wool and symbolize its abundance.

The association of the ram with the number three is conspicuous by its frequency. Figurines are sometimes marked with tri-lines or triple chevrons, and some sacrificial vessels have a triangular form crowned by three ram heads. In addition, some rams are shown with three horns, or three horns serve as handles on dishes. The importance of the number three continues in the convention of three ram heads decorating vases of the Aegean, Proto-Geometric, and Geometric periods and beyond.

FIGURE 120

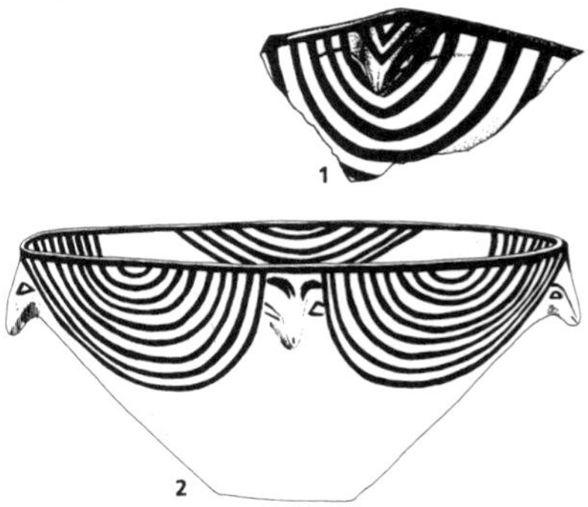

FIGURE 120 Here, ram heads are associated with concentric arcs. (1) Dish fragment painted black on red. (2) Reconstruction of a dish with four ram heads. Dimini ((1) Dimini and (2) Larisa, Thessaly; 4800–4600 B.C.) (1) H. 5 cm. (2) H. 7.4 cm.

FIGURE 121

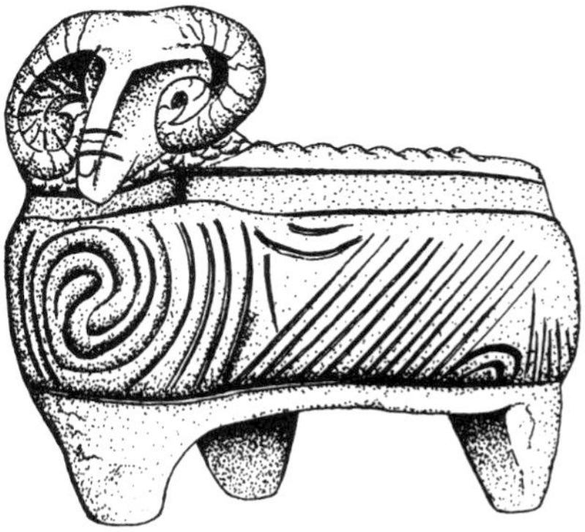

FIGURE 121 This ram-shaped container has a snake coil on the front and stream motifs on the sides. Note that it is three-legged and its nose is marked with three lines. Karanovo (Jasa Tepe, Plovdiv, C Bulgaria; 5000–4500 B.C.) H. 10.6 cm.

FIGURE 122

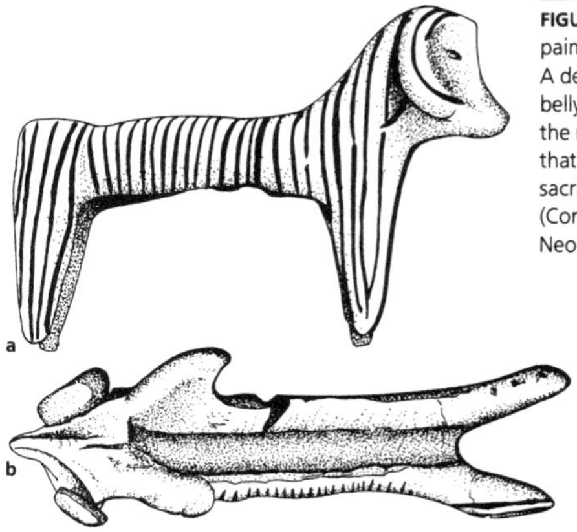

FIGURE 122 Ceramic ram painted with red stripes. A deep ridge along the belly and an incision at the neck may indicate that this represents a sacrificial animal (Corinth, Greece, Late Neolithic). H. 11.5 cm.

9.3 *Fused with Bird Goddess features in one image*

The Goddess's animal sometimes appears in her place or with its features fused with hers. This hybridization led to the creation of peculiar mythical images: figures with a bird's head or beak and ram horns. Examples of this type are known from Hotarani, a Vinča site of c. 4500 B.C. in southwestern Romania. Reproduced here is an altarpiece or replica of a temple façade decorated with an indented meander design; there is a large beaked ram's head in the center and two smaller ones above "stair" motifs on either side. (FIGURE 124)

A relief of a huge ram's head with spiralling horns and an owl's beak majestically covers one of the walls of a rock-cut tomb at Perfugas, Sardinia, dated tentatively to the 4th millennium B.C. (FIGURE 125)

From the Funnel-necked Beaker culture in Poland come vases with handles ending in ram's heads. (FIGURE 126) The rest of the handle is incised with a motif of bird's feet, repeated in vertical bands next to the handle.

FIGURE 123

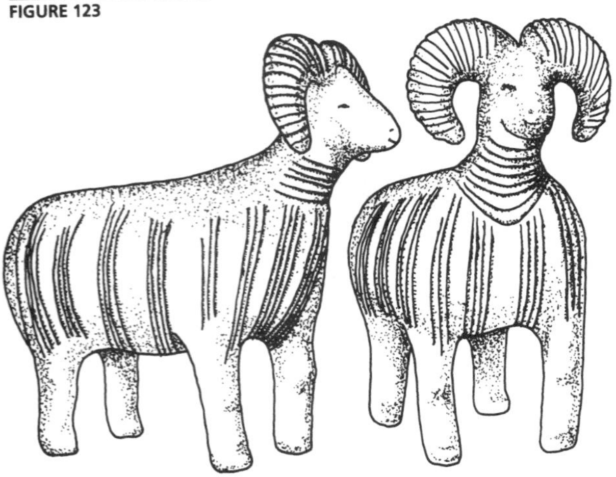

FIGURE 123 Rams are also marked with groups of parallel lines, as is this fine terracotta figurine. The stream motif's symbolic meaning of "abundance" is perhaps here applied to the ram's wooly fleece. Late Lengyel (Jordanów [Jordansmühl], Silesia; c. 3700–3500 B.C.) H. 13.5 cm.

FIGURE 124

a b

FIGURE 124 Altarpiece or temple replica decorated with excised and white-encrusted meanders; it is topped by a large divine head that is both beaked and horned. There are smaller such heads on either side, with large "stair" motifs underneath. Vinča-Vădăstra IV (Hotarani, SW Romania; c. 4500 B.C.) H. 13.5 cm.

FIGURE 125

1 2

FIGURE 125 This larger-than-life relief on the wall of the rock-cut tomb called "Domus dell'Ariete" bears witness to the importance of the ram/bird hybrid. The ram's head with its spiralling horns has an owl's beak. Sardinian Late Neolithic Ozieri culture, early phase (Perfugas, Sassari; c. 4000 B.C.) (1) H. 38 cm.

Bird's heads with ram's horns appear on bird-shaped vases of the Early Helladic II period. These beautifully shaped and burnished vases continue to be misleadingly called "sauceboats." Their water-bird shape is obvious, and the addition of ram's horns to some of their heads suggests their important role in the cult of the Goddess.

There are also winged rams; such portrayals appear on Late Minoan seals from Kato Zakros in Crete. (FIGURE 127) The intimate link between the ram and the Bird Goddess is clear. The ram-headed serpent, according to Anne Ross, is the most expressive and typical of the Celtic cult animals (Ross 1967: 344).

Portrayals of this sacred animal are consistently marked with the signs of the Goddess (V's, chevrons) and with symbols of fertility, abundance, well-being, or source (snakes, multiple parallel lines, nets, checkerboards) for millennia. Furthermore, the Goddess herself fuses with the ram (the ram-horned Goddess on altar screens, ram-headed creatures with bird's feet, askoi with ram horns).

9.4 *In later times and in European folklore*

The ram's role in myth did not die out during the ensuing Indo-European era, despite some transformations and differing associations. In addition to being a sacred animal of the Bird Goddess, the ram also became a sacrificial animal of the new ruling male gods, such as Zeus. In Ancient Greece, the ram continued its traditional role by being sacred to Athena. The sacrifice of rams to her is shown in vase painting. For instance, on one black-figure vase, a big owl (the Goddess) perches on the altar toward which a ram is being led to sacrifice (*Journal of Hellenic Studies*, XXXII 1912: 174, fig.1).

Especially in folktales, the ancient symbolism is transparent; here the ram appears as an animal with magical properties. The chance acquisition of a magical ram, or a taste of its meat, brings ever-increasing wealth and happiness. This mysterious animal is the mascot of the Goddess as Fate, Giver-of-All, Apportioner. In this aspect, the ram is not the Indo-European symbol of the sun or the associated golden fleece.

The ram's head—Aries—as the astrological sign for the beginning of spring, governing the period from around March 21 to April 19, may have its roots in the symbolism of Old Europe.

Up to the middle of the 20th century, terracotta ram figurines were buried in the ground in Lithuania at springtime to secure happiness and material well-being, in apparent memory of an ancient ritual. Ram-roasting feasts are still held today in Britain on May Day or Whit Monday. In earlier days, a ram was sacrificed at a granite menhir at Holne in Devon followed by celebration with dancing, games, and wrestling (Bord 1983: 48). Thus the Old European symbolic meaning of the ram survived to modern times. The Basque Goddess still can be seen mounted on a ram; sometimes she is spinning skeins of golden thread using the horns of her ram as bobbins (Frank and Metzger 1982: 67).

FIGURE 126

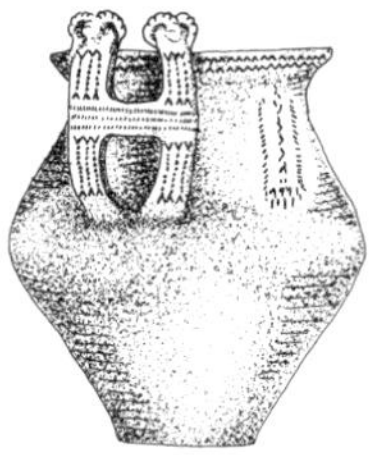

FIGURE 126 Another kind of ram/bird hybrid is represented by this vase whose handles are topped by ram's heads and decorated with stylized bird's feet. This is repeated around the vase's upper portion. Funnel-necked Beaker (Cmielów, near Tarnobrzeg, S Poland; c. 3500 B.C.) H. 33.9 cm.

FIGURE 127

FIGURE 127 Later still, the ram/bird hybrid is anthropomorphized, the result being this whimsical winged ram-man on a Minoan seal. The drawing is from an impression (Kato Zakros, E Crete; 1500–1450 B.C.). H. 2.5 cm.

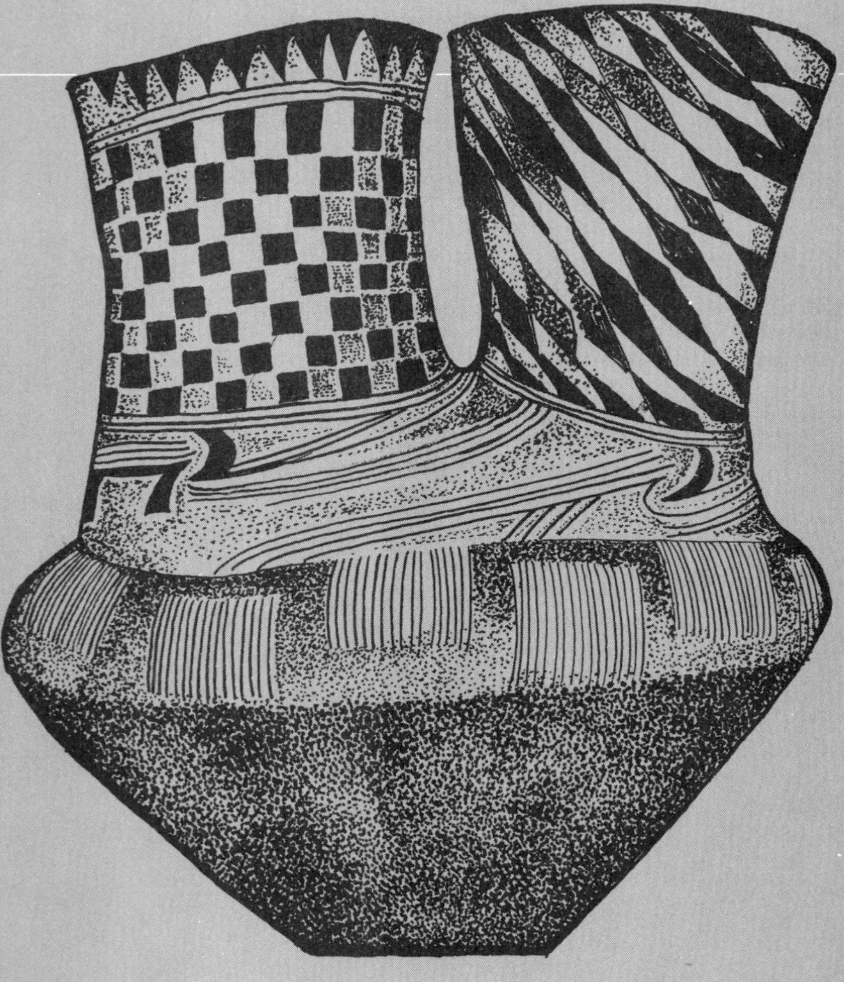

Gumelniţa vase with checkerboard and net patterns. See figure 135, page 84.

10/ *Net Motif*

In the Early Neolithic, the net motif and pottery painting emerge at the same time; the net's symbolic importance is indicated by the thick borders that frame it from the beginning—bands, lozenges, triangles, squares, or circles. Signs associated with the framed net—parallel lines, zig-zags, tri-lines, M's, and chevrons—place it within the aquatic symbol family. The net/water metaphor is clear when rain streams are depicted as net-patterned diagonal bands.

On the other hand, the framed net also appears with symbols of becoming: egg, vulva, uterus, fish bladder forms, and plant leaves. This implies that the net is linked with aqua-cosmogony, the life source, and the birth of human, animal, and plant life. The intimacy of the net with the pubic triangle, uterus, and egg suggests it symbolizes an embryonic substance capable of giving life. (FIGURE 128) In other words, it must have been a symbol of the "water of life" well known to us from myths. The net design over Neolithic figurines probably emphasizes the life-giving power of the Goddess. (FIGURE 129)

FIGURE 128

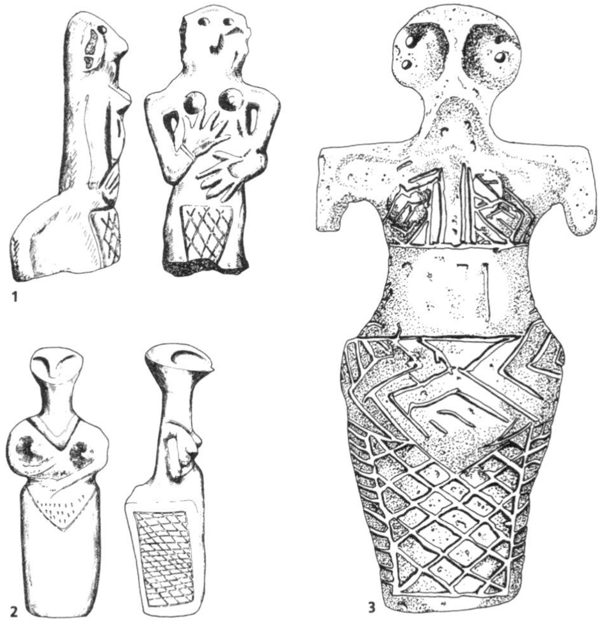

FIGURE 128 On these figurines, the connection between the net motif and the pubic triangle or lower body of the Goddess is clearly made. (1) Tisza (Tiszafüred-Majoros Hunyadihalom); (2) Karanovo IV; and (3) Vinča (Gradešnica, NW Bulgaria; 5000–4500 B.C.). (1) H. 11.2 cm. (2) H. 14.92 cm. (3) H. 16 cm.

FIGURE 129 The net motif sometimes covers the whole or only the lower half of the figurine. Note the prominent breasts on (1) and the characteristic arm stumps and enormous posterior on (2). Starčevo ((1) Starčevo, near Belgrade, Yugoslavia and (2) Sofia, Bulgaria; 5800–5500 B.C.) (1) H. 7.6 cm. (2) H. 10.4 cm.

10.1 *In the Upper Paleolithic*

Limestone slabs and antler or bone objects engraved with a net pattern date from the Magdalenian epoch. As in the Neolithic, the design is organized in square panels, lozenges, triangles, ellipses, and fish bladder or uteri forms. Examples were found in the cave of Parpalló at Valencia, Spain (Pericot-Garcia 1942; Marshack 1972: 204) and in a number of Middle and Late Magdalenian caves of southern France from the period of 12,000–9,000 B.C. (Marsoulas, Laugerie-Haute, Laugerie-Basse, Le Placard and Lortet: Chollot-Varagnac 1980, 198–209). On the

FIGURE 129

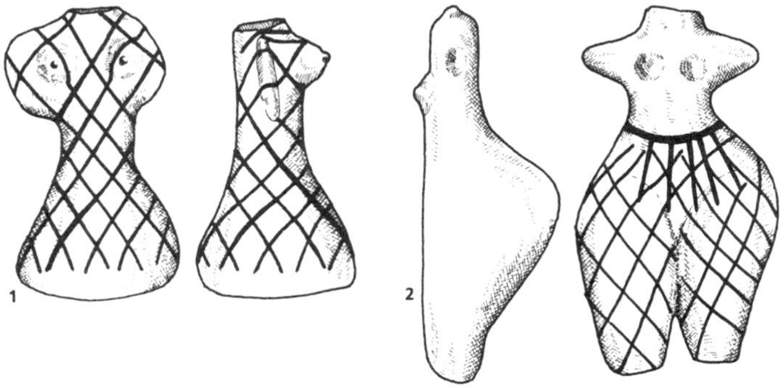

FIGURE 130

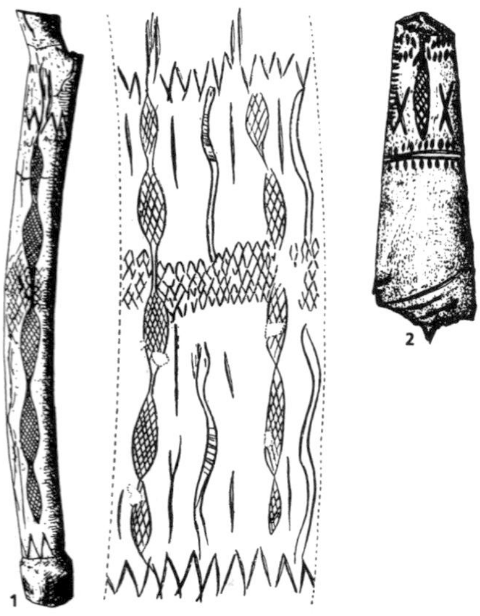

FIGURE 130 The net linked with fish and uterine forms and associated with X's and tri-lines emerges during the Upper Paleolithic, as these objects from the Magdalenian epoch indicate. (1) Reindeer antler "baton" decorated with interconnected fish or uterus forms alternating with a serpentine design (La Madeleine, Dordogne, S France; c. 10,000 B.C.). (2) Fragment of a bone tool engraved with net-patterned ellipses flanked by X's, a tri-line around the lower part (Marsoulas, Haute-Garonne, S France; c. 10,000 B.C.). (1) H. 31.7 cm. (2) 10.1 cm.

ceilings and walls of French Magdalenian caves, the net pattern appears in association with clusters of parallel lines and X's. These caves yielded, alongside unframed criss-cross lines, a great number of squares with a cross or criss-crossed lines. Usually they are in the proximity of bisons, horses, and other animals. The criss-crossed squares seem to have a symbolic meaning related to that of net-patterned squares and are emblematic of the worship of the regenerating Goddess in caves.

On mammoth ivories from Timonovka and Eliesevichi, late Upper Paleolithic sites in the Ukraine, the net design is used in representations of fish (FIGURE 130); it also appears as a symbolic pattern in panels next to zig-zag panels probably symbolic of water (Marshack 1979). Here we find the association of the fish, net, and water. (On the fish and uterus homology, see Part III, section 23.3.)

FIGURE 131

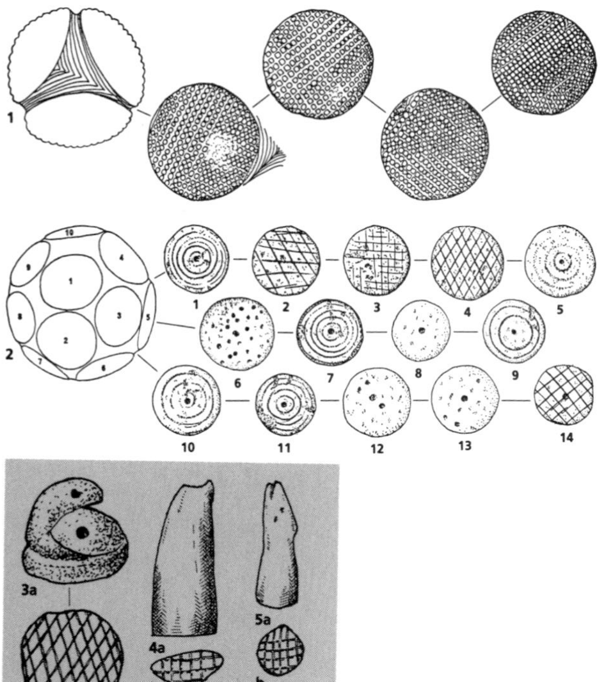

FIGURE 131 (1) and (2) Carved stone balls, probably amulets, with knobs and interspaces engraved with symbols. The net is either associated with female triangles marked with chevrons or is interchangeable with cup-marks and concentric circles (Late Neolithic; Scotland; approx. end 4th or 3rd mill. B.C.). (3) and (4) Middle Minoan seals with snakes for handles ((3) Kalanthiana, S Crete and (4) Cave of Trapeza, N Crete; early 2nd mill. B.C.). (1) H. 3.3 cm. (2) H. 3.6 cm. (3a) H. 1.6 cm. (4a) H. 2.5 cm, (5a) H. 2 cm.

10.2 *Net-patterned squares in Neolithic caves*

Squares with net patterns or parallel lines or marked with a cross or X that appear with an hourglass form are engraved on the rocks of Post-Paleolithic caves. About 2000 caves with such engravings are reported from France, concentrated in the area of Paris, in the districts of Seine-et-Marne, Seine-et-Oise, and Loiret (König 1973). Some of them are known as "Caves of the Fairies" (*Grottes aux Fées*). They are reminiscent of a womb or uterus and probably were as sacred in prehistory as similar caves with miraculous wells are in historic and modern times. Hourglass and cross symbols alongside net-patterned squares are known from the Neolithic subterranean tombs (hypogea) of Sardinia and also on Neolithic ceramics. The chronology of most of the Paris basin caves bearing such signs is likely to be Neolithic. These mysterious places were surely sacred to the Goddess, the owner of life-water, the Giver of Life.

10.3 *On amulets, seals, lids, and vase bases*

The symbolic character of the net pattern is evidenced by its consistent appearance on amulets, seals, lids, and vase bases from the earliest Neolithic to the Bronze Age. Illustrated here are a few examples of carved stone balls with knobs, probably amulets with magical properties, from Scotland. Their knobs and interspaces are marked with symbols. Symbolic associations are revealing: the net on the knobs appears linked with the female triangle and chevrons engraved on the interspaces, or the net is interchangeable with cupmarks and concentric circles with a cupmark in the center. (FIGURE 131, 1, 2) The net in conjunction with the snake occurs on Minoan seals, whose handles are in the shape of one or two serpents. (FIGURE 131, 3, 4)

10.4 *The framed net: lozenges, circles, eggs, uteri, and vulvas on ceramics*

Net-patterned bands, lozenges, triangles, and circles were painted on Neolithic vases from the end of the 7th millennium B.C. and throughout the Copper and Bronze ages. (FIGURES 132, 133) Examples from the central Balkans and Aegean Neolithic, the Cucuteni culture, and the early Minoan II period cover a time span from about 6000 B.C. to 2500 B.C.

Net-patterned squares or lozenges are often the sole motif on globular jars and spouted water jugs. On a lidded globular Late Cucuteni vase with a zig-zag column in the center of the lid, there are painted net-patterned lozenges divided by three lines. Net-patterned circles, ovals, and uteri continue to appear on Minoan and Mycenaean vases. (FIGURE 134)

FIGURE 132

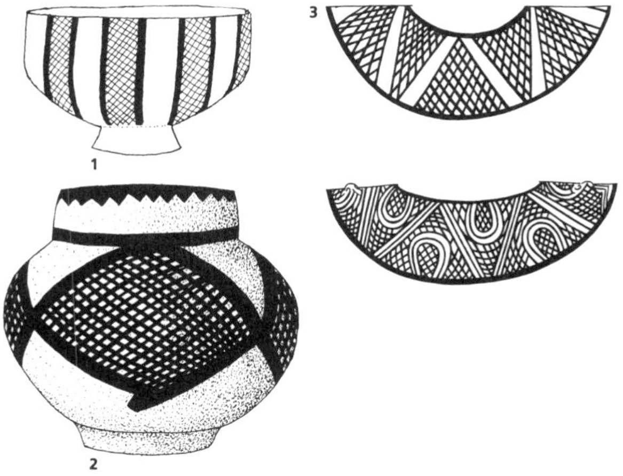

FIGURE 132 The net framed by vertical bands, lozenges, triangles, and uteri is a long-lived convention of Old European ceramics. Painted (1) brown on orange, (2) red on white, and (3) reddish brown on cream. (1) Starčevo (Tečić, near Kragujevac, C Yugoslavia; 5700–5500 B.C.). (2) Late Sesklo (Chaeroneia, C Greece; 5800–5500 B.C.). (3) Cucuteni (Drăguşeni, NE Romania; c. 4200–4100 B.C.). (1) H. 10.9 cm. (2) H. 30.6 cm.

FIGURE 133

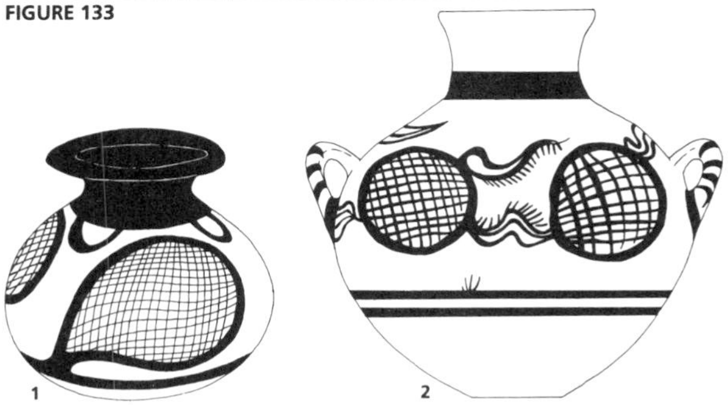

FIGURE 133 The net also fills uterus- or egg-shaped forms, as on these Mycenaean vessels. There thus appears to be an embryonic aspect to the net's symbolic meaning. Painted in dark brown (borders) and light brown (net) on cream. ((1) Prosymna, Late Helladic II and (2) Berbati, Late Helladic III; 1500–1300 B.C.). (1) H. 12.6 cm. (2) H. 21.4 cm.

FIGURE 134

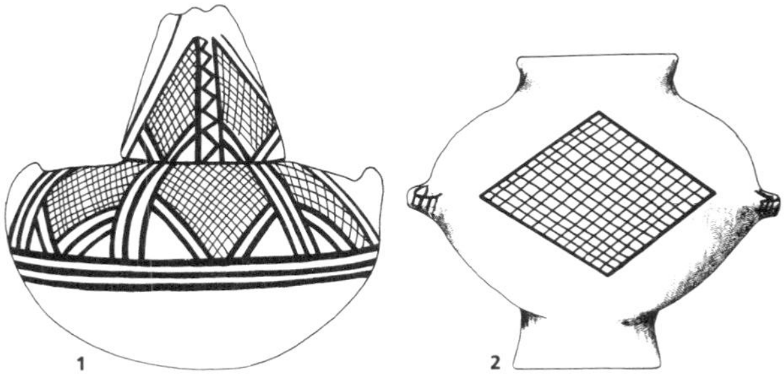

FIGURE 134 Net-patterned lozenges often appear on water jars. (1) On this Cucuteni globular jar, lozenges are divided by tri-lines; there is a zig-zag column on the tall lid. Painted black on cream. (Brailiţa, S Moldavia; 3600–3400 B.C.). (2) This Early Minoan II amphora of a thousand years later is also decorated with the net-patterned lozenge (Haghia Photia, Crete; c. 2600 B.C.). (1) H. 35.8 cm. (2) H. 15.4 cm.

10.5 *Net and checkerboard*

The checkerboard alternates with the net in association with the same series of symbols and appears to be synonymous. It may, however, be a variation of the net, representing a slightly different but related concept. Often the two appear together; numerous vases are painted with checkerboard panels next to net-patterned panels. Examples range from a lower Danube Gumelniţa vessel of c. 4500 B.C. (FIGURE 135) to a Drakhmani II vase from Central Greece, c. 2800 B.C. (FIGURE 136) The double-throated Gumelniţa vase has a checkerboard design on one neck and a net on the other; parallel lines, water streams, and a beak motif are painted below. The Drakhmani specimen features a net pattern flanked by checkerboard panels, an amplification of the symbolic content. Even in the Iron Age, the net and checkerboard appear together (see the doe-shaped vase from Kerameikos, Athens, 925–900 B.C., fig. 182).

FIGURE 135

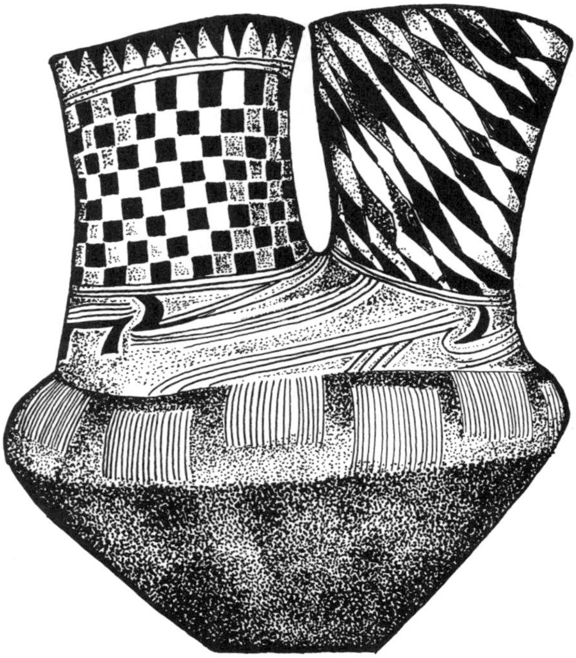

FIGURE 135 Checkerboards and nets often appear together; they are probably related or identical in meaning. A graphite-painted checkerboard is on one neck of a Gumelniţa vase, and a net design on the other (Gumelniţa, near Bucharest, Romania; c. 4500–4300 B.C.) H. 22.4 cm.

10.6 *On spouted and anthropomorphic vases, figurines, and zoomorphic containers*

The character of the vases, figurines, and zoomorphic containers on which the net pattern appears provides some clue to the underlying symbolism of this sign. First, the net is regularly found on jars and spouted vases. During the Early Bronze Age, the net-patterned square, lozenge, and column are depicted on spouted jugs, some of which have modeled breasts or nipples. (FIGURES 137, 138) Furthermore, the net motif frequently appears on Neolithic and Copper Age anthropomorphic images.

FIGURE 136

FIGURE 136 On an Early Bronze Age vase, a net-patterned triangle is flanked by a semicircular framed checkerboard motif; net-patterned triangles encircle the neck. Drachmani II (Phokis, C Greece; early 3rd mill. B.C.) H. 39.6 cm.

FIGURE 137

FIGURE 137 The net motif frequently appears on spouted vessels such as this egg-shaped jar. A net-patterned band encircles the middle, random rectangles of net are scattered over the upper part, and a large quadrangle dominates the center. Painted brown on cream. Early Bronze Age (Phylakopi, Melos; early 3rd mill. B.C.) H. 40.2 cm.

FIGURE 138

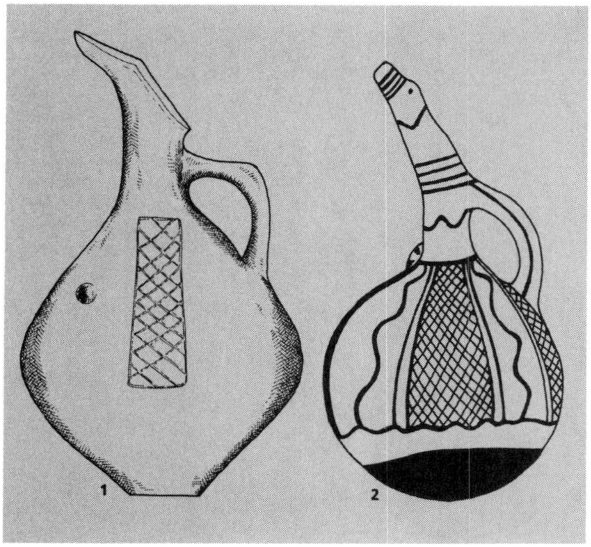

FIGURE 138 These jugs with birdlike spouts are decorated by isolated net-patterned panels. Early Bronze Age ((1) Beycesultan, W Anatolia and (2) Lapithos, N Cyprus; mid-3rd mill. B.C.) (1) H. 59.5 cm. (2) H. 56 cm.

FIGURE 139

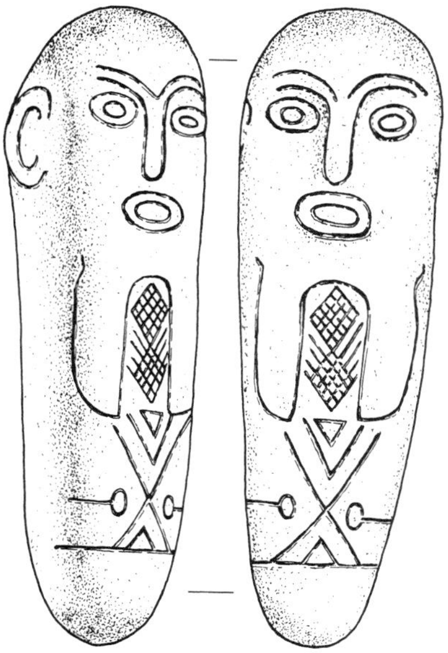

FIGURE 139 On this figurine carved on a pebble, net-patterned lozenges are strategically placed between her pendulous breasts and above chevrons (Gaban shelter, near Trento, Italy; Neolithic of N Italy: Square-mouthed Pottery culture). H. 13.4 cm.

A schematic fish-shaped figurine from the earliest Neolithic stratum of the Gaban shelter in northern Italy features two net-patterned lozenges on the chest between the breasts of the Deity. (FIGURE 139) A triangle, V's, and a cross-band are incised directly beneath the net-patterned squares. The face has the inhuman round mouth of a fish and large staring eyes. A symbolic relationship to the Gaban figurine is seen in the egg-shaped sculptures with half-human/half-fish facial features of Lepenski Vir, northern Yugoslavia, which sometimes are decorated with water stream motifs (see fig. 377).

Further aspects of the framed net symbolism are revealed in the rich details of a sculpture from the Early Minoan II site of Myrtos in southern Crete. (FIGURE 140) The hollow, barrel-shaped terracotta has human facial features, a long cylindrical neck, and perforated breasts that serve as spouts. Her snakelike arms wind around the neck of a water jug marked with parallel lines. Net-patterned squares are painted on the front and back of the vase; a net-patterned pubic triangle is at center front. The net-patterned squares and triangle may symbolize reservoirs of the water of life.

A Mycenaean "kourotrophic" figurine holding an infant in her snake arms embodies the same concept. (FIGURE 141) Snake stripes cover the body of the image; chevrons adorn her crown and arms. A net-patterned disc on her left shoulder seems semantically related to the net squares and triangles painted on Minoan images of the Deity.

One of the most eloquent images of the Goddess with a net-patterned square is the figurine from around 700–675 B.C. from Boeotia in central Greece. (FIGURE 142) A large net-patterned square surrounded by zig-zags and parallel lines covers almost the entire front of the bell-shaped figure. On each side stands a bird with net-patterned body holding a zig-zag snake in its beak. Atop the square are a brush and whirls, which also cover the sides; swastikas (whirls) dot the arms.

FIGURE 140

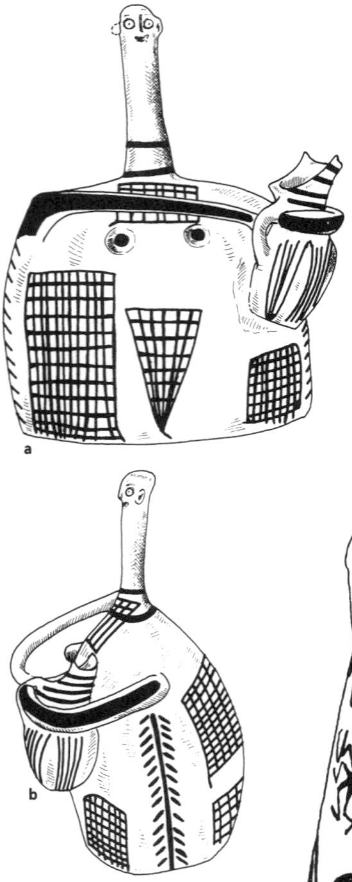

a

b

FIGURE 142

FIGURE 141

FIGURE 140 The net is again associated with the pubic triangle on this anthropomorphic vessel with serpentine neck and arms; perforated breast-spouts indicate its ritual use. The net-patterned rectangles which cover the body may represent reservoirs of life-water. Painted red on gray/buff. Early Minoan II (Myrtos, S Crete; 2900–2600 B.C.) H. 18.8 cm.

FIGURE 141 This snake-striped terracotta figure holds an infant in her serpentine arms; the disc attached to her left shoulder is covered with a net pattern. Painted red on cream (Mycenae; 14th cent. B.C.) H. 20.8 cm.

FIGURE 142 This symbolically rich terracotta provides ample evidence for the connection between the Goddess and the net or water of life in her womb. Note the birds marked with nets with snakes in their mouths, the sprouting branches, and the energy whirls (Boeotia, central Greece; c. 700 B.C.).

A necklace circles the throat, and chevrons decorate the top of the head. There is no mouth, the long neck resembles a phallus or snake, and the breasts are ringed with concentric circles. Plants grow from her body and from the body of the birds at her right. On another Boeotian amphora of the same period the image of the Goddess is shown with a net-patterned fish in her womb (see figure 405) suggesting the intimacy between the net, fish, amniotic fluid, and uterus. This is a portrayal of Artemis, Mistress of Wildlife, who contains her own life source. Significantly, Artemis Diktynna-Britomartis of Crete was associated with fishing nets; one of her titles is "The Lady of Nets," and her myth and ritual are related to childbirth.

The fact that countless images of the divinity bear the net symbol leads to the conclusion that she is the source and container of life-generating and life-sustaining water. In this aspect, she is the youthful Goddess, the Life-Giver.

The association of the net with the ram is apparent from the Neolithic into the Iron Age. This connection is evidenced on Hacilar and Sesklo vases, ram-headed lamps, or vessels of the Starčevo and Vinča complexes and in the symbolic art of Crete and Cyprus during the Bronze and Iron ages (FIGURE 143); it is also apparent during the Greek Mycenaean, Geometric, and Archaic periods. (FIGURES 144, 145)

Why the ram and the net? One explanation might be that ram hair and pubic hair were symbolically interchangeable. Sheep hair is still considered a sexual symbol in Lithuanian folk belief; a handful of wool is laid in the bed of a newly married couple (Greimas 1979: 272).

FIGURE 143

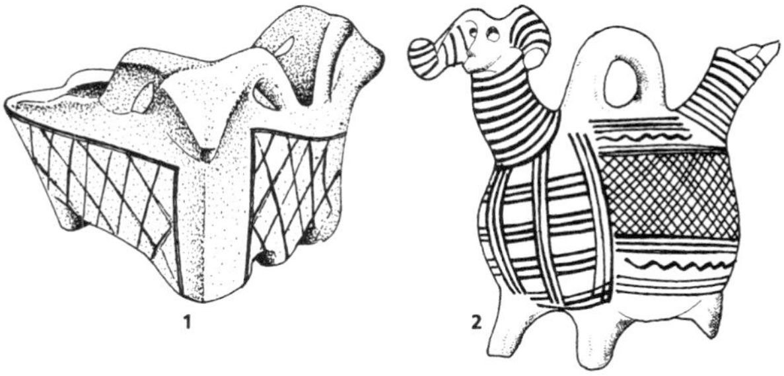

FIGURE 143 (1) Ram-headed protomes on a miniature Vinča container with white-encrusted decorations (Fafos I, near Kosovska Mitrovica, S Yugoslavia; 5000–4500 B.C.).
(2) Spouted ram-shaped vase of the Cypriot Middle Bronze Age, decorated with net-patterned panels, tri-lines, and parallel lines (Vounous cemetery, tomb 9, Cyprus; 1775–1575 B.C.)
(1) H. 7.8 cm. (2) H. 11.6 cm.

FIGURE 144

FIGURE 144 In later vase painting, ram horns extending from net-filled lozenges are a common motif, as illustrated by this particularly handsome detail. Painted brown on buff. Archaic Greek (Cyprus; 700–600 B.C.) H. 7.5 cm.

FIGURE 145

FIGURE 145 On this protome of a vase, a lozenge-shaped net is the central symbol. The spirals at the base imitate ram horns. Painted brown on buff. Late Helladic IIIC (Mycenae; c. 1100 B.C.) H. 10.7 cm.

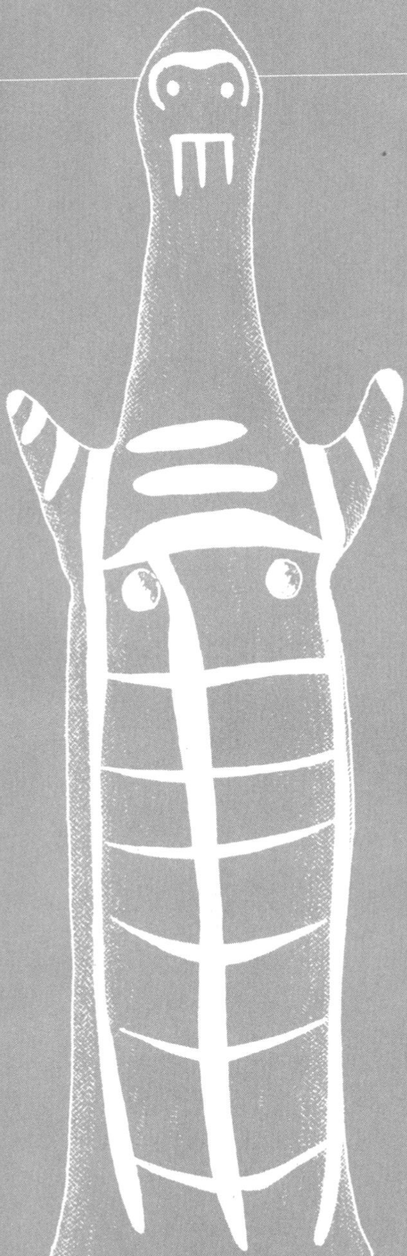

Mycenean figurine covered with stripes that echo the tri-line at the mouth. See figure 158, page 95.

11/ *Tri-Line and Power of Three*

11.1 *On Upper Paleolithic images*

The tri-line, three parallel lines, must have had symbolic meaning from Upper Paleolithic times. It appears concurrently with fish, net, zigzag, snake or serpentine line, bi-line, and parallel line symbolism and in association with the image of the Goddess. One of the most eloquent examples of tri-line symbolism is the figure of the Goddess engraved on a bone point of the Late Magdalenian period from Dordogne. (FIGURE 146) The image is marked in the center with two tri-lines connected at the ends by dashes. The upper sign is between two abstract breasts; the lower is in the abdominal area, above a double-lens-shaped vulva. Three snakes are engraved on a plaque of a mammoth tooth found at Mal'ta, an Upper Paleolithic site in central Siberia. Three snakes obviously expressed greater power than one.

11.2 *On seals, figurines, and vases*

The tri-line occurs as an independent symbol on Neolithic seals and on figurines and vases in all the culture groups of Old Europe. In the Near East, this sign is known on pebbles from the aceramic Neolithic.

Beaked figurines are marked with this sign from the Early Neolithic into the Aegean Bronze Age. (FIGURE 147) Three incisions or dashes occur singly or in groups on the neck, over the shoulders and arms, beneath the eyes, on the forehead, between the breasts, or across the back and abdomen. Possibly the same symbolic meaning is expressed by three or six (two sets of three) holes on the necks of figurines, and by little knobs on the front and back. (FIGURE 148) When intact, the heads of these figurines are beaked.

The tri-line and chevron are seen on eight figurines placed in an open shrine model discovered in the Neolithic tell of Zarkou near Larisa, Thessaly (Gallis 1985). (FIGURE 149) The largest figurine in the left room of the shrine (probably the main Goddess) was carefully marked with three lines between the breasts and over the cheeks and with a chevron on the back. Three other, somewhat smaller, figurines (lower in hierarchy?) were similarly marked. The remaining were poorly preserved but clearly belong to the same category. The model is a replica of an Old European two-room shrine consisting of an altar room and a workshop. It was found below the floor as an offering to the Bird Goddess on the occasion of the foundation of the house or shrine.

At times, the tri-line is the sole decoration on a vase body or base. Tri-lines ending in circular depressions constitute a design typical of Linear Pottery and Tisza pottery in central Europe. (FIGURE 150) Tri-lines not infrequently decorate askoi, spouted vases, and ornithomorphic vases dating from the 5th to 3rd millennia B.C. (FIGURE 151)

FIGURE 146

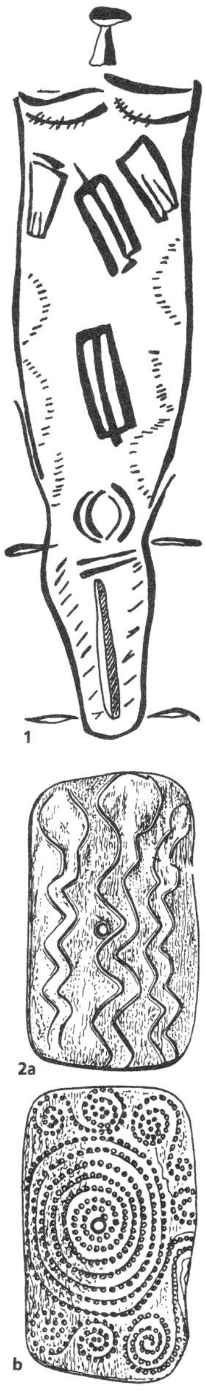

FIGURE 146 The tri-line symbol emerges in the Upper Paleolithic, when it is often associated with aqueous signs.
(1) This abstract female image is engraved on a bone point and is marked with two tri-lines, one between the breasts and the other above the vulva. There are serpentine lines incised around the edges. Late Magdalenian (Abri Mège near Teyjat, Dordogne, S France).
(2) Three snakes wind across one face of a plaque, and a snake coil with spirals is on the other. Engravings on a mammoth tooth from Mal'ta, Siberia (approx. 24,000 B.C.).

FIGURE 147

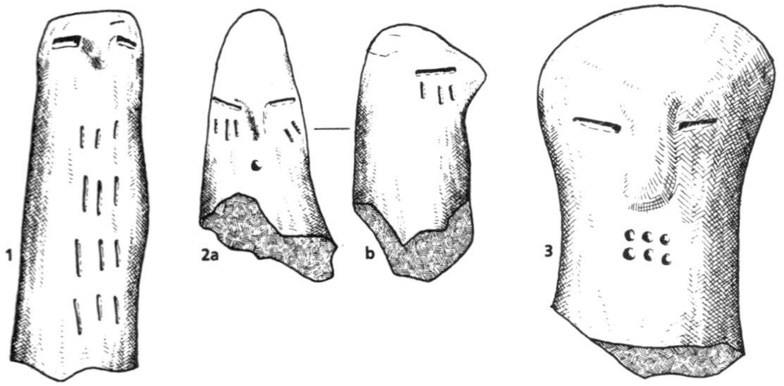

FIGURE 147 From the Early Neolithic into the Bronze Age, beaked figurines are marked over the cheeks and all over their bodies with tri-lines and groups of three dots. (1) and (2) Tri-lines under the eyes and down the neck. (3) Six holes (2 x 3) in place of the mouth. (1) and (2) Sesklo (Tsangli and Achilleion, Thessaly, Greece; 6000–5800 B.C.). (3) Starčevo (Anza, Macedonia; 5800–5600 B.C.). (1) H. 5.4 cm. (2) H. 3.8 cm. (3) H. 5.5 cm.

FIGURE 148

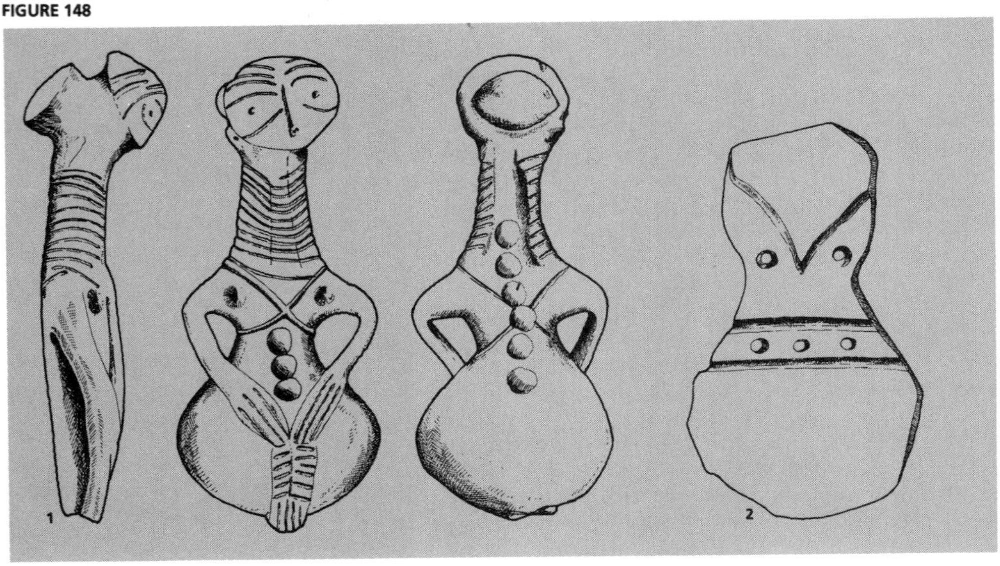

FIGURE 148 A motif related to the tri-line is a group of three or six depressions or holes marking beaked and mouthless figurines. (1) A seated figurine wearing a cross-band and twelve necklaces, with a bowl-shaped protuberance (crown?) behind her masked face. She has three depressions on the abdomen and six on the back. (2) An owl-faced marble figurine with three depressions between bands across the front. (1) Anatolian Early Bronze Age I (Nudra, district of Isparta, central Turkey; early 3rd mill. B.C.). (2) Troy IV (Troy, W Anatolia; end 3rd mill. B.C.). (1) H. 8.7 cm. (2) H. 7.3 cm.

FIGURE 149

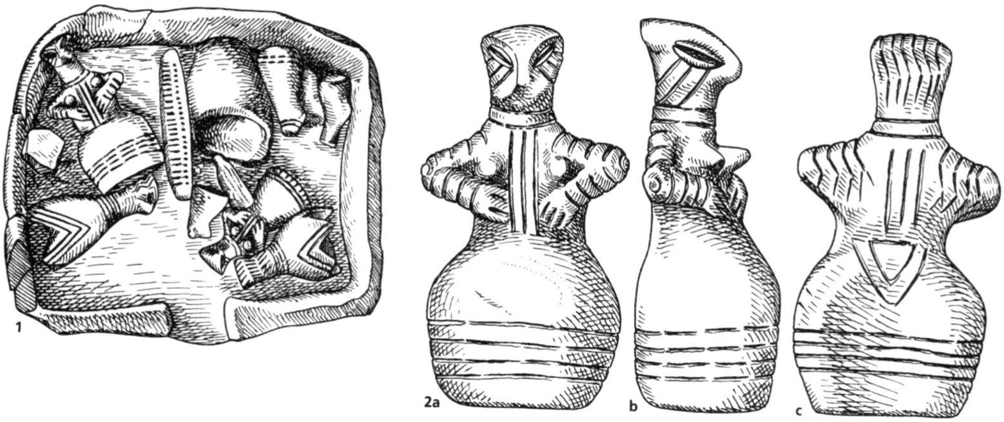

FIGURE 149 This open shrine model of two rooms (1) contains Bird Goddess-type figurines marked with tri-lines and chevrons. The largest figurine (2) occupied the left room together with a smaller schematized figurine; six were placed in the second room around the oven. The sizes and placement of the figurines suggest a hierarchical order. Dimini culture, Tsangli phase (Zarkou at Larisa, Thessaly; early 5th mill. B.C.) H. of figurine 8.6 cm.

FIGURE 150

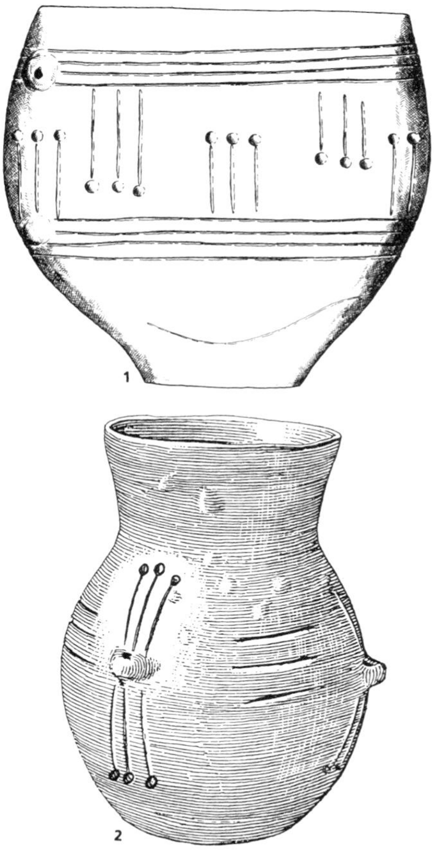

FIGURE 150 Tri-lines ending in circular depressions are a common motif on the Neolithic ceramics of central Europe. (2) was found in a grave above the skull. Linear Pottery Culture ((1) Rybniky, Mor. Krumlova, Moravia and (2) Nitra, Slovakia; c. 5000 B.C.)
(1) H. 13.8 cm.
(2) H. 14.7 cm.

FIGURE 151

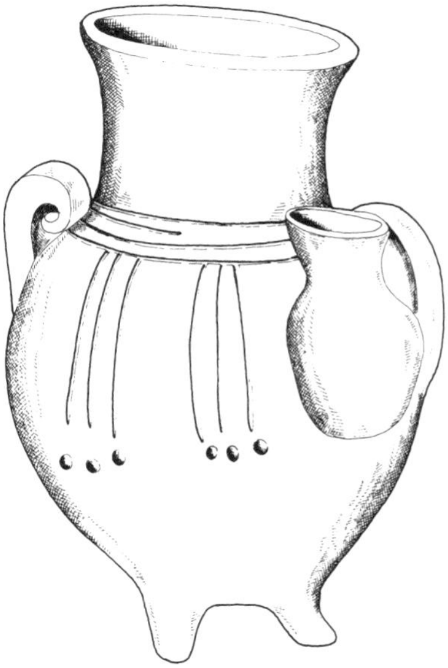

FIGURE 151 Tri-lines are particularly associated with askoi and ornithomorphic vases. This wing-handled vessel seems to be cradling an "infant" jug on one side. Troy IV (Troy, W Anatolia; end 3rd mill. B.C.)
H. 42 cm.

11.3 *Associations with the symbolism of "beginning" and "becoming"*

The most expressive renderings of tri-lines are found on friezes ornamenting Cucuteni vases or on the interior of dishes. Three lines are the sole design on the inner side of a dish, or the tri-line is encircled or framed at regular intervals within decorative bands. (FIGURE 152) Such framing circles may be spaced at intervals and connected by a band which is flanked by two lines and beaks. In rectangular panels, the tri-line is placed vertically or diagonally against a background which is either empty or filled with vertical and horizontal lines, possibly symbolizing sky or clouds. The arc in the lower register probably represents the earth, above which a divine dog trots. (FIGURE 153)

The tri-line is also encountered in the center of a whirling pattern on the inside of dishes, its position giving the impression that it generates the whirling. (FIGURE 154)

Further semantic relationships with "becoming" are indicated by the association of the tri-line with uteri, seed or fish bladder forms, crescents, ram horns, snake coils, and snake spirals. A quartered design on a dish from Sipenitsi in Galicia shows a uterus sign containing three lines in each section. A dish from Ruse, northern Bulgaria, has a tri-line flanked by crescents, the motif repeated in four concentric bands. (FIGURE 155) The crescent also alternates with the tri-line in friezes on Cucuteni amphorae.

FIGURE 152

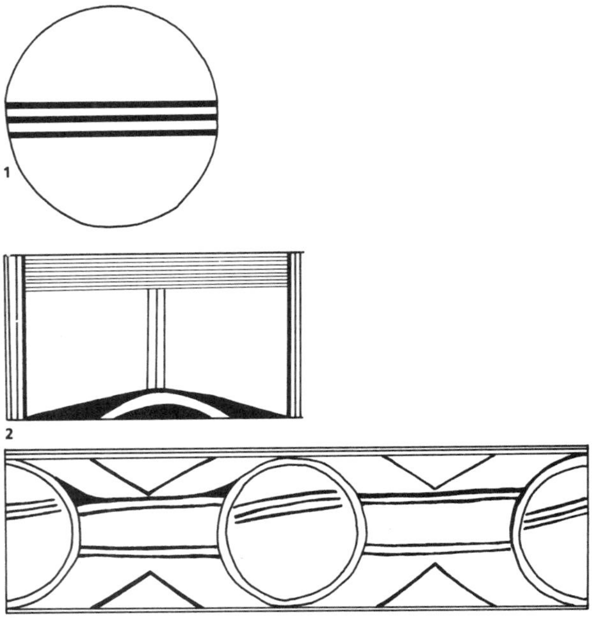

FIGURE 152 Cucuteni ceramics provide insight into the meaning of this tri-line symbol. (1) On the interior of a dish. (2) On a frieze decorating a bowl, stretching between sky and earth. (3) Within circles (eggs?) connected with bands flanked by V-shaped beaks. Black painted on red (Sipenitsi, Galicia, W Ukraine; 3700–3500 B.C.).

FIGURE 153

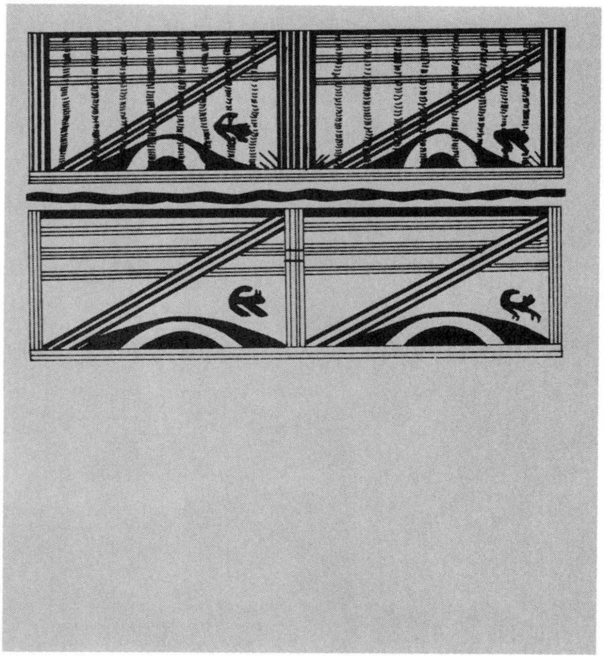

FIGURE 153 Diagonal tri-lines again cross the sky between horizontal lines (perhaps clouds) and the earth below. Rain seems to be falling in the upper frieze. Over the earth bounds a supernatural dog. Late Cucuteni (Sipenitsi; 3700–3500 B.C.)

FIGURE 154

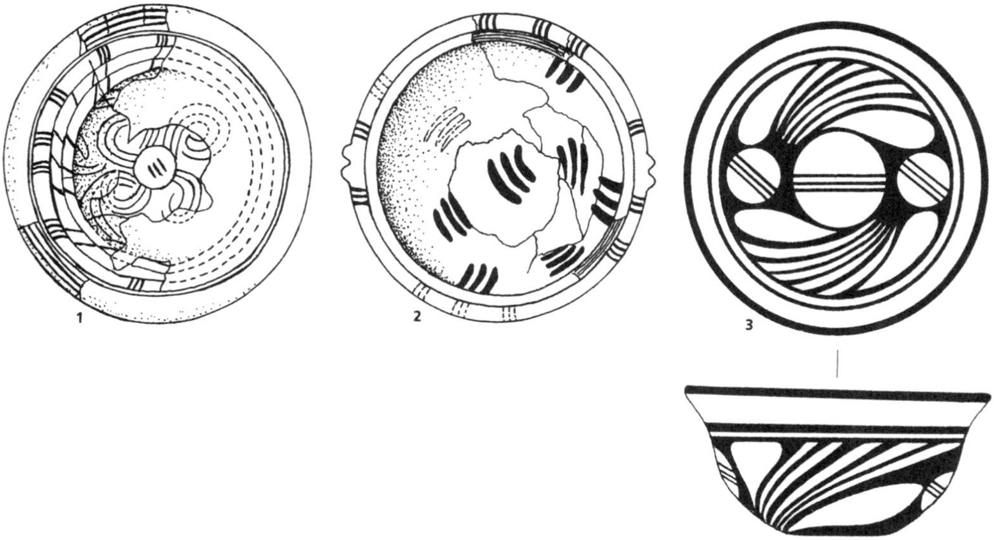

FIGURE 154 The tri-line is associated with energy symbols like the whirl, as on the insides of these dishes. At the center is a tri-line, surrounded by other spinning tri-lines, spirals, and streams.
(1) and (2) Petreşti B (Pianul de Jos, Alba, Transylvania; 4500–4200 B.C.). (3) Late Cucuteni (Valeni at Piatra Neamţ, NE Romania; 3800–3600 B.C.).
(1) DIA. 33.9 cm. (2) DIA. 32.7 cm. (3) DIA. 36.5 cm.

FIGURE 155

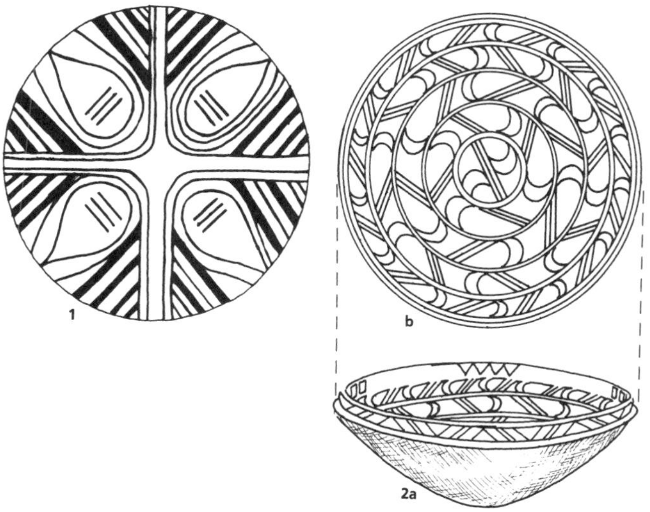

FIGURE 155 The tri-line is related to symbols of "becoming": (1) contained within uteri or seeds and (2) alternating with crescents. Note the chevron or continuous V motifs on each.
(1) Late Cucuteni (Sipenitsi, Galicia; 3700–3500). (2) Karanovo VI (Ruse, on the Danube, N Bulgaria; 4500–4300 B.C.).
(1) DIA. 39.6 cm.
(2) DIA. 39.6 cm.

FIGURE 156

1

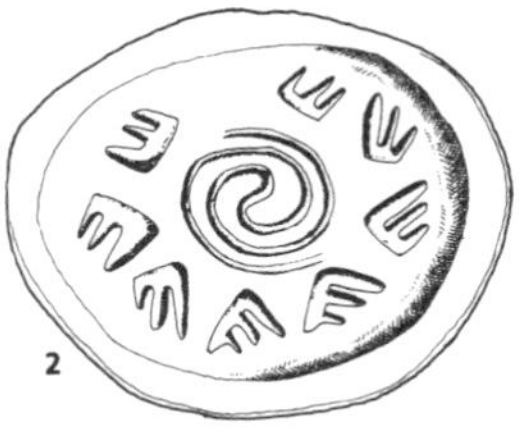

2

FIGURE 156 Other symbols of becoming with which the tri-line is associated include the snake and ram horns. (1) On the inner surface of a dish, tri-lines and ram horns stand at the four quarters around a snake coil. Painted black on red. (2) Joined tri-lines spin around a snake coil on a cylindrical ivory seal from a tholos tomb.
(1) Dimini (Rakhmani III, House Q, Thessaly; 4500–4000 B.C.). (2) Middle Minoan Ia (Vorou, Mesara Plain, S Crete; c. 2000 B.C.).
(1) DIA. 37 cm.
(2) H. 4.6 cm.

Tri-line and ram horn symbols are positioned around a snake coil in the center of a dish from Rakhmani II in Thessaly. A whirl design of tri-lines around a snake appears on Middle Minoan Ia seals in Crete. (FIGURE 156) The tri-line is frequently found on representations of sacred or sacrificial animals, the ram and pig.

11.4 *Emanating from the mouth of the Goddess*

The connection of the tri-line with the Goddess is evidenced by portrayals in which three parallel lines suspended from a horizontal bar (a connected tri-line) represent the Goddess's mouth. The horizontal bar is the mouth proper; the three suspended lines may symbolize the sacred springs streaming from it. The consistency of this sign confirms its symbolic character as, for example, on an anthropomorphic vase from Kenézlö, eastern Hungary, with a masked face on the neck. (FIGURE 157, 1) Two chevrons flank a tri-line on the forehead; the mouth is depicted by a horizontal bar from which flow three vertical lines. Panels of tri-lines, zig-zags, and meanders complete the rich symbolic ornamentation. Analogous is a pottery relief recovered at Turdaş near Cluj, an early Vinča site dating to the end of the 6th millennium B.C.; a connected tri-line covers the mouth of the figurine, which bears chevrons beneath the breasts. (FIGURE 157, 2)

The continuation of this symbolic tradition is observed in Anatolian and Mycenaean figurines. One such example shows the tri-line mouth on a figure with three horizontal lines and three dashes painted on each arm stump. (FIGURE 158, 1) Further analogies are found in Bronze Age figurines from Cyprus. (FIGURE 158, 2)

FIGURE 157

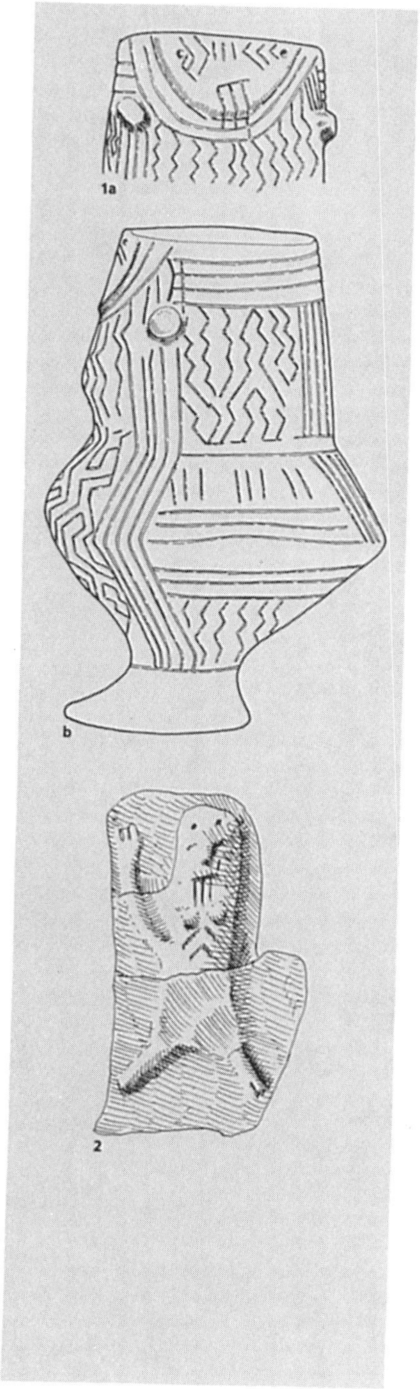

FIGURE 157 One common motif is the tri-line joined by a horizontal bar, which takes the mouth's place on effigies of the Goddess. (1) This anthropomorphic vase is decorated in meander, zig-zag, and parallel line panels. Note the tri-line necklace and chevrons and tri-lines on the face. (2) This figurine in relief on a potsherd is marked simply with a joined tri-line at the mouth and two V 's under the breasts.
(1) Bükk (Kenezlö, NE Hungary; c. 5000).
(2) Early Vinča (Turdaş, at Cluj, Transylvania; 5200–5000 B.C.).
(1) H. 17.2 cm.
(2) H. 5.5 cm.

FIGURE 158

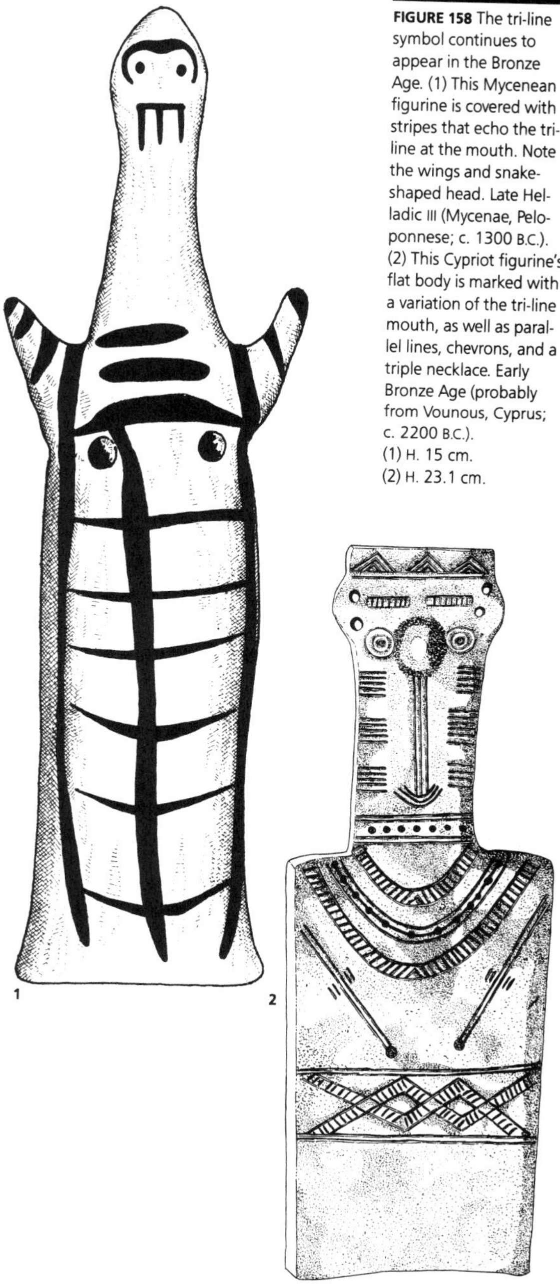

FIGURE 158 The tri-line symbol continues to appear in the Bronze Age. (1) This Mycenean figurine is covered with stripes that echo the tri-line at the mouth. Note the wings and snake-shaped head. Late Helladic III (Mycenae, Peloponnese; c. 1300 B.C.). (2) This Cypriot figurine's flat body is marked with a variation of the tri-line mouth, as well as parallel lines, chevrons, and a triple necklace. Early Bronze Age (probably from Vounous, Cyprus; c. 2200 B.C.).
(1) H. 15 cm.
(2) H. 23.1 cm.

FIGURE 159

2

FIGURE 159 Triple snake coils, perhaps representing a triple life source, appear at Newgrange on a stone wall at the main chamber's entrance and on the stone in front of the tomb's entrance. Irish Passage Grave culture (Newgrange, Boyne River Valley, county Meath; c. 3200 B.C.) (2) View of the chamber and passage looking outward from the end-recess. (1) L. approx. 350 cm.

The tri-line also emanates from the Goddess's eyes or body. We have already discussed Vinča masks and lids on which eyes are emphasized by three parallel lines (see section 6.2). Three (or two) lines below the eyes are a characteristic feature of the Neolithic and Copper Age masks of southeastern Europe, as well as on schist plaques portraying the Owl Goddess from Portuguese megalithic tombs.

The tri-line connected by a dash appears independently on spindle whorls, altars, sacrificial vessels, large and miniature vases, zoomorphic and anthropomorphic vessels, and pebbles or pendants.

The tri-line or number three, as we have seen, repeatedly appears engraved or painted on the body of the Goddess, most often emanating from her eyes. She is marked with chevrons, X's (chest-bands), and meanders; she typically wears one or more necklaces and her head or mask is beaked. These characteristics mark her as the Bird Goddess.

Three parallel lines are a frequent decoration on askoi, spouted vases, miniature pots, and vases with ram-head decoration, all evidently the paraphernalia of ritual activities linked with the Goddess. Painted dishes of the Karanovo and Cucuteni cultures disclose the association of the motif with snake coils, crescents, and ram horns. Three lines appear in the center of a whirling pattern, in the center of a cosmic egg, and as connections between sky and earth.

The tri-line sign seems to symbolize a triple (or multiple) life substance of dynamic quality which flows from the body of the Bird Goddess, the Giver and Sustainer of Life.

The triple source is linked with the triple Goddess, an astonishingly long-lived image documented as early as the Magdalenian epoch (cf. the relief of three colossal female presences with exposed vulvas at the Abri du Roc aux Sorciers, Angles-sur-Anglin, Vienne, France: Campbell 1982: 110). This tradition is continuous throughout the whole of prehistory and history, down to the Greek Moirai, Roman triple Mātres or Matronae, Germanic Nornen, Irish triple Brigit, three sisters Morrígna and the triad of Machas, Baltic triple Laima, and Slavic triple Sudičky or Roženicy. Even in tombs triple signs and triplicity are present, where they seem to symbolize the Goddess as owner of the triple source of life energy necessary for the renewal of life. In the grand megalithic tomb-shrine of Newgrange, Ireland, the repetition of threes is striking (FIGURE 159): three-sided cells; three stone basins; engravings of triple snake spirals, coils, arcs, and brow-ridges above the snake spiral oculi of the Owl Goddess; and three cartouches (an oblong figure enclosing symbols) each with three cupmarks (see below, fig. 370). James Mellaart remarks on the frequency with which objects are found in groups of three in the shrines at Çatal Hüyük. For example, there were three bull's heads beneath the sculptured goddess in Shrine VI.B.10, a row of three bull's heads in Shrine VI.B.8, three horn cores on a bench in Shrines VI.14 and VI.A.50, three bull's heads together in Shrine VII.9 and three rows of triangles in Shrine VII.21. The importance of the number three is also visible in Maltese temples, the earliest of which were trefoil in shape. In later temples, which are anthropomorphic in outline, such as the Tarxien, doorways and passages all use the trilithon principle. Triple shrines and triple columns are common in the Minoan culture.

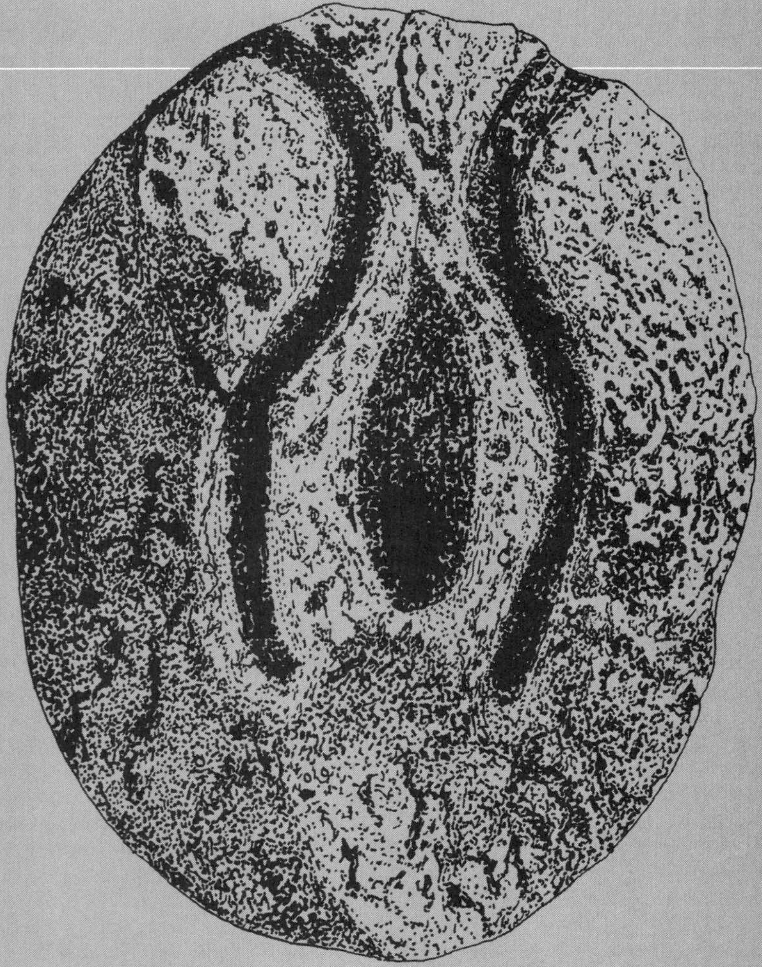

Egg-shaped stone sculpture with vulva as flowerbud engraved on one side; from Lepenski Vir. See figure 164, page 101.

12/ *Vulva and Birth*

12.1 *Earliest portrayals*

Long before the advent of agriculture, people were reproducing the vulva and seeds or sprouts in art. The earliest representations of the female divinity were vulvas as *pars pro toto* engraved on rocks during the Aurignacian period of some 30,000 years B.C. They were found engraved on rocks in the caves of Abri Blanchard, Abri Castanet, and La Ferrassie in the valley of Vézère, in the vicinity of Les Eyzies, Dordogne, S France (Delluc 1978). (FIGURE 160)

The Aurignacian vulva is, in most instances, abstract and schematic. Characteristically, it is semicircular, triangular, or bell-shaped with a dash or dot to indicate the vaginal opening. The emphasis on vulvas in the figurine art of later epochs makes it clear that those of the Upper Paleolithic are not merely "female signs" (so termed by Leroi-Gourhan 1967)—simple expression of physiology—but instead symbolize the vulva and womb of the Goddess.

From Upper Paleolithic times the vulva is portrayed either as a supernatural triangle associated with aquatic symbolism, as a seed and sprout, or as an oval vulva swollen as in preparation for birth. Each category has its own meaning: the first is the cosmic womb of the Goddess, the source of the waters of life; the second is the sprouting of life; the third is the giving of birth.

FIGURE 160

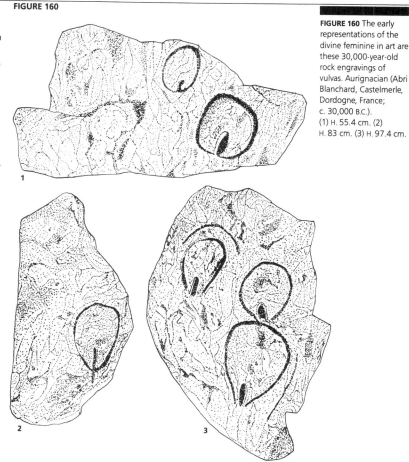

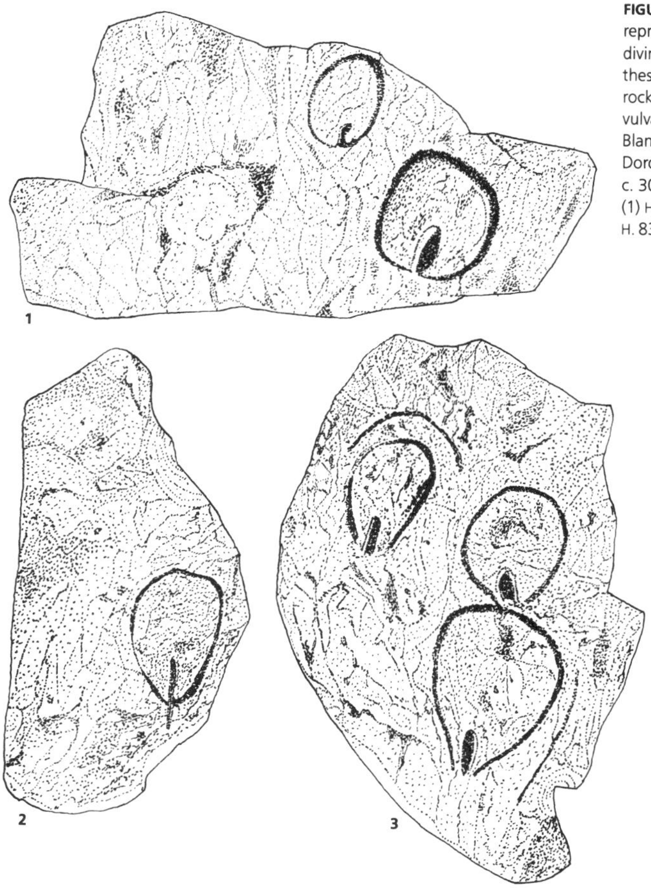

FIGURE 160 The early representations of the divine feminine in art are these 30,000-year-old rock engravings of vulvas. Aurignacian (Abri Blanchard, Castelmerle, Dordogne, France; c. 30,000 B.C.). (1) H. 55.4 cm. (2) H. 83 cm. (3) H. 97.4 cm.

FIGURE 161

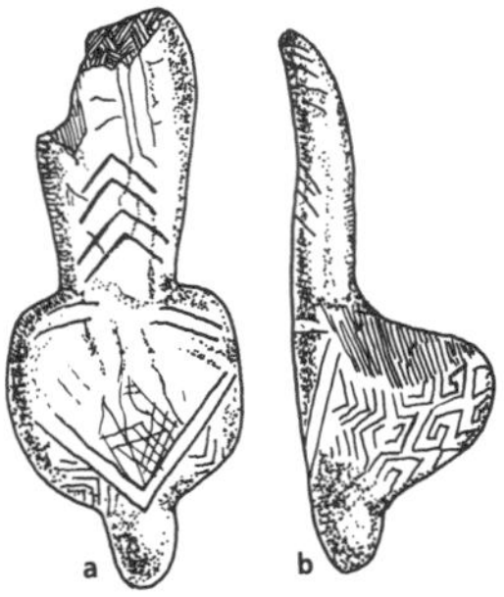

FIGURE 161 An enormous pubic triangle fills the front of this ivory waterbird, also marked with Bird Goddess and aquatic symbolism. Here bird, goddess, and human vulva are symbolically connected. Upper Paleolithic (Mezin, R Desna, Ukraine; c. 18,000–15,000 B.C.) H. 8.67 cm.

FIGURE 162

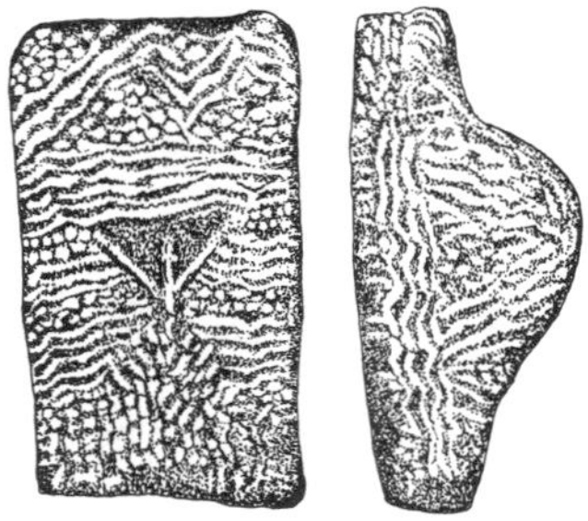

FIGURE 162 The vulva continues to appear amidst aquatic symbolism in later epochs, as on this Neolithic clay figurine. It is the source of or gateway to the waters of life. Lengyel (Křepice, district of Hrotorice, Czechoslovakia; 6th mill. B.C.) H. 7.7 cm.

FIGURE 163

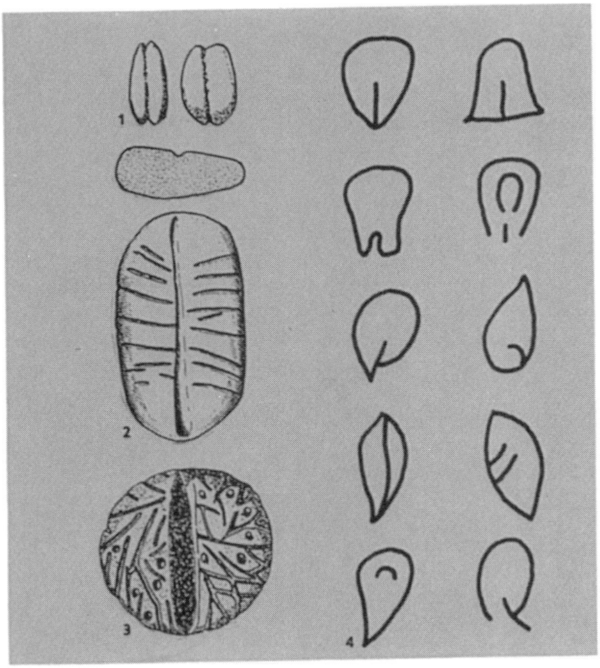

FIGURE 163 The vulva is also associated with the seed of wild fruit; this ancient fertility symbol, similar to the ubiquitous cowry shell, occurs throughout prehistory. It is found here on (1) and (2) Natufian grooved pebbles (Mallaha, Israel; c. 10,000 B.C.); (3) a central Anatolian clay seal (Çatal Hüyük; mid-7th mill. B.C.); and (4) Upper Paleolithic rock engravings (S France; various sites). (1) H. 1.4 cm. (2) H. 3.9 cm. (3) H. 2.9 cm. (4) H. each approx. 1.9 cm.

12.2 *In association with aquatic symbols, seeds, and sprouts*

Ivory figurines from Mezin in the Ukraine, c. 18,000–15,000 B.C., are hybrids of the human female with large vulva and the waterbird. (FIGURE 161) An engraved vulva covers nearly the entire front of the body while the long neck and protruding posterior are characteristic of a waterbird. Large chevrons on the throat are symbols of the Goddess; meanders, zig-zag streams, and parallel lines on the back and sides belong to the aquatic symbolic system. The vulva itself is marked with a net pattern.

The pubic triangle frequently appears amidst parallel lines, meanders, and streams on Neolithic and Copper Age figurines. (FIGURE 162)

Oval pebbles with a groove in the center and parallel lines on both sides were recovered from Natufian sites in Palestine, c. 10,000–9,000 B.C. (FIGURE 163) They are probable representations of a wild fruit seed, symbol of the vulva. Their configuration—a roundish form with central groove and parallel lines on either side—is evidenced not only on round and oval pebbles or bits of clay but also on seals, plaques, pots, and figurines. Its power of giving birth, well-being, or protection is analogous to the magical properties attributed to similarly formed cowry shells, which are frequently found in Neolithic deposits around the Mediterranean.

FIGURE 164

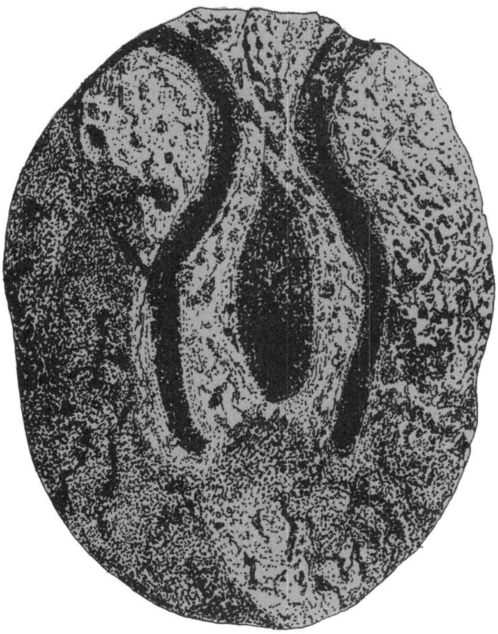

FIGURE 164 This egg-shaped stone sculpture has a vulva as flowerbud engraved on one side. It was placed at the head of a stone altar at Lepenski Vir. (Iron Gates region on the Danube, N Yugoslavia; c. 6000 B.C.) H. 20 cm.

FIGURE 165

FIGURE 165 Germinating seeds commonly occur in Cucuteni vase paintings. On (3), sprouting seeds (lower part) are associated with a tri-fingered figure (the Goddess with bird's feet instead of human hands) within a seed which is surrounded by streams; note the snakes of the upper and central bands. Painted black on red. (1) and (2) Cucuteni AB (Verem'e, W Ukraine; c. 4000 B.C.). (3) Cucuteni B_1 (Luka Vrublevetskaya, W Ukraine; early 4th mill. B.C.). (1) H. 24.2 cm. (2) H. 22.7 cm. (3) H. 38 cm.

A vulva carved on an egg-shaped stone at Lepenski Vir resembles a flower bud. (FIGURE 164) Seeds with a dot in the center or sprouting seeds are encountered in Cucuteni vase painting. (FIGURE 165) They are in rows and in panels, single or double, as on a vase from Verem'e, dated to c. 4000 B.C. Sprouting as a symbol of the birth process is shown on a painted vase from Tomashevka of the Cucuteni B period. In the lower portion is the primary symbol, a sprouting seed. The upper band contains an anthropomorphic figure within a lens or seed, perhaps the Goddess (note the tri-fingered bird's feet); on either side of the lens are water streams.

Vulvas and plants are associated on Cycladic platters of the Aegean Bronze Age which have been given the misleading description of "frying pans." In reality, they are anthropomorphic objects. They stand on two legs and have a large vulva. The illustrated platter from Syros (FIGURE 166) is decorated with interlocking spirals and a ship with a fish and bird's feet in front. The association of anthropomorphic features with plant motifs and the water sphere conveys the idea of regeneration. The fish and the feet of a bird of prey stand here as symbols of the Goddess of Death and Regeneration, whose main epiphany is as bird of prey (vulture, owl, or other) and as fish (see Part III, sections 18, 23). These platters, found in tombs and sometimes in association with the Cycladic marble figurines portraying the stiff Goddess of Death, must have been important in death rituals. Middle Minoan seals depict a seed-shaped vulva connected on all four sides to double spirals. (FIGURE 167) This combination may imply stimulation of the vulva (or seed) to bring about birth-giving or sprouting. The same symbol is known from the earliest Neolithic; compare the illustrated clay seal from Çatal Hüyük.

FIGURE 166

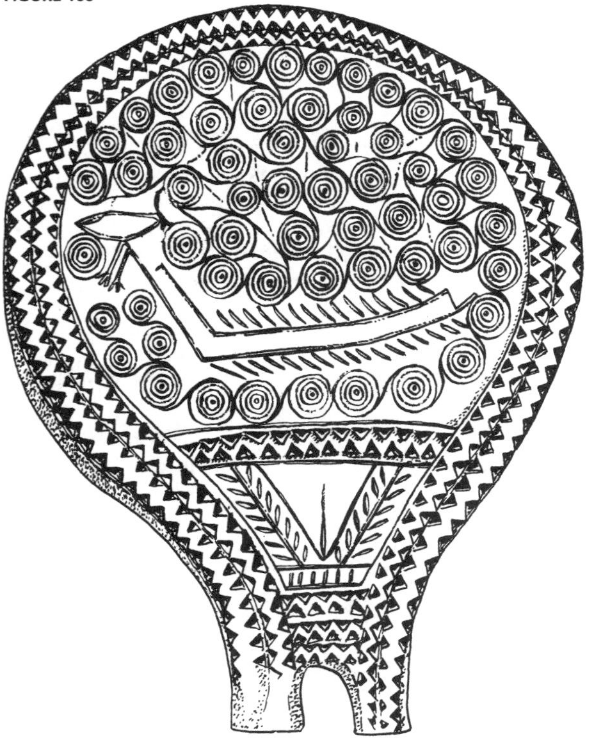

FIGURE 166 This characteristic Cycladic artifact is a platter whose lower part is anthropomorphic; above the legs is a vulva flanked by branches. Note the central drawing of a ship with fish and bird's feet on its prow (left) sailing across a spiral sea. See also fig. 350. Early Cycladic II (Chalandriani, Syros; mid-3rd mill. B.C.) H. 63 cm.

FIGURE 167

FIGURE 167 Perhaps symbolizing the stimulation of growth and life, four spirals surround a seed-like vulva on seals from two different cultures. (1) Central Anatolian Neolithic seal (Çatal Hüyük EIV; mid-7th mill. B.C.). (2) Middle Minoan ivory cylinder seal (tholos tomb Dra Kones, early 2nd mill. B.C.). (1) H. 2.8 cm. (2) H. 2.2 cm.

A seed or plant is incised on figurines in place of the vulva in various culture groups of Old Europe during the 6th and 5th millennia B.C. (FIGURE 168) Up to this century in many countries, peasant women exposed their genitals to the growing flax and said, "Please grow as high as my genitals are now" (cited by Franz 1972: 38). Popular belief in Malta claimed that the mother was delivered of her child as soon as the branches of a dried plant (passion flower) placed in water opened out (Cassar-Pullicino 1976: 217).

12.3 *Exposed vulva and birth-giving posture*

Portrayals of nude females with accentuated pubic triangles or swollen vulvas continue throughout the Paleolithic, Gravettian-Périgordian, and Magdalenian periods, c. 25,000–10,000 B.P. The vulva is exposed on several Gravettian "Venuses." A miniature with vulva portrayed as in preparturition is a Périgordian figurine from Monpazier, Dordogne. (FIGURE 169, 1) Another figurine from Moravany, western Slovakia, is depicted with a swollen mons veneris (Delporte 1979: 154, figs. 102, 103). At Angles-sur-l'Anglin, Vienne, a frieze of four sculpted nudes with exaggerated vulvas was found near a Magdalenian III habitation site. The focal point of the portrayals is the vulva; neither the upper torso nor the feet are featured (Delporte 1979: 87, fig. 49).

Facial features are never detailed in figurines with emphasized pubic triangles. A figurine from Le Placard, Charente, France, probably of the Magdalenian I or II period, is sculpted with an exposed swollen vulva and outspread legs, but the upper part of the body is phallus-shaped (see fig. 357). This may signify a belief that combining the vulva and phallus in one image strengthens the life force.

FIGURE 168

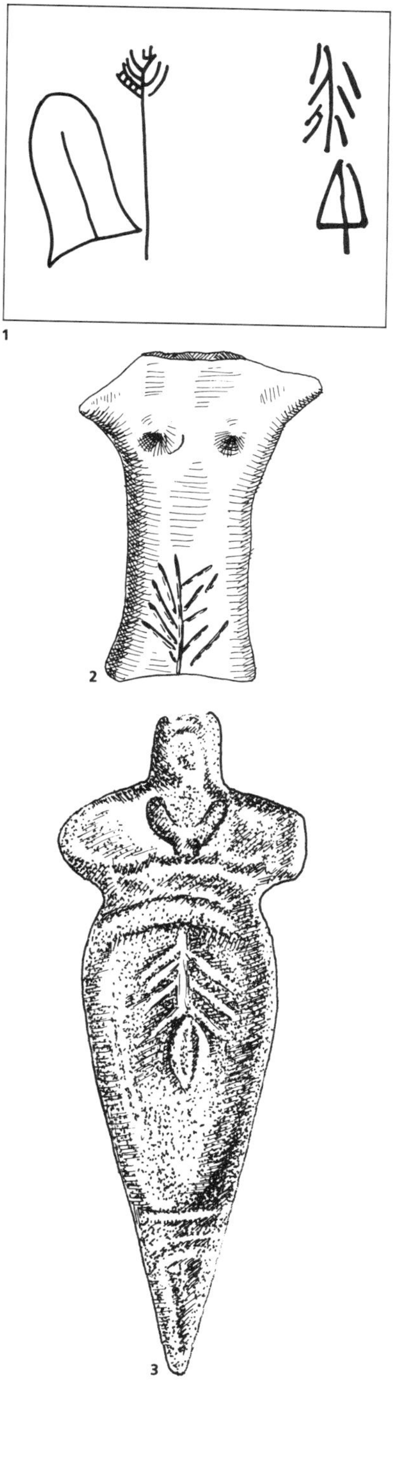

FIGURE 168 Sprouting seeds and young plants are paired with vulvas or take their place on figurines. (1) Paired vulvas and branches from Upper Paleolithic caves (El Castillo, N Spain, and La Mouthe, S France). (2) Early Vinča terracotta figurine (Jela, N Yugoslavia; c. 5200 B.C.). (3) Bone plate figurine from Neolithic Italy; note the crescent (or bull horns?) below the neck (Gaban cave, near Trento, N. Italy). (1) H. 3.7 cm. (2) H. 5.3 cm. (3) H. 5 cm.

FIGURE 169

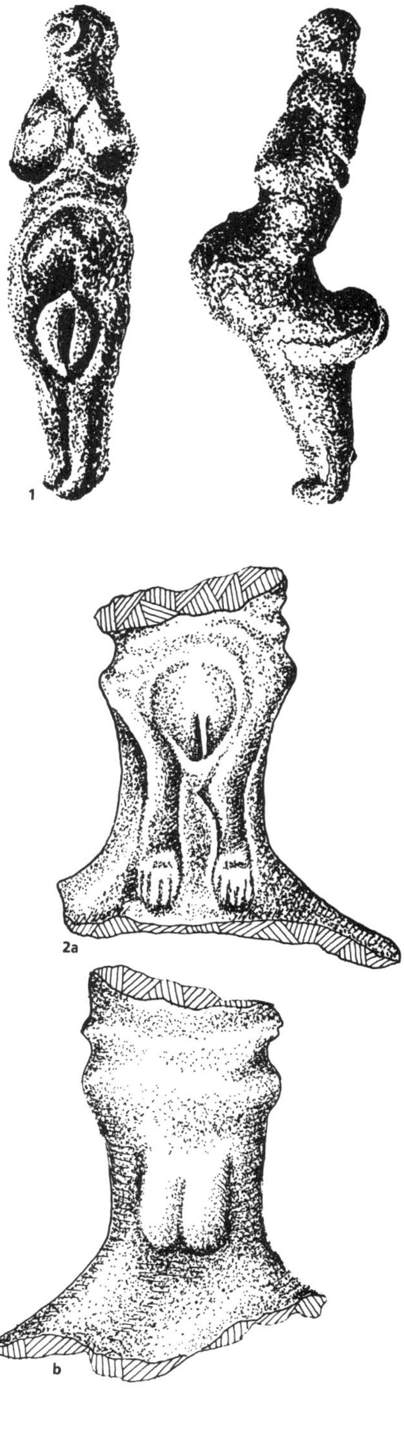

FIGURE 169 (1) A swollen vulva as in preparturition is common on Upper Paleolithic figurines and continues to be portrayed for 20,000 years. Limonite figurine with an enormous vulva, pregnant belly, and exaggerated buttocks. Gravettian-Upper Périgordian (Monpazier, Dordogne, S France, 23,000–21,000 B.C.). (2) Fragment of a lid handle portrays a woman with exposed vulva in front; her buttocks are on the reverse side. Hunyadihalom Copper Age group (Tiszafüred-Majores, SE Hungary; mid-4th mill. B.C.) (1) H. 4 cm. (2) H. 7.2 cm.

A series of Upper Paleolithic figurines place both hands on the pubic triangle. These are known from Grimaldi, Liguria, Italy (Delporte 1979: 106, fig. 59); Parabita, Apulia (ibid.: 115, fig. 66); Avdeevo, the Ukraine (ibid.: 172, fig. 110); and Mal'ta, Siberia (ibid.: 198, fig. 121). We conjecture that this widespread figurine stereotype is related to the exposed vulva type and that both represent the birth-giving aspect of the Goddess in the sense of her protecting, promoting, and aiding the act of birth.

Swollen vulvas continue to be portrayed throughout the Neolithic and Copper ages. A woman with exposed vulva and buttocks sculpted on a lid handle from the Copper Age of southeastern Hungary (FIGURE 169, 2) conveys the same symbolic message as that of the Monpazier figurine produced many thousands of years earlier.

Occasionally vulvas are shown in the very center of a figurine as high up as the location of breasts. For instance, the ingeniously sculpted limestone figurine in a squatting posture from Cyprus dated to around 3000 B.C. has breasts shaped like a triangle. Perpendicular lines in relief across the arms extend the triangle, making it look enormous and powerful. (FIGURE 170)

Of considerable interest is a vase in the shape of the lower part of a seated nude from Drenovac, a mid-Vinča site in central Yugoslavia, dating from the period around 4500 B.C. (FIGURE 171) The rounded buttocks are shown supported by a stool with a groove at the base in the shape of a vulva (see the third view). Such a vase perhaps was produced to celebrate a birth. It also testifies to the practice of birth-giving in a seated posture, as do the following illustrations portraying the birth-giving posture of the Neolithic and Copper ages. This posture is portrayed by figurines with bent legs, sometimes with one upraised arm and an exposed vulva. The earliest portrayals, sculpted or engraved, date from the Upper Paleolithic, c. 21,000 B.C.

FIGURE 170

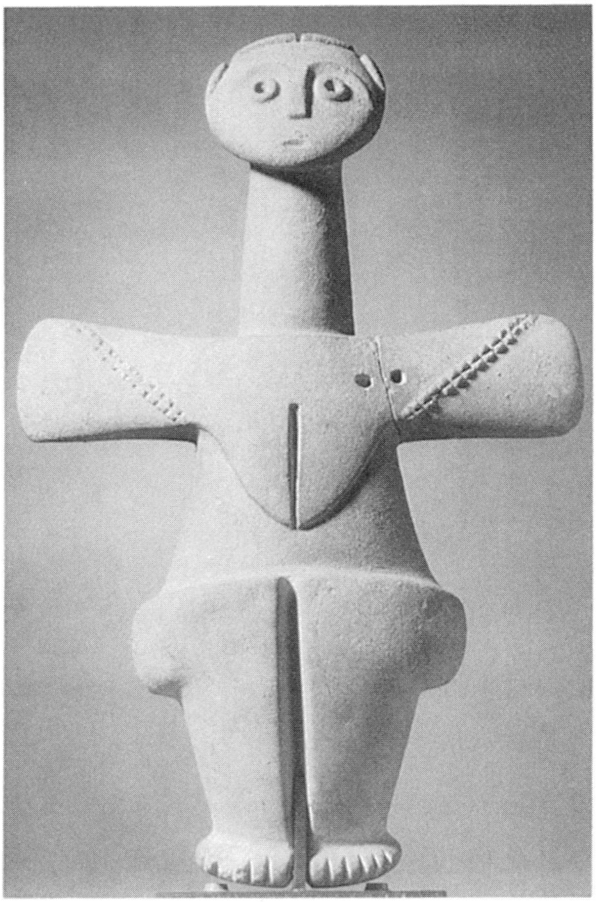

FIGURE 170 Figurine in a squatting posture. The focus is the female triangle in the center of the sculpture portrayed with tightly closed and pointed breasts and perpendicular lines across the arms. Limestone. Chalcolithic Cyprus (Provenance unknown; approx. 3000 B.C.). H. 39.5 cm.

FIGURE 171

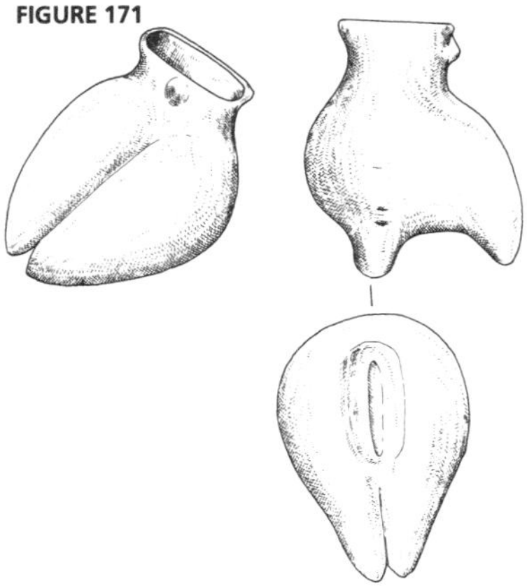

FIGURE 171 Perhaps manufactured to celebrate a birth, this cult vase is shaped like the lower half of a woman's body. She is seated on a stool in the form of a swollen vulva. Mid-Vinča (Drenovac, at Svetozarevo, central Yugoslavia; c. 4500 B.C.) H. 9.8 cm.

Calcite figurines from Tursac and Sireuil, Dordogne, southern France, with short, bent legs most probably represent women in the birth-giving posture. (FIGURE 172) The Tursac figurine actually has a cone-shaped protrusion at her vulva. The sculpture was found at a cave wall, 35 cm from two bovine bones (radius and ulna, probably of a young bison), in a seemingly intentional association. Discovered in a well-established stratigraphic position, the figurine is assigned to the Périgordian V_c period, radiocarbon dated to 21,000 B.C. The Sireuil figurine is regarded on typological grounds as contemporary with that of Tursac (Delporte 1979: 53).

The so-called "reclining women" with one arm and both legs upraised, sculpted in relief in the cave of La Madeleine, France, from c. 10,000 B.C. (FIGURE 173) do not seem simply to be in "unique" postures reflecting a "nonchalant freedom" of portrayal, as described by Leroi-Gourhan (Leroi-Gourhan 1967: 347). Rather, they are seriously motivated expressions of a woman (and symbolically the Goddess) in labor. The association with a bison and a mare in the cave, both apparently pregnant, strengthens this symbolic content. An earlier engraving of a woman "en position gynécologique," in a birth-giving posture (according to the excavator, Gaussen), is from the cave Le Gabillou, Dordogne. It is presumed to belong to the Magdalenian III period, 13,000–12,000 B.C. (Delporte 1970: 86–87).

In the figurine art of Old Europe, the birth-giving posture is quite well evidenced for various culture groups and periods. Illustrated examples are from the Sesklo culture of Greece (c. 6300–6200 B.C.), Vinča culture (c. 4500 B.C.), and the Hağar Qim temple of Malta (end 4th mill. B.C.). (FIGURES 174–176) Schematic figures in birth posture considered to be from the Neolithic were painted in the caves of Spain (Breuil 1933, vol. 3: 41, 85, 105, 109).

FIGURE 172

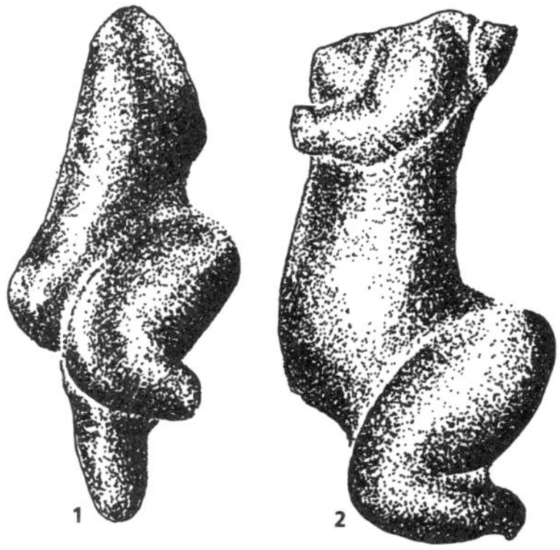

FIGURE 172 These amber-colored calcite Upper Paleolithic figurines seem to be in a birth-giving posture; (1) has a cone-shaped protrusion at her vulva marked with a chevron. (1) Périgordian Vc (Tursac, Vézère valley, France; c. 21,200 B.C.). (2) Périgordian (Sireuil, at Eyzies-de-Tayac, La Beune Valley, France; date possibly close to (1)). (1) H. 8.1 cm. (2) H. 9 cm.

FIGURE 173

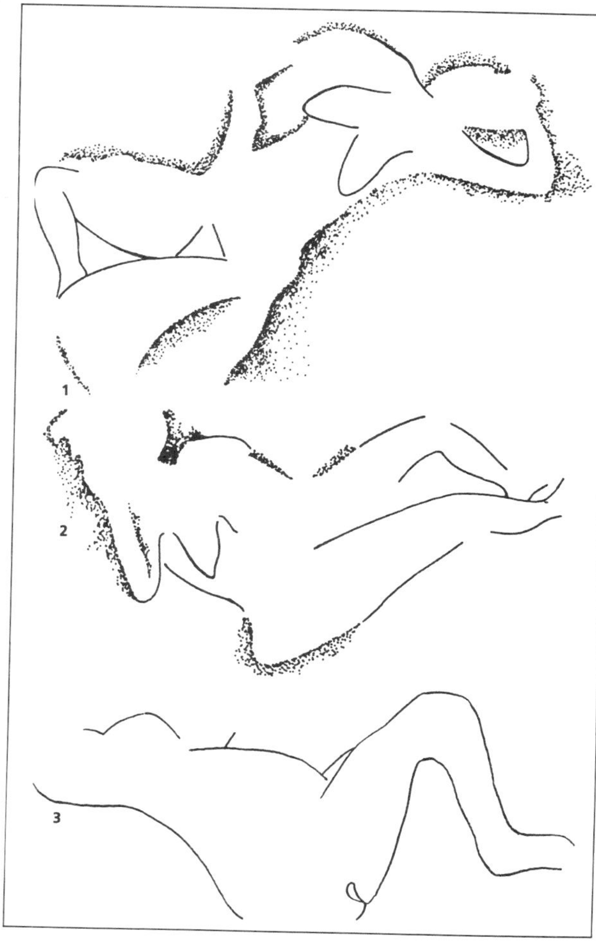

FIGURE 173 These well-known "reclining women," sculpted in relief to enhance the natural contours of Magdalenian cave walls, probably protray women in birth-giving posture. The length of the figures is about 1 m. (1) is next to a bison on the first chamber of La Magdelaine cave; (2) is next to a mare in the same cave. ((1) and (2) La Magdelaine near Penne du Tarn, Tarn, France; c. 10,000 B.C. (3) An engraving from Le Gabillou, Dordogne, France; c. 13,000–12,000 B.C.).

FIGURE 174

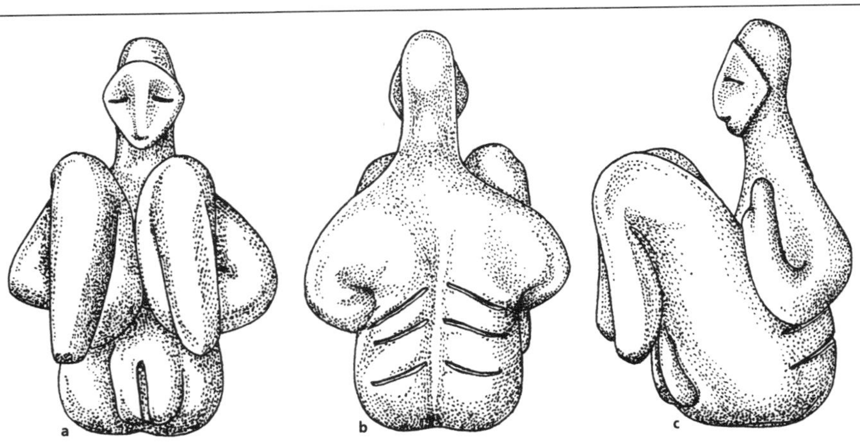

FIGURE 174 In the Neolithic, the birth-giving posture is sitting. This terracotta figurine, which has been reconstructed by the author, lifts up her legs to expose her swollen vulva. Note the tri-lines on her back. Early Sesklo (Achilleion II, near Farsala, Thessaly, Greece; 6300–6200 B.C.) H. 7.1 cm.

FIGURE 175

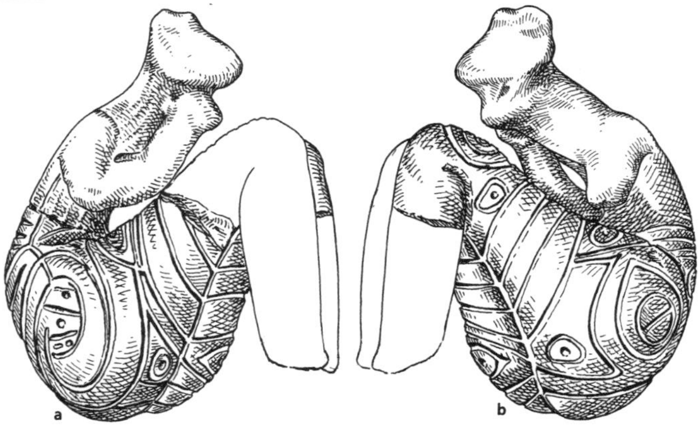

FIGURE 175 Testimony to the stereotype's longevity, the sitting posture occurs almost 2000 years after the Sesklo on this terracotta figurine. Her legs and left arm were broken. Vinča (Medvednjak, central Yugoslavia; c. 4500 B.C.)

FIGURE 176

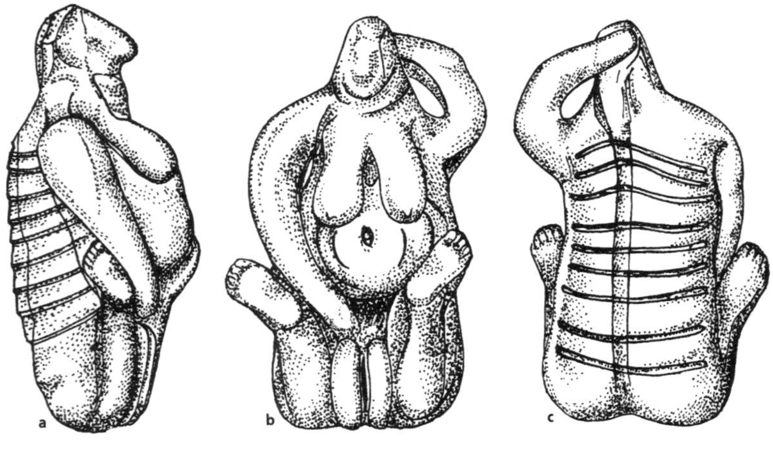

FIGURE 176 With upraised legs, pregnant belly, and hand at swollen vulva, this figurine appears ready to give birth. Do the nine lines across her back represent the nine months of gestation? Drawn in reconstruction, as she was found with right leg broken and face damaged. Maltese temple period (Haġar Qim, Malta; 4th mill. B.C.) H. 6.6 cm.

Another series of birth-giving Goddesses are sculptures of enthroned corpulent females flanked by male animals. A terracotta figurine from Çatal Hüyük, Level II shrine (c. 6000 B.C.) portrays a corpulent woman, the head of an infant emerging from between her ample thighs. (FIGURE 177) She is seated on a birth throne flanked by two felines. This sculpture was recovered from a grain bin. A close parallel to the above is known from Vădăstra, southwestern Romania, dated to c. 5000 B.C. (FIGURE 178) It is a fragment of an enthroned Goddess (the upper portion missing) with an infant's head between her legs.

The portrayal of the Goddess in a birth-giving posture for some 20,000 years demonstrates that this aspect of the Deity was a constant focus of attention.

12.4 *Birth shrines*

Some Neolithic shrines could have been specially assigned for the celebration of birth—both rituals and actual birth-giving took place there. In this respect a shrine at Çatal Hüyük (Shrine VIII.31) is of great interest as it is strikingly different from the others. Called the Red Shrine by Mellaart it differed from all found so far in being provided with a red-burnished lime-plaster floor. All the walls were painted red as well as platforms and benches. Above the low doorway into the shaft the false beams joined a molded porthole which permitted standing in the shaft to look into the room, a feature without parallel so far. Long red plastered runnels ran along the edge of the later platforms (Mellaart 1966: 180–82; Cameron 1981a: 22 ff.).

FIGURE 177

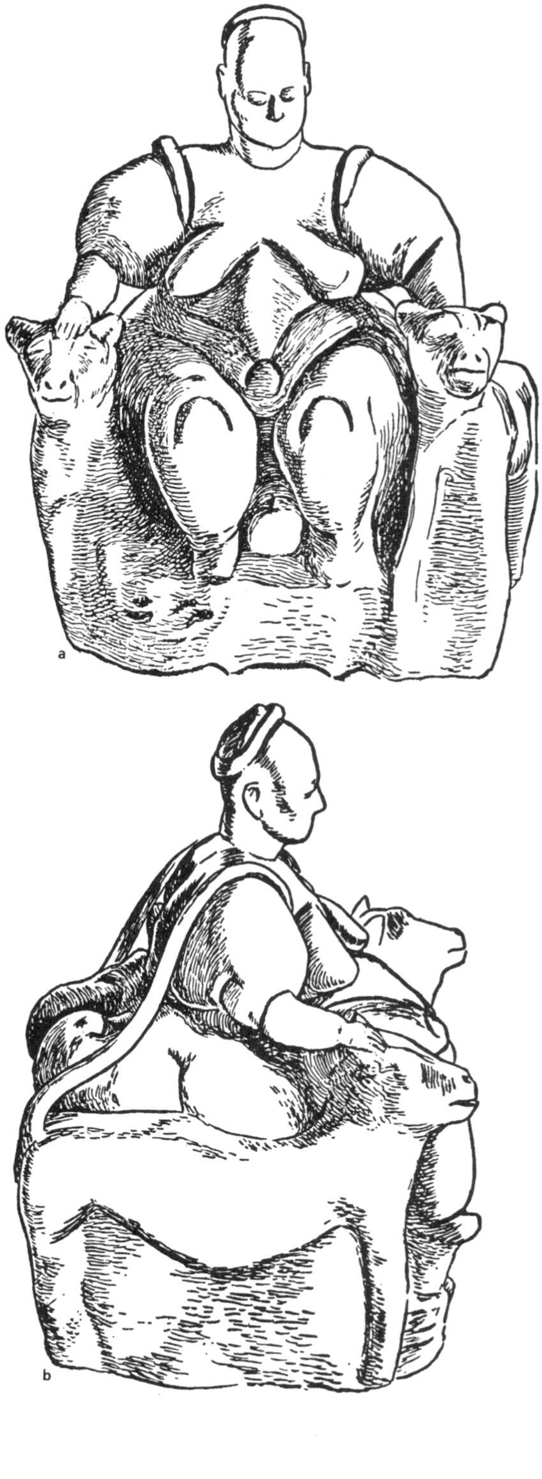

a

b

FIGURE 177 This majestic enthroned Goddess, flanked by felines, is giving birth to the child who emerges from between her legs. She was found in a grain bin. Head reconstructed. Central Anatolian Neolithic (Shrine in Level II, 1, Çatal Hüyük; c. 6000 B.C.) H. 11.8 cm.

FIGURE 178

FIGURE 178 The fragment of a similar figure depicts a goddess seated on a throne, a baby's head emerging from between her legs. Vinča culture. Vădăstra II (Hotărani, SW Romania; c. 5000 B.C.) H. 10 cm.

FIGURE 179

1

2

FIGURE 179 Great Goddess as a Queen of Mountains and Mistress of Animals in representations of Minoan art from Knossos, Crete, and Akrotiri, Thera. (1) Goddess on a mountain peak flanked by lions. Seal impression from Knossos, 16th cent. B.C. (2) Goddess seated on a tripartite platform and flanked by two exotic animals, a monkey and griffin (winged dog). Women are picking the flowers in a rocky landscape and place them in baskets as offering to the Goddess. Sketch of the fresco by Nanno Marinatos (1984). Northern and eastern walls of the mansion Xeste 3, room 3. Akrotiri, Thera, end 16th cent. B.C.

All the symbols represented in this shrine appear to be connected with the birth process. On the west wall three circles were painted in yellowish-white with a red center and outlined in red. Underneath this was a thick line in the same cream color, also outlined in red. As Dorothy Cameron observed, they could be a representation of the cervix, the ring of muscle below the uterus through which the fetus begins its journey to birth. Medical textbooks show the center of the cervix as dark red and the outer rim surrounded by a dark muscular ring. The cream-colored line painted horizontally underneath these circles may be meant to represent the umbilical cord which has to be severed after birth. In actual fact the umbilical cord is about a meter in length. The wavy lines painted across the circles and the yellow line may represent the amniotic fluid in which the baby is suspended during pregnancy.

Mellaart describes in detail the furniture of the shrine, which must have been most impressive, painted entirely in red. "Below the long narrow bench that extended in front of the main northwest platform in the later phases of the building a raised platform, about 2 ft. long, 1 ft. wide and about 8 in. in height was found, resembling a tombstone or altar table in the center of the room. Immediately adjacent was a rectangular panel of orange lime plaster broken by a circular hole that had been replastered in greenish-white clay, an arrangement suggestive of a chthonic libation hole. The east and south sides had been painted, but in the relaying of the floor the paintings were truncated and those of the south side almost entirely obliterated. The east side showed three panels painted in orange red on a fine cream background between polychrome borders with zig-zag lines in red and black." The red-painted platforms were probably the actual accouchement area. A painting on the east side of the red platform was composed of figures in the birth position, stylized open legs with the oval shapes in between surely representing parturition. The birth-giving figures are subdivided by a column of multiple chevrons (Mellaart 1966: pl. XLIX). On the northern wall of this shrine there were two bull's heads modeled with their horns and painted with geometric motifs.

The northern European saunas in which delivery took place as late as the early 20th century are the remnants of birth shrines or birth huts of a millennial tradition. In between the magnificent Çatal Hüyük birth-shrine of the 7th millennium B.C. and modern times there are known many other prehistoric shrines or their models which very likely were devoted to childbirth. Models of couches, figurines in the birth posture, and also imitations of fetuses in clay are found in such shrines. On Malta, for instance, the temple of Mnajdra yielded clay models of low couches, terracotta figurines, and twists of clay. The latter were replicas of two to three months old fetuses (D. Cameron, forthcoming).

12.5 *Mistress of Animals and the Queen of Mountains*

Minoan frescoes and seals of the 16th century B.C. reveal that the Life-giver is not only a goddess of child birth, the ancestress of Artemis Eileithyia, Giver of Birth, but is the incarnation of the fertility of Nature. She is the "Queen of Mountains" portrayed standing on the mountaintop and she is "Mistress of Animals" shown flanked by winged dogs or lions. The Queen of Mountains is known from a seal from Knossos with representation of a goddess on a mountain peak.

(FIGURE 179, 1) The most informative portrayal of this goddess is from the fresco in Acrotiri on the island of Thera, from the sacred mansion called Xeste 3. The Goddess is portrayed seated on a raised tripartite platform and flanked by a monkey and a griffin. She is beautifully dressed and adorned: she wears golden earrings and a necklace with ducks and dragonflies, and her dress is painted with crocus flowers. Her hair is tiered, with a bun on top and with snake-spiral locks in front. Around her throne, girls are picking crocuses and carrying them in baskets to the Goddess as offerings.

(FIGURE 179, 2) On the ground floor, there was a ritual scene of three girls, perhaps an initiation rite, and an altar decorated with a column of life of red lilies and red spirals and topped with horns of consecration. Sketches of full reconstruction of these frescoes by Nanno Marinatos (Marinatos 1984) have shown that much of what we see on other frescoes of Thera and Knossos is very likely linked with the cult of this goddess, for instance, the landscape scene with rivers, mountains, monkeys, and birds, and crocuses, papyri, myrtles, wild roses, iris, olive, rushes, and other plants from the House of Frescoes at Knossos, which is rightly called "an orgy of vegetation." Plant and animal energy is portrayed as bursting forth. This energy is of the Goddess.

12.6 *The Life-giving Goddess in historical times*

The life- and birth-giving aspect of the Goddess is one of the oldest that can be detected and also one of the best preserved to this day in the European subculture.

She is the Fate or three Fates (the Greek Moirai, Roman Fata or Parcae, Germanic Nornen, Baltic triple Laima, Celtic triadic Brighid). The image of a triple Goddess is well evidenced in the sculpture and frescoes of ancient Greece and Rome from the 7th century B.C. to the 3rd A.D. In Ireland and Scotland, she is the triple Brigit (Brighid, Brigid, Bridget) or Bride, the saint of that name has faithfully preserved the character of the Goddess.

12.6.1 *Cretan Artemis Eileithyia, Roman Diana, Venetic Rehtia*

The Cretan Artemis, Eileithyia, whose name means "child-bearing," appears at birthings. This goddess is also known from Greek inscriptions as Dictynna, connected with mountain Dicte on Crete, and as Britomartis, "Sweet Virgin," an epithet of the young and beautiful goddess. Today on Crete and the Aegean islands, she is sometimes seen near caves, in mountains, or bathing in the sea. On the island of Zakynthos, she appears as a tall woman; inhabitants of the island make offerings to her. On the islands of Chios and Skopelos, she is known as the "Queen of Mountains" (Lawson 1964: 164, 170).

Roman Diana presided over childbirth and was called "the opener of the womb." Pregnant women sacrificed to Enodia (another name of Artemis in Thessaly) to ensure her help at birth. Among the offerings to her were clay figurines of the Goddess in a seated position (Willamowitz-Moellendorf, I 1959: 171). Artemis, the beautiful virgin goddess, the protectress of wild animals, was portrayed as a divine huntress armed with a bow and arrow and flanked by hounds and stags. Offerings to her included phalli, dogs, he-goats, stags, spindle whorls, and loom-weights.

The Venetic Goddess Rehtia (Reitia) known from her temple at Este near Padua, northern Italy, of the 6th–4th centuries B.C., is another close parallel to the birth- and health-giving Goddess of the Artemis type. Her name is related to the Greek Goddess Orthia at Sparta and at Epidauros. One of her epithets is connected with the word *akeo*, related to Greek *akéo μai*, "cure." Another epithet *sahnati-*, "straightness," also suggests that she had to do with healing. Her names thus denoted her power of making people erect, especially of restoring women to health after childbirth. The epithet *vrota*, "turner," refers probably to the mode of "presentation" of an infant at birth. Among votive offerings to her were pins with jingling pendants of axe (i.e., female triangle) form, inscribed loom-weights, staghorns, horserider figurines, and alphabetic tablets of lead. The inscriptions on the latter probably were charms or spells intended to secure a safe delivery for women in labor (Conway 1933: 85–93; Whatmough 1937: 171).

The Artemis-type deity of Europe has a close counterpart in Mesopotamia: the Goddess Ninhursaga, one of the most powerful deities of the 3rd millennium B.C. (before she was supplanted by the male Enki in the 2nd millennium B.C.). She was called "Lady of the stony ground" or "Lady of the foothills." Similarly, the Greek surname of Artemis was "The Harsh and Stony One." Ninhursaga was also Mistress of wild animals. As birth-giver, she was called Nintur, which literally means "Lady birth hut" or "cattle pen" (to which cows were taken when they were ready to calve). She is also called "The Lady of the womb" and her emblem, shaped like the Greek letter omega, has been interpreted as a representation of a cow's uterus (Jacobsen 1979: 104–107).

12.6.2 *Irish and Scottish Brigit*

Like Artemis and Diana, Brigit watches over childbirth. She is considered the midwife to the Blessed Virgin and thus the foster mother of Christ. Her feast of purification, Imbolc, is the first of February. This festival celebrated the lactation of the ewes, symbolic of new life and the coming of spring. Milk was poured as an offering on the ground. The dandelion was Brigit's flower; it has a milky juice that was believed to provide nourishment to young lambs.

Special cakes were baked on her day, and dolls in her image were carried by girls in procession through the town. At each household they would stop while the householder made a present to Bride and paid homage to her, the gift could be a pebble, shell, or flower. The mother of each household baked a special cake for her. Finally the girls ended up at one house where they locked all the doors and windows, setting the doll in the window where she might be seen. Then the dancing began which continued until dawn, when they formed a circle to sing the hymn "Beauteous Bride, Choice Foster-Mother of Christ." While the young people were dancing the older women were busy fashioning a cradle, the Bed of Bride. They also made a doll out of a corn sheaf and decorated it with shells, stones, flowers, and ribbons. When the doll was ready one woman went to the door and called, "Bride's Bed is ready." Another replied, "Let Bride come in; Bride is welcome." Then the icon was placed in the bed along with a peeled wand of birch, broom, or bramble white willow (wood being considered sacred). At this point the ashes on the hearth were leveled, for the next morning they hoped to find evidence (footprints) that Bride had visited them, an omen of great prosperity (McNeill 1959: 22–28).

Paying homage to Bride, the presentation of gifts, making dolls, baking of special cakes, welcoming of the Saint in each house, and expectation of her visit as a blessing must have roots deeper than the last centuries of paganism; much of it carries on Neolithic traditions.

This explains still-extant beliefs in the miraculous healing water in wells under churches dedicated to the Virgin Mary and in such famous places as Lourdes, southern France, where Our Lady has a spring of healing water. In Niederbronn, Alsace, where in Celtic times Diana was worshipped as the Goddess of sacred wells, to this day women carry water from the mineral spring to nearby mountains. There, they pour it over stones with circular depressions to ensure pregnancy. In Aargau, Germany, women believed they would become pregnant by bathing in the spring of Verena. (Verena is a Christian saint of the Alemanni who replaced Diana. Duerr 1978: 37.) Holy wells are recorded by the hundreds in 19th century literature. In Ireland, they mostly became St. Brigit's wells, all visited on the first day of spring. Devotees perform the rounds at such wells, washing their hands and feet and tearing off a small rag from their clothes, which they tie on a bush or tree overhanging the well. According to a 1918 written account from Dungiven parish, after performing the usual rounds at the well, devotees proceed to a large river stone which has footprints; they perform an oblation and walk around the stone, bowing to it and repeating prayers as at the well (Wood-Martin 1902: 46). If there are hollows or cupmarks in stones, the country people stoop to drink. As previously mentioned (section 6.4) this water is supposed to possess miraculous curative powers. (The following discussion of Brigit, as well as that on pages 68–69 and page 135, is excerpted from an unpublished paper by Paula Powers Coe, "Fate, Fertility, Spinning, and Stones: A Comparative Study of Two European Goddesses." The author and the publisher regret that the source of this material was not cited in earlier printings of this book.) Annual pilgrimages are still being made to the Irish Brigit's venerated shrine in county Louth at Faughart, an area rich in megalithic tombs. St. Brigit's stone is here, as are numerous large standing stones situated along her stream. An observer of the July 12, 1986, pilgrimage noted that six girls of about seven years of age—*brideoga*—dressed in white with wreaths in their hair, were hauled to the site in a horse-drawn cart. The faithful make circuits of the stones and leave ribbons or strips of cloth from their clothing on nearby bushes, trees, or grass as offerings. "The rag or ribbon, taken from the clothing, is considered to be the depository of the spiritual or bodily ailments of the suppliant. Rags are not merely offerings, or votive, they are riddances" (Wood-Martin, 1902: 158). On the eastern side of Europe, the Russian Mokosh/St. Paraskeviya or Pyatnitsa (Friday) was a patroness of healing springs and menhirs where the paralyzed, the blind, and the deaf offered flax, wool, and sheep.

The *brat Brighide*, St. Brigit's mantle, is a strip of cloth placed on a bush several days before St. Brigit's Eve. Prior to a family dinner on the Eve, the eldest woman of the house would go outside to "fetch in" the cloth and call three times in Irish, "Go ye on yer knees, and close ye your eyes, and let Blessed Bridget in." On the third repetition those in the house cried "Come in, come in, and welcome." She entered and distributed a piece of the *brat* to all present. The cloth was kept to ward off illness and misfortune for the next twelve months (Irish Folk Customs and Beliefs: 63). The *brat Brighide* also functions to protect newborns and nursing mothers from abduction into the Otherworld (ibid., 44).

12.6.3 *Baltic Laima*

In eastern Europe, this Goddess exists into this century as a Fate who allots and absolutely predetermines all events in life. She is the spinner and weaver of human life who attends at birth and determines long life or short, good or bad. She is the owner of an inexhaustible source of life, the miraculous springs located under large stones or in caves. She is the fertility of Nature.

Up to the second half of the 19th century in Latvia and Lithuania, a birth ritual was practiced in the sauna. It was presided over by the grandmother of the family, and only women participated (Biezais 1955: 185 ff.). After the birth, a hen was sacrificed to the Goddess Laima. The grandmother killed it with a wooden ladle. Kneeling down, the participants then ate the chicken. Wooden ladles in the shape of a duck have been discovered at a number of Neolithic sites in Latvia and Lithuania. They may have been cult ladles used in sacrifices to the same Goddess. Before the hen was introduced to Europe, the duck was probably the main sacrificial bird. In Ireland during Imbolc, February 1, the feast of purification, Brigit was propitiated by the sacrifice of a fowl, which was buried alive where three waters met (Sjoestedt 1949: 25, citing A. Carmichael *Carmina Gadelica*, 1900, I: 168). Gifts to the Goddess Laima were linen towels, woven belts, and spindle whorls.

12.6.4 *Recapitulation*

Greek Artemis Eileithyia, Thracian Bendis, Venetic Rehtia, and Roman Diana, as well as the living Fate in European folk beliefs—particularly the Baltic Laima and the Irish Brigit—are unquestionable descendants of the prehistoric Life-giving Goddess. This Goddess has nothing to do with the Indo-European pantheon of gods. She must have survived the process of Indo-Europeanization and was carried over to our times from generation to generation by the grandmothers and mothers of countless families.

The historic and prehistoric Life-giver was a Mistress of mountains, stones, waters, forests, and animals, an incarnation of the mysterious powers of nature. Being an owner of wells, springs, and healing waters, she was a miraculous bestower of health. Through prehistory and history she appeared as a bird-woman, bird, or woman. As a waterbird she was a nourisher of humanity and an increaser of material goods. She was the guardian of the well-being of the family and from Paleolithic times must have been considered to be the ancestress and progenetrix of the family or clan. Bird Goddess was worshipped in house-shrines and temples. She is clearly the main temple goddess in southeastern Europe (as evidenced at Achilleion, Thessaly, in temples dated 6000–5800 B.C.: Gimbutas 1989). That she was a household deity as early as the Upper Paleolithic is suggested by findings in Mal'ta, central Siberia, where Bird Goddess figurines have been found along the inside edges of the circular mammoth-bone dwellings (Abramova 1967: 83). As mistress of animals and of all nature she was worshipped in the open, on mountain peaks. The Life-giver also appeared in a zoomorphic form, as a deer and as a bear. This very archaic aspect will be discussed in the next section.

Bear-legged Danilo rhyton with large ring handle, decorated with aquatic stream, striated triangle, and lozenge designs. See figure 186, page 118.

13/ *Deer and Bear as Primeval Mothers*

The Birth-giving Goddess's mysterious ties with the deer and bear are evidenced in prehistory and recorded in history.

13.1 *The deer, sacred animal of the Birth-giving Goddess*

The transformation of the Birth-giving Goddess into a doe is attested to by historical sources and folk memories. According to Pausanias, the statue of Artemis in the temple of Despoina at Arcadia was clothed in deerskin. Artemis and her companion Taygete assume the form of a deer. She is Elaphaia, "She of the Red Deer," and Elaphebolia, "She Who Strikes or Hits the Red Deer," who at an Attic festival of this name receives a deer sacrifice and honeycakes in the shape of a deer. The Sumerian Goddess of childbirth was also a stag.

The image of a Deer Goddess is preserved in Scottish and Irish fairytales. The supernatural, bigger-than-life women of Scottish tales could turn themselves into deer—or the deer changed into women. The belief in mortal women who can change into deer and who appear in groups is perhaps a folk memory of deer priestesses. There may have been a ritual in which the priestess donned and doffed her vestments, a deer hide with antlers (McKay 1932: 144–74).

In Greece, it was believed that pregnant does swam to an island sacred to Artemis near Colophon to bear their young (Strabo 14.643, cited by Otto 1965: 84).

In northern Asia, the belief in pregnant deer as mother life-givers existed to this century. They were covered with hair and had branching horns (Nganasan myth: Anisimov 1959: 49–50). Among the Evenki, the mother of the universe, called Bugady, was pictured as a doe-elk or reindeer doe (ibid.: 29; Nahodil 1963: 419). Parallels from Siberian hunter tribes suggest the deep antiquity of the cult, whose beginnings were not later than the Upper Paleolithic. During the Late Glacial and early Post-Glacial periods, c. 20,000–12,000 B.C., the hunting people of northwestern Europe sacrificed young by weighting them with stones and throwing them into the waters. Such a practice was observed at the Meiendorf and Stellmoor sites near Hamburg, Germany (Rust 1937, 1943). At Stellmoor 45 such buried carcasses were found. Perhaps Mother Doe, the great life-giver, required sacrifices of young life each year to strengthen her powers to create anew?

At El Juyo, east of Altamira in Cantabrian Spain, recent excavations revealed evidence of a deer cult in the Magdalenian level of the cave site, dating to about 14,000 years ago. Red deer remains lay in a dense mass in an egg-shaped depression about nine feet long, seven feet wide, and one foot deep, filled with the kind of silts that are deposited in ponded water. The depression had been deliberately dug out and encircled by a wall made of packed earth and stone rubble, including blocks and cobbles of sandstone and quartzite that must have been brought into the cave from the outside. Among the contents of this pit or chamber were masses of powdered red ochre; big patties of violet, vermilion, orange, and gray clay (excellent coloring materials); four partly carved deer antlers; a large lamp made from a hollowed out piece of stalagmite; and large grindstones (Freeman, Klein and Gonzales Echegaray 1983). Tito Bustillo is another Magdalenian cave in the Cantabrian region of Spain in which rituals associated with the deer cult and other zoomorphic deities endowed with birth-giving powers might have been practiced. In this cave, an artificial structure consisting of an elongated hole covered with a large stone was discovered. At the base of the hole there was an anthropomorphic sculpture carved in antler around which were clustered several sandstone plaquettes with engravings of deer, reindeer, bison, and horses (Moure Romanillo 1979; 1985). Last stages of this cave are dated to 14,000 B.C. (Moure Romanillo 1986).

FIGURE 180

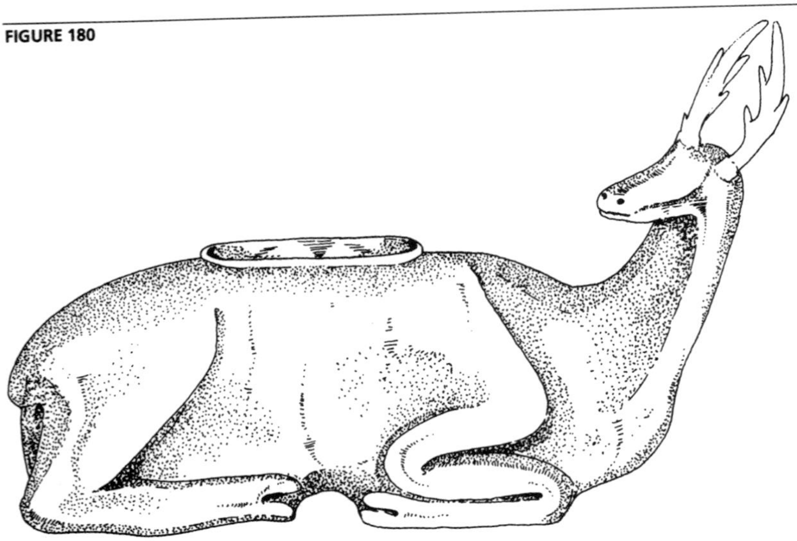

FIGURE 180 Old Anatolian and European cult vases occur in the shape of deer, as does this graceful buff burnished example. (The antlers are reconstructed by the author.) Central Anatolian Neolithic (Hacilar VI; 2nd half of the 7th mill. B.C.) H. 15.6 cm.

FIGURE 181

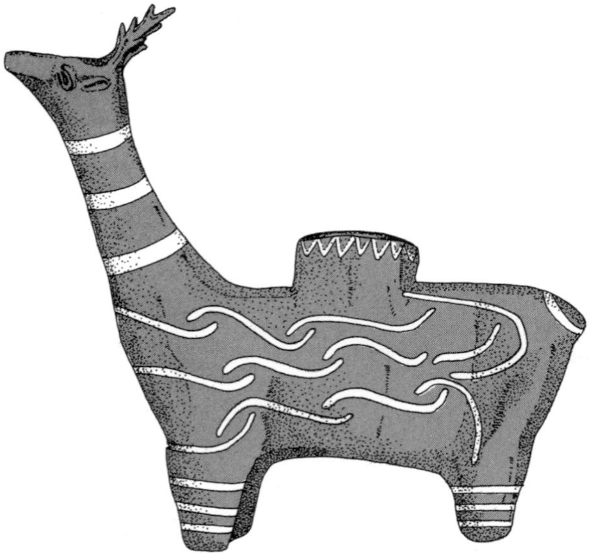

FIGURE 182

FIGURE 181 This zoomorphic vase is testimony to the symbolic connection between the deer and spirals, crescents, and triple bands. Painted white on red. Karanovo I (Muldava, central Bulgaria; c. 5800 B.C.) H. 53 cm.

FIGURE 182 As avatar of the Birth-giving Goddess, the deer is also associated with aqueous symbolism; this doe from a cemetery burial is covered with net, checkerboard, and zig-zag motifs. Greek Proto-Geometric (Grave 10, Kerameikos cemetery, Athens; 925–900 B.C.) H. 20 cm.

Stag dances were performed around the New Year in England, Romania, and Germany by men dressed as women, suggesting a dance in worship of a female deity. A Minoan seal from Zakros on Crete portrays a probable stag dancer with a huge antler for a head, upraised arms, and large breasts. Dancers with stag or deer masks are found in Greek art. The best examples are the terracotta figurines from Cyprus, one removing his stag mask, the other, clad in a rough skin garment, holding his mask in his hand (Lawler 1964: 69). The tradition of stag dances can be traced back to much earlier times. At Star Carr, an Early Post-Glacial camp dating from around 8000–7500 B.C. southeast of Scarborough, England, skulls of stags had been hacked into head-dresses, antlers still in place, the interior of the crania smoothed, the temples punctured for thongs to be passed through (excavated by J. G. D. Clark in 1949–50; a reconstructed head-piece is published by Burl 1981: 33).

Some Romanian Christmas carols, Latin *calendae*, contain archaic elements with no Christian matter in them. Examples are stag carols in which the animal crosses a river carrying a cradle between his big horns. In the cradle is a beautiful girl; she is usually stitching, and keeps warning the stag that, if it does not swim smoothly, he may spoil her work, and then her brothers/hunters will kill him. She further says: "Make my wedding with your flesh, build my house with your bones, roof it with your hide, paint it with your blood, fix your skull on my gate, make good drinking cups of your hooves" (Romania *colinda*, given to the author by Adrian Poruciuc, Iaşi, Moldavia, 1985).

In view of the long-existing deer cult, it is not surprising that exquisite vases in the shape of deer are found in Neolithic southeastern Europe and Anatolia. The earliest examples are from Hacilar in central Anatolia and Muldava, a Karanovo I site, in central Bulgaria. (FIGURE 180) The Hacilar deer is in a crouching position; its antlers are broken. (Mellaart's reconstruction of 1970 depicts bull horns; I have taken the liberty of superimposing deer antlers, using the Muldava deer as a model. There is no doubt that the body of the Hacilar animal is that of a deer.) The Muldava deer was found almost fully preserved. (FIGURE 181) It is in a standing position, painted with spirals and crescents in white on a red background and with three rings around the neck.

Deer portrayals or sculptures of seated women with deer antlers are recorded throughout the Bronze Age and continue into the Iron Age (Markale 1979: 135). (FIGURE 182) The pregnant doe from Kerameikos in Athens, of the Proto-Geometric period (925–900 B.C.), is decorated with panels of checkerboard and net designs over the body and neck. This is an unmistakable Old European style. The association of the net and checkerboard design with the deer suggests the intimate relation with water of life and amniotic fluid symbolism.

In northern Europe, antler-cult staffs with remarkably detailed elk-doe heads were discovered at Šventoji, a Narva site near the Baltic coast, Lithuania. (FIGURE 183) Similar staffs have been found in the graves of the cemetery at Elk Island in Lake Onega, northwestern Russia (Gurina 1956: 214, 215). Figurines or heads of elk-doe carved of antler, bone, and amber are known at a number of Narva sites in Latvia and Lithuania.

The elk-doe cult was not restricted to northern Europe. Similar sculptures, carved of antler, are known from southern Europe. A close analogy to the elk-doe of Šventoji came to light in the Neolithic cave of Gaban near Trento, northern Italy (Graziosi 1973: 251).

FIGURE 183

[redacted]

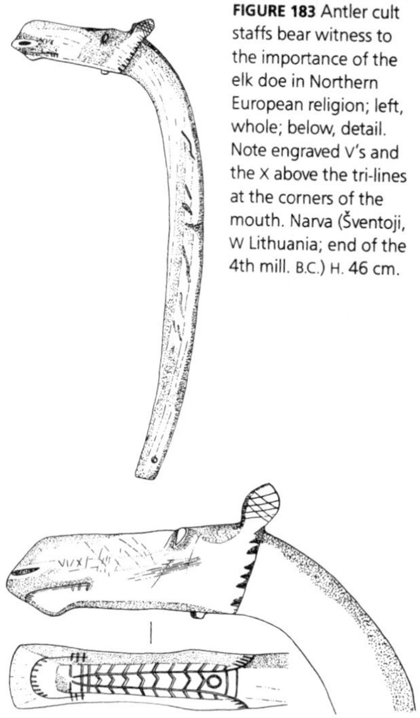

FIGURE 183 Antler cult staffs bear witness to the importance of the elk doe in Northern European religion; left, whole; below, detail. Note engraved V's and the X above the tri-lines at the corners of the mouth. Narva (Šventoji, W Lithuania; end of the 4th mill. B.C.) H. 46 cm.

13.2 *The Bear Mother*

The holiness of the bear, an animal of great strength and majesty, the glory of the forest, is universal in the northern hemisphere. As a vegetation spirit, the male bear was sacrificed once a year to secure the renewal of life in the spring. Upper Paleolithic portrayals of bears with bleeding mouth, nose, ears, and dart marks (Marshack 1972: 237, fig. 121) may be associated with the annual sacrifice of that animal. The other aspect of the bear's holiness, specifically related to the female, is her association with motherhood. Folk memories tell us that the bear was an ancestress, a mother life-giver, like the deer and the elk-doe, and linguistic evidence suggests the association with birth, to carry and bear children, and with child. The Old European root *bher-*, Germanic **beran*, means "to bear children," "to carry." Germanic **barnam*, "child," Old Norse *burdh*, "birth."

Bear feasts were recorded among the Slavs up to the end of the 19th century. Bulgarians prepared a meal on the day of Saint Andrew (November 30), consisting of all kinds of grain, corn, peas, and beans. A part of this meal was thrown through the chimney while someone said, "Be healthy, Grandmother Bear" (*Da si zdrava, baba meco*). The Belorussians believed that the appearance of a bear in a village brought good luck, and so they led them through every corner of the village. Honey, cheese, and butter were laid for them on tables inside the houses. In Bulgaria, a bear was led into the house and seated in the honorable corner by the wall where icons hung—i.e., the sacred corner, the altar place in prehistory. If the bear consumed the food, it was a sign of great good luck. A bear had healing powers, and sick people were made to lie on the floor so that a bear could step over them. Barren women sought the influence of the bear's blessed powers (Moszyński 1934: 575).

Up to the 20th century in the eastern Slavic lands, a newborn baby was laid by the grandmother on a bearskin. The same practice is known from a description by Porphyry, made in the 3rd century A.D. (Uspenskij 1982: 103–104; Marazov 1983: 32). In eastern Lithuania, a woman confined immediately after childbirth is called "Bear" (*Meška*). The name is used when she approaches the sauna for ritual bathing four or five weeks after giving birth. When the women who are preparing the ritual catch sight of the young mother, they exclaim, "The Bear is coming." It sounds like a formula, once part of a ritual, and it is still remembered (Daunys 1980). After bathing, the young mother makes offerings to the Goddess Laima. The gifts include linens and all sorts of woven materials, such as towels and belts, suitable gifts for the Birth-giving Goddess, the weaver of human life.

In contemporary Greece, we also find vestiges of the worship of the Mother Bear. In the cave of Acrotiri, near ancient Kydonia in western Crete, a festival in honor of *Panagia Arkoudiotissa*, "Virgin Mary of the Bear," is celebrated on the second day of February (Thomson 1962). From classical sources we know that in Arkadia the mother of the district's ancestor, Arkas, was changed into a bear shortly before Arkas was born. The mother's name was Kallisto, Megisto, or Themisto, proper epithets of Artemis (Willets 1962: 176–77). We know also that Artemis or her companions assumed the shape of bears and that Athenian girls danced as bears in honor of Artemis of Brauronia. During rites of initiation, the girls became bears. An interesting lead figure from the sanctuary of Artemis in Sparta shows a female dancer wearing a bear mask (Lawler 1964: 68). In Istanbul there is a limestone relief showing a bear-masked dancer (*An. British School at Athens*: 12, 1905–6: 323, fig. 3). In another part of Europe, *Dea Artio*, the Bear Goddess, is known to have been venerated by the Celts. The city of Bern, Switzerland, a cult center of the Celts, identified the bear with the Goddess and chose her as their symbol. An ancient bronze statue of the Bear Goddess was discovered in this city in 1832. She is shown seated before a bear.

"Bear Madonnas" in the form of a woman wearing a bear mask and holding a cub are known from Vinča art of the 5th millennium B.C. (FIGURE 184, 1) Another series of terracotta figurines, portraying women with an animal mask and a pouch on their backs, may represent a mythical Bear Nurse. An especially expressive example is a figurine from Čuprija, central Yugoslavia, of the mid-Vinča period. (FIGURE 184, 2) Hundreds of "hunchback" figurines have been discovered in Karanovo mounds (so far unpublished, probably because of their "ugly" appearance). The earliest such nurses date to the 7th millennium B.C. Several figurines with pouches or shoulder straps have been discovered at Achilleion, where they date from the end of the 7th and early 6th millennium B.C. (author's excavation; Gimbutas: *et al.* 1988).

The association of the mythical bear with the symbols of water and water-of-life is beautifully evidenced by the incisions on the palm-sized Mesolithic amber sculpture found in the bog of Resen in Denmark. (FIGURE 185) Microscopic study by Marshack has revealed that the engravings were made by fifteen different points and at different times. The accumulated signs include net-patterned bands on both sides of the head and body, bands of parallel lines and zig-zags, tri-lines, and other scratches. On one side two zig-zagging snakes can be distinguished. The sculpture is smooth and shows long wear. The symbolically interrelated signs must have been engraved at special occasions over a long period of time.

FIGURE 184

1

2

FIGURE 184 The bear is a ubiquitous cult figure in Europe, often associated with motherhood and nurturing. (1) This bear mother holds her cub in her arms. Vinča culture (Fafos II, Kosovska Mitrovica, S Yugoslavia; c. 4500–4000 B.C.).
(2) This terracotta "bear nurse" wears a bear mask and carries a pouch on her back. Vinča (Čuprija, at Supska, central Yugoslavia; c. 4500 B.C.)
H. 9.2 cm.

FIGURE 185

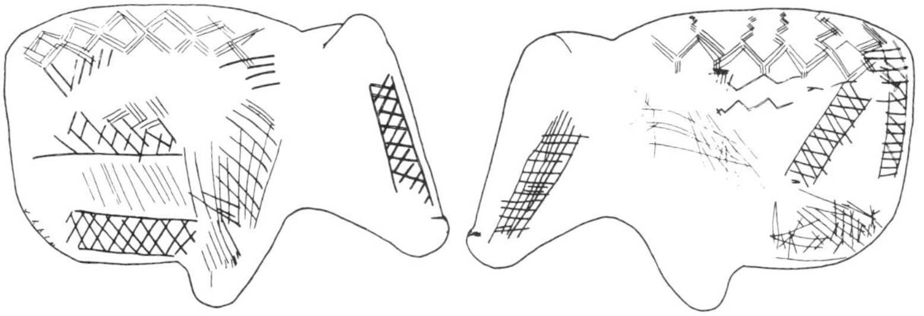

FIGURE 185 Amber bear recovered from a bog is incised with a rich symbology including net panels, snakes, zig-zags, parallel lines, and tri-lines. Maglemose culture (Resen, Jutland, Denmark; 7th–6th mill. B.C.)
H. 17.1 cm.

13.3 *Bear-shaped vases*

The importance of the bear in Old European rituals is attested by bear vases, some of exquisite workmanship, that were produced continuously from the 7th to the 3rd millennia B.C.

Peculiar bear-legged, ring-handled containers decorated with striated or net-pattern triangles and bands and snake zig-zags (FIGURE 186) are found over a wide distribution area comprising Neolithic Thessaly, central Greece, and the Peloponnese; Hercegovina, Dalmatia, and Bosnia in Yugoslavia; Albania; and the Lipari Islands north of Sicily (Korošec 1958: 53–59; Kosmopoulos 1948: figs. 5–6; Weinberg 1962a: 190–95, pls. 64, 65; 1962b: Jovanović 1969; Benac 1972–73: 86; Batović 1968).

Regional variations are noticeable in each area of manufacture, but the ring-handles and fat, zoomorphic legs identify them as of the same type. Strikingly uniform treatments are the use of red-painted borders on ornamental rims, black or gray polished surfaces, and white encrustation of incised designs. These close affinities can well be explained as a shared tradition prescribing the form and decoration of ritual objects.

The repertory of motifs incised on these zoomorphic-legged containers are: net-patterned triangles; net patterns in parallel bands or zig-zag bands; barbed-wire lines or bands; and striped or dotted snakes. This symbolism suggests an association with the snake and water as the life source.

Bear-shaped containers with ring handles seem to die out after 5000 B.C., but the recurrence of the bear in association with symbolic motifs speaks for the continuing importance of the bear in myth over the course of millennia.

FIGURE 186

FIGURE 186 This example of the characteristic bear-legged rhyton with large ring handle, probably a cult vessel, is decorated with aquatic stream, striated triangle, and lozenge designs. Two views. Danilo (Smilčić, at Zadar, Adriatic coast, Yugoslavia; c. 5500 B.C.) H. 17.5 cm.

Well-preserved examples from the 5th, 4th, and 3rd millennia B.C. are a bear vase from Abraham, western Slovakia, of the Lengyel complex (FIGURE 187, 1); one from Sipenitsi of the Late Cucuteni culture (FIGURE 187, 2); and a basin-toting "teddy bear" from the island of Syros, mid-3rd millennium B.C. (FIGURE 188) Bands of parallel lines decorate the Abraham vase, checkerboard motifs cover the back of the Syros bear, and stripes continue over the front portion of the body and legs on the bowl. The vessels must have been used for ceremonial purposes in the worship of the Birth-giving Goddess.

FIGURE 187

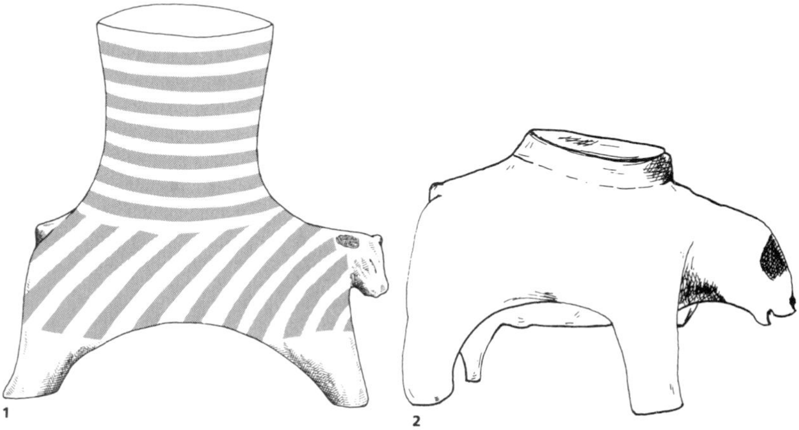

1 2

FIGURE 188

FIGURE 187 (1) This bear-shaped terracotta lamp is decorated with bands of parallel lines. Early Lengyel (Abraham, W Slovakia; 5000–4500 B.C.) (2) Comparatively realistic terracotta bear vase is of Late Cucuteni workmanship. (Sipenitsi, W Ukraine; 3700–3500 B.C.) (1) H. 20.4 cm. (2) H. 11 cm.

FIGURE 188 This charming terracotta bear carries a basin which has an opening into the animal's hollow body. Note the checkerboard patterns on the back and the parallel bands and tri-lines over the bear's body and the bowl. Early Cycladic (Chalandriani, Syros; 3rd mill. B.C.). H. 11 cm.

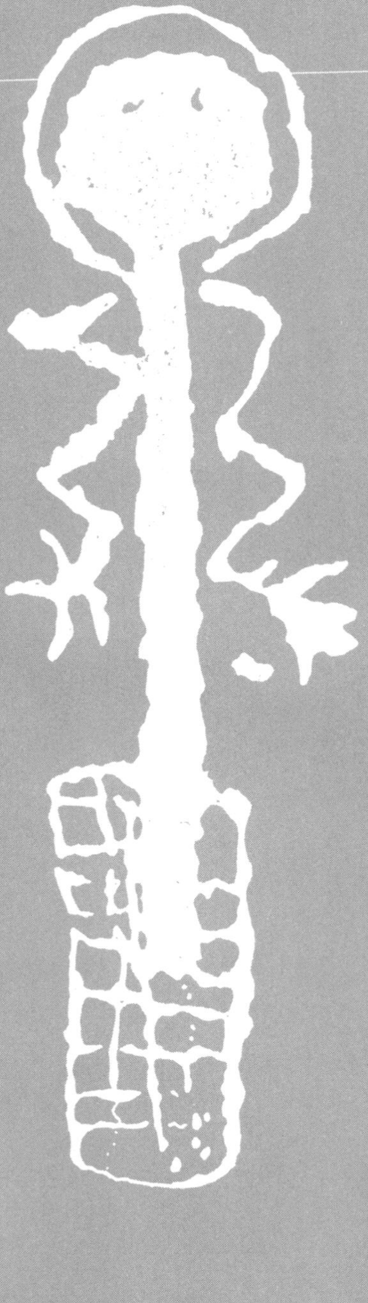

Snake-limbed rock engraving, showing tendency toward abstraction in portrayals of the Snake Goddess. See figure 204, page 127.

14/ *Snake*

The snake is life force, a seminal symbol, epitome of the worship of life on this earth. It is not the body of the snake that was sacred, but the energy exuded by this spiralling or coiling creature which transcends its boundaries and influences the surrounding world. This same energy is in spirals, vines, growing trees, phalluses, and stalagmites, but it is especially concentrated in the snake, and therefore more powerful. The snake was something primordial and mysterious, coming from the depths of the waters where life begins. Its seasonal renewal in sloughing off its old skin and hibernating made it a symbol of the continuity of life and of the link with the underworld.

The symbols surrounding the snake and the anthropomorphic Snake Goddess are the same as those associated with the waterfowl and the Bird Goddess. From the illustrations in this section it can be seen that chevrons, X's, and aquatic symbols—zig-zags, meanders, and streams—accompany snakes. They must have been guardians of the springs of life in prehistory, as they still are in European folklore. The peculiar association of the snake and the ram, the sacred animal of the Bird Goddess, is seen in images of horned snakes, ram-headed snakes, and in the interchangeability of ram horns and snake coils. The intimate relation between waterbird and snake and between Bird Goddess and Snake Goddess continued throughout prehistory and into historic times. In ancient Greece, Athena's attributes are birds and snakes. There is a close connection between the two major goddesses Athena and Hera, the latter a probable descendant of the Snake Goddess. The shrines dedicated to these goddesses often stand together. The snake associated with Athena was seen flying in the air like a bird. The goblins of European folklore who bring treasures to farmers are flying serpents or birds.

The snake is a transfunctional symbol; it permeates all themes of Old European symbolism. Its vital influence was felt not only in life creation, but also in fertility and increase, and particularly in the regeneration of dying life energy. Combined with magic plants, the snake's powers were potent in healing and creating life anew. A vertically winding snake symbolized ascending life force, viewed as a column of life rising from caves and tombs, and was an interchangeable symbol with the tree of life and spinal cord. Similarly, snake coils exuded regenerative force as the moist eyes of the Owl Goddess and as the sun.

The Old European snake is clearly a benevolent creature, except when the death-wielding aspect of the Goddess is represented. Then she is a poisonous snake or appears in the guise of a woman with some features of a snake. In this art we do not find anything that reflects its being evil. This then is the opposite of what is found in Indo-European and Near Eastern mythologies where the serpent symbolizes evil powers. The warrior gods exult in killing serpents and dragons: Vedic Indra kills the serpent Vrtra, Norse Thor kills Midgard, Marduk of Babylon kills the monster Tiamat, and so on. Whirlwinds are dreaded by the Indo-Europeans because the serpent is hiding in them.

On Old European ceramics the "snake theme" constantly grew in importance, reaching its height around 5000–4000 B.C. Its symbolic prominence inspired the development of "snake spiral art," so characteristic of Old Europe in the 5th millennium B.C. The range of decorative possibilities offered by the coil and spiral seemed endlessly to intrigue the European artist. But we shall leave the aesthetics of design aside and deal with winding snakes and snake coils, snake figurines and snake-woman hybrids as the epiphanies of the Goddess. The dynamic energy of the snake as a symbol of regeneration will be discussed in Parts III and IV.

FIGURE 189

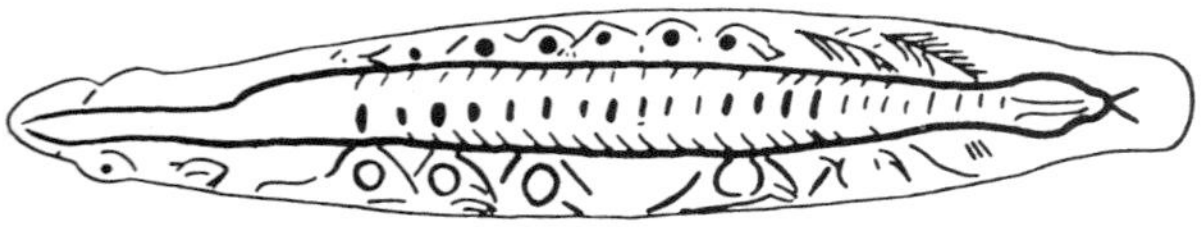

FIGURE 189 Snakes appear in Upper Paleolithic art; this engraved antler is particularly interesting because the serpent is associated with young birds, plants, and a tri-line, implying use in a spring ritual celebrating regenerative growth (Lortet; Middle Magdalenian; c. 12,000 B.C.). H. 2.5 cm.

FIGURE 190

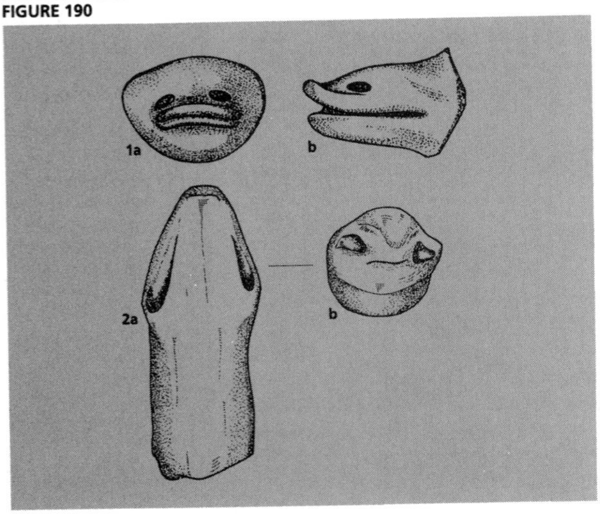

FIGURE 190 These terracotta heads represent the earliest Neolithic snakes so far found in SE Europe. Sesklo ((1) Magula near Tsani and (2) Achilleion IV, Thessaly near Farsala; 5800 B.C.) (1) H. 2.4 cm. (2) H. 6.4 cm.

FIGURE 191

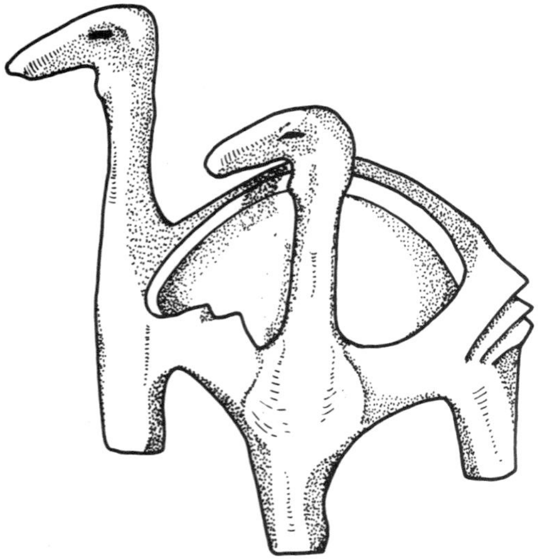

FIGURE 191 The snake appears during the Neolithic in many forms, including as protomes on cult vases. Macedonian variant of the Starčevo culture (Porodin; 5800–5500 B.C.) H. 13.6 cm.

14.1 *The snake and snake coil in the Upper Paleolithic and Neolithic*

Representations of snakes are known since the Upper Paleolithic and continue in the Mesolithic and Neolithic. A considerable number of Magdalenian bone and antler objects are serpent-shaped and marked with zig-zags, winding parallel lines, and interconnected lozenge patterns (see Chollot-Varagnac 1980: 51, 73, 79, 89, 97, 107, 115, 185, 187, 243). Others are incised with snake coils and spirals (ibid.: 227).

A small antler piece (2.5 cm in length) from Lortet, dated to the Middle Magdalenian period, c. 12,000 B.C., is incised with a stretched-out snake associated with rows of young bird heads, branches, and a tri-line. (FIGURE 189) This assemblage of symbols suggests that the object was made for a spring/summer ritual when snakes, birds, and plants regenerate (Marshack 1972: 223).

In the Neolithic of 6500–5500 B.C., ophidian heads with round eyes and a long mouth are sculpted or are featured on jars in southern and southeastern Europe; they continue for centuries as a major design element. (FIGURES 190–192) Snake heads form protomes on vases and are painted or incised on handles, a position of prominence.

Clay stamps bearing a snake coil motif demonstrate that, as early as the middle of the 7th millennium B.C., the coil probably served as the insignia of the Goddess in her epiphany as a snake. (FIGURE 193) Round stamp seals engraved with snake coils are known throughout Old Europe between 6500 and 3500 B.C., and into the Bronze Age of Minoan Crete. The snake coil in relief as an isolated motif on Neolithic vases of the Starčevo and Karanovo complexes is employed not for decoration but as an identifying symbol. (FIGURE 194)

FIGURE 192

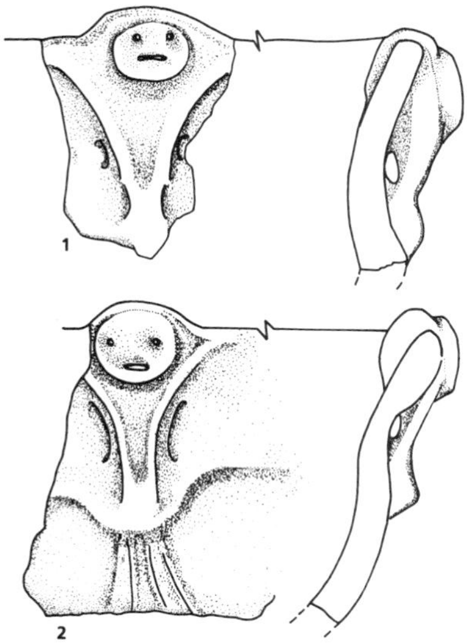

FIGURE 192 These round snake heads peer from the rim of Neolithic vase fragments. Bonu Ighinu culture ((1) Filiestru and (2) Tintirriolu, Mara, Sardinia; end of the 5th mill. B.C.) (1) H. 3.7 cm. (2) H. 4.6 cm.

FIGURE 193

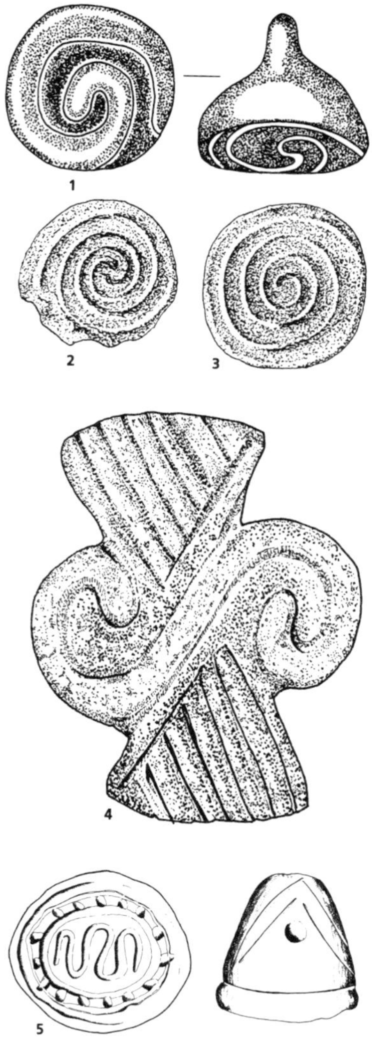

FIGURE 193 Snakes on Neolithic clay stamps. (1) Anatolian Neolithic (Çatal Hüyük VIA; c. 6500 B.C.). (2) and (3) Cucuteni (Frumuşica; c. 4500–4300 B.C.). (4) S Italian Neolithic (Erba; 6th mill. B.C.). (5) Middle Minoan green serpentine seal (Kali Limiones; beginning of 2nd mill. B.C.). (1a) DIA. 3.7 cm. (2) DIA. 3.3 cm. (3) DIA. 3.7 cm. (4) H. 6.7 cm. (5b) H. 2.3 cm.

FIGURE 194

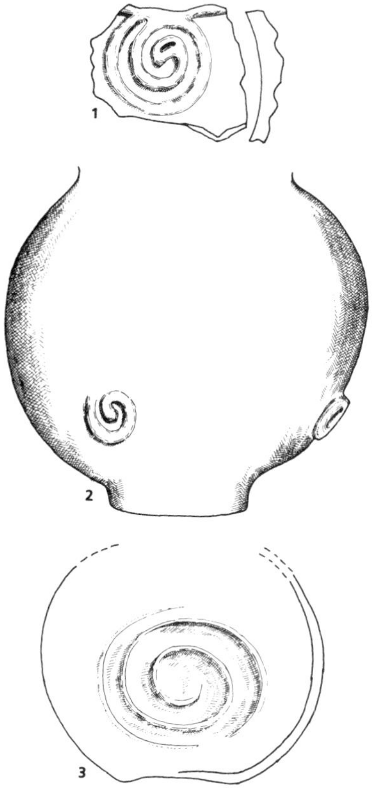

FIGURE 194 Snakes serve to label Starčevo and Karanovo vases of 5800–5500 B.C. ((1) Slatina, Bulgaria; (2) Bukova-puszta, SE Hungary; (3) Lepenski Vir, Iron Gates region) (1) H. 6.6 cm. (2) H. of detail 49.8 cm. (3) H. of detail 17.2 cm.

The snake coil appears on miniature stands—probably tiny temples or altars dedicated to the Snake Goddess—engraved on one face as if to designate the façade; the remaining area is filled with net designs, chevrons, and vertical bands of X's or lozenges (snake skin design?). (FIGURE 195) When the snake coil appears in a panel, it is framed by vertical or horizontal bands and alternates with nets or chevron panels. (FIGURE 196) Sometimes the snake coil is painted or modeled in relief on the inner surface of dishes and bowls produced for ritual use. On the other side of Europe, snake coils are encountered engraved on stone balls from Scotland. They apparently served an amuletic purpose, such as life or fertility insurance. (FIGURE 197) Large snake coils engraved on orthostats of Knowth and Newgrange tomb-shrines, Ireland, are associated with V's, M's, chevrons, and zig-zag bands (Eogan 1986: 150, 193; O'Kelly 1983: figs. 41–55).

FIGURE 195

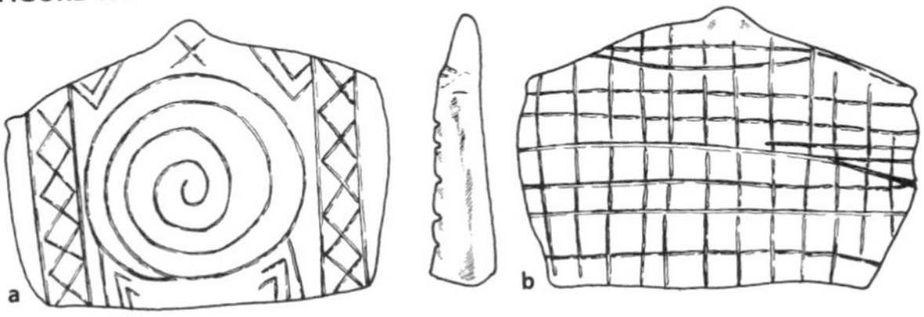

FIGURE 195 Snake coils label miniature clay stands, probable shrine symbols or altar pieces. The central coil is associated with chevrons, X's, and net signs. Karanovo VI (Ruse; 4500–4300 B.C.) H. 8.3 cm.

FIGURE 196

FIGURE 196 Isolated snakes—winding or coiling—appear in panels on the necks or bodies of vases. A snake coil on this vase is flanked by zig-zag columns. Black painted on red. Cucuteni B (Koshilivtsi; c. 3700–3500 B.C.) H. 53 cm.

FIGURE 197

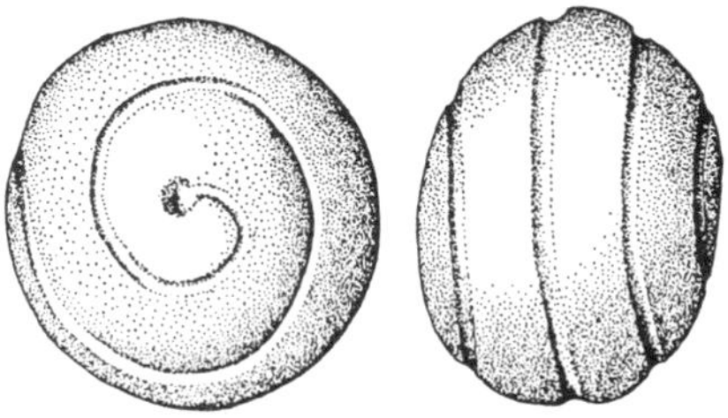

FIGURE 197 Snakes coiling around smooth stone balls. Deep engraving. Late Neolithic Scotland (Aberdeenshire, Scotland; date uncertain, probably 3rd mill. B.C. or before 3000 B.C.) DIA. 3.6 cm.

14.2 *The snake coil in association with aquatic symbols*

The association of the snake with water or stream symbols is visible in ceramic decoration from c. 5500 B.C. on. This symbolism is expressed in isolated snakes, coils, or interlocked snake spirals painted above striated, stabbed, and criss-cross lines or adjacent to parallel lines and meanders.

Examples from 5th and 4th millennia B.C. sites demonstrate the consistent combination of these motifs over an extended time span and wide area. (FIGURE 198) Squares with snake coils alternate with striated squares; snake coils appear rhythmically on net-patterned or striated designs, or are inserted within bands of striated meanders. (FIGURE 199) At times, a snake emerges from a net, meander, or checkerboard pattern. Zig-zags easily become diamond-shaped snake heads, a motif that appears from the Mesolithic through the Iron Age.

Such portrayals convey that, as a symbol of life energy, the snake emerges from the waters.

FIGURE 198

a

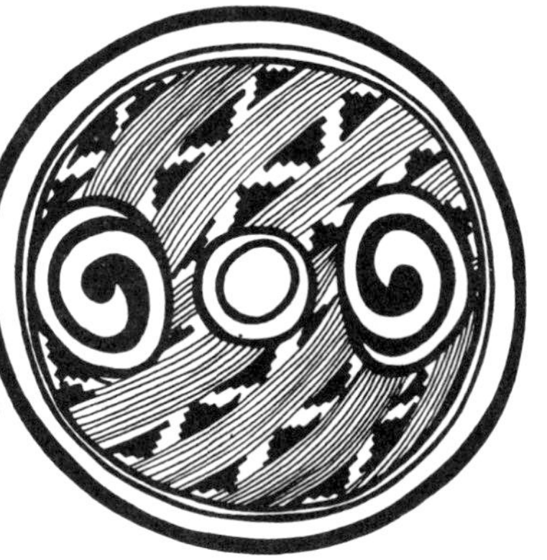

b

FIGURE 198 This dish offers a complex assemblage of snake and water symbols: coils over bands of parallel lines and "stair" motifs, meanders, and checkerboards. Dark brown on cream. Dimini (Sesklo; 5000–4500 B.C.) DIA. 27.2 cm.

FIGURE 199

1

2

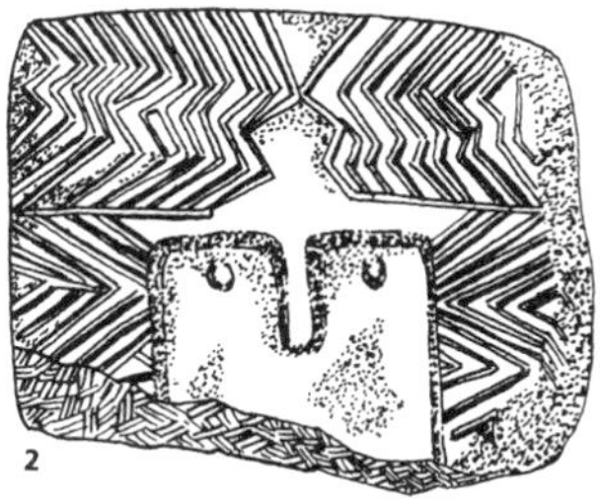

FIGURE 199 Snake heads emerge from meander bands. (1) Snake head emerging from a meander band on a vase. Bükk (Bodrogkeresztúr; 2nd half of 6th mill. B.C.). (2) Snake heads and zig-zags of flowing water above the Goddess's face engraved on a stone stele. S France Late Neolithic (Orgon; 3000–2500 B.C.) (1) H. 7.8 cm. (2) 16 cm.

FIGURE 200

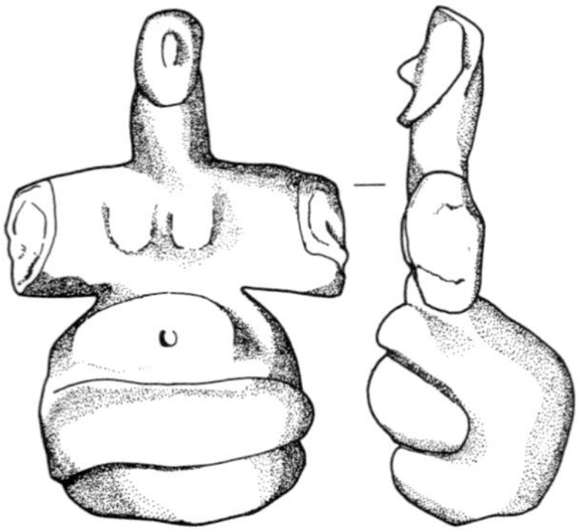

FIGURE 200 Sculptures of an ophidian/human hybrid Snake Goddess, carved of marble or modeled in clay, emerge in Neolithic Crete and the Aegean islands. She is invariably squatting in a yogic posture, and her limbs are snakelike. Her mask has a human nose and sometimes eyes and a mouth, but the mouth is characteristically long. Marble sculpture from Amorgos or another Aegean island. c. 6000–5500 B.C. H. 20.3 cm.

FIGURE 201

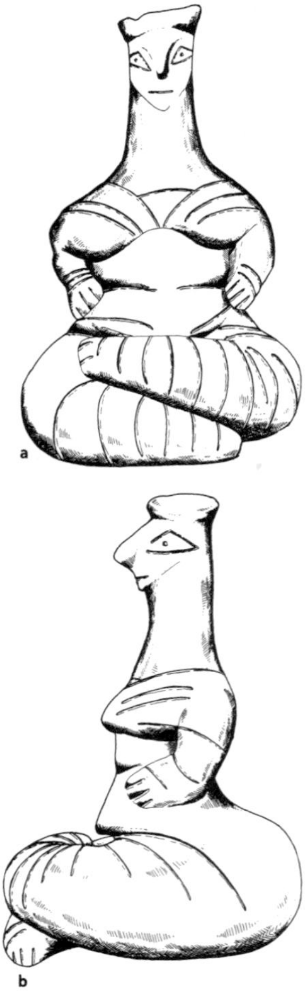

a

b

FIGURE 201 The Snake Goddess from Neolithic Crete. She is portrayed in a yogic posture, with snakelike legs but with human eyes, nose, and mouth. Clay figurine, burnished dark gray and encrusted with white lines (Kato Ierapetra, S Crete; 6000–5500 B.C.). H. 14.2 cm.

FIGURE 202

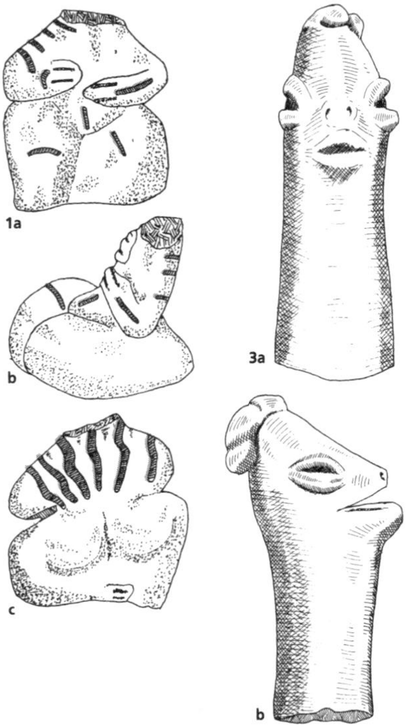

1a b c 3a b

FIGURE 202 Snake Goddess figurines can be identified if they are marked by painted red snakes, or their arms wind around the shoulders like snakes, or they have the characteristic long snake mouth.
(1) Red-painted snakes crawl over the shoulders and back of this squatting figurine. Note that her hands depict profiled snake heads. Sesklo (Achilleion IV; c. 5800 B.C.). (2) This terracotta originally seated on a stool has no human arms. Instead, a snake winds over the neck and shoulders. She has a snakelike head with round eyes and a long mouth. Cucuteni (Traian Dealul Fintinilor, NE Romania; 4800–4600 B.C.).
(3) This example, which is broken off at the neck, has the characteristic long open snake mouth, slit eyes, and crown. Sesklo (Nea Nikomedeia; c. 6300–6100 B.C.)
(1) H. 3.7 cm. (2) H. 6 cm. (3) H. 6.6 cm.

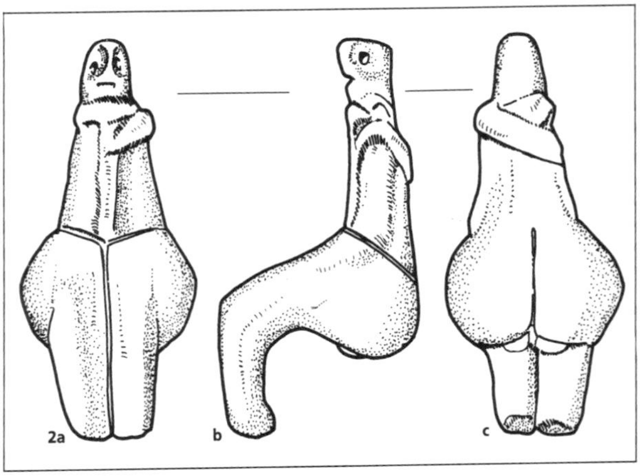

2a b c

14.3 *The anthropomorphic snake of the Neolithic*

Throughout the Neolithic, the Snake Goddess is invariably portrayed in a squatting pose, her arms and legs often lose human form and seem to be actual snakes. Occasionally she has a snake head; if her head is human, she has a characteristic long mouth. (FIGURES 200–203) In schematic representations, her identity can sometimes be detected only by winding snakes on her back, or by dotted bands, checkerboard patterns, or stripes connoting a snake costume.

Images of the Deity exhibit various degrees of anthropomorphism: she may be human with snakelike characteristics or ophidian costume, or she may be predominantly zoomorphic with some human characteristics. The latter aspect is vividly portrayed in the cave paintings of Porto Badisco in Apulia, Italy, where mysterious creatures with limbs ending in snake spirals are painted in black on the cavern walls. (FIGURE 204, 1–4) The figure of Mont Bego in the Alps of eastern France (FIGURE 204, 5) has snake arms, a round head with eyes, and a column instead of a body rising from a checkerboard square.

FIGURE 203

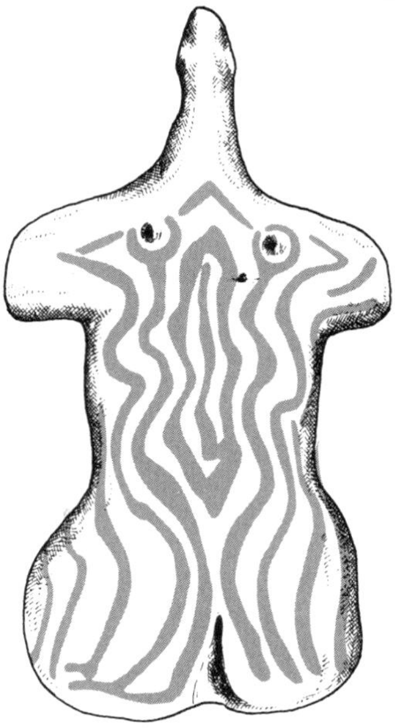

FIGURE 203 Sometimes in schematic representations the Snake Goddess's identity is made known through the snakelike shape of her head, or the wavy (snake) lines painted over her body, representing the life current (*kundalini*). Red painted on cream. Anatolian Neolithic (Provenance unknown; probably 6000–5500 B.C.) H. 9.5 cm.

FIGURE 204

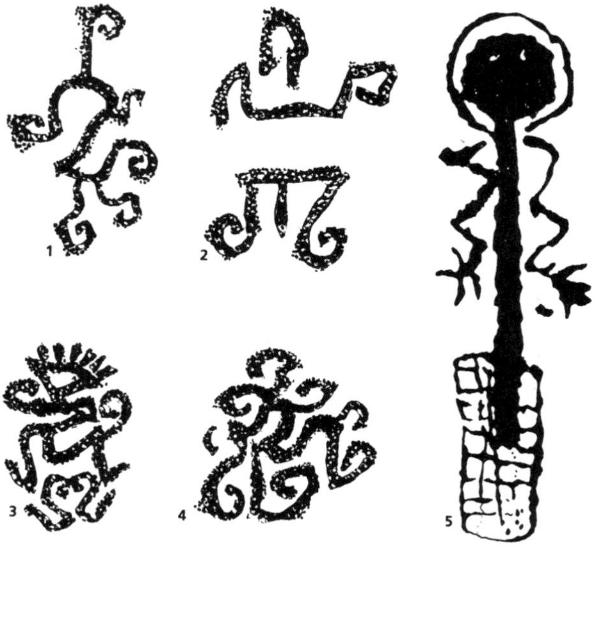

FIGURE 204 These snake-limbed figures (1–4) painted in black on a cave wall and (5) engraved on rock represent an abstracting tendency in some portrayals of the Snake Goddess. (1–4) S Italian Neolithic (Grotta of Porto Badisco; 6th mill. B.C.). (5) Mont Bego rock engraving (Tende, Alpes-Maritimes, E France; date uncertain). (1) H. 5 cm. (2) H. 5.2 cm. (3) H. 3.7 cm. (4) H. 3.5 cm. (5) H. 10.5 cm.

FIGURE 205

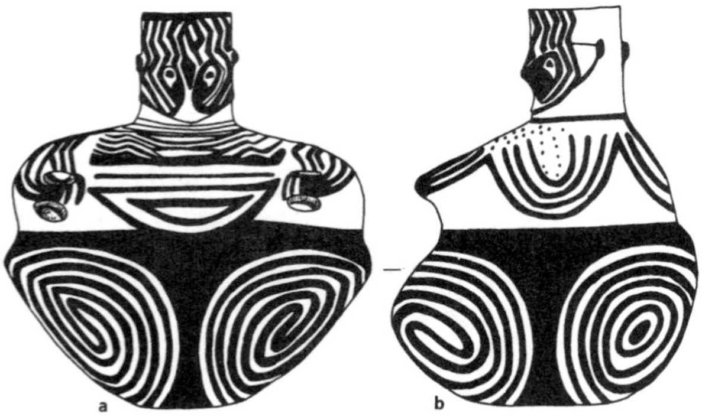

FIGURE 205 The seated Snake Goddess appears frequently in Anatolia, as illustrated by this anthropomorphic vase. She has the zig-zag/snake-head motif on her forehead, obsidian-inlaid eyes, crescents on her chest, and coils for limbs. Painted in red on cream and burnished (Hacilar I; 6000–5500 B.C.). H. 27.8 cm.

FIGURE 206

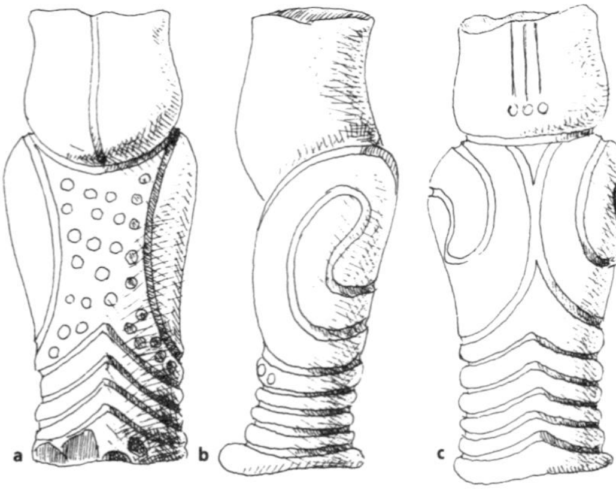

FIGURE 206 The Snake Goddess (or her priestess) has a distinctive costume. This illustration shows examples of aprons and skirts marked with dots and spiral from the 5th and 2nd millennia B.C. (1) Vinča (Beletinci, N Yugoslavia; c. 4500 B.C.); (2) Minoan (Knossos, Crete; 1600–1550 B.C.). H. 7.1 cm.

FIGURE 207

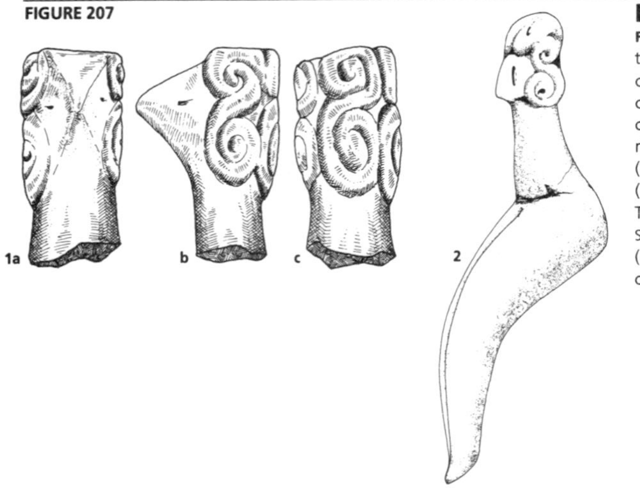

FIGURE 207 The head of the Snake Goddess is customarily crowned or covered by snake-coil curls, as on these figurines. (1) Karanovo VI (Sitagroi III; c. 4500 B.C.); (2) Namazga III (Kara Tepe, Turkmenian SSR c. 3000 B.C.). (1) H. 4.1 cm. (2) H. 15.7 cm.

The snake woman also appears on anthropomorphic vases from Hacilar I, c. 6000 B.C., in central Anatolia. (FIGURE 205) Her legs are painted snake coils and her arms concentric semicircles with dots; zig-zags on her face and chest suggest her association with water. The Deity's eyes of inlaid obsidian stare from the neck of the vessel.

When attired, the Snake Goddess customarily wears an apron denoted by a series of dots, and a skirt distinguished by checkerboard or dotted motifs. (FIGURE 206) Three vertical lines and dots on her back appear to be another identifying mark. The head of the Snake Goddess is usually crowned, or she has snake coils forming anthropomorphic curls.

14.4 *The Snake Goddesses of the Bronze and Iron ages*

During the Bronze Age, the worship of the Snake Goddess continues on Crete, on the Aegean islands, and in mainland Greece. In Crete, the Deity retains her snake arms and the same distinctive attire: a long skirt and apron; and a crown, peaked cap, exquisitely dressed hair, or spiraling curls. (FIGURE 207) An elegantly attired terracotta from Petsofa wears an elaborate peaked hat, a décolleté bodice, and the bell-shaped shirt of the period. (FIGURE 208) A snake crawls around her waist and over the skirt painted with vertical and diagonal tri-lines. The Late Minoan III figurine from the shrine of the Double Axes in Knossos has arms ending in snake heads. Most dramatic of all is the ornate headdress of a Middle Minoan I terracotta head from Kophina. (FIGURE 209) From the front it resembles a tiered crown; from the back it presents a startling mass of writhing snakes in layers above the head.

FIGURE 208

FIGURE 209

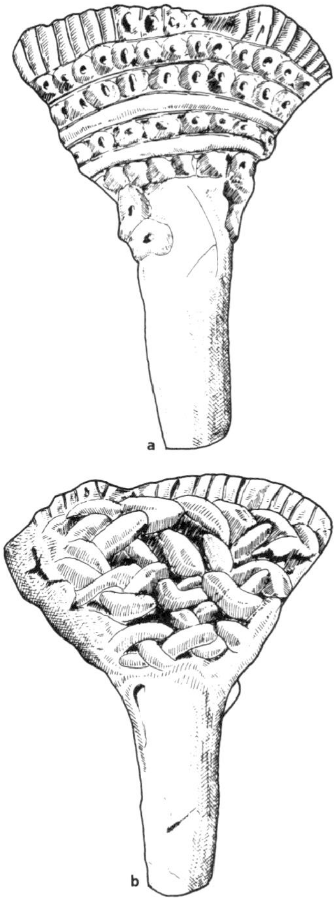

FIGURE 208 The worship of the Snake Goddess continues during the Bronze Age, particularly on Crete. These examples are armless or, like earlier figurines, snake-limbed. Tri-lines decorate their skirts. (1) Middle Minoan I (Petsofas hill sanctuary; 2100–1800 B.C.); (2) Late Minoan III (Knossos). (1) H. 16.3 cm. (2) H. 10.9 cm.

FIGURE 209 During the Bronze Age, the crown on the Snake Goddess is further elaborated. The front is conventional, but the back reveals a mass of writhing snakes. Middle Minoan I (Kophina; c. 2000 B.C.) H. 7 cm.

The most famous Minoan sculptures of Snake Goddesses or her priestesses are the faience statuettes recovered from the underground repository of the Second Palace of Knossos. (FIGURE 210) Their long gowns are adorned with parallel lines and checkerboard and net designs, their aprons festooned with spirals and parallel lines. Serpents crawl over their arms, clasp their waist or abdomen, peer from their headdresses.

Mycenaean terracottas of the 14th and 13th centuries B.C. bear a remarkable resemblance to the Old European Snake Goddess. Diagnostic features are striped bodies, snake arms, pinched noses, exaggerated, staring eyes, crowns, and occasionally a winding snake at the back of the head. During the 8th, 7th, and 6th centuries B.C., there is no observable change in the design motifs which characterize the costume of the Snake Goddess, her shrines, or her attendants. (FIGURE 211) A snake-armed "Dipylon" type figurine recovered from the Argive Heraeum, Hera's temple in Argos, has bands of dotted serpent scales on her body and on her double-stranded necklace. (FIGURE 212) Curious horned-snake appendages, pendant necklaces, and richly decorated snake costumes are worn by standing or enthroned Boeotian figurines of the 7th and 6th centuries B.C. (FIGURE 213) A snake coil (or ram horn?) is silhouetted with zig-zags and dots on their foreheads and polos caps. Panels of running spirals and net patterns, and bands of dotted lines, zig-zags, and vertical winding snakes cover their bodies.

FIGURE 210

FIGURE 211

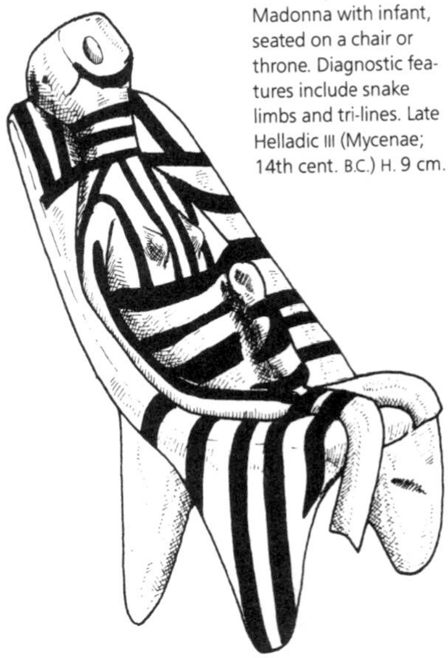

FIGURE 210 Illustrated here is the back of the Minoan faience statuette from the palace of Knossos, 1600–1500 B.C.. Note the spiral design on the figure's jacket and apron. H. 17.3 cm.

FIGURE 211 A motif that appears for millennia in Old Europe is the striped Madonna with infant, seated on a chair or throne. Diagnostic features include snake limbs and tri-lines. Late Helladic III (Mycenae; 14th cent. B.C.) H. 9 cm.

FIGURE 212

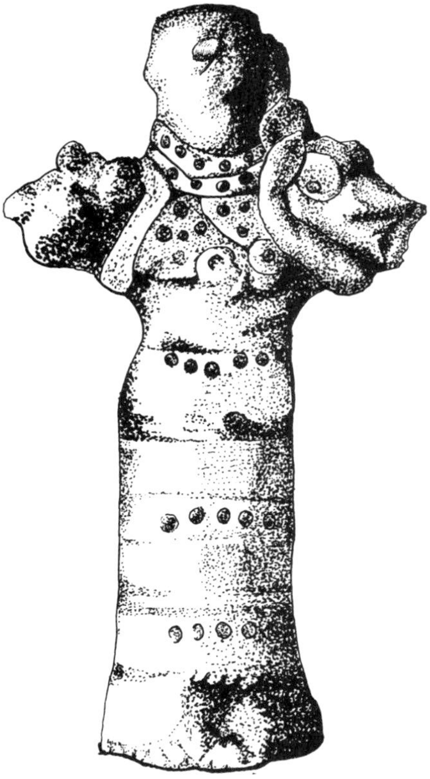

FIGURE 212 The Snake Goddess or priestess continues to appear during the first millennium B.C. in Greece. This "Dipylon" type terracotta figurine is decorated with bands of dots, replicating snake-skin (Argive Heraeum; 8th cent. B.C.). H. 12.3 cm.

FIGURE 213

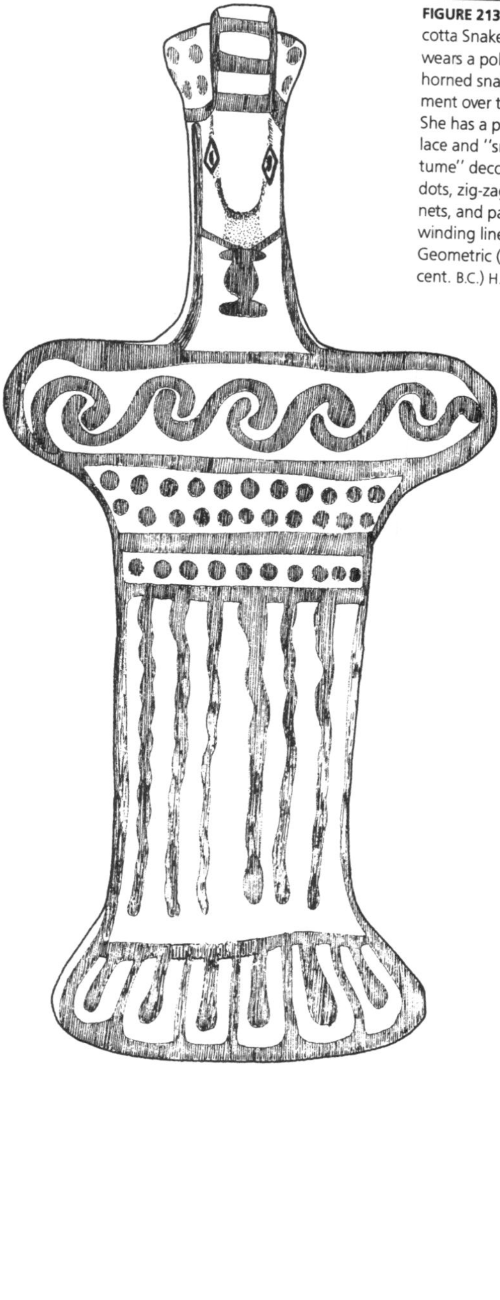

FIGURE 213 This terracotta Snake Goddess wears a polos cap with a horned snake attachment over the forehead. She has a pendant necklace and "snake costume" decorated with dots, zig-zags, spirals, nets, and parallel winding lines. Greek Geometric (Boeotia; 6th cent. B.C.) H. 17 cm.

Outside Greece, the Snake Goddess also continued to be portrayed throughout the Bronze and Iron ages. She can easily be recognized in Celtic art. The illustrated image of an ophidian/human hybrid is sculptured in relief on a golden bracelet discovered in a grave of a princess or queen at Reinheim, southeast of Saarbrücken, western Germany, 370–20 B.C. (FIGURE 214, 1) Characteristically, her eyes have a pronounced snake stare and her legs are snakes, but the nose, mouth and hands are human. She has an owl headdress, and wings (probably of a bee) emerge from her scaley shoulders. Owl heads or masks are again repeated at the ends of the bracelet. The same combination of symbols is familiar in Minoan and ancient Greek art. The bee wings and owl masks or eyes relate this image to the Greek Gorgon. In the later text (see section 18.7) I speak about the likely development of the Gorgon from the death aspect of the Snake/Bird Goddess.

In the north, snake-limbed creatures (Snake Goddesses?) placed in ships or chariots are known from Scandinavian rock engravings and engraved on bronze razors from Denmark and northwestern Germany dating from the Late Bronze Age. At Fårdal, Viborg, Denmark, a figurine of cast bronze with large, round, inset gold eyes and snakelike folded legs came to light together with a bronze-crested serpent and two-horned animal heads (Sandars 1968: 204, fig. 79 and pl. 206). Each object has at the base a tonguelike projection with holes for rivets. The Snake Goddess holding her serpent with a cord originally was in a ship with a horned-animal stern and prow. The tableau is from the eighth century B.C. (see fig. 386, 9).

In the Pictish art of Scotland, the Snake Goddess figure emerges in stone carvings where she has legs as twisted snakes and she holds snakelike hair. (FIGURE 214, 2)

In a slightly modified form the ophidian/human hybrid lives on in modern times in the embroideries of the Aegean islands and Crete, still called "Gorgona." Her snake legs became fish tails which curl up on either side of her body, and which she invariably holds at the thin end before they sprout as a foliage (Greger 1986). Sometimes her body is chrysalis-shaped and has no legs, but her arms are like snakes. She is crowned and from the middle of the head grows a life tree. A related image with ophidian limbs also appears in Russian embroideries but in a severely stylized form (Rybakov 1981: 481–91).

14.5 *The Snake Goddess worshipped in house-shrines*

The shrines in which images of the Bird or Snake Goddess were kept go back to about 6000 B.C. or earlier, as witnessed by the discovery of shrines at Achilleion, Thessaly, northern Greece, a Neolithic tell of the Sesklo culture. A series of shrines in a neat sequence dating from c. 6100 to 5700 B.C. yielded terracotta figurines of Bird and Snake Goddesses in groups from several to fifteen (Gimbutas 1988). From the northeastern corner of Old Europe, a shrine dedicated to the Snake Goddess worship

FIGURE 214

1

2

FIGURE 214 (1) The Snake Goddess (ophidian/human hybrid) on a golden bracelet from a Celtic queen's tomb. She has spiralling snake legs and round eyes. Early La Tène (Reinheim, 15 km SE of Saarbrücken, W Germany; 370–320 B.C.). (2) The Snake Goddess with legs and hair as twisted snakes. Pictish stone carving. (Meigle, Scotland; late Roman period.)

FIGURE 215

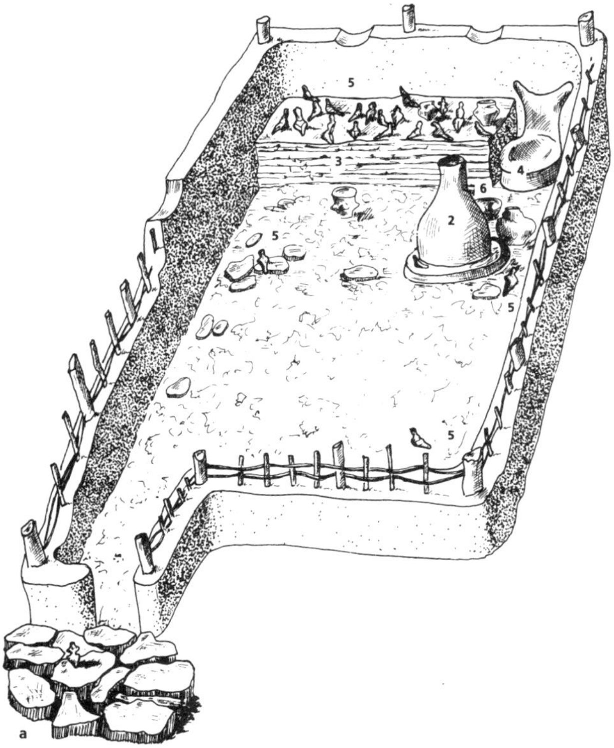

a

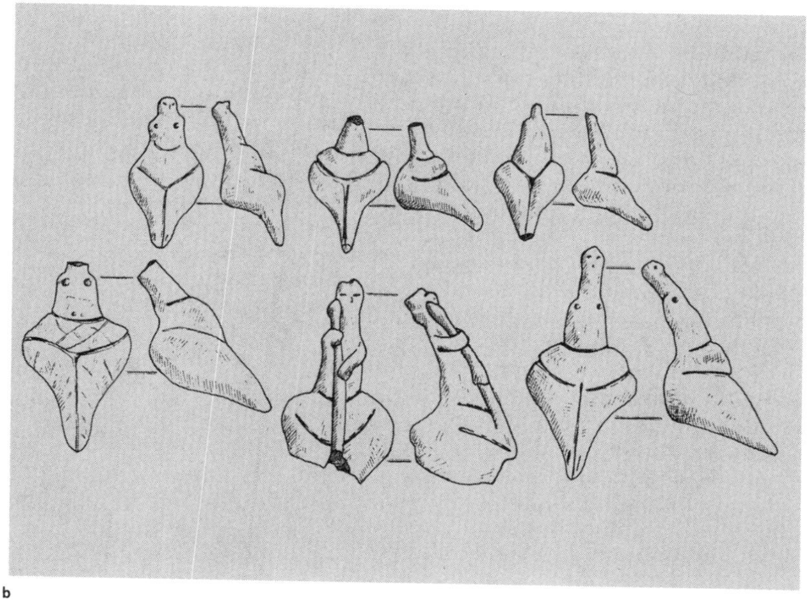

b

FIGURE 215 In Old Europe, Bird and Serpent Goddesses were worshipped in house shrines. (a) This shrine from Sabatinivka dates from the Early Cucuteni (Tripolye) period, 4800–4600 B.C. The building occupied 70 square meters. (1) stone slab floors; (2) oven; (3) dais; (4) clay chair; (5) figurines; (6) groups of vases at the oven.

(b) Several of the 32 figurines found in the shrine of Sabatinivka. The middle one (lower row) holds a baby snake (?); others are armless (probably because they were made in the image of the Snake Goddess). Is this the tableau of a seasonal ritual of renewal?

was discovered at Sabatinivka II in the valley of Southern Bug, Western Ukraine. (FIGURE 215) At the end of this shrine stands an altar, 2.75 × 6 m, covered with layers of plaster, on which sixteen figurines are seated on horned thrones. The figurines have snake-shaped heads and no arms, except for one who holds a baby snake, probably the most important of the group. All are quite schematically portrayed, typical for the early Cucuteni (early Tripolye) phase, c. 4800–4600 B.C. The shrine also includes a bread oven, a dish filled with the burned bones of a bull, and a number of vases. The life-size throne next to the altar apparently was used by a priestess who oversaw the proceedings.

The whole tableau — including anthropomorphized snakes, an oven, and a bull — suggests a mystery of death and regeneration. The baby snake is the bridge, an umbilical cord linking the subterranean womb with the living world. Initiation rites could have been practiced in this shrine.

House shrines with Snake Goddesses or priestesses having round snake eyes, snakes crawling around the waist, and upraised arms are known from the Middle and Late Minoan periods. They were placed on altars together with tripod tables and peculiar tube vessels with snake-shaped and horned handles (Nilsson 1950: fig 14).

14.6 *The descendants of the prehistoric Snake Goddess and other snake deities in history and folklore*

The beautiful Hera, one of the most revered of the Greek Goddesses, is the likely descendant of the prehistoric Snake Goddess. She was called "origin of all things" by Alcaeus, early 6th century B.C. Her name is cognate with Hōrā, "season." Hera's sanctuaries were erected in valleys, at the estuaries of rivers, or near the sea and were surrounded by pastures. In addition to large-eyed figurines with dotted or checkerboard-patterned skirts, votive offerings found in her temples include terracotta snakes, horned animals, and calves. She was associated with pastures and horned animals, more specifically with cows and calves. Homer called her "cow-faced," *boöpis*. Egyptian Hathor was also a cow and is described as the primeval serpent who ruled the world.

Hera appears crowned and possesses magical plants. Coins from Knossos and Tylissos of the 4th and 3rd centuries B.C. show a head of Hera wearing a crown with floral ornaments (Willetts 1962: 252–55). Through the touch of a plant she can create or restore life. (She also created the god Ares through the touch of a plant, as mentioned by Ovid in *Fasti*, 5, 255). In still-existing legends and beliefs, snakes possess magic herbs. An herb placed by a snake next to a dead child restores it to life. An herb or a flower brought by a snake to a newborn baby protects the life of the growing child; he or she will not die in war or in an accident. Hera renews her virginity every year by bathing in the spring Kanathes (Rose 1958: 105). This is allegoric to the yearly renewal of the snake by sloughing off its old skin.

One of the most archaic goddesses related to cows and milk preserved in folklore is the *Marša* or *Maŗa* of Latvian mythological songs. She is called the Mother of Milk, the Mother of Cows, or the Old Shepherdess of Cows. Her own source of milk is a miraculous well. The Cow Marša, or as she is also called, the Fate (Latvian *Laima*) of cows, appears in animal stalls as a black snake, bug, or a hen. Her presence brings fertility to cows; she is responsible for the easy birth of calves and an abundance of milk. If invoked, she can produce large supernatural cows with an inexhaustible source of milk, as well as good pasturelands (Biezais 1955: 243–58). In this symbol system, as opposed to Indo-European mythology, black is not the color of evil but of fertility. An apparent relative of Marša is the Celtic Verbeia in Yorkshire. Her name may mean something like "She of the Cattle" if one can connect it with the Old Irish root *ferb*. She is also associated with sacred springs. Her representations in reliefs show her holding serpents (Ross 1967: 217, pl. 68a; fig. 196). This image is also related to the Irish Saint Brigit who was associated with cattle and was held to be a cowherd (Evans, Estyn 1957: 267).

Since the 7th millennium B.C. the crown is the most constant feature in portrayals of the Snake Goddess. This lives on in European folklore in the belief that some snakes appear crowned; these crowns are the symbol of wisdom and wealth. A person who struggles with a huge white snake acquires a crown that enables one to know all, see hidden treasures, and understand the language of animals. There is a widespread European folktale in which an individual obtains knowledge by eating or tasting the flesh of a white serpent. The crowned snake is "the Queen of Snakes" or "the Mother of Snakes." She rules over her own clan of snakes. In folk beliefs until quite recently snakes were seen to appear in large groups following a crowned leader or having a meeting presided by the Queen. If the Queen is touched or harmed, all attendant snakes are alarmed.

14.7 *The persistence of snake worship to the 20th century*

At the beginning of this century in Lithuania, my own mother observed the greatest respect paid to snakes. They lived under the floors of houses, were fed with milk, and were even allowed to come inside people's homes. (The same reverence is exhibited in Malta, Greece, and the Slavic countries.) To harm a green snake was a great sin. A snake in the house meant happiness and prosperity; it ensured the increase of the family (it was even kept under the bed of a newlywed couple) and of animals, and of the fertility of the soil. They were guardians of the home; they were clairvoyant, knowing the future of family members and the location of hidden treasures. To this day, snakes decorate the corners, windows, and roof of a Baltic farmhouse.

Three hundred years earlier, in 1604, an astonished Jesuit missionary reported on the snake worship in Lithuania: "The people have reached such a stage of madness that they believe that deity exists in reptiles. Therefore, they carefully safeguard them, lest someone injure the reptiles kept inside their homes. Superstitiously they believe that harm would come to them, should anyone show disrespect to these reptiles. It sometimes happens that reptiles are encountered sucking milk from cows. Some of us (monks) occasionally tried to pull one off, but invariably the farmer would plead in vain to dissuade us. . . . When pleading failed, the man would seize the reptile with his hands and run away to hide it" (Mannhardt 1936: 433).

This description vividly portrays the very strong survival of Old European snake worship even in late Christian times. A symbol of concentrated life force so essential to the farmer's well-being could not easily be abandoned.

Into the 20th century in northern and central Europe, a block (the "Yule log") was dragged through villages in winter and then burned. This may not simply have symbolized slumbering vegetation and its destruction, but also the sacrifice of the snake (in the shape of a log) at the beginning of its hibernation cycle. One of the names for the snake in Lithuanian is *kaladė*, "block," which contrasts with the general name for snake, *gyvatė*, meaning "life force." In Greek the word *geras* means both "old age" and "the slough of the snake." Further linguistic associations with the Yule log speak of burning the Old Hag. In the highlands of Scotland the Yule log is called the *Cailléach*, the Old Wife (Hag). By killing the symbolic old snake, its revival was ensured for the spring. It was believed that the ashes of the Yule log could heal cattle, enable cows to calve, and promote the fertility of the earth. This belief is yet another link with the functions of the Snake Goddess.

The symbolic awakening of hibernating snakes took place around February 1. In Scotland a serpent was supposed to emerge from the hills on Imbolc, the Day of Bride (Brigit) ("Today is the day of Bride; the serpent shall come from the hole"). On that day effigies of snakes were made. Carmichael notes that one of the most curious customs of Bride's Day was the pounding of the serpent effigy and records an occasion when an elderly woman put a piece of peat into a stocking and pounded it with fire-tongs while intoning:

This is the day of Bride,
The queen will come from the mound,
I will not touch the queen,
Nor will the queen touch me
(Carmichael 1900, reprint 1983: 169)

In Lithuania, this is the "Day of Serpents" (*Kirmiai, Kirmelinė* from *kirmelė*, "serpent") when "serpents come from the forest to the house." On that day, whose present Christianized equivalent is called *Krikštai* and is celebrated on January 25, people would shake the apple trees in the orchard so that they would be more fruitful and knock on beehives, waking the bees from the winter sleep (Greimas 1979: 317). The awakening of the snakes meant the awakening of all nature, the beginning of the life of the new year. There is a very interesting text from the 16th century by Maletius which relates to the ritual feast "at a certain time of the year"; probably the Day of Serpents.

> *Honoring them as deities, at a certain time of the year they invite them to the table with seer's prayers. Crawling out (from out of their sleep) they lie down on the clean cloth and make themselves comfortable on the table. There, tasting a little every dish, they slither (to the ground) and return to their hole.*
>
> *With the retreat of the snakes, the people happily eat the dishes that have been tasted by them, confident that at that time (i.e., in the coming year) everything will go well for them. And if, in spite of the seer's prayers, the snakes don't break away (from their lair) or do not come to taste the laid-out dishes—then they believe that in those years a huge misfortune will befall them.* (Cited by Greimas 1979: 318)

The tasting of the food by the serpents signified their blessing, which guaranteed the successful continuation of the year. The significance of the beginning is a predestination: the success of the entire year depends on how it starts.

14.8 *Male counterpart of the Snake Goddess*

Although among the prehistoric figurines a male partner of the Snake Goddess has not been identified, in European mythologies and folklore, guardians of the household and multipliers of wealth appear as female and male snakes. Lithuanians have a male *Žaltys*, Poles a male *Wąž*, Greeks had *Zeus Ktesios*, and Romans had male house-snakes as guardians of *penus* (food, provision), called *penates*, known from countless Greco-Roman wall paintings. Russians and other Slavs have *Domovoj* (from *dom*, "house") who lives behind the oven or under the threshold. Considered to be invisible or sometimes imagined as an old man with a bushy head of hair and flashing eyes, the Domovoj's ophidian shape and connection with the underworld are nevertheless clear. The Domovoj is capable of regenerating in the manner of a snake: in the spring he sheds his skin. His other name is *Ded*, *Dedushka* (dim.), "grandfather," "ancestor," and occasionally he even appears in the shape of dead ancestors (Afanasiev 1979: 104).

Related images are known from Basque oral tradition. Such are *Sugaar*, a male snake, and the Black He-Goat, *Akerbeltz* (*beltz*, "black"), who is the protector of the flock, increases fertility of the farm animals, has curative powers, and wards off death and disease. Although the latter inhabits subterranean regions he emerges to the surface and often crosses the sky in the form of a sickle or a flaming crescent moon (as also does the Basque goddess). His passage is an omen of an oncoming storm (Frank and Metzger Ms. 1982). Related to *Sugaar* is the Lithuanian goblin *Aitvaras*, a fiery snake seen in the sky who increases the wealth and fertility of the family (Greimas 1979: 72 ff.). The Basque root *su* means "fire." From the root *su* comes *suga* or *suge*, "serpent." If the *-ar* suffix is added, it means "male" and also "flame of fire." The root *su* is also employed to refer to "heat" in a sexual sense. In Azcoitia, one of the regions of the Basque country, *Sugaar* is called by the name *Maju* and is the husband of the Goddess. Every Friday he visits her and combs her hair. When Maju comes out of his cave and joins the Goddess, they create a tempest causing rain and hail. The highly sexualized fertility imagery of such a storm is clearly evident (Frank and Metzger Ms. 1982).

14.9 *Hermes, snake, phallus, and Asklepios, the Savior-Healer*

There is a pre-Indo-European, pre-Olympian god in Greek mythology associated with the phallus and the snake, who is a likely descendant of Old European phallic figures. This is Hermes, a youthful god, native to Arcadia (a conservative region of the Peloponnese, where ancient features have held the longest). He is a god of luck who gives wealth and increases flocks and herds (Rose 1958: 145). Hermes is likewise connected with human fertility. His cult monument is simply the phallus. *Hermai*—herms—are square pillars, common by the roadside. They are crowned with a human head and have a phallus partway up the front. Hermes always carries his staff or magical wand *kerykeion* with the twin twisted snakes. It is said of him that

> *When he shines forth, the earth blossoms and when he laughs, the plants bear fruit, and at his bidding the herds bring forth young.*
> (Harrison 1962: 296)

He is an attendant to the Goddess: he attends Pandora ("All Gifts") when she rises from the earth.

Hermes is not only a god of fertility who stimulates the growth and the blossoming of plants and the multiplying of animals; he is also a god of the underworld and of ghosts. With his *kerykeion* he summons the souls from the grave. As a snake who comes from a cave he is the very daimon of regeneration. Homer mentions that Hermes puts men to sleep, "lulls to rest," and also wakens them—a good parallel to the hibernating and awakening snake. In Harrison's words, "Hermes was once merely a phallus; that he was also once merely a snake, is, I think, a safe conjecture" (Harrison 1962: 297).

Still another member of the "snake family" deities is the Greek Asklepios (Roman Aesculapius), the Savior-Healer. The snake aspect of this physician is clearly manifest: a snake is coiled around his staff, or he is represented standing next to a snake, or a snake is shown crawling over his body (Harrison 1962, figs. 105–107, 75). The emergence of such a figure in myth is not surprising: that which gives or stimulates life heals diseases. To this day European villagers believe in healing powers of the snake. Tasting a snake's meat even restores eyesight.

14.10 *The snake as a household divinity*

Much that was continuous until recent times in the beliefs concerning snakes in the Greco-Roman world and in the peripheral European villages is paramount for our understanding of the role of the prehistoric snake. The repetition of a number of traits in snake worship through time is quite striking. It certainly speaks of common prehistoric roots.

Of singular interest is the widespread belief in snakes as household gods: they are guardians of the family and domestic animals, especially cows. They assure fertility, increase, and health. Each family and each animal had as a patron divinity a snake whose life energy was the same as of the human or the animal whose patron the snake was. This is manifested in the belief that if a snake is killed, the master of the household, a child, or a cow will die. Thus the life energy of the snake is inseparable from that of humans or animals. Furthermore, the life force of the snake is linked to that of the dead, specifically the ancestors of the family. Thus the snake symbolizes the continuity of life between the generations. The hibernation and awakening of the snake and its renewal through sloughing off the old skin further enhance the belief in the immortality and cyclicity of the snake. The awakening of the snake after winter's sleep meant the awakening of all nature and was celebrated in all of Europe. The return of the snakes was considered to have a profound influence on human and animal well-being for the whole year.

In Old Europe snake effigies and Snake Goddess figurines have been found in house shrines. This testifies to their constant worship as household guardians. It can be conjectured that in prehistory, as later in history, live snakes were kept in houses as symbols of the perpetuation of life, health, and increase.

The image of a crowned snake as a "Queen" or "Mother" of snakes which continues in folklore to the present day dates back to the Neolithic, at least the 7th millennium B.C. Then, as now, this deity had an enormous power: she was a life-giver and was an all-knowing and foretelling goddess like her sister, the Bird Goddess. She was the owner and the guardian of life water and life milk. She was the birth-giver of calves. Magical healing herbs were in her possession.

II

THE RENEWING AND ETERNAL EARTH

In prehistoric art, pregnant women, double eggs, and excited men are not sex symbols in the twentieth century sense. Our European forebears were more philosophical; there was no element of obscenity in their art. Prehistoric fertility symbols are symbols of potency, abundance, and multiplication, concerned with the perpetuation of life and the preservation of life forces constantly threatened by death.

Fertility symbols are seasonal, representing dying and awakening nature. Mother Earth rises as a young goddess in all her splendor in the spring and becomes an old hag in the fall, but her spring/summer pregnancy is the holiest time there is. Male divinities are allegorized as emerging and dying vegetation spirits.

Rising Minoan Earth Mother with upraised arms. See figure 232, page 150.

Pregnant Goddess with hands on her belly, reclining on her large buttocks; from Achilleion. See figure 218, page 142.

15/ *Earth Mother*

Although a great deal of emphasis has been placed on the "Earth Mother" of prehistoric religion, she is but one—albeit an important one—of the aspects of this early Divine Feminine principle. One reason for this emphasis may be that, in the agricultural communities throughout Europe, she survives to the present day. Another is the fact, long accepted by ethnologists, that pre-industrial agricultural rites show a very definite mystical connection between the fertility of the soil and the creative force of woman. In all European languages, the Earth is feminine.

The Old European Pregnant Goddess is the likely prototype of the Grain Goddess, young and old, such as Demeter, and of the Earth Mother of all European folklore. As an Earth Mother she is also Mother of the Dead. How old is she, this symbol of the nutrient earth, fullness, and the cornucopia of the fruitful womb?

It would seem logical to look for the origin of the Earth Fertility Goddess at the dawn of agriculture. Because the Neolithic Goddess had the ability to bring forth all life from her own body, she must have been also endowed with the power to nurture the seeds of the earth. However, the pregnant-type figurine first appears not in the Early Neolithic, but earlier still—in the Paleolithic. The symbol of the fruitful womb is as old as figurine art. We do not know whether it was associated from the very beginning with earth fertility and (uncultivated) plant life. In any case, the Paleolithic motif of a pregnant woman with hands on her abdomen continues into the Neolithic. On the basis of the presently available evidence, the emergence of what can clearly be identified as the Earth Fertility or Grain Goddess and her double, the sow, dates to the 7th millennium B.C. in southeastern Europe.

15.1 *The Pregnant Goddess in the Upper Paleolithic, Neolithic, and Copper Age*

Not all Upper Paleolithic fat ladies, or "fertility goddesses," as they are usually described, are pregnant. Even the famous "Venuses" of Willendorf and Lespugue are probably not pregnant. Their breasts and buttocks are the focus of attention, not their bellies; they hold their hands on their breasts. The images we shall be concerned with here, however, are of pregnant women holding their hands on their bellies.

Good examples of this stereotype are known from Laussel, Dordogne, France; Kostienki I in the Ukraine; and from La Marche, Vienne, France. (FIGURE 216) Laussel is of the Gravettian (Upper Périgordian) age between 25,000 and 20,000 B.C. Kostienki sculptures may date from around 20,000 B.C. (The true chronology may range from c. 21,000 to 12,000 B.C.) The engravings on the stone plaques from La Marche are of the Magdalenian type, c. 13,000–12,000 B.C. Still another image of pregnant woman is known from an engraving on a reindeer bone from Laugerie Basse, a Magdalenian site at Eyzies-de-Tayac, France. She is shown lying under a reindeer or bull. She is nude but wears several bracelets and neckrings (Marshack 1972: fig. 189; Delporte 1979: fig. 23). The buttocks of these pregnant women are not exaggerated and their breasts are normal. If their head is preserved, it is anonymous, possibly wearing a cap or a noticeable hairdo, but without facial features.

Neolithic figurines with hands on their pregnant bellies and enormous pubic triangles are among the most numerous in the corpus of excavated settlements dating from the 7th and 6th millennia B.C. (FIGURES 217–219) They are portrayed in various degrees of schematization and several characteristic postures. Some are seated on a throne, others have buttocks upon which they lean backward in a reclining posture, and still others are stand–type with a flat base. If the head is shown, it is cylindrical and wears a mask, which is not beaked but human, with a normal mouth. Removable masks as found at Achilleion II and IV (c. 6300–5800 B.C.) probably belong to the same Goddess.

The early Neolithic Pregnant Goddesses are marked with two strokes over the shoulders or buttocks. The bi-line probably serves to mark the pregnancy and the power of two—a tradition inherited from the Upper Paleolithic when pregnant mares were painted with two lines over their bodies (see fig. 265).

In Old European settlements, figurines of this type are located on a platform near the oven or other area of grain preparation and under the floor, whereas the Bird Goddess is characteristically found inside house shrines. The earliest evidence for this distribution comes from the Achilleion mound, c. 6400–5600 B.C. (Gimbutas 1989).

In the Copper Age, the Pregnant Goddess remains one of the most revered divine characters. She is the only one portrayed enthroned in a regal posture; her bulging belly and other generous body parts are marked by squares, triangles, snake-coil spirals, meanders, and the numbers 2 and 4. (FIGURE 220)

FIGURE 216

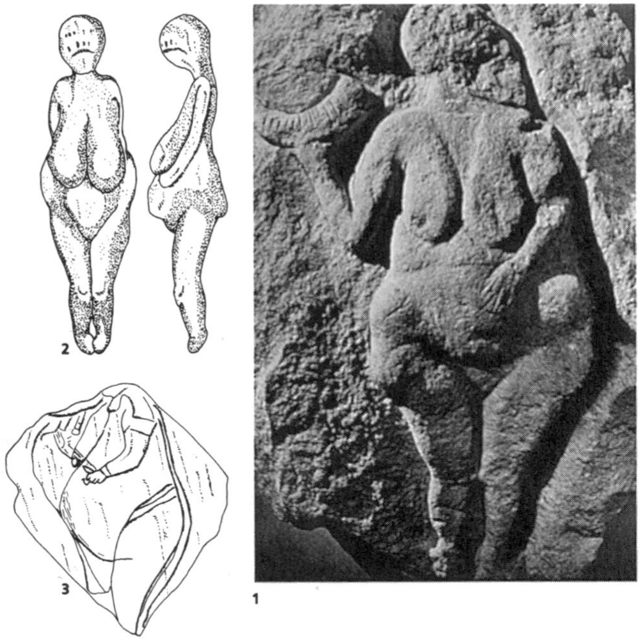

FIGURE 216 Images of the Fertility Goddess as a pregnant woman focus on their bellies, where their hands rest. (1) "Venus of Laussel" in low relief at limestone rock shelter in Laussel, Dordogne, S France. Note her left hand is on the belly and in her right she holds a horn marked with thirteen incisions (Gravettian, Upper Périgordian, c. 25,000–20,000 B.C.) (2) Ivory figurine (Kostienki I, W Ukraine; c. 20,000 B.C.). (3) Engraving on a stone plaque from La Marche, Vienne, S France, Magdalenian III; c. 13,000–12,000 B.C. (1) H. 42 cm. (2) H. 11.4 cm.

In several instances, enthroned figurines of the 5th millennium B.C. are found in hidden alcoves or pits beneath dwelling floors (Tisza culture, Czálog 1943: Table XLIX; Lengyel culture, Dombay 1960: Table LXXXVIII, *2* and Novotný 1958: Table XXXI, *1–2*). The custom of placing the figurine in contact with the earth seems to have originated in the Upper Paleolithic, not the Neolithic; figurines at Kostienki are said to have been placed under the floor of the dwelling (Delporte 1979: 167, citing Abramova 1962).

An open-shrine model from Ghelaeşti-Nedeia, a Cucuteni settlement in Moldavia, shows the Pregnant Goddess in a regal posture seated in front of a hole for libations. (FIGURE 221) A slender figurine is found on either side, one of which is male. Perhaps they represent kouretes worshipping the Goddess? At the front wall of the model a tiny schematic figurine was found—a baby symbolizing new life? (The model is housed in the museum of Piatra Neamţ, Moldavia.)

A very interesting cache of 21 figurines, most probably used for the reenactment of earth fertility rites, came to light in an early Cucuteni shrine at Poduri-

FIGURE 217

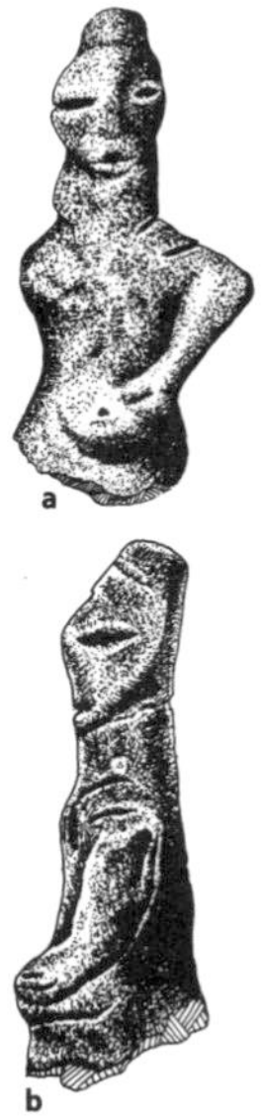

FIGURE 217 The Pregnant Goddess with hands on her bulging abdomen appears in the Neolithic. This masked figurine is marked with two lines on her shoulder; she was originally seated on a throne. Early Sesklo (Achilleion Ib, Thessaly; 6300 B.C.) H. 11 cm.

FIGURE 218

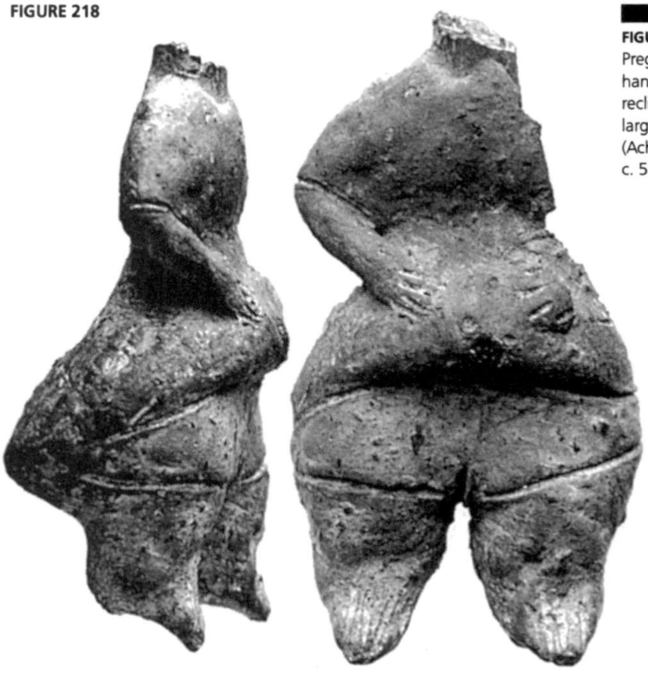

FIGURE 218 Miniature Pregnant Goddess with hands on her belly reclines backward on her large buttocks. Sesklo (Achilleion IV, Thessaly; c. 5800 B.C.). H. 3.8 cm.

Dealul Ghindaru, Moldavia, northeastern Romania (Monah 1982). The figurines were stored in a large vase. In addition there were fifteen chairs or thrones on which larger figurines could sit. The figurines were from 6 to 12 cm in height. The different proportions, workmanship, and symbols painted on the figurines suggest a clear hierarchy in this tableau. The three largest ones are painted in ochre-red with symbols that are typical of the Mother Earth family: antithetic snakes coiling over the abdomen and lozenges on the back, dotted triangles and lozenges over the ample thighs and legs, and cartouches with chevrons over the buttocks. The medium-sized figurines have a striated band across the abdomen and are striped over thighs and legs. The little ones were rather carelessly produced and are not painted with symbols. Such differences may reflect different cult roles ranging from dominant personages (goddesses or priestesses) to assistants and attendants. The upper part of all the figurines is rendered schematically. Only one figurine has arms, with her left hand touching her face or mask and the right clasping the left arm at the elbow. Heads or masks have pinched noses and deeply incised eyes and mouths.

Earth fertility rituals survived for millennia. A cultic festival of the Goddess Nerthus worshipped by Germanic tribes of the lower Elbe area is recorded by Tacitus in *Germania*, A.D. 98. Seven tribes participate in the festival. They

> *... revere in common Nerthus, Earth Mother, and they believe that she intervenes in human affairs and that she rides among their peoples. In an island of the ocean is a sacred grove, and in it a consecrated chariot covered with cloth. One priest is permitted to touch it. He senses that the goddess is present in the inner sanctum and he follows with great veneration as she is drawn away by cows. Days of joy follow, and holidays, in all places that she honors with her arrival and stay.... When she has had enough of the society of mortals, the priest brings the goddess back to her temple. Afterward, the cart, the cloth, and, if you believe it, the Goddess herself are cleansed in a secret lake.* (Tacitus, *Germania*, 40)

FIGURE 219

FIGURE 219 Pregnant Goddess with hands on the belly and enormous pubic triangle is portrayed in a seated posture. Legs are only slightly indicated. Sesklo (Magula near Sofades, Karditsa Plain, Thessaly; 6000–5800 B.C.) H. 4 cm.

FIGURE 220

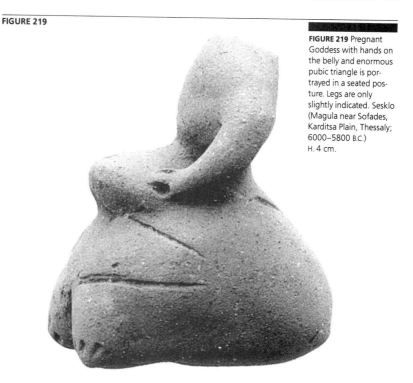

FIGURE 220 In the Copper Age of east-central Europe, the Pregnant Goddess is sometimes portrayed seated on a chair or throne. This one from Bulgaria is marked with a multiple lozenge design over the pregnant belly and two lines across the hips. Karanovo VI, mid-5th mill. B.C. (Selo Kalekovets, district of Plovdiv). H. 10 cm.

FIGURE 221

FIGURE 222

FIGURE 222 These clay seals feature dots within lozenges, symbolic of seeds within the womb or field. They may have been used to stamp this motif on loaves of sacred bread. (3) is perhaps a replica of a bread loaf. Central Anatolian Neolithic (Çatal Hüyük II–IV; 2nd half 7th mill. B.C.) (1) H. 6.2 cm. (2) H. 7.2 cm. (3) H. 8 cm. (4) H. bottom 6.5 cm.

Considerably later, in medieval times, the veneration of Earth Mother among the Germanic peoples continued. In England there is evidence of the rural population's veneration of a plowing and sowing goddess and of her later replacement by the sowing saint Milburga. That Anglo-Saxon peoples invoked Earth Mother at plowing and seeding time is proved by an early medieval plowing charm recorded and preserved in a manuscript in the British Museum (MS. Cott. Calig. A VII, fol. 172b–173a). The ritual has a profoundly pagan aspect. The Anglo-Saxon scribe who recorded the charm set out to relate how the farmer could promote the fertility of his land and protect it from malignant forces. The text offers a prescription for just how this should be done. Before dawn the farmers must remove four strips of turf from four quarters of the land and have priests say masses over them. A sacrificial libation of oil, honey, milk, parts of trees, and holy water should be poured into the ground before the turf is replaced. Then the farmers must recite in Latin the formula "Increase and multiply and replenish the earth" (cited by Berger 1985: 65).

The tie between the fertile soil and Earth Mother is further seen in the continuous veneration of black madonnas to this day. The color black, now commonly associated with death or evil in Christian iconography, was in Old Europe the color of fertility and the soil. The fact that black madonnas throughout the world are focal points for pilgrimages, are regarded as miracle workers, and are among the most highly venerated of all Christian religious symbols indicates that the blackness of these miraculous madonnas still evokes profound and meaningful images and associations for devotees. For instance, the shrine at Częstochowa in southern Poland, known as the Polish Lourdes, housing the black madonna, is the holiest and most visited religious shrine in eastern Europe. It draws thousands of visitors each day and several hundred thousand each August during the Feast of the Assumption.

FIGURE 221 An open-shrine model with the Goddess holding her hands over the pregnant belly and seated in front of a hole for libations. Two slender figurines (a male on the right) and a small unarticulated figurine (not shown in the illustration), perhaps attendants performing ritual, were found together. The model is painted in reddish brown on cream. Cucuteni (Ghelaeşti-Nedeia, Moldavia near Peatra Neamţ, Romania; Cucuteni AB–B_1, c. 4000–3800 B.C.) DIA. 17 cm.

FIGURE 223 This two-part "fruit stand" vase is decorated by seed-within-lozenge and snake-coil designs painted dark and light brown on white. It was found with an assemblage of cult equipment on a tripod table inside a house or shrine. Petreşti B (Pianul de Jos, Transylvania; 4500–4000 B.C.) H. 35.3 cm.

FIGURE 224 The symbolic meaning of the seed-within-lozenge/triangle motif is clear when it appears on the bellies, buttocks, and thighs of terracotta figurines. (1) Early Cucuteni (Poduri, district of Bacău, NE Romania; 4800–4600 B.C.). (2) Early Cucuteni (Novye Ruseshty I, Soviet Moldavia; 4800–4600 B.C.). (3) Middle Cucuteni (Drăguşeni, district of Botoşani NE Romania; 4200–4000 B.C.). (1) H. 12.15 cm. (2) H. 5.6 cm. (3) H. 7.4 cm.

FIGURE 223

FIGURE 224

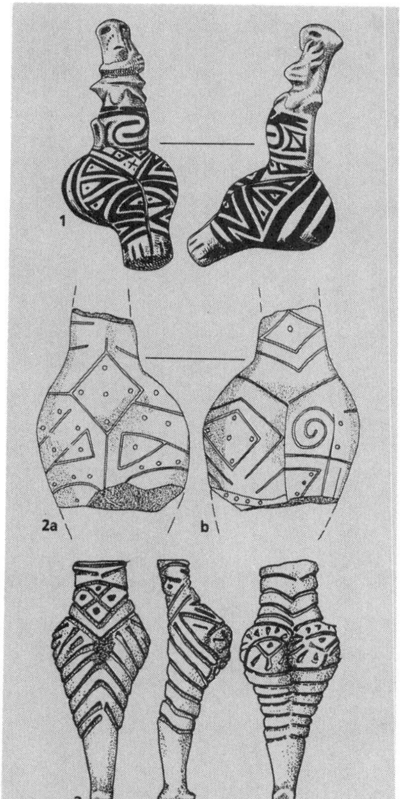

15.2 *Lozenge and triangle-with-dots as symbols of fertility*

The lozenge and triangle with one or more dots are encountered on shrine walls, vases, seals, and typically on the pregnant belly or other parts of the Pregnant Goddess, starting in the 7th millennium B.C. In origin, both glyphs probably are schematized configurations of the vulva and the pubic triangle and relate to the life-source. The dots perhaps represent the seed inside the womb or field.

The presence of the lozenge with a dot in the center or in all four corners, and of a lozenge within a lozenge, on seals and on the Çatal Hüyük and Can Hasan frescoes (Mellaart 1963: Shrine VII, 1; French 1962: House 3, layer 2B) attests to the symbolic importance of the motif. (FIGURE 222) With the beginning of pottery painting c. 6300 B.C. in the Aegean area, the rectangle with a dot and the diamond within a diamond are ornamental designs as prominent on Sesklo ceramics in Greece and on Hacilar and Can Hasan wares of Anatolia as the chevron and triangle motif. The importance of this symbol in design is visible throughout time in all culture areas of Old Europe. Some of the most sophisticated polychrome vases from the 5th millennium B.C. are decorated with lozenges. For example, on the Petreşti fruit stand from Pianul de Jos in Transylvania, found with other painted vases on a tripod table, probably was used for harvest or autumn sowing rituals. (FIGURE 223)

The meaning of the symbol is apparent from its position on the belly of pregnant figurines or fat parts of the body—buttocks and thighs. (FIGURE 224) The lozenge either has a dot in the center or is divided into four equal parts with a dot in each compartment. The enthroned "Lady of Pazardžik" of the Karanovo VI culture (c. 4500 B.C.) is marked by lozenges on her full buttocks and thighs (fig. 220). This suggests that all fat parts of the body were significant, considered to be "growing" or "pregnant." Dotted lozenges on the round portion of globular vessels seem to make a similar statement. Some figurines were impressed with actual grains on buttocks and thighs (Gimbutas 1974: fig. 156).

The lozenge with a dot in the four corners may denote planting "in all four directions," a feature still present in European folk belief. Throughout Europe, sowing in four directions is a ceremony carried out at the winter and spring plantings to ensure that dead vegetation will come to life again. Many dots within a diamond may signify multiplication of the seed, a general resurgence of life in the sown field.

Round vases filled with seeds or decorated with dotted lozenges could have been conceived of as the Mother's womb, and the seeds as the souls of the dead. In ancient Greece, pots with corn seeds kept near the household hearth symbolized the dead who rest in the womb (pot) and are resurrected in the spring. The dead were called "Demetrioi," those who belong to Demeter, the Grain Mother, and who rest, like the corn, in the womb of that Goddess.

15.3 *The sow, double of the Goddess*

The sacred animal of the Pregnant Goddess is the sow. Its fast-growing, rounded body was probably allegorical of seed and field fertility, and its condition must have been regarded as magically influencing the crops. The association of the sow with the Goddess can be observed in figurines of the Pregnant Goddess marked with lozenges and wearing pig masks. Individual sow masks of exquisite workmanship, probably cult paraphernalia, are known from the Vinča and Karanovo cultures (FIGURE 225) and the importance of the sow in cult practice is suggested by the considerable numbers of sow effigies and pig-shaped vases with lids in the shape of a pig's head. Sculptures and vases of sows are known from the end of the 7th to the 3rd millennia B.C. and later from the Early Neolithic in Greece and central Europe to the Aegean Bronze Age (Gimbutas 1974: pls. 213–18). Sculptures were made of clay and even of marble. A beautiful marble container in the shape of a pig from Early Cycladic I, c. 3000 B.C., is in the Goulandris Foundation Museum, Athens.

The lid of a huge vase in the shape of a sow's head, painted white on red and with two copper earrings in each ear, from Gumelniţa of the Karanovo culture (Karanovo VI, mid-5th millennium B.C.) (FIGURE 226) is not unique; sow-headed figures and vases with attached earrings are known from several sites. They show that the animal represented in the sculptural art of Old Europe was an epiphany of the Goddess. The existence of a similar concept is also recorded in the Near East (see sow-headed "Lady" with necklace seated on stool, from northern Syria, 17th–16th centuries B.C., in the Louvre Museum; *Annales Arch. de Syrie* 1933: 240–47).

Sow-masked dancers are found in the reliefs, paintings, and figurines of ancient Greek shrines. Among the eleven female dancers wearing animal masks and hooflike footgear on marble drapery

FIGURE 225

FIGURE 225 The Pregnant Goddess's sacred animal is the sow, whose rapidly growing rotund body was perceived as fertility incarnate. This clay pig mask was probably used in the rituals of her cult. Vinča (Leskovica, near Štip, Macedonia; c. 4500–4000 B.C.) H. 19 cm.

FIGURE 226

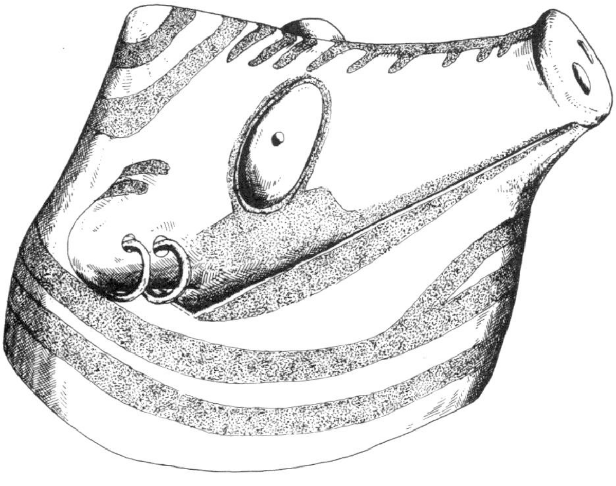

FIGURE 226 This lid, whose design is painted white on red, must once have belonged to a large sow-shaped or anthropomorphic vase. The two copper earrings piercing each ear indicate that the animal is an epiphany of the Goddess. Gumelniţa/Karanovo VI (Gumelniţa tell, S Romania; c. 4500 B.C.) H. 20.4 cm.

from the 2nd century shrine of Despoina, at Lycosura, one wears a sow mask (Lawler 1964: 6, figs. 25, 26). A small terracotta statuette of uncertain provenance, now in the Louvre, depicts a woman with a sow's head and cloven hoofs instead of hands (ibid.: 67).

Suckling pigs were prominent offerings to the Greek Queen of Corn Demeter and her daughter Persephone, as well as to other bread-giving deities of Europe. The festival of Thesmophoria which occurred at the autumn sowing in October in honor of Demeter was performed solely by women and lasted for three days. Women brought suckling pigs, which had been thrown into subterranean caves to rot three months before the festival, and placed them on altars with pinecones and wheat cakes in the shape of male genitals; they were then mixed with the seeds to be used for sowing (Nilsson 1957: 312). The piglet's remains were believed to increase the capacity of the seed to germinate. Herodotus describes a similar rite among the Egyptians. The inhabitants of the Nile delta let pigs trample on seeds and press them into the earth (Herodotus 2, 14). The symbolic relationship between the pig's fattening and seed fertility is reflected in pig figurines impressed with grain known from the early Cucuteni culture (Gimbutas 1974: 211, fig. 165). The Romans sacrificed a pregnant sow and offered flat cakes and grains to Ceres and Tellus (Terra Mater) during the festival Sementiva, the day of sowing. Ovid (in *Fasti*, composed in the first decade of the first century A.D.) gives some details of this celebration (lines 675–94). In the prayer to the goddesses the farmer asks that boundless crops ensue from the seeding and prays for the eventual sprouting of the grain. He requests the goddesses' protection in keeping the fields free from the dangers of birds, ants, mildew, foul weather, and weeds. The rites were to assure the fruition of the grain, and to stimulate the forces of growth.

A black suckling pig was offered to the Lithuanian Earth Mother Žemyna as late as the 17th century A.D. At a harvest feast presided over by a priestess, the sacrificed pig was ritually consumed. A portion of the pig, together with three times nine pieces of bread, was then taken by the priestess to the storage house. There, she prayed alone to the Goddess (Praetorius 1871). Traditionally, three and nine (three times three) were magical numbers used to invoke increase and multiplication. Pork fat is also a fertility symbol; it is used in agrarian rituals, for instance, in the ploughing of the first furrow in the spring. The farmer goes to the fields carrying lard or bacon provided by the housewife, who reminds him to eat some himself and not to forget to apply some to his plough. Thus the ploughman together with his plough which pierces the earth are both smeared with pork fat. Furthermore, in late April (St. George's Day) there is a special ceremony to help the crops grow; during this time the people circle the fields in a procession, burying shells from the Easter eggs and bones from the ham at the boundaries. It is of significance that in Lithuania the custom is preserved of burying the bones of the Easter ham not in one place but at all four boundaries (Greimas 1979: 52). In this way the field is injected with the Goddess's fertility powers on all sides.

15.4 *Sacred bread*

The bread oven was the principal feature of Old European shrines. Some miniature shrine models, such as the one from Popudnia in the western Ukraine, contain one or more figurines engaged in the baking activities of grinding grain and preparing dough (Gimbutas 1974: 70, fig. 23). The inner walls of the model are painted with a multiple lozenge design, clearly linking the shrine with figurines so marked. Bread prepared in a temple was sacred bread, dedicated to a Goddess and used in her rituals.

In later antiquity, bread and cakes for ritual purposes were baked in various shapes—loaf, snake, bird, animal, flower—or had an impressed design. There is no doubt that this custom is Neolithic in origin, and it is highly probable that Neolithic seals with various raised or incised symbols were used to stamp the appropriate design on the breads and cakes assigned to a particular Goddess. Breads marked with multiple lozenges and snake spirals were probably offerings to the Earth Fertility Goddess. Clay models of such loaves are known from various phases and culture groups; the "seal" from Çatal Hüyük illustrated above (fig. 222, 3) is probably such a miniature loaf. The clay model—about 15 cm long and marked with lozenges and spirals—which was discovered at Potporanj, a Vinča site in eastern Yugoslavia, is clearly such a loaf. (FIGURE 227) Another, marked with a meander encircled by inscriptions, was found at Banjica near Belgrade (Todorović and Cermanović 1961: Table XIII, 5).

Memories of the prehistoric bread-giver linger in the image of "Bread Maria" in some European countries. In France, Bread Maria was remembered in processions at harvest time when women gathered flour and baked cakes for her (Galibin 1916). Offerings of bread to the Grain Mother continue to the 20th century in the rural areas of eastern and northern Europe where machines have not intruded into the fields. A loaf or piece of bread is left in a field at the first spring plowing as security for a fertile year, or at the end of the harvest to secure abundance next year. In eastern Lithuania, a piece of bread is placed in a rye, wheat, or barley field at the end of harvest. The mowers must find it and circle it three times. Then they eat a piece of the bread and the rest is buried in the ground (Balys 1948: 19).

FIGURE 227

FIGURE 227 This loaf-shaped clay object is probably a model of sacred bread which has been marked with snake coils and lozenges; both loaf and model were probably offerings to the Pregnant Goddess. Vinča (Potporanj, at Vršac, E Yugoslavia; 5000–4500 B.C.) H. 8.8 cm.

FIGURE 229

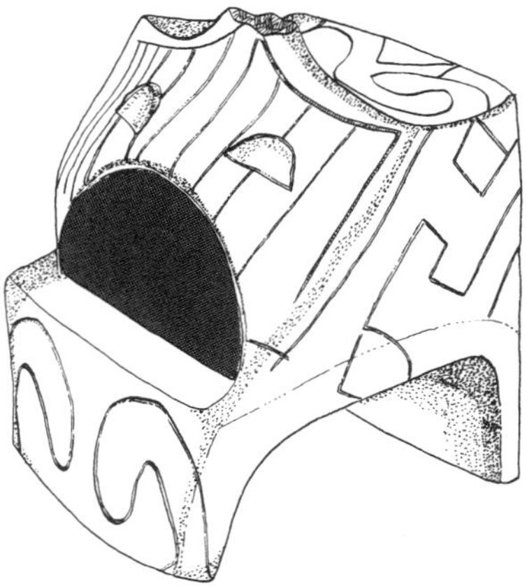

FIGURE 229 The identification of the bread oven with the Goddess herself is clear in this miniature model of an oven with anthropomorphic features. Around the eyes and open mouth are parallel lines, spirals, and meanders. Vinča (Medvednjak, at Smederevska Palanka, central Yugoslavia; 5000–4500 B.C.) W. 10 cm.

FIGURE 228

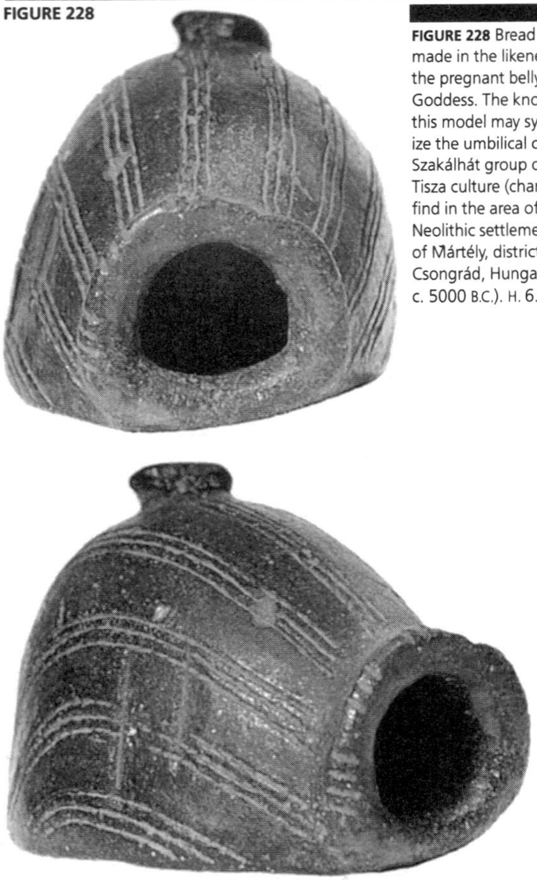

FIGURE 228 Bread oven made in the likeness of the pregnant belly of the Goddess. The knob on this model may symbolize the umbilical cord. Szakálhát group of the Tisza culture (chance find in the area of a Neolithic settlement of Mártély, district of Csongrád, Hungary; c. 5000 B.C.). H. 6.2 cm.

FIGURE 230

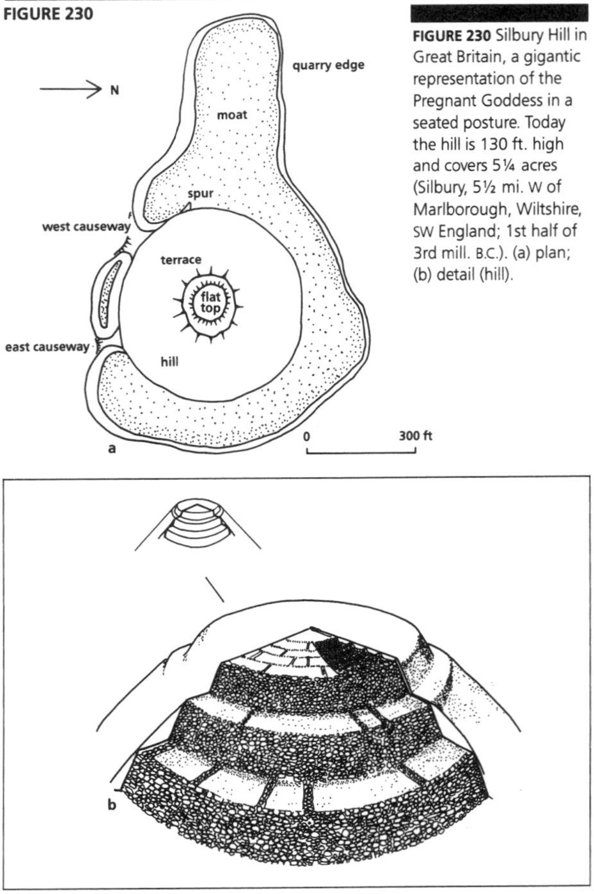

FIGURE 230 Silbury Hill in Great Britain, a gigantic representation of the Pregnant Goddess in a seated posture. Today the hill is 130 ft. high and covers 5¼ acres (Silbury, 5½ mi. W of Marlborough, Wiltshire, SW England; 1st half of 3rd mill. B.C.). (a) plan; (b) detail (hill).

The prehistoric bread oven itself was an incarnation of the Grain Mother. This can be seen from the anthropomorphized miniature models of ovens found in Vinča sites. (FIGURES 228, 229) The Goddess's eyes are indicated above the opening, which is her mouth.

15.5 *Hill and stone (omphalos) as metaphor of the Pregnant Earth Mother*

An identification of the pregnant belly of the Earth Mother with mounds of all kinds, including small ones such as bread loaves and ovens, is also found with regard to large mounds.

Hillocks of rye, wheat, barley, and oats were considered by European peasants to be pregnant bellies of the Grain Mother. During the harvest at the end of mowing, the very top of the hill was left uncut and cleaned of weeds. Then the owner tied a knot of ears of grain (Neuland 1977: 53); this knot or the last sheaf was considered the mound's umbilical cord. In Lithuania, the mower who happened to cut the last portion of rye was called "the cutter of the umbilical cord."

Michael Dames, in his interpretation of the Silbury hill monument in Wiltshire, southwestern England (Dames 1976), assumes that in Neolithic Britain the hill was a metaphor for the Goddess's pregnant belly. (FIGURE 230) (Stage I of Silbury hill is dated by corrected radiocarbon chronology to c. 2750 B.C.) The whole structure—the mound arranged with astounding deliberation and the ditch around it—forms the Goddess. The hill is the belly, the ditch the rest of her body in a seated or squatting position.

The circular summit of Silbury hill is the Goddess's navel or omphalos in which her life-producing power is concentrated. In ancient Greece the omphalos, literally "navel," was held to be the center of the world. Silbury very probably was also considered to be the center of the world. Representations of the omphalos on many Greek vases show a snake within or a crowned Goddess—Gaia, Aphrodite, Semele—who rises from it, bringing new life (see Harrison, *Themis*, 1962 ed.: figs. 113 and 124, and our fig. 246). The omphalos is both the Earth Mother in her young aspect and the snake.

A symbolic hill or the Goddess's pregnant belly with an omphalos on top is also portrayed in Neolithic grave architecture and engraved on slabs in the Megalithic tombs of Brittany. A good example is the passage grave of Île Longue, Larmor Baden. (FIGURE 231) The beehive-shaped chamber topped with a flat stone appears to be a pregnant belly and an omphalos. This symbol—a hill-shaped figure with a small knob at the top—is repeated in an engraving on a slab at the beginning of the passage. (This curious and misunderstood image is, unfortunately, called a "buckler" in archeological literature.) The wavy lines emanating from the upper part of the hill may stand for the resurgence of plant life. The hill and omphalos symbol of Île Longue is not unique; it reappears many times in other passage graves (among them in Barnenez, Le Moustoir, Mane-Lud, Mane-Rutual, Mane-er-H'Roëk, and Gavrinis; see Müller-Karpe 1974: Taf. 580–87).

FIGURE 231

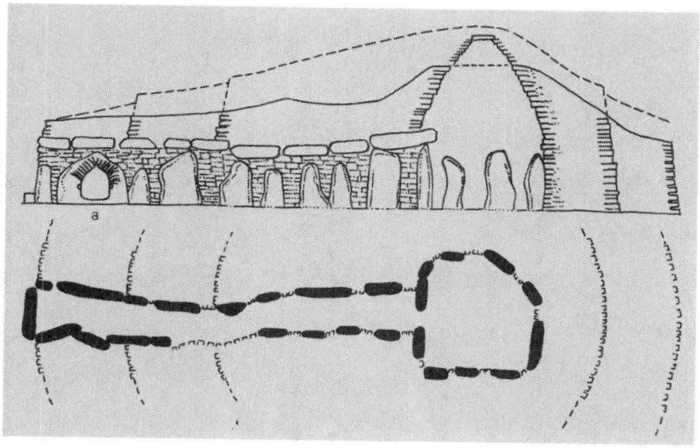

FIGURE 231 In this passage grave, the beehive-shaped chamber (belly of the Earth Mother) is topped by a flat stone (omphalos). A slab at the passage's entrance is engraved with the same mound-and-knob configuration. The lines emanating from the mound may represent resurgent plant life. Armorican Neolithic (Ile Longue, Larmor Baden, Brittany; early 4th mill. B.C.) L. of the grave 14.5 m.

Among the Minoan goddesses there is a distinct type with a cone-shaped protrusion from the masked head surrounded by fruits, poppies, and birds; the illustrated Goddess head is from a Post-Palatial shrine at Gortyn. (FIGURE 232) Sometimes a bird nestles at the edge of the mask or close to the ear or cheek. Figurines with this type of head decoration—an abstract rendering of earth fertility concentrated in an omphalos—have upraised arms. Fruits, birds, and upraised arms suggest that the image portrays a blessed emergence of the Earth in all her splendor. She is the same Goddess as the one who appears on seals and signet rings seated beneath her tree receiving offerings of poppy-heads and flowers, symbols of her bounty.

Sacred hills were venerated in history up to the 20th century. The worship of the Earth Mother was celebrated on mountain summits crowned with large stones. Such practices are recorded for both Minoan and modern Crete in the south, the British Isles in the west, and the East Baltic area, in various historic periods. For instance, the sacred hill called Rambynas on the Nemunas River in western Lithuania has been mentioned ever since the 14th century. Even in the 19th century offerings were made by newlywed couples seeking fertility at home and good crops in the field. A 16th century source says that women coming to Rambynas seeking fertility should be very clean (Balys 1948: 21; Gimbutas 1958: 95).

Those stones of the Earth Mother having the power to bestow fecundity on allegedly barren women usually have a polished surface. In Germany and the Scandinavian countries, a flat stone with polished surfaces is widely known as

FIGURE 232

2

FIGURE 232 The rising Earth Mother and the omphalos. (1) An interesting variation on the omphalos theme is represented by this Minoan Goddess with a cone-shaped headdress over her masked face. Post-Palatial Crete (Gortyn, Crete; c. 1400–1100 B.C.). (2) The rising young Earth Mother with upraised arms. Above her head is a cone decorated in front with poppy heads. Post-Palatial Crete (Gazi, probably late Minoan IIIA, c. 1350 B.C.)

FIGURE 233 Infant was buried in an egg-shaped bread oven, the very womb of the Mother. Salcuţa variant of Karanovo (Curmatura, district of Dolj, S Romania; c. 4000 B.C.)

FIGURE 233

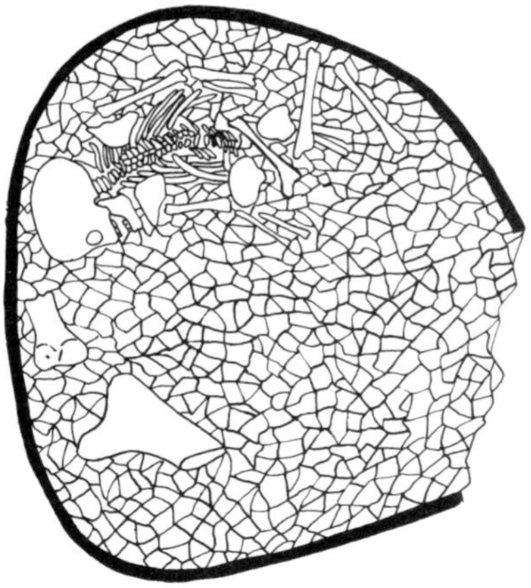

Brautstein, or bridestone. Young brides used to visit these stones to sit on them or crawl over them, seeking fertility. *La glissade*, "sliding" in French, secretly practised in France in the 18th and 19th centuries, involves contact of the hindparts of the person with the stone itself. Inclined stones are best suited for this purpose. Because of the oft-repeated ceremony by numberless generations the surface of such stones became polished.

Rubbing the bare navel or stomach against a menhir (standing stone) and especially against a projection, a round knob, or an unevenness of the stone assured marriage and fecundity and helped a happy delivery (Sébillot 1902: 79 ff.). A round knob and even an unevenness on a menhir was considered to be a spot where divine energy was concentrated—in other words, an omphalos. Seeking blessings from stones in this manner is widely recorded in Europe and the Near East, and in each place this custom is said to be "ancient."

Large stones with flat surfaces dedicated to Ops Consiua, a Roman Goddess of Earth Fertility, were kept in holes in the ground (*sub terra*) covered with straw. They were uncovered only once a year during a harvest feast (Dumézil 1969: 293–96). About 1500 years later, the same tradition is recorded in northern Europe. In Lithuania, the Jesuit annals of A.D. 1600 describe large stones with flat surfaces dug into the earth and covered with straw; they were called *Deives*, "Goddesses" (*Annuae Litterae Societatis Jesu*, anni 1600; cited by Greimas 1979: 215). Thus we learn that the stone is the Goddess herself.

European folktales contain memories of magical hills which open if one knocks at the entrance. Usually a beautiful lady leads the hero of the tale to the hill and knocks three times or knows a magical opening formula; the hill opens and inside sits a Queen in full splendour (Duerr 1978: 209). She is the prehistoric Earth Fertility Goddess, the Queen who holds the secrets of plant life.

15.6 *The tomb is womb*

"The earth under which men [sic] are buried is the mother of the dead. The object of the tomb builder would have been to make the tomb as much like the body of a Mother as he was able. The same idea seems to have been carried out in the internal arrangements of the passage grave, with the burial chambers and passage perhaps representing uterus and vagina" (Cyriax 1921, cited by Dames 1977: 30).

This fairly recent quotation of an interpretation aired more than half a century earlier shows that the "tomb is womb" theory is not a new one. The "Mother" should be understood as the Goddess, and the grave as her body or uterus. The "Mother of the Dead" continues to live in folk memories. In Latvian mythological songs, she is called "Mother of the Grave" or "Mother of the Sand Hillock."

The caves, crevices, and caverns of the earth are natural manifestations of the primordial womb of the Mother. This idea is not Neolithic in origin; it goes back to the Paleolithic, when the narrow passages, oval-shaped areas, clefts, and small cavities of caves are marked or painted entirely in red (Leroi-Gourhan 1967: 174). This red color must have symbolized the color of the Mother's regenerative organs. In southern and southeastern Europe, Neolithic graves were oval in shape, symbolic of an egg or womb. These, as well as pithos graves (interment in an embryonic position inside an egg-shaped vase) and oven-graves, express the idea of burial in the mother's womb. (FIGURE 233) Burial in the womb is analogous to a seed being planted in the earth, and it was therefore natural to expect new life to emerge from the old.

FIGURE 234

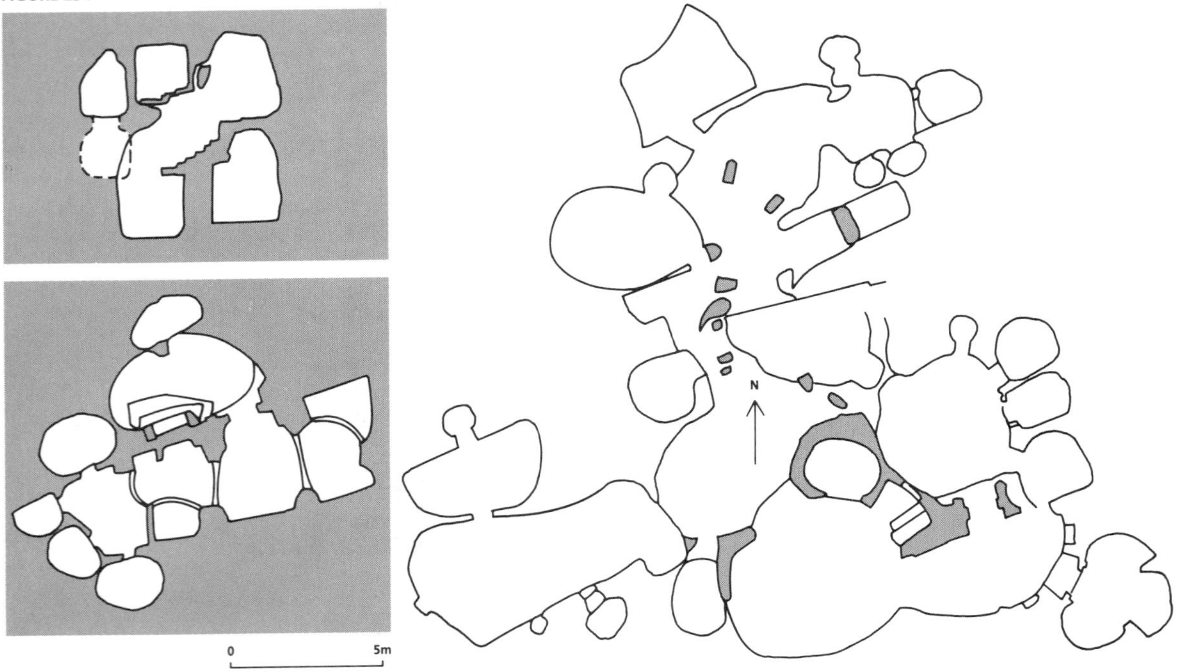

FIGURE 235

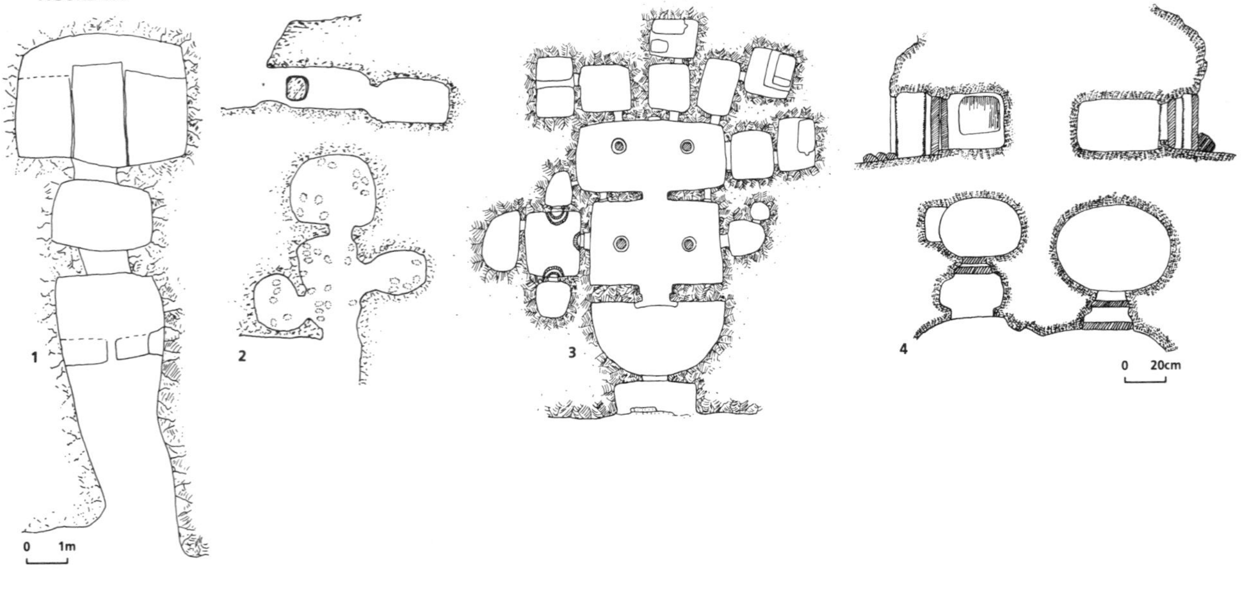

The rock-cut tombs and hypogea (subterranean tombs) of Malta, Sicily, and Sardinia are usually uterine, egg-shaped, or roughly anthropomorphic. (FIGURES 234, 235) In western Europe where large stones were used in grave architecture, the body of the Goddess is magnificently realized as the megalithic tomb. (FIGURE 236) The so-called "cruciform" and "double-oval" tombs are unmistakably human-shaped. (FIGURE 237) The stone temples of Malta share the same contours as terracotta and stone figurines of the Goddess.

Some monuments replicate the ample contours of the Pregnant Goddess figurine. For example, a small stone grave from Mierzyń, western Poland, closely resembles an obese seated figurine from Malta. (FIGURE 238)

The earliest form of grandiose megalithic architecture is the passage grave, consisting of a corridor and principal chamber. The natural cave with its connotations of the Goddess's womb (vagina and uterus) was probably the inspiration for erecting monumental structures

FIGURE 236

FIGURE 234 Floor plans of the three underground stories of interconnected tombs at Hal Saflieni, Malta. Some of the large halls and side niches are egg-shaped. This hypogeum was used during the 4th and early 3rd millennia B.C. DIA. of centered tombs approx. 30 m.

FIGURE 235 In these Sardinian and Sicilian subterranean and rock-cut tombs, some of the outlines are roughly anthropomorphic and the side chambers are egg-shaped. Circles in (3) are contours of columns. (1)–(3) Ozieri culture of Sardinia ((1) Montessu, Villaperuccio; (2) San Benedetto, Iglesias; (3) San Andrea Priu, Bonorva; c. 4000–3500 B.C.). (4) Early Bronze Age Sicily (Castellucio, Noto; 3000–2500 B.C.).

FIGURE 236 The entire body of the Goddess is represented in the megalithic tombs of W Europe, whose shape sheds an interesting light on the later cruciform cathedrals of Europe. Plans of tombs inside cairns. The Neolithic Passage-grave culture of Ireland (Carrowkeel, County Sligo, NW Ireland; 2nd half 4th mill. B.C.) (1) L. 7.5 m.; (2) L. 6.3 m.; (3) L. 5.8 m.

FIGURE 237

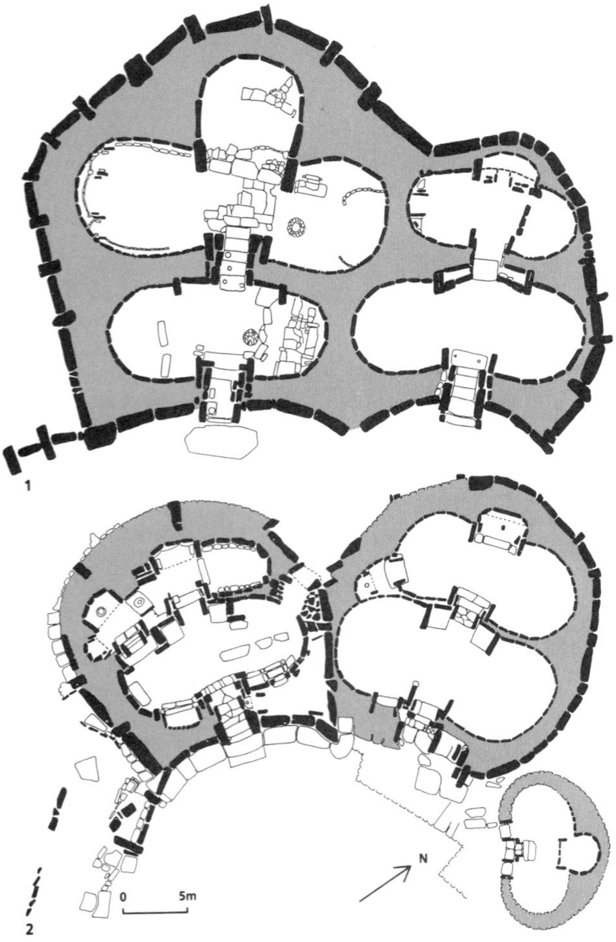

FIGURE 238

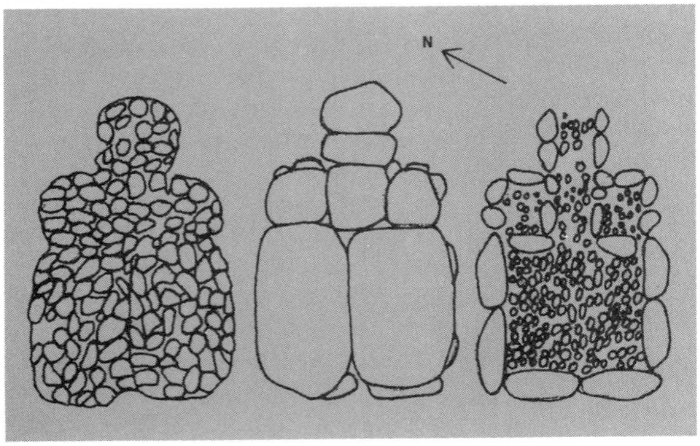

aboveground. The basic form—a shorter or longer passage and a round chamber with a corbelled roof—dates to the 5th millennium B.C. in Brittany. In the course of the 4th millennium, passage graves developed many variants, which typically featured three or five projecting niches.

The interior structures of many Irish Neolithic "court tombs" of the 4th millennium B.C. are outlined in a clearly anthropomorphic form. In addition to the large oval abdomen (pregnant belly?) and head, some have legs and even eyes. (FIGURE 239) The name "court cairns" or "court tombs" comes from their semicircular entrance built of large stones. In many instances, the court and one or more chambers attached to its middle are all that remain of the cairn (De Valera 1960: pls. II–XXX). However, better-preserved examples show that the court marks the inner contour of the anthropomorphic figure's open legs; the chambers or a corridorlike structure next to it leading into the very center of the mound is the vagina and uterus. (FIGURE 240)

FIGURE 237 The stone temples of Malta are more generously proportioned versions of the Goddess. Note that one temple is slightly smaller than the other. ((1) Ġgantija, Gozo; mid-4th mill. B.C. (2) Mnajdra, Malta; end 4th mill. B.C.) DIA. 65 m.

FIGURE 238 From Poland as well comes an example of graves built of large stones in the shape of a seated corpulent Goddess. Havel group of Funnel-necked Beaker (Mierzyń, W Poland; 3500–3000 B.C.) H. 2.8 m.

FIGURE 239 These so-called "court cairn" tombs are actually representations of a standing or seated Goddess. All have large abdomens; notice the prominent eyes in all three. Irish Neolithic ((1) Ballyglass, Co. Mayo; (2) Deer Park or Maghezaghannesh, Co. Sligo; (3) and (4) Creevykeel, Co. Sligo; early 4th mill. B.C.).

FIGURE 240 Other "court cairn" tombs show that the "court" is the space between the Goddess's open legs; the corridor or chambers beyond are her vagina and uterus. Irish Neolithic ((1) Shanballyemond, Co. Tipperary; (2) Clady Haliday, Co. Tyrone; (3) Ballymarlagh, Co. Antrim; early 4th mill. B.C.) L. of tombs approx. 10 m.

FIGURE 239

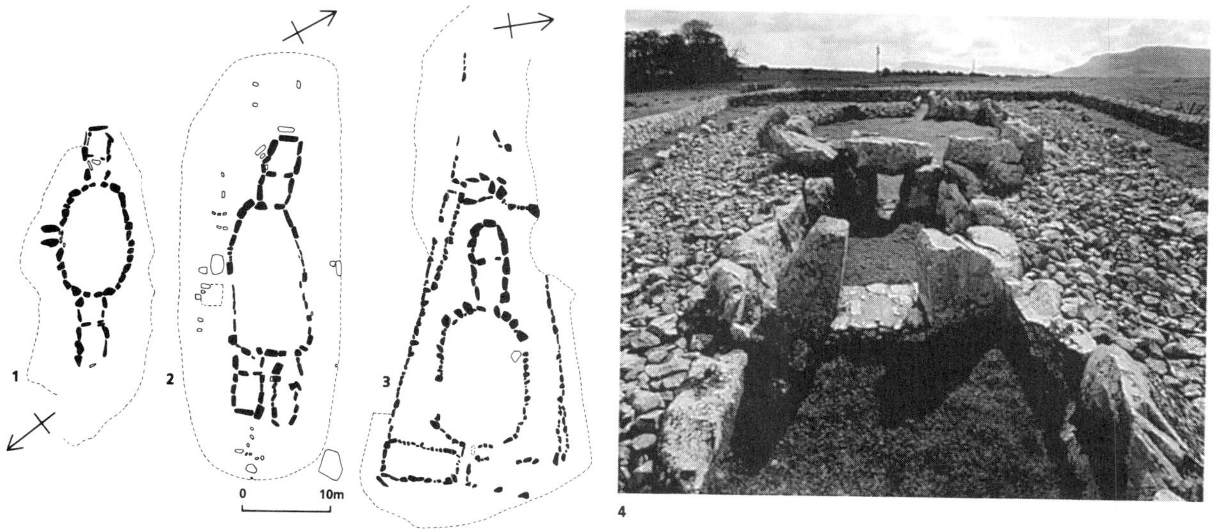

FIGURE 240

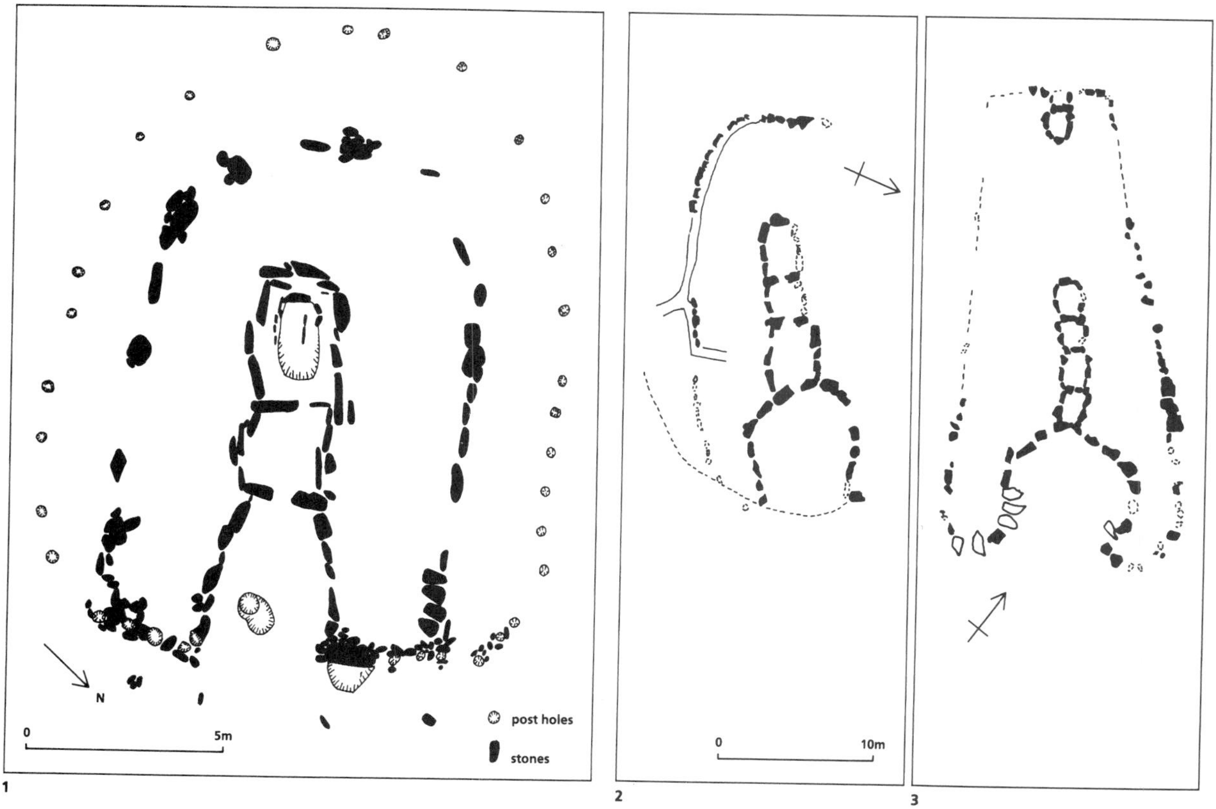

FIGURE 241

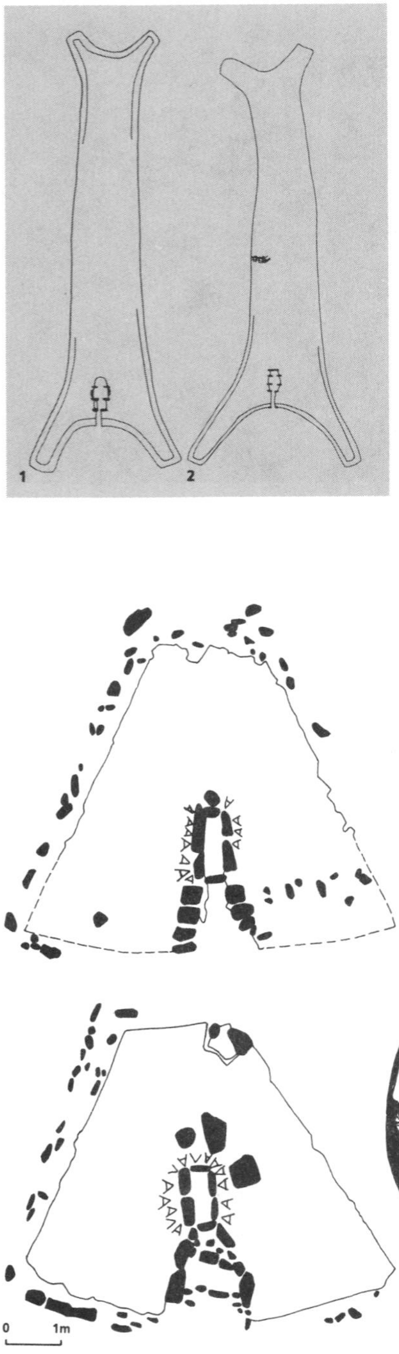

FIGURE 242

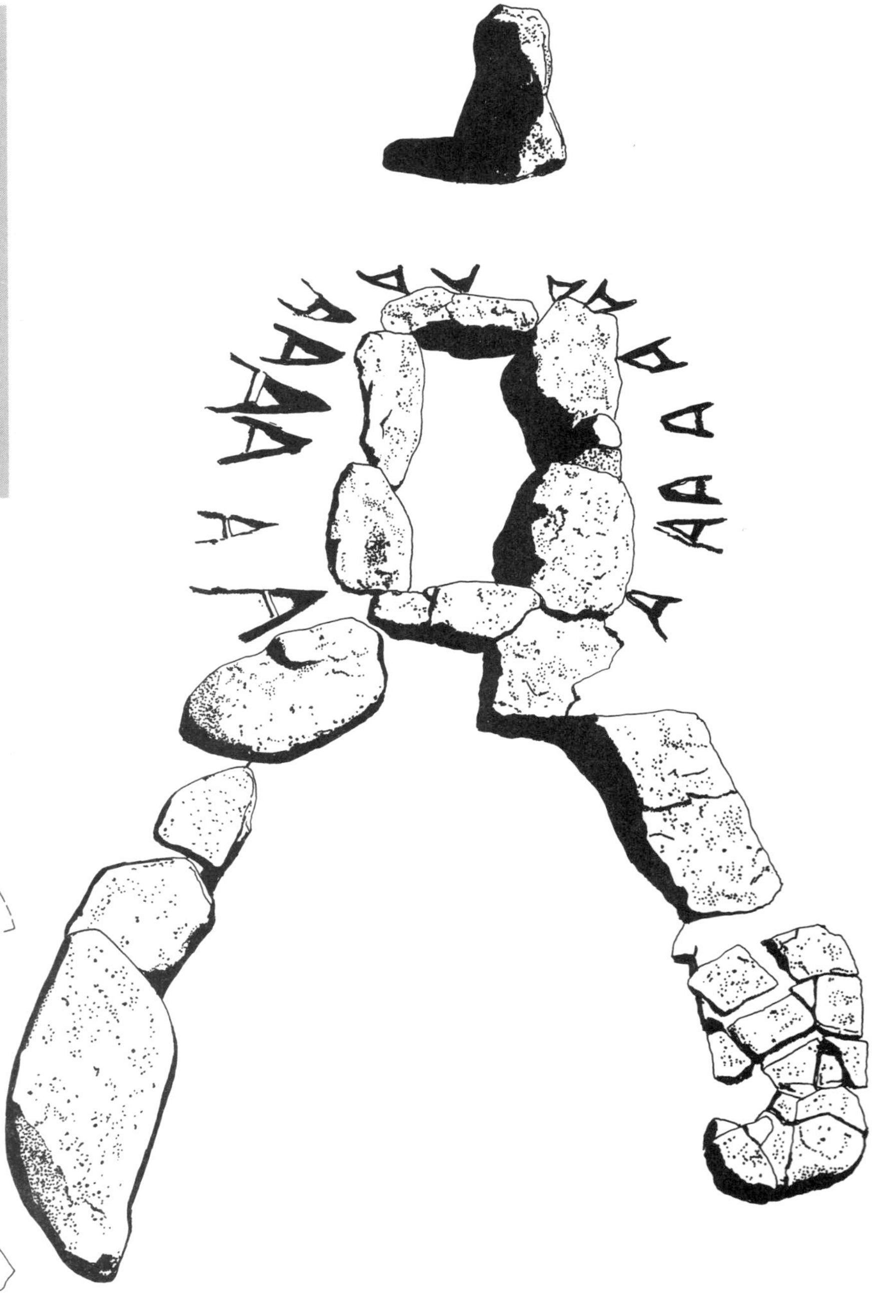

FIGURE 241 Some long barrows are precisely in the shape of the Old Hag's bone of death. (South Yarrows, Orkney; end of 4th mill. B.C.) L. approx. 66 m.

FIGURE 242 Plans of Lepenski Vir shrines in the Iron Gates region, northern Yugoslavia. The two rows of stones forming the entrance symbolize the Goddess's open legs; these lead to the generative part of the body, represented here by a rectangular stone altar outlined with thin stone slabs set vertically in a pattern of continuous triangles. Quite regularly, a large stone sculpture (usually egg-shaped or an anthropomorphic Fish Goddess) stands next to the end slab of the altar (see detail). About 7 m wide. (Lepenski Vir shrines nos. 4 and 19; Phase Ic and Id, c. 6000 B.C.)

FIGURE 243

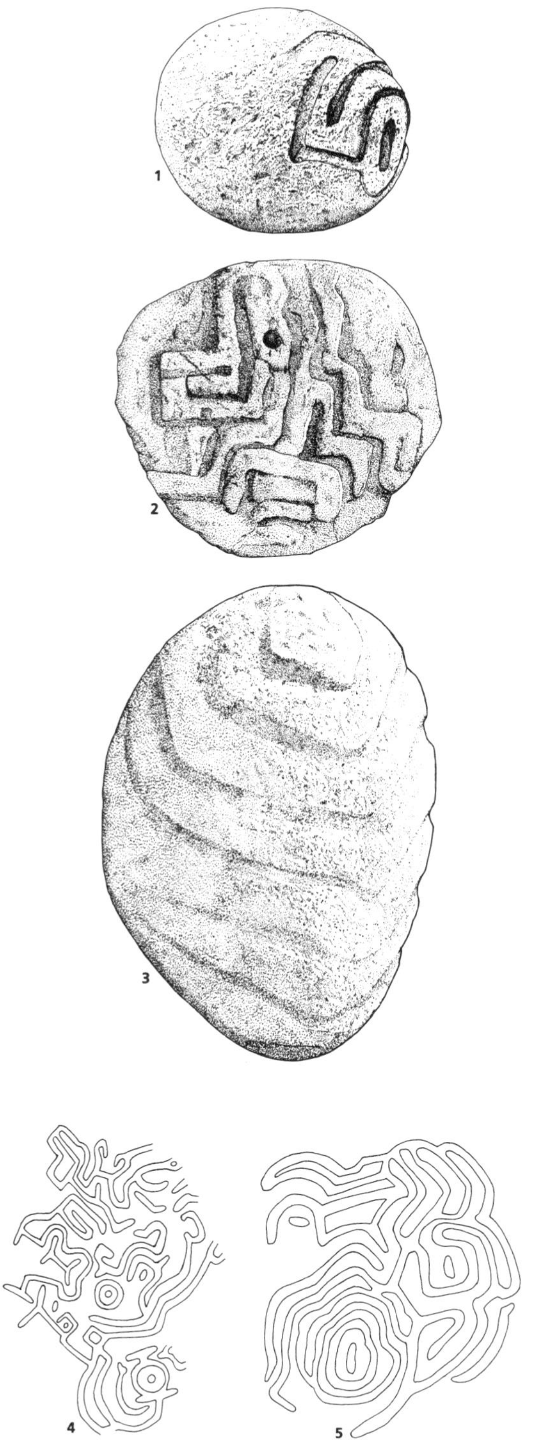

FIGURE 243 Labyrinthine designs were engraved on Lepenski Vir egg/fish-shaped stone sculptures placed at the head of the altar (see figs. 407, 408). Sculptures were painted red. Lepenski Vir Ib-II; (1) shrine 37; (2) found dislocated from the original position; (3) shrine 21; (4) shrine 38; (5) shrine 28; end of 7th and early 6th mill. B.C. Scales: (1) 19 × 14.2 cm; (2) 31 × 27 cm; (3) 14 × 15 cm.

The other type of grave is a barrow with a long corridor, resembling a bone or the lean bonelike Goddess in her death aspect (FIGURE 241). (See discussion on Old Hag, dry bones, and winter, section 18.9.)

Closely related symbolism appears in Lepenski Vir shrines and graves, discovered on the Danube in the Iron Gate region during the excavations of 1965–68 (Srejović 1972: Srejović and Babović 1983). The trapeze-shaped (i.e., triangular with the narrow end cut off) structures with red-lime plaster floors of Lepenski Vir, dated to the second half of the 7th to early 6th millennium B.C., were dug into an amphitheater-like recess in the bank of the Danube. (FIGURE 242) The essential feature of the shrine is the rectangular altar built of stones, with an entrance in the shape of the Goddess's open legs, just as in Irish "court tombs" (compare with fig. 240). At the end of the altar stood one or two sculptures representing the Fish Goddess (see below figs. 407, 408), a round or egg-shaped stone engraved with a labyrinthine/uterine design (FIGURE 243), or a sacrificial container.

The dead were buried in similar triangular structures; they were placed on the red floor with their heads in the narrow end and positioned so that their navels were in the very center of the structure. (FIGURE 244) In the shrines this is the location of the sculptures. The character of the finds within the shrines and faunal analysis of the bones in the altars (identified bones were of large fish, dog, boar, and deer) show that Lepenski Vir shrines served funerary rituals. The site itself was a sacred burial place; 170 skeletons and many fragments were found in the area. The process of excarnation of the dead very likely took place in front of the shrines.

15.7 *Holed stones*

In the megalithic dolmens, passage and gallery graves, stone slabs or partition walls sometimes have round holes. Their meaning is apparent once we note the continuing veneration of stones with holes. Belief in the miraculous power of holed stones occurs in Ireland, Scotland, England, France, and many other European countries. Crawling through an aperture of a sacred stone brought regeneration; diseases were healed. Weak and feeble children were passed through the hole under a firm conviction that it would give them health. The children were introduced head first into the hole from the outer side (Sébillot 1902: 88). Some holed stones taken to the crypts of Christian churches are still regarded as performing miracles (Wood-Martin 1902: 226–34).

Trees with holes play a related role. In a North German example, the object of veneration is an aged oak where the postulant, after creeping through the hole of a decaying trunk in the prescribed manner, completed the rite by burying a silver coin in the ground under the roots of the tree (Wood-Martin 1902: 228).

Typically, the entrances to the tombs are narrow and often vulva-shaped. (FIGURE 245) One enters by either crawling or crouching through a narrow passageway of stone. The mouth of the entrance is supported on both sides by a wall of large curbstones to form a forecourt. Perhaps this is a replica of the narrow and difficult entry to the Mother's womb?

Crawling through the aperture of a stone or tree is as difficult a struggle as that through the birth canal. In Megalithic tombs, one is crawling into the Earth Mother's womb and giving oneself to her. Strengthened by her powers, a person is reborn. This rite actually is an initiation similar to sleeping in a cave—that is, "sleeping with the Mother," which means to metaphorically die and be resurrected. A well-known sculpture of a sleeping lady from the Hal Saflieni hypogeum in Malta, dating from approximately the end of the 4th millennium

FIGURE 244

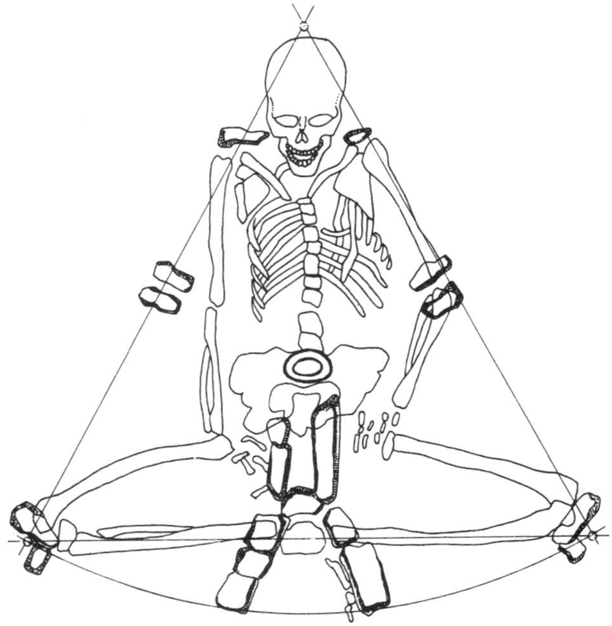

FIGURE 244 Graves and shrines were triangular at Lepenski Vir. Skeleton found placed on a triangular red lime plaster. In the shrine, the central point is the locus of sculpture; in the grave, this point coincides with the navel of the human body. (Lepenski Vir, grave No. 69)

FIGURE 245

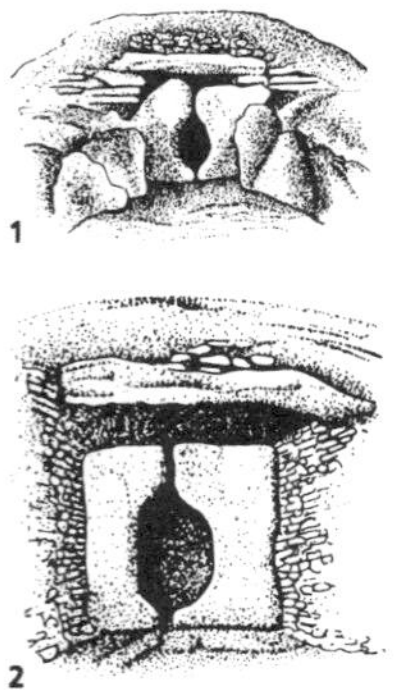

FIGURE 245 The long barrows of Neolithic Britain have narrow vulva-shaped entrances. ((1) Norn's Tump and (2) Windmill Tump, Gloucestershire, England; c. 3000 B.C.).

FIGURE 246

FIGURE 246 The design on an ancient Greek "Anodos" vase portrays "The Bringing up of Semele (Gaia)." The young goddess is shown in an artificial mound which very likely represents an omphalos. A life-tree springs from the mound, surrounded by Satyrs, a Goat-man, and Dionysos.

B.C., most likely represents such an initiation rite. Even in the 2nd century A.D., in Artemidor of Daldis's book of dreams, the expression to "sleep with the Goddess" means to die (Duerr 1978: 203).

15.8 *The eternal Earth Mother*

What we have described so far is the fertility aspect of the prehistoric Earth Mother—her pregnant belly, her miraculous womb emitting life energy and receiving it back at death. However, as is known from written records, legends, tales, and deeply rooted folk beliefs, she is more than that.

Indeed she is earth fertility incarnate: moist, mysterious, strong. She is pure and immaculate, creating life from herself, from her moist womb. She continually performs the miracle of magical transformation. Everything born from the earth is brimming with the life force. Flower, tree, stone, hill, human, and animal alike are born from the earth, and all possess her strength. Sacred groves, meadows, rivers, leafy trees, and gnarled, contorted trees growing together from several stumps are particularly charged with the mystery of life. The Earth Mother creates a cover for the earth that is lush, blossoming, and enchanted. In 17th and 18th century Lithuanian prayers to the Earth Mother Žemyna, equivalent to Greek Gaia and Thrako-Phrygian Semele, she is addressed as the "Blossomer" and the "Bud-Raiser."

In her anthropomorphic shape, the Earth Mother is a metaphor of the human mother. "Mother, I come from you, you carry me, you nourish me, and you will take me after my death" is a phrase still heard in European villages.

The Earth Mother is regarded as being pregnant in the spring and thus has to be protected and respected. Especially on her "nameday," the 25th of March, it was a very grave sin for the peasants of the western Ukraine and Byelorussia to strike the earth, or to spit, dig holes, or plough (Moszyński 1934: 510). There is a saying in Poland and Russia that "to strike the earth is the same as striking your own mother." If the Earth Mother is insulted, she will moan and groan.

In ancient Greece, there was a ceremony for Herois or the "bringing up of Semele" which was celebrated by women. It was a joyous event, charmingly described by Pindar in his spring Dithyramb:

> *Then are flung over the immortal Earth lovely petals of pansies, and roses are amid our hair; and voices of song are loud among the pipes, the dancing floors are loud with the calling of crowned Semele.* (Pindar, 5th century B.C.; Harrison 1962: 418)

The magnificent queen is crowned. She is portrayed on the "Anodos" vase illustrated here as the spirit of the earth incarnate rising to bring new life, surrounded by Satyrs and a goat-daimon. (FIGURE 246) This young Goddess, Kore or Pherophatta, represents the youthful aspect of Gaia/Semele.

The triumphant days of the Earth Mother are in August. The 15th of August, now the Feast of the Assumption of Mary (into heaven), is a feast of herbs, flowers, and corn richly celebrated to this day in all Catholic countries between Ireland, Lithuania, and Malta. Bouquets of corn ears, flowers, and herbs are brought to church to be blessed by the Goddess, and on this day is made a fat Corn Dolly, in Scotland called "the fatling of Mary," *Moilleán Moire*. It is made of ears of corn plucked early in the morning then laid on a rock to dry. When dry they are husked in the hand, winnowed in a fan, ground in a quern, kneaded on a sheepskin, and formed into a bannock (flat cake). This is toasted before a fire of rowans or some other sacred wood. Then the husbandman breaks the bannock and gives a bit to his wife and children, and the family raises "The Paean of Mary Mother," who promises to shield them. While singing thus, the family walks sunwise round the fire (Ross 1976: 141). The custom of baking fatlings of Mary seems to be inherited directly from the Neolithic. Baking fatlings in imitation of the crop deity is also encountered on the other side of Europe. The Lithuanians of East Prussia, on the occasion of the harvest feast, would bake a cake in the shape of a woman referred to as *Bobas-puppe*, "the doll of Boba," i.e., the image of the Old One of the Rye (Balys 1966: 94). The Fat Ladies of the Neolithic and Copper Age perhaps were also produced at harvest to celebrate and symbolize the bounty of the Earth Mother.

The Earth is also Justice, social conscience, as represented by the Greek Themis, Russian Matushka Zeml'ja and Lithuanian Žemyna. The wide distribution of this idea points to its roots in prehistory. For centuries, Slavic peasants settled legal disputes relating to landed property by calling on the Earth as a witness. If someone swore an oath after putting a clod of earth on his or her head or swallowing it, that oath was considered binding and incontestable. The Earth Mother listens to appeals, settles problems, and punishes all who deceive her or are disrespectful to her. She does not tolerate thieves, liars, or vain and proud people. In legends and tales, sinners are devoured by the Earth along with their houses or castles; the Earth closes over them, and a lake or a mountain appears on the site.

The Earth is the holiest there is. One cannot joke with her. Sacrifices to her are of the utmost importance, and grave consequences are expected if offerings—bread, ale, black animals or birds—are not made at regular intervals. In such cases, as recorded in 1582 in eastern Lithuania, a family member or an animal of the household may become paralyzed, or a huge snake will obstruct the entrance to the house (Ivinskis 1950).

Earth Mother remained part of humankind's religious history for millennia. The transformation of the Grain Protectress from Goddess to Saint (in western Europe to Radegund, Macrine, Walpurga, Milburga) or to the Virgin Mary is vividly presented in the informative book by Pamela Berger, 1985.

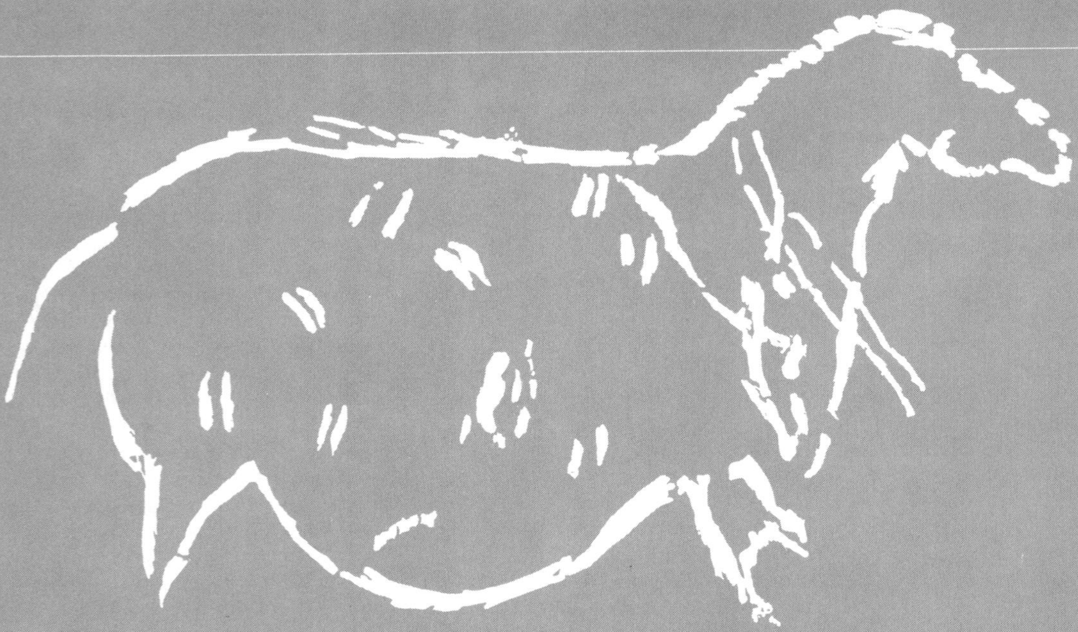

Painting of pregnant mare marked with bi-lines, from Magdalenian cave of La Pileta, near Gibraltar. See figure 265, page 168.

16/ *Power of Two*

To express intensification, the cultures of Old Europe used images of doubles to indicate progressive duplication, and hence potency or abundance. This can be seen in the frequent use of double images of caterpillars or crescents, spirals, snakes, birds, and even goddesses. Dualism is also expressed by two lines on a figurine or in the center of an egg, vulva, or seed, and by a double-fruit symbol resembling two acorns.

16.1 *Doubles*

The use of duplication—in this case a double yolk, caterpillar, nautilus, phallus, snake, bird, or crescent—is well manifested in Cucuteni vase painting (4500–3500 B.C.) and on Minoan vases and seals (2000–1500 B.C.).

Two caterpillars or snakelike forms, a larger and a smaller, flanked by mythical dogs, are painted inside a large conical bowl of the Cucuteni B Culture. The vessel's rim is decorated by ovals (eggs?) with two vertical dashes in each center. Another dish from the same site shows two pairs of caterpillars in a double compartment. (FIGURE 247) A related theme on other vases is expressed by bands of egg-shaped or half-egg-shaped panels containing a double-seed/yolk motif.

The interior of dishes and conical bowls is frequently painted with a double-egg motif, sometimes with a snake stretched across it. (FIGURE 248) On Cucuteni figurines the strengthened fertility concept is expressed by twin embryos in the belly, or by a double line within a double egg on the buttocks and belly. (FIGURE 249)

The double-egg or double-yolk motif is familiar in the art of Thera and in Minoan art of the early 2nd millennium B.C., especially on spouted and egg-shaped

FIGURE 247

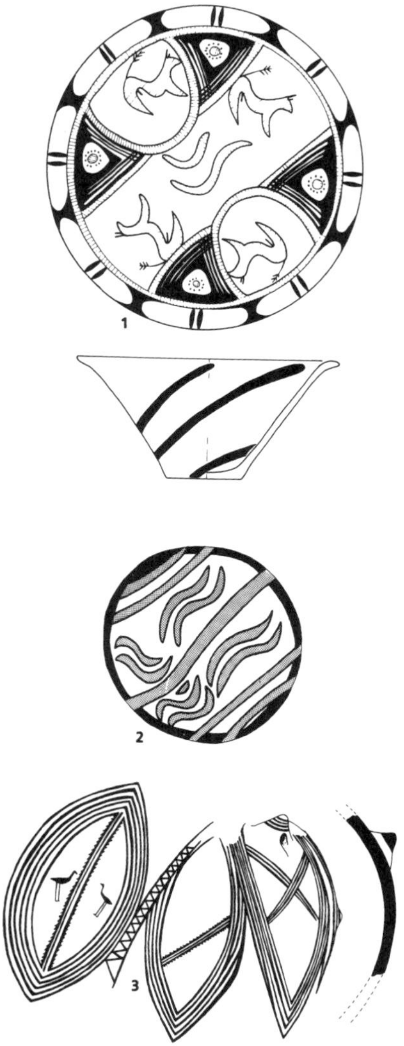

FIGURE 248

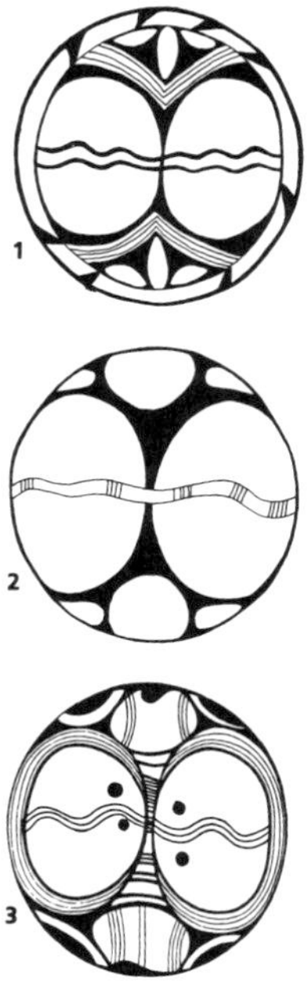

FIGURE 247 On the interior of this conical bowl (1) two pairs of dogs stand at the four corners around two caterpillars. The rim is painted with elongated eggs, each containing a pair of lines. Note that the exterior of the dish is marked with a tri-line. Inside another conical dish (2) two pairs of caterpillars are in each of two separate compartments. Cucuteni B_2 (Valea Lupului, NE Romania; c. 3500 B.C.) (3) Two cranes stand in the bipartite ellipse or seed painted black on red on a Cucuteni B vase (W Ukraine; 3700–3500 B.C.). (1) DIA. 61 cm. (2) DIA. 32.75 cm. (3) H. of detail: 17.2 cm.

FIGURE 248 Cucuteni ceramics are also painted with double eggs crossed or joined by a snake, symbol of becoming. Painted black on red (Tomashevka, near Uman, W Ukraine; c. 3500 B.C.) (1) (2) (3) DIA. 51 cm.

FIGURE 249

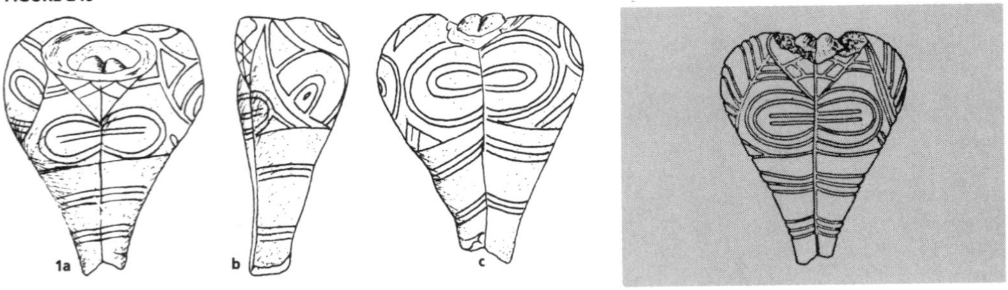

FIGURE 249 Abundant fertility is symbolized by twin embryos in the womb and a double egg on buttocks and thighs. The double eggs often contain two straight lines across both halves. Classical Cucuteni (Novye Ruseshty I, Soviet Moldavia; c. 4500 B.C.) (1) H. 10.2 cm. (2) H. 9.2 cm.

FIGURE 250

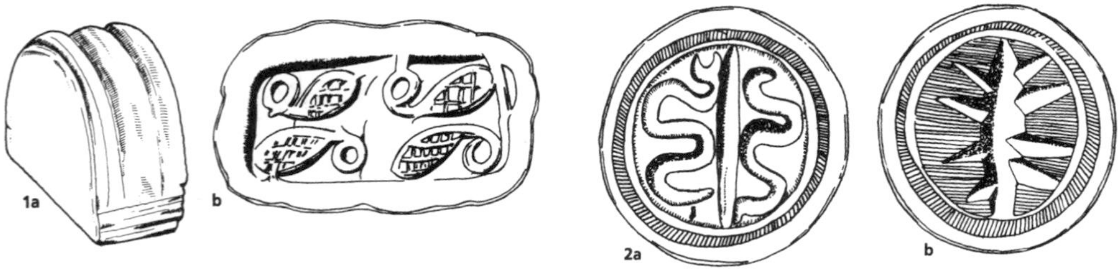

FIGURE 250 Double snakes or nautili are common on ivory seals from tholos tombs. Middle Minoan (Platanos, Mesara Plain, S Crete; early 2nd mill. B.C.) (1b) H. 2 cm. (2) H. 2.4 cm.

FIGURE 251

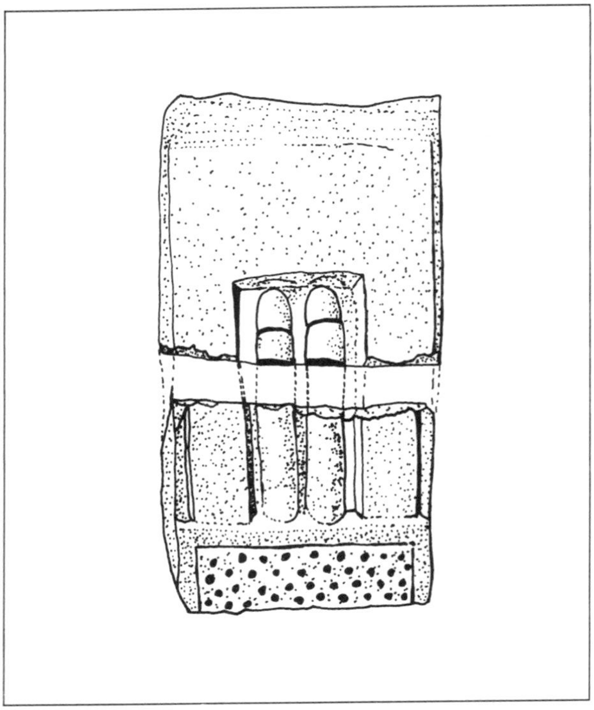

FIGURE 251 Sculpted pair of phalli found in a temple niche. Maltese temple period (Tarxien, Malta; early 3rd mill. B.C.) H. 8.3 cm.

FIGURE 252 This extraordinary mammoth-ivory sculpture conflates breasts and buttocks into a zone of eggs circling the figure's middle. Gravettian-Upper Périgordian (Des Rideaux, at Lespugue, Haute Garonne, France; c. 21,000 B.C. Breasts-buttocks in front were found damaged; here they are shown in reconstruction). H. 14.7 cm.

FIGURE 252

vases. Double pairs of snakes or nautili are among the typical design motifs on Middle Minoan ivory seals. (FIGURE 250) The Minoan "figure-eight shield" belongs to the same "power of two" family of symbols.

The sculptured pair of phalli in a niche of the Tarxien temple in Malta is another example of the use of doubling to express intensification. (FIGURE 251)

16.2 *Double-egg-shaped buttocks*

The question of the steatopygia (extreme accumulation of fat on the buttocks) of Upper Paleolithic and Neolithic "Venuses" has long haunted archeologists and art historians, who have struggled for many years to explain the exaggerated buttocks and abnormal proportions of the female body typical in sculptures, reliefs, and engravings of some 20,000 years ago. According to earlier researchers, the phenomenon expressed a "peculiar ideal of beauty" resulting from "barbaric taste," or was a realistic portrayal of a physical condition caused by a special (grain) diet in the Neolithic. (But what of the obese "Venuses" of the Upper Paleolithic?) It is my opinion that in this ancient configuration of the Deity, the exaggerated buttocks are a metaphor for the double egg or pregnant belly: intensified fertility. Centers of similar significance and potential were the pregnant belly and other fat parts of the Goddess.

The symbolic linking of the double egg with the buttocks can be traced to Gravettian sculptures of the Upper Paleolithic. One of the best examples is an ivory figurine with double-egg breasts and exaggerated, egg-shaped buttocks from Lespugue in France. (FIGURE 252) An ivory carving of two winding snakes, recovered with the Gravettian figurine, may have had a symbolic connection; a snake or double snake often winds over the buttocks and pregnant bellies of Copper Age figurines.

After the introduction of a food-producing economy, the double-egg buttocks metaphor continues for five millennia in southeast Europe and Malta. A striking similarity of perception is evident in the form of the Lespugue figurine and that of much later figurines from Starčevo, Karanovo, Cucuteni, Vinča, and Lengyel—a form which is a long-fixed, conventional expression of the fertility metaphor. A double figure emerging from egg-shaped buttocks, a relief figure on a Cucuteni vase from Truşeşti, probably also symbolizes intensified fertility. (FIGURE 253)

It is interesting to note that in the Neolithic, the nourishing aspect of the Deity is not a dimension of her fertility; the breasts of figurines with exaggerated, egg-shaped buttocks are insignificant or completely absent. Many figurines from Starčevo and Cucuteni are no more than buttocks with abstractly rendered upper torsos and feet (FIGURE 254)—another traditional form descended from the Upper Magdalenian (12,000–9000 B.C.). Many such schematic figurines, some elegantly abstract in form, were found at Feldkirchen-Gönnersdorf, on the Rhine in southwestern Germany (c. 12,000–11,000 B.C.), engraved on plaques or carved from antlers (see fig. 73). They all have greatly exaggerated buttocks, but, except for occasional breasts, no other anatomical details (Bosinski and Fischer 1974).

Fertility symbolism is evident in bone and stone pendants and amulets in the form of buttocks. Such an amulet was found among a number of terracotta figurines and reliefs, also with egg-shaped buttocks, at the hypogeum of Hal Saflieni in Malta in an egg-shaped, rock-carved subterranean room with red-painted snake spirals on the ceiling. (FIGURE 255) The placement of such amulets and figurines in subterranean tombs perhaps indicates a belief in the strengthening of life power at the moment of death.

Similar intensification can be seen in energy symbols—whirls and double snake spirals—on the egg-shaped buttocks of figurines from the Karanovo,

FIGURE 253

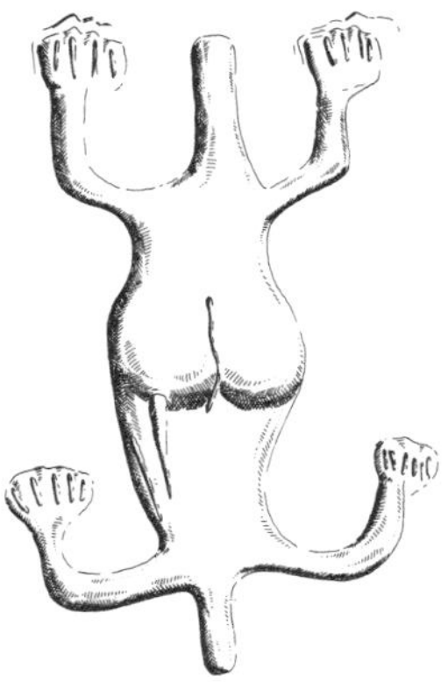

FIGURE 253 A double anthropomorphic figure and a single pair of female buttocks in the center. Arms are outstretched and with enormous hands which express magical potency. A relief on a large Cucuteni vase (Truşeşti, NE Romania; Cucuteni A_2 phase, c. 45th to 44th cents. B.C. H. 9.5 cm.

FIGURE 254

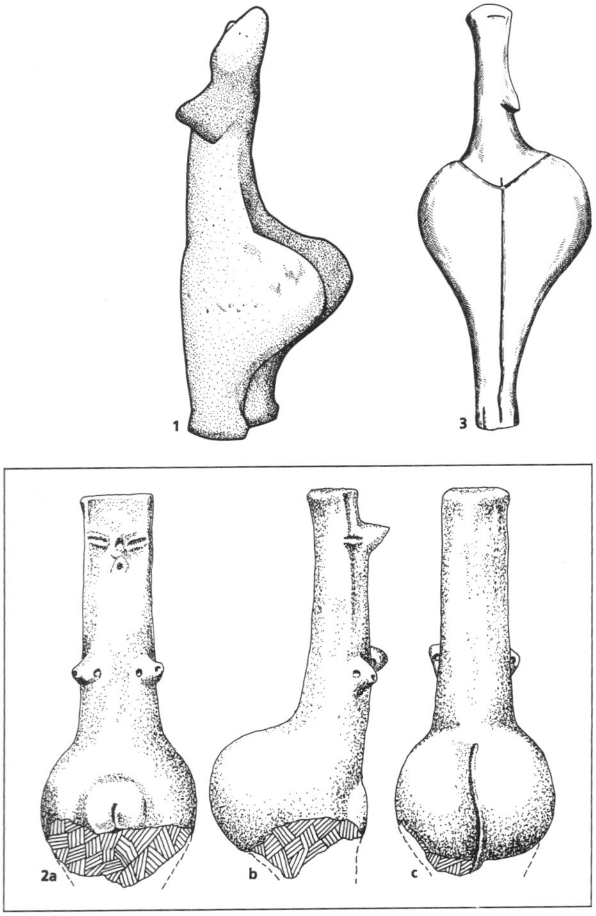

FIGURE 254 The buttocks as a metaphor for a double egg continued to appear on Neolithic and Copper Age sculptures. These terracotta figurines have schematized upper torsos and grossly enlarged egg-shaped buttocks. (1) and (2) Starčevo-Körös (1, Méhtelek, upper Tisza, NE Hungary; 2, Szajol-Felsőföld, SE Hungary; c. 5500 B.C.). (3) Cucuteni (Tirpeşti, NE Romania; "Pre-Cucuteni III" phase, c. 4600–4500 B.C.) (1) H. 16.2 cm. (2) H. 17 cm. (3) H. 18.2 cm.

FIGURE 255

1 2 3

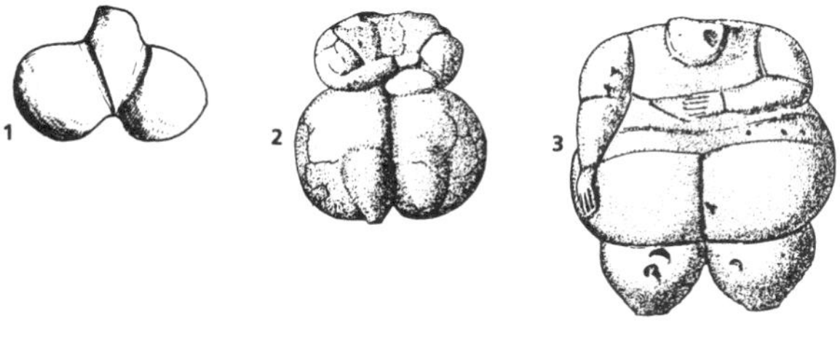

FIGURE 255 This (1) buttock-shaped amulet was found together with (2), (3) terracotta figurines displaying egg-shaped buttocks. They were in a subterranean egg-shaped room painted with red snake spirals, possibly connecting the power of life or fertility with death (Hal Saflieni hypogeum, Malta; end of 4th mill. B.C.). (1) H. 1.5 cm. (2) H. 4.2 cm. (3) H. 6 cm.

Cucuteni, and Vinča groups. (FIGURES 256, 257) Another fertility symbol—with implications of field fertility—is the lozenge. This sign, sometimes quartered or in a panel, often marks the front and back of figurines with exaggerated buttocks, as in the illustrated specimen from the Vinča culture.

On the basis of the foregoing discussion, it should be obvious that, in the prehistoric era, fat female posteriors had quite other than erotic significance. This symbolism expressed reverence for supernatural potency, expressed by the doubling device, the "power of two."

FIGURE 256

1 2

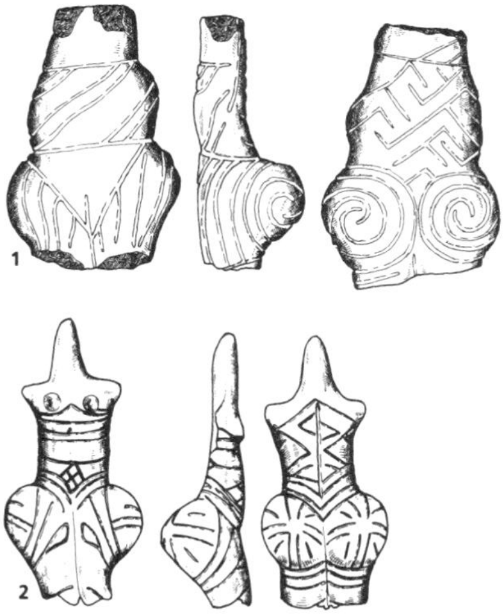

FIGURE 256 Egg-shaped buttocks are decorated with energy symbols: antithetic snake spirals, whorls, and concentric circles. (1) Karanovo IV (Kalojanovec, near Nova Zagora, central Bulgaria, 5200–5000 B.C.). (2) Cucuteni (Novye Ruseshty I, Soviet Moldavia, c. 4500 B.C.). (3) Cucuteni (Vladimirivka, W Ukraine, c. 4000–3900 B.C. (1) H. 5.56 cm. (2) H. 11.7 cm. (3) H. 5.6 cm.

FIGURE 257

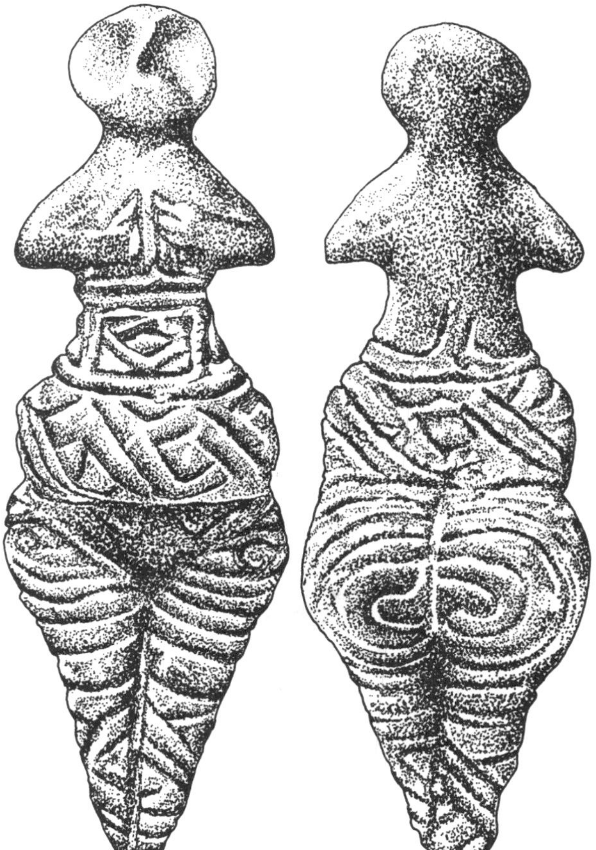

a b

FIGURE 257 This terracotta figurine graphically demonstrates the connection between double-egg buttocks and lozenges, which circle the abdomen and appear in a rectangle. There are two lines between the breasts and on the back. Vinča (Gradešnica, NW Bulgaria; 5000–4500 B.C.) H. 16.46 cm.

FIGURE 258

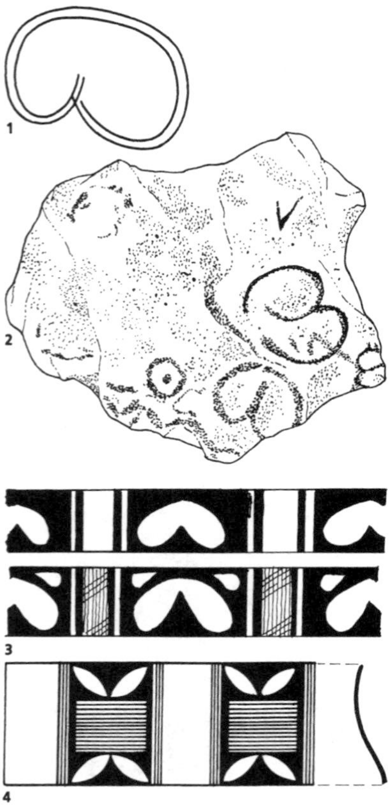

FIGURE 258 The double fruit sign represents plant fertility as a particular concern of the Divine Feminine.
(1) Upper Paleolithic engraving (Pech-Merle, Lot, S France; probably Early Magdalenian),
(2) Stone engravings probably from a passage-grave site (Ardmulchan, Co. Meath, Ireland; late 4th mill. B.C.). (3) Painted panels on Cucuteni B vases (Cucuteni site; 3900–3700 B.C.).
(4) Cucuteni B (Miorcani at Botoşani, NE Romania; 3900–3700 B.C.).
(1) H. 3.05 cm. (2) H. 90.5 cm. (3) H. 9.1 cm. (4) H. 8.2 cm.

FIGURE 259

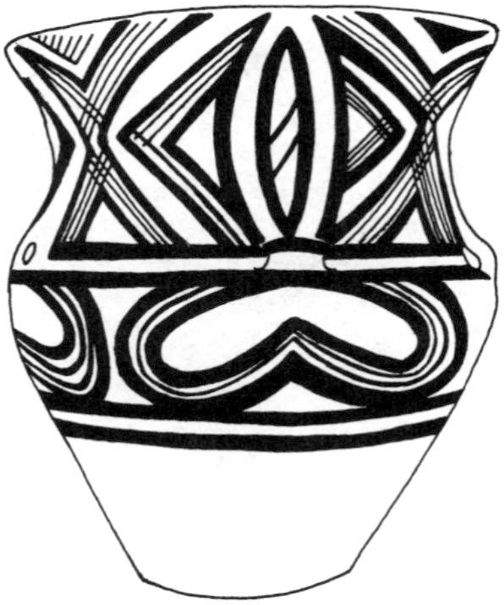

FIGURE 259 This double-fruit glyph decorates Cucuteni vases where it is associated with lens-shaped vulvas within lozenges containing bi-lines, chevrons, and eggs. Cucuteni (Ghelaeşti-Nedeia, district of Neamţ, Moldavia; early 4th mill. B.C.) H. 25.2 cm.

16.3 *The double-fruit or double-grain glyph*

A glyph of two ellipses connected at one end—double grain, double fruit, or abstract buttocks—can be seen on ceramics, seals, and megaliths throughout the duration of Old Europe. (FIGURE 258) The sign may have been retained from the Upper Paleolithic: Magdalenian parietal art includes a sign of two connected ovals much like buttocks. Similar signs are engraved on Irish megaliths. In the Neolithic, the sign acquired an elongated form resembling a double acorn. Its presence on pregnant-type figurines—fertility incarnate—seems to focus on vegetation fertility as an attribute of the Deity.

The glyph which we shall for convenience term the *double fruit* usually appears around the neck or on the lower register of richly decorated Cucuteni vases. (FIGURES 259, 260) It is one of a fairly large number of motifs at the potter's disposal. Depending on the desired "message" which controls their use and combination, the range of possible symbolic associations is rather extensive. Such associations are always purposeful and often consistent—and when consistent, meaningful.

The double-fruit glyph continues to be significant in Minoan ceramic art. (FIGURE 261) By the Middle Minoan, it can be seen in association with a tree and a sprouting bud.

The mystique of the power of two is a heritage from Old Europe which lingers in European folk tradition, especially in the East Baltic countries which have remained a depository of ancient beliefs and traditions. Latvians have preserved to this day the word *jumis* and the deity of the same name. The meaning of the word is "two things grown together into one unit, such as apples, potatoes, etc." *Jumis* and *jumm*, Finnish and Estonian words considered to be ancient borrowings from the Baltic, mean "two things or beings joined together; bundle of flax; divinity which gives wedding luck" (Neuland 1977).

FIGURE 260

FIGURE 260 This egg-shaped vase has double-fruit symbols on the neck and sprouting seeds or buds and lozenges in the central panel, connecting the double fruit with plant fertility. Cucuteni (Cucuteni-Dîmbul Morii, NE Romania; c. 4000 B.C.). H. 26 cm.

FIGURE 261

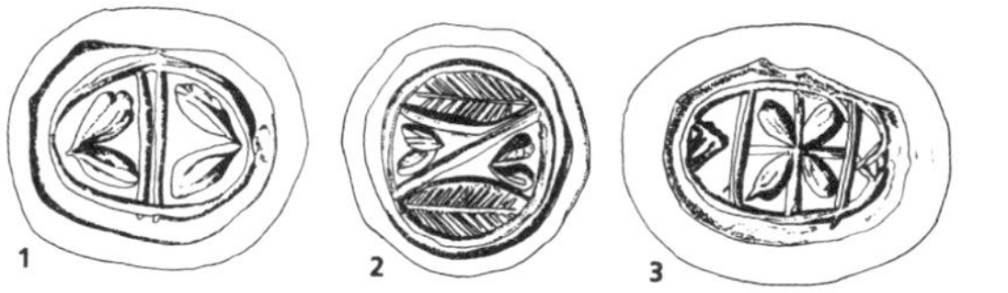

FIGURE 261 Double fruits continue to appear on Minoan seals. Note their placement (1) and (3) within an egg shape, (2) in association with leaves, and (3) in a quadripartite design. (1) and (3) white faience; (2) white steatite. Middle Minoan ((1) and (2) Kali Limiones, (3) Landa; early 2nd mill. B.C.). (1) H. 2.4 cm. (2) H. 2.3 cm. (3) H. 2.4 cm.

FIGURE 262

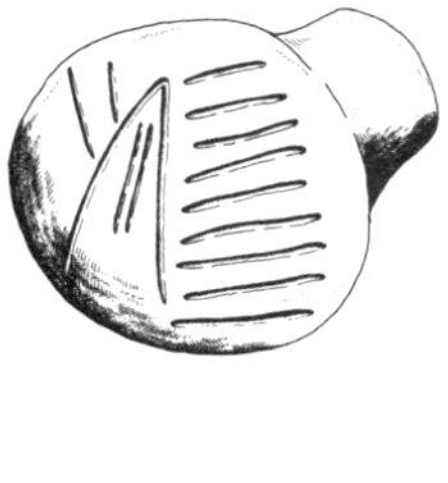

FIGURE 262 This clay stamp is marked by a vulva; there is a bi-line within and on one side, and multiple parallel lines on the other. It is tempting to read from left to right that "two" undergoes the alchemy of the vulva to become "many." Starčevo (Porodin, W Macedonia; 5800–5500 B.C.). H. 5.7 cm.

FIGURE 263

FIGURE 263 For centuries, the bi-line within an egg was a favorite ceramic motif. (1) Arapi phase of Dimini culture (Thessaly, N Greece; early 5th mill. B.C.). (2) Late Cucuteni (Sipenitsi, W Ukraine; 3900–3700 B.C.).

Twin ears of rye, barley, or wheat—a fairly rare phenomenon—are a manifestation of *Jumis*. When a double ear is found at harvest time, it is brought home by the reaper and put in a place of honor on the wall beside the table. The following spring, the *jumis* is mixed with the seed and sown in the field. In the case of winter rye, this occurs the following fall when winter rye is sown (Latkovski 1978 and Neuland 1977). *Jumis* is a force which increases wealth and prosperity by giving the desirable weightiness characteristic of double ears, double fruit, and double vegetables.

The power of two belief is also demonstrated in proverbs such as: "Double does not break apart" (German *Doppelt reisst nicht*) or the adjuration of the Latvian shearer who strikes a shorn ewe lightly with a rope and repeats the formula, "Grow long and bring back a couple (of lambs)" (Latkovski 1978). Special power is ascribed to a twin pair of oxen in ritual plowing in the spring. At the end of the 19th century, it was believed in Lithuania that if a field were ploughed in a circle by a pair of twin, black oxen and if the plowman were also a twin, the field would be protected from hailstorms, thunderstorms, diseases, and other disasters (Basanavičius 1899: 25).

16.4 *Two lines across a vulva, seed, egg, and the face, body, or buttocks of the Goddess*

Two parallel lines constitute a sign which at times is the central mark on a seal or vase. This bi-line is probably the abstract symbol of the "power of two" concept discussed above. (FIGURES 262, 263)

The distinctly symbolic function of the bi-line is clear from its use on some figurines and engraved or painted images where it is the only decoration. Marking the buttocks with two lines, parallel or crosses, is a tradition as old in western Europe as the Magdalenian, illustrated here by schematic female figures from the cave of La Roche at Lalinde and Fontales, southern France. (FIGURE 264) The pregnant mares and bisons of Paleolithic cave paintings were quite consistently marked with bi-lines and P signs (FIGURE 265), which probably are signs of pregnancy (Leroi-Gourhan 1967: 334, 508, 509, Chart XLII; Sauvet and Wlodarczyk 1977).

In the Neolithic, images of the seated goddess are frequently marked with two dashes over the hips or arm stumps or between the breasts. Schematic figurines of the Copper Age are marked by two lines inside a square (FIGURE 266) and the pubic triangle of the seated pregnant type figurine may show two or four painted lines.

Often two horizontal or vertical lines are painted or incised across the mask of the Goddess, as on the illustrated examples from Vinča and Cucuteni sites. (FIGURE 267) Owl-faced menhir statues of France and Iberia usually have two lines engraved across the cheeks. (FIGURE 268)

A double line on the forehead over the eyes marks images of the Snake Goddess, as on the relief image from a large pithos from Hodoni, western Romania. (FIGURE 269) Here there are also two pairs of bi-lines over the breasts just below the shoulders; two more pairs emanate from both sides of the head.

FIGURE 264

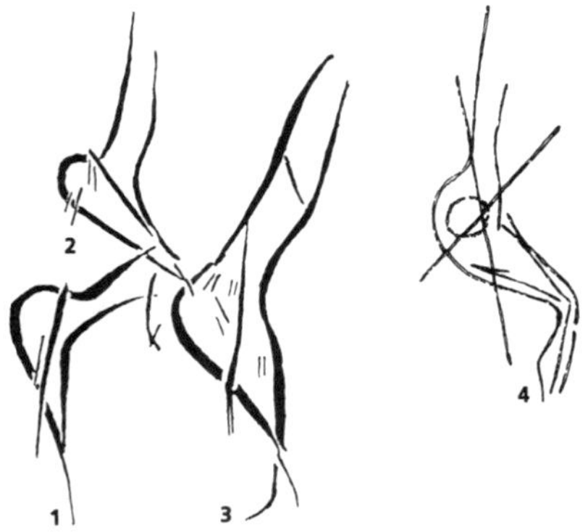

FIGURE 264 Engravings on stone slabs portray abstract female forms whose primary features are buttocks; they are marked with one or two lines, or an egg and crossed lines. Late Magdalenian ((1)–(3) Lalinde and (4) Fontales, S France; 11,000–9000 B.C.) H. of the largest figurine 20 cm.

FIGURE 265

FIGURE 265 This painting of a pregnant mare marked with bi-lines is from the cave of La Pileta, near Gibraltar, c. 10,000 B.C. Each set of fingermarks was made by a different person, using red and brown paint. (2) This engraving of a pregnant bison is marked with two sets of bi-lines and a vulva. (Bernifal, S France; Middle Magdalenian, c. 13,000–11,000 B.C.) L. (1) and (2) approx. 50 cm.

FIGURE 266

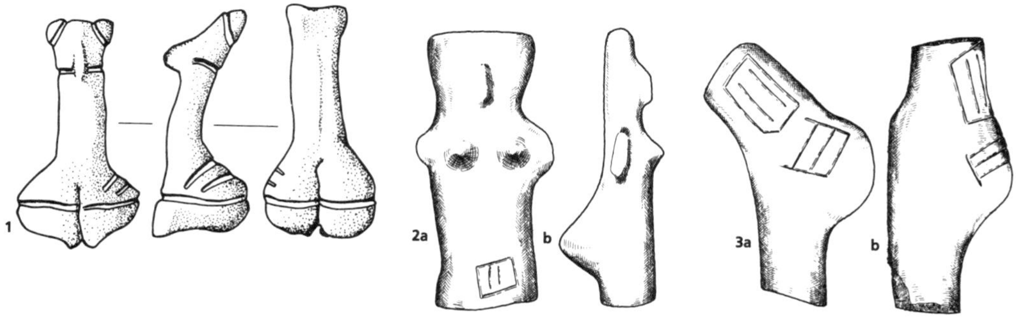

FIGURE 266 On one type of schematic figurine, the vulva or buttocks is marked by bi-lines. (1) Beautifully schematized Neolithic terracotta figurine in a seated posture. Two excised dashes are on the left buttock. Eyes, headgear or crown, and a hip-belt are marked by excision and white paste filling. Starčevo (Anza II, central Macedonia; 5800–5600 B.C.) (2) Early Vinča (Matejski Brod, at Zrenjanin, N Yugoslavia; 5200–5000 B.C.). (3) Early Cucuteni (Tirpeşti, N Moldavia; 4800–4600 B.C.). (1) H. 3.9 cm. (2) H. 6 cm. (3) 6.3 cm.

FIGURE 267

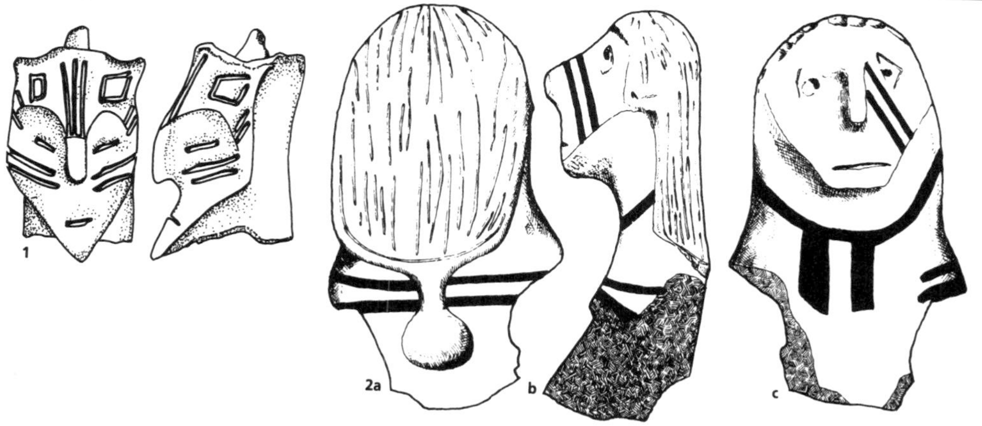

FIGURE 267 Bi-lines are often painted or incised on the masked head of figurines. (1) Clay mask with bi-lines below the eye and over the temples, a vertical tri-line across the forehead. Vinča (Slatino, Kiustendil district, W Bulgaria; early 5th mill. B.C.). (2) Terracotta figurine with bi-lines across the cheek, over the throat, and across the shoulders. Late Classical Cucuteni (Vladimirivka, S Bug basin, Ukraine; c. 4000–3900 B.C.) (1) H. 4.6 cm. (2) H. 6.9 cm.

FIGURE 268

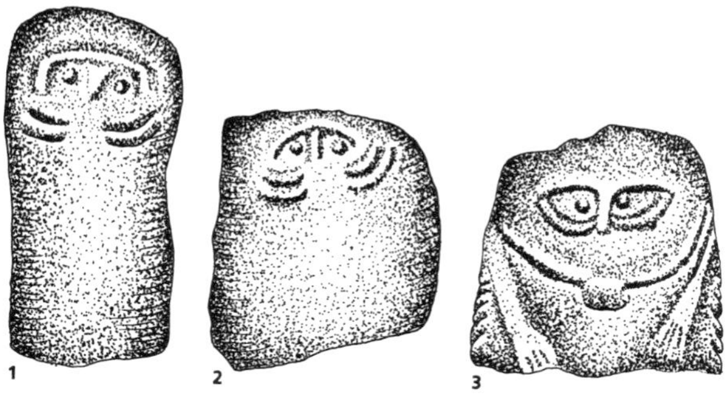

FIGURE 268 In W Europe, owl-faced stone stelae usually bear bi-lines on the cheeks. (3) has vestigial arms, parallel lines down the sides, and a necklace with a single bead. ((1) Braguassargues, (2) St. Theodorit, and (3) Le Colombier, Languedoc, S France; c. 3000 B.C.).

FIGURE 269

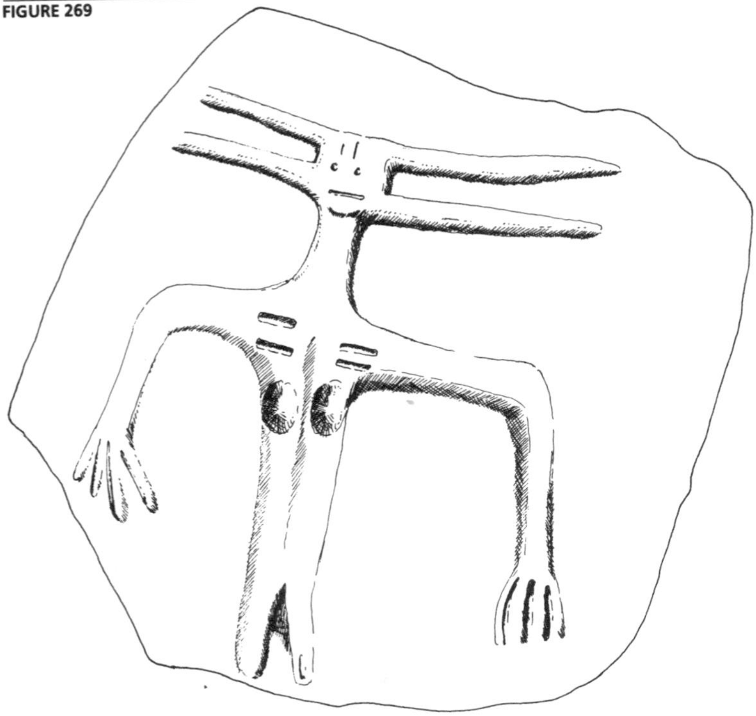

FIGURE 269 A bi-line on the forehead marks the Snake goddess, as on this sherd of a large pithos. The figure in relief also has bi-lines above the breasts and two curious parallel lines emanating from each side of her head. Tisza (Hodoni, W Romania; c. 5000 B.C.) H. 22.6 cm.

FIGURE 270

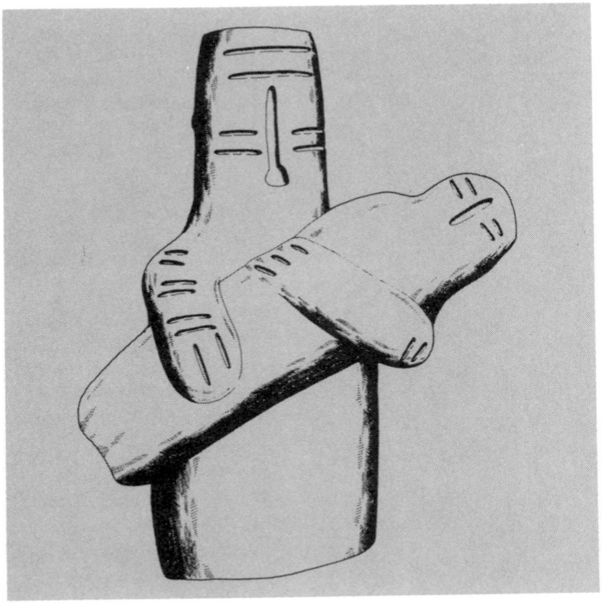

FIGURE 270 The bi-line is a typical feature of mother and child images, illustrated here by a highly schematized figure holding a cocoon-like infant. Bi-lines appear on the forehead in place of the eyes, and on the arms. Slipped in brownish red with white-filled incisions. Early Cypriot (provenance unknown; 2300–2000 B.C.) H. 9.3 cm.

The bi-line also typically marks mother and child figurines, such as the Vinča madonna whose Bird Goddess mask has two lines deeply incised above the eyes (Gimbutas 1974: 132). There are almost always more than one bi-line on Cypriot Bronze Age figurines holding babies. (FIGURE 270) The marking of mother-and-child effigies with the bi-line further suggests connotations of resurgence and new life.

16.5 *The double-headed Goddess and Mother-Daughter images*

Figurines of "Siamese twins" and of "Mother-Daughter" (larger and smaller) pairs are known throughout the Neolithic and Copper Age. The earliest example is a double-headed figurine with two pairs of breasts recovered at Çatal Hüyük, c. 6500 B.C. (Mellaart 1967: pl. 70). Numerous figurines with two heads on a single body are known from various phases and sites of the Vinča culture (Gimbutas 1974: pls. 86, 90, 100, 101). The heads of these figurines are beaked and masked; the bodies are marked by chevrons, meanders and cross-bands. These attributes identify the image as the Bird Goddess. In most instances, one head is slightly larger or positioned higher than the other—a relationship which represents either a major and minor aspect of the Goddess or a mother-daughter pair, or two sisters. (FIGURE 271) Two goddesses as two sisters are known to early history and to folklore. Some of the prehistoric pairs very likely are representations of two divine sisters and not necessarily mother and daughter. In Anatolia and the Aegean area, two-headed figurines continue into the Archaic Period of Greece.

FIGURE 271

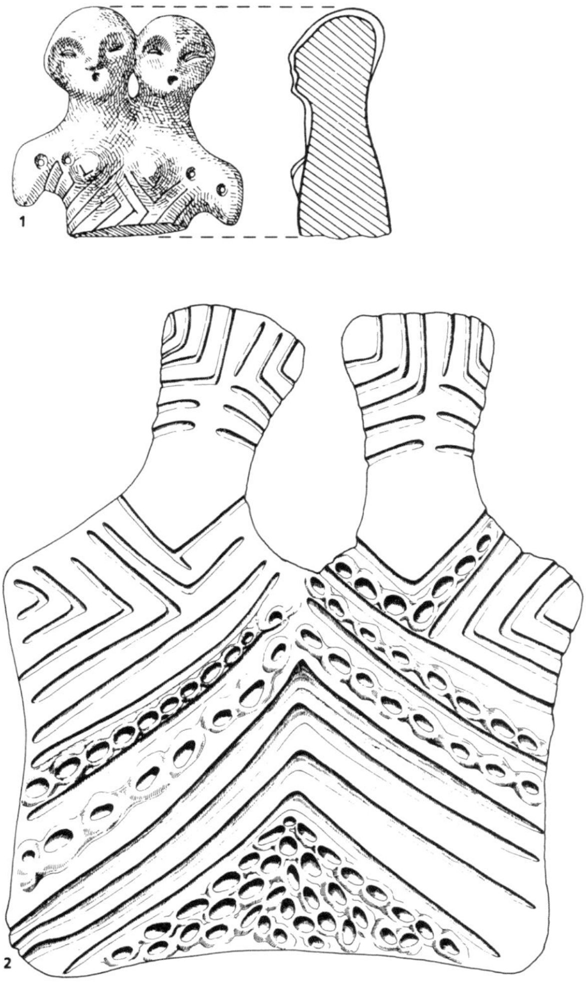

FIGURE 271 (1) A double-headed figurine from the Vinča culture with one head slightly larger than the other (Rast, near R. Danube south of Craiova, S Romania; c. 5000–4800 B.C.). (2) The two-headed goddess continues to appear during the Bronze Age, as this elaborately decorated flat figurine attests. Bi-lines mark the eyes while chevrons cover the crowns of the heads and the arm stumps; the bodies are joined by an enormous chevron in the center. Connected lines and a honeycomb of egg-shaped depressions complete the symbolic pattern. Anatolian Early Bronze Age II (Çaykenar type, provenance unknown; c. 2600 B.C.) (1) H. 4.5 cm. (2) H. 9.1 cm.

The twin aspect of the Goddess is also expressed in the Early Bronze Age in the Aegean, Crete, and Malta by double-bodied or double-necked vessels. Furthermore, there are two major temples of Neolithic Malta, one larger and the other slightly smaller, both in the anthropomorphic (Goddess) shape. This is beautifully revealed in Ġgantija on Gozo and Mnajdra, Malta (see fig. 237). This suggests the cyclical character of the Goddess with her summer and winter—young and old—aspects. Two aspects of the same goddess are expressed by representations of larger and smaller pairs of breasts on the walls of the gallery graves of Brittany (fig. 70). Such portrayals cannot be accidental; they are recorded in a number of gallery graves (an identical cartouche with two unequal pairs of breasts like those illustrated in fig. 70 is known from the gallery grave of Prajou Menhir, Plemeur-Bodou (L'Helgouach 1957; Twohig 1981: fig. 152).

The beginning of the double Goddess goes back to the Upper Paleolithic, some 25,000 or more years ago. There is a representation of a double figure among those in low relief on stone slabs at Laussel of the Gravettian (Upper Périgordian) period: two female bodies are shown opposed in a configuration of an egg from which a circular head projects at either end. One figure is more voluminous than the other. (FIGURE 272)

16.6 *The summer/winter duality*

The symbolic affinity between the double egg, the snake, and the resurgence of plant life is documented by an unusual discovery made in 1970 at Nedeia, near the village of Ghelaeşti in northeastern Romania. The find was recovered from the southeast corner of a centrally located structure in an excavated village of the Cucuteni AB to B period (c. 4000–3600 B.C.). Because it yielded only ritual equipment, the building was determined to be a shrine.

FIGURE 272

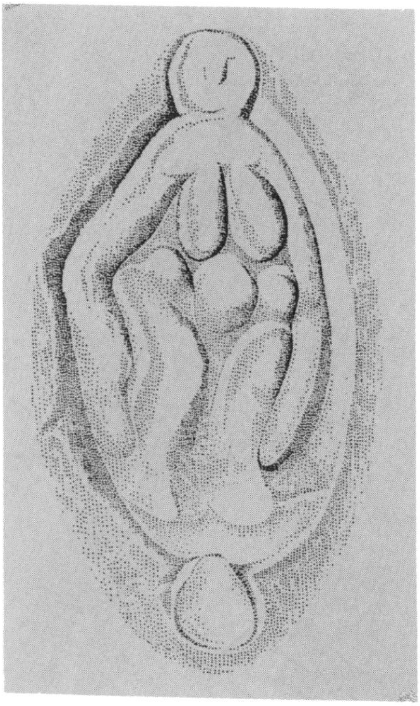

FIGURE 272 Double-Goddess (?) from the Upper Paleolithic, c. 25,000 ago. Deeply incised oval from which a circular head projects from either end; figure shown head up is female having pendulous breasts, strongly projected belly, raised thighs, arms extended the length of body, hands appearing to be beneath lower limbs; second figure, with head projecting from lower end of oval, is in opposite position but symmetrical to the figure described above; chest of second figure carefully sculpted, rest of body seeming to disappear under that of the first (Laussel, Dordogne, S France). H. 20 cm.

FIGURE 273

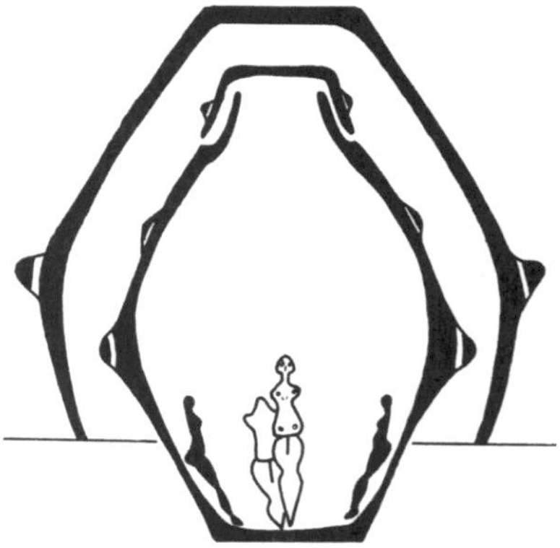

FIGURE 273 A large vessel placed over an egg-shaped vase. Inside the vase were four figurines of two distinct types, placed at the cardinal points. The vase itself is decorated in snake spirals and double fruits. This ritual complex clearly shows the idea of duality, particularly in relation to seasonal and temporal cycles. Cucuteni B_1, Nedeia, at Ghelaeşti, district of Neamţ, NE Romania; c. 4000–3800 B.C.) H. of egg-shaped vase approx. 50 cm.

FIGURE 274

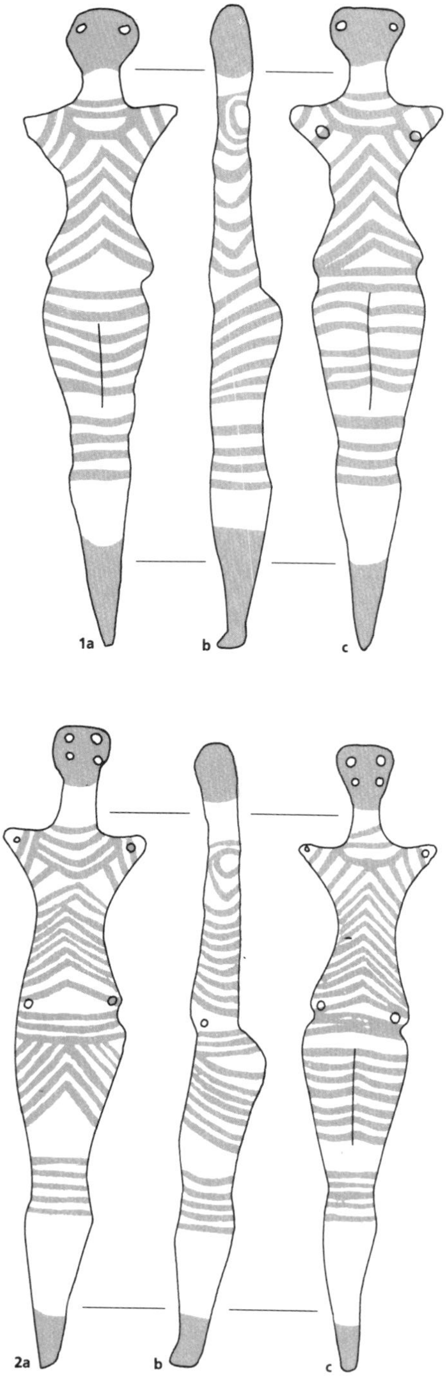

FIGURE 274 Two of the four figurines from the Nedeia ritual complex have black-painted heads and feet; the bodies are decorated with chevrons and parallel lines. The other two are unpainted but bear traces of red ochre. H. 12.6 cm.

The ritual find, assigned to the Cucuteni B1 phase (Cucoş 1973), consists of six painted vases arranged in a circle around a large vessel intentionally placed over an egg-shaped, lidded vase. (FIGURE 273) At the base of the vase, four figurines had been placed at the cardinal points. Two were unpainted but bore faint traces of red ochre; the heads and feet of the other pair were painted black and the bodies carried an overall parallel line pattern. (FIGURE 274)

The excavator interpreted the black-headed figurines as representing the chthonic (earth) sphere and the unpainted ones the uranian (sky) domain. Further, the entire arrangement was instrumental in seasonal fertility rites dedicated to the resurgence of plant life. Symbolic designs on the vases support this supposition: the egg-shaped pot containing the figurines is decorated with a broad band of snake spirals above which are symbols of double seeds/fruits. The double-fruit sign is repeated on the lid of a piriform vase and appears four times in separate panels on another pot. Four other vases are decorated with the egg and seed symbol flanked by snake spirals. The design on the eight vases is remarkable for its thematic unity and the use of the traditional "power of two" device—repetition—in the conventional way to express (and to invoke) fertility.

However, more notable is the fact that the concept of dualism had advanced from simple replication to a more complex cognition of opposition—life and death, summer and winter—which accepts the cyclicity of nature and the life/death relationship. The cosmological orientation of the shrine in its centrally located structure is revealed by the placement of the figurines at the cardinal points. This is an extraordinary revelation which affords a glimpse into the organization and sophistication of the culture.

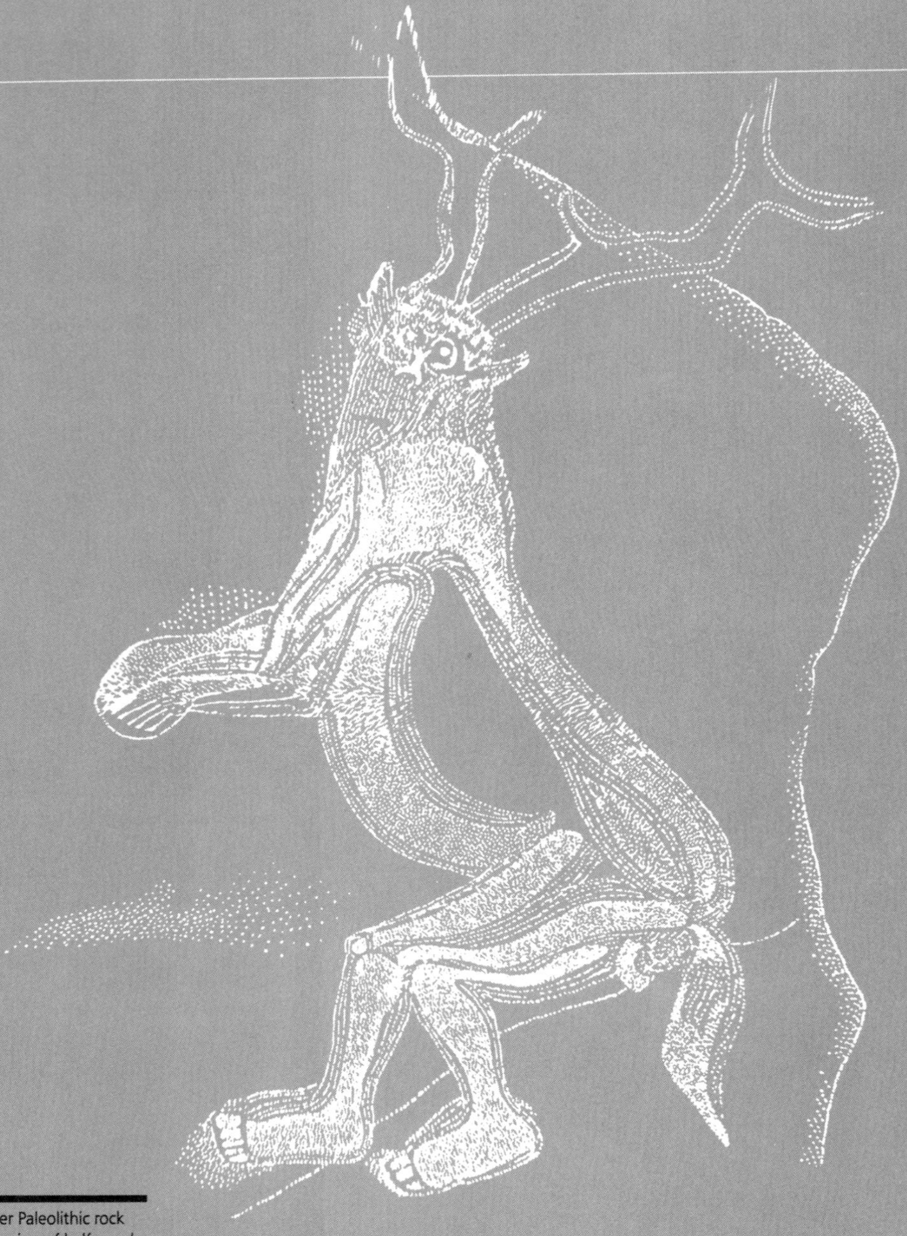

Upper Paleolithic rock engraving of half-man/half-animal, probably a protector of animals and forests. See figure 275, page 176.

17/ *Male Gods and Daimones*

The natural rhythm of the male is a phallic one of rise and fall. . . . The myths would, therefore, quite naturally tell stories in which the male is the climactic, tragic figure of flourish and vanish. (William Irwin Thompson, 1981)

Indeed, most of the male figures in Near Eastern and Old European art are symbols for the flourishing but limited and ultimately vanishing body. They are metaphors of rising and dying vegetation, or they are youths and consorts of the Goddess—ephemeral and mortal figures. The male God is also a parallel to the hibernating and awakening snake.

Male figurines constitute only 2 to 3 percent of all Old European figurines, and consequently any detailed reconstruction of their cult role is hardly possible. However, from the consistent appearance of certain stereotypes through millennia and in a variety of culture groups, we can speculate about the existence of certain long-lasting categories of male figures. These include horned animal- or bird-masked and ithyphallic men, some clearly participants in rituals; creatures who are half-animal/half-man (centaurs); enthroned vigourous men; and pensive and sorrowful men, seated on a stool or throne, with hands on knees or supporting their heads.

Some of these categories have roots in preagricultural times, such as animal-masked and hairy men and bird-masked participants in ritual scenes. Others, such as centaurs and sorrowful figures, belong to the agricultural era, associated with rising and dying vegetation.

Forest spirits and gods, dying and self-renewing vegetation gods known from the myths of historic times, may have their antecedents in deep prehistory. The very ancient features and behavior of some of these mythical men speak for their continuity from prehistory to history.

17.1 *Master of Animals: animal-masked and robed men*

Male figures in Upper Paleolithic art are known from engravings and paintings, but not from sculptures. Most of them are fantastic composite beings arising from the imaginative pairing of man and horned animal. A number of them are grotesque and enigmatic figures and rather carelessly engraved.

Horned, nude, and usually ithyphallic figures occur in Final Périgordian, Middle and Final Magdalenian, and Epipaleolithic cave engravings and paintings of France and Spain (Los Cesares, Teyjat, La Pasiega, Les Combarelles, Les Trois Frères, Le Gabillou, La Madeleine, Lascaux, Addaura, and La Pileta). (FIGURE 275)

The most interesting and well known in archeological literature are two bison-men and the so-called "sorcerer" with stag antlers from the cave of Les Trois Frères (Ariège), France. One of the two bison-men is reproduced here (fig. 275, 1). He has a bison's head with large horns and a hairy pelt with a tail. He has human legs and animal arms; he is walking or dancing in an upright position. A curious object between his mouth and right arm is perhaps a wind instrument. This bison-man is portrayed driving before him a herd of animals, a female reindeer and a bison. The thrilling hybrid figure of a man with antlered head, round eyes, a long beard, animal (lion?) paws instead of hands, the tail of a wild horse, and his sexual organ placed beneath the tail (fig. 275, 7) seems to be a more important personage than a "sorcerer," as he is called. This creature was painted separately, four meters from the floor and above an opening in the vicinity of a small rotunda ending in a well. Abbé Breuil was right to call him the "God of Les Trois Frères" (Breuil 1956: 170). The three male figures from Les Trois Frères and others from Teyjat and Le Gabillou are shown moving, probably dancing. All other figures of hybrid bison-men are standing still, although most of them are in an excited state.

One of the clues to the symbolic meaning of the bison-man at Les Trois Frères is his association with the animal herd. Was the bison-man a Master of Animals, a divine figure well known among the hunting peoples in the Americas and northern Eurasia? The wide distribution of a mythical figure with similar features suggests its prehistoric roots. Among the American Indians the Master of Animals is one of the most distinctive mythic ideas. He is a supernatural ruler whose function is to exercise stewardship over the wild animals, especially the animals hunted by men (Hultkrantz 1961: 54 ff.).

FIGURE 275

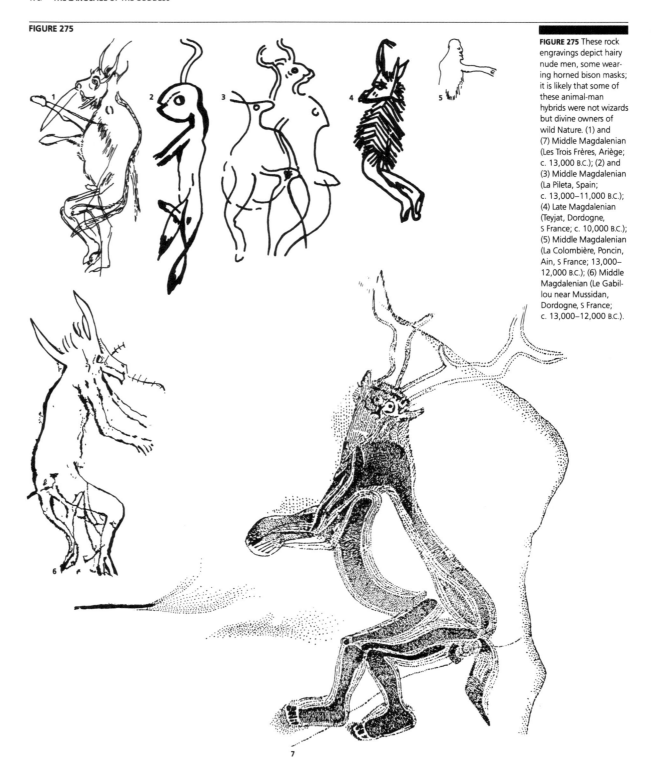

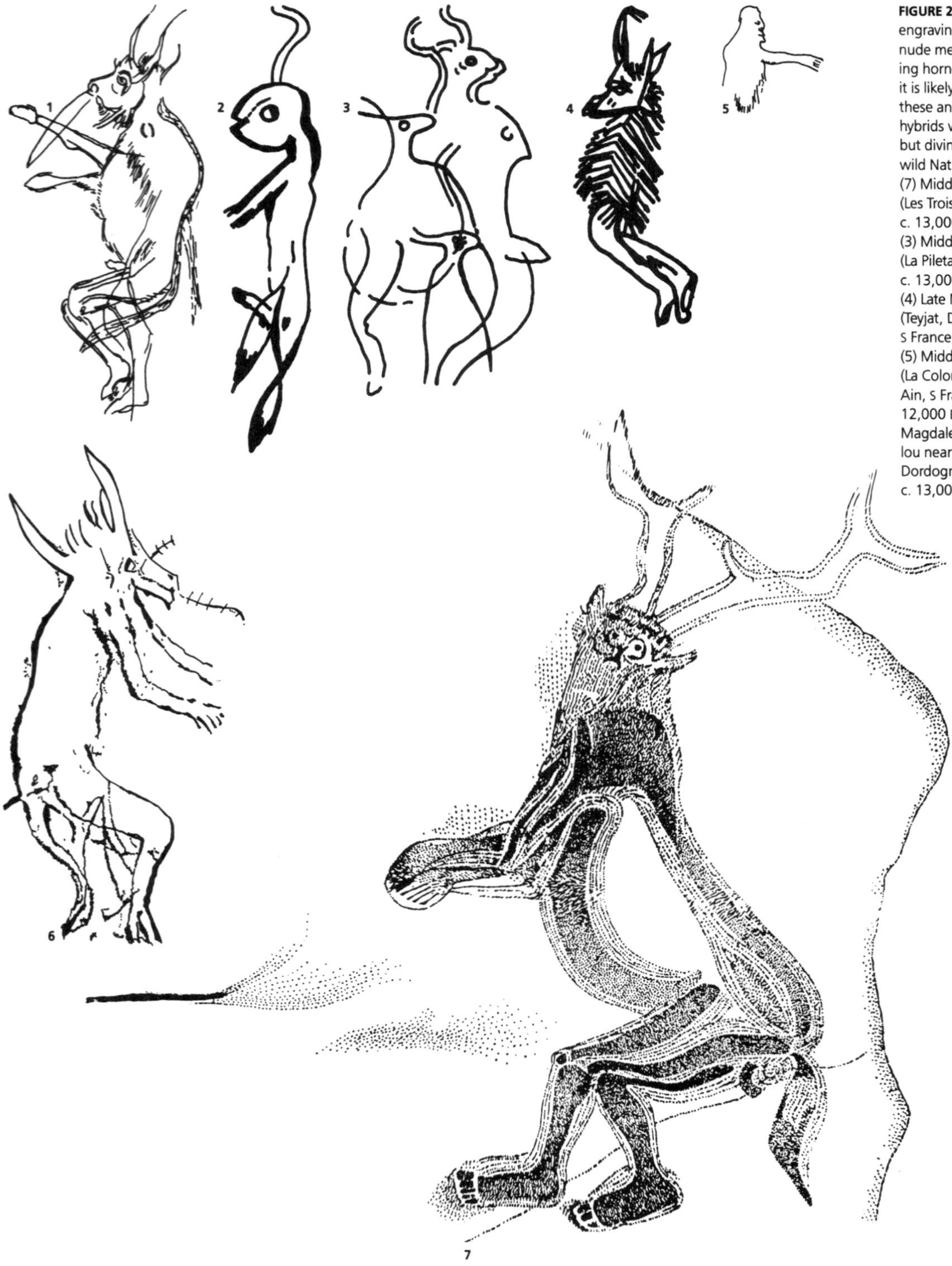

FIGURE 275 These rock engravings depict hairy nude men, some wearing horned bison masks; it is likely that some of these animal-man hybrids were not wizards but divine owners of wild Nature. (1) and (7) Middle Magdalenian (Les Trois Frères, Ariège; c. 13,000 B.C.); (2) and (3) Middle Magdalenian (La Pileta, Spain; c. 13,000–11,000 B.C.); (4) Late Magdalenian (Teyjat, Dordogne, S France; c. 10,000 B.C.); (5) Middle Magdalenian (La Colombière, Poncin, Ain, S France; 13,000–12,000 B.C.); (6) Middle Magdalenian (Le Gabillou near Mussidan, Dordogne, S France; c. 13,000–12,000 B.C.).

In Scandinavian folklore divine guardians of animals, forests, mountains, and seas are called *rå*. The name is of neuter gender and is used for both male and female owners of animals, forests, and mountains; in 10th century written records, the words *radlrod* appear, meaning "ruling power." The Lapps have the word *Radien* for "God" or "Lord," from *råda* "to rule" (Liungman 1961: 72 ff.). The original meaning of this word was probably not restricted to the ruler of animals but must have referred to a broader spectrum, such as a ruler of many aspects of wild nature. I would think that the repetitiously portrayed Paleolithic "sorcerers" or "shamans" were divine owners of animals and forests.

In the religion of the agricultural communities, the Master of Animals and Forests must have lost his distinctiveness. The Neolithic figurines do not clearly support the existence of this mythical figure, but it must be remembered that statistics of Neolithic sculptures are based on what was found within the houses, shrines, or temples, and the God of Wild Nature must have been worshipped in the wild. Nevertheless, owners, protectors, or spirits of animals, forests, and mountains are documented in Europe through time in written records and folklore. In the Greek and Roman cultures, related mythical figures are known under the names of Pan, Faunus, Silvanus, and others. Greek Pan was a mortal god of the forest. He was a shepherd and believed to be the protector of wild animals, beekeepers, and hunters. He was linked with a syrinx (Pan's pipes), a shepherd's crook, and a pine tree twig. Roman Faunus was identified with Pan, and both are related to other deities with different names: Roman Silvanus (featured with a syrinx) and Illyrian Vidassus, god of forests and pastures, identified with Silvanus (Markotić 1984). There are more than 100 recorded cult places associated with Pan's name in ancient Greece. This seems to indicate that he was popular and widely worshipped, although he was outside the pantheon of great gods and goddesses.

These beings were believed to have strange sounding voices and the ability to prophesy. Pan and Faunus caused sudden panic. These features are also characteristic of forest gods and spirits known to the folklore of the 19th and 20th centuries, for instance Russian Leshy (from *lesŭ*, "forest, wood"), the guardian of forests. Appearing in human and animal guise, he is an old man with long hair and beard, flashing green eyes and a body covered by a thick coat of hair. His stature depends on the height of the trees in the forest he inhabits; in the fields he is no taller than the grass. Usually there is only one Leshy in each wood. When he roams through the wood, a rustling of the trees accompanies him. He rocks upon the boughs, whistles, laughs, barks, lows, neighs, and leads wanderers astray, luring them into thickets and morasses. Huntsmen and shepherds make offerings to him. Hunters leave for him the first game they take; shepherds sacrifice a cow to secure his protection for their flocks (Machal 1964: 261–62).

An analogous image is recorded in Lithuanian mythology. The 16th century sources (the chronicle of Stryjkowski, 1582) mention a shepherd god Ganiklis (Lith. *ganykla*, "pasture"), Master of Forests and Animals. Bulls, horses, goats, and other animals were sacrificed to him on a large stone and the following prayer was said: "As this stone is calm and does not move, so you, our god Ganiklis, make that wolves and other beasts of prey do not move and harm our animals without your knowing" (Mannhardt 1936: 331). In Celtic legends, traces of a forest deity have also survived. In Wales he is Myrddin (the Merlin of the Medieval Romance) and in Ireland, Suibhne Geilt, or Mad Sweeny. Both were made Wild Men of the Forest, wandering in woods, befriending trees and animals, uttering prophecies, and shunning human society.

The shepherd's crook (crozier) or hook represents a further link between Greek and Roman gods (Pan, Kronos, Faunus, Silvanus) and the Neolithic and Copper Age enthroned male figures holding this symbol.

An Old European masterpiece is the Tisza figure from Szegvár-Tűzköves, southeastern Hungary, of a seated masked man holding a hook in his right hand. His thin arms, adorned with a number of bracelets, tightly press against his chest. The only indication of dress is a broad belt with zig-zag design incised around the middle of his body (Gimbutas 1974: pls. 46, 47). This image somewhat recalls the Roman god Silvanus, lord of forests and pastures, typically depicted with crozier in hand. He is also related to the pre-Greek god Kronos, whose representations show him as a majestic old man holding a curved object. The *Kronia* festival was a harvest festival (Rose 1958: 43, 68).

In the hands of the God of Vegetation, the hook is probably a symbol of renewal, not an emblem of regnant power. Its presence signified that he would awaken after the barren winter season.

Another pre-Hellenic god was Hyakinthos (eventually overshadowed by the Indo-European Apollo), whose festival, the Hyakinthia, was celebrated at Amykla in Lakonia, Peloponnese. His name is not Indo-European, having the suffix *-nth* which belongs to the language of the country's indigenous inhabitants. His cult statue depicts him as a mature bearded man (James 1961: 135). Figures of a bearded god on a bull were found in Çatal Hüyük, 7th millennium B.C. (Mellaart 1964: fig. 29). Bearded men are also known from Copper Age Old Europe — for instance, from the Cucuteni culture. (FIGURE 276) Unfortunately, only broken heads — not whole sculptures — are preserved. Similar images are evidenced in the Bronze Age. In Cyprus, a large terracotta plank-shaped idol of a bearded figure was discovered at a Middle Bronze Age site of Nicosia-Ayia Paraskevi. The figure is decorated with a painted linear motif, dots, and solid red paint (Karageorghis 1976: 116, fig. 83). Pan and Faunus also had beards.

17.2 *Participants in rituals*

Bird-masked men appear as participants in rituals. Some Upper Paleolithic representations, notably from Addaura, Monte Pellegrino at Palermo, Sicily, are clearly of ritual scenes. (FIGURE 277)

The Addaura composition presents at least twelve superbly drawn bird-masked male figures engaged in a ritual drama. Two ithyphallic men lie on the ground bound neck to ankle. Near them, five men in an ecstatic state seem to be performing a ritualistic dance. Two are shown with arms raised high, others with half-raised or lowered arms, their motion vivid. Seven figures below this dance scene are also engaged in some activity, perhaps in connection with the stag (a sacrifice?) shown next to them. One of the dancing figures in the upper part is drawn on top of the stag's head, which suggests a later date for the dancer than for the animal; thus, the contemporaneity of the men and stag is questionable. Although we shall never be certain what this scene portrays, we may conjecture that the dance around the two bound men is a spring or summer ritual, perhaps a scene of the mock sacrifice of males in an aroused state to ensure the flourishing of life forces.

FIGURE 276

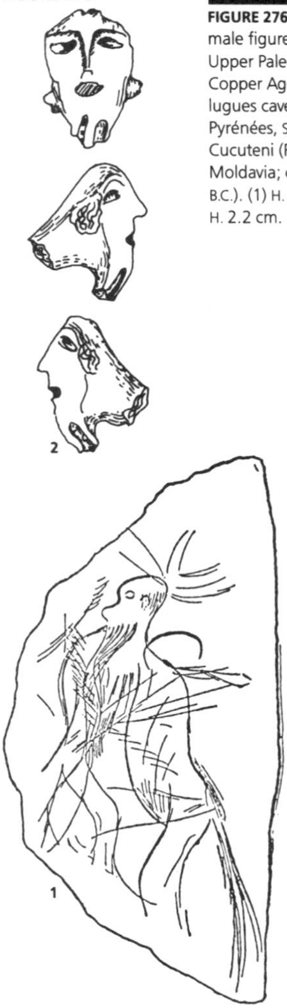

FIGURE 276 Bearded male figures from the Upper Paleolithic and Copper Age. (1) Espélugues cave, Haute-Pyrénées, S France. (2) Cucuteni (Rusheshty I, Moldavia; c. 4500–4300 B.C.). (1) H. 14.5 cm. (2) H. 2.2 cm.

Another ritual scene with the participation of a bird-masked man is known from the shaft of the cave of Lascaux, Dordogne, France, dated to c. 15,000 B.C. (Leroi-Gourhan 1967: Color illus. 74). The ithyphallic man with outspread arms (possibly bird's feet) and signs of the highest excitement is painted next to a large and vigorous bison; on his other side is a pole with a bird perching on it. A stick with a barb and a vulva of concentric ovals are shown at the hind part of the bison.

Masked ithyphallic men are encountered among Neolithic and Copper Age figurines (Gimbutas 1974: pls. 227, 229). Their postures and gestures suggest that they are participants in the ritual worship of a numinous power. Some of the ithyphallic nude figures however may represent a phallic god interchangeable with the snake, ancestral to Greek Hermes, discussed above (section 14).

17.3 *Fertility daimones*

Some of the portrayals of ithyphallic, youthful, strong men, as well as bull-men and goat-men, dating from the 5th millennium B.C. in the Balkans (see fig. 221), are very likely the antecedents of the Satyrs, Sileni, Kouroi or Kouretes (the projections of marriageable youths), centaurs, and the young Dionysos of Greek mythology. They are fertility daimones whose function is to magically help the Earth Maiden rise from underground at spring, or to stimulate life powers in general, particularly the growth of plants. In Greek vase painting from the Proto-Geometric to Archaic periods, Satyrs and centaurs — creatures having a human male head and sometimes torso, and goat or horse body — are

FIGURE 277

FIGURE 277 Bird-masked males performing rituals. (1) Two engraved figures from the cave of Altamira, N Spain; Magdalenian, probably 13,000–11,000 B.C. Scale 1/8 to 1/12. (2) Ritual scene deeply incised in rock. Gravettian or Epipaleolithic (Grotta dell'Addaura, Monte Pellegrino, Palermo, Sicily) (1) H. approx. 116 cm. (2) H. of detail 96.7 cm.

portrayed in association with plants and water symbols, net-patterned panels, and M's. (FIGURE 278) They either hold branches in their hands or flank life trees or life columns, as do he-goats in many Copper and Bronze Age representations.

The centaurs of the Vinča culture are bull-men wearing a large human mask marked with an M sign. (FIGURE 279) In front, on the chest, there is a tri-line or a life column. (FIGURE 280) The huge front legs are marked either with snakes or uterus forms. Some of the horned masked sculptures from the same culture may represent goat-men (the name *centaur* comes from *centron*, "goat"), which suggests that the early form of half-man/half-animal images was a goat-man. The grafting of male beast to male human doubled the strength and influence of fecundity and regeneration.

Bull-men with human masks, sometimes bearded and horned, are known from Crete and Cyprus, found in the Ayia Triada and Enkomi sanctuaries of the 11th century B.C. In the sanctuary of Ayia Irini in Cyprus, which belongs to the archaic period, centaurs have been found in association with the bronze statue of a horned god (Dionysus?) and large numbers of terracotta bull figurines (Karageorghis 1965).

Orgiastic winter and spring festivals dramatizing the seasonal sequence of death and rebirth in nature, a sequence critically important to agrarian peoples, is attested to in Old European cultures by phalli, phallic stemmed cups, and ithyphallic figurines of masked men. The importance of the seasonal sequence continues undiminished in the Post-Neolithic. This long-lasting tradition remained vigorous in ancient Greece in such orgiastic winter and spring festivals as the Anthesteria, the Lenaia, and the Greater Dionysia.

The image of centaurs still lingers in Greek folklore. Now called Callicantzari, they are usually black (the color of fertility) and covered with a coat of shaggy hair. Their faces are black and their eyes have a red glare; they have the ears of a goat. They are neither wholly anthropomorphic nor wholly theriomorphic, but

FIGURE 278

FIGURE 278 Illustration from the neck of a large pithos found in a cemetery shows the centaur holding up a life-tree next to a net-patterned column. Note the similarity to representations of he-goats (see figs. 365–69). Sub-Geometric (Kameiros, Rhodos; c. 700 B.C.)

FIGURE 279

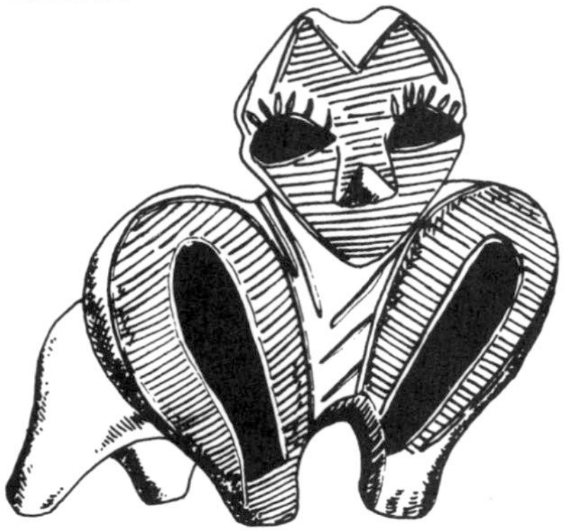

FIGURE 279 From an earlier age, these terracotta Vinča centaurs are masked bull-men. They are incised with an M at the forehead, a tri-line on the chest, and uteri over the forelegs. Painted red and black. (Valač, near Kosovska Mitrovica, S Yugoslavia; c. 5000–4500 B.C.) H. 11.7 cm.

FIGURE 280

FIGURE 280 The centaur is here portrayed as a terracotta goat-man wearing a mask whose horns have broken off. There is a red-painted chevron on his chest. Vinča (Valač, near Kosovska Mitrovica, S Yugoslavia; c. 5000–4500 B.C.) L. 12.3 cm.

a blend of the two. Clay statuettes of centaurs and Satyrs of the Classical Greek period, now in the National Museum in Athens, were identified by peasants as Callicantzari (Lawson 1964: 190–92).

Phallic cult articles are discussed in section 20, below. They do not represent a male god but rather a vivifying and fructifying force of nature appearing as an aspect of life column symbolism; or they are fused with the divine feminine body and subsumed to the power of the Goddess. (For more on phalli, see my earlier work, Gimbutas 1974: pls. 219–226.)

17.4 *The Year God: a strong and dying vegetation god*

There are two types of enthroned male figures: one youthful and strong with an erect phallus, the other ancient and peaceful. Both types probably belong to the series of a Year God. The first, brimming with virility, represents the revival of nature, the second symbolizes dying nature. The enthronment of both types of male figures speaks for their important role in cult.

Only a few sculptures of the first type are known. The most impressive example is a large one (49 cm high) from the Late Neolithic culture of northern Greece, discovered in the region of Larisa. (FIGURE 281) A nude and vigorous male with an erect phallus is shown in a seated posture. His right arm is lifted and with the left hand he holds his phallus. He wears a necklace with pendant beads. Above his genitals, an arc is incised with parallel lines inside.

The other type of male figurine, the peaceful ancient with signs of worry on his face or mask (if the head is preserved) is a probable vegetation god of mature age. The earliest sculptures of this type date from the end of the 7th and early 6th millennium B.C., from the Sesklo culture of Thessaly. (FIGURE 282) This god is portrayed seated on a stool or throne, hands on knees, and legs fused with the front legs of the stool.

FIGURE 281

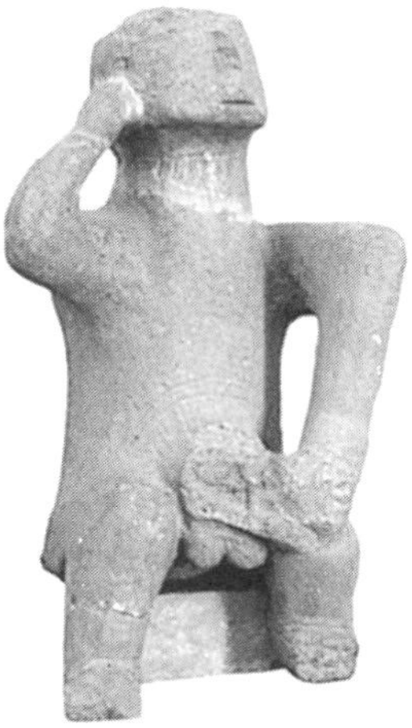

FIGURE 281 Vigorous ithyphallic figure of a seated man with right hand at the cheek and left hand holding phallus; a Year God symbolizing revival of nature (?). Presumed to belong to Dimini culture (found near Larisa, N Greece; (1st half of 5th mill. B.C.). H. 49 cm.

FIGURE 282

a

b

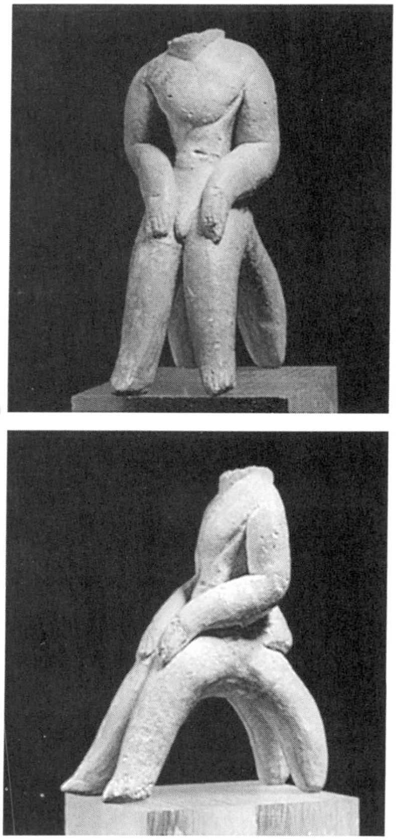

FIGURE 282 This enthroned male god is an example of the "Sorrowful Ancient" vegetation god of Old European tradition. Painted in red on the back and front. Sesklo (Pyrasos, near Volos, Thessaly; c. 5900–5700 B.C.) H. 7 cm.

At Çatal Hüyük, a white marble sculpture of a male god seated on a stool with hands on knees was found in the Vulture Shrine VI.A.25 (Melaart 1967: pl. 84)—an obvious association with the aspect of death.

To this series of unquestionably male figurines from Thessaly belongs a little sculpture of an androgyne: a seated nude male in the same posture as the others, but with female breasts. (FIGURE 283) Do we see here an Old Hag and a dying Vegetation God in one?

A thousand years later, these two deities appear as a pair, female and male together but differentiated, in two sculptures of the Hamangia culture on the Black Sea, Romania. (FIGURE 284) This figurine of the "Sorrowful God" from the Cernavoda cemetery (c. 5000 B.C.) is seated in an appropriately doleful pose. Elbows on knees, he supports his masked head in his bent arms. His companion is a seated female, also masked and marked with a large pubic triangle, her arms resting on the knee of a drawn-up leg. This remarkable pair was obviously rendered by the same masterful hand; they represent a unique instance of a divine couple in the archeological record of Old Europe. One of many possibilities is that they represent a male and a female deity with similar functions: the Old Hag (the aged aspect of the Earth Fertility Goddess) and the Dying God.

The dying god has descendants in ancient Greece and in European folk beliefs and customs, in the flax- or corn-god who is born out of the earth in the form of flax or corn and whom we find tortured, dying, and resurrected out of the earth. This god is known by the names *Linos* in Greek, *Vaižgantas* in Lithuanian, *Barleycorn* in Scottish, and others. It is not so much the image of the god but his torture, death, and lament in annual ceremonies that are preserved in texts from Homer and Hesiod to modern folklore (for a detailed study see Eisler 1951). The "Linos dirge" or "Linodia" is first mentioned by Homer in the *Iliad* in the description of the "Shield of Achilles" (*Iliad*, XVIII: 569 ff.). In the midst of the harvesting and dancing scene a boy plays a lyre and sings "Lovely Linos" (*kalòs Línos*) with a delicately modulated voice. A related harvesting and dancing scene in visual art can be recognized on a black steatite vase from Aghia Triada, 14th century B.C., portraying a dance of harvesters carrying stalks of corn and shaking sistra. Hesiod, in the middle of the 7th century B.C., speaks of Linodia, telling us that all singers and lyre players recite the Linos song at banquets and dances. Other sources mentioning the lament of Linos (*oi tò Línon*) are Pamphos, a pre-Homeric poet, and Sappho, c. 600 B.C., as noted by Pausanias (9,27,2). Aeschylus, Sophocles, and Euripides also speak of "Ai Linon," translatable to "Doom-Linos" or "woe-Linos." Murr in 1890 (Eisler 1951: 118) was the first to explain Linos and the Linos dirge as a personification of plants comparable to Hyakinthos, Narkissos, and other vegetation spirits whose "premature" death was lamented in annual ceremonies similar to the mourning of Adonis and the wilting of his potted gardens.

There is a common word for flax in European languages: Greek *linon*, Latin *linum*, Old Irish *lin*, Old German *lin*, Gothic *lein*, Lithuanian *linas*, Old Slavic *linu*, Albanian *l'ini*. The presence of the word among the European Indo-European languages suggests the European roots, i.e. the European substratum language. This would harmonize very well with the fact that flax fibers in Old Europe and Old Anatolia are known from early Neolithic times (Barber 1988). Fragments of linen cloth preserved at Çatal Hüyük are dated from the 8th millennium B.C.

17.5 *Passion of the flax and the dying god*

The "passion of the flax" is a widely spread motif in European folklore and is best known from Hans Christian Andersen's children's story (1843) telling the sad experiences of the flax: how the seed is buried in the dark earth, thence to raise its head and penetrate to the light of the sun; how its blue flower has to withstand the sun's heat and lashing by the sweeping rain, until one day wicked people come and pull the poor plant, root and all, out of the ground by its hair. Then they torture it by drowning in water, roasting over a fire, beating with sticks, breaking and dressing it, heckling and combing it with hackle-combs and thorns, spinning it to thread, weaving it into linen, cutting it, piercing it with needles, sewing it into shirts which are worn till they are rags, drowned and pulped and calendered and dried into the paper upon which its story is written. Before the paper-making motif was introduced, the suffering of the flax ended in shirt making. The flax had to be pulled, rippled, retted, swung, spun, woven, bleached, and then sewn into a shirt. In a Danish version, a fairy tale of the type of "The Grateful Dead," a troll who wants to enter a house is told "You may come in, but you will have to suffer the Rye's Pain (*Rugen's Pine*)." He asks, "What is the *Rugen's Pine*?" and is told, "In the autumn you will be sown, deeply buried in earth; in the spring you will rise; in the summer you will be parched in the sun, drenched in the rain, then cut and dried, carted to the barn and threshed; yes, and carted to the mill and ground." "What?" "Yes, ground, sieved and bagged." When he hears this the troll explodes and breaks up into flints (Eisler 1951: 123).

The association of the flax god with the dead is clear from the description of a Lithuanian autumn festival called *Ilges*, in honor of the flax-god Vaižgantas, during which he is offered *sikes*, the food of the dead (Greimas 1979: 62). *Sikes* are prepared from flax seeds.

The European flax- or corn-god has a close relative in the Near Eastern corn-god Tammuz known from cuneiform tablets. In the text found at Ras Shamra, in the ancient Phoenician city of Ugarit, the Death Goddess Anat kills the corn-god, called *Mot*, "Death":

Seized Mot, the divine son.
With a cutting blade (bhrb) *she cuts him,*
With the winnowing sieve (bhsr) *she winnows him,*
With fire she roasts him,
With the mill (stone) she breaks him,
In the fields she scatters his flesh,
For the birds to eat.
(Cited by Eisler, 1951: 123)

In folk art, a "sorrowful Christ" is a well-known figure in central and northern Catholic Europe. This is particularly true for Lithuania, where thousands of "worrying Christs" have been carved in wood and preserved to this day. This image is neither Christian nor Indo-European but a continuing Old European stereotype. In this forested part of Europe, wood-carving traditions persisted for millennia in portrayals of the dying God, originally the Spirit of Vegetation. It was an image which even traumatic upheavals in religious thought were unable to uproot; it survived in the dying Christ. In present folk belief, he is the "sorrowful God" who worries over the tragedies of mankind.

FIGURE 283

FIGURE 283 A very interesting light is shed on the Sorrowful Ancient stereotype by this hermaphroditic figure. As in other entirely masculine images, she/he sits on a stool with hands on knees, with female breasts and male genitalia. Sesklo (Magula no. 94, near Larisa, Thessaly; 6000–5700 B.C.) H. approx. 7 cm.

FIGURE 284 A remarkable pair of polished brown figurines. The masked male god (left) sits in a pensive posture and has been dubbed "The Thinker." Hamangia (Cernavoda, Black Sea, Romania; c. 5000 B.C.) H. (male) 11.5 cm.; (female) 11.3 cm.

FIGURE 284

III

DEATH AND REGENERATION

Although our theme is death and regeneration, there is much more emphasis on regeneration than death in iconography. This reflects the belief that out of every death new life grows.

The Goddess of Death and Regeneration is also the Bird Goddess, the nocturnal aspect of the Life-giver. However, she can appear in countless epiphanies. As death she is a bird of prey—vulture, owl, raven, crow, hawk; or she is an animal—boar or dog. But at the same time these symbols of death have powers of regeneration. The symbol closest to death is a bare bone. Stiff nudes as images of death were the color of bone, made of marble, alabaster, and bone itself. And yet they were shown with supernatural pubic triangles or round owl eyes like suns, impregnated with life-creating moisture. As the promoter of the beginning of the life cycle, the Goddess appears as a tiny mysterious fetus or uteruslike animal—the frog or toad, lizard, turtle, hare or hedgehog, and fish. The bucranium (skull of the bull) is also a symbol of the uterus, an amazing Old European/Old Anatolian creation derived from the observation of the similarity between the horned head of a bull and a woman's uterus and fallopian tubes. The connection with new life is made in the form of a bee or butterfly emerging from the bucranium.

Caves and tombs are interchangeable with womb, egg, and uterus symbolism. Columns of life, trees, snakes, and phalli as embodiments of the life force rise from the Goddess's womb, cave, or tomb. The Goddess herself rises from the deep in the elemental shape of a triangle or an hourglass (two triangles). The bird's feet attached to hourglass forms reveal her identity.

Butmir ceramic vase with typical life column, fish, and triangles. See figure 352, page 229.

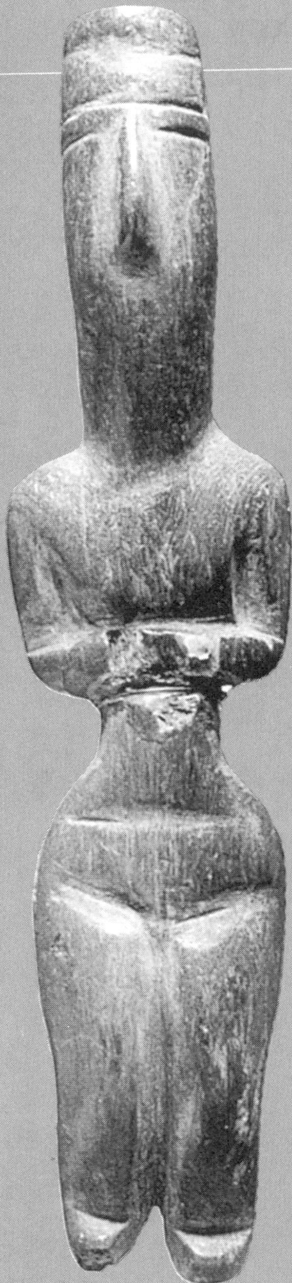

Stiff Nude of carved bone; from Sardinia. See figure 316, page 201.

18/ *Symbols of Death*

The principal images of death that can be detected in prehistory and which still play a part in folk beliefs are the vulture, owl, cuckoo/hawk, dove, boar, the White Lady and her hound, and the dry bone.

18.1 *Vulture*

A direct connection between the vulture and death can be seen in the paintings on shrine walls at Çatal Hüyük. The earliest such representation is on the east wall of a shrine in Level VIII, 8, in which large vultures attack an apparently lifeless human with extended arms. (FIGURE 285) In the "Vulture Shrine" on Level VII, 8, seven vultures are depicted swooping down on six headless humans. In yet another shrine on Level VII, 21, a huge vulture with human legs stands beside a decapitated human. (FIGURE 286)

The bird is identified as the griffon, or Old World vulture, *Gyps fulvus*. Completely black, it is a very impressive bird, especially in flight with its nine-foot wingspan; however, it is entirely nonaggressive and feeds exclusively on carrion (Turner 1973; Cameron 1981). It is this trait which is responsible for the griffon-vulture's special association with death.

The human legs of the vulture in the Level VII, 21 shrine imply that it is not simply a bird but rather the Goddess in the guise of a vulture. She is Death—She Who Takes Away Life, maleficent twin of She Who Gives Life—ominous in flight on great, outspread wings. Despite the incarnate presence of Death, the vulture scenes of Çatal Hüyük do not convey death's mournful triumph over life. Rather, they symbolize that death and resurrection are inseparably linked.

This philosophical concept is symbolically expressed in many ways. The headless corpses are shown with extended legs and arms. Significantly, the vultures are not black but red, the color of life (Mellaart 1964: 64). The vulture fresco in Shrine VII, 21 is immediately adjacent to one which features a huge bull's head, symbolic of the vital life force, below which rests a human skull. Here is direct assurance that resurrection follows death. At the fateful moment, the Vulture Goddess "snatches the soul," but the head from the fresco's decapitated body is carefully placed in contact with the regenerative bull.

The relation of the Vulture Goddess to the life force is dramatically revealed by structural details in Shrine VI B, 10. On the eastern wall between a large bull's head and one of the supporting posts, a pair of human breasts above a red niche is modeled in relief and painted red. Griffon-vulture beaks emerge from the open nipples. A complete vulture skull was found inside each breast (Mellaart 1976: pl. 28, figs. 38, 39).

We recognize here that the breasts are a component of the Bird Goddess in her Vulture aspect, as the breasts in French megalithic gallery graves are a component feature of the Owl Goddess. This discovery provides a cross-confirmation of the motherly personality of the Deity. We might add that the picture of a vulture in Egyptian hieroglyphics stands for "mother"; further, among Siberian Yakuts, the word for "vulture" equals "mother." Pliny the Elder (1st century A.D.) tells us that vulture feathers help birth-giving.

The sacrifice of vultures or the offering of their wings is an old tradition. At Ksar Akil, Lebanon, vulture bones appear throughout the sequence from Mid-Paleolithic to Epipaleolithic (Hooijer 1961: 9–11). Avian remains have been found in the Upper Paleolithic Magdalenian deposits of France and in the cave of Adaouste Bouches-du-Rhône. At Isturitz, Pyrénées atlantiques, wings of the Alpine chough (related to the jackdaw and the jay) were similarly deposited (Solecki 1981, based on Bouchud 1953). Possible representations of vultures or other birds with large wings are known from Upper Paleolithic caves (Castillo, Gabillou, Pileta, and others). (FIGURE 287)

A burial of the head and neck of a large bird was found in the Siberian Upper Paleolithic site of Mal'ta on the River Belaja northwest of Irkutsk, dated to approximately 16,000–13,000 B.C. This site also yielded a number of ivory and reindeer figurines of Stiff Nudes, portraying the Goddess in her Death aspect, and ivory figurines of birds or bird-women hybrids (fig. 1). This association does not seem to be accidental.

FIGURE 285

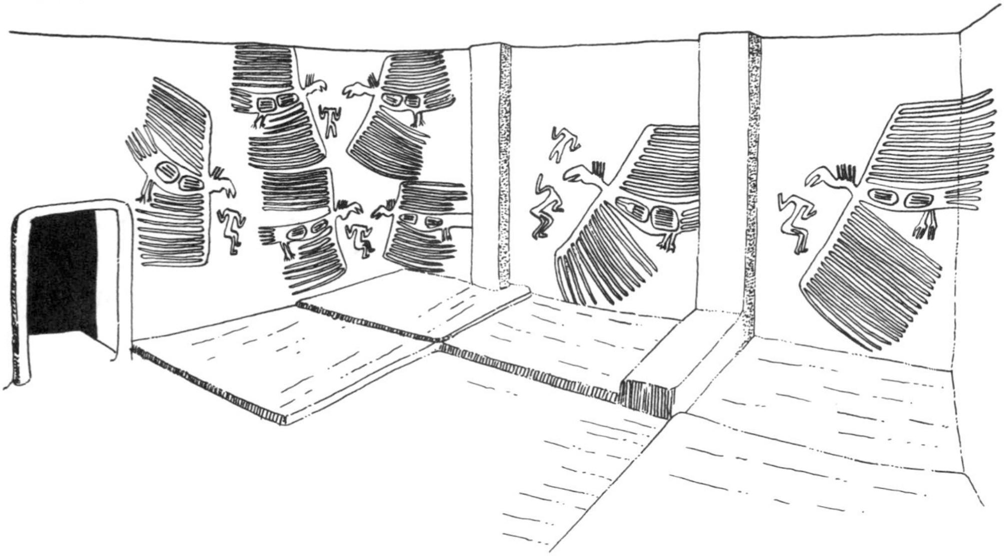

FIGURE 285 Vultures with wings like brooms swoop down on headless corpses. Significantly, the birds are not black but red, the color of life. W Anatolian Neolithic (Çatal Hüyük; fresco of shrine Level VII, 8; early 7th mill. B.C.)

FIGURE 286

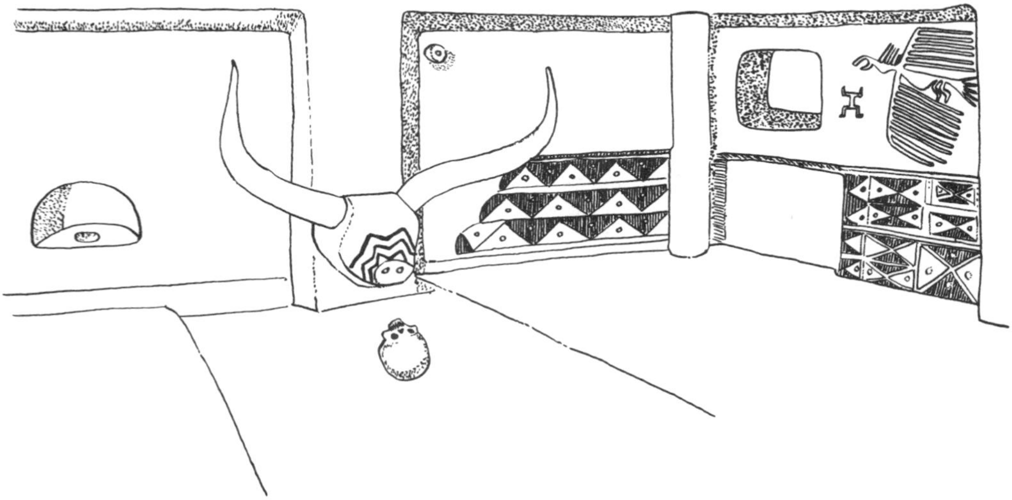

FIGURE 286 Vulture with gaping maw and human legs overshadows a decapitated figure. Nearby, a skull (from the headless corpse?) rests below a large bull's head, symbol of regeneration. (Çatal Hüyük shrine in Level VII, 21; early 7th mill. B.C.)

A very interesting deposit of large bird bones was discovered at the Proto-Neolithic site of Zawi Chemi Shanidar in northern Iraq, dated by radiocarbon analysis to 10,870 ± 300 B.P. (Solecki 1981). It included a minimum of seventeen birds of five species: four bearded vultures (*Gyptaeus barbatus*), one griffon vulture (*Gyps fulvus*), seven white-tailed sea eagles (*Haliaetus albicilla*), one great bustard (*Otis tarda*), and four small eagles. All except the bustard are carrion feeders. It is significant that 90 percent of the bird bones are wings. Slice marks indicate that they were carefully cut from the body and carefully deposited in a heap. Excavations in 1987 at Nemrik on the river Tigris, northern Iraq, by Warsaw University yielded stone sculptures of vulture heads, dated also to approximately 10,000 years ago (*Daily Gulf Times*, Nov. 18, 1987, Qatar, Doha).

Large birds were also buried in the megalithic tombs of western Europe. Recent excavations have uncovered a large deposit in a chambered tomb at Isbister in Orkney. In all there are 725 identifiable bird bones, most of which were shown to belong to the period of the tomb's use. By far the greatest number of bones (88 percent) come from the white-tailed eagle (*Haliaetus albicilla*), representing fourteen or more individual birds. Others were from short-eared owls, great black-backed gulls, rooks or crows, and ravens (Hedges 1983; see the description of bird remains by Branwell). All of these birds feed on carrion.

The fact that all parts of the skeleton are present suggests that the bird remains were deposited as complete carcasses. Their burial, similar to that of the large birds mentioned above, was very likely sacrificial. It must have been an offering to the Goddess of Death, who in the Scottish islands manifested herself not as a vulture (there are no vultures in Scotland) but as other large birds with awe-inspiring wingspreads—in Isbister's case, as an eagle, great gull, owl, crow, and raven.

It is clear that for millennia, large wings had enormous symbolic importance. The vulture wings of Çatal Hüyük have a supernatural appearance; they resemble rectangular brooms rather than actual wings, which are curved differently. The broom or brush sign repeatedly marks the vultures bodies; perhaps it denotes the energy and power of the Death Goddess, as does the witch's broom of European folklore (on the brush as an energy sign see Part IV, section 26.3).

The transformation of the Goddess into a vulture is well known from Egypt and Greece. The Egyptian Neith was sometimes depicted in vulture form, and the Goddess Mut wears a vulture's head; in *The Odyssey*, Athena once changes into a vulture. One of the names of the Celtic Triple Goddess in Ireland was *Badb*, which means "crow," and the Morrígan (seemingly a generic term) is described in one text as *an badb catha*, the battle crow. The same Morrígan can appear as a hag, a beautiful woman, or a crow or raven. (The names of the goddesses appear in the cycle *Tuatha Dé Dannan*, "People of the Goddess Danu," referring to a race inhabiting Ireland before the arrival of the Milesians.) In Gaul, a related goddess has another name, Nantotsuelta, "winding river," represented in reliefs with her raven and dovecote symbols (Ross: 219, 244). The Germanic Valkyrie is identified with the raven, the dark bird of the dead, which is called *waelceasig*, "corpse-choosing," a term which exactly accords with *waelcyrge* or Valkyrie (Ninck 1967: 183).

In their bird-of-prey/woman form, the ancient Greek Sirens and Harpies—also known as the Keres (Fates) of Death—must have descended from the Old European/Anatolian Vulture Goddess (or some other Bird of Prey Goddess). The Siren is endowed with the power to lure by her song; in the Harpy, the ravening, snatching nature of a carrion eater is emphasized. They have human heads but vulture's feet, and as both Fates and birds they appear in threes or in flocks. In Hellenistic and even medieval times they are portrayed as women with bird's feet

FIGURE 287

FIGURE 287 Interest in the vulture goes back to the Upper Paleolithic, as shown by these possible representations of vultures or other birds with enormous wings, painted and engraved on the walls of caves. (1) Red painted. Magdalenian (Castillo, N Spain; more exact chronology unknown); (2) Associated with geometric signs. Middle Magdalenian (Pileta, S Spain; c. 13,000–11,000 B.C.) L. of vultures approx. 50 cm.

and are an image of obsession, nightmare, and daydream (the terror of the midday sleep in a sun-smitten land).

In Harrison's definition, the bird-woman became a death demon, a soul sent to fetch a soul, a *Ker* that lures the soul. The Siren's song is seductive; the end of her song is death. Horror, Harrison says, is kept in the background, seduction to the fore (Harrison 1922: 198–99).

In the Basque country of northern Spain, a main repository of Old European beliefs, Mari or the Lady of Amboto (Goddess of the Mountain) appears in some caves as a vulture. (In others she is a crow or a woman with the feet of a bird.) She and her female companions appear as vultures in the great cave of Supelegor in the mountain of Itzine. According to the account recorded by Manuel de Ugarriza of Orozco in 1922, the female companions of the Goddess — the vultures — act as her representatives and do her bidding. This also illustrates that as late as 1922, the Goddess was still feared:

A shepherd constructed his hut near the cave. Fearing the nearness of the dwelling place of the Goddess, he fixed crosses and blessed candles on either side of the mouth of the cave. But then a flock of vultures came, and alighting on the roof of his hut, told him that he was to take the blessed objects away from the cave. They continued to insist until the shepherd, fearing some act of vengeance, gave in to their demands. (Barandiarán 1974, I: 290; quoted in English by Frank and Metzger MS 1982)

The cinereous vulture does not inhabit territory farther north than southern Europe, and so its symbolic association with death is assumed in the iconography of prehistoric Europe and European folklore by the owl, as discussed below.

18.2 *Owl*

From prehistoric times to the present day the owl has been considered a harbinger of death. A still-held belief in many European countries is that a family member will die if an owl alights on the roof of the house or on a nearby tree. The owl was the hieroglyph of death for the Egyptians. In Pliny's time (1st century A.D.) it was believed that the appearance of an owl in a city signified destruction. To many writers of later times, the owl was ominous, ugly, miserable, hated by all other birds. To Chaucer the owl was the portent of death and Spencer called the bird "death's dreadfull messengere whom men abhorre and hate" (Rowland 1978: 119). In spite of the gloomy aura which surrounds it, the owl has also been endowed with certain positive qualities. It is credited with profound wisdom, oracular powers, and the ability to avert evil. Its eyes are regarded as having sacred power because it seems to surpass all other creatures in visual acuity. This ambivalent image is a dim reflection, diffused through time, of the owl as an incarnate manifestation of the fearsome Goddess of Death. She was revered as a divinity and perhaps respected for her grim but necessary part in the cycle of existence.

As an artistic image, the owl has a long history. In fact, the earliest representation of a bird identifiable by species is that of snowy owls engraved in the gallery of an Upper Paleolithic cave at Trois Frères, southern France. (FIGURE 288) The Goddess in the guise of an owl is an image prominent from the Neolithic through the Early Bronze Age. In the East Mediterranean, the anthropomorphized owl is portrayed in stone and clay as early as the Pre-pottery Neolithic B, the end of the 8th and the first half of the 7th millennium B.C. (FIGURE 289) She is present in the form of urns in Danubian Europe, the northern Aegean, and western Anatolia in the 4th and 3rd millennia B.C.; in western Europe, her image is engraved on statue menhirs, on the orthostats of passage and gallery graves, and on schist plaques and bone phalanges laid in graves (see figs. 91–93). In northern Europe, her owlish features are recognizable on amber figurines and wooden posts from the East Baltic Narva culture, 4th millennium B.C. (FIGURE 290) As a bird identified with the Goddess, she survives in representations of Athena in Greek art.

In Mycenaean Greece, this goddess is represented in gold sculptures found in tholos tombs (Kakovatos, Pylos) and in shaft graves (Peristeria) of the 15th century B.C. (Marinatos 1968: pl. 58). The Owl Goddess is also richly represented in terracotta figurines in the Cypriot Bronze Age of the 14th and 13th centuries B.C. She is portrayed with a beaked nose, large round eyes, gigantic earlobes with ringed earrings, and a huge pubic triangle (Spiteris 1970: 69). In Mesopotamia she is known as Lilith, whose name means "screech owl."

Beautiful examples of owl-shaped burial urns dating from c. 3000 B.C. come from the Baden culture in Hungary, from Poliochni on the island of Lemnos, and from Troy. (FIGURES 291, 292) They have wings, the characteristic owl beak connecting arched brows, and sometimes a human vulva or a snakelike umbilical cord, symbols of regeneration. The tradition of urn burial and the shape of the urn persisted in east-central Europe even after Indo-Europeanization, apparently carried on by the substratum population. (FIGURE 293)

FIGURE 288

FIGURE 288 These three snowy owls are engraved in the portion of an Upper Paleolithic cave known as the "Gallery of Owls." Middle Magdalenian (Les Trois Frères, Ariège, S France; 13,000 B.C.)

FIGURE 289

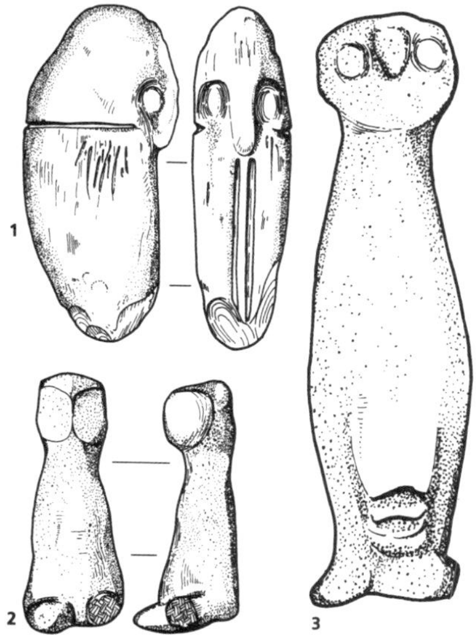

FIGURE 289 These Prepottery Neolithic B (1) stone statue and (2) and (3) clay figurines from the Near East were apparently made in the likeness of the Owl Goddess. ((1) and (2) Mureybet III, upper Euphrates, Syria; 8000–7500 B.C. (3) Munhata 6–3, Jordan; 7000–6500 B.C.). (1) H. 8.3 cm. (2) H. 6.2 cm. (3) H. 9.2 cm.

FIGURE 290

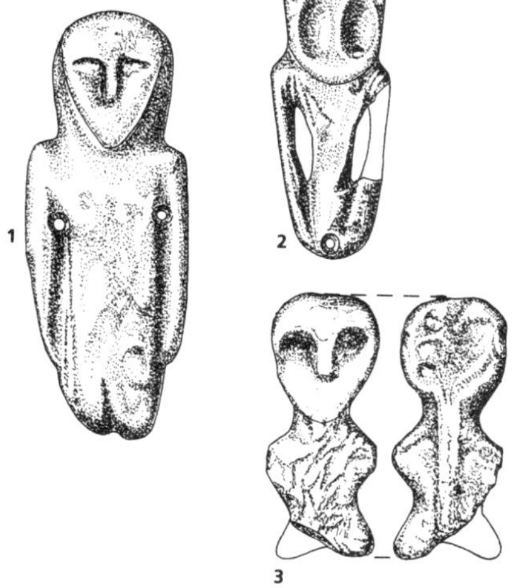

FIGURE 290 These schematized anthropomorphic figurines carved in amber with facial features resembling an owl's are probably amulets in imitation of the Owl Goddess. Two (1, 2) have perforations, perhaps for attachment to another object; the third (3) has hair, perhaps braids, indicated on the back. Narva culture (Juodkrantė, Kuršių nerija-Courish lagoon at the Baltic Sea, W Lithuania; c. end of 4th mill. B.C.) (1) H. 11 cm. (2) H. 7 cm. (3) H. 6.8 cm.

FIGURE 291

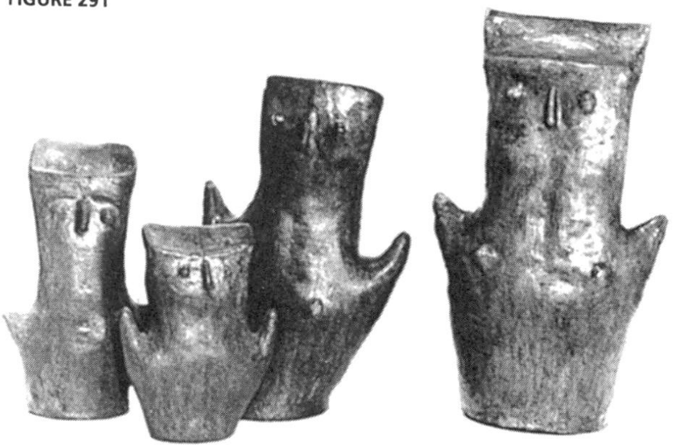

FIGURE 292

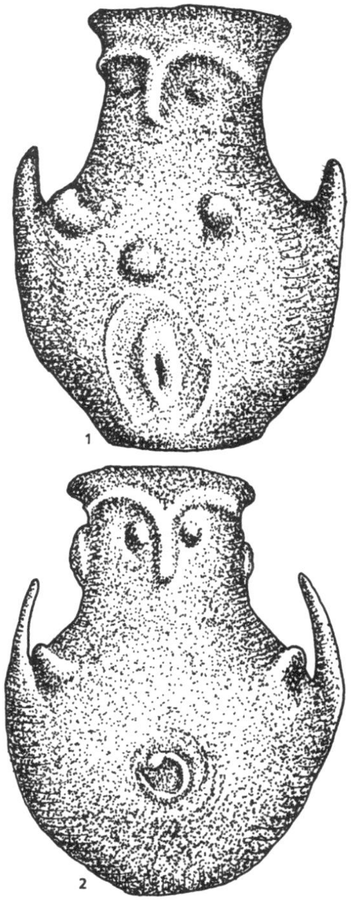

FIGURE 291 Owl-shaped urns containing cremated remains of an adult (mother?) and children. Baden culture (Center, NE Hungary; c. 3000 B.C.) H. largest 48.4 cm.

FIGURE 292 Striking owl-shaped burial urns are a tradition throughout Europe and Anatolia. They have the universal Owl Goddess face and breasts; regeneration is emphasized by large vulvas or serpentine umbilical cords. N Aegean/W Anatolian Early Bronze Age ((1) "Green Phase" of Poliochni, town on Lemnos; c. 3000–2500 B.C. (2) Troy II–III; 3000–2500 B.C.). (1) H. 24.3 cm. (2) H. 23.1 cm.

The characteristic features of the owl—round eyes and beak—can be seen on the statue menhirs of southern France and Iberia, and in reliefs and charcoal drawings in the hypogea of the Parisian basin. (FIGURES 294, 295) The stereotype varies only slightly in style from region to region and from phase to phase: it is schematized as a T shape or has only eyes and brows, or a square head among chevrons in the center of the forehead.

A series of stelae and drawings of the Owl Goddess from Brittany and the Paris basin are depicted with breasts and one or more necklaces. Stelae from Portugal and Spain (usually only 40–50 cm high) have round eyes and a pronounced beak or a straight, sticklike nose. (FIGURES 296, 297) The images of the Owl Goddess on schist plaques in the passage graves of Portugal have a prominent nose or beak, schematized arms, horizontal lines across the cheeks, occasional indications of a vulva, and a chevron design on the back. Occasionally total abstractions of this goddess appear engraved on megalithic tomb walls. For instance, at Locmariaquer, Brittany, the body of the Owl Goddess is no more than a large oval vulva. Only the round eyes and beak betray her identity. (FIGURE 298)

The Goddess's owl face on a very fine sculpture discovered at Knowth West, Ireland, is immersed in a labyrinthine design probably symbolic of life-giving waters, in the center of which is a vulva. (FIGURE 299) This image resembles Vinča figurines from the other side of Europe, with wings and owl mask, marked with a labyrinthine design. (FIGURE 300)

FIGURE 293

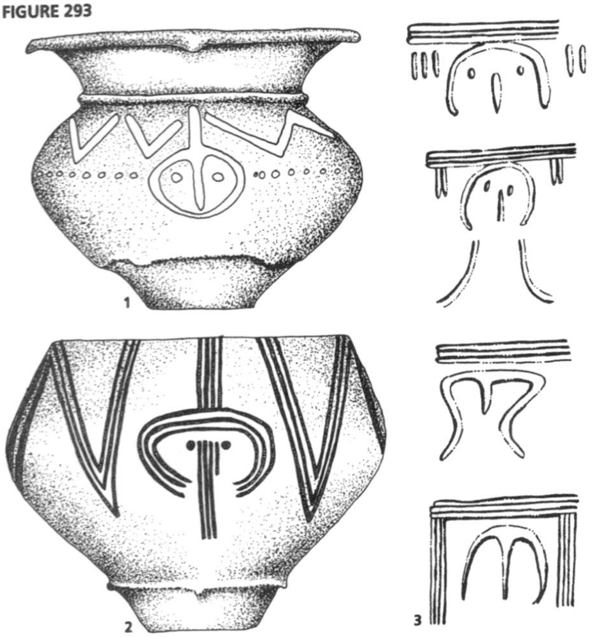

FIGURE 293 The tradition of urn burial and its association with the Owl Goddess survived Indo-Europeanization in some parts of Bronze Age Europe. So apparently did the symbolic meaning of the V and chevron. (1) and (2) Monteoru culture (Cindeşti, Vrancea district, NE Romania; 1800–1500 B.C.). (3) Schematic owl faces on other vases of the Monteoru culture, Romania. (1) H. 19.5 cm. (2) H. 20.5 cm.

FIGURE 294

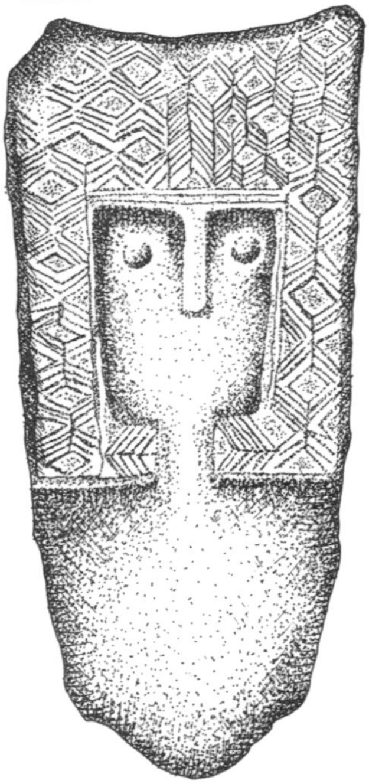

FIGURE 294 The Owl Goddess of western Europe appears in many variations on an unwavering theme; on this stone stele her face is surrounded by a squared-off border of opposed chevrons. Late Neolithic of Provence, Final Chasséan culture (Lauris-Puyvert, Bouches-de-Rhône, S France; c. end of 4th mill. B.C.) H. 30.1 cm.

FIGURE 295

FIGURE 295 This drawing in charcoal is from the left wall of the antechamber to a Paris basin hypogeum. In a common convention, the Owl Goddess wears a necklace over her knoblike breasts. Shafted axes were drawn on both sides of the entrance to the main chamber. Final Neolithic, SOM (Seine-Oise-Marne) culture (Razet cemetery, Coizard, Arr. Apernay, Marne, France; 3000–2500 B.C.) H. 127.5 cm.

FIGURE 296

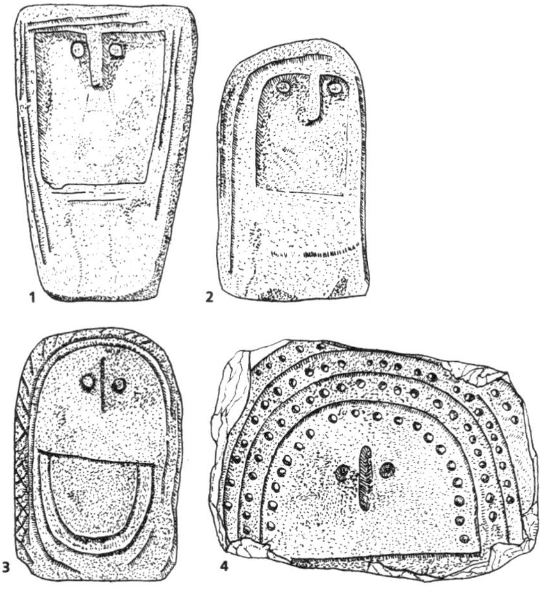

FIGURE 297

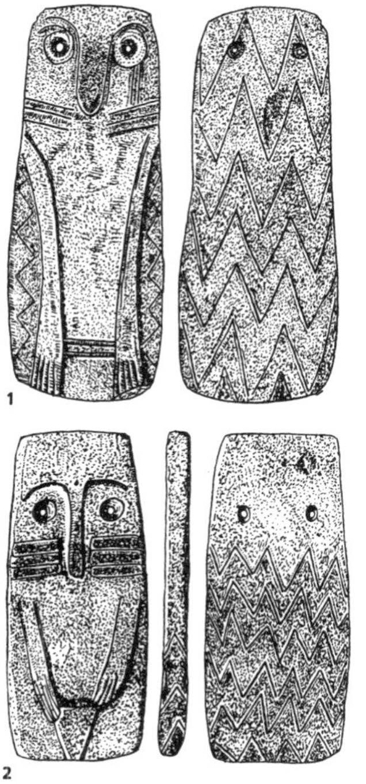

FIGURE 298

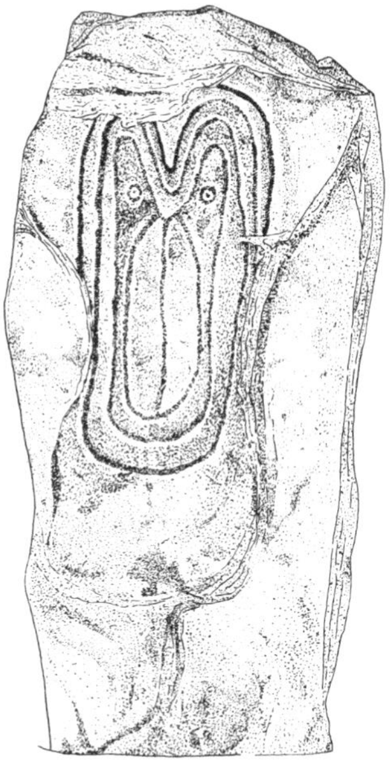

FIGURE 299

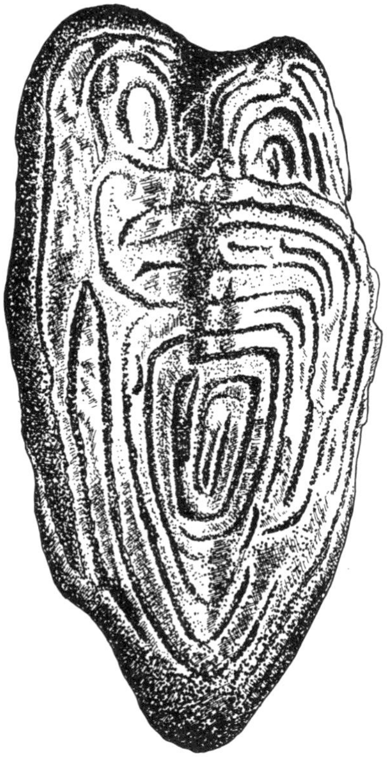

FIGURE 296 Illustrated here are typical Late Neolithic owl stelae from Spain and Portugal. (1) Asquerosa, province of Granada, Spain; (2) Central Portugal; (3) Crato, central Portugal; and (4) Arronches, E Portugal. Although they are not from certain archeological contexts, they date from about the end of the 4th or early 3rd millennium B.C. (1) H. 60.3 cm. (2) H. 50.9 cm. (3) H. 50.8 cm. (4) H. 50.3 cm.

FIGURE 297 Schist plaques from megalithic passage graves. ((1) Horta Velha do Reguengos, province Alentejo and (2) Vega del Guadancil, province Careres, Portugal; c. mid-4th mill. B.C.) (1) H. 7.2 cm. (2) H. 6 cm.

FIGURE 298 The characteristic beak-and-eyebrow motif of the owl is joined with a large oval vulva on an engraving within a panel on a stone slab of a megalithic tomb. Final Neolithic of Brittany: Angled Passage Grave period (Les Pierres Plates, Locmariaquer; c. 3000 B.C.) H. 180 cm.

FIGURE 299 Owl-faced image engraved on a stela from an Irish passage grave, found just to the right of the tomb. (Knowth West, County Meath, Ireland; second half of the 4th mill. B.C.) H. 48.1 cm.

FIGURE 300

FIGURE 300 Vinča figurine with an owl mask and wings. The design is incised and white encrusted on the polished black body. (Gradešnica, NW Bulgaria; 5000–4500 B.C.) H. 13 cm.

FIGURE 301 In France, the Owl Goddess is associated with the hook, which usually lies across the upper part of her body. ((1) La Gayette, (2) and (3) Mas de l'Aveugle, Collorques, Gard, and (4) Aven Meunier I, S France; isolated finds probably originating from hypogea of the Fontbuxian culture, early 3rd mill. B.C.).
(1) H. 141.4 cm.
(2) H. 182.4 cm.
(3) H. 163 cm.
(4) H. 164.1 cm.

FIGURE 302 Owl Goddess on miniature vase found in the Encantada III megalithic tomb (Almizaraque, Almeria, SW Spain; c. 3000 B.C. or earlier). H. 7.5 cm.

A glyph associated with the Owl Goddess in France is a hook which usually lies across the body near the arms and emphasizes her regenerative force. (FIGURE 301) Another glyph with related meaning, particularly frequent on orthostats of the megalithic graves of Brittany, is the axe. (Both symbols are discussed in more detail in Part IV.) It is usually triangular, as at Gavrinis where axes appear within a labyrinthine design. In the several hypogea of Razet in the Paris basin, axes in low relief are found on either side of the entrance to the main chamber, the blades turned toward the opening.

The Owl Goddess on vases from Almeria in Spain is at times associated with a maze of V's, M's, Y's, and lozenges as in the decoration of a miniature vase from an Encantada tomb. (FIGURE 302) Such a maze of various angular forms occurs repeatedly over the millennia in association with images of the Old European divinity. The Goddess at Çatal Hüyük Shrine VII, 23 (see fig. 363) is covered with this design, which extends even beyond her body. This is the sacred "script." The meaning of the signs was probably related to the "life source" category of symbols.

The review made here of the symbols associated with the Owl Goddess—snake

FIGURE 301

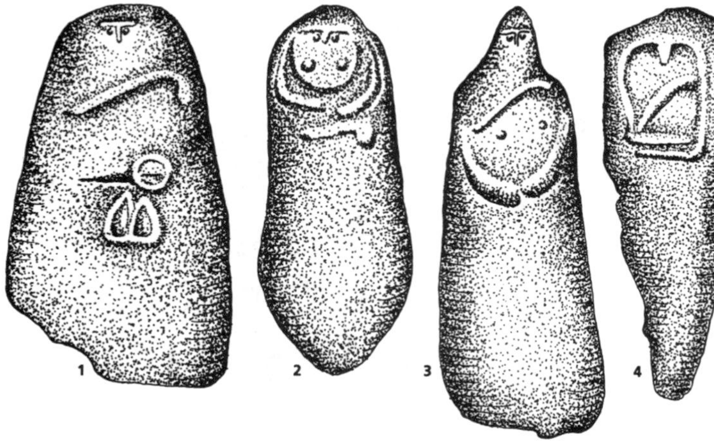

FIGURE 302

as umbilical cord, vulva, triangle, hatched or zig-zag band, net, labyrinth, bi-line, tri-line, hook, axe—shows them to be life source, energy, or life-stimulating symbols. Their association with the Owl Goddess of Death serves to emphasize regeneration as an essential component of her personality. The agony of death which we take so much for granted is nowhere perceptible in this symbolism.

18.3 *Cuckoo, hawk, and dove*

The Goddess can also change into any small bird, most frequently a cuckoo or dove. From early history we know that Athena and Hera assume dove form in the writings of Homer. Germanic Holla and Freya also appear in the guise of doves. The cuckoo is one of the incarnations of Baltic Laima, the Fate, and of Polish Živa, the life-giving Goddess of Spring. Up to our century, the cuckoo and dove were believed to be prophetic birds, omens of death, and spirits of the dead.

The cuckoo, swallow, lark, and dove are birds of spring. The cuckoo's familiar cry was especially welcomed as a sign of spring. In the winter, the cuckoo was believed to transform into a hawk, and this wintertime cuckoo/hawk is associated with death. It is still believed from England to Lithuania that if a cuckoo is heard after midsummer it may be a portent of death. In Wales it is considered unlucky to hear the cuckoo before the 6th of April (Armstrong 1958: 202–206). This cyclical appearance and transformation link the bird with the Goddess, the overseer of the cycles of time, life and death, spring and winter, happiness and unhappiness.

Small birds were sculpted, engraved, and painted throughout prehistory. In Minoan Crete they appear perching on shrines, pillars, and the Goddess's head. Unfortunately, it is not possible to recognize the species of the birds portrayed, except in a very few cases. A mottled one perches upon an obelisk crowned with a double-axe in the famous funeral scene on the painted sarcophagus from Aghia Triada, Crete, of c. 1400 B.C. (Long 1974). The bird may portray the soul of the dead man. The bird as the reincarnation of the soul has a close connection with burial places. Wooden posts topped with a bird are known to have existed in village cemeteries in the early part of our century. In Russian, *golubec* means "grave marker," from *golub* "dove, pigeon" (Oinas 1964). In eastern Siberia, after a Gilyak cremation, a wooden cuckoo is placed above the effigy representing the dead man (Armstrong 1958: 206). In Lithuanian and Latvian folksongs, the cuckoo is the main incarnation of the dead mother.

18.4 *Boar*

The wild boar is a scavenger and like the vulture eats corpses. Not surprisingly it has acquired a symbolic association with death. Paintings of boars from the caves of the Magdalenian epoch are known from Altamira, Spain, and from other locations. At Altamira, galloping boars flank the ceiling composition at left and right and the very large head of a third boar appears at upper center, in the midst of a group of bison forming the majority of the figures in the composition (Breuil 1952: fig. 4; Graziosi 1960: pl. 254). The placement of the animal in association with the female bison must have had a special significance. Unfortunately, portrayals of the boar do not abound in Upper Paleolithic and Neolithic art, and the evidence is too thin to elaborate on the early symbolic role of this beast. However, later mythology affords many clues to the basic symbolic character of this animal.

In Near Eastern and European myths, the boar is a beast of death who kills the male vegetation god (Egyptian Osiris, lover of the Goddess Isis; Syrian Tammuz, Aphrodite's lover; Diarmuid, lover of the Irish Gráinne, daughter of the King of Tara). An unknown god disguised as a boar kills Ancaeus the Arcadian king, a devotee of Artemis (Graves 1972: 210). According to a legend from the north of Ireland, an enormous boar

> *committed great devastation throughout the country; so much so that all the hunters of the kingdom assembled, determined to pursue the animal until they succeeded in killing it. His pursuers stood around leaning on their spears, viewing with amazement the huge proportions of the body, as also the length and strength of the bristles with which it was covered. One of the hunters incautiously stroked them the wrong way, thereby causing a venomous bristle to prick his hand, and fell down writhing in agony.* (Wood-Martin 1902: 131–32)

The boar was magical, and because of his poison and the devastation he caused was held in great dread.

That the boar played a role similar to that of the vulture during the Neolithic is convincingly evidenced at Çatal Hüyük Shrine EVI8; here breasts cover the lower jaws and tusks of enormous boars (Mellaart 1963: 80). In the next shrine, as already mentioned above, breasts cover vulture skulls. Once again, death is juxtaposed with life; the breast contains the beast of death. However, the jaws and tusks do not cover the breast; rather, the breasts enclose the tusks. Life triumphs.

The magical tie between the boar and the Goddess is revealed by a figurine, discovered in the Neolithic stratum of the Gaban cave in the northern part of Italy, made from the third lower molar of a boar. (FIGURE 303) The underside of the tooth was used for the image. The section containing the roots was scraped clean, leaving an even surface but with some hollows and protuberances, which became a uterus and breasts. The figure resembles the type of figurines which I call the Stiff Nude, with closed arms and

FIGURE 303

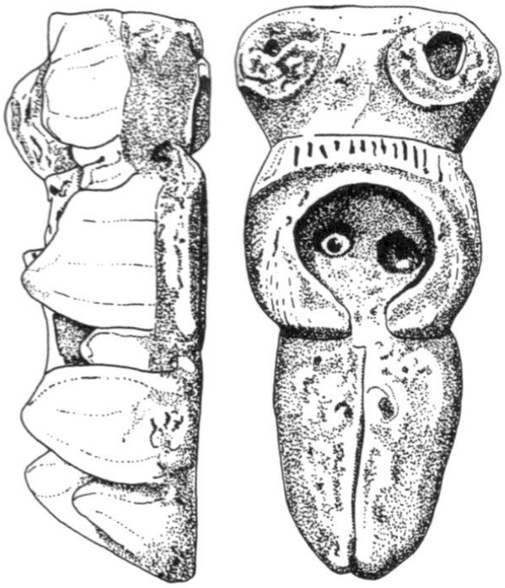

FIGURE 303 Figurine made from the molar of a boar. The underside resembles an anthropomorphic figure. Neolithic of northern Italy: Square-mouthed Pottery culture (Gaban cave near Trento). H. 10.2 cm.

FIGURE 304

1

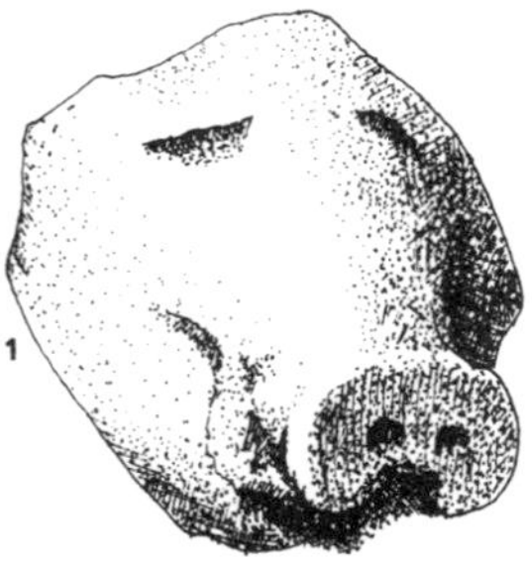

2

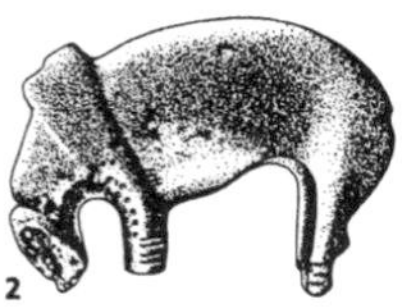

3

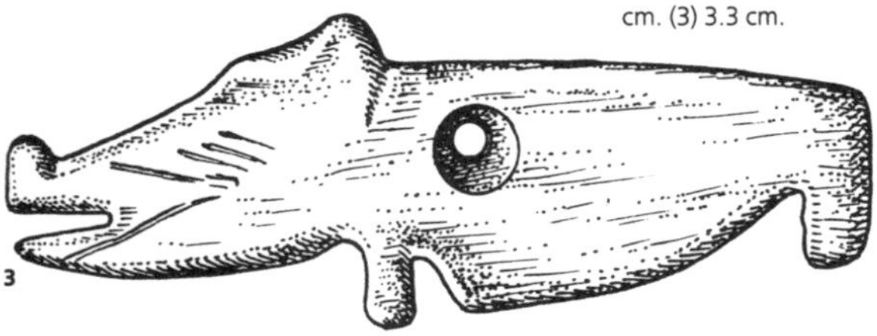

FIGURE 304 Like the vulture, the carrion-eating boar is symbolically associated with death. Its cultic significance is testified to by (1) a terracotta figurine from east central Europe (2) an amber figurine from the southern Baltic area, and (3) a bone carving from the northern Baltic area. (1) Cucuteni (Novye Ruseshty I, Soviet Moldavia; 4500–4400 B.C.); (2) Funnel-necked Beaker (or Baltic Mesolithic) culture (Stolp, N Poland); (3) East Baltic Narva Culture (Tamula, Estonia; second half of 3rd mill. B.C.). (1) H. 6.3 cm. (2) c. 8.8 cm. (3) 3.3 cm.

FIGURE 305 Boars on Minoan seals. (1) Middle Minoan IB–II (Mallia; c. 2000 B.C.); (2) and (3) Middle Minoan II (Phaistos; 1800–1700 B.C.)

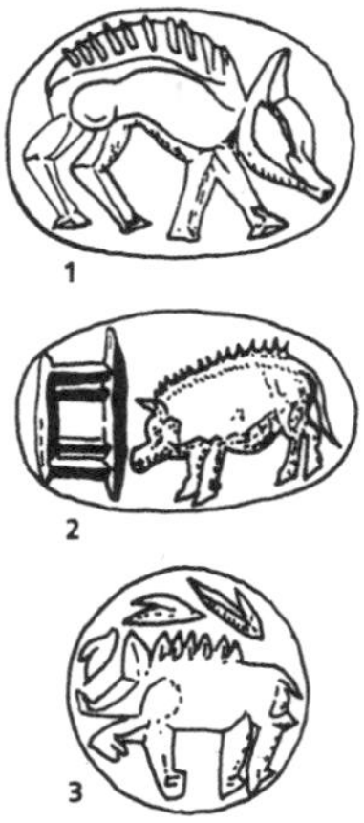

legs and an emphasis on the womb, described below. There are thirteen incisions above the uterus, perhaps a counting of the lunar months in a year or the number of days of the waxing moon. The same layer of the Gaban cave yielded a boar's humerus incised with symbolic design. Its decoration, subdivided into four sections, features from top to bottom a frog-shaped figure, a triple zig-zag band, a net, and a uterus placed on bands of streams. (Graziosi 1973: III.) We see here an agglomeration of symbols on the theme of regeneration: uterus-frog-water (or amniotic fluid). Again, symbols of life rule over the bare bone, symbol of death.

The lower jaws and tusks of a boar are not uncommon in Old European graves from the 6th to the 4th millennia B.C., best evidenced in the Copper Age cemeteries of Hungary (Bognár-Kutzián 1963; Skomal 1983). They were placed in the graves of adults and children of both sexes, perhaps as objects having apotropaic qualities, similar to those of an owl carcass in the European villages of our times. In western Europe, lower jaws of boars were found in front of megalithic tombs or in mortuary houses. For instance, in front of Hetty Pegler's Tump, a megalithic tomb in the Cotswolds, England, two human skeletons and the jaws of several wild boars were discovered. Further north in Yorkshire, at Hanging Grimston, four heaps of jaws from young boars were found in a mortuary house under the round barrow dated to about 3540 B.C. The points of most of the tusks had been broken off (Burl 1979: 79; 1981: 56). The custom of placing the jawbone of a boar in a grave is of great antiquity, preceding the Neolithic and even the Upper Paleolithic. At Mount Carmel in Israel, a cemetery of Neanderthal burials was excavated, in which the jawbone of a large wild boar had been placed by the right hand of one of the adult males (illustrated by Campbell 1983: 51, fig. 71). This practice thus is one of the earliest manifestations of ritual, dating to the period between 100,000 and 40,000 B.C.

The cultic importance of the boar is attested by boar figurines, large sculptures, and boar-shaped vases. Figurines of boars were found among sacrificial goods with the burials under the shrine floors at Çatal Hüyük. Other deposits were eggs, grain, flints, and auroch's skulls (Mellaart 1967: 77). Other terracotta figurines of boars come from the Copper Age cultures of east-central Europe as well as by portrayals on Middle Minoan seals. (FIGURES 304, 305) The role of the supernatural boar continued during the Bronze and Iron ages, as numerous sculptures with exaggerated bristles in central and western Europe, particularly in Celtic and Roman Britain, suggests. Cornelius Tacitus in *Germania*, chapter 45, A.D. 98, writes that the tribes of the Aestii (Old Prussians, that is, the western Balts) worship the mother of the Gods and as the symbol of their religion they carry figures of boars. They believe that, without weapons or protection of any kind, this charm preserves a devotee of the Goddess from harm even among his enemies. In Norse mythology, Freya, Goddess of Death and Regeneration and who has qualities of a mother of the dead, is closely associated with the boar. Perhaps therefore she was nicknamed *Syr*, "Sow."

18.5 *Howling dog*

The howling of dogs as a harbinger of death was a universal belief in the ancient world and in European folklore. Even very recently farmers believed that if a dog is heard howling near the house of a sick person, death is near and all hope of recovery is abandoned. In ancient Greece, dogs howled at the approach of Hekate, a nightmarish lunar goddess. The hound is her animal and her epiphany; dogs were sacrificed to Hekate. In Hellenistic relief plaques this goddess is shown accompanied by a hound. The Germanic Hel (Holle, Holla) escorts the dead to the otherworld and her wolflike dogs nip the flesh of the corpse.

The dog's eminent role in Old European religion is shown by its prolific portrayals in marble, rock crystal, and terracotta, by vases in the shape of dogs, and by pictorial painting. Sometimes dog sculptures appear wearing a Goddess's mask. (FIGURE 306) The dog was one of the most prominent sacrificial victims in association with funerary rites. At Lepenski Vir, sacred burial place on the bank of the Danube in northern Yugoslavia (see section 23.3), whole skeletons of dogs were found in rectangular hearths in the center of triangular shrines.

Pictorial portrayals of dogs are known from the Late Cucuteni culture. They appear on vases as fantastic mythical creatures masterfully schematicized. Leaping or flying in space with upraised tails, ferocious hounds are associated with crescents, caterpillars, and full moons. As was his Mistress, the hound was an overseer of cyclical time. In addition, dogs were guardians of life and very influential in the awakening of slumbering vegetation and in stimulating the rise of plant life. This latter role comes forth beautifully in paintings on Cucuteni vases, to which we shall return in the section on regeneration below (see section 20.5).

FIGURE 306

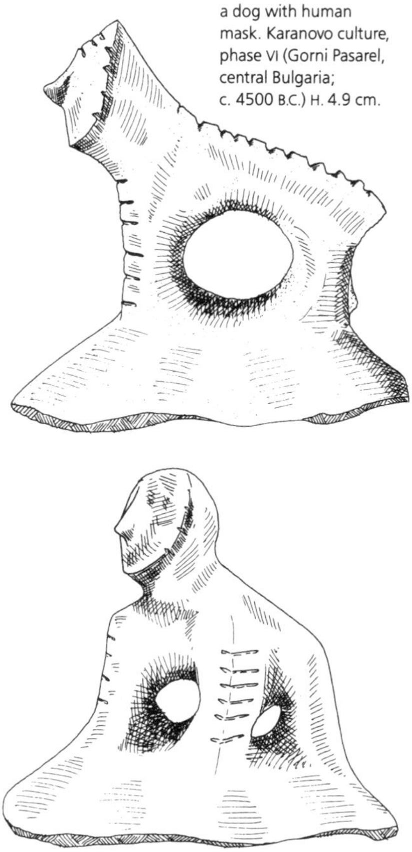

FIGURE 306 Goddess in her epiphany of a dog: lid handle in the form of a dog with human mask. Karanovo culture, phase VI (Gorni Pasarel, central Bulgaria; c. 4500 B.C.) H. 4.9 cm.

FIGURE 307

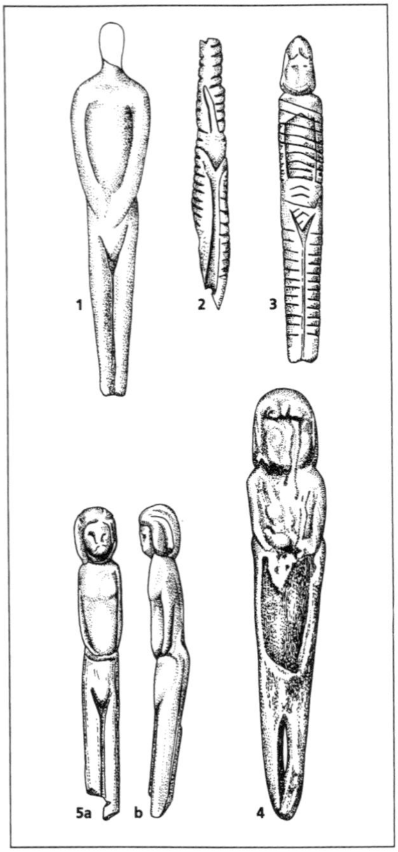

FIGURE 308

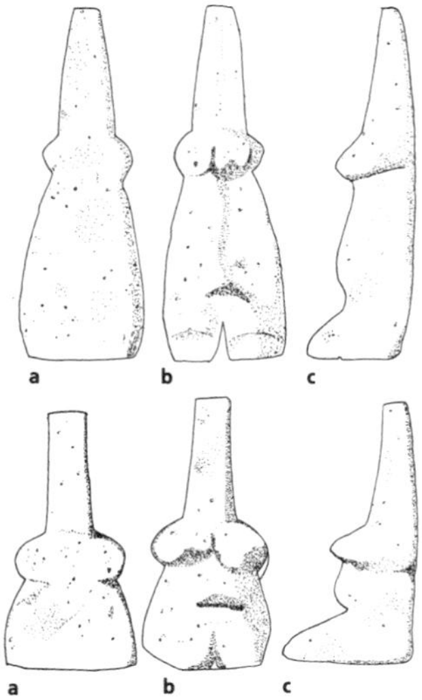

FIGURE 309

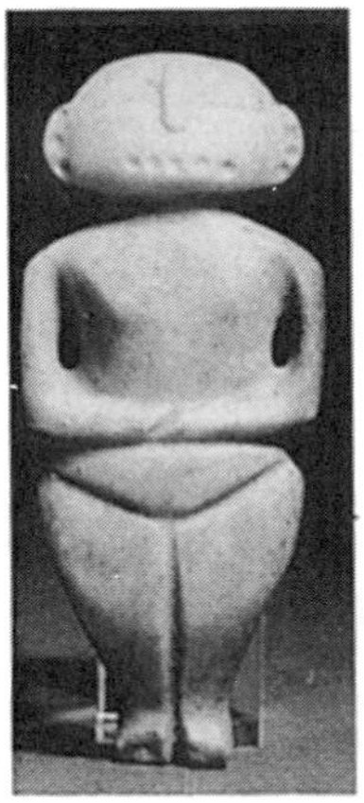

FIGURE 310

FIGURE 307 Categorically different from the corpulent figurines with large breasts and buttocks are stiff nudes or cocoon-shaped images of the Upper Paleolithic as these ivory figurines from Mal'ta, Siberia, indicate (16,000–13,000 B.C.). H. largest, 13.6 cm.

FIGURE 308 The "Stiff White Lady," anonymous and the color of bone, is a stereotype that appears from the Upper Paleolithic through the Bronze Age. These Neolithic terracotta figurines with flat backs and long cylindrical necks were found in the graves of the Golovița cemetery. Hamangia (Baia, Danube estuary; c. 5000 B.C.)

FIGURE 309 Marble figurine with rigid posture, folded arms, and a large vulva. Karanovo VI (Sulica, Stara Zagora, central Bulgaria; c. 4500 B.C.)

FIGURE 310 Bone figurine with an enormous pubic triangle; the upper body is totally reduced and copper plates cover the legs. She has a long mouth and the round eyes of a snake. Karanovo VI (Lovets, at Stara Zagora; 4500–4300 B.C.)

18.6 *Stiff White Lady*

A distinct stereotype in figurine art is the nude with folded or extended arms, a supernatural vulva, a long neck, and no face, or with a masked head and polos or diadem. The media are marble, alabaster, amber, light-colored stone, bone, and sometimes clay. The light color is the color of bone—that is, of death. The anthropomorphic female Death of European folklore to this day is imagined as tall, bony-legged, and dressed in white. No doubt she is inherited from the Old European substratum when death was bone white, not black like the terrifying Indo-European male god of death and the underworld.

Made of bone, ivory, or reindeer antler, schematized stiff nudes with arms folded or pressed to the sides, a large pubic triangle, and tapering legs appear in the Upper Paleolithic. They are categorically different from the famous Willendorf-Lespugue type with large breasts, belly, and buttocks, and from the Sireuil-Tursac type representing birth-giving. They seem to be the prototypes of the Neolithic stiff nudes. Such figurines are known, for instance, from the Pechialet and Laugerie Basse caves in Dordogne, France, made of bone and ivory; from the upper Périgordian and Magdalenian epochs (Delporte 1979: 54, figs. 20, 21); and from Mal'ta, Siberia (FIGURE 307) made of ivory and reindeer antler (Abramova 1962: pls. 45, 46).

The stiff nudes of the Neolithic, Copper Age, and Early Bronze Age are best evidenced where cemeteries or single tombs have been excavated, since this type of figurine was deposited in graves. They are abundant in the Hamangia, Karanovo, and Cucuteni culture groups and are unquestionably a dominant type among the pre-nuraghic sculptures of Sardinia and the Early Bronze Age Cyclades. Isolated examples very probably come from destroyed tombs.

FIGURE 311

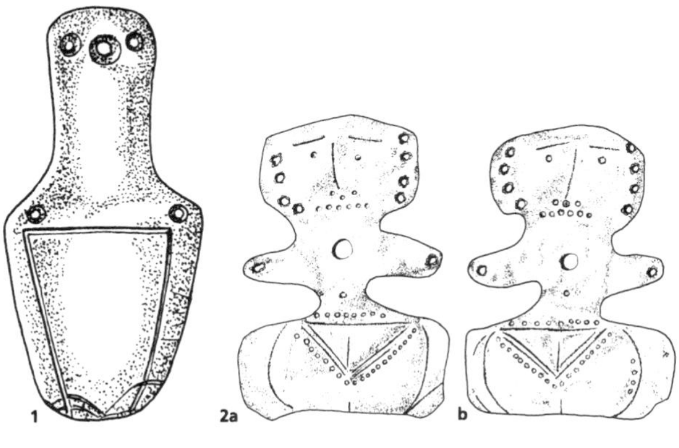

FIGURE 311 Stiff Lady figurines from the Baltic Sea coast and Bulgaria. (1) Amber figurine with an enormous pubic triangle. Narva (Neidenburg, East Prussia, end-4th mill. B.C.); (2) Gold-plate figurine with emphasized vulva; the broad mask has perforations for earrings and the dots in the mouth area stand for fangs. Karanovo VI (Ruse, N Bulgaria; mid-5th mill. B.C.) (1) H. 5.6 cm. (2) H. 7.3 cm.

FIGURE 312

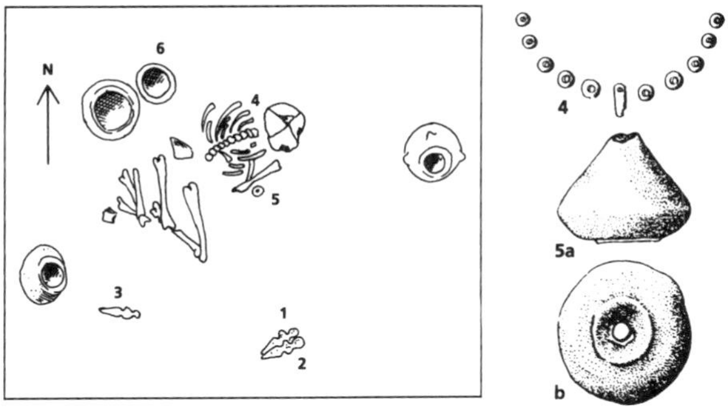

FIGURE 312 A group of three Stiff White Ladies was found in the grave of this nine to ten year old girl. Her grave goods consist of (1)–(3) terracotta figurines, (4) shell beads, (5) a spindle whorl, and (6) vases. Late Cucuteni (Grave No. 5, Vykhvatintsi cemetery, Soviet Moldavia; c. 3500 B.C.) (1) H. 16.7 cm. (2) H. 9.4 cm. (3) H. 14.2 cm. (4) H. 4.1 cm. (5a) H. 5.6 cm.

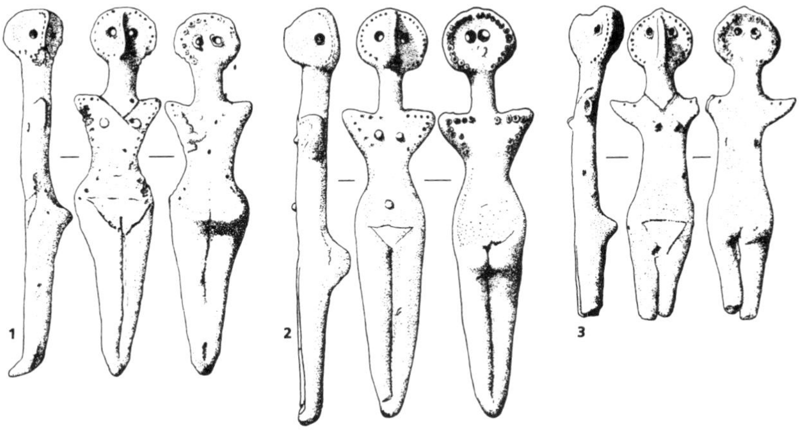

18.7 *Stiff nudes of the Hamangia, Karanovo, and Cucuteni cultures*

The largest Neolithic deposits of this type of figurine were found in the Cernavoda and Golovița cemeteries near the Black Sea, Romania. Both belong to the Hamangia culture, c. 5000 B.C. (FIGURE 308) At Cernavoda, 400 of the 600 graves were excavated (Berciu 1966). The oval-shaped graves yielded flat-backed statuettes of marble, clay, and bone in either a standing or seated posture.

Variant on this same tradition is the Copper Age Karanovo VI figurine of the mid-5th millennium B.C., with a broad mask with earrings, a large mouth, and teeth that are indicated by depressions or round holes below the mouth. (FIGURES 309, 310) The arms are folded or, in more schematic versions, not shown at all; the legs, tightly pressed together, taper at the end. Horizontal groups of lines and dots incised or drilled around the legs give it the appearance of a pupa or cocoon. This type of figurine was produced in bone, marble, gold plate, and, in the Baltic area, in amber. (FIGURE 311)

The Cucuteni (Tripolye) nudes of 4500–3500 B.C. are more gracile, with arms sometimes totally neglected, and legs tapering to a cone. They have a round mask with holes as eyes and a raised ridge for a nose. (FIGURE 312) In the cemetery of Vykhvatintsi, Soviet Moldavia, such figurines were found in threes in the graves of young girls (9 to 10 years old). Other graves, both male and female, contained single terracotta figurines of the same type and also of an entirely schematized type carved in bone. Painted vases from this cemetery are decorated with symbols elaborating on the theme of becoming: four-cornered designs, uteri, and seedlike compartments with snakes or pairs of caterpillars.

18.8 *Stiff nudes of Sicily, Sardinia, the Cyclades, Crete, and Turkey*

In Sicily, the image of a stiff nude was sculpted on smooth river pebbles. Their feminine form is scarcely sketched, exploiting the natural shape of the pebble. Deeper incisions delineate the head or mask, breasts, pubic triangle, and parting of the legs. Two little sculptures on pebbles were discovered in the Neolithic necropolis of Cozzo Busone, Agrigento. (FIGURE 313)

The Sardinian variant of the stiff nude is known from oven-shaped tombs of the Neolithic Bonu Ighinu culture, mid-5th millennium B.C. She is rotund, not obese, and the treatment of the upper and lower parts of her body displays an amazing sculptural harmony. In the center is the pubic triangle fused with the belly. She is seated or standing with arms folded or, more often, pressed to her sides. Her massive cylindrical head is masked and topped with a polos. (FIGURES 314, 315) These masterpieces of this Sardinian Goddess are made either of alabaster or soft rock. The sculpture from Cuccuru S'Arriu (Oristano) wears a polos with triple scallop side attachments outlined in double ribbons and decorated in a geometric design of four rows of zigzag lines (see fig. 314). Carved of bone, Stiff Nudes became elongated and quite slender, but they portray the same rigid posture of the Deity. (FIGURE 316) The illustrated bone figurine is from Monte Miana cave at Santadi, where a number of such images came to light, dated to the second half of the 5th millennium B.C.

As the excavations at Cuccuru S'Arriu have shown, the figurine was placed in front of the dead who lay in a contracted (fetal) position covered with red ochre. (FIGURE 317) In Tomb No. 387, a dish placed next to the figurine contained two valves of an opened shell filled with red ochre, the color of life. The same position in graves has also been observed in the late Neolithic oven-shaped tombs of Apulia. At Arnesano near Lecce, a

FIGURE 313

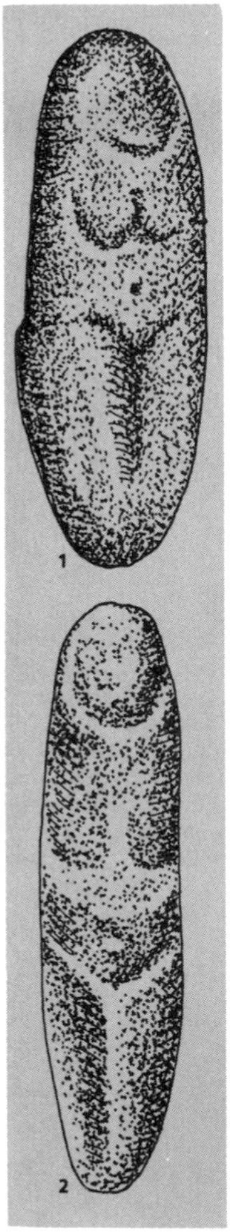

FIGURE 314

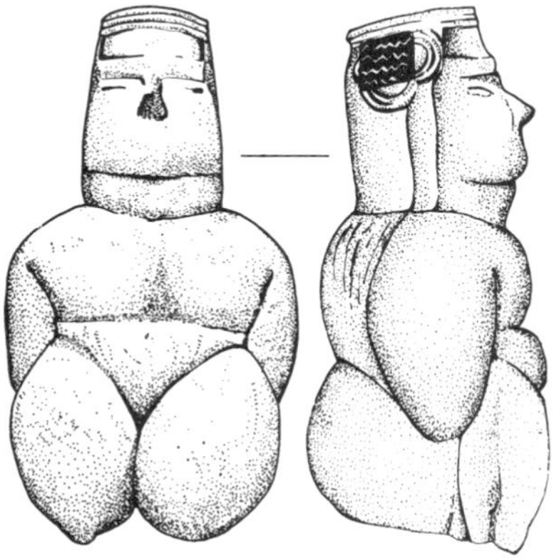

FIGURE 315

FIGURE 313 In the Mediterranean area, river pebbles are lightly sculpted into stiff nudes; these were discovered in oven-shaped graves in the Eneolithic necropolis of Cozzo Busone. Sicilian Eneolithic (Agrigento, S Sicily; early 4th mill. B.C.) (1) H. 6 cm. (2) H. 16.1 cm.

FIGURE 314 This Sardinian Neolithic nude displays an amazing sculptural harmony. She is rotund and stiff with arms pressed to her side. Her polos has triple side attachments. Long hair falls on her shoulders. Bonu Ighinu culture (from an oven-shaped tomb at Cuccuru S'Arriu, Oristano, central W Sardinia; mid-5th mill. B.C.) H. 18.4 cm.

FIGURE 315 Another example of this type is the "Dea di Olbia," a rotund nude in a rigid posture with arms pressed to her sides carved of soft stone. Her abdomen and pubic triangle are fused; she wears a polos and a mouthless mask. Bonu Ighinu (Santa Mariedda, at Olbia, N Sardinia; mid-5th mill. B.C.) H. 8.3 cm.

FIGURE 316

FIGURE 316 This Stiff Nude is beautifully carved of bone. Her head is large and supernatural, with incised eyes but no mouth. She wears a polos. Sardinian Neolithic (Monte Miana cave, Santadi; 4500–4000 B.C.) H. 7.35 cm.

FIGURE 317

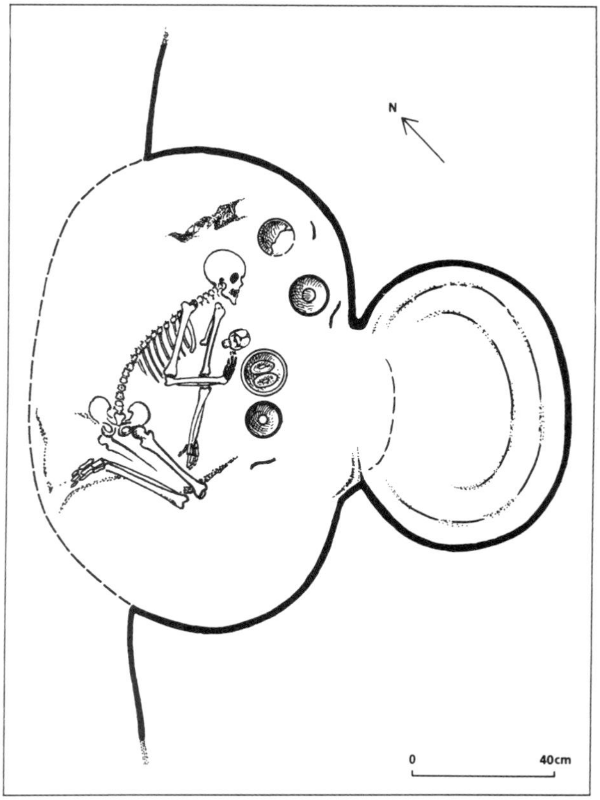

FIGURE 317 Plan of an oven-shaped tomb shows the placement of a stone figurine of a "Stiff White Lady" in front of the body, which lies in a fetal position. Five vases surround them. (Tomb No. 387, Cuccuru S'Arriu, Oristano, Sardinia; mid-5th mill. B.C.)

stone figurine with an owl mask, a chevron under it and the lower part of the body reduced to a stump (FIGURE 318) was placed in the same relationship as at Cuccuru S'Arriu to the contracted skeleton. Next to the statue stood beautifully burnished monochrome red vases of the Diana-Bellavista style, typical of southern Italy and Sicily around 4000 B.C.

Figurines from the succeeding Ozieri culture of Sardinia (second half of the 5th to the early 4th millennium B.C.) lose the earlier roundness; they become flat and are schematized into a T shape, with the upper torso and arms fused into a solid rectangle and the lower body into a cone. Facial features are totally neglected except for a beaklike protrusion for a nose. Small breasts and a V collar are usually indicated. The best-known example of this type, many times reproduced in art books, is the 44 cm high marble statue from Senorbi. (FIGURE 319, 1) This elegantly schematized image seems to have continued throughout the 4th and into the 3rd millennium B.C. However, most of the figurines are isolated finds, and their chronology is established mainly by stylistic comparisons. To the post-Ozieri end of the series belongs the Porto Ferro type, similarly schematized but with a more detailed upper part and cut-outs for arms. (FIGURE 319, 2) The lower body remains reduced to a cone or occasionally to a semi-oval. The rounded mask has a nose but no other facial features. Such figurines were found in Sardinian subterranean tombs.

FIGURE 318

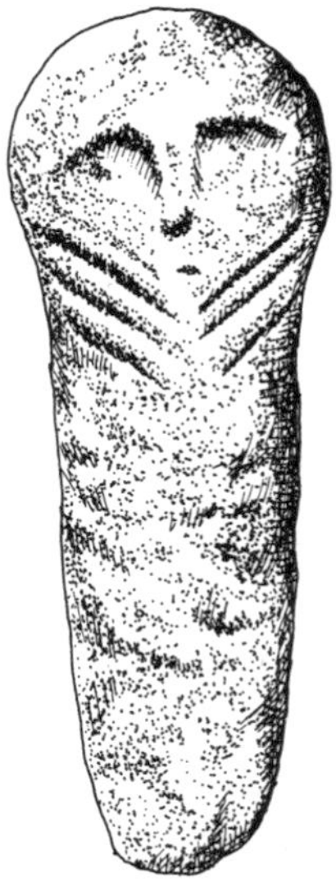

FIGURE 319

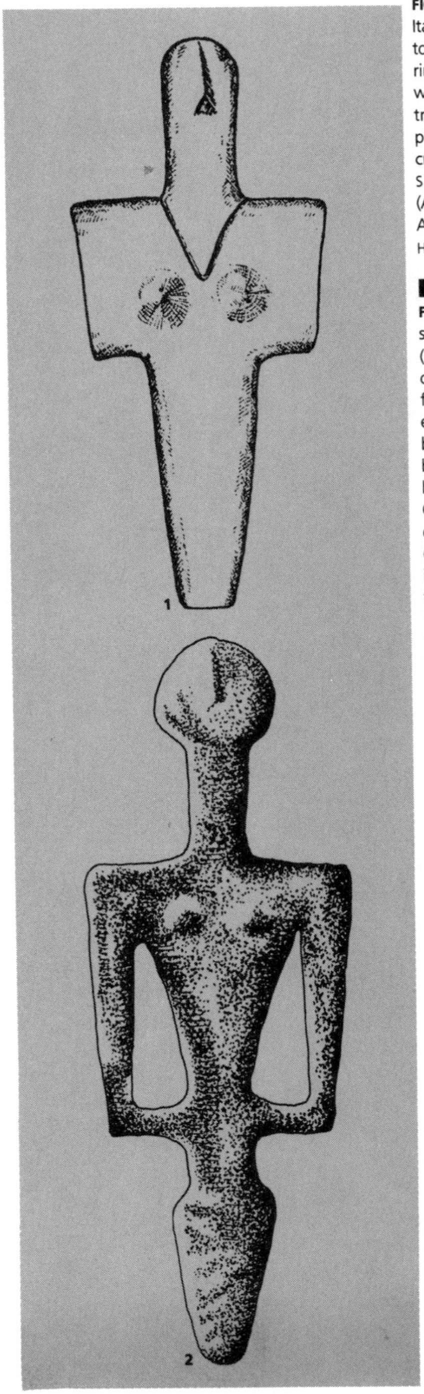

FIGURE 318 In a south Italian oven-shaped tomb, a cylindrical figurine of calcareous rock with an owl mask and a triple chevron was placed in front of the crouched skeleton. S Italian Late Neolithic (Arnesano, ner Lecce, Apulia; c. 4000 B.C.) H. 35 cm.

FIGURE 319 Alabaster sculptures from Sardinia. (1) A schematized image of the Goddess with folded arms; V sign engraved above the breasts; face represented by nose alone; the lower body is a cone. (Senorbi; Ozieri culture. Tentative date: end 5th mill. B.C.) (2) This statuette found in a hypogeum also has the cone-shaped or "chrysalid" lower body, long neck, and blank face of the Stiff White Lady tradition; her arms, separated from her body, represent a local stylistic variation. Late or post-Ozieri (Porto Ferro, Sardinia; tentatively late 4th mill. B.C.) (1) H. 44 cm.

FIGURE 320 Marble statuette, example of the famous Cycladic figurines. Early Cycladic II (Syros, Cyclades; 2800–2500 B.C.) H. 0.00 cm.

FIGURE 321 In western Anatolia, some marble figurines portraying Stiff Nudes are winged and wear large (probably owl's) masks. Early Bronze Age II mid-3rd mill. B.C.). Asia Minor, exact provenance unknown. H. 9.9 cm.

The celebrated marble idols found in Cycladic and Cretan graves dated to c. 3500–2500 B.C. (FIGURE 320) continue the Neolithic/Copper Age tradition: a supernatural vulva, rigid posture with folded or no arms, schematically rendered or no legs, cylindrical neck with a mask or without, and a nose indicated by a raised ridge. Even bands of parallel lines were incised as on Karanovo idols. Many have an incised V sign below the neck, and on some, red paint marks are preserved on the mask or chest. Although they share the same features, they differ in dimensions, proportions, and degree of schematization. Some western Anatolian examples have wings. (FIGURE 321) They are most often from 10 to 30 cm high but with some lifesize exceptions (now on display in the National Museum of Athens). A good number of Cycladic and Cretan idols were found in oven-shaped and round or rectangular tombs at Naxos, Amorgos, Syros, Thera, and Crete, dated to Early Cycladic/Early Minoan I and II.

FIGURE 320

FIGURE 321

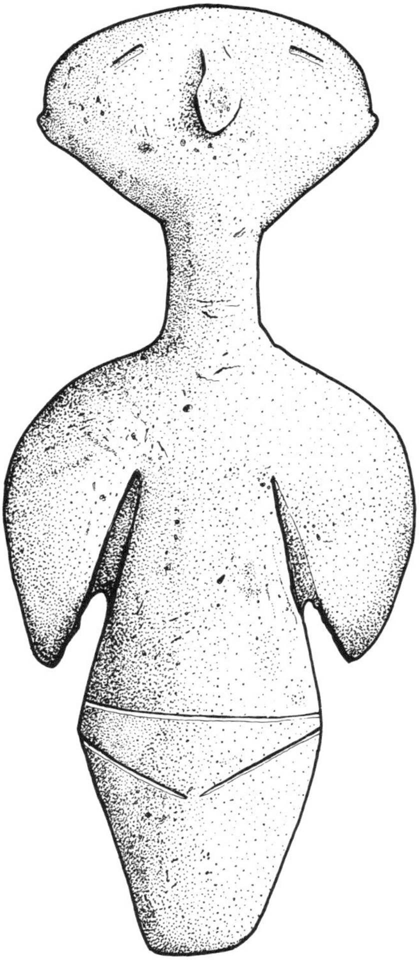

18.9 *Stiff nudes of Spain and Portugal*

In Spain, related images were carved of ivory. (FIGURE 322) Some statuettes portray slim, flat, very stiff fleshless figures. More than others they convey the fearsome image of bony Lady Death.

Bone phalanges from the passage graves of Spain and Portugal—most of which are undecorated but some of which have owl eyes surrounded by multiple arches and are engraved with nets, zig-zags, and net-patterned triangles (see fig. 91)—must have served the same function. Similar bone figurines with large round eyes recently emerged in graves of the Linear Pottery culture in the upper Rhine area. The illustrated example, with glaring inlaid eyes of shell, is made of a young animal bone and was placed in the grave of a child about three or four years old (fig. 92).

18.10 *Stiff nudes in Danubian Bronze Age graves*

The Bronze Age funerary monuments of the middle and lower Danube region also include a deity whose icons are richly marked with symbols of becoming, but of an entirely different form and style unique to this area. From the 2nd millennium to the 13th century B.C., the agriculturalists along the Danube in Yugoslavia, Romania, and Bulgaria retained Old European traditions. In fact, they formed an island surrounded on all sides by thoroughly Indo-Europeanized peoples. In their cremation cemeteries, vases and sculptures are decorated with encrustrations of white paste; figurines are placed either inside the urn or on its shoulder. Such figurines never occur in settlements, indicating their association with funerary rituals only.

The figurines are clothed in long skirts; some wear necklaces, a diadem, and a belt. (FIGURE 323) The human form is abstracted, without naturalistically rendered heads, arms, hands, or legs. A button-shaped protrusion for the head and vaguely marked arms are discernible on most figurines. The flat chest area between the arms and the bell-shaped or cylindrical lower part of the body serve as surfaces for the encrustation of symbols.

The dominant motifs are snake coils, double spirals, helices, and whirls. Typically, spirals and helices turn in opposite directions, one descending, the other ascending. The repeated combination of snake coils and spirals with whirls, crescents, and snakelike lines conveys a message concerning the regenerating life force or the cyclical change between death and life. Also frequent are triple lines and triple triangles (vulvas).

One figurine of this type from Glamija in northern Yugoslavia (related to the one reproduced in fig. 323, 1) was found in a double vessel together with a modeled ornithomorphic vase. This grave included three urns and five smaller vessels containing the bones of a fowl and black sand (Letica 1973: 93), indicating the sacrifice of a waterfowl to the Goddess.

In sum, the rigid White Lady was portrayed for millennia, from the Upper Paleolithic to the Bronze Age. She is nude, stiff as bone, with a supernatural pubic triangle, and masked. She is slim, except for the Neolithic, when she is massive or rotund but not obese. In figurine art this aspect of the Goddess cannot be confused with the Bird Goddess of the large breasts and posterior or the Pregnant Goddess. However, she also is a Bird Goddess, a nocturnal one, a bird of prey. Her link with the owl is obvious. The owl's beak and arched, merging browridges of an owl are indicated. Sometimes even wings are shown as on marble

FIGURE 322

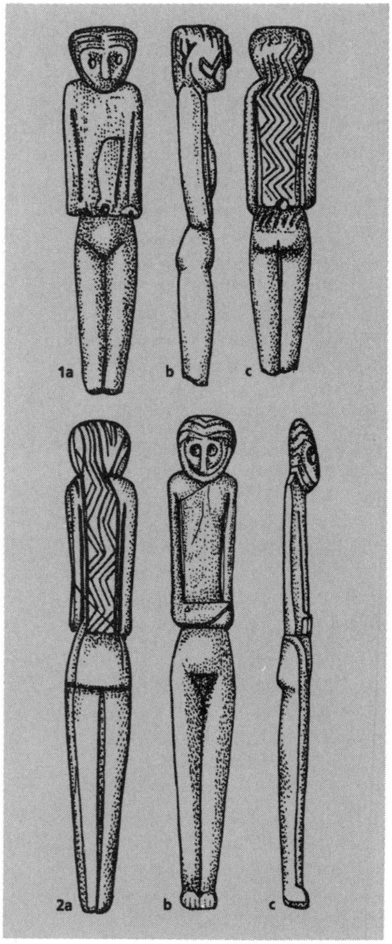

FIGURE 322 Very stiff and slim ivory figurines with folded arms are also known in Spain. Their heads are engraved with chevrons and V's; long hair flows like water in chevron bands down the back. The cavities of the round eyes were once inlaid with shell or some other material. Copper Age Spain ((1) grave at Jaen, (2) Cave at Torre del Campo, prov. of Jaen; c. early 3rd mill. B.C.) (1) H. 5.8 cm. (2) H. 8 cm.

FIGURE 323 Related but stylistically distinct figures come from the Bronze Age cremation cemeteries of the Danube. Their symbols of becoming are encrusted with white paste and include spirals—probably abstracted snake limbs—whirls, crescents, and triple triangles/vulvas. ((1) Glamija, E Banat, Serbia; (2) Cirna, S Romania; (3) Kladovo and (4) Korbovo, Iron Gates region, N Yugoslavia; 17th–13th cents. B.C.) (1) H. 12.31 cm. (2) H. 10.4 cm. (3) H. 8.59 cm. (4) H. 7.93 cm.

FIGURE 323

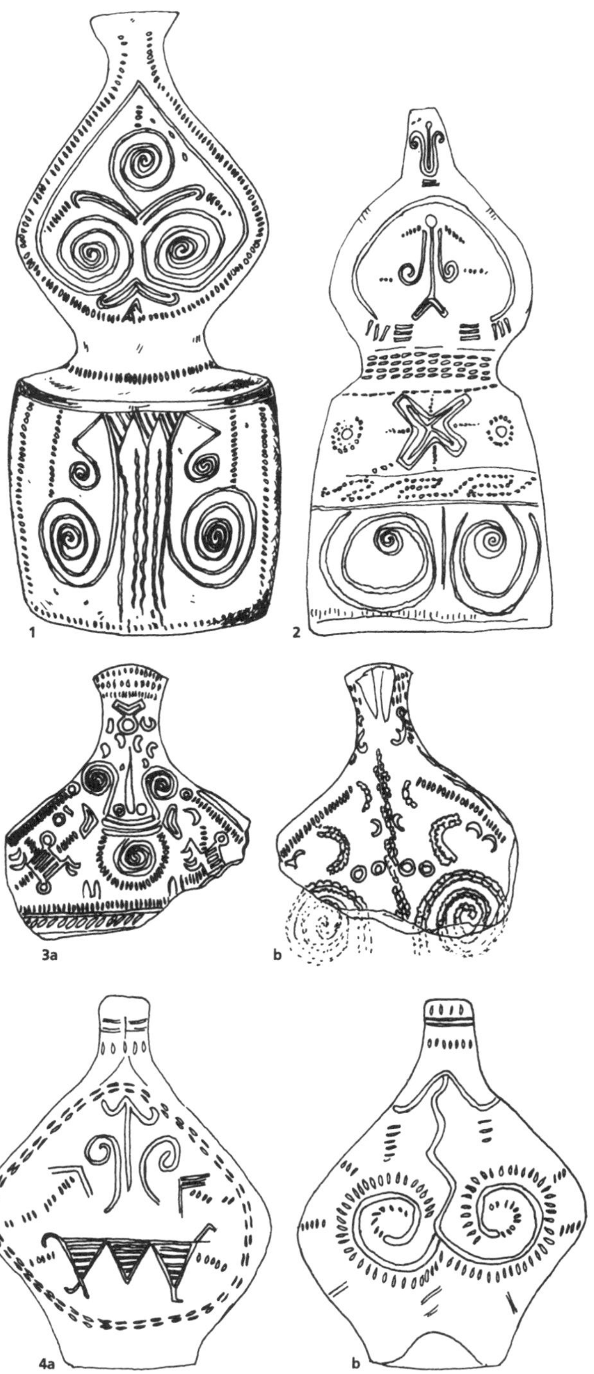

figurines from western Anatolia dating from the Early Bronze Age II, first half of the 3rd millennium B.C. (Thimme 1977: Nos. 560–66). The Owl Goddess's identity can also be deciphered from the numinous round eyes on schematic effigies of bone and stone from the megalithic tombs of Iberia. In the East Balkans and the Danubian plain, often she is not the bird of prey but a serpent. There is a good possibility that the round eyes and a long mouth of the Karanovo Stiff Ladies and her masks are those of a serpent, i.e., of the Snake Goddess in her poisonous or death aspect (see fig. 310). The Bronze Age examples with a button-shaped protrusion for the head and snake coils emanating from the central life column shown in the middle of the skirt (see fig. 323, 1) are also likely portrayals of a Snake Goddess. Images on Etruscan sarcophagi from the 6th and later centuries B.C. represent this goddess with snake legs and bee wings (necropoli of Cerveteri: Villa Julia Museum, Rome; other: Grosseto Archaeological Museum). Her placement in graves perhaps opened the entrance into the subterranean womb and secured cyclical regeneration.

18.11 *Burial of the Goddess's mask (gorgoneion)*

The 1972 discovery of the rich Karanovo VI cemetery of the mid-5th millennium B.C. at Varna, Bulgaria, sheds new light on this specific category (Gimbutas 1977; Ivanov 1978). Among the 81 graves excavated in 1976, 16 were mask graves; that is to say, they contained no human bones, only a lifesize clay mask decorated with gold. (FIGURE 324) The eyes of such a mask are convex, round plates, the mouth an elongated plaque, and the teeth gold studs. A diadem covers the forehead; earrings are attached to pierced clay earlobes. At the chin are ring-shaped pendants with "eyes" (two holes at the top of the ring) and a protrusion representing a head.

FIGURE 324

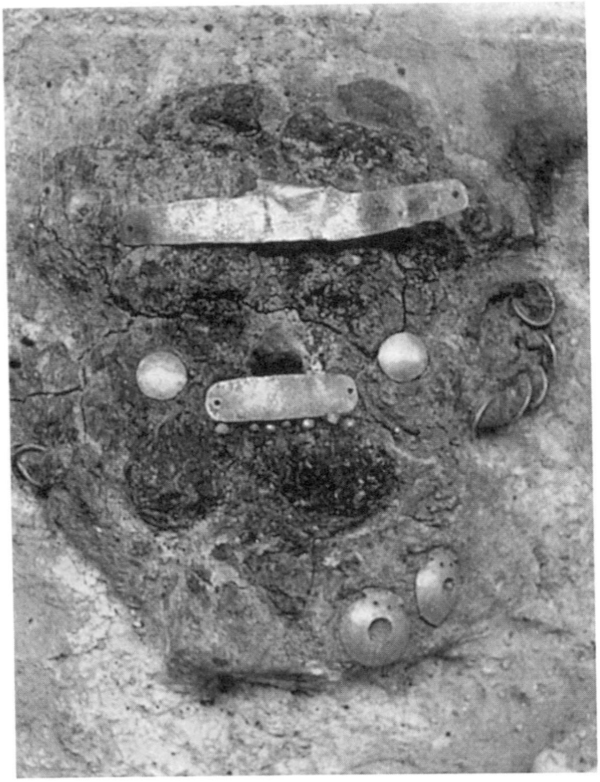

FIGURE 324 This life-size clay mask from the Varna cemetery has a diadem, round plates for eyes, a long plate for a mouth, seven studs for teeth, five earrings, and a pair of pendants with "eyes," all made of gold. Karanovo VI (Bulgaria; mid-5th mill. B.C.)

FIGURE 325

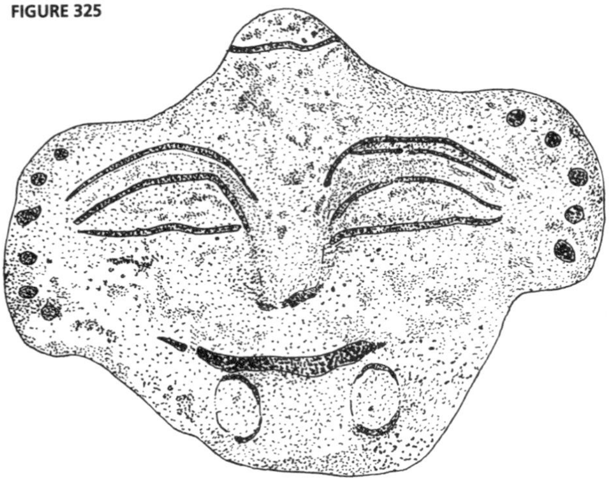

FIGURE 325 A similar terracotta figurine mask has a diadem, large eyes, huge perforated earlobes, and two pendants on each side of the chin. Karanovo (Karanovo tell near Nova Zagora, central Bulgaria; c. 4500 B.C.) H. 8 cm.

The mask's features match those of the nude figurines with supernatural vulva and folded arms. A figurine mask from the Karanovo mound with the same facial features is illustrated here for comparison. (FIGURE 325) The golden ring-shaped pendants attached to the chin of the Varna mask, which are also known from many other 5th millennium B.C. sites of east-central Europe and Greece, seem to be schematic versions of the Goddess with her womb (the round hole) being the essential part.

The masks are accompanied by a profusion of gold, colored stone, and shell beads, gold and copper ornaments, marble and ceramic dishes decorated with egg and whirl motifs, and flint tools. A marble figurine with a strange semicircular head was among the offerings with the illustrated mask from Grave No. 3. The eyes, breasts, and vulva are indicated by attached convex plates of gold. Other gifts include red ochre, marble and ceramic dishes, and triangular bone pendants, obviously symbolic of the vulva, in the possibly magical number of 27 (3x9).

Ugly-looking figurines of marble and bone are found in mask and other rich graves of the Varna cemetery, and in other sites of the Karanovo culture. (FIGURE 326) The protruding sides of their strange heads are perhaps symbolic of the dishevelled hair of an Old Hag; they seem to be replicas of winter corn dolls. A related, elongated bone figurine in the shape of a spatula is known from the Vinča culture. In a woman's grave (No. 41) at Varna, such a bone figurine was found associated with a tiny statuette portraying a stiff nude with a large vulva made of beautifully polished bone.

Also in this grave were a bone pin with a double-egg head, a deer's tooth, a marble dish, rhyton with the remains of red color, stone pestle for ochre crushing, a copper needle, a spindle whorl, obsidian and flint knives, and thousands of gold and shell (spondylus and dentalium) beads. Much in this grave emphasizes the life force (e.g., red ochre, double-egg, large vulva). From the combined presence of life and death symbols, we sense here the underworld or dark moon

FIGURE 326

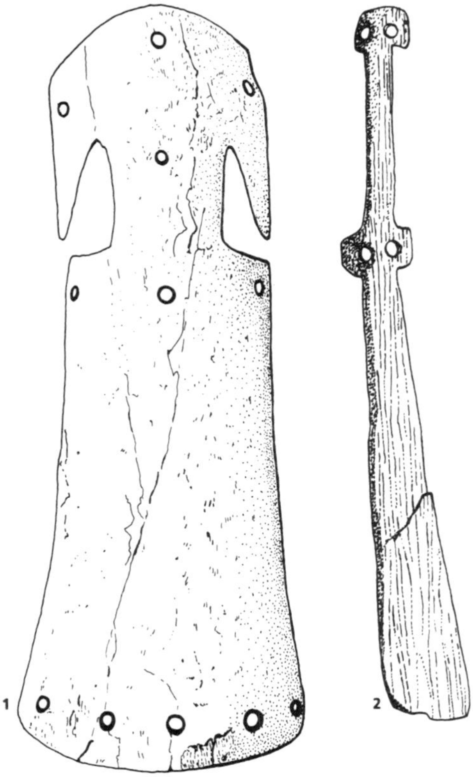

FIGURE 326 These bone figurines may be winter dolls. (1) The protruding sides of the head may symbolize the dishevelled hair of an Old Hag. The perforations suggest it was attached to a larger object. Karanovo (Woman's grave No 41, Varna, E Bulgaria; mid-5th mill. B.C.). (2) Vinča (Krameniti Vinogradi at Aradac, Serbia; 5000–4500 B.C.). (1) H. 16.4 cm. (2) H. 21.5 cm.

FIGURE 327

FIGURE 327 Anthropomorphic vase as the Goddess of Death and Regeneration. Painted white on buff. Karanovo VI (Sultana near Oltenița, S Romania; mid-5th mill. B.C.) H. 32.3 cm.

aspect of the cyclical cosmic mystery of life, death, and rebirth.

It is impossible to determine exactly when the interment of a mask took place. It could have been seasonal, at the annual harvest festival or on the occasion of a human death. Since stiff nude figurines are not found in graves (except the above-mentioned woman's grave), it can be assumed that the burial of a life-size mask took the place of a figurine. Both portray the same broad, ugly face with large mouth and fangs.

The same face reappears on an anthropomorphic vase from Sultana, southern Romania, which was perhaps used in a death ritual. (FIGURE 327) She holds her left hand at her lower lip or lolling tongue (its end covered by the hand). The ten holes above the tongue are fangs. The two loops on both sides of the chin probably portray the ring-shaped pendants. A vulva flanked by crescents is central on the vase's rounded body. On the back are two spirals, (bird's?) feet, a double egg, and U shapes—symbols of potential regeneration. She is clearly the same character no matter what we call her: Death, or the magician Goddess of Regeneration.

Was the frightening face of the Goddess a prototype of the later Gorgon heads? In the Bronze Age vase painting of the Cyclades and Crete, there appear nightmarish phantoms with masks having either an owlish face or a snake face, two rows of fangs, and bird claws. (FIGURE 328) They are the intermediaries between the Copper Age and ancient Greece.

The Gorgon Medusa is essentially a grinning mask with glaring eyes and pendant tongue. Her stare can turn men to stone. She is capable of taking the breath away. If a body is appended to this mask, it has the wings of a bee. In some portrayals, Gorgons have the heads of bees and snakes in place of antennae and the first pair of legs. (Two such Gorgons are known from a painting on a Proto-Attic krater found at Eleusis, c. 675–650 B.C., now in the Eleusis Museum. Richter 1959: 286, fig. 405; Richards-Mantzoulinou 1980: 91.)

FIGURE 328

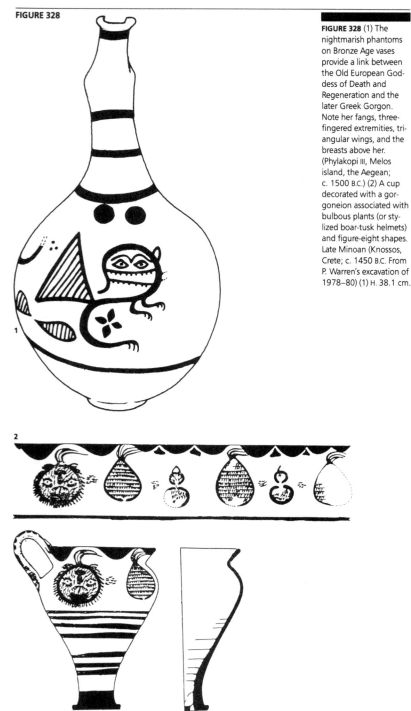

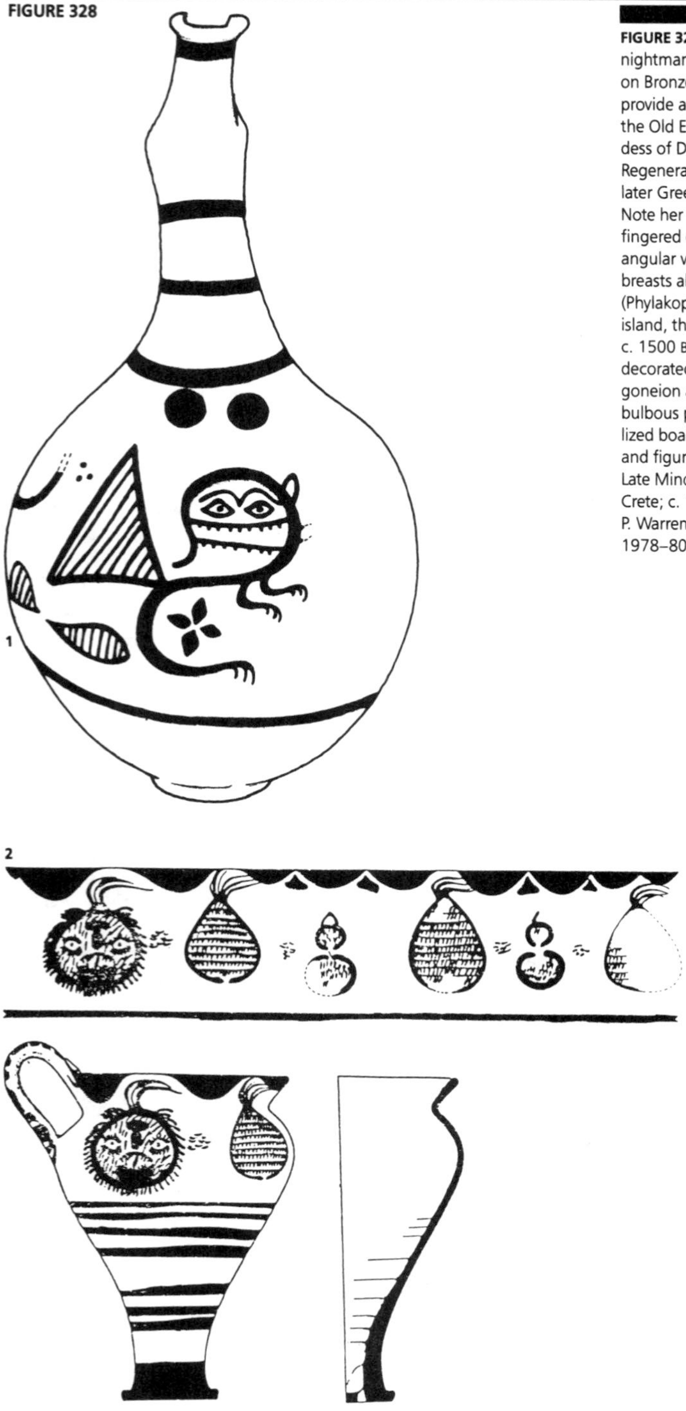

FIGURE 328 (1) The nightmarish phantoms on Bronze Age vases provide a link between the Old European Goddess of Death and Regeneration and the later Greek Gorgon. Note her fangs, three-fingered extremities, triangular wings, and the breasts above her. (Phylakopi III, Melos island, the Aegean; c. 1500 B.C.) (2) A cup decorated with a gorgoneion associated with bulbous plants (or stylized boar-tusk helmets) and figure-eight shapes. Late Minoan (Knossos, Crete; c. 1450 B.C. From P. Warren's excavation of 1978–80) (1) H. 38.1 cm.

Why bee wings and snakes? The answer to this peculiar combination of symbols comes from the fact that both snakes and bees (and, as known from Greek myths, honey as well), were connected with regeneration. Like the Varna masks and their associated objects, again we see a fusion of the symbols of death and rebirth.

The early Gorgon was a potent Goddess dealing with life and death, not the later Indo-European monster to be slain by heroes such as Perseus. Images of her with the wings of a bee surrounded by whirls and flanked by cranes and lions (which replaced earlier Old European dogs) or holding cranes and geese in her hands (such as on a plate from Rhodos: Harrison 1922: fig. 33; Hampe and Simon 1981: fig. 104) betray her identity as the "Mistress of Wild Things," or Artemis. Her frightening mask indicates that she is the Erinys side of Artemis, the dangerous one. In other words, she is Hekate, whose temples and altars stood at gates, entrances, or in front of houses in ancient Greece. In the earliest historic records which mention her, she is linked with Artemis. Artemis and Hekate are one, a lunar Goddess of the life cycle with two aspects: one standing at the beginning of the cycle, the other at the end; one young, pure and beautiful, connected with young life, and the other gruesome, connected with death. No wonder that the Orphics saw the moon's face as a Gorgon's head. Hekate is described as traveling above graveyards with her hounds, collecting poison and then mixing deadly potions (Willamowitz-Moellendorf 1959: 170). She is a remorseless killer appeased only by bloody sacrifices. Her eerie howl conveys the presence of death.

The Gorgon lived throughout ancient Greece. Her hideous features—lolling tongue, projecting teeth, and writhing snakes for hair—were believed to be protection against the Evil Eye. As a prophylactic mask the Gorgon was depicted on shields, portable ovens, town walls, buildings, etc. On the western pediment of the Artemis temple on Corfu,

c. 580 B.C., she is portrayed with snakes emerging horizontally out of her head; she is girdled by two snakes with hissing opposed heads exuding powerful energy.

18.12 *The White Lady as Death Messenger in European folk traditions*

There are two images in folk traditions that clearly go back to the prehistoric Goddess of Death and Regeneration: 1. the White Lady as death messenger, and 2. the Killer and Regeneratrix, degraded to a witch in historical times. Both are anthropomorphic, but with some characteristics of a bird of prey or of a poisonous snake. They fly as birds or are heard as birds' screeching, screaming, or interjecting sounds, or they are sensed as snakes' sliding. In the Basque area, as was already mentioned, this goddess continued to exist as a vulture until the first half of the 20th century. In early Ireland, she was Morrígan (single or triple) or a Crow Goddess (*badb*) until the 18th century, when this image gradually merged with that of a banshee, an anthropomorphic fairy (Lysaght 1986: 106 ff.). The White Lady is directly associated with death; she is a death forboder. The Killer acts on a cosmic plane: she balances the life energy of humans, animals, plants, and even of the moon. Her domains are night and winter, whereas the death messenger presents herself at the occurrence of death, night or day.

In Irish folk tradition of the last centuries, the death messenger usually appears as a little woman dressed in white or gray, but occasionally she is tall, slim, and ugly. If she is beautiful, her beauty is especially due to the long yellow or golden hair. She manifests herself outside the house of the dying person, in the garden, in the orchard, at the turf stack, but more often at the openings or entrances to the house, especially at the windows. The presence of the death messenger is not so much seen as it is heard. The sound is described either as birds' cry or as "lonesome" and "mournful." The sound is also compared with the howling of dogs or foxes. It heads for and encircles the house of a dying person. Frequently it is repeated three times. Although Patricia Lysaght, in her study on the Irish Banshee of 1986, has shown that the image of a death messenger as a crow—well attested in the literary accounts—has dwindled in the last centuries, the memory of the death messenger as a bird still lives. For instance, the banshee appears in the shape of a bird and sits on the windowsill of the room in which the person lies ill. She comes regularly for about a week before the person dies (Lysaght 1986: 107). To some people, interviewed about the banshee as late as 1976, it was nothing else but a bird: "She was a bird, you'd hear the flutter of the wings. . . . And they say it is a bird, not a woman, a bird" (Lysaght 1986: 108, 109). The death messenger also manifests herself as a washerwoman. In legends she beats the winding sheet. In the Scottish-Gaelic tradition, the supernatural washer-woman, the *bean-nighe*, is also a foreboder of death. In early Irish sources the washing activity is ascribed to the goddess Badb or Morrígan (Lysaght 1986: 128–33; 198, 199). Why washing? Perhaps because water is a link with the other-world.

In Lithuanian folk tradition she is the double or "sister" of the Birth-giving Fate. When the time of death comes, she is there at the dying person's head. Gates and fences do not mean anything to her; doors open by themselves. As a woman, she is slim and tall and has an insatiable appetite. She has a poisonous, lolling tongue like the pre-Vedic Indian goddess Kālī. Dressed in a white sheet, she collects poison from corpses buried in graves. If she licks a person with her tongue, that person will instantly die (recorded at the end of the 19th century in Lithuania: Basanavičius 1903). The name of the Lithuanian Death Goddess *Giltinė* derives from the verb *gilti*, "to sting," and is related to *geltonas*, "yellow." (Yellow is still considered the color of death because it is the color of bone).

From her activities and her name it can be judged that Giltinė originally was not a vulture or crow but a poisonous snake, the deadly aspect of the Snake Goddess. She can also change her shape into any form she wants, including inanimate objects, such as a woodshaving, a basket, a stick. As in other areas of Europe, she appears as one or three (three young girls dressed in white) and occasionally as a larger group of young girls. As in Ireland, she is more frequently heard than seen. The sound, however, is more mysterious than moaning, lamenting or birds' cry. It is like the splashing of water or running of ale, tapping at the door or table, striking with a whip, rattling of glasses, or a shudder in the body, usually repeated three times. This subdued sound or sensation seems to be related to a snake's creeping or sliding. A white dog or hound is Giltinė's animal. The howling of a dog or appearance of a white dog running from the direction of a cemetery forebodes death (Gimbutas 1984; 1985).

18.13 *The Killer-Regeneratrix or Witch, an image continuing to the 20th century*

The second image, that of a Destroyer and Regeneratrix, is colorfully preserved to this day in the Baltic and Slavic folk tradition. She is Ragana in Lithuanian and Latvian folklore and Baba Yaga in Russian tales. This image is familiar in Grimm's fairy tales: a crooked Old Woman, yellow and lean, with a large hooked nose, the point of which reached her chin. The nose is hooked like the beak of a bird of prey. She is none other than the Goddess Holle degraded to a witch.

The name of the Baltic Ragana is related to the verb *regėti*, " to know, see, foresee," and to the noun *ragas*, "horn, crescent." The name itself reveals her essential characteristics: she is a seer, she "knows," and she is associated with the moon's crescent. In appearance she can be a beautiful woman or a nightmarish creature. She can transform herself into myriad shapes, primarily of a toad, hedgehog, and fish. She is also a bird since she flies, rarely walks; or else she rides on a stick or a stump (a symbol of dead nature). At the winter solstice, assemblies of Raganas fly at night to a special meeting place on a hill. One of the group is called "Lady." In the winter, Raganas bathe in ice-holes or sit in birch trees and comb their long hair. The killer instinct of Ragana manifests itself not in the winter but in the summer, especially when nights are shortest and plants thrive. She prevents plants from thriving; she may tie the ears of rye into knots and pluck pea blossoms. She takes milk from cows and shears sheep; she spoils brides at weddings and turns bridegrooms into wolves, and she kills newborn babies. She even cuts the waxing moon in half. Her destructive actions seem to be nothing else but a control of the cyclic life power. She stops growth, waxing, blossoming, productivity, and fertility lest life powers flourish forever. She reminds us that nature is mortal and that there is no life without death. Thus, she is essentially concerned with regeneration. The uterus, placenta, and the newborn babies belong to her. The blood of the newborns perhaps is an offering to her, necessary for the renewal of the cycle.

Baba Yaga, the ancient Goddess of Death and Regeneration in Slavic mythology, is well preserved in folk tales (mainly Russian) in a degraded form, i.e., as a witch. She might be depicted as an evil old hag who eats humans, especially children, or as a wise, prophetic old woman. In appearance, she is tall, bony legged, pestle headed, and has a long nose and disheveled hair. At times she is a young woman; at other times, she appears as two sisters, one young and one old. Baba Yaga never walks; she either flies in a fiery mortar or lies in her hut on bird's legs. The fence around the hut is made of human bones and topped with human skulls with eyes intact. The gate is fastened with human legs and arms instead of bolts, and a mouth with sharp teeth serves as a lock. The hut can turn around on its axis like a spindle and is, in fact, Baba Yaga herself. Her primary theriomorphic image is a bird or snake, and she can turn instantly into a frog, toad, turtle, mouse, crab, vixen, bee, mare, goat, or into an inanimate object.

Linguistic analysis of her compound name reveals prehistoric characteristics. The Slavic etymon *baba* means "grandmother," "woman," "a mythic cloud woman" (who produces rain), and "pelican." The latter suggests Baba Yaga's avian nature (Shapiro 1983: 109 ff., 125–26). Russian *Yaga*, Polish *Jędza*, Proto-Slavic **(y)ęga*, connotes "disease," "fright," "wrath" in Old Russian, Polish, Serbo-Croatian, and Slovene, and is related to the Lithuanian verb *engti*, to "strangle," "press," or "torture."

The Breton Ankou or "Death," commonly found in folktales and sometimes referred to as Maro "Death," and Irish Morrígan identified with Ana, a "Guardian of the Dead" also mentioned as "Mother of the Gods" (Doan 1980: 35), is surely related to Russian Yaga (Proto-Slavic Enga). Welsh *angeu* means "death." Near Eastern Anat of the Ras Shamra texts, a Goddess who can turn into a bird of prey, is another member of the same tradition of Death (or Vulture) Goddess.

The ancient Killer-Regeneratrix is known to all European folklore. However not as a formidable goddess but as a witch; her original is but a loathsome caricature thanks to enormous energies spent by missionaries and inquisitors to fight this powerful goddess. Flying witches on broomsticks or monsters, old women casting spells surrounded by animals or changing into animals or stones, gathering herbs, preparing potions, etc., are well-known images from stories and book illustrations starting in the 16th century. The images and activities of "witches" described in inquisition times are still full of reminiscences of actual characteristics of the Goddess. I shall cite here a report to the Inquisitor of a soldier who fell into the hands of "witches."

Sir, they command the sun and it obeys them, they change the stars in their courses, and they take away the light from the moon and restore it again at their will. They cause clouds to form in the air, and make it possible to tread on them, and they travel about the country. They cause fire to grow cold and water to burn. They turn themselves into young girls and in the twinkling of an eye into old women, or sticks, stones or beasts. If a man pleases them they have the power to enjoy him at will; and to make him more willing they can change him into various animals dulling his senses and his better nature. They have such power by reason of their arts that they have only to command and men must obey or lose their lives. For they like to move freely by day and night along roads and valleys and over mountains about their business, which is to cast spells, gather herbs and stones and make pacts and agreements (Baroja 1975: 149).

Even if somewhat dramatized, this image in its core is not an exaggeration. Witches were greatly feared since they continued to represent the powers of a formidable Goddess on earth. Her role as a commander of the atmospheric changes and controller of growth of moon, sun, and fire can be reconstructed from the recorded activities of the Basque Mari, Irish Morrígan (or three sisters, Neman, Macha, and Morrígan), German Frau Holle, Lithuanian and Latvian Ragana, and Russian Baba Yaga (Polish Jędza). All of them create clouds, tempestuous winds, pulling them out of caves or abysses. They shed showers, fog, and hailstorms. They can be seen as a sphere or a stick of fire in the sky. The Basque Mari appears as a sickle or half-moon emitting flames or as a woman whose head is encircled by the moon. Ragana is known to cause eclipses of the sun and to control the growth of the moon. All of these goddesses are shape-changers and can change humans into animals. They also have powers over human and animal sexuality and fertility.

18.14 *Killer-Reneratrix as Old Hag, dry bones, and winter*

Funerary monuments and their symbolism reveal a close link between the grave type, Old Hag, dry bones, and the death of nature in winter. Folk stories associate megalithic tombs with a fearsome goddess. Some cairns are said to be composed of stones dropped from the apron of the "Old Hag." At least forty chambered tombs in Ireland are nicknamed "Dermot and Grania's Bed" (because a young man and his girl, who were eloping, were supposed to have made a bed of stones every night as they fled). But Grania's name suggests deeper roots than the story itself. The original meaning of gráinne is "ugliness." Thus, Grania is the Old Hag of Celtic myths (Burl 1981: 66). The other meaning of gráinne is "grain, seed," which suggests association with regeneration. The passage grave at Knockmany, County Tyrone, Ireland, is called "Annia's Cave," the home of the hag Ana or Anu, guardian of the dead. Grania, Annia, Anu, and other goddesses associated with bones, death, winter, and ugliness are related to the above described Killer-Regeneratrix. In folk tales, Berchta (the winter aspect of German Holle), Ragana and Baba Yaga appear as "bones" or "bony-legged hags." Ragana's white bones "sparkle in the snow" in the winter when the sun shines. "Sparkling snowflakes" mean "witches bones" in Lithuanian tales.

The bone and the hag are symbolically related. Custom required that corpses be reduced to bare bones to become "Death." In western Europe, this result was achieved by allowing birds of prey to remove the flesh. Only then were the bones brought to the tombs. Where excarnation of this sort was not practiced, the dead had to be cremated. However, large bones were preserved and buried. In ancient Greece, large bones, called "white bones," were smeared with fat before their burial. They must have been regarded as a bridge between death and new life. The power of regeneration of the Goddess remained in them.

Moisture remaining in the bones after death had to be removed, as the bone marrow and moisture were symbolic of life. The Greeks believed that the spinal cord of a dead man turned into a snake when the marrow decayed, or that the moisture of the marrow produced serpents (Harrison 1962: 268). Only clean and dry bones were placed in the tomb chambers.

Skulls were treated with special care, as can be seen from tidy collections of skulls placed separately from other bones. For instance, at the Knowe of Yarso, in the Orkney Islands, 29 skulls were meticulously positioned along the tomb wall, facing the passage and the entrance. At Isbister, also in the Orkneys, skulls were placed in pairs, in the corners and cell openings (Burl 1981: 74).

Human death was thought to be similar to nature's death in winter, when the sun's power is weakest and the days are short and nights long. It is not surprising to discover that many west European tomb-shrines have been constructed so that the entrances align with the winter solstice. (This is true at Gavrinis in Brittany, Newgrange in Ireland, and Maes Howe, Mainland, Orkney Islands, Scotland: see Thom and Thom, 1978; also Heggie 1981 and Ruggles 1984.) The winter solstice marks the time when the days start to become longer and life begins again. The alignment of tomb entrances according to the moon's position at the winter solstice suggests the importance of lunar influences on burial customs.

Symbols carved on the orthostats and curbstones of large megalithic tombs speak for a preoccupation with measuring the length of the year and counting lunar phases (see Part IV). These carvings even include sundials. One of the best is on a curbstone at Knowth, a giant tomb-shrine near Newgrange in Ireland (Brennan 1983: 158 ff.). Megalithic tomb-shrines were not built to serve as solar and lunar observatories, as claimed by Thom (1971), Thom and Thom (1978), and a number of other scientists writing on the importance of megalithic astronomy. Rather, their orientation according to solar and lunar phases served essentially for the regeneration of life. Rebirth was in the power of the Goddess. In megalithic symbolic art, we see the link between the time-measuring symbols of lunar cycles and the symbols of Her regenerative power, and between sundials and Divine Eyes, symbols of the life-source and rebirth. All other associated symbols—multiple arcs rising in vertical columns, trees, serpent forms, bands of wavy lines or zig-zags—are expressions of regenerative aquatic or plant force.

An English herbal of the 12th century (ms. in British Museum, Harley 1585: 12v–13r; cited by Hull 1928: 24; also by Graves 1972: 73), includes a prayer to the Goddess. The prayer addresses the Deity with these words: "Divine Goddess Mother Nature, who generatest all things and bringest *forth anew the sun* which thou has given to the nations; Guardian of sky and sea and of all Gods and powers; through thy influence all nature is hushed and sinks to sleep. . . . Again, when it pleases thee, thou sendest forth the glad daylight and nurturest life with thine eternal surety; and when the spirit of man passes, to thee it returns. Thou indeed art rightly named Great Mother of the Gods. . . ." She is here the same Regeneratrix—Ana, Ankou, Holle, also addressed as "Mother of the Gods." Surely this prayer embodies a memory of a once omnipotent goddess who had the power to regenerate the sun. German Holle regenerates the sun, and she is herself the sun, addressed as "The Mother of all Life" and "The Great Healer" (Rüttner-Cova 1986: 78).

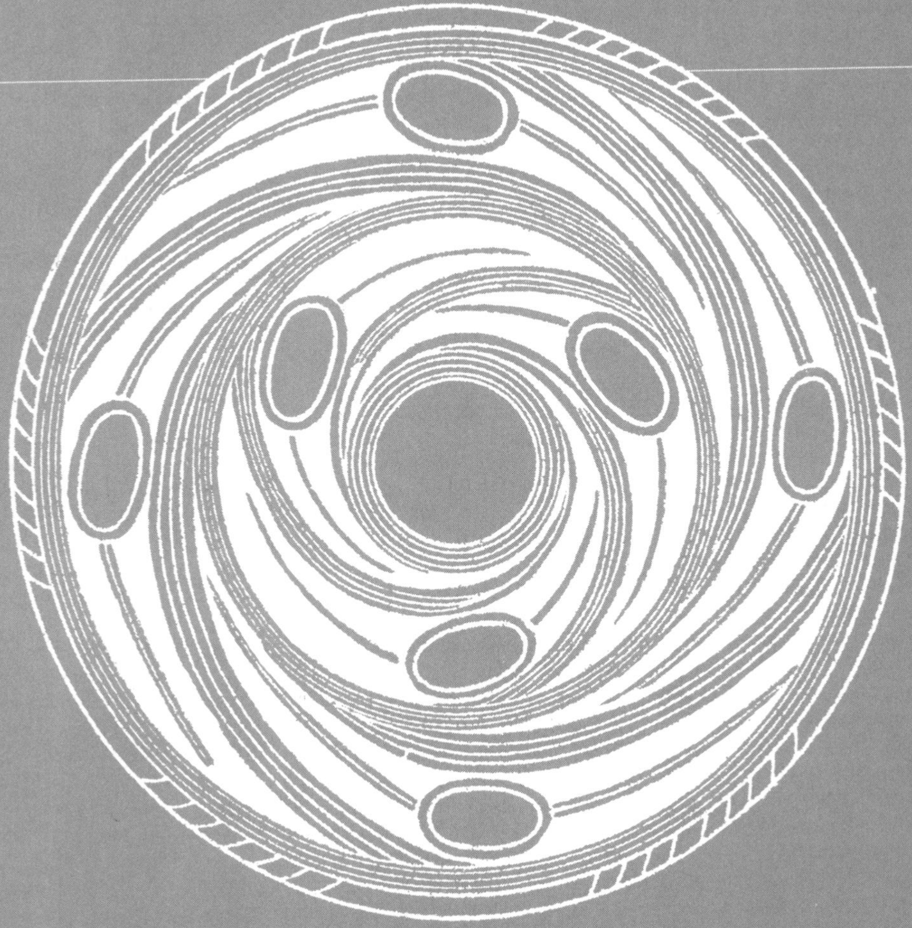

Egg forms part of whirling compositions on interior or this graceful dish; Karanovo, N Bulgaria. See figure 338, page 218.

19/ *Egg*

The significance of the egg is clear from the earliest stages of the Neolithic in Europe and Anatolia. It appears in egg-shaped vase forms, painted decorative motifs, and in the frescoes forming a heritage for the later Dionysian and Orphic mysteries. This symbolism is splendidly illustrated in Cucuteni and Karanovo vase painting of the 5th and early 4th millennia B.C. It continues with great richness of expression in the Aegean and Mediterranean area to 1500 B.C. and beyond into the Mycenaean culture.

The symbolism of the egg bears not so much upon birth as upon a rebirth modeled on the repeated creation of the world (Eliade 1958: 414). In our own time, this is manifested in the ritual use of eggs at New Year's and Easter in European villages (Easter is a Christianization of more ancient spring regeneration rituals). Eggs painted with red and black whirls, spirals, snakes, crescents, and plant motifs are carried around and given to each family at Easter in the Baltic and Slavic countries to celebrate the coming of spring. To ensure the renewal of vegetation, eggs are placed in the ploughed earth.

Furthermore the egg plays a role in feasts of the dead and is placed as an offering in graves to prompt regeneration. This is an ancient association; from the early Neolithic onward, burial pithoi (jars) are egg-shaped, symbolizing the womb of the Goddess from which life would re-emerge.

Egg forms—circles, ovals, ellipses—as meaningful symbols go back even further, into the Upper Paleolithic. In Magdalenian art, circles and ovals are engraved over female buttocks and the bodies of bulls. (FIGURE 329) The latter association will continue throughout prehistory.

There are several categories of egg symbolism, which may be reconstructed through the observations of symbolic association. The first comprises birds carrying a cosmogonic egg, the second links the egg with water and the bull as life-generators, and the third associated eggs with symbols of becoming—spirals, crescents, horns, whirls, crosses, X's, snakes, and sprouting plants.

FIGURE 329

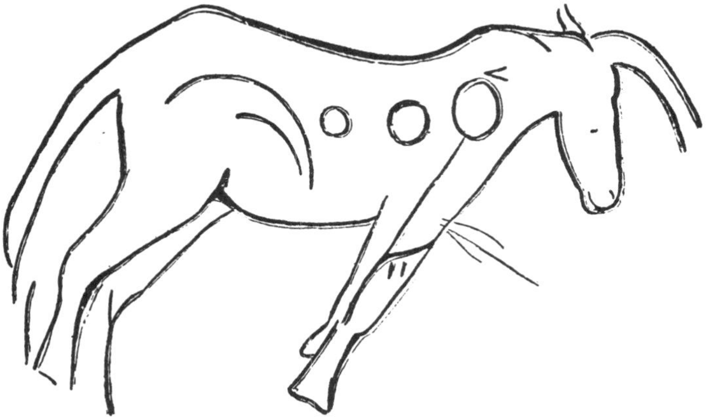

FIGURE 329 The egg, symbol of regeneration and rebirth, appears in the Upper Paleolithic, in this case on a bull painted on a cave floor; note the large crescent behind the three eggs. Middle Magdalenian (Niaux, Ariège, Pyrénées, S France; c. 12,000 B.C.) H. 64.5 cm.

19.1 *The cosmogonic egg*

The bird-shaped vase of the Neolithic and later ages is possibly linked to a universal myth in ancient civilizations, that of the cosmic egg laid by a sacred waterbird. (FIGURE 330) This idea takes graphic form on Minoan, Cycladic, and Helladic vases as a bird who carries within her an egg, usually painted red. (FIGURE 331)

FIGURE 330

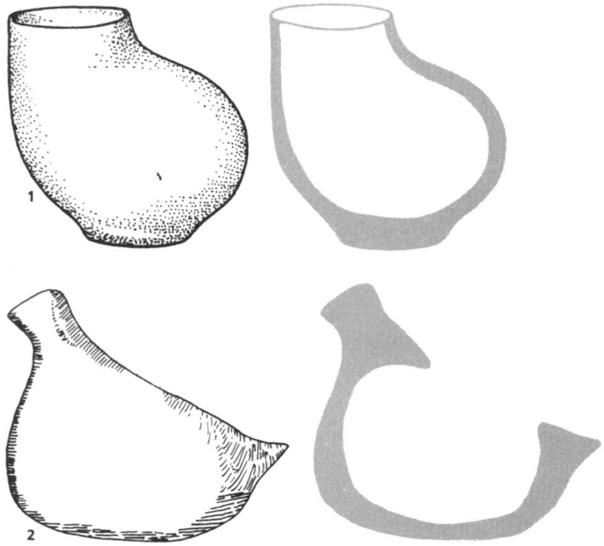

FIGURE 330 Throughout the Neolithic and Copper Age, askoi—bird-shaped vases with egg-shaped interior spaces—are common. (1) Sesklo (Nea Nikomedeia, Macedonia, N Greece; c. 6300–6200 B.C.). (2) Megalithic passage grave (Mesa de Las Huccas, Portugal; 4th mill. B.C.). (1) H. 13.1 cm. (2) H. 15.8 cm.

FIGURE 331

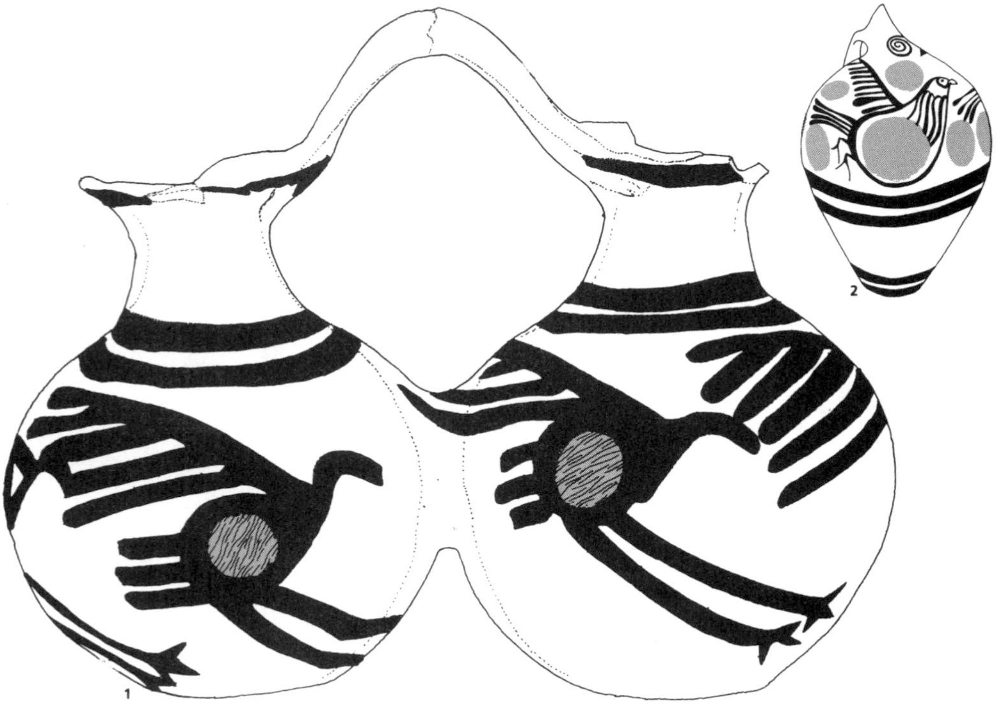

FIGURE 331 Helladic and Minoan vases, where a bird carries an egg, usually red, in her belly. (1) Middle Helladic (Asine, near Argos, Greece; early 2nd mill. B.C.). (2) Late Minoan (Knossos palace repository, Crete; 16th cent. B.C.). (1) H. 34.8 cm. (2) H. 37 cm.

19.2 *Egg and uterus*

On Maltese vases, the dotted or striated ground in which the eggs sit indicates a link with the watery sphere. (FIGURE 332) This association is also seen on Cucuteni and Minoan vases. Many representations seem to depict the egg as mushy and fluid, as a bubble or a drop of water, or they are synonyms of uteri. Egg and water are further linked with the bull and horns. Not infrequently bull heads or horns alternate with eggs in vase decoration. (FIGURE 333) The conceptual relationship between water, egg, and bull symbolism is reflected in representations on vases where all three appear in association, as on a dish from the Hal Saflieni hypogeum of Malta. (FIGURE 334) On one side are bulls with enormous horns; on the other side, eggs connected by striated lines seem to float in primeval waters.

FIGURE 332

FIGURE 332 On a knobbed lid, these eggs, symbols of rebirth, float on a striated background probably representing the waters of life. Pre-Cucuteni (Izvoare, near Peatra Neamţ, NE Romania; c. 4600–4500 B.C.)

FIGURE 333 The egg is associated with bulls and bull horns, symbols of regeneration. On this footed bowl, eggs alternate with horns. Pre-Cucuteni III (Traian-Dealul Fintinilor, Moldavia; 4600–4500 B.C.). H. of fragment 13.6 cm.

FIGURE 333

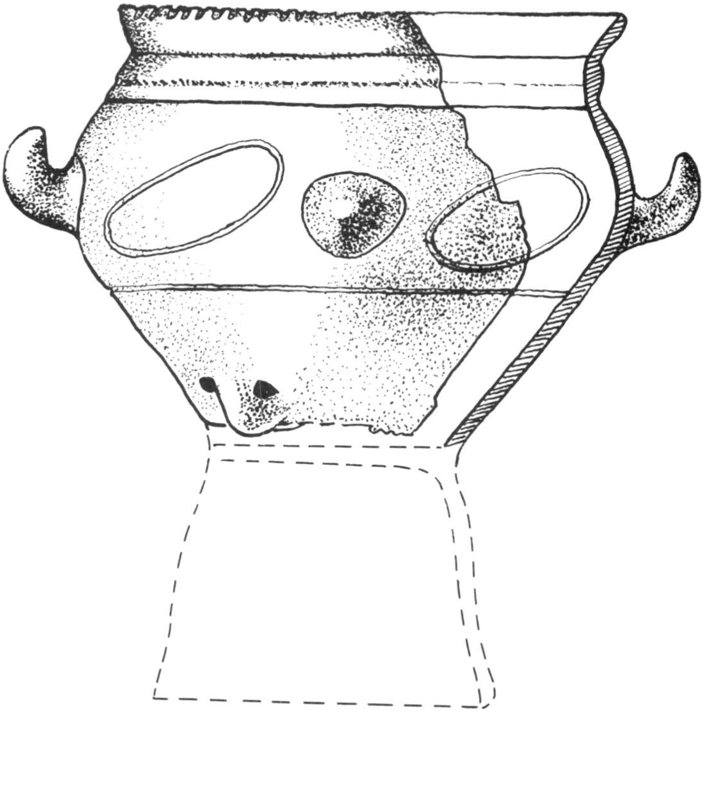

FIGURE 334

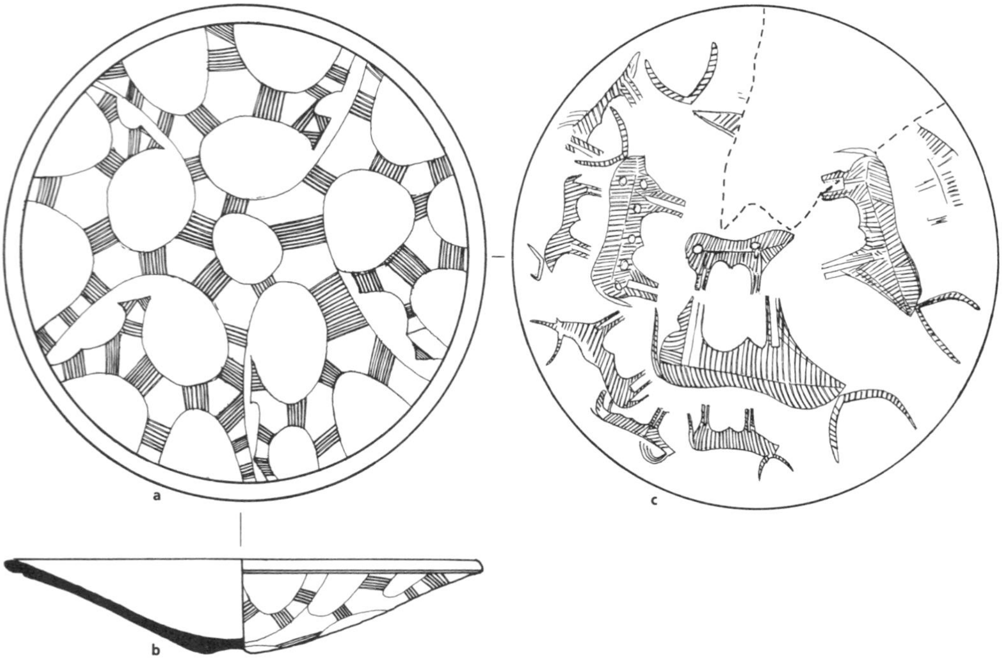

FIGURE 334 Egg, water, and bull combine on this Maltese dish. Note the tadpole-like forms of some of the eggs, and the eggs on the bodies of some of the bulls on the interior. (Tarxien, Hal Saflieni hypogeum, Malta; c. 3000 B.C.) DIA. 26.1 cm.

FIGURE 335

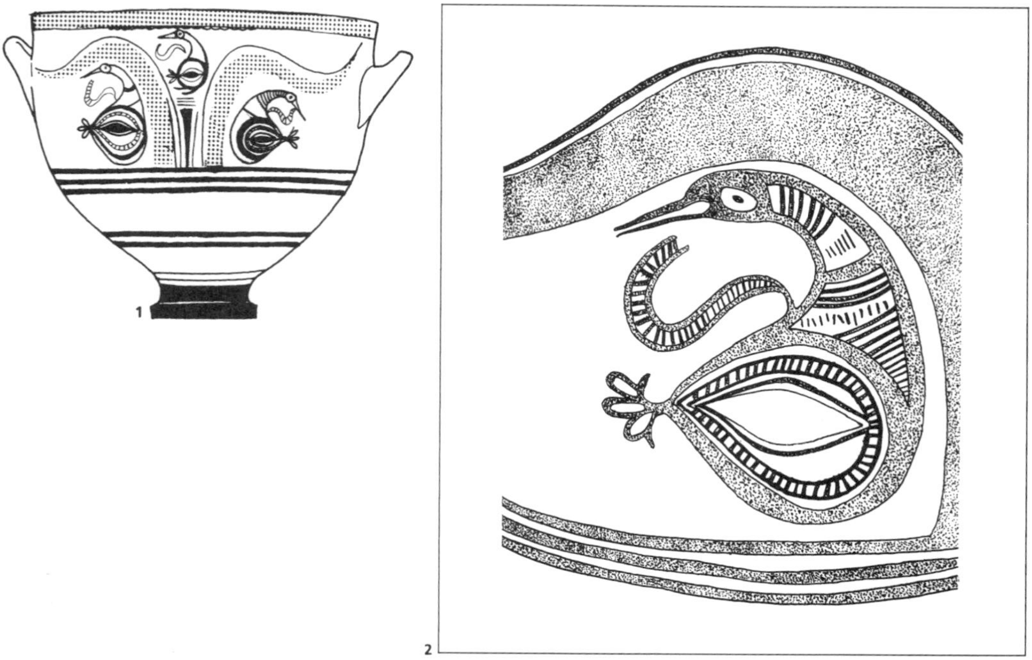

FIGURE 335 Bulls, birds, and eggs form a tableau of "becoming" on this vase. Waterbirds with sprouting eggs in their bellies and a snake or caterpillar below their beaks surround a large pair of bull horns. Vase (1) and detail (2). Painted red and dark brown on cream. (Knossos, Crete; Sub-Minoan krater; 14th cent. B.C.) H. 19.8 cm.

FIGURE 336

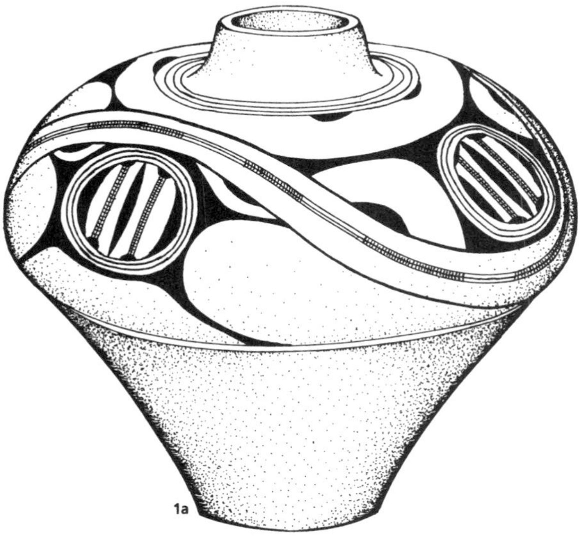

1a

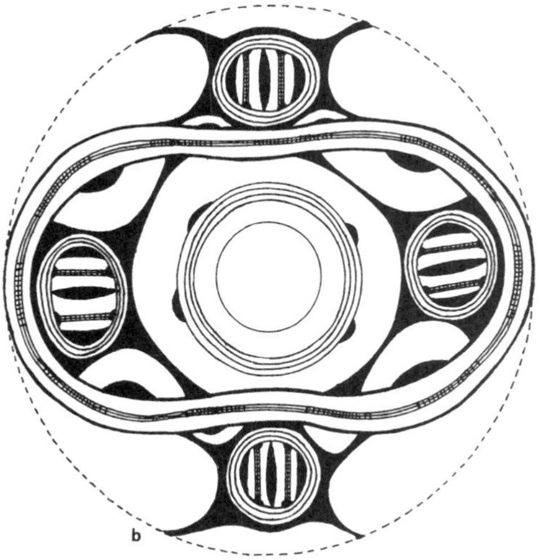

b

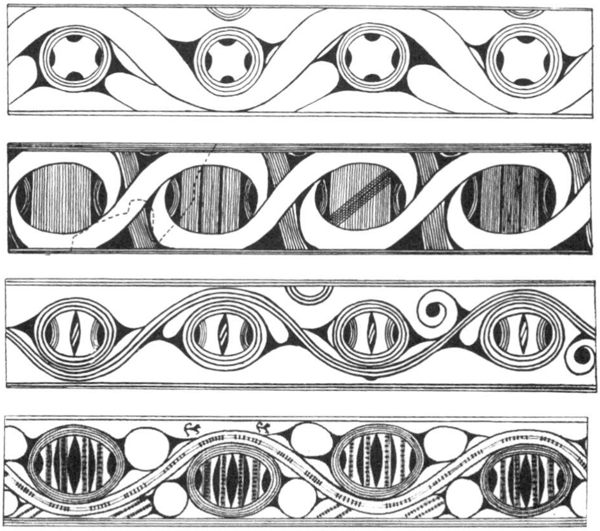

2

FIGURE 336 The common ancient myth featuring a cosmogonic egg and a snake may be represented in Late Cucuteni vase painting. Snakes wind around eggs filled with lenses and net columns. (1) Painted black on red. Vase (a) and view from top (b). (Kriszczatek, upper R. Dniester, Bukovina; c. 3900–3700 B.C.). (2) Designs over the bodies of four vases painted black on red (Sipenitsi; c. 3900–3700 B.C.). (1) DIA. 41.6 cm.

The process of "becoming" is well expressed by a Late Minoan vase on which an egg in the belly of a waterfowl is represented as a sprouting seed. (FIGURE 335) The birds are placed in between and underneath a pair of bull horns.

Judging from compositions on Cucuteni vases where a gigantic undulating snake winds around four eggs placed in the cardinal directions, there is also a link between the egg and the water- or world-snake. (FIGURE 336) Such portrayals very likely reflect a connection with those creation myths featuring a cosmogonic egg and snake at the beginning of the world.

19.3 *Egg and symbols of "becoming"*

A spiral, cross, or X signifies the energy inherent in the egg. Bands of eggs marked with an X or cross, alternating with vertical columns of parallel lines, decorate Cucuteni vases. (FIGURE 337) The egg also figures in whirling compositions; see the exceptionally dynamic whirl painted on the interior of a Karanovo dish from Hotnica, Bulgaria, c. 4500 B.C. (FIGURE 338) In sum, prehistoric art reveals that the egg in the Old European belief system stands for becoming, regeneration, and recreation.

FIGURE 337

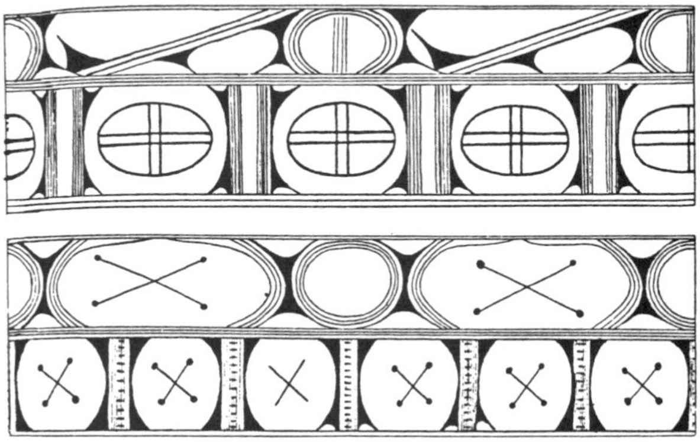

FIGURE 337 A cross, X, or whirl represents the inherent regenerative energy within the egg. In these decorative bands from the shoulders of Cucuteni B vases, the eggs often alternate with life columns. (Sipenitsi, W Ukraine; 3900–3700 B.C.)

19.4 *The tomb as egg*

This symbolism is strikingly clear in the tomb shape itself, particularly in the central Mediterranean area where egg-shaped tombs were cut in rock. In the Balearic Islands, Corsica, Sardinia, central and southern Italy, Sicily, and Malta oven-shaped rock-cut tombs appear singly (see fig. 217) or in pairs resembling kidneys. Larger cemeteries, such as Anghelu Ruju near Alghero in Sardinia, consist of groups of egg-shaped niches linked by a corridor (Atzeni 1981: xxxii).

The most amazing monument is the Hypogeum of Hal Saflieni in Malta, an enormous labyrinthine underground ossuary-sanctuary laid out on three stories reaching 30 feet below the surface of the rock. It is an aggregate of many variously sized egg-shaped chambers connected by passages and stairways. There were also two large cisterns for collecting water. The many burial chambers were not cut all at once but possibly over several centuries (Evans 1959: 130). When it was excavated in 1904–11 by Zammit, in front of the entrance were found traces of a megalithic building, perhaps a temple originally connected to the Hypogeum.

FIGURE 338

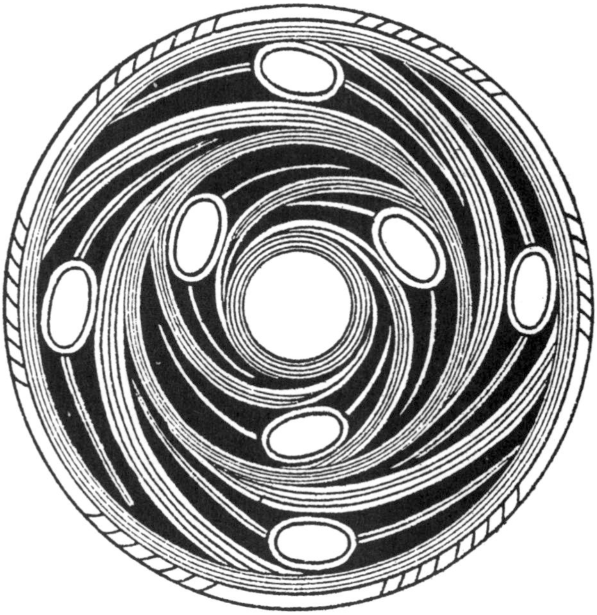

FIGURE 338 The egg also forms part of whirling compositions, as on the interior of this graceful dish painted in red and graphite. Karanovo VI (Hotnica, N Bulgaria; 4500–4300 B.C.) DIA. 63.6 cm.

The entrance to the underground was through a trilithon (three stones) leading to the first level; the most elaborate oval halls are on the second level. They have ceilings painted in red spirals, or rather a vine appears to spring up from the floor and meander upwards and outwards, interweaving with a honeycomb pattern whose hexagonal cells each contain either a red circle with a small red central disc or else a spiral and a disc (Ridley 1976: 78). Traces of paint in most chambers show that originally tombs were either painted solidly in red or had symbols painted in red; the exception is one wall where a checkerboard pattern was painted in black and white. Altogether bones of 7000 individuals were recovered from this huge catacomb oven. The bones were found in disorder, which suggests that they were collected after the flesh had decomposed and were laid to rest in these red-painted egg-shaped burial chambers for incubation and regeneration.

The oval architecture, life and energy symbols painted in red, votive offerings of miniature sleeping women comfortably lying on couches, a fish on a dish-like support, vases decorated with eggs and crescent-horned bulls (fig. 334)—all inform us that Hal Saflieni Hypogeum was not merely a necropolis, but a place of sacred mysteries concerning dying and rebirth akin to the Eleusynian mysteries of ancient Greece. Here in the moist darkness of the womb, Earth's powerful energy and the mystery of life's beginnings in death was experienced through a state of heightened consciousness. As at Eleusis and hundreds of other sacred grottos used from the Neolithic to the present day, sick people sought health, barren women sought pregnancy, and devotees congregated and slept in womb-shaped chambers. Strengthened by the Earth powers and probably by a priestess's divination and acoustic conjuring reverberating through the vaults, the pilgrims were born anew.

Seed corn, sacred to the Corn Goddess, the fat Lady of Tarxien, could also have been stored in the Hypogeum to make it fertile before sowing. This would correspond with ancient cults associated by the classical Greeks with Demeter, their goddess of corn and fertility (Ferguson 1985).

The belief in the intertwining of death and birth still lingers in 20th century Malta, northern Africa, and in most of Europe. A Maltese proverb runs that "a woman's grave is open from the day she has conceived till the fortieth day after her deliverance." The forty days are extremely dangerous for the baby. The *Zagaz*, *jnuns*, and *janas*, wicked genies or witches, kill or snatch the newborns or exchange them for their own ugly children. The sacrifice of a fowl and preparation of a special hen-meal for the mother are to appease the Goddess ruling over death.

After birth, the midwife must carefully obliterate all traces of the child's birth, and she personally buries the placenta or throws it into the sea. And what she says while burying it is most striking: "It is not thee that I am burying, O afterbirth, it is the Zagas" (Cassar-Pullicino 1976: 234–41). That is to say, the placenta is a homologue of the Goddess of Death. The obliteration of the placenta arrests the power of death and secures a smooth transition to life, a transition from darkness to light. The killing or devouring of newborns by Hekate, Ragana, Baba Yaga, and other goddesses of death and regeneration do not literally describe their cannibalistic nature; their behavior is symbolic, since after birth the child is still in the hands of the dark powers. To protect the living from the Goddess of Darkness the newborn babies were buried under the floor of the house. This custom is well documented by the excavations of Neolithic houses and it is known to have continued to the 19th century A.D. (recorded among the Slavs: Afanasiev 1867: 113).

The cosmic egg as the womb of the world likely is the underlying idea of the ground plans of Newgrange, Knowth, and Dowth, the gigantic round mounds of Ireland. Covered with white quartz, Newgrange looks like a huge egg-shaped dome. The color of the quartz must have been of great significance. Quartz is not found near Newgrange, so hundreds of tons had to be transported to the site, probably from the Wicklow mountains about forty miles to the south. It is unlikely that the Newgrange builders undertook such a vast project for purely decorative reasons. The white quartz and the egg-shaped plan possibly meant to suggest the surface of an egg (the idea proposed by Brennan 1980: 18).

Large quartz stones were also found in a number of cairns (round mounds of stones over graves). In the passage grave of Baltinglass in County Wicklow they were so plentiful that they speckled the cairn like daisies. Quartz stones or white pebbles were found strewn around cremations (Burl 1981: 93). The latter may also suggest a link with the egg, the obvious symbol of the compacted potentia of regeneration. The deposition of white chalk balls in ditches or henges of Windmill Hill, Stonehenge, Avebury, Newgrange, and other cult places of England and Ireland (Burl 1981: 45) likewise may be associated with egg symbolism. Further, the color of the egg is also the color of bone, another reason for its association with the dead and tombs. We deal here, it seems, with polyvalent symbolism, with that of both death and rebirth, tomb and womb, at once.

Gavrinis orthostat covered with vertical columns of concentric arcs radiating from central vulvar opening. See figure 344, page 225.

20/ *Columns of Life*

In the philosophical system of Old Europe, the life column was regarded as an embodiment of the mysterious life force, the link between nonbeing and being. This nuclear life force was believed to be inherent in the egg, snake, water, and the body of the Goddess—specifically her womb—which is actualized in a cave, underground crypt, or megalithic structure.

20.1 *Within the egg*

Judging from its position within the cosmic egg, the column of parallel line, checkerboard, or net pattern is the form in which the germinating life force of the primordial substance becomes manifest. In Old European symbolism, the seed or a sprouting plant alternates with the column to represent the life force coming into being. This is reinforced by flanking egg/uterus forms, crescents, helices, horns, and half or "splitting" eggs, symbols of becoming.

Within horizontal bands on Cucuteni vases, the central "world egg" containing a vertical life column is flanked by helixes. (FIGURE 339) (The diagonal column between the motifs seems to be a variant of the vertical column.) Eggs, half-eggs, or splitting eggs rhythmically repeat the main idea in the lower bands. The life column motif is also painted inside dishes, themselves probably a metaphor of the cosmic egg, so that the vessel resembles a cross-section study of the process of regeneration. (FIGURE 340)

Occasionally the egg contains a tree or beanlike plant, its stem a column of parallel lines or net patterns. Two or more such eggs, equally spaced around a vase and connected by an undulating snake, is a common decoration on Cucuteni, Minoan, and Mycenaean vases. (FIGURE 341) On a multifaceted Minoan seal, the life column is flanked by nautili on one face; there is a sprouting plant on another, and a whirl or star on the third. (FIGURE 342)

The tree as outgrowth of an underground column appears in Minoan art. On a gold ring from Phaistos (Alexiou 1969: 89), a tree rises from a pillar contained in an enclosure or shrine. This is a symbolic rendering of the emergence on earth of the chthonic life force.

20.2 *Within the cave and crypt*

In Europe, pillar shrines and the ceremonial use of caves with stalagmites and stalactites date from the 7th millennium B.C. and continue into the 5th and later, but the beginnings of life-column symbolism in caves must have been considerably earlier. Clay phalli have been found in Upper Paleolithic caves (in the upper Périgordian shelter of Laussel, Dordogne, and in the Magdalenian cave of Tuc d'Audoubert, Ariège, France).

FIGURE 339

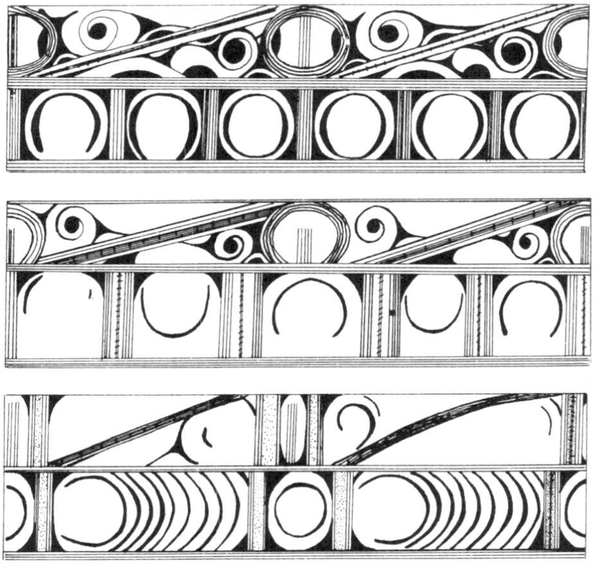

FIGURE 339 The column of life, manifestation of the life force, appears with eggs, spirals, and other symbols of becoming. Note that columns of parallel lines occur both inside (upper registers) and next to the world eggs. Painted black on red on the shoulders of piriform vases. Cucuteni B (Sipenitsi, Bukovina; 3900–3700 B.C.)

FIGURE 340

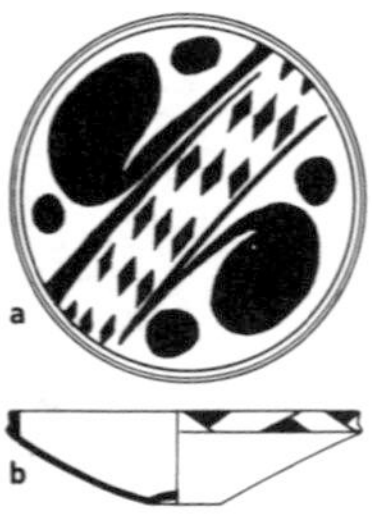

FIGURE 341

FIGURE 342

FIGURE 340 In a cross-section of the process of regeneration, a dish represents the cosmic egg, complete with life column inside and flanked by uterus forms and eggs, discs, or moon phases. Karanovo VI (Gumelniţa A_2, S Romania; c. 4500 B.C.) DIA. 33.5 cm.

FIGURE 341 Sometimes the life column within an egg takes the form of a tree or beanlike plant. The eggs are connected by undulating snakes; the discs probably represent moon phases. (1) Cucuteni B (Koszylowce, Galicia, W Ukraine; c. 3500 B.C.). Painted black on red. (2) Mycenaean (Mycenae, Peloponnese; 14th cent. B.C.). Painted brown on red. (1) H. 28.6 cm. (2) H. 19.6 cm.

FIGURE 342 This multi-faceted Middle Minoan seal is carved with a life column and nautili, a sprouting plant, and a whirl or eight-pointed star, all symbols of regeneration. (Platanos, Mesara Plain, Crete; early 2nd mill. B.C.) H. 1.4 cm.

Womblike caves, filled with stalagmites and stalactites and sheltering sacred water at the bottom, were sanctuaries. At Scaloria in Manfredonia, southeastern Italy (unpublished; excavated by Gimbutas and Winn 1977–80), cultural remains date to 5600–5300 B.C. More than 1500 whole and fragmented vases painted with egg, plant, snake, triangle, hourglass, V, and chevron motifs were recovered there. Some were standing at the base of stalagmites, deep in the narrow lower cave. One hundred and thirty-seven skeletons, most of which were in a mass burial and had traces of peculiar cuts at the base of their skulls, were found in the upper cave close to the entrance to the lower cave. Perhaps Death and Regeneration Mysteries were celebrated here. The cycle of regeneration is mirrored in the cave's uterine shape, the life water below, and the stalagmites in a constant process of formation.

In the analagous vagina-uterus-shaped cave of Koutala on the Cycladic island of Serifos, the sacred water in the bottom contains a rock on which a stalagmite appears in the form of a female figure. In front of it were the remains of offerings —Neolithic dishes, animal bones, and charred material (Petrocheilou 1984).

The Neolithic cave of Porto Badisco in Apulia includes not only drawings of snake-limbed creatures (see fig. 204) but also columns of interconnected lozenges, checkerboard columns, and firlike trees, probably symbolic of underground columns of life (Graziosi 1973: 160; and idem. 1980).

Another cave where sacrifices took place is from the Linear Pottery culture at Jungfernhöhle near Bamberg, Germany, c. 5000–early 5th millennium B.C. (Kunkel 1955). Thirty-six girls and women between one and 45 years of age and two men were found here believed to be sacrificial victims. The vases deposited in the cave were decorated with hourglass and triangle motifs, suggesting that the sacrificial ritual was connected to regeneration.

A dark subterranean crypt with a square central pillar was a common feature of most Minoan settlements and temple-palaces. Inside these symbolic wombs, hundreds of cups—some still filled with the carbonized remains of vegetable matter—were found scattered among animal bones around the pillar. This verifies the focal position of the life-force pillar in religious ceremonies.

In the western wing at Knossos, rooms above the crypts contain round columns. Pillars in the subterranean rooms and the related columns on the floors above are frequently marked with double axes (the horizontal hourglass or butterfly of resurrection) and sacral knots, emblems of the Goddess. It seems probable that pillar crypts symbolized the womb of the Goddess Creatrix, where transformation from death to life took place and where initiation rites were performed. The participants returned to the womb—that is, "died"—and after the ceremonies were reborn again.

Analogues in the wild are sacred Minoan caves with stalagmites and stalactites. These include the Cave of Eileithyia (Goddess of Childbirth) east of Herakleion, and those at Psychro, Arkalokhori, and other localities where offerings, including double axes, were found. Like pillars, the stalactites and stalagmites probably symbolized the embryonic, concentrated life force materializing in the womb of the Goddess.

20.3 *Within the tomb/womb*

Life columns appear engraved on stones in womblike tombs of Brittany, Ireland, and Spain, and in the temples of Malta. Rising columns of multiple arcs, triangles, lozenges, and ferns or fir-tree motifs are quite frequent on the orthostats of passage graves. Their associations are with life-water symbols (cupmarks, bands of wavy lines) and energy symbols (spirals, hooks, axes). Not infrequently, life columns are combined with anthropomorphic features—vulvas, snake-coil oculi, and eyes and eyebrows of the Owl Goddess. A "potted plant" pattern beautifully carved on a block holding a basin was found in the Hağar Qim temple of Malta. Its lowest branches are bent downward so as to form the eyes and brow-ridges of the Goddess. This block is part of a ritual installation which also includes a slab carved in relief with an oculi motif (Evans 1959: pls. 78, 79).

In Neolithic Sardinia, Corsica, and Malta, as well as in the Etruscan culture of the first half of the 1st millennium B.C., phallic pillars were connected with tomb and temple architecture. I interpret their presence as vital for sustaining life and assuring regeneration; they were not standing in front of tombs as symbols of sexual procreation.

One of the richest megalithic monuments in Brittany, remarkable for the excellence of its relief engravings, is the Late Neolithic passage grave of Gavrinis. Even its location has religious implications. Surrounded by water, the primordial life source, it now occupies a small island (earlier a peninsula) in the Gulf of Morbihan; it is aligned to the rising sun at winter solstice, but the main orientation of the passage is toward an extreme rising position of the moon.

Engravings within the sanctuary completely cover the surface of 23 orthostats, giving an impression of overall symbolic unity. (FIGURE 343) Extensive use of wavy and concentric arc motifs harmonizes with the surrounding watery element. The dominant symbol is the concentric semicircle, interconnected with or surrounded by multiple wavy lines and serpentine forms. (For more illustrations see Twohig 1981: 172–75, figs. 110–22.)

FIGURE 343

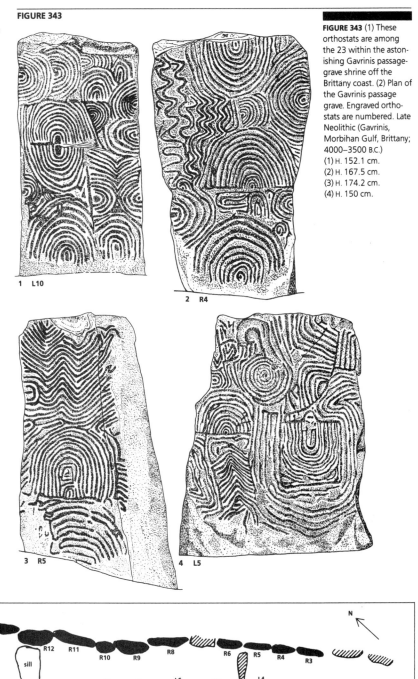

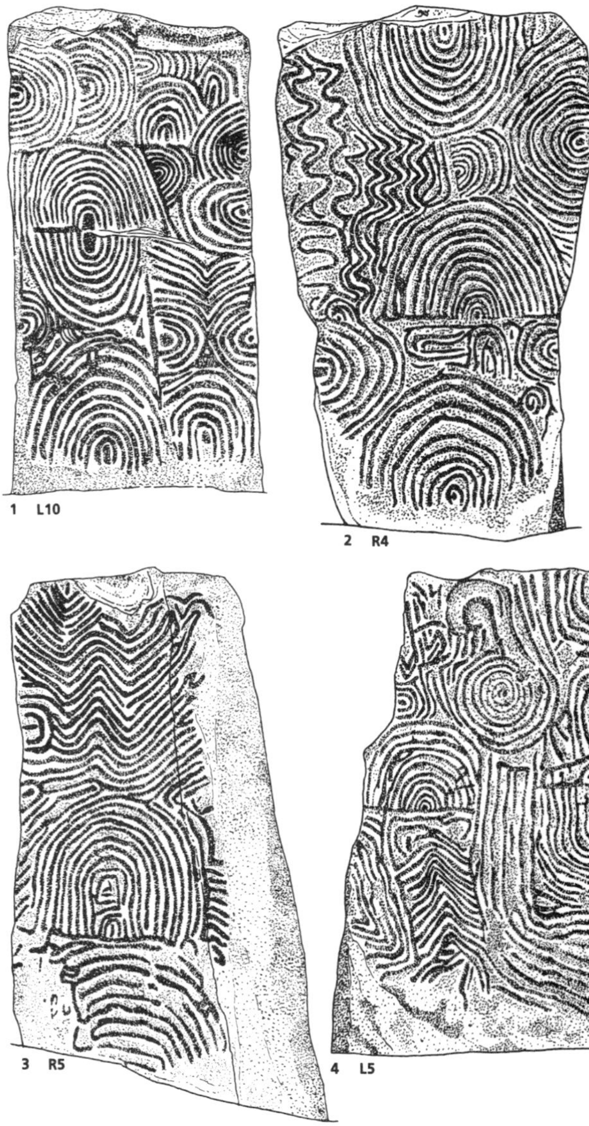

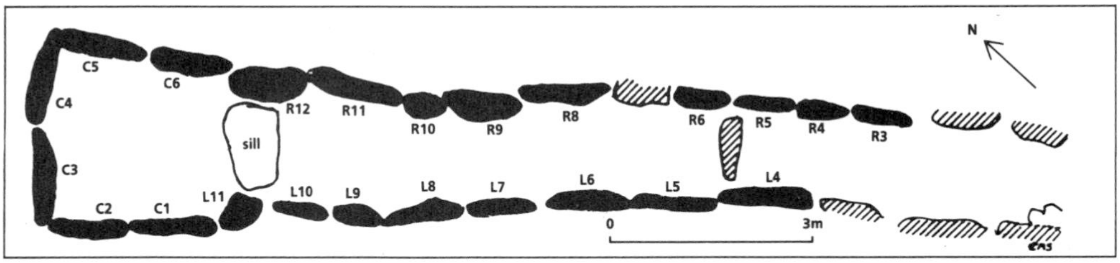

FIGURE 343 (1) These orthostats are among the 23 within the astonishing Gavrinis passage-grave shrine off the Brittany coast. (2) Plan of the Gavrinis passage grave. Engraved orthostats are numbered. Late Neolithic (Gavrinis, Morbihan Gulf, Brittany; 4000–3500 B.C.)
(1) H. 152.1 cm.
(2) H. 167.5 cm.
(3) H. 174.2 cm.
(4) H. 150 cm.

FIGURE 344

1 R9

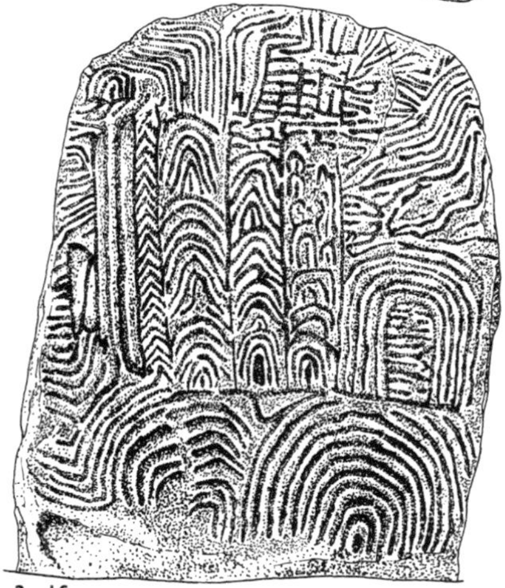

2 L6

FIGURE 344 Some Gavrinis orthostats are covered with vertical columns of concentric arcs which radiate from a central vulvar opening; the protrusion at the top (in central columns) are omphali. This glyph probably represents the rising generative force of the Goddess.
(1) H. 145.8 cm. (2) H. 156.8 cm.

Several orthostats are decorated with concentric arcs piled one on top of the other in vertical columns. (FIGURE 344) Those in central positions are larger than the rest and have an omphalos-like protrusion. In my opinion, this image is a symbol of rising generative force. Emphasis is given to the vaguely anthropomorphic vulva sign in the center, which actually is a "symbol of the center." Although executed with great minuteness of detail, the Gavrinis symbolism at its core is essentially the same as that of the Aurignacian vulvas engraved on rocks 30,000 years ago. The piled-up signs seem to say that the creativity of the Goddess is inexhaustible and comes from the cosmic deep, which is implied by a variety of adjacent aquatic configurations.

"Becoming" is a central concept of the cosmology which inspired the artists of the Gavrinis "Cathedral of Regeneration." The Goddess Creatrix shares her fundamental generative potential, expressed at Gavrinis by its metaphoric form, unique and significant locale, and engraved signs.

Regeneration is clearly the main theme on the orthostats and curbstones of Newgrange, Knowth, and Dowth in the Boyne Valley, Ireland. As in Gavrinis, multiple arcs and wavy lines or bands of zig-zags and serpentiforms speak for the belief in the generative potential of water and the connection between the snake and the mysterious power of stone. These signs are often associated with natural hollows and cupmarks, dots-in-circles or concentric circles, snake coils, eyes (snake-coil oculi), and the number three (see figs. 159, 370; also O'Kelly 1983: 152 ff.; Eogan 1984: 156 ff.). Cupmarks and dot-in-circle motifs are most numerous of all and usually hidden (engraved on stones lowered into the ground), and are therefore seminal. There is a clear affinity in symbolism between the life column within the egg/cave/womb and the cupmark (or dot)-in-circle or concentric circle. The former symbolizes the rising force, the latter the source or center of this force.

One of the orthostats in the chamber of Dowth is almost solidly covered with columns of lozenges, triangles, and winding snakes. The triangle is a symbol of the Goddess's regenerative vulva (see below, section 21). The diamond in megalithic tombs seems to be a doubling of triangles (two triangles joined at their bases). Engravings of multiple triangles and diamonds as on this illustrated stone from the tomb of Dowth evoke or strengthen the Goddess's power of regeneration. (FIGURE 345, 1) An aggregation of symbols which affirms the affinity of water, the regenerative vulva, concentric arcs, the sun, and winding serpents are pecked out on a ritual stone basin recovered in the right recess of the tomb-shrine at Knowth. (FIGURE 345, 2)

Several thousand years later, essentially the same symbolism of the Goddess's regenerating power rising from the cosmic deep reappears on Late Minoan III sarcophagi (Khania Museum, western Crete). Reproduced here is a sarcophagus from Armenoi at Rhetymno, Crete, portraying a snake-armed Goddess; her body is composed of piled-up concentric semicircles resembling those of Gavrinis. (FIGURE 346) A checkerboard design stands for the lower body or skirt of the deity, a probable metaphor of the water sphere. Wavy tri-lines flank the image. On other sarcophagi there appears a stick figure with human legs, but whose arms and head are snake spirals. This figure can also be a totally abstracted image whose body is a net-patterned square with spirals emanating from each corner. Such figures are painted in panels flanking a central life column composed of piled-up sacred horns. Large snakes wind vertically along the legs of the sarcophagus and moon crescents decorate the roof.

FIGURE 345

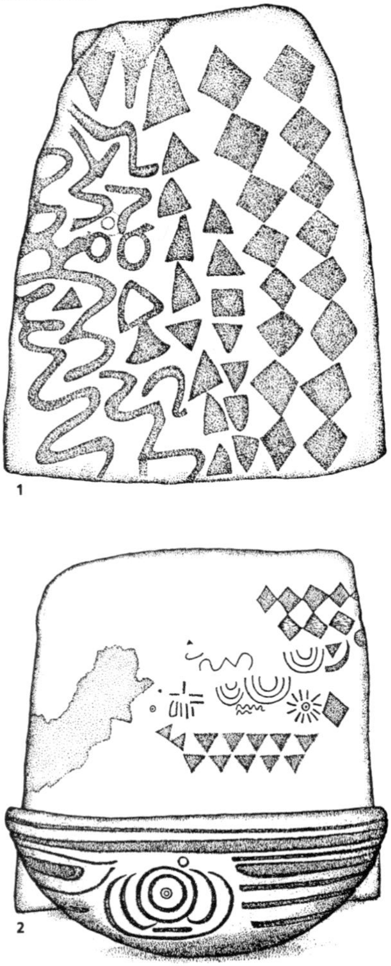

FIGURE 345 Columns of serpents, triangles, and lozenges (double triangles) in Irish megalithic tombs repeat the theme of regeneration.
(1) These symbols engraved on an orthostat in the tomb chamber (Dowth, Stone 5, Boyne Valley; c. 3200 B.C. or earlier). (2) Symbols of regeneration are here associated with a ceremonial basin in the recess of the tomb-shrine at Knowth. The basin is marked in front with a dot-in-double-circle, a symbol of center or concentrated life power and concentric arcs emanating from it. Irish Neolithic (Boyne Valley; 3500–3200 B.C.)

In the 9th century B.C., a related image is painted beneath the handle of an urn found in the cemetery of Fortetsa at Knossos. (FIGURE 347) The "skirt" of the deity is a rectangular panel similar to that of the figure on the Armenoi sarcophagus. Here too, a pair of snakes peer from the corners of the panel. The upraised arms suggest a Goddess rising from her own aquatic sphere.

In addition to this rising Goddess with serpent characteristics on the funerary ceramics of the Late Minoan Bronze Age, c. 1400–1200 B.C., there also appears a deity in the form of an octopus. (FIGURE 348) The Goddess's head may be portrayed as an octopus with the creature's arms metaphoric of winding curls, or else the octopus's elongated head becomes the body of the Goddess with its big eyes serving as her breasts. The illustrated figure has upraised horn-shaped arms ending in spirals, and the serpentiform octopus's tentacles emerge in several rows from the body. In this ingenious composition, the symbols of becoming are fused with the mysterious body of the octopus.

The snake is constantly present on tombs and funeral "hero-reliefs" of Indo-Europeanized Greece. On reliefs of the funeral banquet type, a snake appears twined about a tree or drinks from a cup in the reclining hero's hand (Harrison 1962: figs. 87, 89; *Id. Prolegomena*: figs. 97–100, 105, 106, 112).

FIGURE 346

FIGURE 347

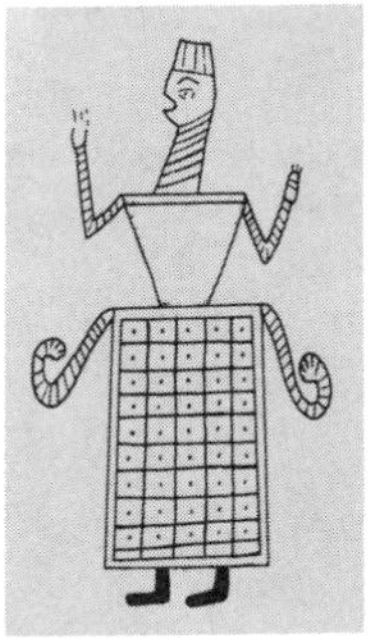

FIGURE 346 The Post-Palatial Cretan sarcophagus portrays a snake-limbed goddess whose body is covered with wavelike concentric arcs; she is flanked by watery tri-lines. Painted brown on buff. Post-Palatial Crete, Late Minoan III (Armenoi, at Rhetymno, W Crete; 14th–13th cent. B.C.)

FIGURE 347 Stylized figure painted in a panel beneath the handle of an urn found in a cemetery. She rises up from the checkerboard field of her skirt, a symbol of life-giving waters (compare fig. 346). Early Hellenic Crete (Fortetsa, at Knossos; 9th century B.C.)

FIGURE 348

FIGURE 348 Related to the rising Snake Goddess and obviously associated with the cosmic deep is the rather whimsical "Octopus Goddess." Her tentacles cover the whole of a bathtub-shaped sarcophagus; her arms extend like horns and end in spirals. Post-Palatial Cretan (E Crete; c. 14th cent. B.C.)

20.4 *As snake and phallus in painting and sculpture*

Seventh millennium B.C. paintings in several shrines at Çatal Hüyük contain a column of life with a pattern of lozenges, perhaps the snakeskin design or a metaphor of a spinal cord. (FIGURE 349) Three such columns in Shrine E VI A, 50 are flanked by horns and whirls. On the north wall of Shrine VIII, four columns with a lozenge design and bull horns are separately framed as panels (Mellart 1964: pl. XIII).

The convergence of life force symbols with the snake symbol can be seen at the shrine of Căscioarele, southern Romania (c. 5000 B.C.). Here, two hollow clay columns, originally containing tree trunks, are painted with a winding-snake design. (FIGURE 350) Small fragments of poorly preserved frescoes on the walls show the usual association of egg, spiral, and snake motifs. Over the shrine's entrance is a bichrome snake coil in relief. (FIGURE 351) The prominence given the snake in this decor shows that it and the tree of life are considered alternate symbols with the same meaning. Later in history, in the Graeco-Roman world, a snake appears twined about a tree on countless reliefs of the funeral banquet type.

On ceramics, snake columns around the upper portion of a vase or on its handle appear as zig-zag bands or as dotted "snake pillars." (FIGURE 352) A phallus-shaped vase from Nebo, a Butmir settlement in Bosnia, is decorated with four such zig-zag columns flanked by dotted fish and triangle motifs. On a spouted vase with snake arms from southern Crete, c. 2000 B.C., three columns of life with snakeskin design rise up the center of a Snake Goddess image. (FIGURE 353)

The early palace art of Crete abounds in decoration featuring the column of life flanked by crescents, nautili, helices, and spirals. The motif is also popular on mainland Greece and is a consistent decorative element of Mycenaean art. A vase from Berbati, Attica, is painted with a central column of wavy lines flanked by

FIGURE 349

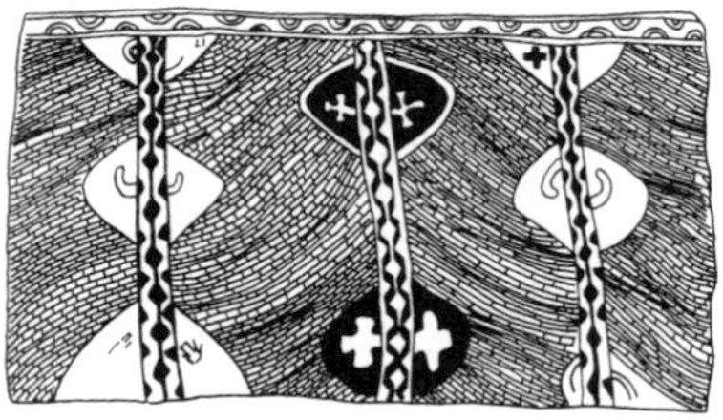

FIGURE 350

FIGURE 351

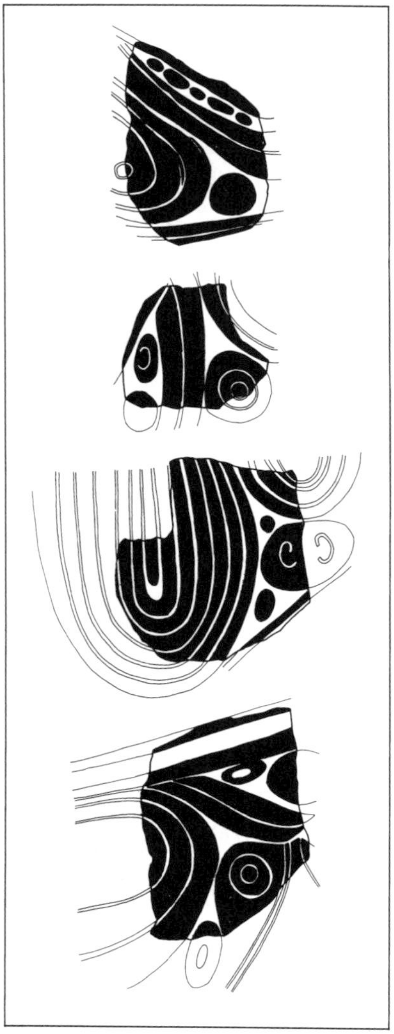

FIGURE 349 The shrines of Çatal Hüyük are decorated in frescoes which testify to the connection between the life column, symbol of the life force and the snake. Anatolian Neolithic (Shrine E VI A, 50, Çatal Hüyük; end-7th mill. B.C.)

FIGURE 350 This clay column is one of two built around tree trunks in an island shrine. It is painted reddish-brown on a cream background in a winding snake design. Karanovo culture (Căscioarele, lower Danube; c. 5000 B.C.)

FIGURE 351 The interior walls of the Căscioarele shrine in southern Romania were painted red on cream. The dominating motifs are eggs, spirals, rising concentric arches, and concentric circles. The theme of regeneration harmonizes with the central symbol of the shrine, the life column decorated with a winding snake design (see fig. 350).

FIGURE 352

FIGURE 352 The life column often appears on Old European ceramics. Here four zig-zag columns on the shoulders are surrounded by dotted diamonds (fish) and triangle (vulva) motifs. Black with white-encrusted excisions over a red background. Butmir (Nebo, at Travnik, Bosnia, W Yugoslavia; 4900–4700 B.C.) H. c. 40 cm.

FIGURE 353

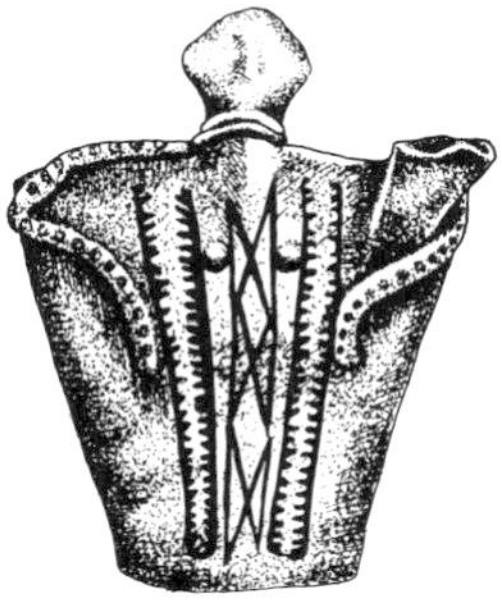

FIGURE 353 An interesting spouted anthropomorphic vase has snake arms in relief and cross-hatch life columns up the center of the body; found in a sanctuary, it probably represents the Snake Goddess. Painted brown and red on cream. Middle Minoan Ia (Koumasa, S Crete; c. 2000 B.C.) H. 14.92 cm.

FIGURE 354

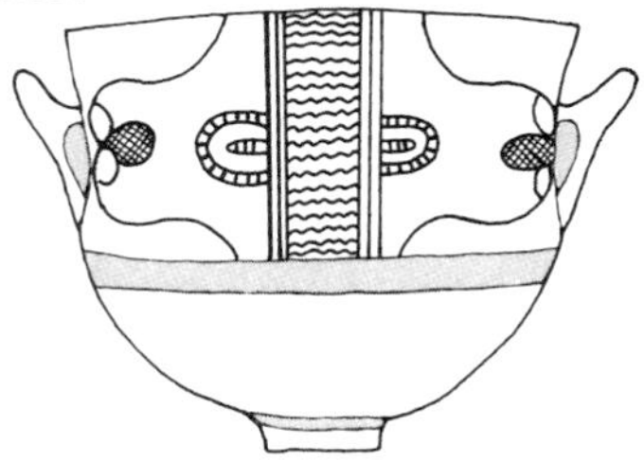

FIGURE 354 The life column on this vase appears to be made from or filled with water; it is flanked by two half-eggs, each of which also contains a life column. Next to the handles are two sideways pairs of bull horns with phallic life columns rising from their centers. Late Helladic III (Berbati cemetery, Peloponnese; 14th cent. B.C.) H. 13.5 cm.

FIGURE 355

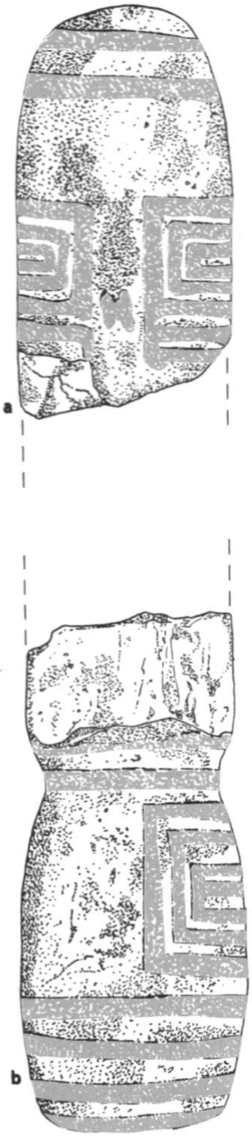

a

b

FIGURE 355 Marble phallus is decorated in red with angular meanders and a butterfly, linking the phallus/life column with the aquatic sphere and regeneration. Sesklo (Sesklo; early 6th mill. B.C.) (a) H. 6.7 cm. (b) H. 8.5 cm.

FIGURE 356

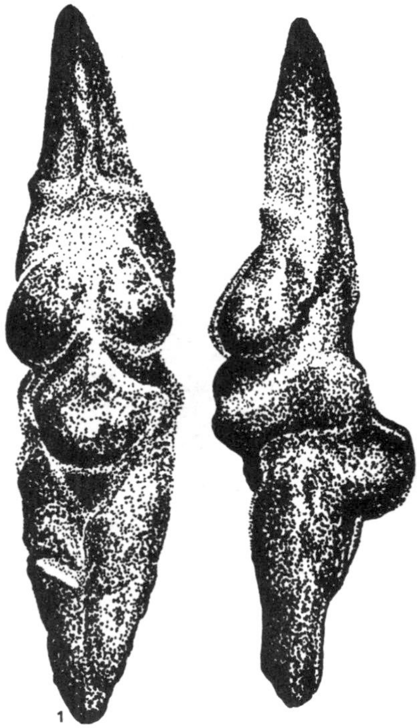

1

2

FIGURE 356 The phallus is often used with the female body, whose inherent power is enhanced by the life force manifested in the column. (1) On this Upper Paleolithic figurine of steatite (or serpentine marble), the head is replaced by a featureless phallus. Gravettian/Grimaldian (Savignano, border between Bologna and Modena, N Italy; c. 20,000 B.C., but chronology uncertain). (2) This tiny figurine of calcite was found in an ochreous deposit in the cave. On top of the phallus there is a small circular depression. Upper Périgordian/Gravettian (Cave of Weinberg near Mauern, Bavaria, c. 23,000–21,000 B.C.) (1) H. 22.9 cm. (2) H. 7.2 cm.

half-eggs and bull horns. (FIGURE 354) Similar compositions are common on Mycenaean pottery from Cyprus. Columns of life are patterned with lozenge, zig-zag, net, and checkerboard designs (for more examples see Furumark 1972: fig. 62).

In the southeast European Neolithic and Copper Age, phalli occasionally are decorated with spiralling snakes or with meander and net motifs, the latter suggesting a relationship with the aquatic sphere. Illustrated here is a marble phallus from Sesklo (early 6th millennium B.C.), painted in red meanders over both the upper and lower portions. (FIGURE 355) The butterfly between meanders on the upper part resembles the symbolic configuration of a butterfly atop a pillar or between bull horns found on Minoan vases of the first half of the 2nd millennium B.C.

The Old European phallus is far from being the obscene symbol of our days. Rather, it is close to what is still found in India, the *lingam*, a sacred cosmic pillar inherited from the Neolithic Indus valley civilization.

One of the earliest such representations in Europe is a fusion of the phallus with the divine body of the Goddess, which begins in the Upper Paleolithic. Some of the "Venuses" of this period have phallic heads with no facial features. (FIGURES 356, 357) They have been found in Savignano and Lake Trasimeno, northern Italy (assumed to be Gravettian), in the Weinberg Cave near Mauern, Bavaria, of the upper Périgordian or Gravettian period, and in Placard, Charente, France, of the Magdalenian I–II period. The same phenomenon is encountered in southeastern Europe during the Neolithic until about 5000 B.C. Clay and marble figurines from the Sesklo and Starčevo cultures often have long phallic necks. Some are amorphous; others have pinched noses or wear masks.

Among the Starčevo figurines of the mid-6th millennium B.C. are some whose form is that of male genitals: the upper part is phallic and the lower buttocks are shaped like testicles. (FIGURE 358)

FIGURE 357

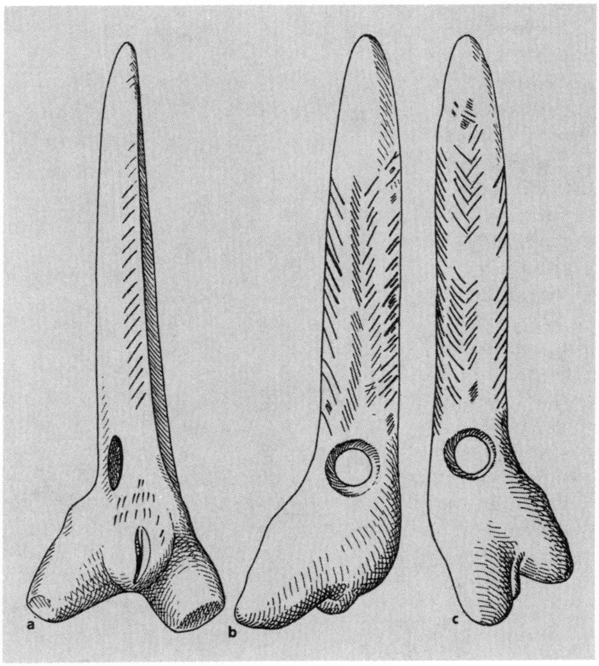

FIGURE 357 This abstractly anthropomorphic figure carved from a reindeer antler has a prominent vulva and long phallic neck. As determined by Marshack's microscopic analysis, the strokes are of different lengths and rhythms. Magdalenian I–II (cave of Le Placard, Charente, France; 15,000–13,000 B.C.) H. 15 cm.

FIGURE 358

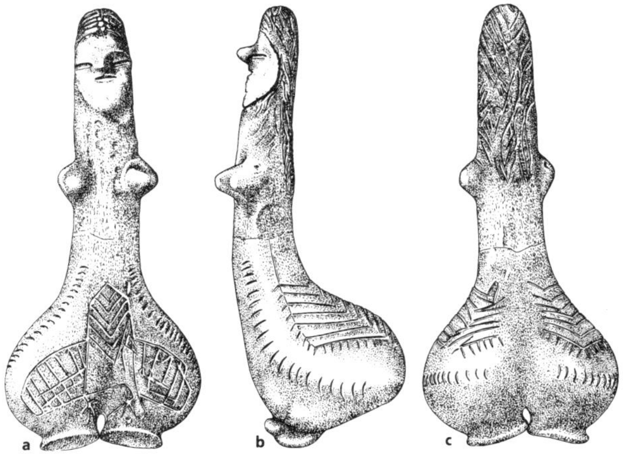

FIGURE 358 This female figurine has a phallic head whose lower part may be shaped like testicles. The engraving in front is a bird (note the vulture's claws) marked with chevrons and a net. The locks of hair on both sides of the head were painted red, and the chevrons incised on the back are white-encrusted. Starčevo (Endröd-Szujóskereszt, Körös Valley, SE Hungary; c. 5600–5300 B.C.) H. 19 cm.

Although the male element is attached, these figurines remain essentially female. They do not represent a fusion of two sexes but rather an enhancement of the female with the mysterious life force inherent in the phallus. The Goddess figurine creates a base from which the phallus, understood as a cosmic pillar, rises. It comes from her womb in the same way that stalagmites and stalactites grow from her womb in the cave.

A limestone figurine from Chalcolithic Cyprus conveys a similar idea. (FIGURE 359) The seated female figure is related in style to many other female figurines of the same period, but unlike the others it has a high cylindrical neck with a "mushroom" head on top and no facial features (a, b). When viewing the object from the back (c) we see an anatomically correct rendition of the male genitalia, an erect penis and scrotum with the genital ridge represented by a deep groove (Swiny 1983: 58). When viewed from top and bottom (d, e), however, the sculpture resembles female genitalia. The Cypriot sculptors of around c. 3000 B.C. were quite inventive; one cannot expect such resemblances to be accidental.

From later times, the Middle Minoan period of Crete, there is an exciting seal which portrays a phallus sprouting from the head of a deity and flanked by horns. (FIGURE 360) The anthropomorphic head has a long mouth and round eyes—unmistakably those of a Snake Goddess. Her upraised arms are not human; the three-fingered right hand is clearly a bird's foot. This portrayal is a characteristic combination of a series of symbols of regenerative energy: serpent, phallus, horns, bird's feet. The Vulture Goddess here seems to be hybridized with the Serpent Goddess.

FIGURE 359

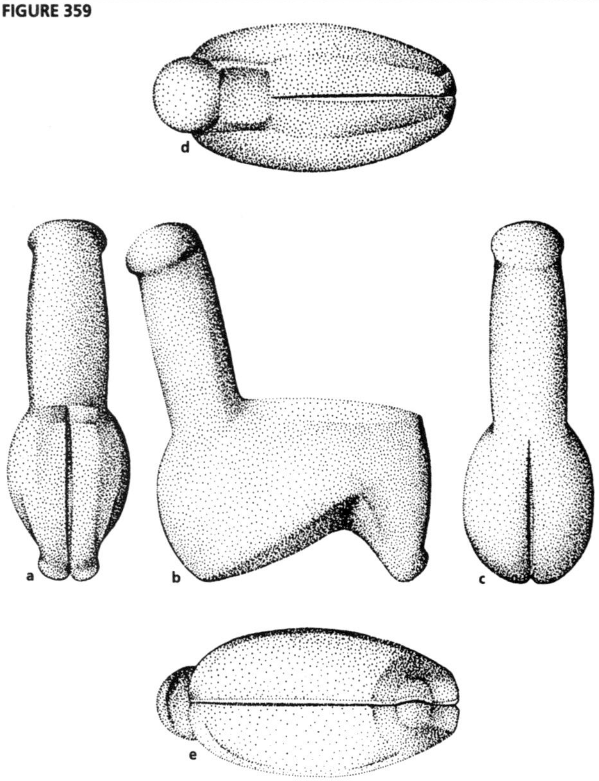

FIGURE 359 A seated human figure of white limestone embodies both feminine and masculine characteristics; (a) front; (b) side; (c) back; (d) top; (e) bottom. Surface find stylistically related to figurines of Chalcolithic Cyprus (Sotira Arkolies, west of Limassol; probably c. 3500 B.C.) H. 14.7 cm.

FIGURE 360

FIGURE 360 A pair of horns or hooks and a phallus sprout from the head of a Snake Goddess on a Middle Minoan seal. (Mochlos, Crete; early 2nd mill. B.C.) DIA. approx. 3 cm.

20.5 *Dogs and goats flanking the column of life*

Through millennia dogs and he-goats appear in art in ways that show their involvement with the process of becoming as energetic stimulators of the life force. They promote the lunar cycle and plant growth.

The dog's role in the symbolism of becoming is apparent in Cucuteni vase painting where it flanks life columns and is associated with spirals, crescents, moons, snakes, caterpillars, and the number three. (FIGURES 361, 362) The dog's most frequent depiction with crescents and full moons bespeaks its influential role in the promotion of moon cycles or the change of moon phases; see the illustrated Cucuteni vases from Ghelaeşti, Truşeşti, and Valea Lupului. This ancient symbolic connection comes down to us today in the potent image of a wild dog howling at the full moon.

On other ceramics, ferocious hounds with upraised tails and three-clawed paws seem to fly in space. On the vases from Sipenitsi, they flank the tree of life symbol as guardians of new life. (FIGURE 363)

The dog is prominent in Bronze Age compositions of becoming, most notably in heraldic postures flanking the Goddess, column of life, or sacred tree. Early in the 3rd millennium B.C., however, the lion begins to replace the dog in heraldic compositions, frequently appearing on Minoan seals in a spinning pattern around a whirl.

The he-goat is also well known from Old European and Near Eastern plaques, seals, rings, and vase paintings. It figured as a sacrificial animal in rituals of death and resurrection and was prominent in compositions with the sacred tree.

The earliest European pictorial association of the goat with the tree comes from the sacrificial pit of Tartaria, near Cluj, Transylvania, dated c. 5200–5000 B.C. (FIGURE 364) Three plaques were recovered from the pit along with scorched human bones, 26 figurines of the Early Vinča type, an anchor-shaped

FIGURE 361

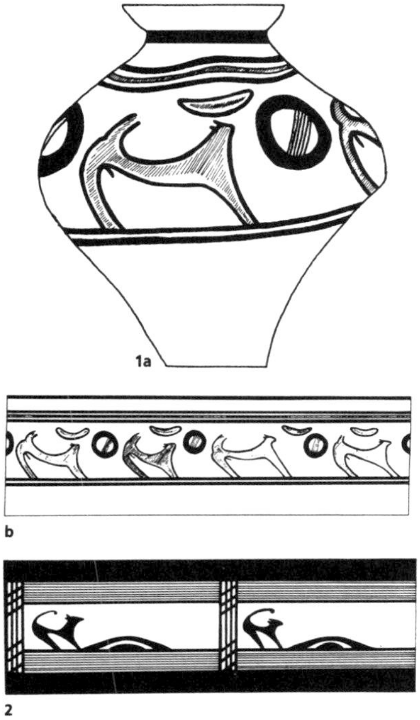

FIGURE 361 As a dynamic symbol of becoming, the dog stimulates plant growth and the lunar cycle. On panels from painted Cucuteni B vases, dogs stand alertly next to the crescent and full moon. Painted black on red. ((1) Truşeşti, NE Romania; 3800–3600 B.C. (2) Nedeia at Ghelaeşti, NE Romania; early 4th mill. B.C.). (1) H. 54.2 cm.

FIGURE 362

FIGURE 362 In a virtual riot of "becoming," two Cucuteni B_2 craters are similarly decorated with snakes as life columns alternating with panels of dogs, caterpillars, and tri-lines. Below are net-patterned life columns surrounded by crescents, uteri (fish bladder forms), and double eggs. (Valea Lupului, NE Romania; 3800–3600 B.C.) (1) H. of vase 50 cm.

FIGURE 363

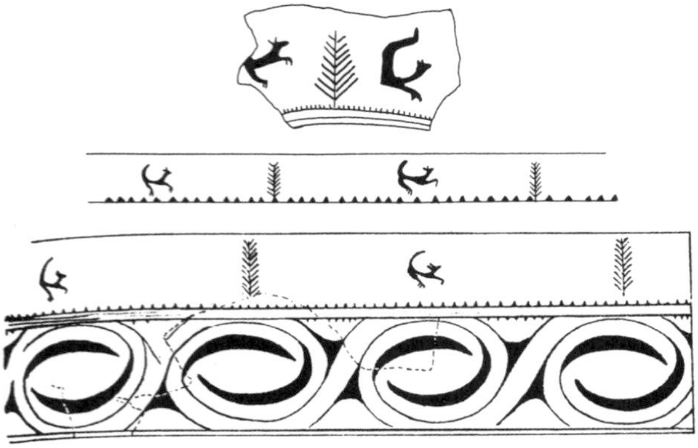

1

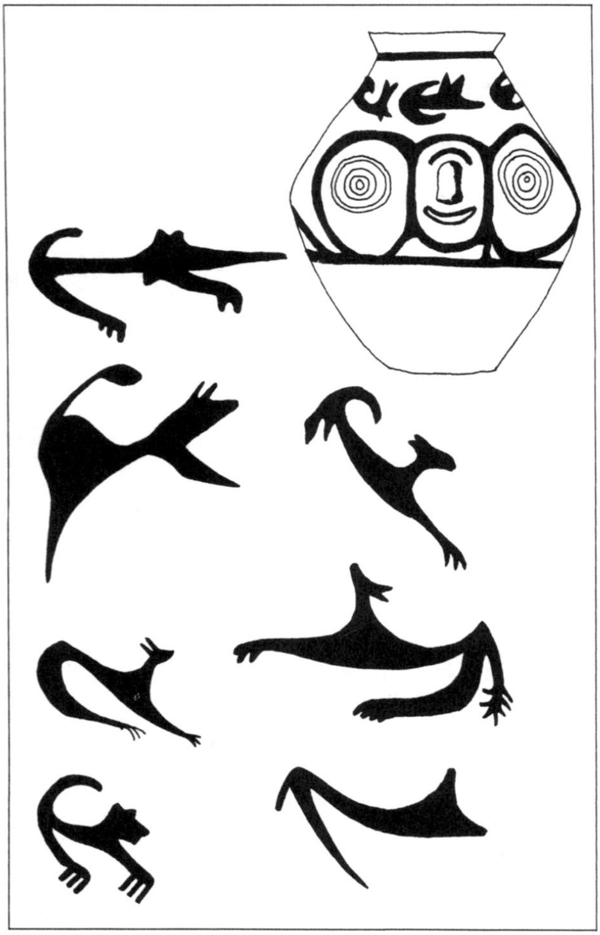

2

FIGURE 363 Flying hounds act as guardians of the new life symbolized by sacred trees on Cucuteni vases. (1) Note the spiral and opposed crescent motif below. (Sipenitsi, W Ukraine; 3900–3700 B.C.).
(2) Flying hounds on other Cucuteni vases of the same period.

FIGURE 364

FIGURE 364 Goats are synonymous with dogs as life-stimulator symbols of becoming. On this plaque recovered from a sacrificial pit, two goats (or a goat and dog) flank a central life-tree. The goat was sacrificed in rituals of death and regeneration. Presumed to be Early Vinča (Tartaria, near Cluj, W Romania; 5200–5000 B.C.) H. 2.8 cm.

FIGURE 365

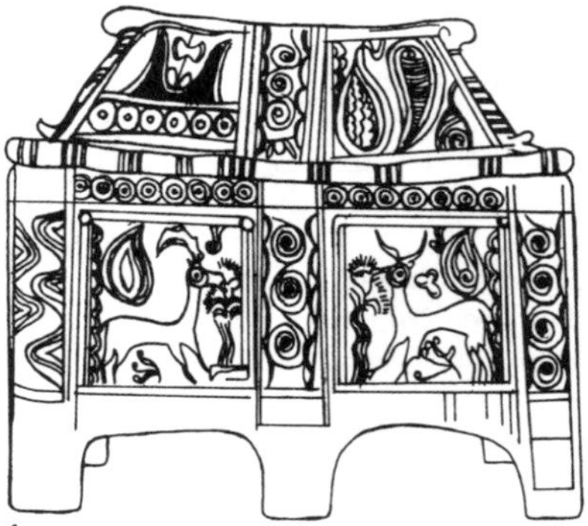

1

2

FIGURE 365 Because horned animals are symbols of regeneration, it is not surprising to find them on sarcophagi.
(1) Here a he-goat and bull with flowers and fish bladders (uteri) flank life columns made of spirals. The roof panels are decorated by sacred horns and a butterfly (left), and uteri. Late Minoan III (Armenoi, Crete; 1300–1100 B.C.).
(2) Like the dog, the goat is associated with the moon. Here two goats flank a column of life filled with four discs of different sizes and designs, probably representing lunar phases. Painted light and dark brown on cream. Proto-Geometric (Knossos, Crete; 10th cent. B.C.) H. 16.8 cm.

object, and a spondylus shell bracelet. One plaque is incised with a tree and two animals in silhouette; one is clearly a goat.

Goat figures appear on Minoan and sub-Minoan ceramics and stone seals, frequently associated with moons, plants, and the life tree. (FIGURES 365, 366) On a seal from Platanos, a sacred tree is carved on two faces, a goat on the third, and a column flanked by moons on the fourth. On a double-faced seal, one side shows a sacred tree and copulating goats. On the other side, a human couple is similarly engaged, in what is probably a sacred marriage scene or a ritual meant to recharge the energy of rising life or the Goddess through cosmic sexual power and flow.

A gold ring of Minoan workmanship recovered at Mycenae depicts a he-goat with a plant sprouting from its back, standing with a youth beside an enclosed sacred tree. (FIGURE 367) Does this tableau represent a later version of this early myth? In any case, the equation between the sprouting life column and the sprouting goat is made, clearly demonstrating the role of the goat in plant regeneration.

Ithyphallic men who stand at a life tree associated with crescents and bull horns on Minoan seals and bronze plaques show that the sexual power of men was considered equally as influential as he-goats on the process of becoming.

The life-stimulating role of goats continues into later times. Scenes of goats on both sides of a burgeoning plant are frequently encountered in the Proto-Geometric and Geometric art of Greece, especially on funerary vases. Sprouting plants and jumping ibexes create a very dynamic scene on a vase from the necropolis of Kameiros, Rhodos. (FIGURE 368)

Similar motifs survive in European folk art to this day, although in folk beliefs the symbolic role of the he-goat has clearly merged with that of the Indo-European Thunder God. The goat is, alongside the bull, the principal representative of his sexual, generative power on earth.

FIGURE 366

1

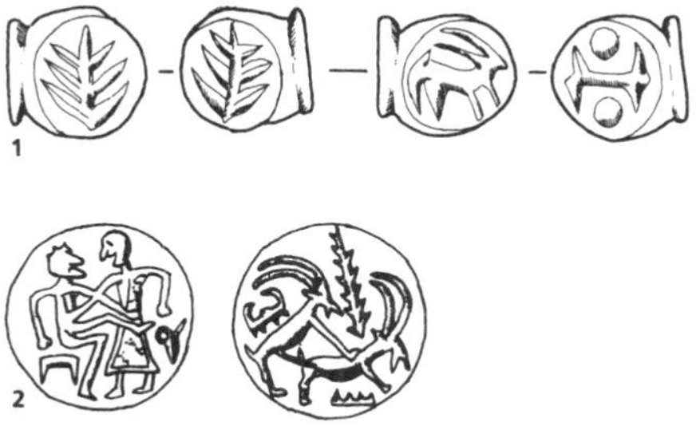

2

FIGURE 366 (1) On a four-faced Minoan seal of black steatite, there are two life trees, a he-goat, and a column flanked by moons. (Tholos B, Platanos, Mesara Plain, Crete; c. 2000 B.C.). (2) On a double Minoan seal, a human couple copulates on one side, as a pair of goats do likewise under a life tree on the other. (Middle Minoan; early 2nd mill. B.C.)
(1) DIA. 1.2 cm.
(2) DIA. 2 cm.

FIGURE 367

FIGURE 367 A gold ring is decorated with a he-goat from whose back sprouts a plant, and a youth standing beside an enclosed (that is, chthonic) column of life with a similar plant sprouting from it. (Mycenae; 16th cent. B.C.) DIA. approx. 3 cm.

FIGURE 368

FIGURE 368 The goat's special symbolism survived for millennia. In this design of a funerary vase, three life-trees of net-patterned triangles and lozenges, and spirals—the central one topped by a flowering plant—are flanked by a pair of leaping ibexes and a bird. (Necropolis of Kameiros (Camiros), Rhodes; 8th cent. B.C.)

Hourglass-shaped figure engraved on rock; Neolithic Spain. See figure 376, page 241.

21/ *Regenerative Vulva: Triangle, Hourglass, and Bird's Claws*

The triangle is the vulva (pubic triangle), and the hourglass is two triangles joined at their tips. These geometric forms become anthropomorphic shapes if a head or breasts, arms, and legs are added. However, it is not human arms but bird's claws that are attached to hourglass figures. The triangle and hourglass are symbols of the Goddess in her epiphany as a bird of prey; they are typically found in caves and sepulchral monuments. In vase painting, anthropomorphic hourglass figures are portrayed in the context of waters or are associated with serpents and marked with nets.

21.1 *Triangle*

A triangular stone as a symbol of the Goddess or her regenerative power may be as old as the Lower Paleolithic. Naturally formed or intentionally chipped triangles of flint, some with breasts or with crudely outlined head at the tip of the triangle, are encountered in the Acheulean/Heidelbergian deposits of western Europe (Musch 1986: 19). (FIGURE 369) In the Middle Paleolithic Mousterian period, skulls were buried under triangular stones. For instance, at La Ferrassie, Dordogne, France, L. Capitan and D. Peyrony excavated six Mousterian graves in 1909–22. At the back of the cave the contracted skeleton of a child lay in a pit, but the skull was one meter away under a triangular limestone block on which small hollows had been ground out. There were nine smaller and one larger hollow, all artificially made, reminiscent of cupmarks (Müller-Karpe 1966: 265, Taf. 35, *L*). In the Neolithic, large triangular stones were used as backstones or entrance stones in Irish court tombs and the passage graves of Brittany. They are there as seats of the Goddess (some have vulvas and energy symbols engraved on them; see fig. 456). The cairns of Irish courttombs are triangular in plan.

The meaning of the regenerative triangle is made clear in the wall painting of the Vulture Shrine (Level VII) at Çatal Hüyük (see fig. 286) by the presence of a row of red and black triangles, each with a central circle, perhaps representing a birth canal. This painting is next to the huge sculpture of a bucranium under which a human skull was found (Cameron 1981: 30).

On the walls or curbstones of the megalithic tombs of Ireland (Newgrange and Knowth), the triangle either stands alone, sometimes encircled by multiple arcs as on the curbstone at the entrance to Newgrange, or it appears in rows and pairs joined at the tips or at their bases. (FIGURE 370) Such rows of triangles typically decorate hooks and stone plaque images of the Goddess of Death and Regeneration deposited in the megalithic graves of Portugal. (FIGURE 371) Triangular amulets of stone, clay, or bone are found in graves and caves through time. At Varna (mid-5th millennium B.C.), 27 bone triangles appeared in a grave in association with the mask of the Goddess

FIGURE 369

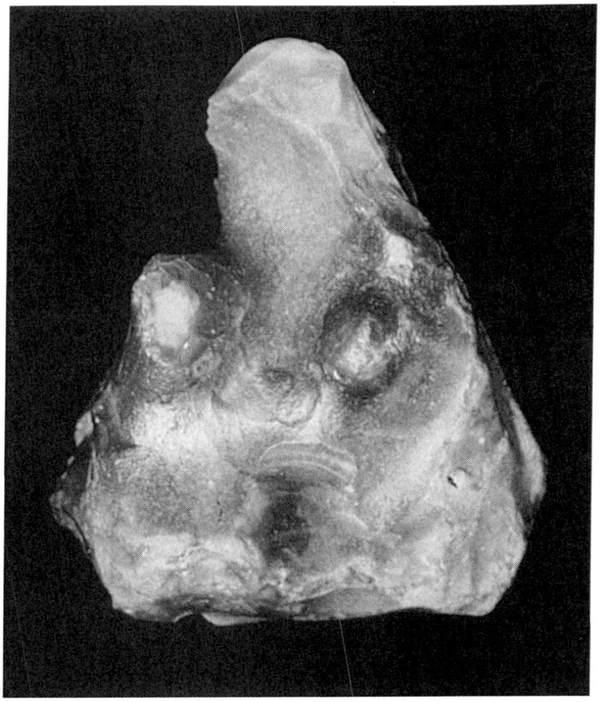

FIGURE 369 This Lower Paleolithic triangular figure of flint knapped from the nodule has breasts and shows traces of intentional chopping to mark the head, breasts, and vulva. Natural protrusions have been chipped to form the breasts. The figurine can stand on a flat surface. (Assumed to be Heidelbergian; dated on the basis of association with tools possibly as early as 500,000 B.P.)

FIGURE 370

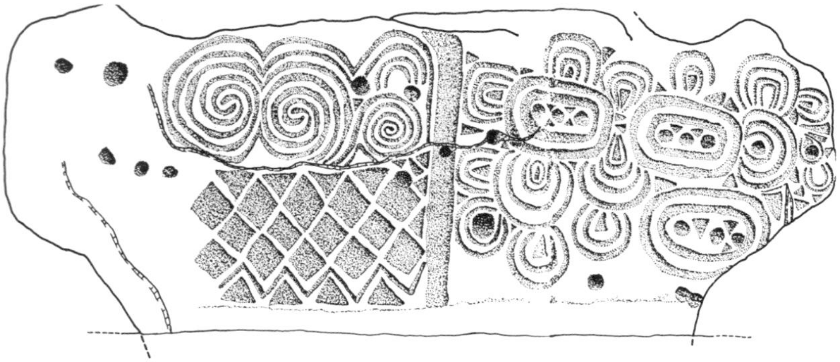

FIGURE 370 In this composition on the curbstone of Newgrange (right panel), triangles and cupmarks as concentrated Goddess energy seem to be semantically interrelated: both are within multiple arcs or in double cartouches. There are also snake-spiral oculi with triple eyebrows above diamonds (left panel). Irish Neolithic Passage Grave culture (curbstone 52 of the tomb-sanctuary at Newgrange, Co. Meath; c. 3200 B.C.) L. 3.4 m.

FIGURE 371

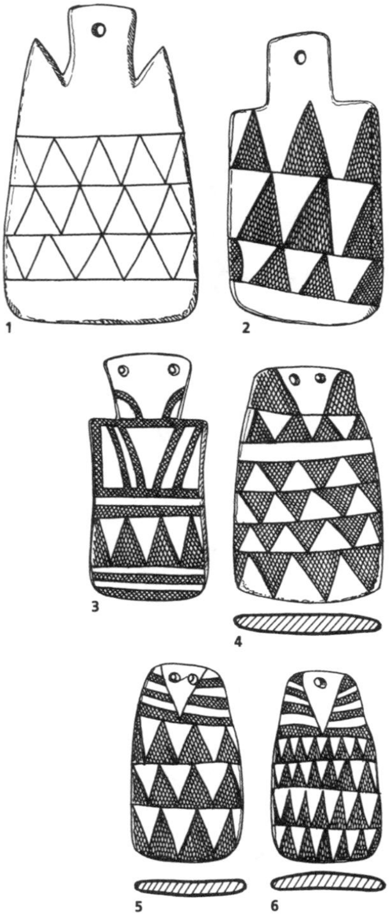

FIGURE 371 Portuguese megalithic tombs of the tholos type yield considerable numbers of stone plaque idols decorated with rows of triangles, usually net-patterned. Their heads are also triangles. All have one or two perforations, perhaps for attachment to garments. Neolithic of Portugal ((1) Carrajola; (2) Sobreira; (3) "Marquesa"; (4) Horta Velha do Reguengos, province Alentejo; (5) and (6) Cabeco da Arruda; c. 3500–3000 B.C.) (1)–(6) H. from 8.5 to 5 cm.

FIGURE 372

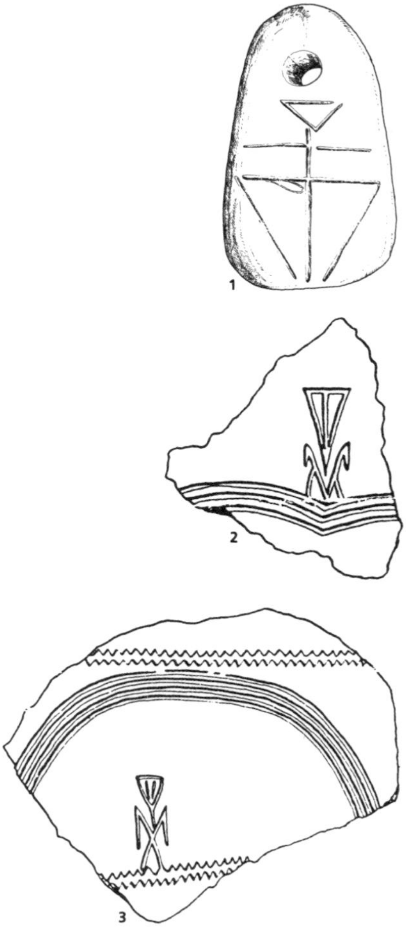

FIGURE 372 (1)The Goddess composed of two joined triangles is engraved on this loom-weight. Karanovo (Gumelniţa; mid-5th mill. B.C.). (2) and (3) Stick figures with triangular heads on earliest Maltese funerary pottery. (Zebbuġ rock-cut tombs; 2nd half 5th mill. B.C. (1) H. 8.7 cm.

(see fig. 324). The triangle and an anthropomorphic image made of two triangles are frequent motifs on loom-weights, suggesting the Goddess's "weaving the body tissues anew." (FIGURE 372, 1) Figures with heads as triangles (vulvas) with a dash in the middle or two dashes for eyes appear on the earliest Maltese funerary ceramics from the Zebbuġ tombs of the 5th millennium B.C. (FIGURE 372, 2, 3)

The vulva's intimacy with regeneration and transformation can be seen on anthropomorphic platters from the Aegean area. On these cult objects, the triangular vulva is associated not only with water and plant symbols (see fig. 166), but also with the ship, snake, fish, and bird's claws (see fig. 385). The claws are those of a bird of prey, the main epiphany of the Goddess in her aspect of death and rebirth.

21.2 *Hourglass*

In Cucuteni vase paintings (c. 4000 B.C.) (FIGURE 373) the vertical double-triangle form is enclosed in a seedlike compartment or column, or it is surrounded by large snake spirals and meanders; as our study of the associated signs now allows us to "read," this symbolizes the Goddess of Death and Regeneration. On a rectangular vase from southeastern Hungary (Szakálhát group, c. 5000 B.C.), the double-triangle central figure has V-shaped arms, bird's claws for hands, and a head represented by three lines. (FIGURE 374, 1) The lower triangle (the womb) is also marked with three lines. Associated with the figure are Y signs and dots (sprouting shoots and rain?). On another panel, the association is given further emphasis by a large vulva among the dots. The link with the Bird Goddess is also shown by the indication of a crest on a double figure of the Sesklo culture composed of two triangles and heads with red-painted crests. (FIGURE 374, 2)

FIGURE 373

FIGURE 373 The hourglass Goddess in Cucuteni vase painting. (1) On this vase, the Goddess, whose body is an hourglass, is encapsulated within a seedlike compartment that is surrounded by water meanders. In other words, represented here is the Goddess about to be (re)born from the waters. (2) On another Cucuteni vase of similar imagery, flanked by snake spirals and surmounted by large meanders. The hourglass form symbolizes the subterranean or subaqueous life force of the Goddess and imminent rebirth. Note: her hands are bird's claws. Painted white, red, and dark brown. Cucuteni AB (Traian dealul Fintinilor, NE Romania; c. 4000 B.C.)

FIGURE 374

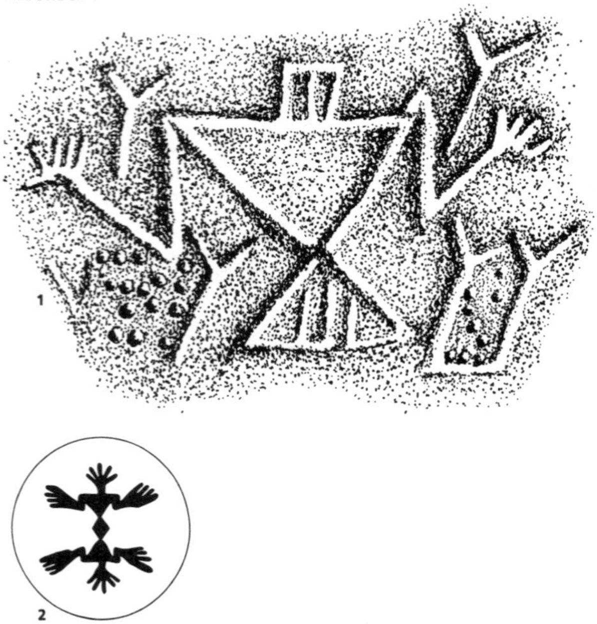

1

2

FIGURE 374 Here are examples of hourglass figures with bird's claws or wings. (1) The Goddess has V-shaped arms and hands which are bird's claws; her head and lower triangle are made of three parallel lines. She is associated with Y-signs and dots, perhaps representing sprouts and rain. On the opposite panel of the vase is a vulva sign surrounded by dots. Linear Pottery (Szelevény, E Hungary; c. 5000 B.C.). (2) A double hourglass figure with bird's wings (or feet). Painted on the interior of a dish, her head has a red crest. Sesklo (c. 6000 B.C.)

FIGURE 375

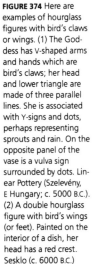

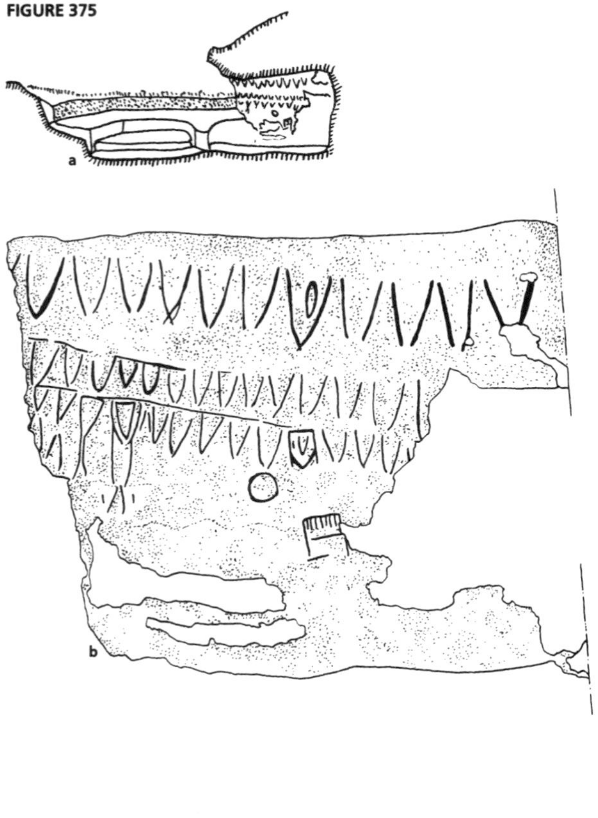

a

b

FIGURE 375 The hourglass (double triangle) is associated with the vulva on the walls of Sardinian hypogea. Lines of vulvas are interspersed with several hourglass and anthropomorphic forms in the bottom row, left. Sardinian Late Neolithic (Tisiennari, Bortigiadas, N Sardinia; 4th mill. B.C.) H. 84.2 cm.
(a) cross-section.
(b) detail.

It is important to note this juxtaposition of the triangle (or vulva) sign and the Goddess's hourglass form. Apparently these two elements in combination represent a specific meaning, as in the wall painting of the Tisiennari hypogeum, north Sardinia. (FIGURE 375) Three triangles are painted in red over a pair of horns in one chamber; three rows of triangular vulvas are painted on a wall of the adjoining room. Among the vulvas in the bottom row are several hourglass signs and one clearly anthropomorphic figure, an indication that the two are closely related, even interchangeable, symbols. Three triangles or three hourglass signs are engraved also on stones of Newgrange and Knowth, Ireland (see fig. 370). Furthermore, they are probably semantically interrelated with three dots or depressions, three chevrons, triple V's, three spirals, and the triple eyebrows and eyes of the Owl Goddess.

Small stone figurines of hourglass shape (FIGURE 376, 1), sometimes with triangular heads, are frequently found in Iberian megalithic tombs of the Los Millares type (circular with a corridor), dating from the end of the 4th or early 3rd millennium B.C. (Müller-Karpe 1974: Taf. 542–48). Groups of hourglass figures also appear painted on Spanish cave walls. These are assumed to be of the Neolithic or Copper Age period (Beltran 1985). In painting, figures are sometimes portrayed with limbs and with additional attributes that identify the deity represented. One of the most revealing hourglass figures is from Los Organos, southern Spain. (FIGURE 376, 2) That it is a woman and bird hybrid is shown by bird's feet. The head has antennae of an insect and protruding circular eyes, perhaps of a bee. Three horizontal lines emanate from the face on both sides. These are the same as face markings with tri-lines on shist plaque figurines of the Owl Goddess in Portuguese passage graves (see fig. 297). In this powerful image we can recognize the Goddess of Death and Regeneration who is at once a woman, a bird of prey, and a bee.

In French caves with engravings of allegedly Neolithic age, the hourglass

FIGURE 376

1

2

FIGURE 376 (1) These hourglass-shaped figurines of schist plate are found in megalithic tombs. Los Millares (El Pozuelo, Prov. Huelva, Spain; c. 3000 B.C.). (2) This figure painted on a cave wall in southern Spain has bird's feet and hands, a triangular head with tri-lines emanating from the cheeks, protruding circular eyes of an insect, and antennae. Neolithic Spain (Los Organos, Despeñaperros, Jaén; probably 4th mill. B.C.). (1) H. 11.2 cm.

interchanges with an X sign, triangle, and X framed within a rectangle (König 1973: figs. 105–10). All seem to be homologues. The hourglass framed within a rectangle appears on Irish megalithic stones together with triangles, lozenges, circles, and an array of other symbols related to regeneration or perpetual renewal—life trees, vertically winding serpents, coils, cupmarks, concentric arcs and circles.

Ritual dances performed by the Goddess's maidens in the shape of hourglasses appear painted on Sardinian, Sicilian, and Cucuteni vases dated from the early 4th millennium B.C. (FIGURES 377, 378) Maidens dance in a ring, singly, or in pairs; one hand is at the head and the other at the hip, or they are holding hands above their heads. The Cucuteni dancing figures are portrayed within lenticular vulvas in association with dogs, snakes, and whirling signs. The completely preserved design on a frieze of one Cucuteni vase consists of six vulvas: two include dancing figures and the others columns of life. The skirts have tassels that look like brushes, energy symbols. The figures on Sardinian vases of the Ozieri culture are clearly shown with bird's claws for hands.

FIGURE 377

1

FIGURE 377 Scenes painted on Sardinian Ozieri ceramics. ((1) Dish from Monte d'Accodi between Alghero and Sassari, N Sardinia; (2) vase from Grotta di Sa Ucca de Su Tintirriolu di Mara, N Sardinia; 4000–3800 B.C.)

2

Dancing hourglass-shaped figures with hands above their heads and assisted by nude ithyphallic men (FIGURE 378, 5) were found painted on the walls of the Magurata cave in northwestern Bulgaria (Anati 1969). Other contemporary paintings in this cave include anthropomorphized suns surrounded by axes and other geometric symbols (see fig. 459), clearly associated with the idea of regeneration. The shape of axes corresponds with that of actual copper axes of the Vinča and Karanovo cultures dated to 4500–4000 B.C. I assume the Magurata paintings to be of this age and since this area of northwestern Bulgaria belongs to the distribution territory of the Vinča culture, the paintings most likely were done by the Vinča people. Very similar dancing figures with upraised arms appear portrayed painted on sarcophagi and molded of clay on sacrificial vases of the Minoan and Mycenaean cultures. One such scene from the end of a Late Mycenaean sarcophagus from Tanagra, central Greece, is shown in figure 378, 6. Many authors have interpreted such dancing figures as "mourning" figures, which, I think, does not reflect the real meaning. Dances of hourglass-shaped figures were portrayed in an identical manner for more than 3000 years in Old Europe; they witness energetic regeneration rites, not mourning or wailing of women.

In Sicilian Copper Age vase painting, the hourglass appears in association with snakes and nets, or the symbol itself is net-patterned, as on the illustrated vase from the cave of Chiusazza near Syracuse. (FIGURE 379) The net places the hourglass close to the "water of life" symbols; the snakes accentuate rebirth, or they have a lunar-calendrical connotation. On a Cucuteni vase, two hourglass figures in a dancing posture also have two winding snakes above them. All these scenes seem to portray ritual dances, perhaps in connection with funeral rites or the regeneration of dying Nature.

This sign, which likely originated in the Paleolithic from the triangular vulva

FIGURE 378

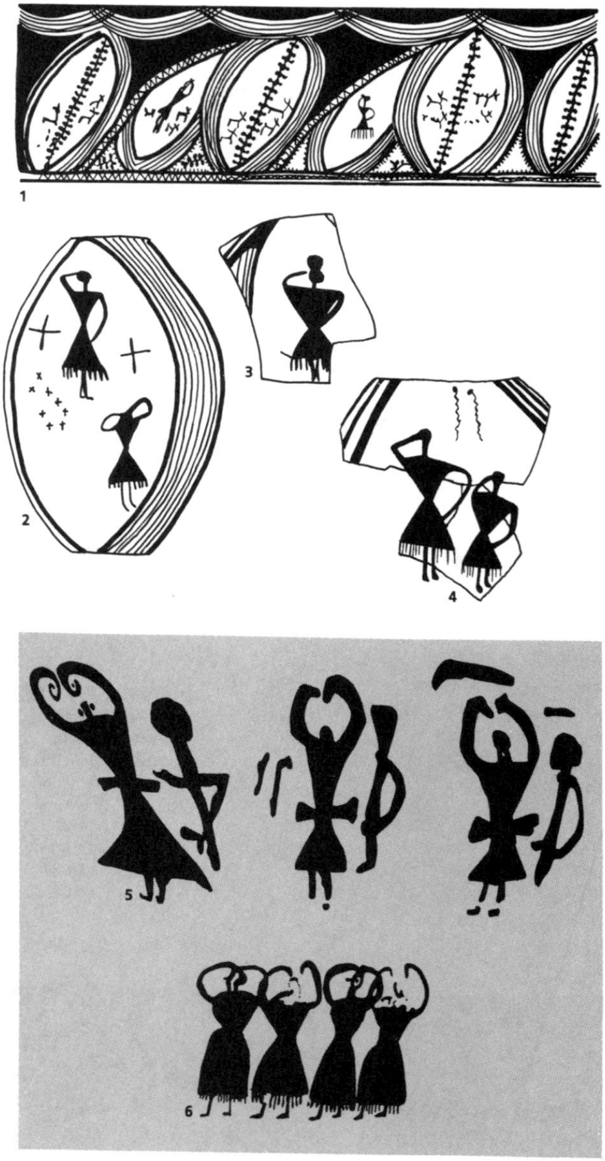

FIGURE 378 (1)–(4) A ritual dance is again performed by one or two hourglass-shaped figures portrayed within a vulva/seed. The figures are associated with dogs, crosses (whirls), and snakes. In (1) there is a life column flanked by animals (probably dogs or goats) within each larger vulva. Vase painted black on red. Late Cucuteni (Brinzeni-Tsiganka, W Ukraine; c. 3800–3600 B.C.). (5) These dancing hourglass-shaped figures have male companions. The tiny head of the figure on the left has two small discs or earrings on the sides. The projections in the middle of the figures which look like double axes probably are portrayals of special ritual belts. Vinča culture (Magurata cave sanctuary, NW Bulgaria; exact chronology unknown; most probably 4500–4000 B.C. on the basis of associated painted axe forms; see fig. 459). (6) Dancing figures painted on a sarcophagus (below these is a scene of women placing a dead man into sarcophagus). Late Mycenaean (Tanagra, Thebes, Boeotia, Tomb 22; 14th cent. B.C.) (1) H. 7.9 cm. (2) H. 8.2 cm. (3) H. 4.3 cm. (4) H. 5.7 cm.

symbol, and which as an anthropomorphic hourglass figure is evidenced on Early Neolithic ceramics of the mid-7th millennium B.C. (see Hourmouziadis 1969: fig. 1), continues to appear for a very long time. Such figures are found in the Bronze Age and even on Iron Age funeral ceramics (for instance on Hallstatt ceramics of 750–500 B.C.).

In Bronze Age vase decoration, a geometricized hourglass (with no indication of the Goddess's head and limbs) appears in vertical columns and is usually net-patterned. This motif is common on matt-painted Middle Helladic pithoi of the early 2nd millennium B.C. The vertical columns of piled up hourglass forms relate to the life column.

FIGURE 379

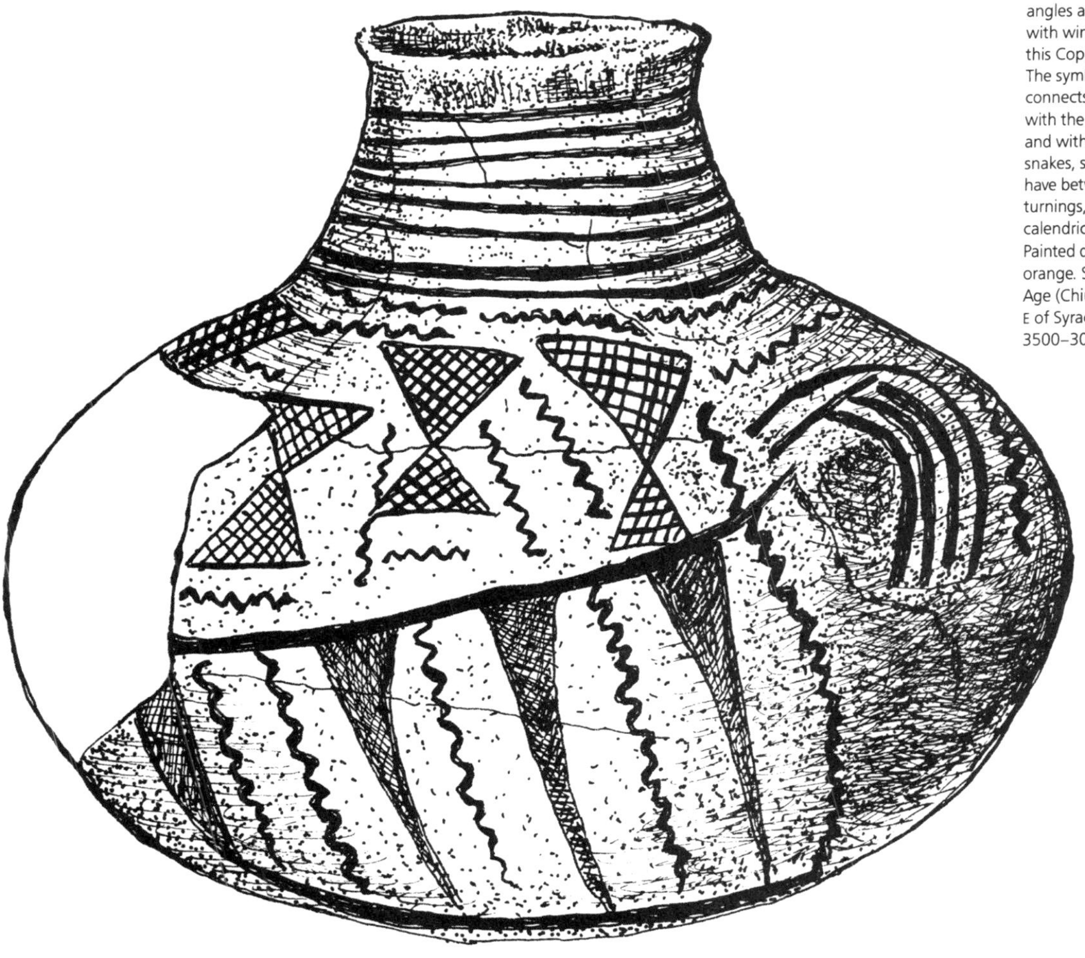

FIGURE 379 Net-patterned hourglass forms and elongated triangles are interspersed with winding snakes on this Copper Age vase. The symbol association connects the hourglass with the water of life and with rebirth; the snakes, some of which have between 14 and 17 turnings, may also have calendrical significance. Painted dark brown on orange. Sicilian Copper Age (Chiusazza Cave, E of Syracuse, SE Sicily; 3500–3000 B.C.)

FIGURE 380

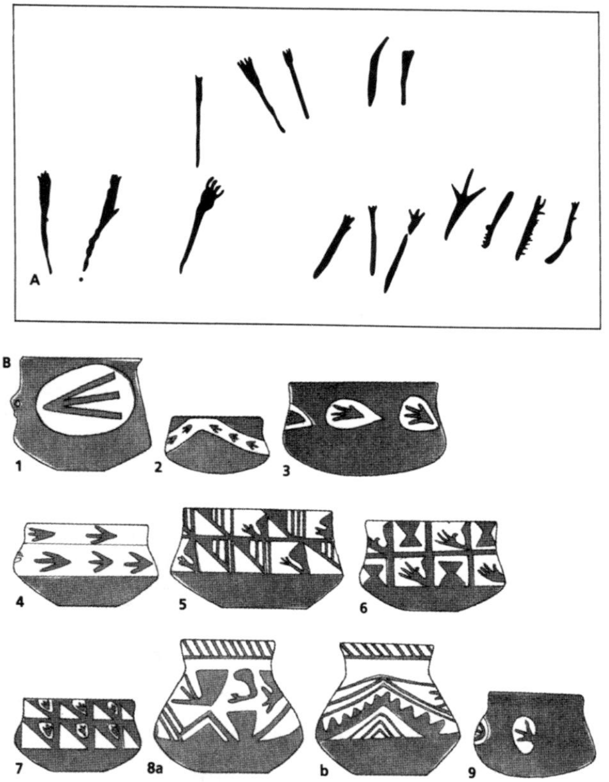

FIGURE 380 Bird's feet in the Upper Paleolithic and Neolithic paintings. A. Bird's feet in the Late Upper Paleolithic cave at Santander, N Spain. B. Bird's feet as the Goddess's hands appear as a design on vases. Note the association with triangles (5, 7) and with hourglass shapes in separate panels (6). Painted red and white. Hacilar V–II (Hacilar, central Anatolia; early 6th mill. B.C.) (1) H. 12 cm. (2) H. 6 cm. (3) H. 9.8 cm. (4) H. 8.8 cm. (5) H. 10.6 cm. (6) H. 9.6 cm. (7) H. 7.6 cm. (8) H. 14 cm. (9) H. 8.8 cm.

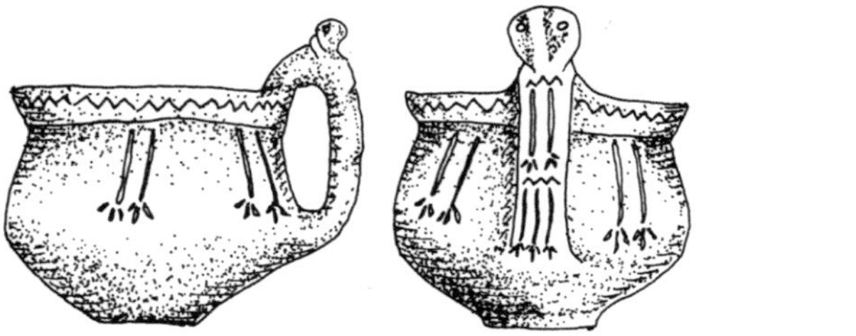

FIGURE 381 The bird-foot motif decorates a cup whose handle is topped by a mask of the Bird Goddess. Funnel-necked Beaker (Cmielów, S Poland; c. 3500 B.C.) H. 14.2 cm.

21.3 *Bird's claws*

Whence came these feathers and these feet of birds?
Your faces are the faces of fair maids.
(Ovid, *Metamorphoses*, v. 552)

The three-fingered "hands" of the Goddess that appear in all Old European phases starting with the Early Neolithic and survive in current folklore are actually bird's feet. In folk-tales witches and fairies related to ancient Goddesses often have bird's feet. The Russian Baba Yaga lives in a hut standing on a chicken leg; Lithuanian Laumes (fairies) have chicken legs.

The mythical importance of the bird's feet motif (and of the Bird of Prey Goddess) goes back to the Upper Paleolithic. At Santian, Province of Santander, northern Spain, red-painted bird's feet were found on the walls of a narrow cave with stalagmites and stalactites. (FIGURE 380, A) Here the red color stands for life, not death. Like the regenerative triangle and hourglass, isolated bird's feet were also symbols imbued with the potency of regeneration.

Bird feet motifs appear on Neolithic and Copper Age vases in Europe and Anatolia. For instance, Hacilar V–II vases bear this motif in bands or panels. (FIGURE 380, B) Here only the feet are of importance, not the entire figure of the deity, but it is significant that they alternate in panels with triangles and hourglass figures. Bird's feet sometimes are a vase's sole decoration. An indication of their divinity comes from masks of the Goddess attached to such vases, as on the illustrated vessel from the Funnel-necked Beaker culture of Poland. (FIGURE 381)

Bird feet as *hands* of the Goddess are engraved on Minoan seals and painted on Greek Geometric and Archaic pottery. Two seals from the Cretan sites of Mallia and Phaistos are reproduced here; the three-fingered creature on the seal from Mallia has a body made of two triangles and frog's legs. (FIGURE 382)

In the Iron Age, bird's feet appear on northern European anthropomorphic urns of c. 525–500 B.C. The illustrated urn from the area of Gdańsk, northern Poland, has the facial features of an Owl Goddess and bird's feet for arms. (FIGURE 383) She wears a cap, triple earrings with amber beads, a broad collar, and a spiral-headed pin. On other urns from the same area, bird feet form a design motif around the shoulders of the vase or appear on the cap.

Bird claws identify the hourglass figures with the Vulture, Owl, and other Bird of Prey Goddesses, who, as we know, is the Goddess of Death and Rebirth. The main component of her image—the triangle (vulva)—secures regeneration. A related image is the butterfly and "double axe" (a horizontal hourglass), also an epiphany of the same Goddess. To her we shall return in the pages below.

FIGURE 382

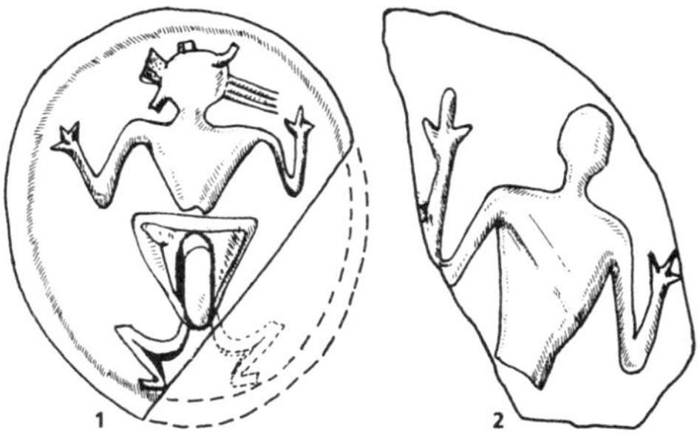

1 2

FIGURE 382 The figure with bird's feet for hands appears on Middle Minoan seals ((1) Mallia and (2) Phaistos, Crete; early 2nd mill. B.C.) (1) H. 4.5 cm. (2) H. 4.7 cm.

FIGURE 383

1

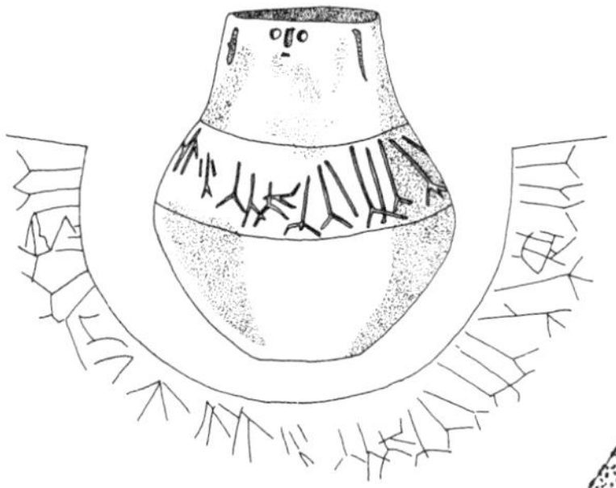

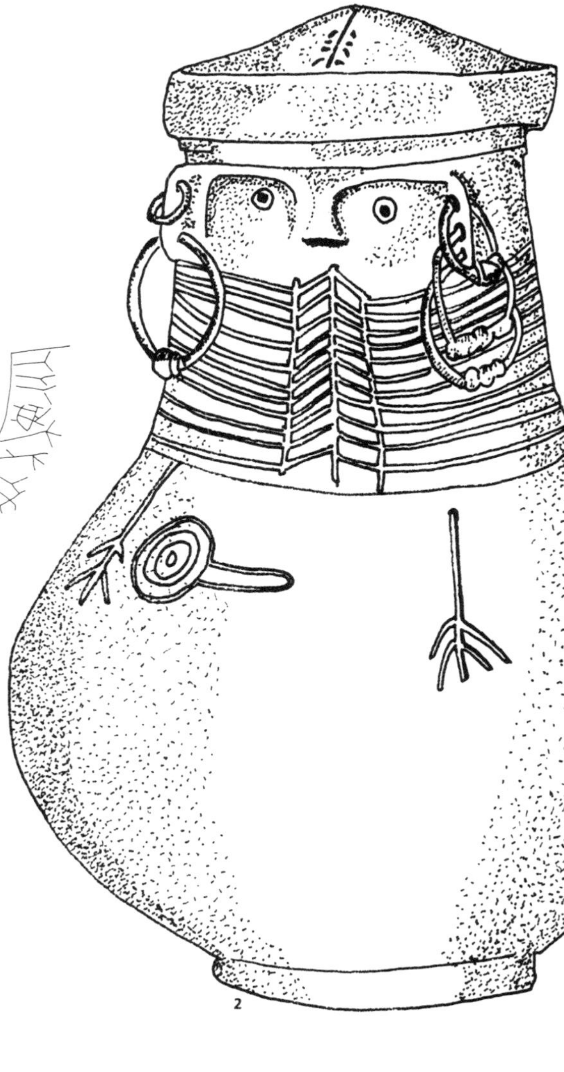

2

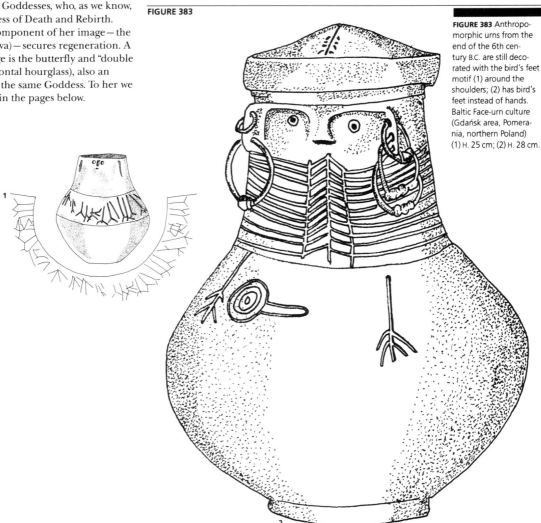

FIGURE 383 Anthropomorphic urns from the end of the 6th century B.C. are still decorated with the bird's feet motif (1) around the shoulders; (2) has bird's feet instead of hands. Baltic Face-urn culture (Gdańsk area, Pomerania, northern Poland) (1) H. 25 cm; (2) H. 28 cm.

Cupmarks and trees of life on "ship of renewal" in Scandinavian rock carving. See figure 386, page 249.

22/ *Ship of Renewal*

Engravings of ceremonial ships in Europe are known from megalithic tombs in Brittany and Ireland, the Maltese temples, and the Cycladic tombs of the mid-3rd millennium B.C.; from Minoan portrayals on seals and rings; and from the Scandinavian rock pictures of the 2nd millennium B.C. The fact alone that they were engraved on inner tomb walls speaks for their connection with the cult of the dead or rituals associated with the death of Nature. All depictions of ships are highly abstracted; some are just a row of vertical lines connected by a bar at the bottom. (FIGURE 384) However, frequently there is a zoomorphic or spiral head, probably a serpent's, on the keel. What the vertical lines represent is not clear—perhaps human beings (souls? people performing certain ritual functions?) or life columns. Several portrayals from the gallery graves of Brittany show an abstracted image of the Goddess being pulled by a snake; that is, she is on the ship with a spiral or serpent head (fig. 384, 4 and 5).

The Cycladic anthropomorphic platters of the Keros-Syros culture throw more light on ship symbolism. The middle part is usually decorated by interconnected spirals symbolizing water (the sea) with a ship in the middle, or there is a radiant sun or snake coil design. The handle is a pair of legs with a triangular vulva above, surrounded by plant motifs, zig-zags or striations (see fig. 166 above). Why vulva and ship on the same cult object? Let us note that there are bird's feet and a fish attached to the prow. (FIGURE 385) The feet indicate the presence of the Goddess herself, and the fish is one of her basic epiphanies as the Goddess of Regeneration. Thus we can read the symbolism as: the Goddess in the guise of a bird of prey or a fish pulls the boat across the waters. And who is on or above the ship? Some are marked with

FIGURE 384

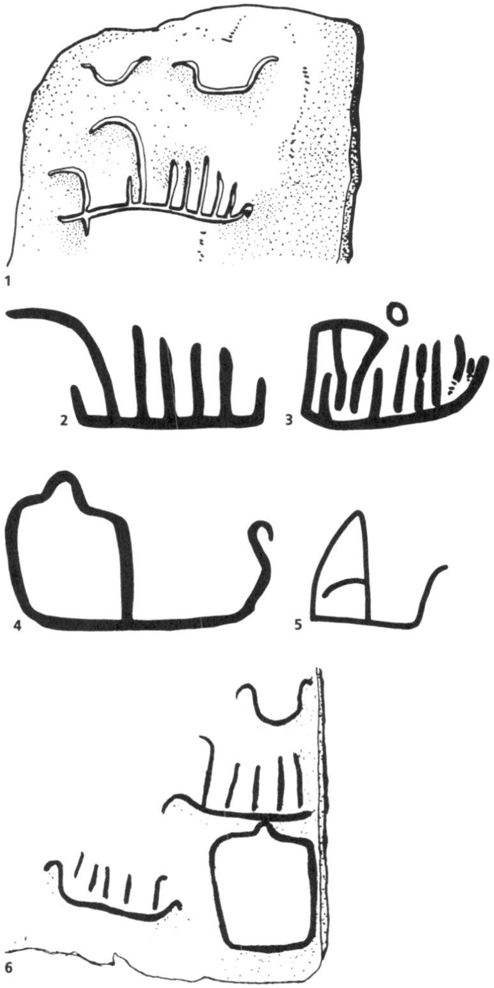

FIGURE 384 These portrayals of ceremonial ships are engraved on the stones of megalithic tombs. The keels appear serpentlike. In (4)–(6) the Goddess in a schematic (or nuclear) form is on the ship or surrounded by ships. On (1) and (6), the smaller engravings probably are reduced versions of ships, not "yokes" as they are called. (1), (2), and (4)–(6), megalithic graves of Brittany. (1), (2), (6) Mané Lud dolmen; (3) Newgrange, Ireland; second half of 4th mill. B.C.; (4) Petit Mont, 4th mill B.C.; (5) Barnenez; mid-5th mill. B.C..

striations which may represent oars, but others carry a zig-zagging snake along the whole length of the craft, or a zig-zag (a symbol of a snake) is shown on the body of the boat. Such representations link the ship with the serpent. Are they interchangeable symbols? Very likely.

A surprisingly similar juxtaposition of winding serpent and ship appears both in Egypt and on Scandinavian rocks. In Egypt, the serpent above the boat symbolizes a cosmic snake, giver of life to Earth and gods; it is a very distinct symbol of renewal (Almgren 1934: 74 ff.). Such serpents are associated with the dying and resurrecting god Osiris or his son Horus. Frequently a sign of life (♀) (a uterus with a dash under the loop) is placed next to the head of the snake. In some portrayals the snake springs out of a lotus flower. The association of ship and serpent occurs frequently on the rocks of Sweden; either the keel is shaped like a snake, or a long serpent winds along the whole length of the ship. (FIGURE 386) These parallels allow us to assume that the schematized portrayals of ships in megalithic tombs also represent "serpent ships." If the ship and serpent are interchangeable symbols, then many winding and zig-zagging serpents engraved on tomb walls and curbstones are life renewal symbols. It is not accidental that some of the zig-zags or winding serpents in Knowth and Newgrange are joined to a triangle or lozenge, the special signs of the Goddess of Regeneration, just as the bird's feet are attached to the prow of the ship on Cycladic platters. On the ship of cast bronze from Fårdal, Denmark, dated to the 8th century B.C., the Snake Goddess is shown pulling her serpent with a cord (fig. 386, 9).

In addition to the frequent depiction of a serpent head on the ship's keel in Scandinavian rock engravings, other animals also appear—deer, elk, and perhaps swan or duck. (Horses and figures of Thor holding a gigantic axe or hammer and of Odin holding a supernatural spear are Indo-European additions to this rock art.) A life tree, a sun wheel, or signs like cupmarks may be shown on the ship; Scandinavian rock art also includes

FIGURE 385

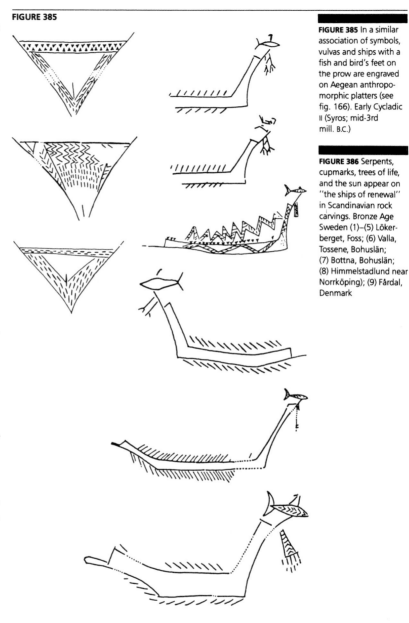

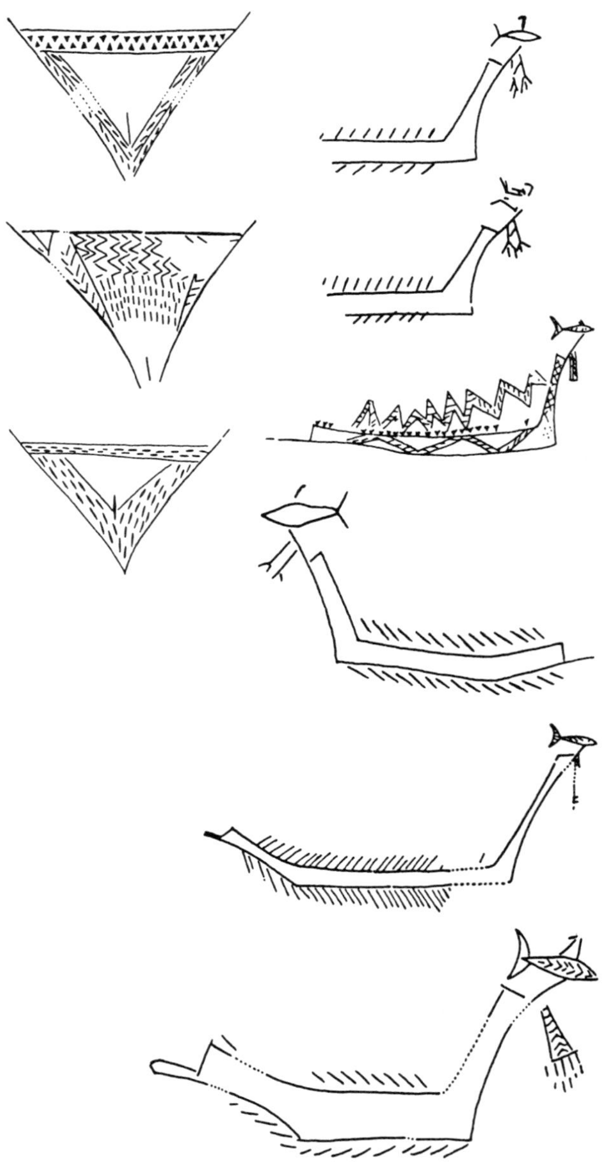

FIGURE 385 In a similar association of symbols, vulvas and ships with a fish and bird's feet on the prow are engraved on Aegean anthropomorphic platters (see fig. 166). Early Cycladic II (Syros; mid-3rd mill. B.C.)

FIGURE 386 Serpents, cupmarks, trees of life, and the sun appear on "the ships of renewal" in Scandinavian rock carvings. Bronze Age Sweden (1)–(5) Lökerberget, Foss; (6) Valla, Tossene, Bohuslän; (7) Bottna, Bohuslän; (8) Himmelstadlund near Norrköping); (9) Fårdal, Denmark

FIGURE 386

ships with lura players, dancers, or acrobats, figures with upraised arms or holding axes, and sacred marriage scenes. (The lura is an instrument similar to the trumpet.) In the south there is a Late Minoan gold ring from the island of Mochlos at Crete depicting a ship with a Goddess seated in the middle next to a tree of life (an olive tree). A deer or horse head is on the ship's prow (Alexiou 1969: 113, fig. 51).

The ship portrayals from north and south Europe are witness to very rich ritual practices connected with the idea of the renewal of nature at the winter solstice or at the crisis of human death.

In Roman times, the goddesses Isis and Nehalenia are portrayed with the ship, or with one leg in a ship. Greek Dionysos, brimming with the vital forces of blossoming vegetation, appears from the sea on a boat in February and with him come also the souls of the dead. The water is clearly a link between this world and the netherworld. The dead are "those below" or "those beneath the bosom of the Queen of the underworld" as we hear from the funerary text on a gold plate from Thurii, south Italy, of the 4th–3rd centuries B.C.: "I have sunk beneath the bosom of the Mistress, the Queen of the underworld" (cited by Eliade 1974:41).

The symbolic importance of the ship has not yet died out; in some parts of Europe, Germany, Belgium, and France, it reappears at spring carnivals. Even a "Queen of Queens" with her whole entourage is seated in a boat and drawn around on wheels or a sled. (A photograph of a Queen of Queens on a ship in Paris, dated to March 12, 1921, can be seen in Almgren's book of 1934: 19.) Ships were regarded as female (and still are), named after women or goddesses; and ship's prows (figureheads) were frequently portrayed in the form of women.

Middle Minoan vase with a uterus or bladder shape hanging from mouth of a fish. See figure 409, page 262.

23/ *Frog, Hedgehog, and Fish*

The frog or toad, hedgehog, and fish were both funerary and life symbols at the same time. Their peculiar relationship—even equation—with the uterus of the life-giving, regenerating, and transforming Goddess accounts for their prominent role in Old European symbolism.

23.1 *Frog and toad*

More recent beliefs concerning frogs and toads illuminate those of prehistory. To this day European peasants believe that a toad is a portent of pregnancy. There is a good deal of evidence from both folklore and history (Egyptian, Greek, Roman, and later) that the toad was regarded as an epiphany of the Goddess or her uterus. Hence the belief in the "wandering womb," found in Egyptian and classical sources as well as from present day folklore. Both Hippocrates and Plato described the uterus as an animal capable of moving in all directions in the abdomen (Ekenvall 1978). In many countries, the croaking of frogs in springtime is said to resemble the cries of unborn children; the frog itself, therefore, represents the soul of the not-yet-incarnate child. (For the association of woman, uterus, child, and frog in sculpture and painting through history, see Deonna 1952.) In the Jungian psychology of dreams, this creature, not yet a human being, represents an unconscious impulse that has a definite tendency to become conscious (Franz 1972: 24).

The frog-woman image may be as old as the Upper Paleolithic. On one of the engraved bones found in the cave of Les Trois Frères in southern France there is a series of strange engraved creatures with frog-shaped legs. (FIGURE 387, 1) Another frog-woman with V-shaped limbs, a human rib cage, and a human/frog head is engraved on a bone from Fontales, southern France. (FIGURE 387, 2) In the site of Laugerie-Basse, a figure of an anthropomorphized lizard appeared engraved on bone objects. (FIGURE 387, 3)

FIGURE 387

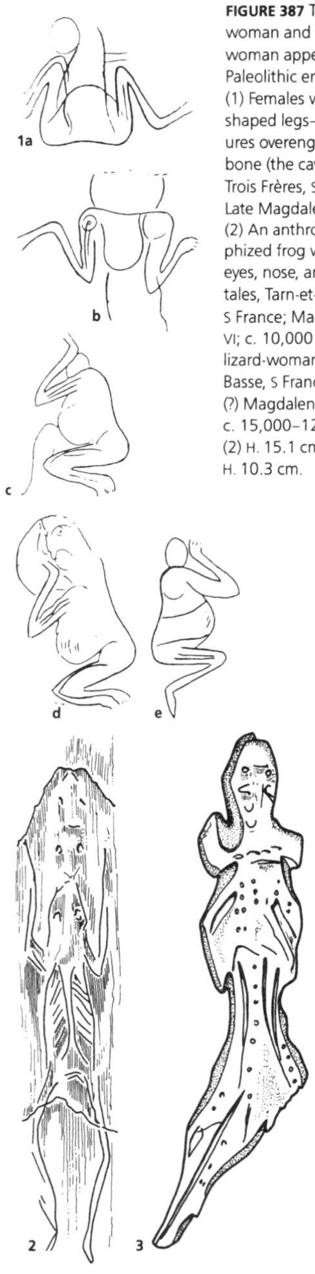

FIGURE 387 The frog-woman and lizard-woman appear in Upper Paleolithic engravings. (1) Females with frog-shaped legs—several figures overengraved on a bone (the cave of Les Trois Frères, S France; Late Magdalenian). (2) An anthropomorphized frog with human eyes, nose, and ribs (Fontales, Tarn-et-Garonne, S France; Magdalenian VI; c. 10,000 B.C.); (3) A lizard-woman (Laugerie-Basse, S France; middle (?) Magdalenian; c. 15,000–12,000 B.C.). (2) H. 15.1 cm. (3) H. 10.3 cm.

From the earliest Neolithic, the frog is represented in carved stone—marble, alabaster, green or blue stone—in clay, and engraved or incised on stone and ceramics. (FIGURES 388, 389) Sometimes the body of a naturalistically rendered toad/frog is perforated for the insertion of a head, presumably anthropomorphic. A ceramic Frog Goddess with human head intact is found at Hacilar, Anatolia. (FIGURE 390, 1) In most cases, the effigy is a woman/toad hybrid, characteristically with human vulva. An Early Neolithic (late 7th millennium) example with perforations for suspension illustrated here is from Achilleion, Thessaly. At times, the figure is completely animal in form except for the anthropomorphic element of a large pubic triangle. In the Copper Age, frog figurines are made of stone and clay, beautifully modeled (see the example from Vinča, fig 389).

Figures with outstretched legs and arms appear in relief on the walls of Çatal Hüyük shrines. Such a Frog Goddess from a shrine in Level VII, 23 is covered by a red, black, and orange painted veil whose honeycomb design (or interconnected signs of sacred script) extends beyond her body. (FIGURE 390, 2) Her navel is marked with concentric circles, above which rises a framed life column of multiple lozenges. The head was not preserved. The honeycomb design, life column, concentric circles, and the association with bucrania in the shrine link this figure with the theme of regeneration. Thus it appears that the image does not represent, as often hypothesized, a birth-giving posture; rather the shape is that of an anthropomorphized frog which is connected by its symbolism to regeneration.

The same theme reappears through the millennia in prehistory and history. For instance, the toad on a Minoan amphora from Phaistos of the Early Palatial period (early 2nd millennium B.C.) is painted below a uterus sign. (FIGURE 391) Frogs or toads painted on a kalathos (a vase shaped like a fruit basket) from Kouklia, Cyprus, c. 1100 B.C., are portrayed in panels alternating with panels including life

FIGURE 388

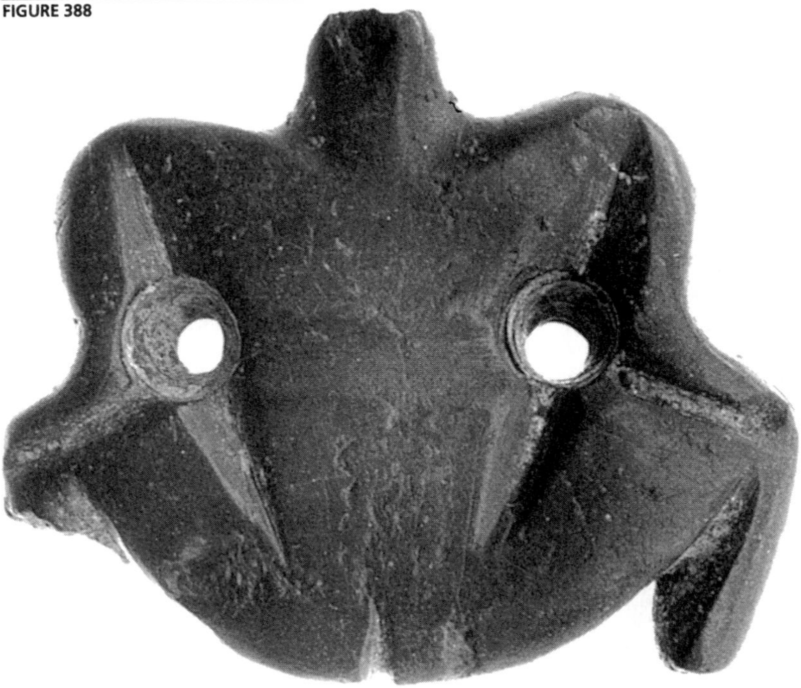

FIGURE 389

FIGURE 388 A major Old European archetype is the Frog Goddess. This amulet carved of black stone has perforations suggesting that it was meant to be attached to something else. Early Sesklo (Achilleion Ib, Thessaly; c. 6300 B.C.). H. 3.2 cm.

FIGURE 389 This terracotta frog is in a standing posture. Classical Vinča (Vinča; 1st half of 5th mill. B.C.) H. approx. 6 cm.

FIGURE 390

1

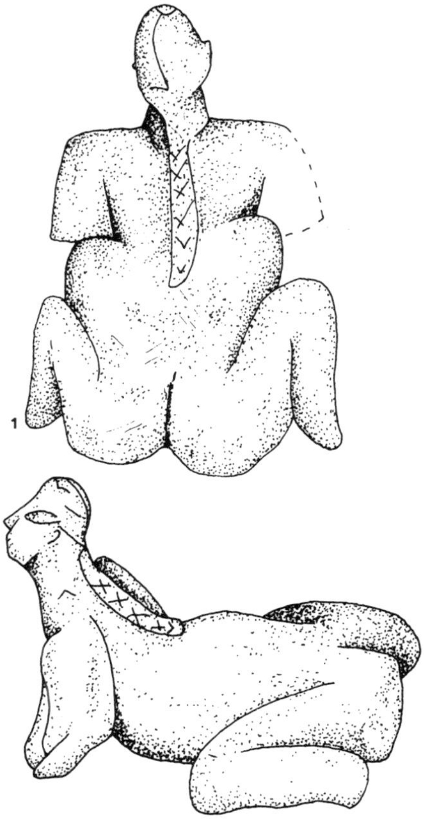

2

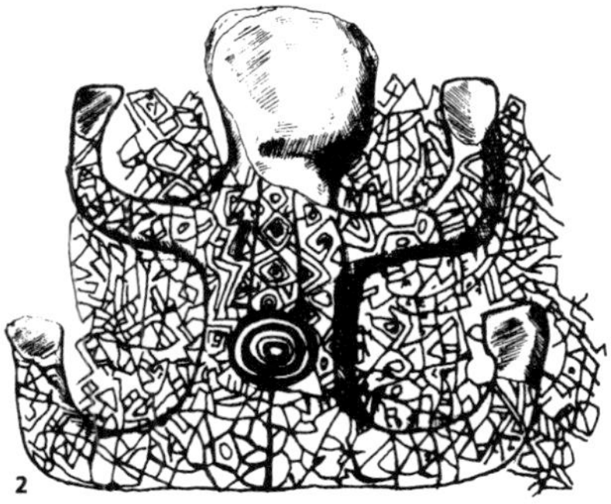

FIGURE 391

FIGURE 390 Frog/woman hybrids, symbols of regeneration, are quite common in Anatolia. (1) Like most, this ceramic example has a human head and vulva, with a froglike body. Central Anatolian Neolithic (Level VI, House Q.VI.5, Hacilar; end of 6th mill. B.C.). (2) One of the most characteristic Çatal Hüyük motifs is a figure of the Frog Goddess sculpted in relief on a temple wall, richly painted in red, black, and orange. There is a framed column of lozenges on her chest and concentric circles around her navel, symbols linking her with regeneration. Her face has not been preserved. Central Anatolian Neolithic (Shrine VII, 23, Çatal Hüyük; mid-7th mill. B.C.) (1) H. 7.5 cm.

FIGURE 391 Frog or toad painted on an amphora, reminiscent of the widespread belief that the womb is an animal which wanders about the body. Middle Minoan I (first palace at Phaistos, Crete; early 2nd mill. B.C.) H. 12.5 cm.

FIGURE 392

FIGURE 392 The frogs on this kalathos vase are associated with life columns; their heads are portrayed as whirls. Late Bronze Age Cyprus (Grave 9, Kouklia, Palaipaphos, Cyprus; c. 1100 B.C.) H. 14.1 cm.

FIGURE 393

1

2

FIGURE 393 Here is testimony to the longevity of the frog-woman/goddess-vulva association. (1) This arresting votive tablet from Bavaria, dated A.D. 1811, includes a frog with vulva on its back next to the Madonna. (Alpine region, Bavaria, S Germany; A.D. 1811) (2) This ex-voto frog with a human face, of silver plate, is from the end of the 19th cent. A.D. (found in the Andechs Monastery, on Ammersee, Alpine region).

FIGURE 394

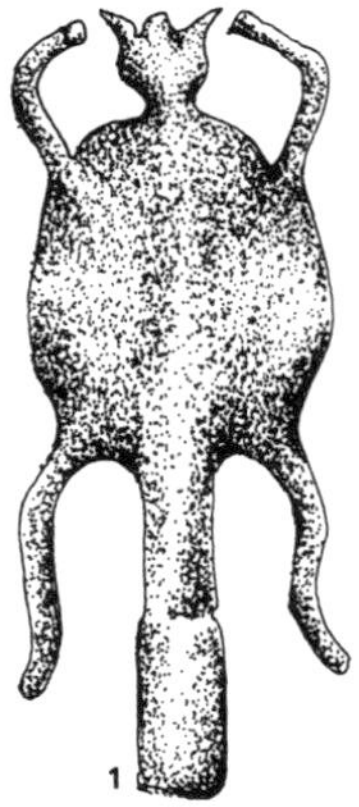

1

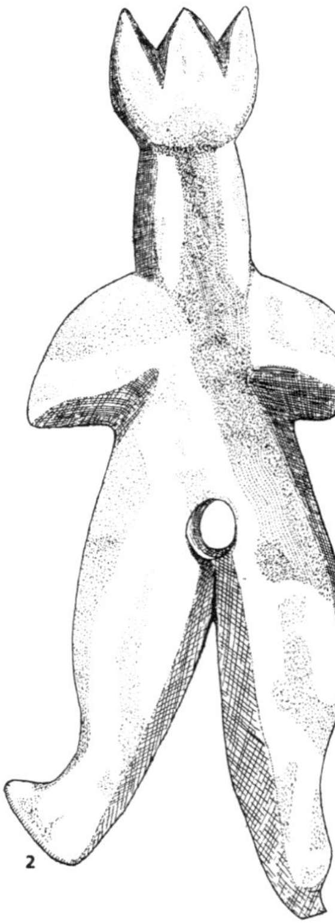

2

FIGURE 394 Nearly 8,000 years separate these toads whose heads are sprouting lilies, symbol of regeneration. (1) Wooden tombstone (Nida, Kuršių nerija, W Lithuania; end of 19th cent.). (2) Sesklo terracotta figurine (Sesklo; c. 6000 B.C.). (1) H. approx. 1.6 m; (2) H. 4.5 cm.

columns of net-patterned lozenges and zig-zags. (FIGURE 392) Quite amazingly, on a votive tablet dated A.D. 1811 found in a church in Bavaria, a toad with a human vulva on its back appears together with the Madonna. (FIGURE 393, 1) In Germany up to the 20th century, women suffering from uterine problems presented images of toads to the Virgin Mary. (FIGURE 393, 2)

In 19th century Lithuania, wooden tombstones were constructed in the form of a toad with a lily (symbolic of new life) sprouting from its head. (FIGURE 394, 1) In northeastern Siberia, the Nikhs (Gilyaks) of Sakhalin in the lower Amur area made pictures of a toad with buds at each extremity, for use in the course of the commemoration feast held for the dead (Black 1973). Truly startling evidence of this long-lived symbolic association between the toad and the bud—at least as old as the Early Neolithic—is the toad-shaped figurine with a budlike or flower-shaped head, discovered at Sesklo, c. 6000–5800 B.C. (FIGURE 394, 2) The frog's association with life-generating forces is preserved in the functions of the German Frog Goddess, Holla/Holle, inhabiting wells, ponds, bogs, and caves. Holla in the guise of a frog brings back to earth the red apple, symbol of life, which when ripe falls down into the well (Rüttner-Cova 1986: 79).

Stylized stick-figure frogs are encountered on ceramics throughout prehistory. The stylization even went so far as to form a design distinct from anthropomorphic frogs. (FIGURE 395) This geometricized motif is particularly common on the Neolithic pottery of southern Italy, Linear Pottery vases of central Europe, and on those of Early Bronze Age Crete. (FIGURE 396) Together with the tiny amuletic sculptures of frog women, the frequency of these designs testifies to the considerable role of the Frog Goddess in the Old European belief system.

Portrayals in historic times of froglike, stooping women with hands on their pudenda, such as the famous Sheila-na-gigs found in Irish, Scottish, and English medieval churches and castles, usually displayed by the entrance (Murray

FIGURE 395

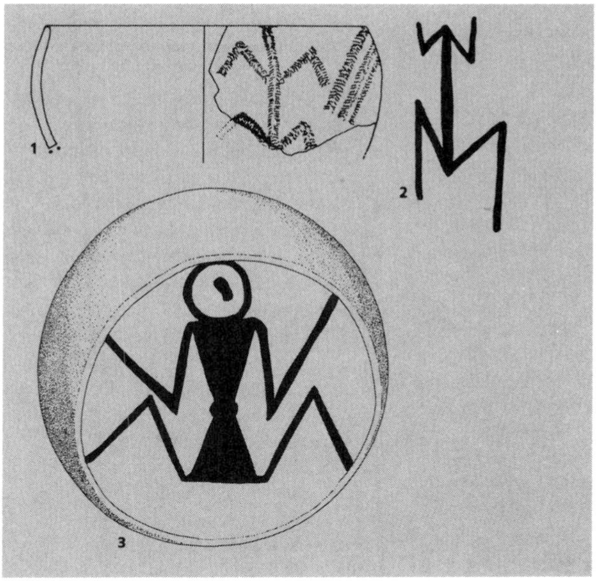

FIGURE 395 Schematic stick-figure frogs occur on ceramics throughout Old Europe. (1) Rocker-stamped jar from the second period of the Impresso culture (Rendina, near Melfi, SE Italy; 1st half of 6th mill. B.C.). (2) Vase painting from a Pre-Palatial tholos tomb (Lebena, S Crete; mid-3rd mill. B.C.). (3) Painting on the base of a Late Minoan III vase (Myrsini, Siteia, E Crete; 14th century B.C.). (2) H. 5.7 cm. (3) H. 5.8 cm.

FIGURE 396

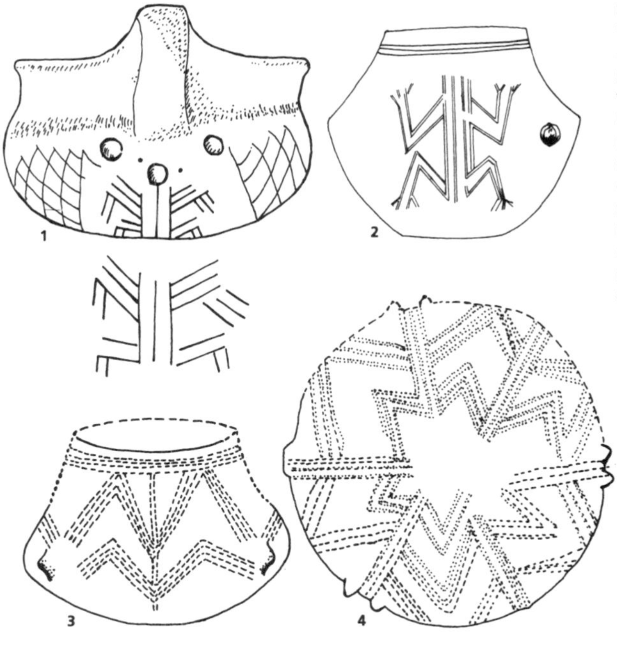

FIGURE 396 These vases from central Europe are also decorated with stylized frogs. Linear Pottery ((1) Halle-Trotha, E Germany; (2) Nová Ves, near Kolín, Bohemia; (3) Lockwitz, E Germany; (4) Dresden-Mokritz, E Germany; early 5th mill. B.C.) (1) H. 4.4 cm. (2) H. 10.2 cm. (3) H. 11.2 cm. (4) H. 21.2 cm.

1934: 93) probably have roots in the prehistoric Frog Goddess. The Egyptian Goddess Creatrix Haquit was portrayed as a woman with the head of a frog, and this animal was her hieroglyphic sign (Deonna 1952: 239). Hekate of ancient Greece has an epithet "Baubo," i.e. Toad (ibid., 238). The names given to the toad link it with the Goddess in many European languages. *Hexe* in German, *fata* in Italian dialects, *czarownica* in Polish, *bosorka* in Ukrainian, *gatalinka* in Serbo-Croatian, *mantis* in Greek. They mean "witch" or "prophetess" (Alinei 1987: 265).

The toad was sacred to Ragana, the Lithuanian Goddess of Death and Regeneration and was her main epiphany. If not properly treated, the toad, it was believed even in the early 20th century, can be as dangerous as the Goddess herself. If someone should spit on it, and the toad should catch the spittle, that person will surely die. If one makes a toad angry, she can blow herself up and then burst, releasing a virulent poison. If her venom lands on an exposed part of the body, that person will be poisoned. Often sores will develop and the skin will crack. Beware of killing a toad with your bare hands—your face will become blemished, rough, and pimpled like the skin of the toad. As a messenger of death, the toad can crawl onto the chest of a sleeping person and suck the breath from his or her body, causing certain death. On the other hand the toad has healing properties. Placed on a sore, the toad may heal it (Gimbutas 1984; 1985). There is still a folk belief in modern United States that toads can cause warts to appear. In the Alpine zone of Bavaria it was believed to the present century that toads had a special healing power if killed on Virgin Mary's days, August 15 and September 8. They were deadly if killed on other days. Caught on these holy days the toads were kept nailed on doors of houses and stalls for the protection of the animals and humans from illness and death (Rüttner-Cova 1986: 163).

Because the toad was incarnated with the powers of the Goddess of Death and Regeneration, her functions were both to bring death and to restore life.

23.2 *Hedgehog*

A nocturnal and hibernating animal, a spiny ball that can best be found on moonlit nights, the hedgehog has been endowed with mystery from time immemorial. Much of what is credited to the moon by folk beliefs is also credited to the hedgehog: it rejuvenates and beautifies, heals wounds (if they are rubbed with hedgehog fat), and has a considerable influence on sexual life. Images of hedgehogs were placed in graves in the early 20th century and in antiquity. Spiny balls made of wood and painted red, produced in the southern Tirol in this century and found deposited in graves and churches, were called "uteri" (Kriss 1929; Gulder 1962). (FIGURE 397) The connection with the uterus—and hence with renewal, regeneration, and the Goddess—is reinforced by the German words for a cow's uterus, which after parturition remains swollen and is covered with warts; it is known as *Igel*, "hedgehog," or *Igelkalb*, "hedgehog's calf." From the latter expression we sense the link between the hedgehog and the Goddess. A Maltese proverb says "We are all the children of the hedgehog" (Cassar-Pullicino 1976: 170).

The hedgehog/uterus connection is very old, probably earlier than the beginning of agriculture. Uterus-like signs, some with spikes, some marked with bi-lines, are known from several Upper Paleolithic caves, including La Pileta in Spain and Font-de-Gaume in France. (FIGURE 398) Whether they are hedgehogs and uteri in one remains to be answered.

The presence of the hedgehog in Old Europe is firmly established. Figurines of hedgehogs and hedgehog vases with anthropomorphic lids—i.e., vases with warts and with the Goddess's face on the lid—are known from the Lengyel, Tisza, Vinča, Karanovo, and Cucuteni culture groups. The best examples come from the Karanovo VI (Gumelniţa) culture. (FIGURES 399–401)

FIGURE 397

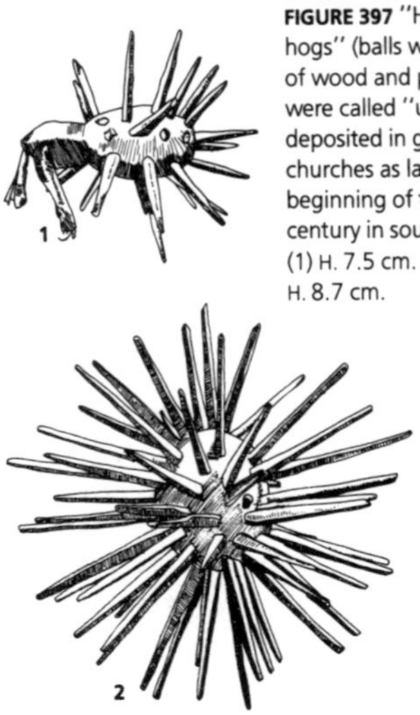

FIGURE 397 "Hedgehogs" (balls with spikes) of wood and painted red were called "uteri" and deposited in graves and churches as late as the beginning of the 20th century in southern Tirol. (1) H. 7.5 cm. (2) H. 8.7 cm.

FIGURE 398

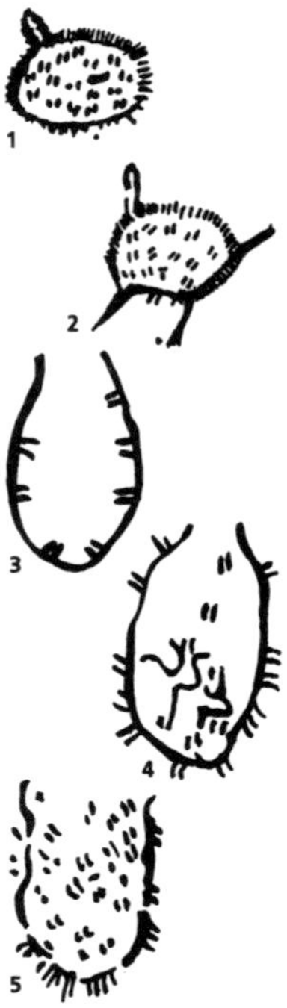

FIGURE 398 The intimate connection between the hedgehog and the uterus in the symbolism of regeneration may go back to the Upper Paleolithic. These designs from cave walls are uteri, hedgehogs, or a hybrid of the two. (La Pileta, near Gibraltar, Spain; c. 10,000 B.C.)

FIGURE 399

1
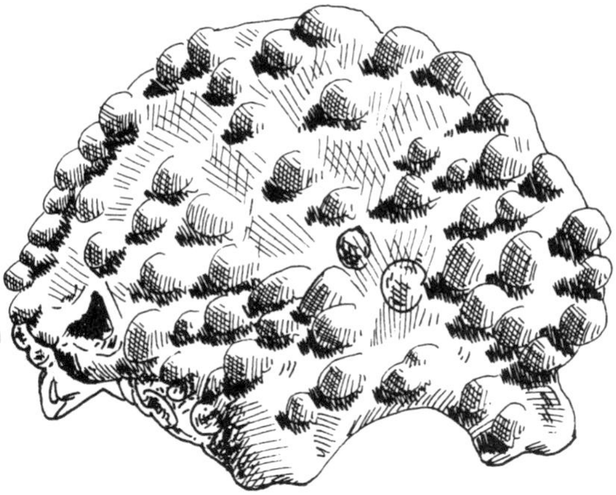

2
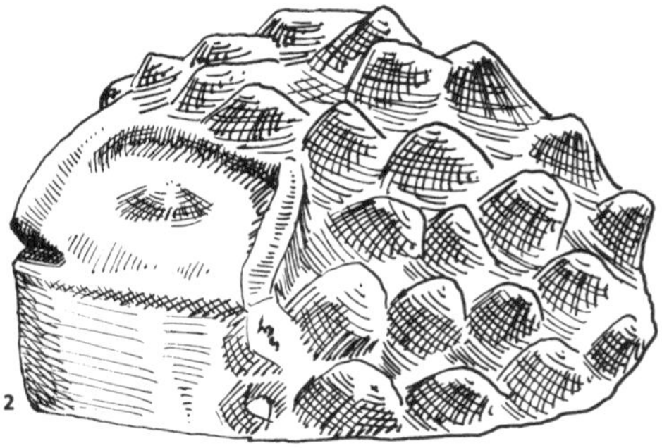

FIGURE 399 Figurines and vases in the form of a hedgehog or Hedgehog Goddess are common in Old Europe. (1) Terracotta figurine and (2) lid with the Goddess's face and a surface covered with warts in imitation of hedgehog's spikes. Karanovo VI/ Gumelniţa ((1) Radaşeni and (2) Căscioarele, S Romania; mid-5th mill. B.C.) (1) H. 7.86 cm. (2) H. 5.1 cm.

FIGURE 400

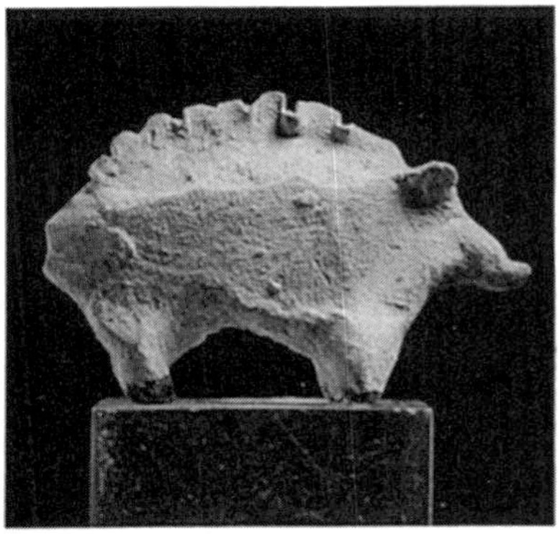
1

2

FIGURE 401

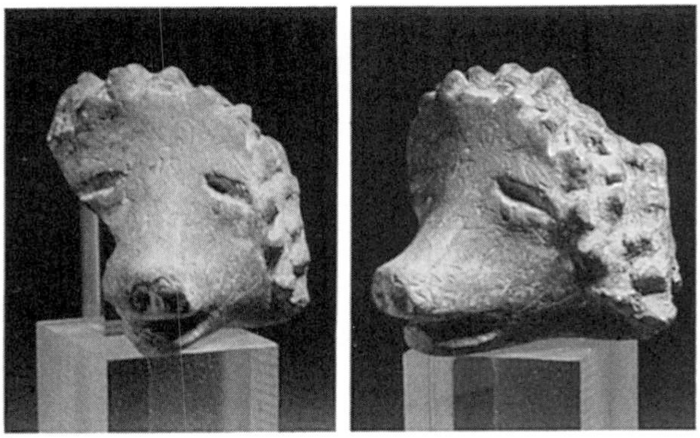
1

2

FIGURE 400 Hedgehogs associated with the uterus appear throughout Old European art. (1) Spiny-backed creature made of fine brown terracotta. Karanovo VI/ Gumelniţa (Radaşeni, S Romania; mid-5th mill. B.C.). (2) Terracotta figurine of a probable hedgehog. Cucuteni A_2 (Frumuşica, NE Romania; 45th to 44th cents. B.C.) L. approx. 8 cm.

FIGURE 401 These hedgehogs are (1) a terracotta head and (2) a lid with the Goddess's face and a surface covered with spikes (see fig. 399, 2). (1) Vinča (Crnokalačka Bara, near Niš, SE Yugoslavia; 5000–4500 B.C.). (2) Karanovo VI/ Gumelniţa (Căscioarele, S Romania; mid-5th mill. B.C.).

In Minoan and Mycenaean art, stylized hedgehogs appear as terracotta figurines or in vase decoration. (FIGURE 402) A beautiful hedgehog-shaped vase with two heads, decorated with running spirals, has been discovered at Ras Shamra in a cemetery of the 14th century B.C. (FIGURE 403) From the 9th to 6th centuries in Greece, Rhodes, and Etruria, hedgehog-shaped vases served as pithoi, especially for infant burials. (FIGURE 404) Once again, through the intermediary symbol of the hedgehog, the identity of the womb and regenerating tomb is established.

23.3 *Fish*

Throughout prehistory the fish was homologized with the Goddess's uterus. This peculiar association is obvious when the fish is placed within the womb of the Goddess, as in the case of the Artemis painted on a Boeotian vase around 700–675 B.C. (FIGURE 405) On other vases, instead of a fish the same Deity features a net-patterned rectangle, symbolizing life-giving uterine moisture. Such alternating representations suggest that fish, net, and moisture are conceptually interrelated. The moistness of the fish and of the uterus may have been homologized in deep prehistory.

On Upper Paleolithic objects the fish is depicted in association with aquatic symbols (zig-zag bands, streams, nets) and with the phallus. (FIGURE 406) (See fig. 130; for more illustrations from the Upper Paleolithic, Epipaleolithic, and Mesolithic eras see Marshack 1972: figs. 194, 198; also Marshack 1981, Cologne Symposium MS). The fish also appears in a seasonal context representative of early spring—new shoots, kids, and ibexes (Marshack 1972: 169–79).

FIGURE 402

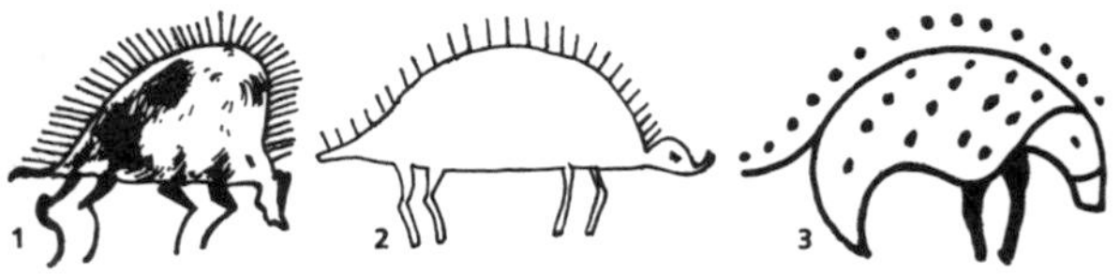

FIGURE 402 Stylized hedgehogs also appear in Mycenaean art, as in these Mycenaean IIIC1 vase paintings of the 12th century B.C.

FIGURE 403

FIGURE 403 This two-headed hedgehog vase is covered with graceful running spirals. Mycenaean (Ras Shamra, E Mediterranean; 14th cent. B.C.) L. approx. 20 cm.

FIGURE 404

FIGURE 404 In a later era, the connection between the hedgehog and uterus is still apparent in the use of hedgehog-shaped burial pithoi, particularly for infants. Greek Geometric (Kameiros, Rhodos; 8th century B.C.) H. 16.2 cm.

FIGURE 405

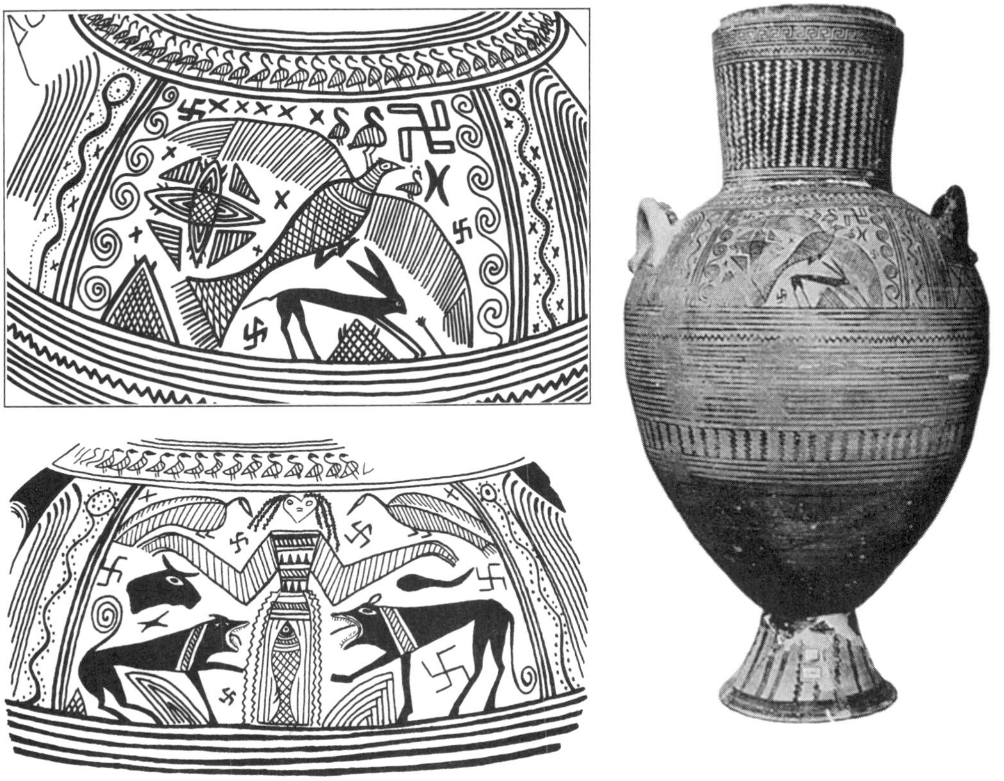

FIGURE 405 The equation of fish with womb of the Goddess is clear on this Boeotian egg-shaped amphora. Found in a tomb, it is decorated with scenes of regeneration. In one panel the Goddess, with a fish in her womb, is surrounded by animals, birds, whirls, a bull's head, a uterus, and chevrons; snakes and multiple arcs rise to either side of her. On the other side, this goddess appears in the epiphany of a bird with widespread wings whose body is a net-patterned fish. She is also surrounded by whirling signs, birds, running spirals, crescents, net-patterned triangles, and a hare. Sub-Geometric/ Early Archaic (near Thebes, central Greece; 700–675 B.C.) H. of vase 86.5 cm.

FIGURE 406

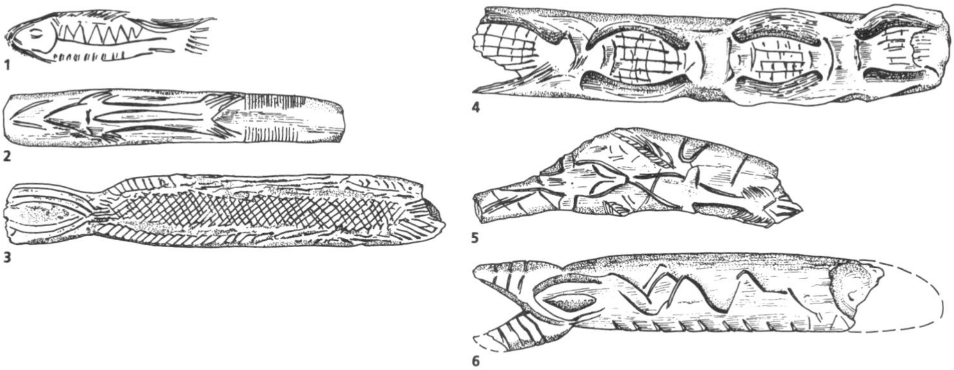

FIGURE 406 Because the fish is a symbol of becoming, it is associated very early with the vulva, uterus, net, zigzag, spiral, parallel lines, and plant shoots, as can be seen on these engravings on bone or antler from Upper Paleolithic Magdalenian sites in southern France and northern Spain. ((1) and (4) La Madeleine, Dordogne; (2) Le Souci; (3) El Pendo, Santander; (5) Laugerie-Basse, Dordogne; (6) Le Mas d'Azil, Ariège.) (1) H. 1.3 cm. (2) H. 2.1 cm. (3) H. 1.8 cm. (4) H. 2.4 cm. (5) H. 1.7 cm. (6) H. 2.2 cm.

FIGURE 407

As we have already seen, the net pattern most frequently appears in uterine forms, pubic triangles, and diamonds (see figs. 133–40). The fish is also shaped like a lozenge/diamond in a number of Epipaleolithic and Mesolithic representations engraved on stone, antler, or bone. The angularization of its rounded body may have emerged because of the symbolic equation of the fish with the vulva or uterus as lozenge (two pubic triangles joined together). The same interrelationship is seen on a fish-shaped and fish-faced pebble figurine from the cave of Gaban in Italy (fig. 139) that is engraved with an X under the net-patterned lozenges. Repeated net squares and X's appear in the hypogea of Sardinia and caves of the Paris basin.

The anthropomorphized Fish Goddess is splendidly represented at Lepenski Vir in the Iron Gate region of northern Yugoslavia, dated between the middle of the 7th and the early part of the 6th millennium B.C. (the triangular shrines of this site are discussed above; see figs. 242–44). Fifty-four *red* sandstone sculptures were placed in the *reddish* lime-plaster triangular floors at the head of vulva/uterus-shaped altars. Most of them were twice as large as a human head and carved of naturally egg-shaped river boulders. Some are undecorated, others are engraved with labyrinthine and aquatic designs, and fifteen reveal half-human, half-fish features. (FIGURE 407) Their staring eyes and open mouth with slightly downward-drooping corners are strikingly fishlike. (FIGURE 408) Several of these sculptures are engraved below the face with interconnected diamond bands and columns of chevrons or zig-zags.

Was the Fish Goddess a primeval creatrix in whose power was the renewal of life? The animals sacrificed and the labyrinthine design on sculptures and other cult objects indicate that she was the Mistress of Life and Death, a generative womb. The people's main activities at Lepenski Vir were ritual sacrifice and the carving and engraving of sacred sculptures and cult objects in association with burials. It was astonishing to paleozoologists to find a very high

FIGURE 407 This Fish Goddess with bird's feet for hands, vulva, and breasts is the presiding deity at Lepenski Vir, a sacred site on the Danube linked with funerary rituals. Sculptures are of reddish sandstone. (Lepenski Vir II, Iron Gates region, N Yugoslavia; 6000–5800 B.C.) (1) H. 51 cm.

FIGURE 408 A considerable number of Lepenski Vir fish-faced sculptures were engraved with labyrinths. The area of the design is painted red, the color of life. (Lepenski Vir I c and II, shrines 28 and 47; 6000–5800 B.C.) (1) H. 36.5 cm; (2) L. 27 cm.

FIGURE 408

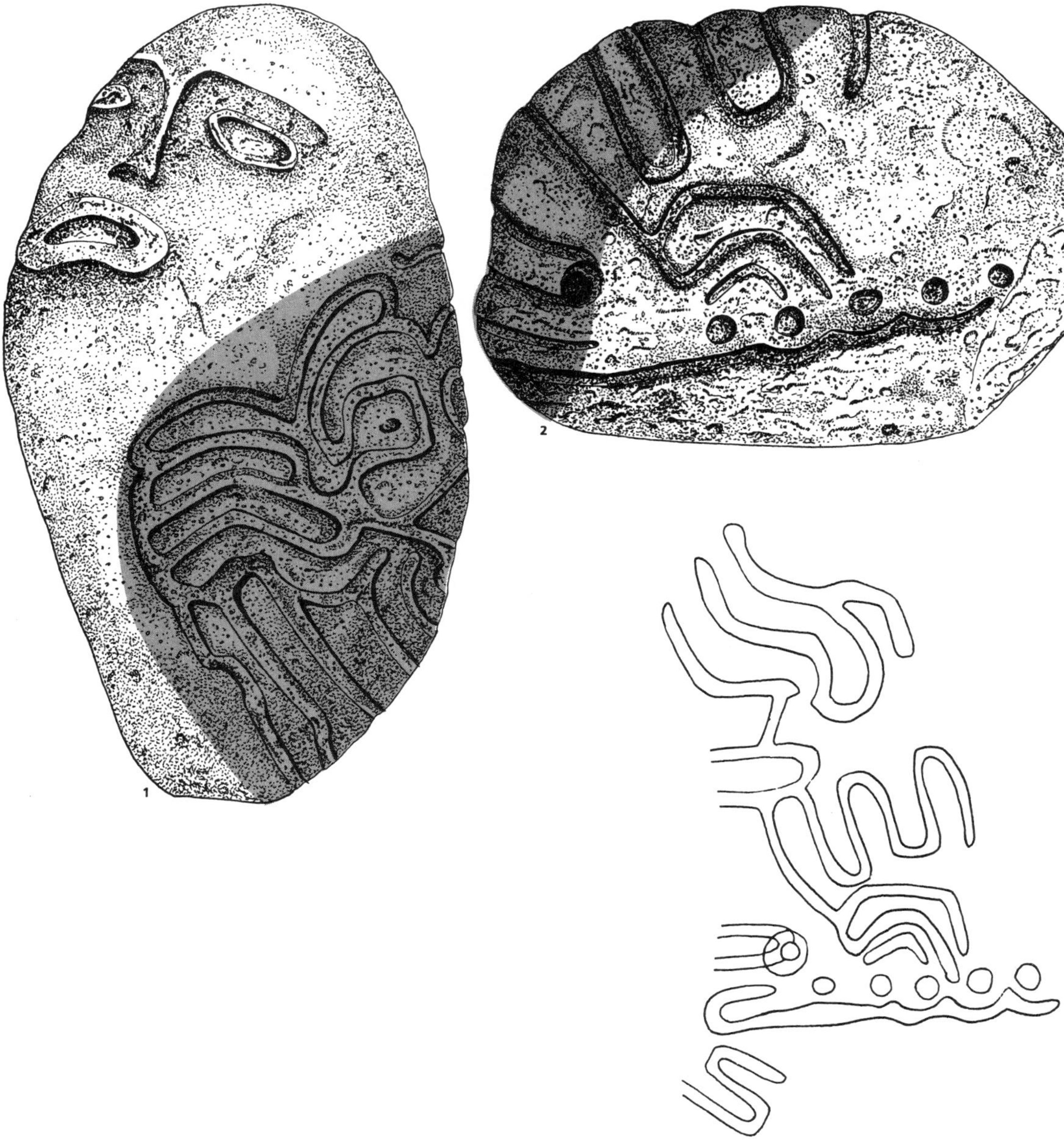

proportion of dog bones in the early phases of the site, when there were no herds to be watched by dogs. The bones were not broken up, indicating that dogs were not used for meat, and the often intact skeletons lay in anatomical order (Bökönyi 1970). Large fish bones (carp, catfish, sturgeon, pike) were identified in almost all structures; one exceptionally large catfish may have weighed 140–180 kg—about 300–400 pounds! Twenty shrines contained a red deer skull or shoulder blade, which often was associated with the bones of dogs and boars.

Thus, the sacrificial animals at Lepenski Vir were fish, deer, dogs, and boars—the animals known from prehistory and early history to be associated with the life-giving aspect of the Goddess (deer, fish) and with her death aspect (dog, boar). The main deity worshipped was the Fish Goddess, appropriate to a place right above a rich source of fish and in front of a mysterious whirlpool (*vir*). Names such as Adam, Chronos, Merman, Danubius, Barbarian, and The Founder of the Tribe given to the Lepenski Vir sculptures by D. Srejović since their discovery in 1965 show disregard of their fish and uterine forms, ochre paint, breasts, and the regenerative meandroid mazes decorating a large number of them.

At Vlasac, an earlier Mesolithic settlement (early 7th millennium B.C.) 3 km down the Danube from Lepenski Vir, 28 egg-shaped and spherical boulders from 8 to 14 cm in diameter and painted with red ochre were found (Srejović and Letica 1978: 153). Although not engraved with features of the Deity, they very likely were related to life-renewing uterus or egg symbolism. The painting of an egg-shaped boulder in red must have been symbolically close to the practice of sprinkling the dead with ochre. Similar symbolism is seen in the placement of red-painted spiky balls, called "uteri" or "hedgehogs," in 20th century graves.

FIGURE 409

FIGURE 409 Much later and far away, this Middle Minoan vase is decorated by a fish with a winding snake along its body; from its mouth emerges a bladder-shaped figure (uterus?). Note the aquatic symbolism (running spirals, wavy lines) and in particular the uterine form attached to the left-hand spiral. Painted white and yellow on gray-brown. (Early Palace, Phaistos, Crete; 2000–1700 B.C.) H. 34.7 cm.

Naturalistic uteri in clay alongside triangular vulvas, viscera, livers, and phalli were laid in Etruscan tombs of the 3rd to 2nd centuries B.C. (such ex-votos are on display in the museums of Vulci, Tarquinia, and Villa Julia in Rome).

Fish-uterus-moisture symbolism continues into later times, but not monumental sculptures of the Fish Goddess. So far, the Lepenski Vir statuary is unique. However, the importance of the fish in the cult of the Neolithic and Copper Age is occasionally attested to by cult vases in the shape of a fish (an example from the Vinča culture is reproduced in Gimbutas 1974: fig. 74). In the Hypogeum of Malta, a fish modeled in clay was placed on a miniature platform similar to the famous Sleeping Ladies. At Buggiba, a temple of the Tarxien period, a fish was engraved on an altar stone (Archaeological Museum, Valletta).

The fish-uterus-water association is clear on Minoan vase and sarcophagus painting. A good example is a painting on a large vase from Early Palatial Phaistos. A uterus form charged with embryonic life force hangs from the mouth of a fish; the net-patterned upper and lower portions of the uterus imply life-giving moisture. (FIGURE 409) The figure is flanked by running spirals to which small uteri or bladder forms are again attached. On a dish from the end of the 13th century B.C. (Mycenaean III B) discovered at Kition, Cyprus, fish, zigzags, and net-patterned lozenges circle around a snake coil in the center (Courtois 1969: XXI).

Fish and uterus motifs are common on Post-Palatial sarcophagi. (FIGURE 410) They appear as single images in a panel and often are associated with sacred horns, butterflies, plants, and shells—all symbols asserting rising life power at the moment of death.

The existence of the apparent semantic link between the Greek *delphis*, "dolphin," and *delphys*, "womb," also may support the intimate relationship between the womb/uterus and fish.

FIGURE 410

FIGURE 410 The fish/uterus motif occurs frequently on Minoan sarcophagi. On this example, panels with columns of running arcs and spirals and panels featuring the number three flank the fish. Post-Palatial (Armenoi, at Rhethymno, W Crete; c. 1100 B.C.)

Late Minoan sarcophagus with joyful signs of a regenerated life. See figure 431, page 274.

24/ *Bull, Bee, and Butterfly*

The identity of the bull with uterus and regenerative waters accounts for its role as the principal sacrificial animal in the drama of creation. From the bucranium or body of the sacrificed bull, new life emerges in an epiphany of the Goddess as flower, tree, column of watery substance, bee, or butterfly.

There are indications that long before the Neolithic, the horns of large bisons held symbolic meaning. In the Périgordian/Gravettian cave sanctuary of Laussel, Dordogne, nude women (representing a Pregnant Goddess) are depicted holding a bison horn in upraised hands (see fig. 216, 1; also Leroi-Gourhan 1967: 303, figs. 270–74; Delporte 1979: 60–66). Other Paleolithic representations show bison heads in association with plants, seeds, and double seeds or nuts (see engraved bone objects from the site of La Vache, Ariège, final Magdalenian, Marshack 1972: 174, fig. 67). As illustrated above, bison horns were most frequently depicted as moon crescents (see fig. 434). As Leroi-Gourhan noted, the importance of bisons in Paleolithic art is suggested by the fact that a painting of a bison always appears on the main panel in the center of the cave. Its central position probably derives from the intimate relationship between the bison and the Goddess; the fact that the woman and the bison both have a pregnancy of nine months may help account for this connection.

With the advent of sedentary life, horns, bucrania, bull figurines, and taurmorphic vases become omnipresent in the art of the Near East and Old Europe. Miniature clay bucrania are known from early farming village occupation layers of the 8th millennium B.C. at Tepe Guran, Iran (Meldgaard, Mortensen and Thrane 1963: 119). Çatal Hüyük shrines of the 7th millennium B.C. are dominated by the bull (Mellaart 1967: 101 ff.).

Why is the role of the bucranium so prominent among the symbols of becoming? And why such close association with the Goddess? It seems that the key to this question lies in the extraordinary likeness of the female uterus and fallopian tubes to the head and horns of a bull, as noticed by Dorothy Cameron in her book on *Symbols of Birth and Death in the Neolithic Era* (Cameron 1981a: 4, 5. She gives a diagram of the female reproductive organs from a medical textbook, here reproduced). (FIGURE 411) This similarity, Cameron believes, is likely to have been discovered with the development of the excarnation process of burial. Turning to figure 411, it can be seen how the female uterus and the fallopian tubes form a simulacrum of the head and horns of the bull. The fallopian tubes are thrust forward in the female body and can be turned up or down, normally downward. However, when the body is

FIGURE 411

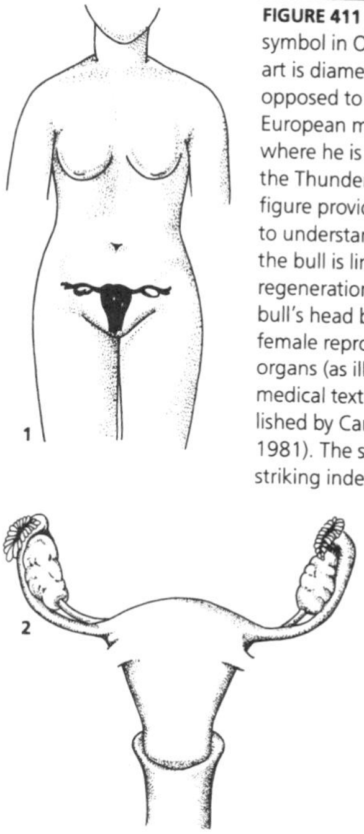

FIGURE 411 The bull as symbol in Old European art is diametrically opposed to that of Indo-European mythology, where he is an animal of the Thunder God. This figure provides the key to understanding why the bull is linked with regeneration: it is not a bull's head but the female reproductive organs (as illustrated in a medical textbook published by Cameron 1981). The similarity is striking indeed.

laid flat they would be turned upwards, as they would have been observed during the excarnation process. If we note that some representations of the bull's head in Neolithic art show the horns capped with rosettes or stars, then the similarity is even greater. This does confirm some basic knowledge of anatomy. Whether this occurred in the Early Neolithic or even earlier will be difficult to prove with certainty. However, the bull/uterus motif is clearly present in Çatal Hüyük frescoes, most clearly represented in still unpublished illustrations. Here are cleverly composed bull's heads and horns within the female figure (Cameron, forthcoming).

On anthropomorphic vases a bull's head is placed where it belongs—below the abdomen (see the marble vase from the Cyclades). (FIGURE 412) Bucrania engraved on rocks are sometimes encircled in a roughly anthropomorphic form or an oval and often in association with cupmarks (as in Monte Bego, the Alpine slopes on the border of Italy and France; Conti 1972: 47).

In the end, it has become clear that the prominence of the bull in this symbolic system comes not from that animal's strength and masculinity, as in Indo-European symbolism, but rather from the accidental similarity between its head and the female reproductive organs. The bull is not a god but essentially a symbol of becoming. Its intimacy with the uterus further explains the bull's association with symbols of regeneration and becoming such as life water, moon, eggs, and plants.

The Egyptian hieroglyph for uterus depicts the two-horned uterus of the cow. It is clear that models for such symbols were slaughtered animals.

FIGURE 412

FIGURE 412 The bull's head as uterus is placed below the abdomen on this anthropomorphic marble vase from the Cyclades. Early Cycladic I (provenance unknown; c. 3000 B.C.). H. 10.5 cm.

FIGURE 413

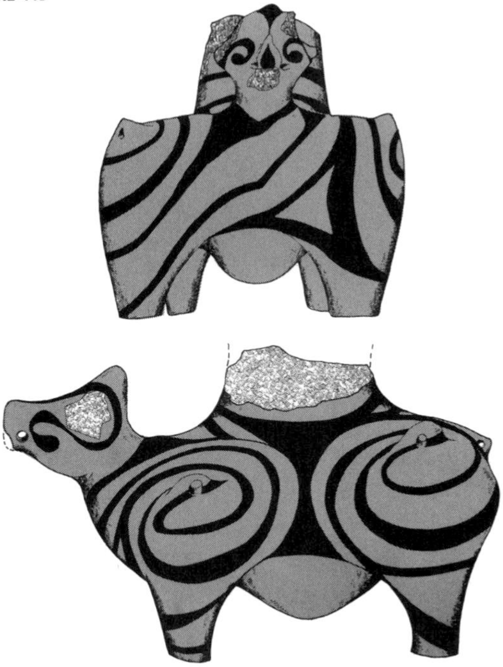

FIGURE 413 The eyes of this tauroform lamp are coiling snake heads; its haunches are covered with huge snake spirals. This symbolic association is repeated on many Old European ceramics. Painted black on red. Karanovo (Sitagroi III, Drama Plain, NE Greece; 4500–4300 B.C.) H. 10.6 cm.

24.1 *The bull and symbols of "becoming"*

The role of the bull in regeneration—an immediate transformation from death to life—is most impressively revealed by large bulls or aurochs in Çatal Hüyük frescoes covering whole walls of the shrines, three-dimensional bull heads attached to the walls, and horn cores set in benches. They are associated either with vultures (see figs. 285, 286) and boar jaws, symbols of death; or with triangles, diamonds, honeycombs, caterpillars, bands of multiple zig-zags (water), hands, brushes, whirls, and eggs, symbols of becoming and regeneration. Bulls are incarnated with the generative force of the Goddess. It is therefore not surprising to see the bulls portrayed with vultures' heads. Such appear on Minoan sarcophagi of the 14th to 13th centuries B.C. (Khania Museum, western Crete).

In the ceramic art of Old Europe, bull sculptures or horns in vase painting are consistently allied with energy symbols—snake coils, concentric circles, eggs, cupmarks, antithetic spirals, and life columns.

Look at bull lamps and bull-shaped containers of the 5th millennium B.C. A spiralling snake winds over each massive rump of the bull from Sitagroi, northeastern Greece. (FIGURE 413) Snake heads represent the animal's eyes. A crouching bull from Gumelniţa is graphite-painted with concentric circles below the masked head, and two juxtaposed snake coils mark the back of the bull. (FIGURE 414, 1) A recently discovered vase with a bucranium in front at Poieneşti, district of Vaslui in Moldavia, a Cucuteni A_3 site (4300–4100 B.C.), is decorated by antithetic snake head and uteri motifs (Niţu and Mantu 1987). A tiny bull vase from Hienheim in Bavaria, a Linear Pottery site, is also decorated with a concentric circle motif over the rounded parts of the vessel. (FIGURE 414, 2) Four dots on the forehead which are repeated over the concentric circles may stand for moon

FIGURE 414

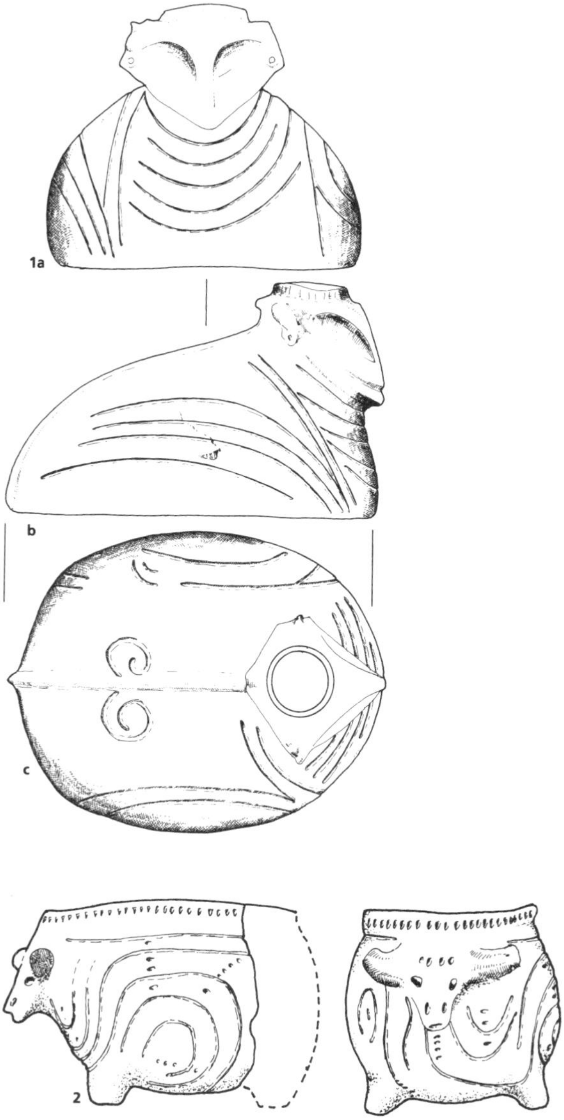

FIGURE 414 Bull vases are marked with symbols of regeneration and energy. (1) Concentric semicircles in front and on the sides and along the spine are painted in graphite. Karanovo (Gumelniţa, lower Danube; c. 4300 B.C.). (2) The concentric arc motif is repeated on this tiny bull vase; the four dots on the forehead and over the circles may represent lunar phases. Linear Pottery (Hienheim, Bavaria; c. 5000 B.C.) (1) H. 11.1 cm; (2) H. 6.6 cm.

FIGURE 415

a

b

FIGURE 415 Bull horns surround a quartered disc representing the moon in the left center of this tripartite frieze of becoming. The out-stretched design from a Cucuteni vase (see b) is filled with running spirals, opposed spiral heads shown as uteri shapes, and double-fruit symbols in the lower band. Painted dark brown on cream. (Podei, at Targu-Ocna, NE Romania; 3700–3500 B.C.)

phases. Minoan bull sculptures are painted with crescents and triangles. The triangle over the head or forehead links the bull with the generative force of the Goddess (see the hourglass symbol between the bull horns in the Sardinian hypogeum of fig. 447, 1).

Huge crescent horns in relief with the full moon symbol between them are seen in the center of a Late Cucuteni vase from Podei, Moldavia. (FIGURE 415) The horns are surrounded by energy-generating opposed spirals.

24.2 *Bucrania in subterranean tombs*

Hundreds of subterranean tombs (hypogea) have been discovered in northwestern Sardinia; some are radiocarbon dated to the 4th millennium B.C. while others probably belong to the 3rd (Tanda 1977). In these tombs, bucrania in a variety of shapes and degrees of schematization are modeled in low relief on the inner walls, usually above or on either side of an entrance or false door. (FIGURE 416) Sometimes there is an egg or moon between the crescent-shaped horns; at others, the bull's head is marked with a concentric circle (a full moon?). (FIGURE 417)

The placement of one to four bull skulls with horns under the floor of the houses next to infants' or children's burials in Neolithic villages probably had a symbolic significance: rebirth. Such were found in recent excavations at Herpaly, east Hungary. In the same site, stylized clay bull horns were discovered clustered on the inner surface of side walls of the houses and pairs of horns were also found on the corners of the clay ovens (Kalicz and Raczky 1984: 135).

Bucrania or horns in tombs or under the floor insure the rebirth of the dead.

FIGURE 416

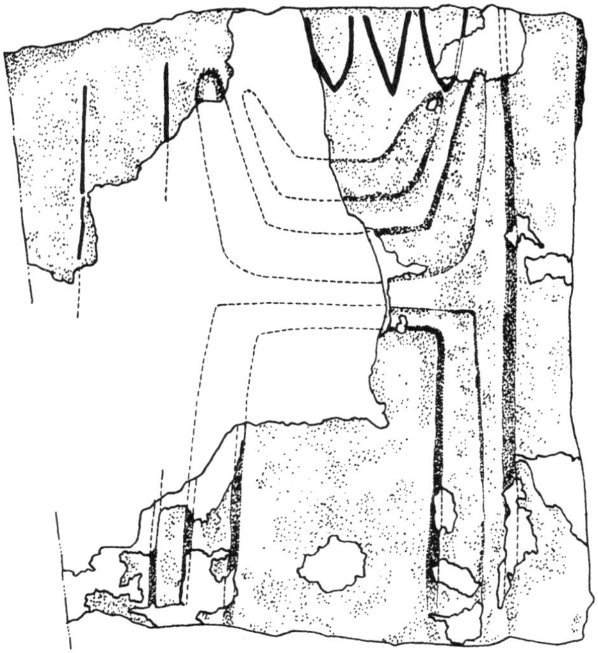

FIGURE 416 Bull horns or bucrania are often found in subterranean tombs to ensure regeneration. These horns in relief are portrayed above false doors. Three vulvas are painted in red above the bull horns. Sardinian Late Neolithic (Tisiennari, Bortigiadas, N Sardinia; late 4th mill. B.C.) H. of door 50 cm.

FIGURE 417

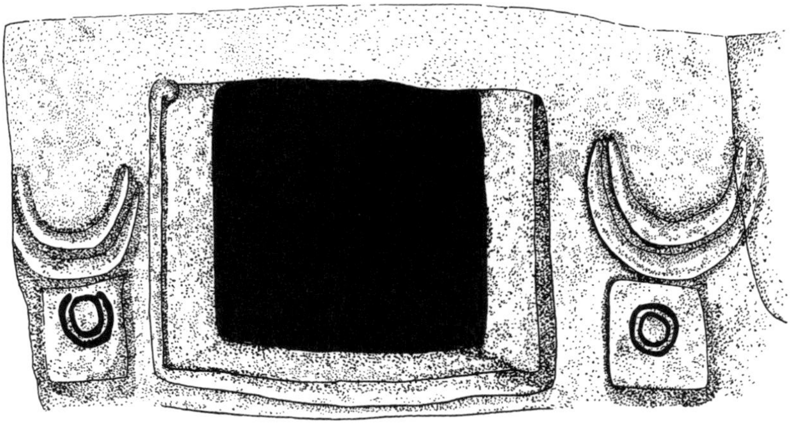

FIGURE 417 In this subterranean tomb, crescent-shaped bull's horns appear on both sides of the entrance and associated with double circles. (Anghelu Ruju, Alghero, N Sardinia; late 4th mill. B.C.) H. of detail 98.5 cm.

24.3 *The bull and the waters of life*

The bull is a mystical life-source, an earthly manifestation of the cosmogonic primordial waters. The taurian nature of lakes and rivers is attested to in Greek myths and in European folklore. River gods were constantly portrayed as bulls (Nilsson 1972: 10, 11; Oxford Classical Dictionary: River Gods).

According to Lithuanian folklore, lakes follow bulls; wherever the bull stops, a lake appears. A lake can be created when a bank of dark clouds rests in a meadow. The clouds are drawn down only when invoked by the chance use of the proper word, which is the name of the lake. The names of such bull-lakes are of great semantic interest for the connections they reveal between the bull, the moon, water, drones, peas, and snakes. Among the words which will invoke a lake is that for drones, *Bitinėlis* (from *bitė*, "bee"); *Bamblys* and *Pilvinas* (fat drones with a round, drumlike stomach); *Samanis* and *Kamanys* (masculine forms of "wild bee"); *Avilys* ("beehive"); *Žirnis* ("pea"); and *Žaltytis* ("grass snake") (Kerbelytė 1973). These word associations were obviously inherited from the bull symbology of deep antiquity. Some are metaphors for the moon, which is represented by the growth and contours of the drone or pea.

The identity between the bull and water can be seen in Minoan sculptural art and Mycenaean vase painting, in which bulls are frequently marked solidly with a net design or with striated or net-patterned, egg-shaped forms, probably symbolic of uteri filled with life-giving or amniotic water. In the Vinča, Lengyel, Polgar, and Cucuteni cultures, small bull figurines were found standing at the edge or in the middle of water basins. Round basins with a miniature bull inside continued to be made in the Minoan culture.

24.4 *"Bull flowers"*

The life power inherent in the bull manifests in plants and flowers springing up from the bull's body. This belief is recorded as late as the 16th century A.D. It occurs in Simon Grunau's *Old Prussian Chronicle* 2.4.1., compiled between 1517 and 1521. The author tells of a fabulous ox whose body is made in part of plants and which, when killed, gives birth to plants:

> *there one finds the wild ox called "Auroxhs" which is unbelievably huge. This beast must be slain by an arrow in its mane, for its flesh is such that it is covered with garlic, which in the wilderness blooms into an herb called "wild lilies"*. . . . (Lincoln 1986: 199).

Bovine sculptures with holes in their heads known from the Cucuteni culture may have been decorated to represent bulls with plants or flowers emerging from their heads. In Myceneaen art, flowers grow out of life columns or between two bull horns. The "bull flowers" are not realistic; they are made of net-patterned, sometimes horn-shaped buds or concentric semicircles. (FIGURES 418, 419)

The so-called "horns of consecration" from the Palatial period of Minoan Crete originated some 3000 years earlier. Horned stands are known from many Vinča, Karanovo, and Cucuteni sites of the 5th and 4th millennia B.C. Their association with the rites of seasonal regeneration is indicated by a perforation between their horns for the insertion of perishable material such as flowers and foliage, symbolizing new life.

24.5 *Bull-begotten bees and butterflies*

The concept of regeneration was dramatically perceived as the birth of young life from a sacrificed bull. This was a seasonal function of the life-giving waters which the bull symbolized; its particular form may have been suggested by an observable, albeit mysterious, natural phenomenon: the sudden appearance of a swarm of insects in the carcass of an animal. This notion of spontaneous generation was not laid to rest until the mid-19th century of our era.

This connection between insects, the bull, and emergent life occurs in Roman times in the writings of Ovid, Vergil, and Porphyry (Ransom 1937: 107–14). The latter unknowingly echoes religious ideas as old as the Neolithic in his comment:

> *The moon (Artemis), whose province it was to bring to the birth, they (the ancients) called Melissa (bee), because the moon being a bull and its ascension the bull, bees are begotten of bulls. And souls that pass to the earth are bull-begotten*. (Porphyry, *De ant. nym.*: 18)

The epiphany of the Goddess as a bee is engraved on a bull's head carved of bone from the Cucuteni site of Bilcze Zlote, c. 3500 B.C. (FIGURE 420) The Goddess's body is an hourglass whose upraised arms are bifurcated and whose head is a dot. But the tradition of her epiphany as bee or butterfly was already thousands of years old by this time. A butterfly sign next to a bull's head is flanked by whirls on a wall painting of Çatal Hüyük's Shrine A VI, 6, c. 6500 B.C. The butterfly sign in combination with whirls is also incised on Linear Pottery dishes of central Europe from c. 5000 B.C. (FIGURE 421)

FIGURE 418

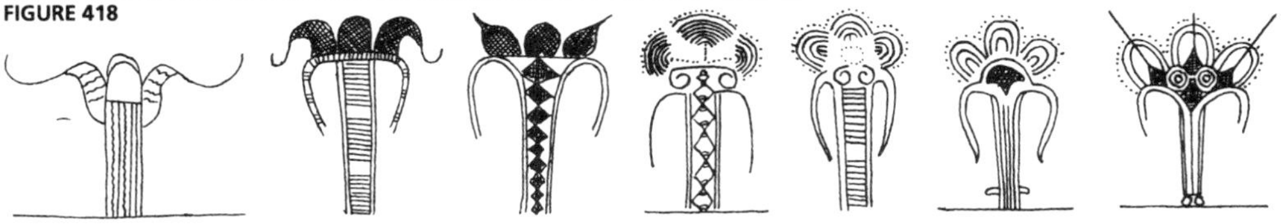

FIGURE 418 These "bull flower" images from Mycenaean vases are completely abstracted; the flowers are net-patterned or made from concentric semicircles, symbols of becoming. Mycenaean IIIA (14th cent. B.C.)

FIGURE 419

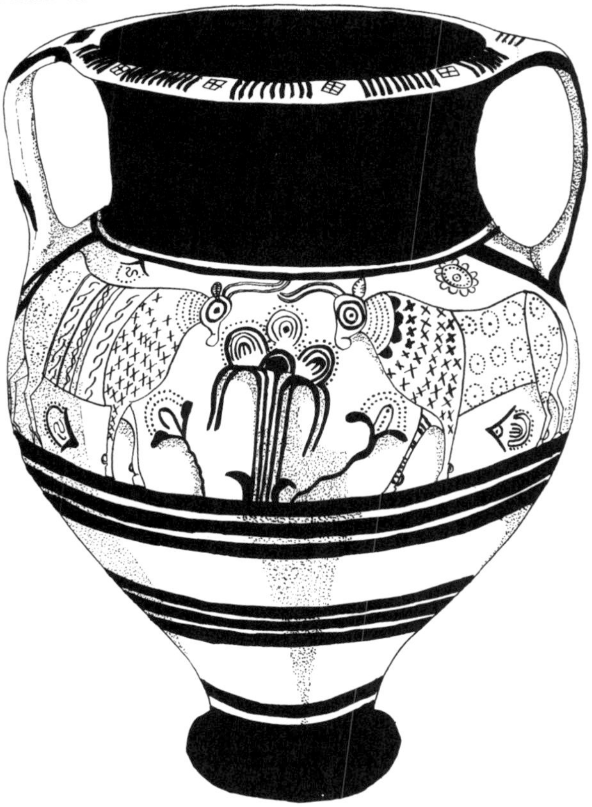

FIGURE 419 Like other sacred animals, bulls may flank a column of life, appearing on this Mycenaean krater as a "bull flower." Note the symbolic markings on the bulls: circles, semicircles, X's, dots, and bands of spirals; fish and uterus forms are painted under them. (Cyprus; Palaepaphos; 13th–12th cents. B.C.) H. 43 cm.

FIGURE 420

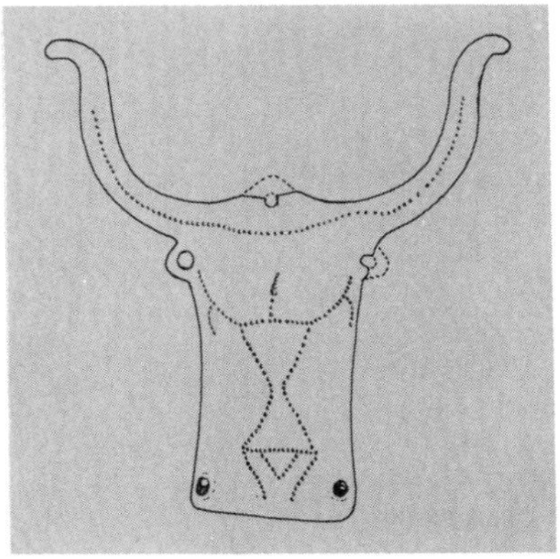

FIGURE 420 Punctate silhouette of the hourglass-shaped Bee Goddess rendered on a bull's head carved of bone plate. Cucuteni B (Bilcze Zlote, upper Seret valley, W Ukraine; 3700–3500 B.C.) H. 17 cm.

FIGURE 421

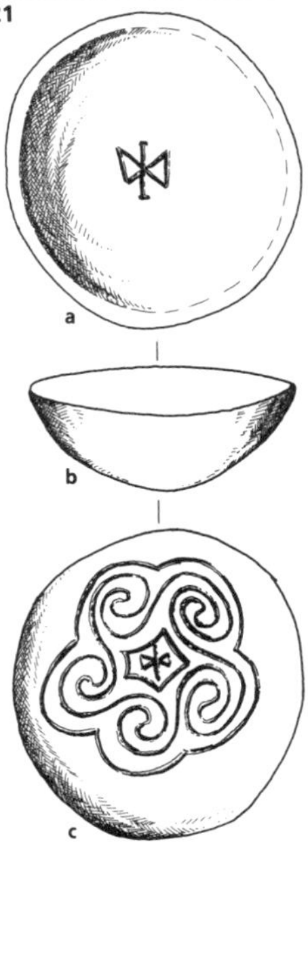

FIGURE 421 A geometricized double-axe shaped butterfly appears within a whirling design on the exterior of this Linear Pottery dish; there is another butterfly inside. (Statenice, Bohemia; c. 5000 B.C.) (a) interior; (b) profile; (c) exterior.

Strange beelike creatures with uplifted arms or antennae, nonhuman heads (usually a dot, stick, or cylinder), and protrusions from the lower body resembling a tail or stinger (FIGURES 422, 423) are known from the Hacilar I, Sesklo, Starčevo, Tisza, Linear Pottery, and Cucuteni cultures, c. 6500–3500 B.C., and from the Late Neolithic tombs of Corsica and Sardinia, c. 3500–2500 B.C. (FIGURE 424) (Lanfranchi and Weiss 1973: 150–53; Lo Schiavo 1980: pls. 15–17).

Later seals and gemstones from Minoan Crete often depict the bee on one face and a bull or dog, familiar of the Goddess, on the other. (FIGURE 425) An onyx gem from Knossos depicts the Goddess, who is flanked by winged hounds, as a woman with the head and eyes of an insect; between the double bull horns above her head is a double-axe-shaped butterfly. (FIGURE 426)

Variations of the bee/woman image continue in the Proto-Geometric, Geometric, and Archaic periods of Greece. From Rhodes and Thera of the 7th to 5th centuries B.C. come figures on gold plaques with human heads, the bodies and wings of a bee, and human arms beneath the wings. On the handle of the famous François vase (7th century B.C.) in the Archaeological Museum of Florence, the Deity is otherwise anthropomorphic, but she has the wings of an insect.

FIGURE 422

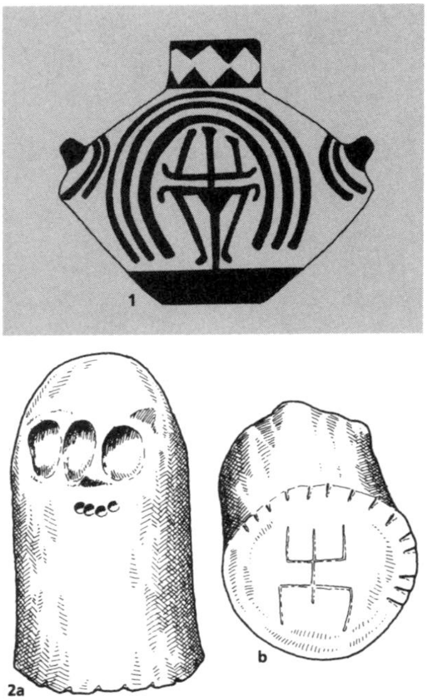

FIGURE 423

FIGURE 422 (1) On a vase painting from Hacilar, an anthropomorphized bee is within a concentric circle. (Central Anatolia, Level 1; mid-6th mill. B.C.). (2) This stand or stamp seal has an incised "Bee Goddess" on the base. Note the three and four depressions on the handle and 14 notches on the base. Karanovo (Vidra, southern Romania; c. mid-5th mill. B.C.)

FIGURE 423 The Goddess in her epiphany as a bee appears on a cave wall of Bue Marino, Dorgali, Sardinia (Late Neolithic). H. 30 cm.

FIGURE 424

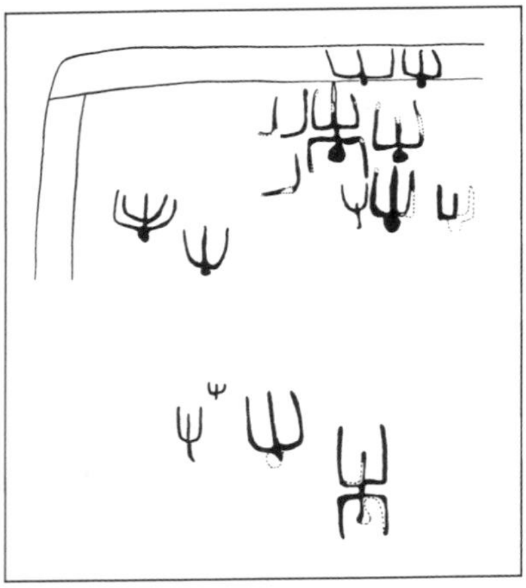

FIGURE 425

FIGURE 424 Anthropomorphized bees or other insects are engraved on the wall of a hypogeum. Sardinian Neolithic (Tomba dell'Emiciclo di Sas Concas, Oniferi, NU; end 4th mill. B.C.) H. (bottom right) 2 cm.

FIGURE 425 Bees also appear on Middle Minoan seals. (Early 2nd mill. B.C.) H. 2.1 cm.

24.6 *The Minoan butterfly*

The double axe of the Bronze Age was originally an hourglass-shaped Goddess of Death and Regeneration. Epiphany of the Goddess in her aspect of emergent life, the butterfly rises from the body or skull of the sacrificed bull in a tableau symbolic of both seasonal fertility and fructifying waters. The butterfly is, in short, the embodiment of the principle of Transformation.

In Minoan art, a harmonious context is consistently provided for the butterfly symbol by its association with signs of becoming. A polychrome vase from the palace of Phaistos, c. 1700 B.C., is decorated with demi-rosettes and opposed fish bladders which create torsion around the focal element, a double-axe sign enclosed like an embryo within an egg. (FIGURE 427) A jug from Aghia Triada, c. 1400 B.C., shows a similar association: a rising anthropomorphic butterfly flanked by fish bladder (uterine) forms. (FIGURE 428)

FIGURE 426

FIGURE 427

FIGURE 428

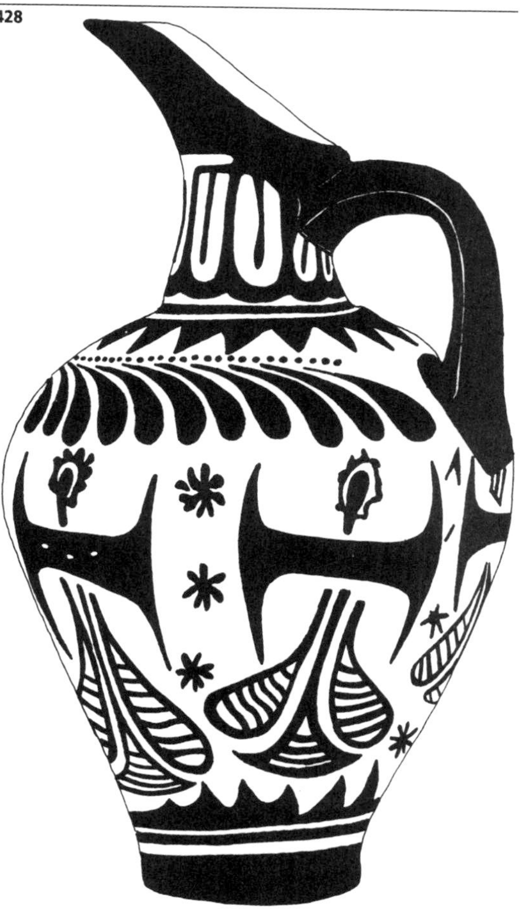

FIGURE 426 The Goddess as bee has two sets of bull horns and a double-axe-shaped butterfly. The winged dogs that flank her reinforce the theme of becoming. Late Minoan II (Knossos, Crete; 15th cent. B.C.) DIA. 3 cm.

FIGURE 427 A seemingly decorative motif from a polychrome vase yields rich symbolic association upon examination. Representing new life, a double-axe-shaped butterfly appears within an egg, flanked by "uteri" and rosettes. Middle Minoan II (Palace of Phaistos, S Crete; c. 1700 B.C.)

FIGURE 428 Epiphany of the Goddess as a butterfly is represented by abstract figures surrounded by uterus or fish bladder forms and rosettes. Painted brown on buff. Late Minoan (Aghia Triada, S Crete; c. 1400 B.C.)

On a Late Minoan vase from Mochlos, the Deity as half-woman/half-butterfly is depicted with a stemlike columnar body, upraised arms, and butterfly wings. (FIGURE 429) The figure is flanked by fish bladder forms, and the head is enveloped by a whirl. Her upraised arms are vulture's feet. On a Late Minoan pithos from Pseira, the central butterfly has widespread wings sectioned by bands of parallel lines, and a head of concentric circles. (FIGURE 430) Floral motifs and bull heads with butterflies like flowers between the horns surround the figure; the symbolic context is further enhanced by bands of butterflies, circles, spirals, concentric circles, and double-spiral flowers.

Scenes of regeneration and hymns to rising life are portrayed on Late Minoan III (c. 1300–1100 B.C.) sarcophagi from the area of Rhetymno and Khania, western Crete. One of the most beautifully executed sarcophagi housed in the Khania Museum features panels of sacred horns with rising butterflies, shells, and buds. The motifs are duplicated, triplicated, and multiplicated, placed in horizontal and vertical bands. The whole composition is graceful and joyous. Life-reaffirming columns rise as buds, shells, or replicated bull-horn/butterfly motifs. It is a declaration of the triumph of life, in which plants, animals, and sea life participate. (FIGURE 431)

FIGURE 429

FIGURE 430

FIGURE 431

FIGURE 429 Whirling uterus or fish bladder forms spin next to an anthropomorphic butterfly. The theme of emergent life is reinforced by the eggs above and plants below. Painted brown on buff. Late Minoan I (Mochlos Island, E Crete; c. 1400 B.C.)

FIGURE 430 This elaborately decorated pithos reveals the full drama of resurrection as an ancient mystery. A double-axe-shaped butterfly with a head of concentric circles emerges from a vessel of some kind (center); she is flanked by growing plants and bull's heads, from between whose horns emerge lily-headed butterflies. Late Minoan (Pseira, E Crete; 16th cent. B.C.)

FIGURE 431 A joyful celebration of regenerated life—bull-horns-and-butterfly, bud, shell, and spiral motifs—covers this sarcophagus, testimony to the hopes and beliefs of its time. Painted dark brown on buff. Late Minoan III (Khania, Crete; 1300–1100 B.C.)

FIGURE 432

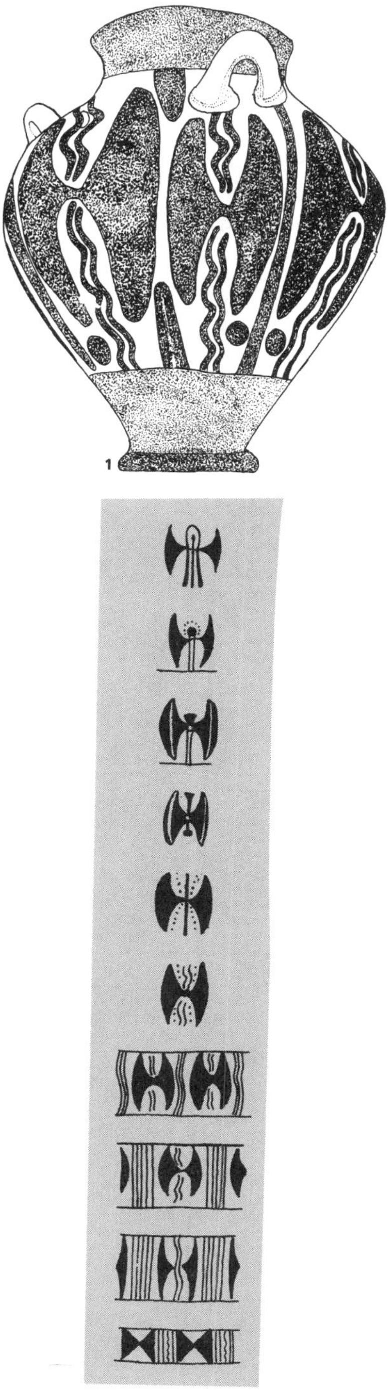

1

2

FIGURE 432 The double-axe-shaped butterfly appears on Mycenaean vases, where the stem often becomes a pair of winding lines, and the whole is flanked by parallel lines. (1) Late Helladic IIA vase painted dark brown on buff (Mycenaean acropolis, Greece; 15th cent. B.C.). (2) Typology of similar motifs from other Late Helladic IIA and III vases.

The Minoan butterfly continues to appear in Mycenaean art. It acquires on vases of the Late Helladic I period (16th century B.C.) a circular or button-shaped head. In Late Helladic II (15th century B.C.), the image is geometricized and becomes more abstract. On the illustrated vase, the stem between the wings, typically rendered by two winding lines, is flanked by three or more parallel lines. Schematic butterflies interspersed with three or more parallel lines remain one of the most frequent design motifs throughout the Proto-Geometric and Archaic periods of Greece. (FIGURE 432)

24.7 *The butterfly in folklore*

The butterfly was one of the many insectomorphic manifestations of the Goddess in whose hands was the magic transformation from death to life. In folk beliefs, the butterfly is considered to this day to be a demoniacal creature. "If you kill a butterfly, you kill a witch," says a Serbian proverb. The witch is, of course, none other than the demonized prehistoric Goddess herself.

Though beautiful and ethereal, the butterfly is a symbol which arouses fear, not because she is a symbol of the deceased's soul or of a soul that is wandering while a person dreams, but because she is the dangerous and frightening Goddess. This ancient meaning of the symbol is preserved in etymology. The Breton and Irish *Maro* means "Death (Goddess)" and Lithuanian *Morė* is "Goddess of Death, Old Hag"; but the Greek, Germanic, and Slavic *mora*, *mara*, or *morava* mean both "nightmare" and "butterfly"; the German *Mahr* and French *cauchemar*, "nightmare," are further derivatives.

Indeed, there is a very thin borderline between life and death, between the butterfly and the Goddess in her destructive aspect. Not neglecting death, Old Europeans sensed the short-lived beauty of life, which was deeply and dramatically manifested in bee and butterfly symbolism.

IV

ENERGY AND UNFOLDING

A large group of symbols can be categorized as those of either energy or cyclic time. These are: spirals, circles, coils, crescents, hooks, horns, four-corner signs, brushes, combs, hands and feet, and animal whirls or processions. These dynamic symbols are either themselves energy incarnate or are stimulators of the process of becoming. Moving up, down, or in a circle, they symbolize cyclical time. The pulse of life demands an unending stream of vital energy to keep it going.

Triangular backstone of a French passage-grave representing the Goddess; vulva at center flanked by four rows of hooks. See figure 456, page 289.

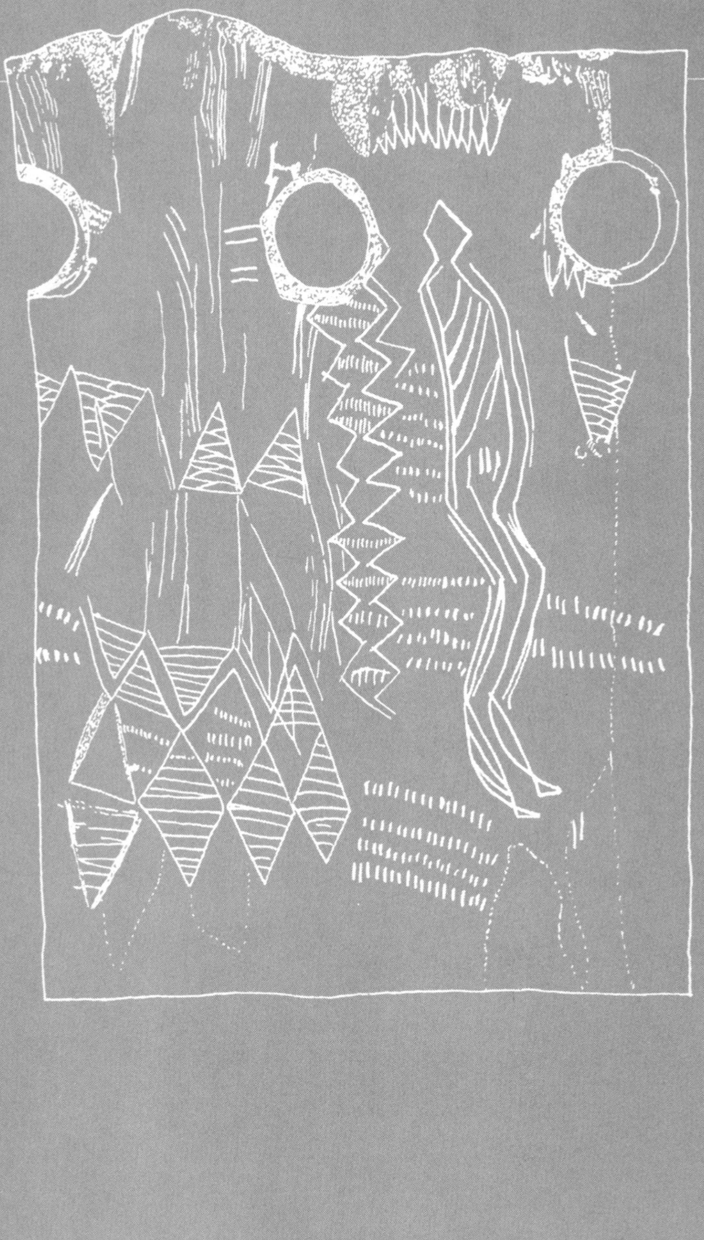

Configuration of renewal on engraved Mesolithic antler axe made up of snakes in association with triangles and diamonds. See figure 451, page 287.

25/ *Spiral, Lunar Cycle, Snake Coil, Hook and Axe*

Spirals appear in Upper Paleolithic caves in association with serpentine forms, zigzags, crescents, and cervids or bovides with crescent-shaped horns. (FIGURES 433–435) These associations continue for millennia afterwards. Horn, snake, and spiral signs are virtually inseparable, the latter being both an artistic geometrization and a symbolic abstraction of the dynamic snake.

25.1 *Spiral*

The spiral as a design on pottery emerges in the second half of the 7th millennium B.C. in southeastern Europe (at Achilleion II, Thessaly, dated to c. 6300 B.C.). It spread to the Danube basin and eastern Balkans between 6000 and 5500 B.C. and became very common during 5500 and 3500 B.C. (FIGURES 436, 437)

Running spirals—painted in relief or excised and white-encrusted—make the ceramics of 5th millennium B.C. Old Europe truly outstanding. (FIGURE 438) S-shaped spirals run in horizontal, vertical, and diagonal bands or float freely on the surface. Exquisite globular vessels with symmetrically interlocking spirals, and large pedestalled or pear-shaped Butmir and Cucuteni vases with freely winding spiral snakes, are masterpieces of Old European ceramic art (see figure 461).

And yet the spiral never entirely breaks free from its conceptual framework. On such ceramics, vigorous spirals move rythmically around the neck and shoulders or float in a free field style brimming with vitality. The energy inherent in the continually moving forms awakens dormant life power and moves it forward. We sense this symbolic meaning when spirals run in bands, are shown over a field of strewn eggs, moons, and bands of parallel lines, or flank life

FIGURE 433

FIGURE 433 The spiral, symbol of energy and cyclic time, appears in the Upper Paleolithic, where it is associated with serpentiforms and horned animals (La Pileta cave, near Gibraltar, Spain; c. 13,000–10,000 B.C.). H. figure at left 80 cm.

FIGURE 434

FIGURE 435

FIGURE 436

1

2

FIGURE 434 The bull is connected with the moon from earliest times, as these bovines with horns as lunar crescents in Upper Paleolithic cave painting and engraving attest. (1)–(4) La Pileta, S Spain; (5) Escural, Spain; (6) and (9) Parpalló, Valencia, Spain; (7) La Pasiega, N Spain; (8) Lascaux, S France; various periods between 15,000 and 10,000 B.C.

FIGURE 435 An intriguing mythical creature is this Upper Paleolithic horned snake, painted in red on the wall of La Pasiega cave. (Santander, N Spain; Early Magdalenian, c. 15,000–13,000 B.C.)

FIGURE 436 The spiral enlivens the ceramic art of Old Europe with its fluid dynamism. Note the association of these spirals with (1) crescents and (2) breasts. Linear Pottery (Brno, Moravia; c. 5000 B.C.)

FIGURE 437

FIGURE 438

1

2

FIGURE 439

FIGURE 437 Since snakes were considered creatures of the water, it is not surprising that symbols of the two are associated on ceramics from the mid-6th millennium B.C. On this Dimini vase, spirals sweep across a striated background representing streaming water. There are chevrons on the handle. Painted brown on buff. (Rakhmani II; end of 5th mill. B.C.) H. 24.15 cm.

FIGURE 438 Illustrated here are two Butmir globular vases. (1) Interconnected S-shaped spirals are modelled in relief. (2) Interlocking spirals, encrusted with red paint, wind around on a black surface (Nebo; 4900–4700 B.C.). H. approx. 15 cm.

FIGURE 439 Spirals are an important design element on some of the most beautiful Old European ceramics. On bands from Cucuteni B vases, large spiral heads flank or seem to pull columns of life or columns of cyclic time (3). Painted black on red. (1) Popudnia; (2) and (3) Sipenitsi, upper Dniester basin, W Ukraine; 3900–3700 B.C.

columns. (FIGURES 439, 440) Spiral heads, like the hooks of a swastika, move the cosmic four corners around. On figurines, spirals sometimes replace the Goddess's eyes, are incised next to her breasts, or are placed in the center of a band on her back. (FIGURE 441) Clearly they are not there for decoration but rather for the enhancement of her energy; the spiral- or serpent-force is the Goddess's energy.

Coiling and uncoiling spiral dances must certainly have been performed in deep prehistory, definitely in the days when this beautiful spiral-decorated pottery was produced. A Greek Crane Dance is known which, according to Plutarch, Theseus introduced into Delos; it was performed around a horned altar and represented the circles that coiled and uncoiled in the labyrinth (Graves 1972: 233).

The life-force power within the spiral is demonstrated pictorially when spirals transform into plants, as leaves branch off from their outer turnings. The spiralling force affects the germination and growth of trees and plants. Beautiful examples of these spiral/plant combinations come from the art of Malta and Minoan Crete. (FIGURE 442) In human life, the umbilical cord is itself a serpentine connection between the mother and new life.

The upward and downward movement of the spiral must have been compared very early to the spiral of the waxing and waning moon. In Karanovo and Cucuteni vase painting, spirals with crescents or with the phases of the moon are a constant theme. (FIGURE 443) The spiral often appears in the center of a dish or bowl, and around it are circles in panels or bands; these usually number twelve and sometimes thirteen, perhaps symbolizing the year cycle with its twelve or thirteen lunar months.

FIGURE 440

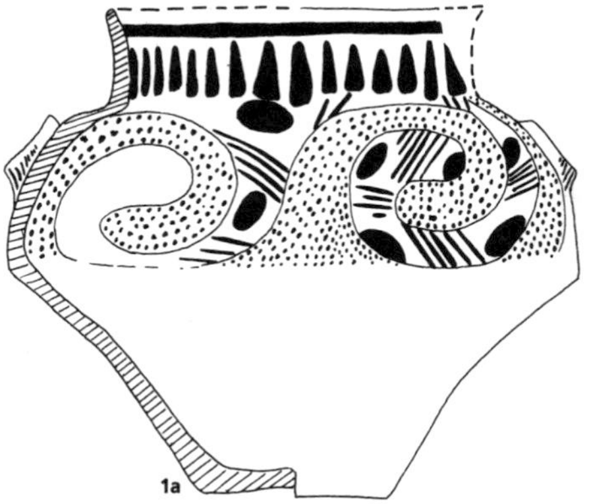
1a

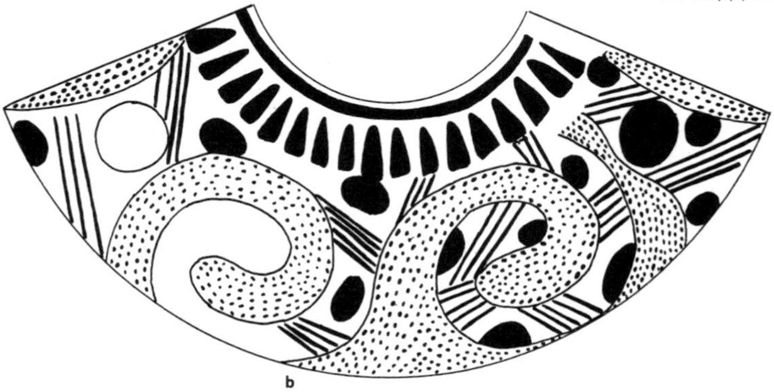
b

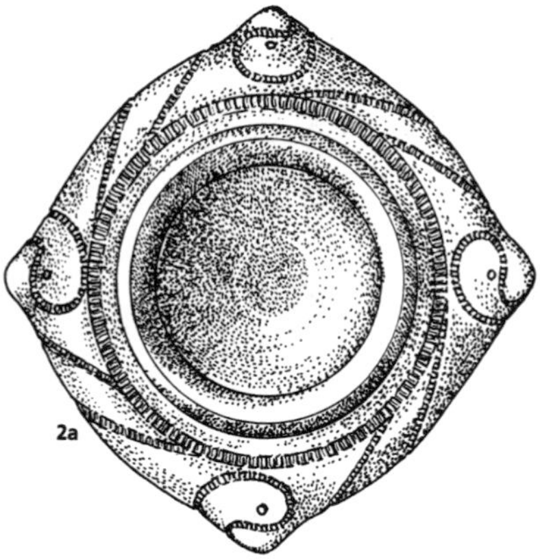
2a

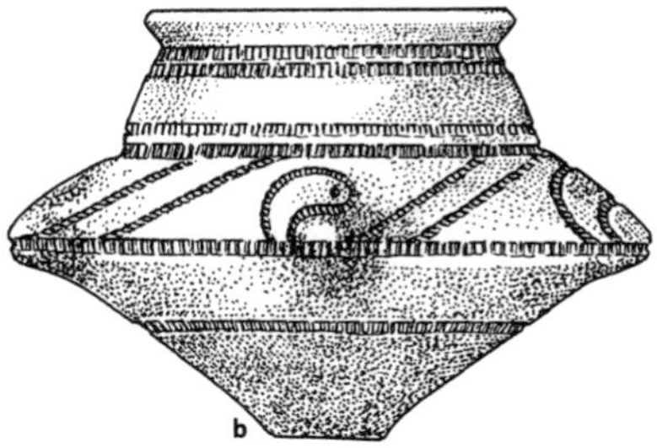
b

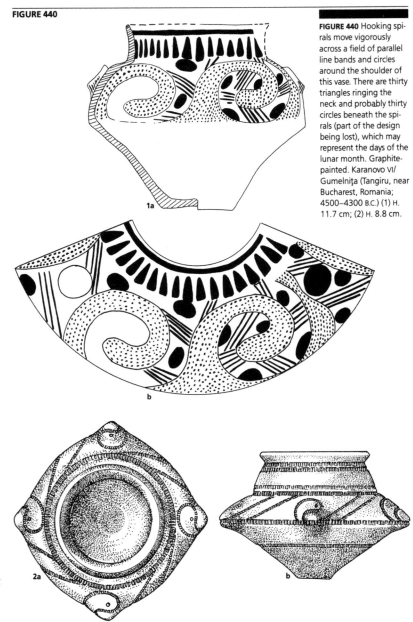

FIGURE 440 Hooking spirals move vigorously across a field of parallel line bands and circles around the shoulder of this vase. There are thirty triangles ringing the neck and probably thirty circles beneath the spirals (part of the design being lost), which may represent the days of the lunar month. Graphite-painted. Karanovo VI/ Gumelnița (Tangiru, near Bucharest, Romania; 4500–4300 B.C.) (1) H. 11.7 cm; (2) H. 8.8 cm.

FIGURE 441

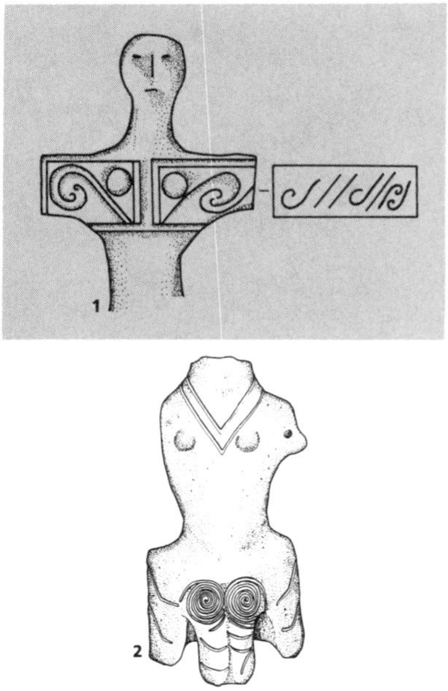

FIGURE 441 On figurines, spirals appear in symbolically potent places: (1) at the breasts, across the back, and (2) on the knees. (1) Karanovo V (Azmak V, central Bulgaria; early 5th mill. B.C.). (2) Vinča (Banjica at Belgrade; 5000–4500 B.C.). (1) H. of detail 6.9 cm. (2) H. 11.1 cm.

FIGURE 442 The life force inherent in the spiral is made manifest by leaves sprouting from its outer ring, and its transformation into a growing plant. These spirals grace temple megaliths of Malta (Tarxien, Malta; c. 3000 B.C.).

FIGURE 443

FIGURE 443 On Cucuteni and Gumelniţa bowls, a central spiral is surrounded by twelve discs, perhaps representing the lunar year. (1) Upper part of a footed bowl, painted red and white with dark brown borders. Cucuteni A_3 (Habaşeşti, Moldavia, NE Romania; 44th–43rd cents. B.C.). (2) Graphite-painted bowl. Karanovo VI (Tangiru, near Bucharest, Romania; 4500–4300 B.C.) (1) DIA. 12.5 cm; (2) DIA. 14 cm.

FIGURE 442

FIGURE 444

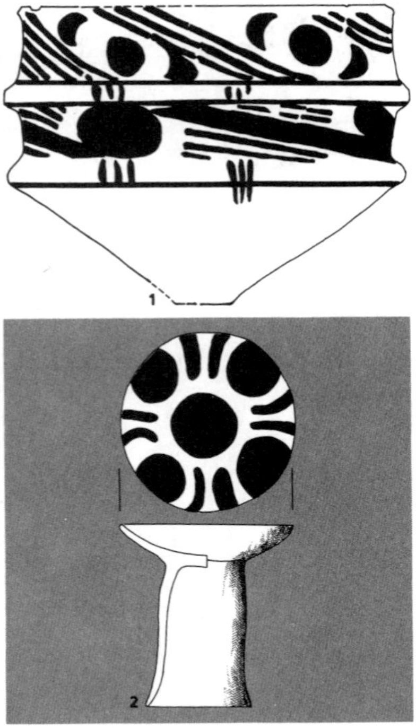

FIGURE 444 The lunar cycle is represented by a right crescent, full moon, and left crescent on Old European ceramics. (1) Upper register of a graphite-painted bowl. Karanovo VI/Gumelniţa (Tangiru, near Bucharest, Romania; c. 4500–4300 B.C.). (2) Around the interior of a footed bowl painted red on white. Cucuteni A_3 (Habaşeşti, Iaşi district, Moldavia; 4400–4200 B.C.). (1) H. 9 cm. (2) H. 26.2 cm.

FIGURE 445

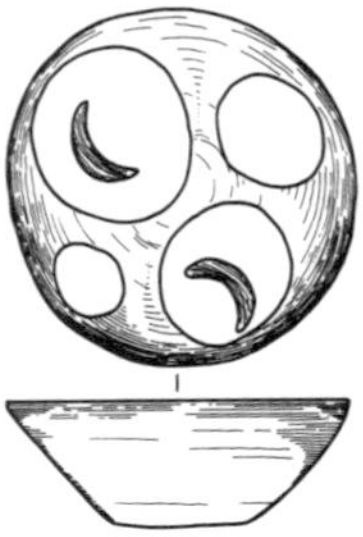

FIGURE 445 The lunar cycle also appears as a unit of four: two opposing crescents, full moon, and new moon (represented here by the smaller disc). Interior of a Cucuteni dish. Tripolye BII (Nezvisko, upper Dniester valley; c. 4000 B.C.) DIA. 19 cm.

FIGURE 446

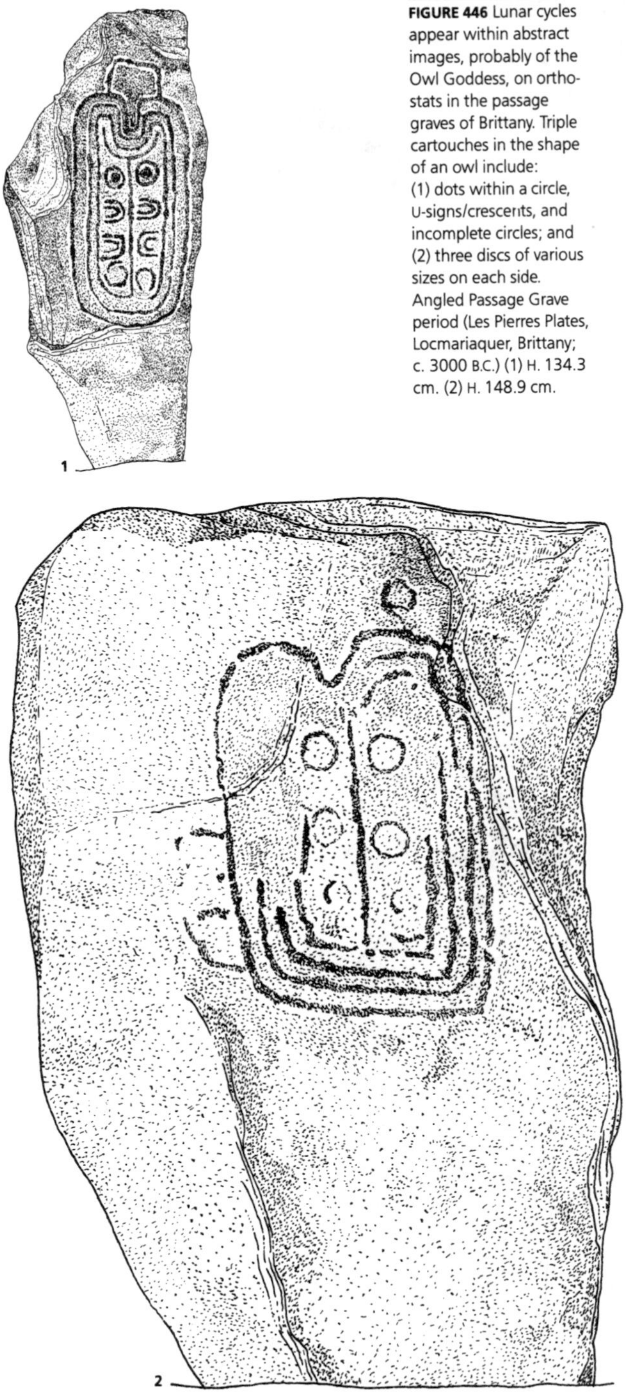

FIGURE 446 Lunar cycles appear within abstract images, probably of the Owl Goddess, on orthostats in the passage graves of Brittany. Triple cartouches in the shape of an owl include: (1) dots within a circle, U-signs/crescents, and incomplete circles; and (2) three discs of various sizes on each side. Angled Passage Grave period (Les Pierres Plates, Locmariaquer, Brittany; c. 3000 B.C.) (1) H. 134.3 cm. (2) H. 148.9 cm.

25.2 *Lunar cycle*

The group of three—left crescent, full moon, and right crescent—is a common motif, not unlike the modern international code of symbols for the moon cycle. (FIGURE 444) Also common are opposed crescents on either side of a large snake coil.

The lunar cycle is also rendered pictorially as four circles: left crescent, full moon, right crescent, and a small circle apparently symbolizing the dark moon. (FIGURE 445) Probable lunar cycles appear on both sides of a column within owl-shaped figures (the Owl Goddess); these images are engraved on orthostats from an angular passage grave at Les Pierres Plates, Locmariaquer, Brittany. (FIGURE 446) On one stone, a dot within a circle (full moon?) is followed in vertical order by a right crescent, left crescent, and incomplete circle (dark moon?). On another orthostat, three circles flank the column on either side.

Above the entrance to the chamber tomb at Mandra Antine, Thiesi, Sardinia (FIGURE 447) is a pair of bull's horns, to each of which is attached three red discs. A brown fourth disc, perhaps the full moon, is attached to a square at either side. In the center of the horns are three hourglass figures (symbols of the Goddess in triplicate nuclear form). The ceiling of the chamber is divided into twenty compartments; preserved in seven of them are signs painted in yellow over a brown background: crescents, half-moons (semicircles), and full moons (snake coils).

These lunar cycles in passage graves and hypogea suggest by their association with images of the Goddess an early philosophical connection between cyclical lunar time and the regenerative role of the Goddess in the cycles of birth, death, and rebirth.

FIGURE 447

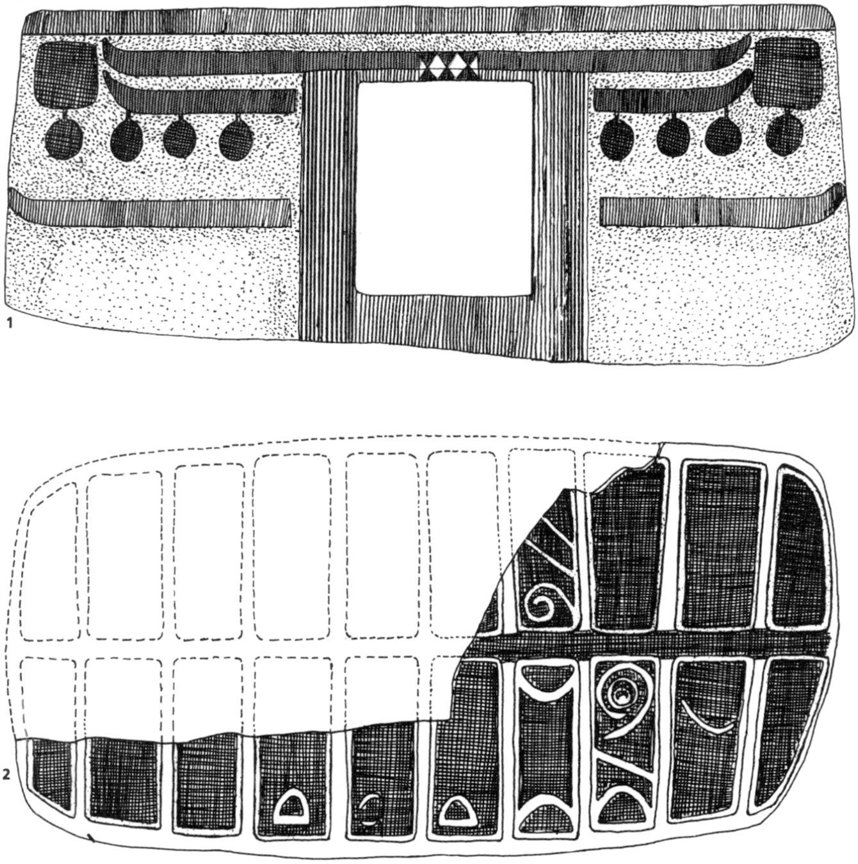

FIGURE 447 Probable lunar cycles in a Sardinian hypogeum: (1) bull horns above a false door. (2) Ceiling designs represent moon cycles. Yellow on brown. (Mandra Antine, Thiesi, the province of Sassari, N Sardinia; c. 4000 B.C.).

25.3 *Snake coil*

A Dimini vase from Sesklo, Thessaly, is decorated with an intriguing design. (FIGURE 448) A snake spiral sits coiled over a semicircle and flanked by two crescents; around this are successive layers of streams or rain torrents, M signs within lozenges, an arcing torrent, and more crescents. Spiral, rain, and lunar crescent are purposefully combined to create what may be a seasonal tableau.

The role of the spiral, crescent, snake coil, and winding snake in time reckoning has been suspected by Martin Brennan on Irish megaliths (Brennan 1983). The exceptional concentration of symbols preserved on the retaining stones of Knowth, Dowth, and Newgrange in the Boyne River valley and several other mounds in northern and eastern Ireland has made it possible to observe the consistent associations and deliberate repetitions of crescents, snake coils, winding snakes, and other symbols.

We learn that both a sphere and a snake coil may represent the full moon. (FIGURE 449) Opposed crescents with a snake coil in the middle, or opposed crescents alone, depict the moon cycle and are frequently encountered on stones, as is illustrated here by symbols on a stone from Knowth. (FIGURE 450) The wavy lines of a winding serpent appear to measure time; each turn is a counting unit of the lunar calendar. Serpentiforms sometimes have between 14 and 17 turnings, the number of days the moon is waxing. After waxing for two weeks, the moon is considered full for three days; on the 17th day it begins to wane. The longest winding snakes have up to 30 turnings, as close a rendering as possible of the 29.5 days in a lunar month.

Such peculiarly winding serpents are encountered not only on Irish megalithic stones, but are also engraved on antler artifacts of the northern European Mesolithic and on the 5th millennium B.C. ceramics of east-central Europe. (FIGURES 451–453) This argues that time

FIGURE 448

FIGURE 448 A snake coils above a half-disc and between crescents, probably representing phases of the moon. The coil is flanked by streams or rain torrents and M signs in lens-shaped compartments; more crescents look down over the entire tableau. Design on a vase flattened out. Painted in dark brown on buff. Lenses: ochre red. (Dimini culture, Arapi phase, at Sesklo; around 5000 B.C.)

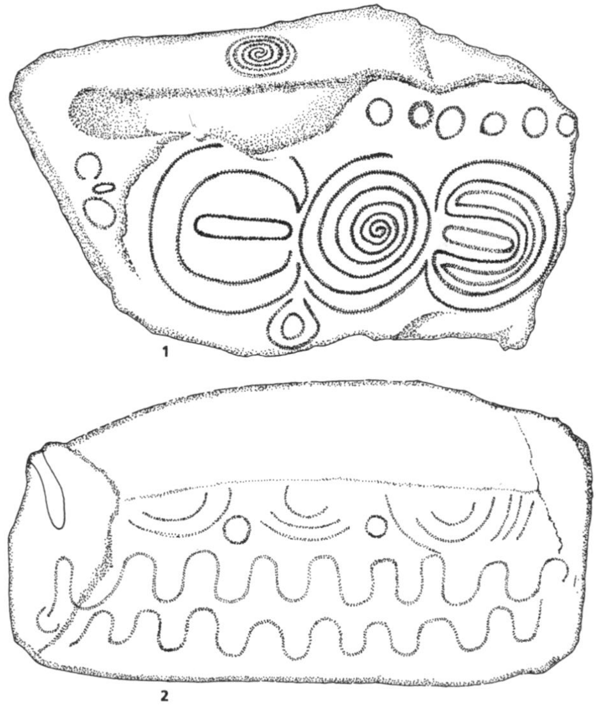

FIGURE 449 Possible lunar cycles as symbols of renewal are engraved on curbstones of Knowth. (1) The full moon is represented by a spiral or snake coil; left and right crescents are differentiated by their design. Note the line of discs across the top and the isolated spiral above. (2) Probable waxing moon symbolism is expressed by winding serpentiforms, whose turns number between 14 and 17, the number of days up to or including the full moon. The upper 17-turn serpentiform on this stone begins with a crescent; note the discs and concentric semicircles above. Passage-Grave culture (Knowth NE 6 and SE 3, Boyne River Valley, Co. Meath, Ireland; middle or 2nd half of 4th mill. B.C.) L. approx. 180 cm.

FIGURE 450

FIGURE 450 Winding serpents, circles, and arcs appear as symbols of renewal with possible lunar configurations. Passage-grave culture (Knowth, Stone NW 4, curbstone 43, middle of 4th mill. B.C.)

FIGURE 451

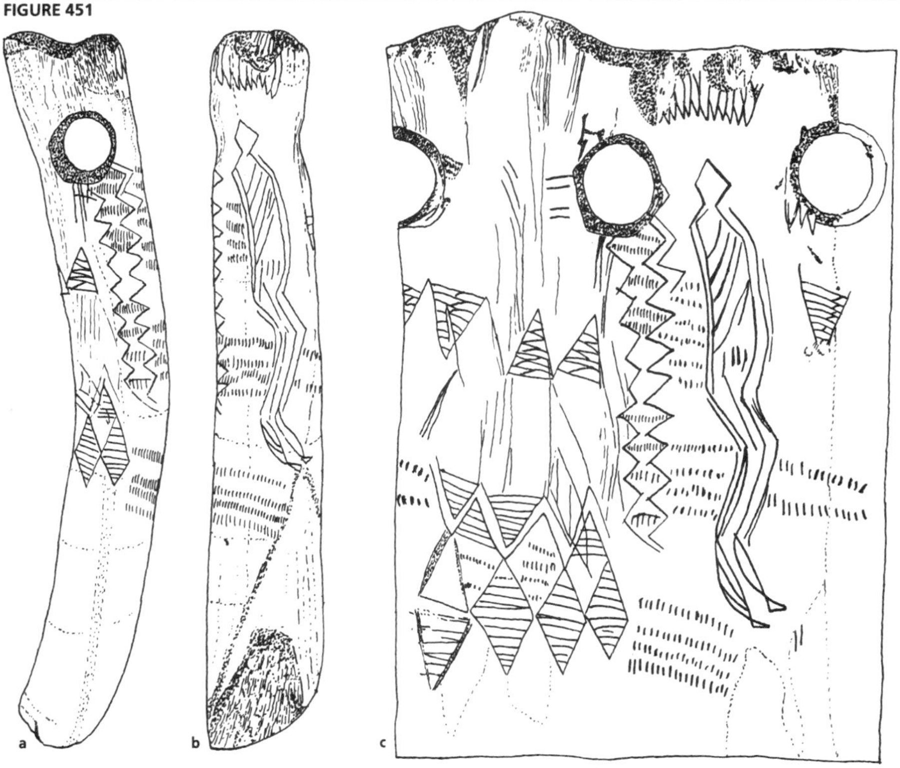

FIGURE 451 On this Mesolithic antler axe, another configuration of renewal is made by engravings of winding snakes and an anthropomorphized serpent in association with triangles and diamonds. Next to an anthropomorphized figure with a diamond head, two zig-zag lines, possibly snakes, have 17 turnings starting at the perforation. Most of the incisions at or below the figure also number from 14 to 17 (see flattened out design). (NW European Mesolithic; Jordløse, Denmark) H. 45.8 cm.

FIGURE 452

FIGURE 452 Such serpentiforms with 17 windings also appear on southeast European ceramics. On this large pear-shaped and polychrome vase (dark brown, light brown, buff), zig-zagging snakes with 17 turns are painted over the shoulders, flanking a quartered disc with a single horn attached, an ingenious combination of regeneration symbols. Cucuteni A_2 (Truşeşti, Moldavia, NE Romania; 4500–4300 B.C.) H. 32 cm.

FIGURE 453

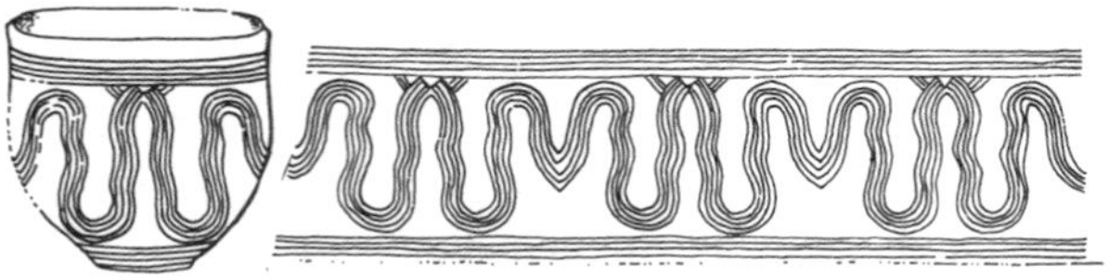

FIGURE 453 A spiral with 17 turns is excised and encrusted with white on the dark brown burnished surface of this Bükk jar (Sarazsadany-Templomdomb, NE Hungary; 2nd half of 6th mill. B.C.). H. 12.4 cm.

FIGURE 454

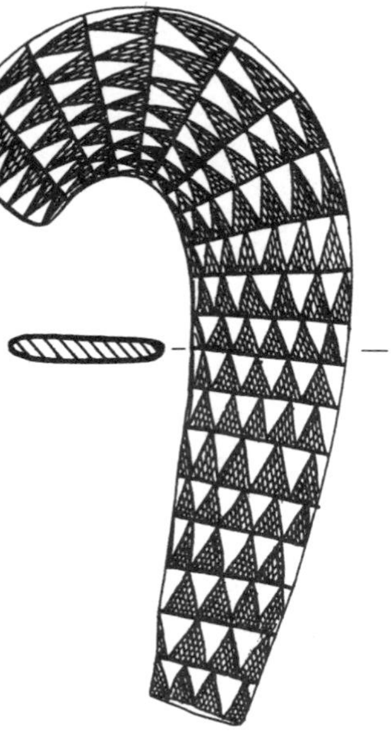

FIGURE 454 Symbols of regeneration, hooks made of schist plate are found in Portuguese megalithic tombs. This example, decorated with rows of net-patterned triangles, is from tholos tomb the "Marquesa" (Marvao, Prov. Alentejo; c. 2nd half of 4th mill. B.C.). H. 18 cm.

reckoning may well have been accomplished by a similar method in all parts of Europe.

This is not surprising, since the tradition was inherited from the Upper Paleolithic. Lunar notations on bone, antler, and stone objects dating from between the Aurignacian and Mesolithic have been convincingly presented by Alexander Marshack (Marshack 1972: 21–108). Bovine or bison horns were also notated with marks. The horn which the "Venus" of Laussel of the Upper Périgordian period holds in her hand is incised with thirteen marks. These may symbolize the waxing days of the moon.

Speaking of time reckoning symbols, we should not forget that they are associated with funeral monuments and the belief in regeneration from death, and that they are made of dynamically winding and coiling snakes. The serpent's life force is at the heart of this symbolism. It influences the renewal of Nature by moving time from the point of death to life, from dark moon to full moon, from winter to spring.

25.4 *Hook and axe*

The hook (crozier) is a simplified single spiral and in origin probably inseparable from it.

From the Neolithic onward, the hook appears as an independent symbol, particularly in western European megalithic tombs. (FIGURE 454) However, it is not confined to western Europe alone; it is universal throughout Old Europe and is well evidenced in Egypt.

On the stone slabs and menhirs of France, the hook appears singly, in rows, and in pairs. (FIGURE 455) In the latter case, the hooks are often turned in opposing directions and resemble horns. In one instance, at Gavrinis, the hook springs from a snake coil, providing grounds for the assumption that it can be grouped with snakes and horns as energy signs (see above fig. 343, 4).

Carved stone hooks found in Portuguese megalithic tombs in association with schist plaques depicting the schematized Owl Goddess are decorated with bands of nets, triangles, striations, and zig-zags, symbols of the aquatic sphere and regeneration. On some orthostats in the megalithic tombs of Brittany, the hook interchanges with spirals, footprints and glyphs of the rising Goddess, snakes, and V's.

On an abstract image of the Goddess as the triangular backstone of the passage grave at La Table des Marchands, Brittany, four rows of hooks flank a vulva, the generating life source. (FIGURE 456) As energy symbols, the hooks, which increase in number from the top to the bottom row, stimulate the Goddess's power.

In east-central Europe, a pair of hooks appears in relief on vases of the 6th and later millennia. At Varna a single hook produced in gold was found in Grave No. 36 (a cenotaph), in association with bull figurines, bull horns, ring-shaped pendants, an astrogalus, an axe, and a diadem, all of gold (Ivanov 1978: 93). The association of symbols in this tomb again suggests that the hook was an essential life-stimulating symbol.

This symbol continues to be used during the Bronze Age, usually in funerary monuments. Ivory hooks from graves of a Pre-Palatial cemetery at Fourni, Arkhanes, Crete, were found associated with marble figurines representing the White Lady (Death), triangular vulva-shaped pendants, and small figurines of birds carved in ivory and gold (Herakleion Museum). The hook is seen occasionally on vases found in Late Bronze Age tombs of the Aegean area (see Irini cemetery, Pecorella 1977: fig. 486).

FIGURE 455

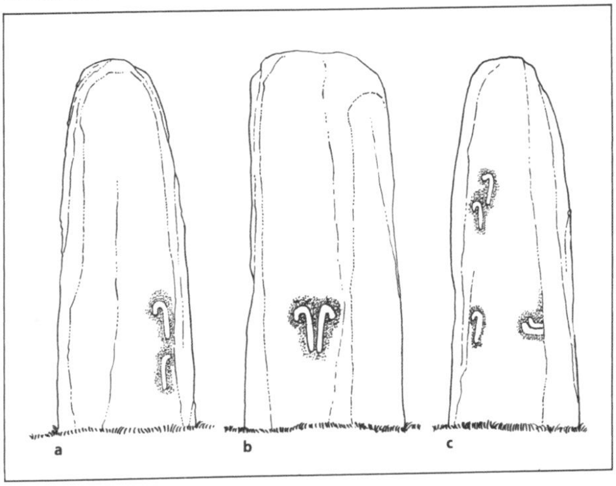

FIGURE 455 The hook is common through Neolithic Europe, particularly in the west. On this French menhir, hooks appear in relief on three sides; note the resemblance to horns of the pair in the center. (Kenmarquer, Morbihan, Brittany; c. 3000 B.C.) H. 587 cm.

FIGURE 456

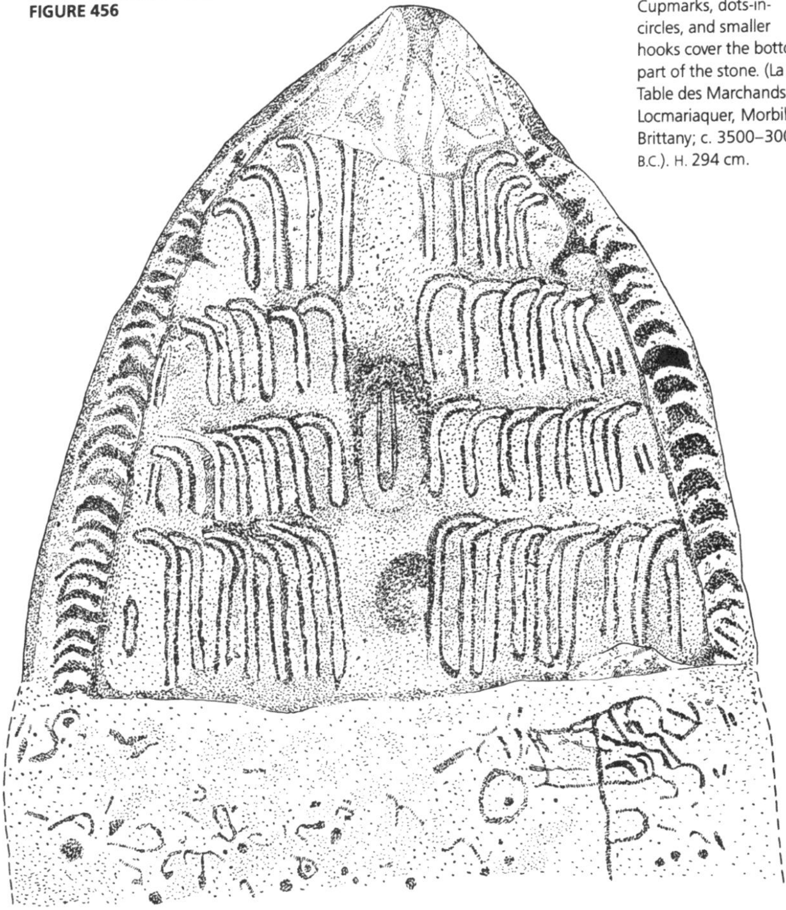

FIGURE 456 Representing the Goddess, the triangular backstone of a French passage-grave has a vulva at its center which is flanked by four rows of opposed hooks. The hooks stimulate the life source or represent emanation of its energy. Cupmarks, dots-in-circles, and smaller hooks cover the bottom part of the stone. (La Table des Marchands, Locmariaquer, Morbihan, Brittany; c. 3500–3000 B.C.). H. 294 cm.

The crooked staff becomes an emblem of power in the hands of the rulers and bishops of later prehistory and history. The earliest such male image in Old Europe is a seated masked god holding a hook in his right hand, from the Tisza culture in southeastern Hungary of c. 5000 B.C. But as we have discussed in section 17, it is doubtful that the curved object is an emblem of regal power in the representation of Old European gods; more likely it is a symbol of the renewal and stimulation of life.

The cultic importance of the axe can be observed from the earliest Neolithic. Tiny greenstone axes of exceptional workmanship and no traces of use, roughly triangular in shape, are found in Greece, Bulgaria, Yugoslavia, southeastern Italy, and elsewhere. In a number of sacred places of the late 7th through the 5th millennia B.C., deposits of axes seem to have been made as offerings. Copper axes from the 5th millenium B.C. in east-central Europe are decorated with chevrons and round depressions like cup-marks. The triangular form links the axe with the vulva. Axes and celts in the Neolithic and Bronze Age of western Europe were decorated with net-patterned triangles and even with quite naturalistically rendered vulvas complete with an indication of pubic hair. (FIGURE 457, 1, 3)

Axes were also made of clay, a convincing indication that such carefully made specimens were not used as tools but were intentionally created for cult purposes. Clay axes are known from the Sesklo culture; at Achilleion II and III (c. 6300–6100 B.C.), they were found in association with Bird Goddess figurines and cult vessels (Gimbutas 1989). In northern Europe, many Funnel-necked Beaker and Narva sites have yielded clay and amber axes (see Klebs 1882; Brøndsted 1957; Gurba 1956).

A strikingly graphic link between the axe and the Owl Goddess is provided by a perforated stone axe from Transylvania. (FIGURE 457, 2) An owl face is engraved on the tip; bird's feet are attached to the eyes. A further link between the Owl Goddess and the axe is attested by their associated portrayals in megalithic tombs, hypogea, and on stelae.

On the orthostats from Gavrinis, two axes are intentionally engraved close together to achieve the shape of a vulva. (FIGURE 458, 1) Such an attempt at transformation made the axe as powerful as the regenerative triangle. Further association of an axe with regeneration is made clear by its placement next to the bulls as can be seen from the engraving on the slab covering the chamber of Gavrinis. (FIGURE 458, 2)

The stela from Mane er H'Roeck, Brittany, features a rising hill-shaped Goddess with an omphalos on the top, surrounded by shafted axes. (FIGURE 458, 3)

Scenes of axes flanking the sun painted on cave walls suggest that the axe was imbued with energy indispensable to the drama of regeneration. An interesting group composed of an anthropomorphic sun surrounded by shafted axes appeared in the cave of Magurata, northwestern Bulgaria (Anati 1969: 99); axes of various sizes were painted on all sides of a sun with oculi face. (FIGURE 459) Here we probably see a winter sun which needs stimulation by the power inherent in axes for its renewal. This composition was the central depiction in this sanctuary. The dancing hourglass-shaped figures in the same cave (see fig. 378, 5) strengthen our assumption of the winter sun perhaps associated with ritual dances which were not only recorded on the wall but were also actually performed.

In the Old European symbol system, the axe is an energy symbol and not a vehicle of the Thunder God's sexual power as in the Indo-European religion.

FIGURE 457

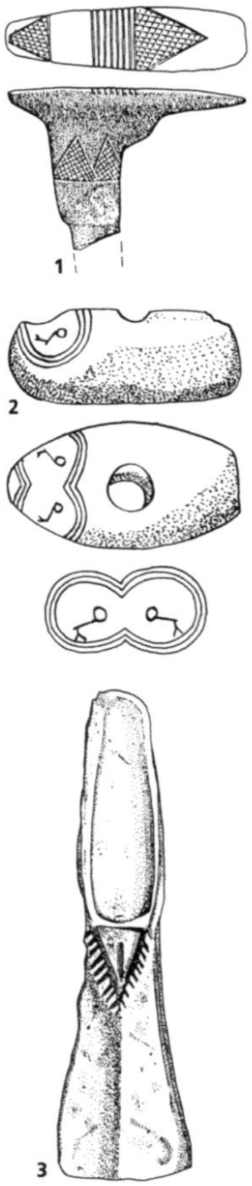

FIGURE 457 Symbols engraved on axes and celts link them with the Goddess of Regeneration. (1) A limestone celt from a megalithic chamber tomb decorated with net-patterned triangles, symbols of regenerative power. Chalcolithic Portugal (S. Martinho de Sintra, Estremadura; 3000–2500 B.C.). (2) The tip of this stone axe is an owl's face whose beak and eyebrows are characteristically joined; a stick with a V sign at the end (a bird's foot?) is incised at the corner of each eye. Probably Petreşti (Transylvania, except provenance unknown; 4500–4000 B.C.). (3) An axe from Middle Bronze Age Brittany decorated with a vulva. (1) L. 15 cm. (2) L. 5 cm. (3) H. 11.3 cm.

FIGURE 458

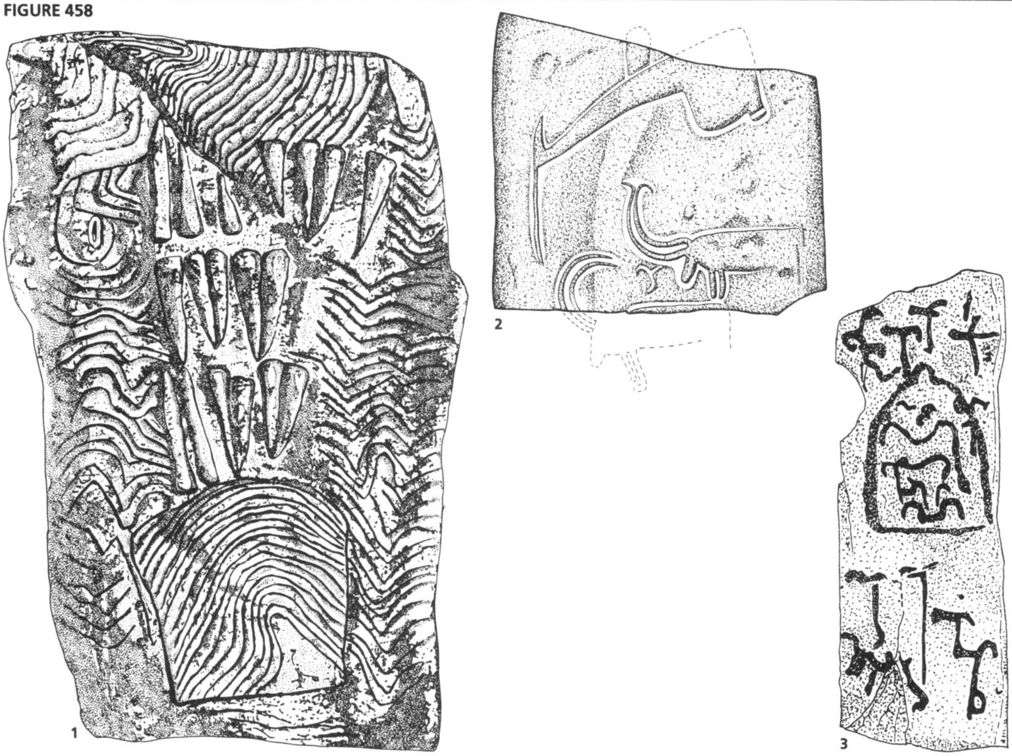

FIGURE 458 Axes as energy symbols surround the rising Goddess or new life in the form of a life column, omphalos, or winter sun. Such compositions are known from tomb walls, stelae, and caves in western and southeastern Europe. (1) One of the orthostats in the passage grave of Gavrinis was engraved with three rows of axes, most of which were paired so as to form a vulva sign. Wavy multiple lines and columns surround them. (Gavrinis, Morbihan, Brittany; c. 3500 B.C.). (2) A gigantic axe and bulls with enormous horns engraved on the slab covering the chamber of Gavrinis. (3) Engraved on this stela is a central hill-shaped Goddess with a knob (omphalos); abstract serpentlike ships are engraved within her body, and she is surrounded by shafted axes. Armorican Neolithic (Mane er H'Roeck, Locmariaquer, Brittany, France; 4500–4000 B.C.)
(1) H. 145.6 cm.
(2) H. 300 cm.
(3) H. 110.6 cm.

FIGURE 459

FIGURE 459 In the Magurata cave sanctuary of Bulgaria, shafted axes are painted next to an anthropomorphized sun, perhaps a winter sun which needs new energy. There are two smaller discs on the sides, and two lines and a checkerboard pattern below. (Exact chronology unknown; probably 4500–4000 B.C. when copper axes of similar shapes were produced.)

Cucuteni figurine with comb, as still worn by European peasants for healing and protection. See figure 481, page 301.

26/ *Opposed Spirals, Whirls, Comb, Brush, and Animal Whirls*

26.1 *Opposed spirals, caterpillars, and snake heads*

Opposed spirals, crescents, and snake heads are configurations intended to stimulate the process of becoming. This motif, universal throughout Old Europe, is encountered on seals, plaques, altars, dishes, elaborately decorated vases, anthropomorphic vases, and figurines. It continues in full strength in Minoan, Cycladic, and Mycenaean art. Its significance as a special symbol is indicated by its independent occurrence on seals and as a primary motif on decorated vases. Opposed snake heads or two pairs of snakes around the mouth of a vase is quite often the sole motif in ceramic decoration. On a vase from Teiu near Bucharest, two pairs of snakes "turn the wheel of life" and are associated with bull figures, symbolic of the life force. (FIGURE 460)

Exquisite examples of opposed snake or spiral heads as a central theme come from Cucuteni vase painting of the Cucuteni A period. (FIGURES 461–465) Pairs of this life-stimulating sign also mark the abdomen, shoulders, and buttocks of figurines and anthropomorphic vases.

FIGURE 460

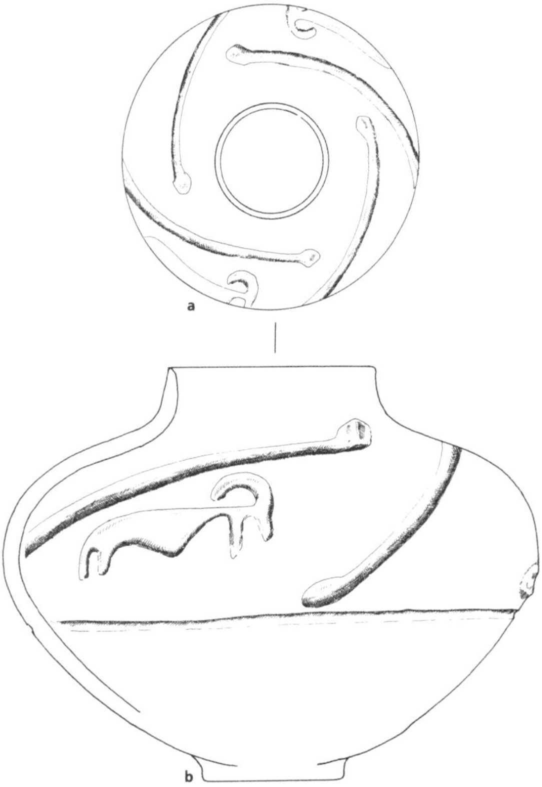

FIGURE 460 Two pairs of opposed snakes spin around the mouth of a globular vase, creating a four-cornered whirl. Bulls, symbols of regeneration, stand between the snakes on two sides; all figures are in relief. Karanovo VI/ Gumelniţa (Teiu, near Bucharest, Romania; mid-5th mill. B.C.) H. 33 cm.

FIGURE 461

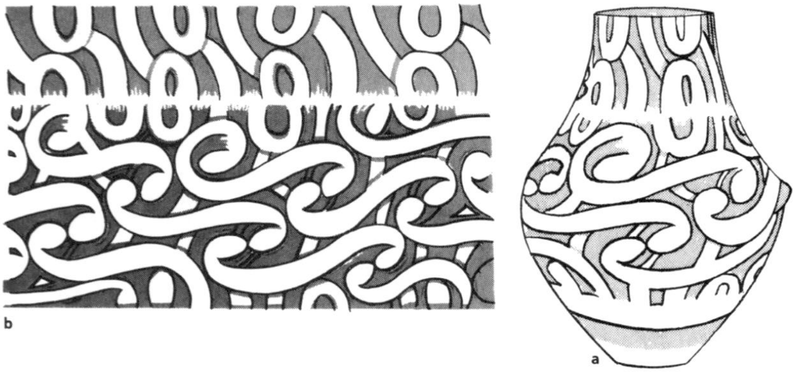

FIGURE 462

FIGURE 463

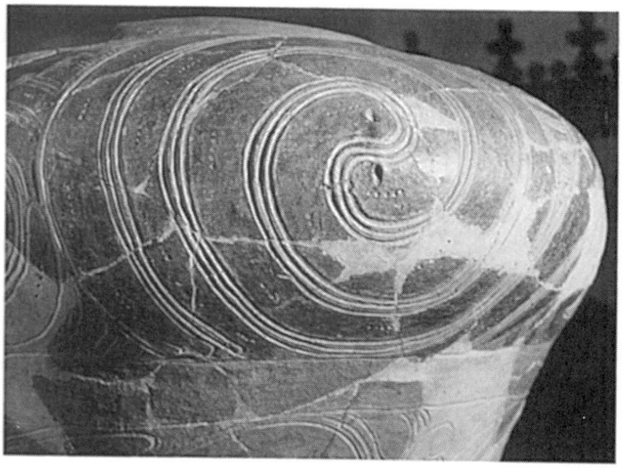

FIGURE 464

FIGURE 461 S-shaped spirals with opposed heads float over the body of a vase whose neck is ringed by U-forms. Cucuteni A_3 (Cucuteni; 44th–43rd cents. B.C.). H. 33.6 cm.

FIGURE 462 Stylized opposed snake heads decorate this Cucuteni A_2 vase. The snakes are painted in three parallel bands of brown and bordered in black. (Frumuşica, NE Romania; 45th–44th cents. B.C.) H. approx. 20 cm.

FIGURE 463 A large piriform vase is decorated with opposed snake coils outlined by grooves filled with white paste. Cucuteni A_2 (Truşeşti, NE Romania; 45th–44th cents. B.C.) Detail.

FIGURE 464 Opposed horns and crescents—some ending in discs, or linked with sprouting branches—spring inside conical bowls. Note the central winding snake and opposed crescents of (4) and (5). Painted black on red. Cucuteni B ((1)–(3) Sipenitsi; 3900–3700 B.C.; (4) and (5) Tomashivka, W Ukraine; c. 3500 B.C.) (1)–(5) DIA. 22.5 cm.

FIGURE 465 This Cucuteni figurine has antithetic spirals on her lower abdomen, as well as her left buttock and the back of her shoulders. Hooks follow the lines of the collarbone, and her tiny breasts are made of U signs; the rest of her body is covered in striations. Cucuteni A_4 (Drăguşeni, NE Romania; 43rd–42nd cents. B.C.) H. 18.6 cm.

FIGURE 465

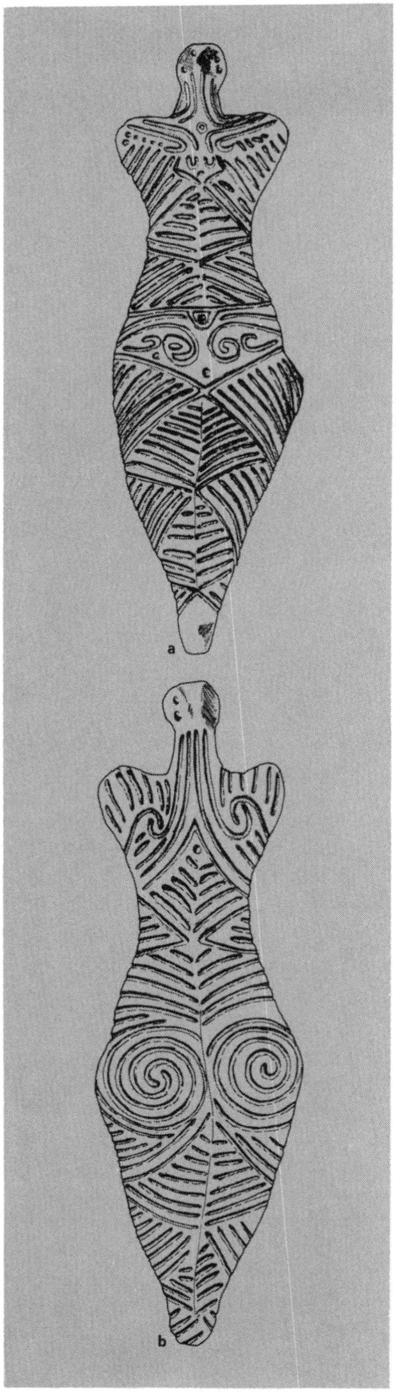

Two abbreviated spirals form a sign which resembles the combination of an upright and an inverted U. (FIGURE 466) On dishes of the 5th millennium B.C., this form alternates with plant motifs; it is profusely employed in decorative bands on vases of the Aegean Bronze Age and of the Greek Geometric and Archaic periods.

26.2 *Whirls and four-corner designs*

"Motion is its ruling characteristic. . . . The decorative designs whirl and turn . . . in a hymn of joy and life," said N. Platon, speaking of Minoan art in 1959 in *A Guide to the Archaeological Museum of Herakleion*. The same words can be repeated in relation to the European art two to three millennia earlier. Symbols that fight stagnation and promote the continuation and perpetual renewal of the cosmic cycle are at the very heart of the Old European farmer's ideology. Whirling signs seem to ensure a smooth transition from one phase to the next, from one cardinal direction to another. These signs—together with spirals, crescents, and hooks—represent life and time, which are cyclical and revolve in a circle or spiral.

Such symbols are necessary at critical moments—for example, at times of human illness and death when life powers are at stake. Funeral vases deposited in graves are regularly decorated by fourfold and whirling signs; these are inseparable from the moon, snake, spiral, crescent, and all other symbols of becoming, such as caterpillars, butterflies, seeds, eggs, and splitting eggs. (FIGURES 467, 468)

FIGURE 466

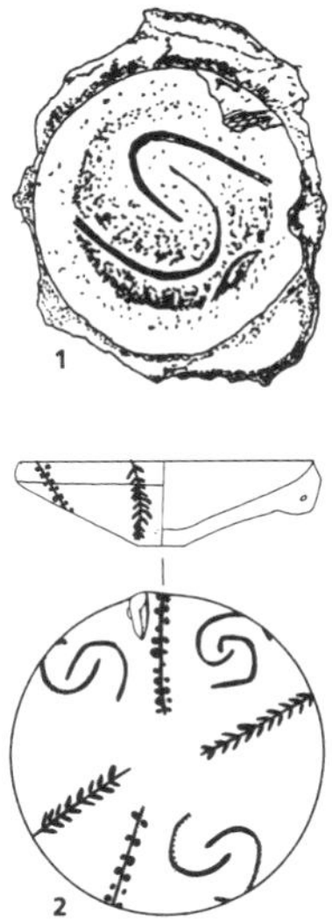

FIGURE 466 Abbreviation of the antithetic spirals motif results in a sign that resembles interlocking U's. (1) Incised on the base of a Karanovo IV vase (Kolojanovec, central Bulgaria; c. 5200–5000 B.C.). (2) Painted on the exterior of a dish next to plant motifs, a common association (Malik II, Albania; mid-5th mill. B.C.). (1) H. 9.6 cm. (2) DIA. 22 cm.

FIGURE 467

FIGURE 467 Whirls and four-corner designs are symbols of becoming and the turnings of cyclical time. This four-corner whirl is painted in graphite on the interior of a Karanovo VI dish (Brailiţa, lower Danube, distr. Galati; mid-5th mill. B.C.). DIA. 32 cm.

FIGURE 468

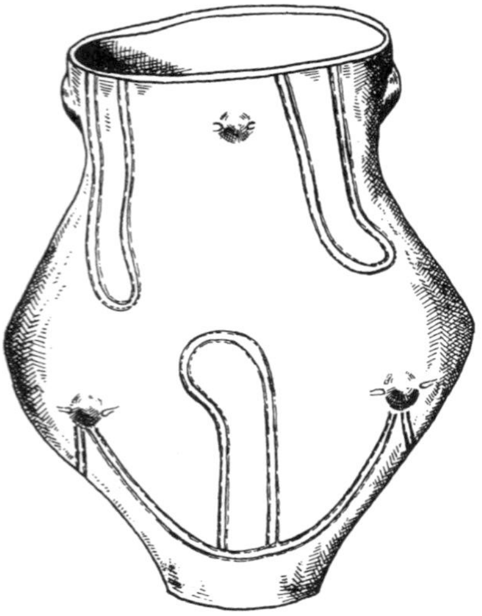

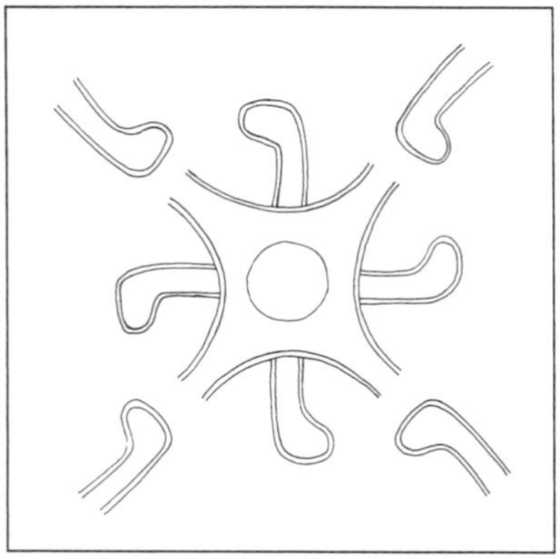

FIGURE 469

FIGURE 468 A four-corner design wraps around the bottom of this vase from a grave in a Lengyel cemetery. Hooks that promote its turning motion thrust out from the four sides. Painted red on cream. (Zengővárkony, W Hungary; early 5th mill. B.C.) H. 10.9 cm.

FIGURE 469 Illustrated here are further examples of quartered circles associated with snakes. (1) White, red, and dark brown design on the inside of a Cucuteni AB bowl (Ghelaeşti, NE Romania; c. 4000 B.C.). (2) Late Cucuteni vase painted black on red (Valea Lupului, Moldavia; c. 3800–3600 B.C.). (1) DIA. 28 cm. (2) H. 35.2 cm.

In painted compositions around the shoulder or bellies of large vases and on the interiors of dishes, we find a circle which is marked in the center with an X sign and placed on the path of a cosmic snake or surrounded by a snake. (FIGURE 469) The quartered circle is a universal human symbol of diverse usage; most simply, it represents the unification of the four cardinal directions of space and the four seasons of time. Its association with the snake in Old Europe also suggests an early prototype of ancient Mediterranean creation myths involving a goddess, a cosmic egg, and a snake (see Graves 1960: 27ff., for a full discussion of this later myth).

Other whirling signs are made of crescents. A whirling composition on a dish from Devetashka cave, central Bulgaria, consists of an inner circle of clockwise and an outer circle of counterclockwise crescents. (FIGURE 470) This gives the impression that the outer circle of crescents invigorates the central whirl, thus expressing the idea of reciprocal forces in the universe.

Four-fold designs are often composed of a central circle with four circles or loops around it, suggesting concepts of the center as cosmic source and of the unification of opposites. (FIGURES 471, 472) Each of the four circles or loops encloses either a cross, M, zig-zag, caterpillar, chick, butterfly, seed, or double-seed. Each is thus shown to contain the spark of life. Associated designs include aquatic symbolism: net, checkerboard, meander, parallel lines, a dotted field.

Miniature sacrificial and funerary vessels are often double or quadruple—that is, made up of two or four sections. The illustrated example of a sacrificial vessel (*kernos*) from Gumelniţa, Romania, has four sections, each covered by a lid. (FIGURE 473) Characteristically, the decoration consists of crescents and rows of zig-zags around the shoulders. The lids are incised with a four-fold sign, opposed crescents, and dots. Such kernoi were very likely used for sacrifices to the Goddess in rituals concerned with regeneration.

FIGURE 470

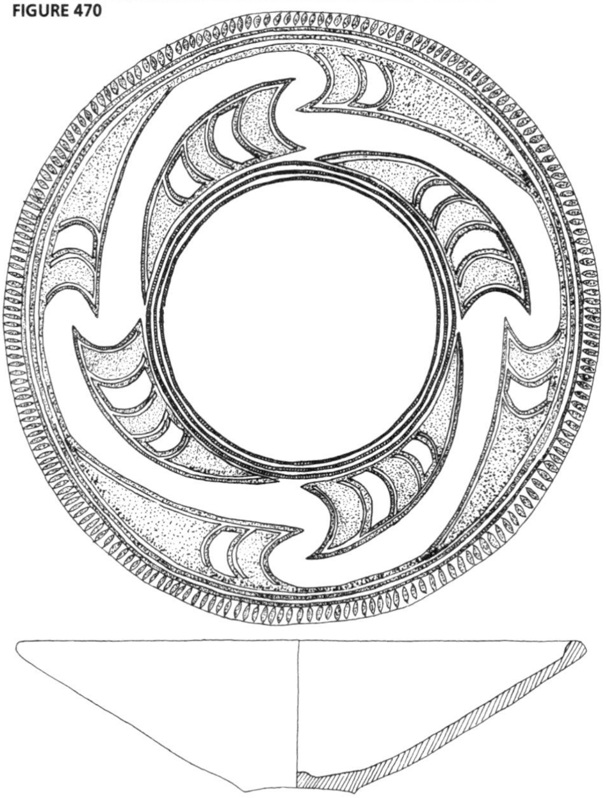

FIGURE 470 The elegant design on the interior of this dish is made up of a central whirl of clockwise-turning crescents around a disc or egg. Four crescents create a counter-clockwise whirl around the outer edge, invigorating the inner whirl. Graphite painted. Karanovo VI (Devetashka cave, central Bulgaria; mid-5th mill. B.C.) DIA. 44.7 cm.

FIGURE 471

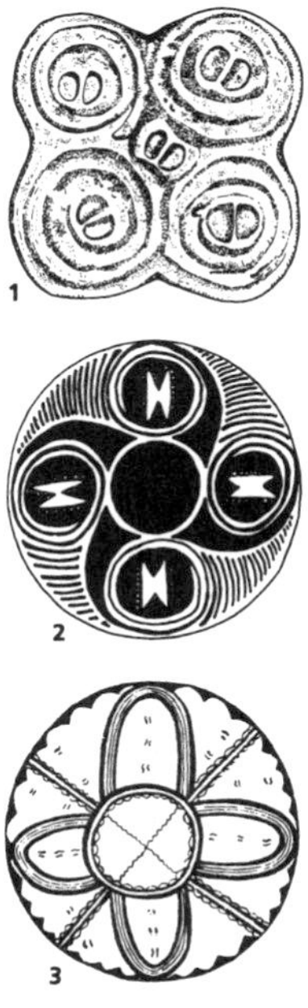

FIGURE 471 Quadripartite designs often consist of a central circle surrounded by four circles or loops; the latter contain such symbols of becoming as a double seed, butterfly, and caterpillar. (1) Terracotta stamp. Middle Neolithic in Italy (Arene Candide, Liguria, NW Italy; 5th mill. B.C.). (2) Interior of a Rakhmani style dish. Dimini (Rakhmani, Thessaly; end of 5th mill. B.C.. (3) Interior of a dish. Cucuteni (Vykvatintsi cemetery, Soviet Moldavia; c. 3500 B.C..
(1) W. 5.1 cm;
(2) DIA. 19.2 cm;
(3) DIA. 17.2 cm.

FIGURE 472

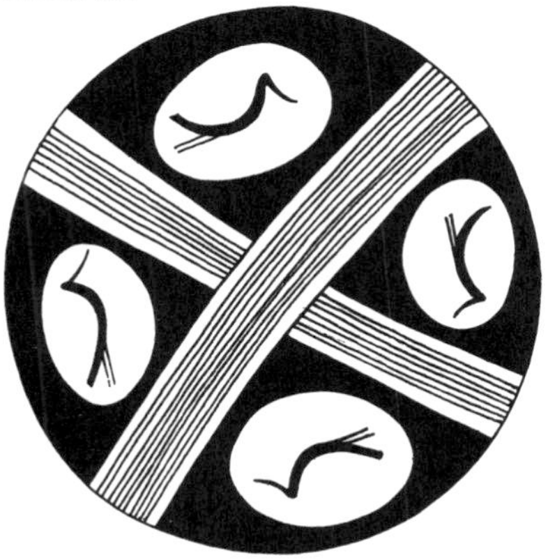

FIGURE 472 Four-fold designs which promote the turning of the great cycles of life are often composed of four circles or eggs around a common center, as on this Late Cucuteni bowl. Chicks in each egg stress the regenerative energy. Cucuteni B_2 (Buznea near Peatra Neamţ, Moldavia; 3700–3500 B.C.) DIA. approx. 30 cm.

FIGURE 473

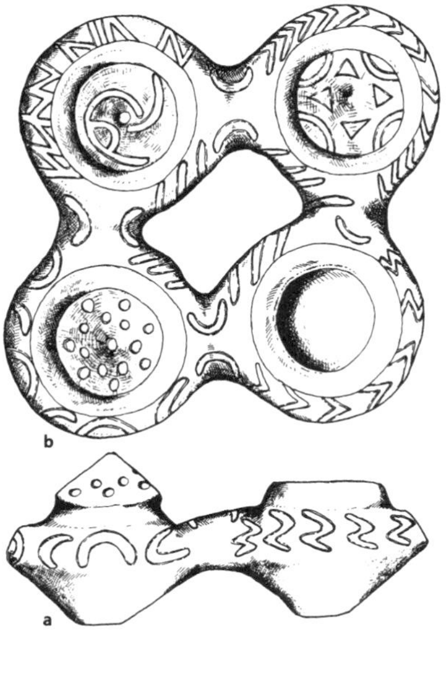

FIGURE 473 This example of a sacrificial vessel in four sections is decorated by white-encrusted excision. There are crescents and zig-zags around the shoulders, and designs of opposed crescents, a field of dots, and four cardinal triangles on the lids. Karanovo VI/Gumelniţa (Gumelniţa, S Romania; mid-5th mill. B.C.) H. 8.4 cm.

The Minoan art of some two thousand years later is still replete with whirls of great variety. Simple whirls and patterns composed of spirals with attached net-patterned loops, of rosettes enclosed in circles, and of spirals and plant motifs occur on seals and vases. The most outstanding ceramics depicting whirl compositions are from the Middle Minoan period, particularly those of the Kamares style from the first palace of Phaistos, early 2nd millennium B.C. Turning and sprouting create a joyous sensation of the triumph of life. The same assertion of renewal is seen in the compositions with whirls, butterflies, and bull horns.

Whirling signs accompany the Goddess in her life-giving function, the Lady of the Beasts of the Artemis type (see fig. 405). In Ireland to this day people make up St. Brigit's Crosses on the eve of her feast on the First of February, putting them up to protect their houses and invoke the blessings of the Saint. Her "crosses" of straw look much more like whirls; the cross-arms are joined by arched lines and the middle part is filled in. "Brigit's girdle," a circle of straw rope about four feet in diameter, plays a similar role. Boys dressed as women go from house to house carrying the girdle; if you pass through the circle you invoke the Saint's protection against physical ailments.

26.3 *Brush and comb*

The brush—a series of parallel lines bound by a bar on one side—appears in the Upper Paleolithic in association with snakes and fish and continues throughout prehistory and history. (FIGURE 474) Its association with whirls, swastikas, wings, and hands suggests that it is an energy symbol. It is obvious that the brush symbolizes the Goddess's regenerative powers when it is shown above or instead of her pubic triangle. This energy promoting renewal is also implied by portrayals of ships with vertical lines across their whole length encountered on megalithic tomb walls in western Europe and on Maltese temple walls; they seem to be interchangeable with or closely related to the brush symbol.

The whirl—a four-cornered sign with parallel lines at the ends of each bar—is seen on Çatal Hüyük frescoes of the 7th millennium B.C. (see Mellaart 1967: pl. 40). The bull heads in Çatal Hüyük shrines are painted with one or two brushes, alone or together with a hand or honeycomb motifs, a meaningful combination of regeneration and energy symbols. (FIGURE 475) A further visible association is of bird wings and brush; the wings of the Vulture Goddess are portrayed as brushes and a comb sign is painted on her body (see above fig. 285).

The brush often appears on the bases or sides of pots during the 6th millennium B.C., and on Bird Goddess figurines from the Vinča, Tisza, Petreşti, Linear Pottery, and Cucuteni cultures, frequently associated with the vulva. (FIGURE 476) It is also common on schematic winged Early Bronze Age Cypriot figurines from the end of the 3rd millennium B.C. and on the vases of Early Bronze Age Anatolia. (FIGURE 477)

FIGURE 474

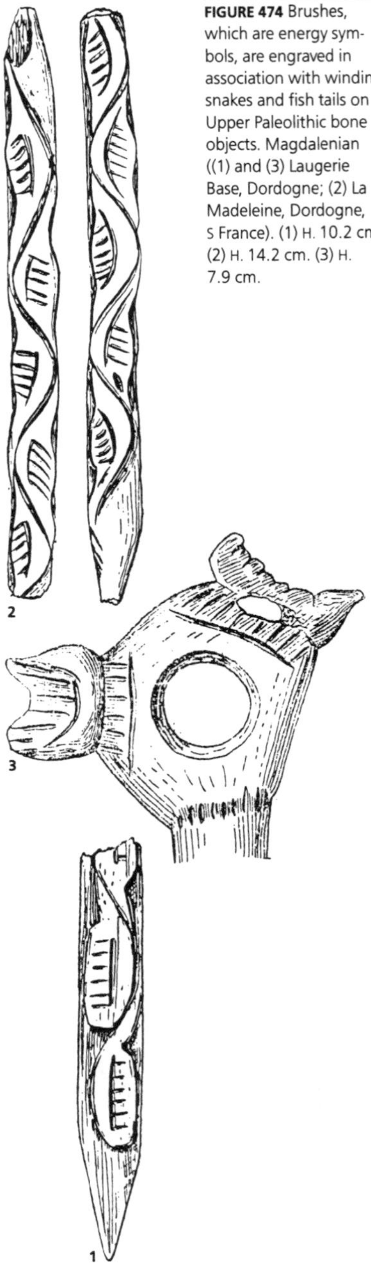

FIGURE 474 Brushes, which are energy symbols, are engraved in association with winding snakes and fish tails on Upper Paleolithic bone objects. Magdalenian ((1) and (3) Laugerie Base, Dordogne; (2) La Madeleine, Dordogne, S France). (1) H. 10.2 cm. (2) H. 14.2 cm. (3) H. 7.9 cm.

FIGURE 475

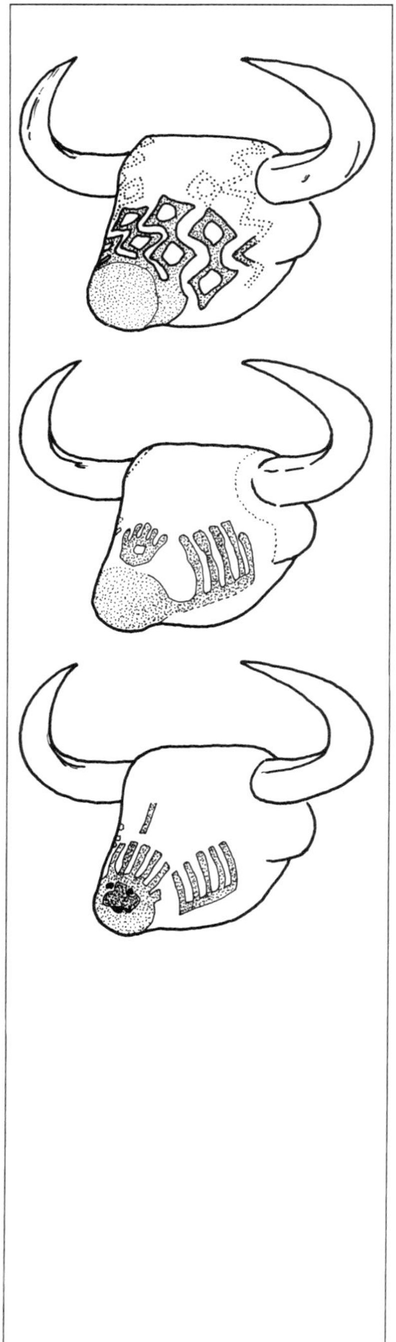

FIGURE 475 Bull's heads in Çatal Hüyük shrines were painted with brush, hand, and honeycomb motifs in successive phases (the First Shrine, E VI 8; approx. 6000 B.C.)

FIGURE 476

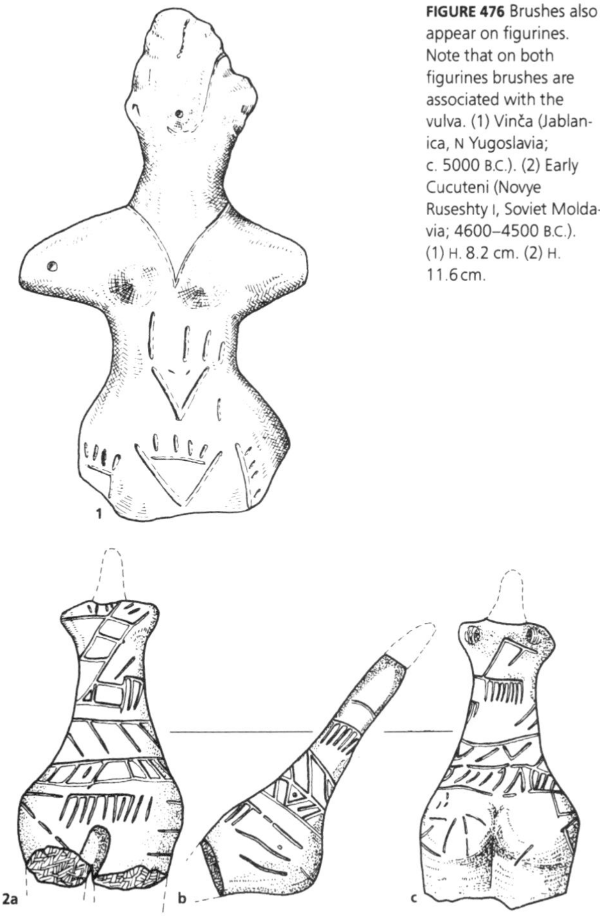

FIGURE 476 Brushes also appear on figurines. Note that on both figurines brushes are associated with the vulva. (1) Vinča (Jablanica, N Yugoslavia; c. 5000 B.C.). (2) Early Cucuteni (Novye Ruseshty I, Soviet Moldavia; 4600–4500 B.C.). (1) H. 8.2 cm. (2) H. 11.6 cm.

FIGURE 477

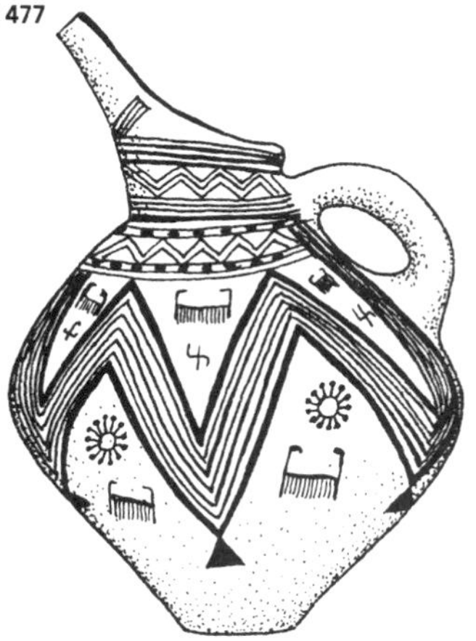

FIGURE 477 A symbol related to the brush, the comb is associated with suns and swastikas on an Early Bronze Age vase from Anatolia (Kültepe, central Turkey; c. 3000 B.C.) H. 21.2 cm.

A coiling or undulating snake is often used in the Cucuteni culture on dishes and spherical objects to create a spin effect. Torsion is indicated by the juxtaposed heads of snakes whose bodies, made of parallel lines like rain torrents, twine in opposite directions. The heads frequently end in horns, three dashes, or a brush crest; in the center of the dish is a brush used as a fixed sign. (FIGURE 478)

The brush on amber pendants of the Ertebølle culture, Denmark (c. 4000 B.C.), may suggest a symbolic relationship between the brush and amber, a substance which emanates energy and has healing potency. (FIGURE 479)

The divine power of the brush/comb can best be perceived in images where the comb appears as a Goddess with breasts and head, as in an anthropomorphic comb-pendant from the Neolithic Cortaillod culture in Switzerland (FIGURE 480) or as an hourglass-shaped image whose lower part is a brush. A similar symbol—a combination of the divine image and a comb—continued in European prehistory down to the Celtic La Tène period in Central Europe.

Combs were worn as a pendant on the front or back of a figurine, such as this Cucuteni example. (FIGURE 481)

To this day, European peasants use the comb for protection against diseases and other evils and for healing purposes. Children and women after childbirth wear a comb pendant on their front or back, a custom inherited from prehistory when it was considered necessary to appease the Vulture (Death) Goddess during the period of her rule in order to secure a safe and healthy life.

FIGURE 478

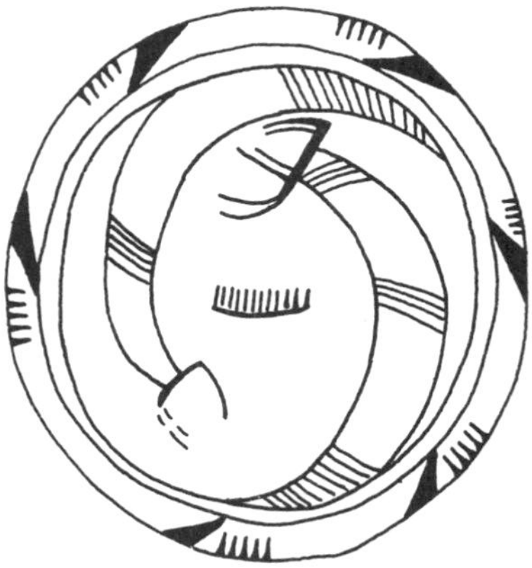

FIGURE 478 As in the Upper Paleolithic, the brush is also associated with snakes in Old Europe. This black-painted design on the interior of a conical bowl portrays two horned snakes spinning around a central brush. Cucuteni B (Staraja Buda, Tomashivka, and Sipenitsi, W Ukraine; 3900–3700 B.C.) DIA. 31.5 cm.

FIGURE 479

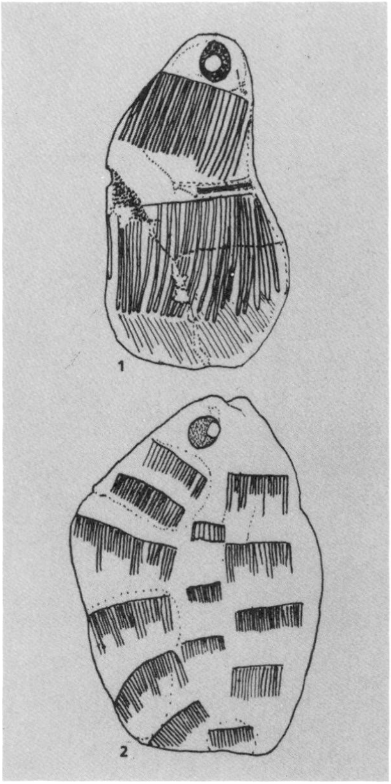

FIGURE 479 In northern Europe, amber pendants are sometimes carved with brush signs. Since, then as later, amber was probably believed to generate healing energy, the brushes may well have been a symbol of that energy. (Ertebølle, Brabrand, Denmark; c. 4000 B.C.) (1) H. 5.35 cm. (2) H. 5.7 cm.

FIGURE 480 The comb can take the form of a divine female figure, as these examples show. (1) Neolithic Switzerland (Cortaillod; c. 4000 B.C.). (2) and (3) La Tène, Iron Age Switzerland. (1) H. 6.5 cm. (2) H. 3 cm. (3) H. 4 cm.

FIGURE 481 The comb is still worn by European peasants for healing and protection in the same way as shown on this Old European figurine. Cucuteni B (Bilcze Zlote, upper Dniester, Ukraine; 4000–3500 B.C.) H. 17 cm.

FIGURE 480

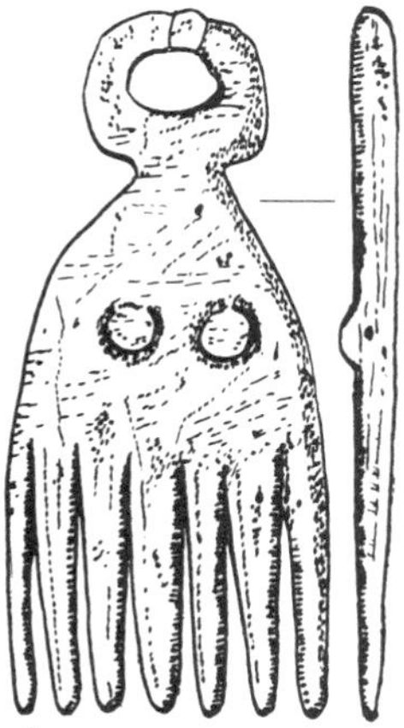

1

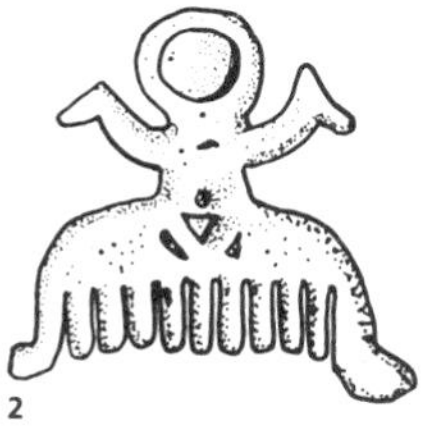

2

3

FIGURE 481

26.4 *Animal whirls and processions*

We are familiar with animal processions as symbols of cyclic time through the omnipresence of the astrological zodiac. The zodiac as we know it is very ancient, but the tradition of animal whirls and processions which stimulate the motions of time is older still.

Animals portrayed as marching in a row of five or more, or whirling around a center, are known from Old European vase paintings, Minoan engravings on seals, and bas-reliefs in Maltese temples. Dogs and goats are primary in such processions, alongside stags, hinds, and caterpillars. Female animals appear next to male: stag and hind, male and female goat. The doubling of sexes probably doubles their force.

In vase painting, animals may belong to a whirl which is part of a larger whirling design. On a large Cucuteni crater from Krutoborodintsi, western Ukraine, the animals—hind, dog, female goat, male goat, and caterpillar—move counterclockwise in a frieze around the vase's shoulder. (FIGURE 482, 1) This frieze is the inner circle of a large four-corner composition with smaller circles placed at each of the cardinal points. On other Cucuteni vases, the procession includes an ostrich-like bird. (FIGURE 482, 2)

FIGURE 482

Animal processions also occur on a large scale. At the Tarxien temple of Malta, goats and a pig led by a ram march in a horizontal line across a carved stone slab. (FIGURE 483)

The symbolic significance of Old European portrayals of animals in a sequential order must have been inherited from Upper Paleolithic traditions. On a number of cave walls of that period (La Pasiega, Les Combarelles, Lascaux, Font-de-Gaume, Les Trois Frères) animals appear in groups consisting of the whole range of types: bison, horse, stag, ox, boar, feline, mammoth. Bison and horse are usually placed at the beginning of the sequence (Leroi-Gourhan 1967: 348, 351, 366). Next to them are geometric signs—such as inverted V's, bi-lines, or a *b*-sign (buttocks)—and occasionally hands, owls, and owl heads.

The meaning of animals in sequential order as portrayed in these caves is not yet well understood. Their association with the symbols of the Goddess (hands, owls, inverted V's) and signs of cyclical time (spirals and crescents) suggest a link with a deity in whose power was the promotion and control of the life cycle from birth to death and from death to regeneration. It is worth remembering that the Lady of the Beasts is a mythological archetype that lasts well into the historical period of Europe. Her animals convey the presence of a primordial life force.

FIGURE 482 Animal processions, particularly those that are circular, symbolize the cyclic motions of time, much as the astrological zodiac does. (1) On this crater, a frieze of hind, dog, she-goat, he-goat, and caterpillar circle the center of a large four-corner design. Painted black on orange-red. Late Cucuteni (Kruto-borodintsi, W Ukraine). (2) The frieze on this Cucuteni vase from Var-varovka, Soviet Moldavia, depicts a procession of stag, deer, hounds, birds (ostriches?), and other young animals (early 4th mill. B.C.). (1) H. 25 cm. (2) H. 29.7 cm.

FIGURE 483

FIGURE 483 On a large stone slab from a temple compound, goats, a pig, and a ram march in zodi-acal procession. Temple period of Malta (Tarxien; c. 3000 B.C.)

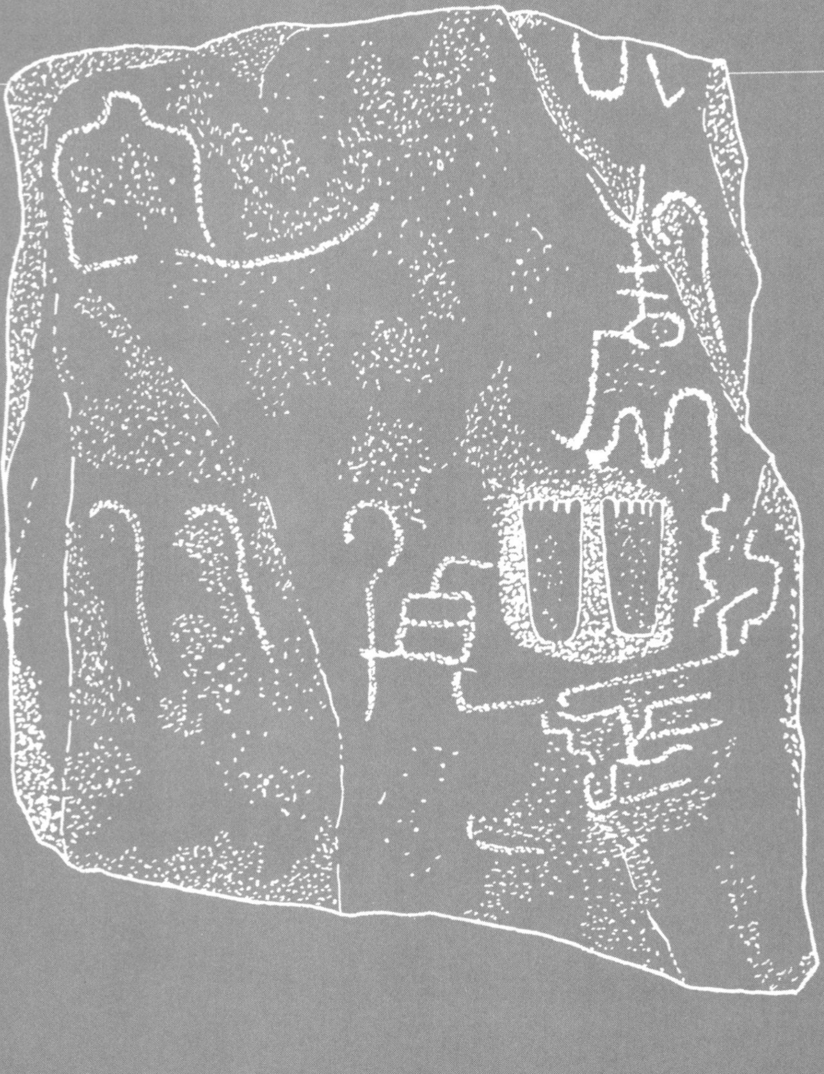

Footprints, hooks, snakes, and rudimentary image of the Goddess (left corner) in megalithic gallery grave. See figure 487, page 308.

27/ *Hands and Feet of the Goddess*

The hands and feet of the Goddess have appeared over the millennia painted on cave, shrine, and megalithic tomb walls and on vases, and carved in stone. Even today, stones with miraculous footprints of the Virgin, Jesus, or the saints are held in deep reverence in the Catholic countries of Europe. They have the power to heal, give strength to feeble children, and protect against evil. Water collected in such footprints can heal and fertilize; hands painted on doors have apotropaic powers. Irish Brigit upon her visits to country hearths leaves her footprints in the ashes. They are a promise of prosperity and abundance (Sjoestedt 1949: 25). Such beliefs hark back to a much more ancient religion; as *pars pro toto*, hands and feet symbolize the touch of the Goddess; they impart her energy.

Red and black silhouettes of hands appear on Upper Paleolithic cave walls continuously from around 20,000 to 10,000 B.C., i.e., from the end of the Gravettian and throughout the Magdalenian epochs (Leroi-Gourhan 1967: illus. 60, 64, 129, 138, 147, 160). The majority of hands painted in positive and negative in the caves are the hands of women. Hands are portrayed singly, in rows, and in groups. Some, as at Pech-Merle, are found in association with a mare's pregnant belly and the bi-line, symbol of pregnancy. Some hands are placed near "quadrangular" and cross signs, as in the cave of El Castillo, Santander; others are near a "tent" or "shrine" which may be an abstract sign of the Goddess, as in Les Combarelles, Dordogne. At La Pileta and El Castillo, Spain, hands appear in association with bovids. (FIGURE 484)

FIGURE 484

FIGURE 484 The hands of the Goddess, symbols of her energizing touch, appear on the walls of Upper Paleolithic caves. In the cave at La Pileta, near Gibraltar, Spain, hands are painted above a bovide with crescent-shaped horns and in association with groups of parallel lines, most of which are double and triple lines. The types of animals below the ox are uncertain (13,000–11,000 B.C.). H. 179 cm.

FIGURE 485

FIGURE 485 The hands of the Goddess also appear on the walls of Neolithic shrines. At Çatal Hüyük, hands of red (the color of life, represented in this figure as gray) and black (fertility) are joined by a honeycomb or net. A horizontal panel. (Shrine in Level VII,8, central Anatolia; mid-7th mill. B.C.)

Red and black panels of hands are found in many Çatal Hüyük shrines. Their association with bull heads, honeycombs, whirls, chrysalises, bees, and butterflies places them among symbols promoting the process of becoming. Further, the colors used—red (of life) and black (of fertility)—must have been chosen for their symbolic significance. Hands are shown with four or five fingers in positive and negative impressions, placed vertically and horizontally.

Of utmost symbolic importance are hand panels in Shrines VII, 8, and E VI, 8. (FIGURE 485) The wall painting in the former is composed of two horizontal rows pointing to the right. Seven red and black hands alternate in the top row and seven red hands line the bottom. All have an open area on the palm which is filled with one or more dots. Between the two rows is a honeycomb or net design.

In Shrine E VI, 8 the two-hand-motif panels are below three bull heads, each marked with a honeycomb pattern. (FIGURE 486) The top register of the upper frieze contains egg- or fish-shaped ovals enclosing two hands joined at the fingertips in positive and negative design. The central portion is covered with circle, whirl, crescent, and caterpillar or insect symbols. The bottom register is made up of vertical and horizontal hands, positive alternating with negative. The lower panel consists of randomly placed hands in negative design on a red background. The second painting, from an earlier phase, portrays a field of flowers or whirls with chrysalises swaying from boughs (the wavy lines at the top) and insects or butterflies (Mellaart 1963: 80).

Portrayals of hands are not found in European shrines but appear on Neolithic and Copper Age vases (see Gimbutas 1974: pl. 158 for a huge hand in relief as the sole design on a vase from Baniata, Karanovo culture). Figurines occasionally have enormous hands seemingly imparting divine energy or spell.

FIGURE 486 In another shrine at Çatal Hüyük (E VI, 8), the wall is covered with two panels of hands placed under bulls' heads. The upper panel consists of opposed hands in positive and negative design within oval forms; circle, whirl, and insect motifs inside honeycomb-like cells; and a line of alternately vertical and horizontal hands. The lower panel is of hands (right and left) shown in negative design on a red background (end-7th mill. B.C.).

FIGURE 486

FIGURE 487

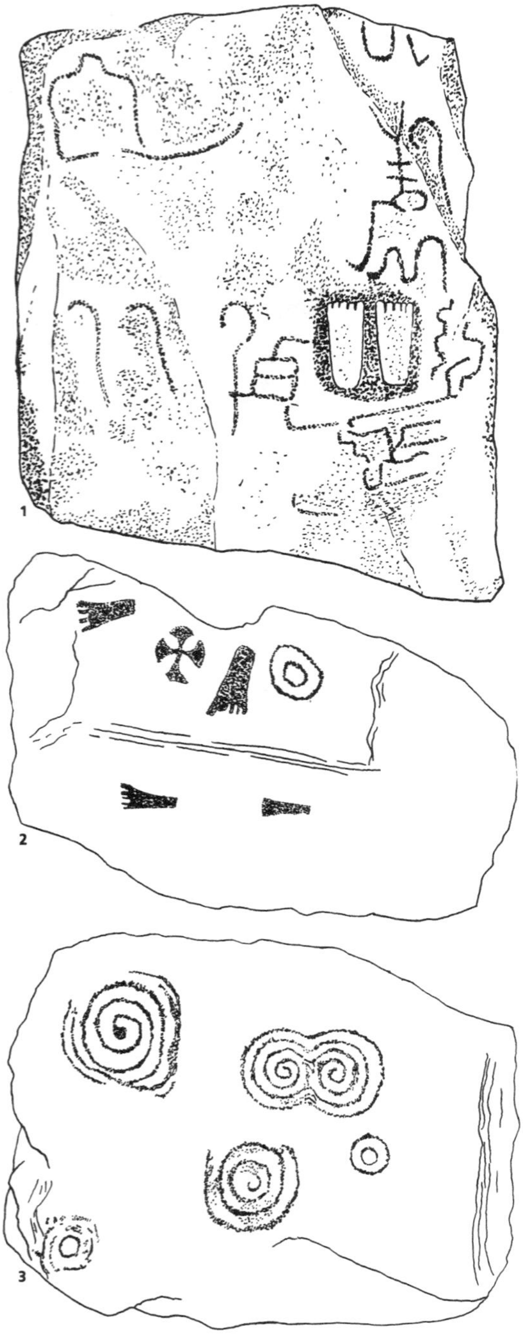

FIGURE 487 Feet also appear in megalithic graves. These footprints are from (1) an orthostat in a gallery grave, and (2) probably a passage grave. They appear with life-stimulating symbols—whirls, hooks, and snakes—and images and symbols of the Goddess. ((1) Petit Mont, Arzon, France; c. 3000 B.C. or earlier. (2) and (3) Calderstones, Liverpool, England.) (1) H. 114 cm. (2) H. 91.5 cm, (3) 103 cm.

FIGURE 488

FIGURE 488 These extremely interesting seals leave a foot-shaped pattern of chevrons, linking the foot with the Bird Goddess. (1) Early Sesklo (Sesklo tell, Thessaly; c. 6500–6300 B.C.). (2) Starčevo (Gura Valii, Western Romania; c. 5500 B.C.). (3) Karanovo VI (Djadovo, near Nova Zagora, central Bulgaria; c. 4500 B.C.). (1) H. 3 cm; (2) H. 3.3 cm; (3) H. 2.2 cm.

The Goddess's footprints occur on orthostats in French gallery graves. (FIGURE 487) It is significant that her feet appear not in isolation but in association with life stimulating symbols, hooks, crosses, concentric circles, oculi motifs, and snakes.

Vases and seals in the form of human feet appear from early Neolithic phases to beyond the Copper Age. (FIGURE 488) The illustrated foot-shaped seals bear chevron and zig-zag signs linking them with the Bird Goddess.

Exquisite vases from the 5th millennium B.C. sometimes have handles shaped like human feet. It seems a bit peculiar to find feet and not hands as handles, but this is indeed the case. Interesting symbolic associations can be discerned on a black-burnished vase with four feet on four sides uncovered at Střelice, an early Lengyel site (c. 5000 B.C.). (FIGURES 489, 490) The symbols used are: four dogs sculpted around the mouth; four human figures with V-shaped arms associated with life columns; caterpillars, snakes, crescents, and plants, all symbols of becoming. This indicates that feet and upraised arms have a related symbolic meaning, that of promotion. The feet, dogs, snakes, and lozenges are meant to promote life. If hands and feet represent the divine touch, then this motif surely imparts the powerful energy of the Goddess.

FIGURE 489

FIGURE 489 Four feet are attached to the middle of this black-burnished vase. Four dogs surround the mouth, and the body is decorated with white-encrusted punctate lines in the shape of four human figures and four lozenges with double spirals. Lengyel (Střelice, near Znojmo, Moravia; c. 5000 B.C.). H. 38 cm.

FIGURE 490 Outstretched design of the Lengyel vase illustrated in fig. 489.

FIGURE 490

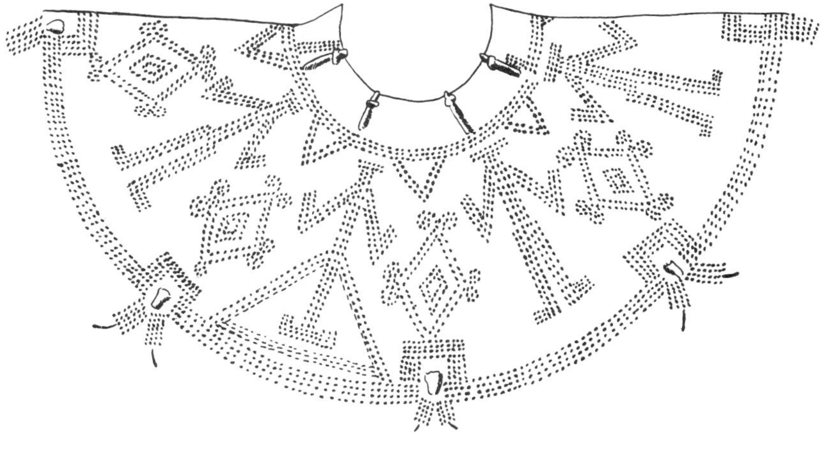

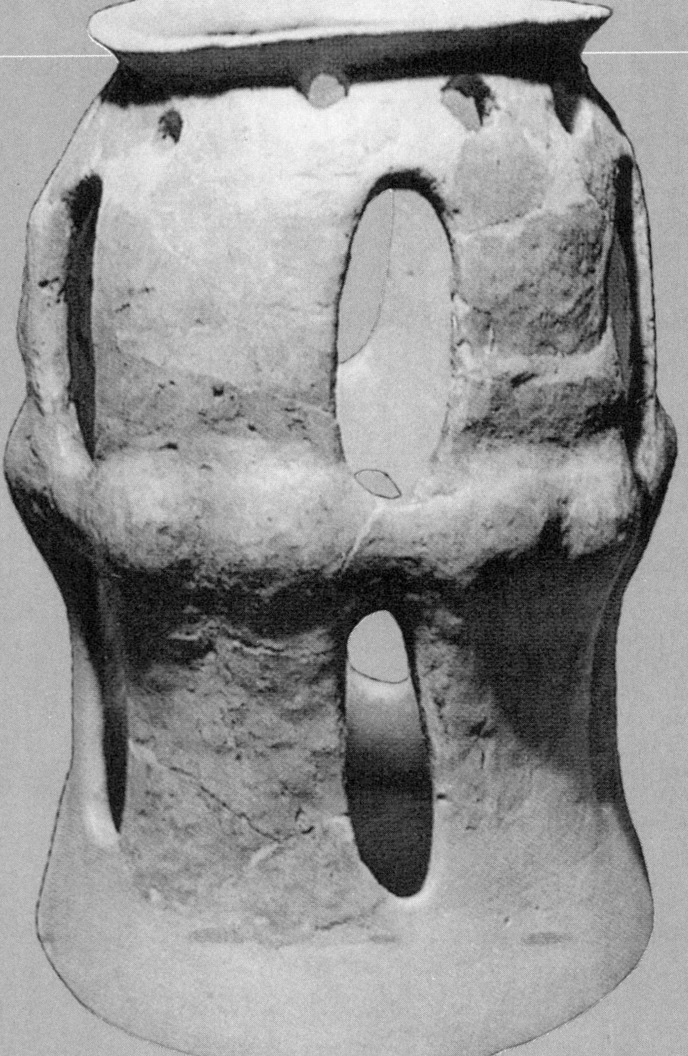

''Ring dance'' vase support of six nude figures connected at shoulders and feet; from Cucuteni. See figure 492, page 312.

28/ *Standing Stones and Circles*

The standing stone (menhir) gives off a mysterious psychic vibration. To this day humans and animals are drawn to menhirs by their magic power. People touch them or go three times around them in order to be cured of illness; sick livestock are brought to rub against them. The menhir is the Goddess.

That a menhir is the epiphany of the Owl Goddess we know from prehistoric stelae in southern France, Spain, and Portugal (figs. 294–97). The Goddess's intimacy with stone is also witnessed in historical times. Greek Artemis was called "the stony one" and Mesopotamian Ninhursaga, "Lady of the stony ground." In folk memories, the menhir is the abode of Irish Brigit and Baltic Laima (Fate) as late as the 20th century. In Lithuania, upright stones surrounded by ditches, which stood along the rivers, were believed to be goddesses and were called *deives* as late as 1836 (Gimbutas 1958: 95). Such stones, usually six feet high, were erected at places sacred to the goddesses who spent their time at the stones spinning the fates of humans.

Menhirs turn around, move, dance, and even speak. Legends say that at midnight stones walk, dip their head into a well, and quietly go back home. In southern England and Wales 39 instances of restless stones were recorded in this century (Grinsell 1976: 59–67). Twenty of them are recorded as going to the nearest body of water to drink or bathe; others are said to turn, move, or dance, and some 27 to go into action at midnight. "Something" comes up the stone avenues on certain days and walks down heralded by the cuckoo's call (recorded in the 19th century Hebrides: Burl 1976: 152). A cuckoo's call is the Goddess's call. Bretons believe that when the cuckoo is first heard a menhir turns thrice (Armstrong 1958: 205).

Prehistoric circles, some with a menhir in the middle, had avenues of stones that led downhill to water. At Callanish in the outer Hebrides, a small stone circle with a menhir in the center had avenues and rows leading downhill towards the bay (Burl 1976: 177); the stones of Carnac, Brittany, go down to the sea (Evans 1895: 25). Sometimes a well, not a stone pillar, is found in the middle of a stone circle, and dances around the well were performed. At Callanish the cuckoo sang its May song of spring from the circle (Burl 1979: 224).

Dances around wells are known from 19th century Scotland and Ireland. One such story took place in Scotland on the first Sunday in May in the 1860s, when two men travelling in the moors near Aberdeen noticed a ceremony around a well. They saw a circle of women with garments tucked up under their arms join hands and dance around the well. An old woman was sprinkling them with the well water as they danced (McPherson 1929: 50–51).

Clearly, the association of standing stones with the sea, rivers, brooks, and wells is richly evidenced in European folklore. The link between the menhir and well is paralleled by the link between the Goddess and water of life. Even the Goddess's names give a clue to this association. Take, for instance, the Slavic Goddess Mokosh-Paraskeva Pyatnitsa (the latter half of her name meaning "Friday"), the dispenser of the water of life and the spinner of the thread of life. The name *Mokosh* is connected with moisture, *mok-* or *mokr-* meaning "wet, moist," and her ritual was called *mokrida*. On the other hand, the root *mok-* appears as a name for stones. In Lithuanian, *mokas* is a "standing stone," always appearing in legends associated with lakes or rivers.

Folk memories of relationships between the menhir, well, and stone ring suggest the interchangeability of the Goddess, ring, and well. Stone rings and ring dances seem to be an extension of the centrally concentrated Goddess energy. Circles with a depression in the middle inscribed on flat stones perhaps convey a related meaning: the Goddess's power is in the deep, in stone and water, surrounded by magic circles. (FIGURE 491)

Fairies, the maidens of the Goddess, are of wells, springs, and rivers, or they originate like flowers with the morning dew. Dancing in a circle, they create a power capable of tearing any man to pieces who happens to enter the sacred ring. Rings of standing stones or rings in green grass meadows are called "fairy rings," *cercles des fées* in French. Swift maidens, naked or in white robes, appear there dancing with linked arms at midnight. The great speed of the dancing sets up a free flow of energies.

Fairy dances are related to the ecstatic mountaintop dancing of the Bacchantes and Maenads in Greek legend. Southern Slavic fairies, *vile* (pl. of *vila*) also dance on mountain tops near lakes and springs. They take offence when a person interrupts their *kolo*, or "ring." They blind him with a mere glance or pull him in and dance him to death (Djordjević 1953: 61).

The circle—be it fairy dance or ring of standing stones—transmits the energy increased by the combination of the powers of stone, water, mound, and circling motion.

FIGURE 491

FIGURE 491 Circles and concentric circles with a cupmark in the middle are engraved on a megalith. Such engravings are semantic relatives of stone circles and ring dances around a well, which is the concentrated life source of the Goddess. Irish Neolithic (found near Loughcrew, Ballinvalley I, Co. Meath; probably end of the 4th mill. B.C.)

The practice of the sacred ring dance can be as old as the Upper Paleolithic and surely continues throughout the Neolithic, prehistory, and history. Ring dances of naked women are portrayed in Cucuteni ceramics of the second half of the 5th millennium B.C. A series of vase supports from the classical Cucuteni culture are shaped like naked women in a ring with joined arms. Romanians call them "Hora vases," from the *hora* or "ring dance" still alive today. (FIGURE 492) Minoan seals and vase paintings are also witness to the practice of ring dances.

The abundance of folklore regarding the prehistoric henges and rings of western Europe must reflect their importance in prehistoric rituals. They are believed to be inhabited by fairies or witches; music and laughter are heard there and dances are seen in the moonlight. The association of henges and

FIGURE 492

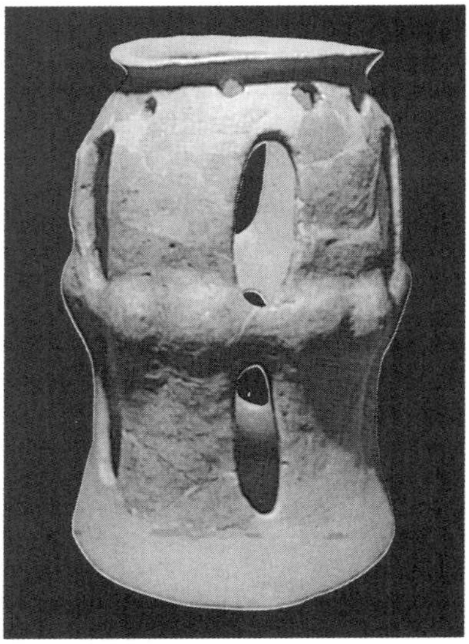

FIGURE 492 This "ring dance" vase support is made up of six nude figures connected at shoulders and feet. Cucuteni A_2 (Frumuşica near Peatra Neamţ; 45th–44th cents. B.C.)

rings with megalithic tombs and standing stones speak of their link with death and regeneration rituals.

Prehistoric stone circles and henges are largely a phenomenon of the British Isles dating to the period between 3300 and 1500 B.C. More than nine hundred circles still exist in the British Isles. They are found in river valleys or near water in low-lying areas (Burl 1976: 4–21). Their use as places of rituals is borne out by the lack of habitation artifacts. In pits at Maumbury Rings, outside Dorchester, antler picks, a huge chalk phallus, and sherds of grooved ware were found. The phallus rested alongside an antlered stag's skull (Burl 1981: 44).

The henge and rings of Stennes and Brogar in the Orkney Islands are good examples of such impressive sacred sites. Stennes henge is 61 m in diameter and has one entrance to the north. A circle of twelve stones with a diameter of about 30 m is set inside the henge. In the center is a rectangle of four flat stones, 2 x 2 m in which cremated animal bones and flint flakes were found. The Brogar ring of 60 stones has a diameter of 103.7 m and is surrounded by a rock-cut ditch with two entrances in the northwest and southeast (Renfrew ed. 1985: Appendix, 263–74). They are contemporary with megalithic tombs (Maes Howe) and dated c. 3100 B.C.

To the same period belongs Stonehenge I, the best known monument of England. Its henge is 320 feet in diameter with 56 shallow pits, called Aubrey Holes, located around its inner circumference. Larger and smaller henges, such as Durrington Walls and Woodhenge two miles away, contained timber buildings inside their enclosures made of concentric circles of wooden posts supporting a cone-shaped roof (Wainwright 1968; 1970). A circular building may also have stood at the center of Stonehenge I (Atkinson 1956; 1979). Since Aubrey Holes yielded cremation deposits, the central building most likely was a temple associated with the funerary or regeneration rituals. The pits in which only small amounts of cremated remains were found as token representations, were laid out around the solar axis of the site. The solar and lunar Station Stones were symmetrically placed among the pits. From this arrangement the general nature of the ritual, as proposed recently by Ray, was an attempt to coordinate the solar and (possibly) lunar cycles with the spirits of the dead represented by the token cremations (Ray 1987: 270). The period of Stonehenge II and III, of considerably later date, may have seen a shift away from the dead toward sky-oriented religion since the monument is focussed upon the midsummer sunrise (Atkinson 1979: 173) due to the influence of the Indo-European religion.

According to Thom and Thom (1978: 122–37), stone rings were lunar and solar observatories. Alexander Thom, who measured hundreds of circles and alignments, believes that the geometry of the stone circles is derived from the extreme positions of the moon and sun as they cross the horizon. Large stones acted as markers (Thom 1971). From astronomical associations we can deduce that the builders of tombs, rings, henges, and avenues developed a considerable body of astronomical knowledge for what were, ultimately, ritual purposes. There was an undeniable interest in the winter solstice, and in particular in marking the position of the moon at that point. This suggests the practice of winter rituals when the sun is at its weakest and seen as dying. Rituals that apparently are inseparable from the lunar Old Hag and the burial of the Old Year's bones are still practiced today (cf. McNeill 1961: 113–25). The purpose of such rituals essentially is the regeneration of life powers, made possible through energetic ring dances combined with the powers of stones standing in a circle. The stone circles are not fully activated unless the calendrical events are accompanied by human rituals and dance. To this day, New Year's celebrations in villages have much to do with magic life-giving water, going round the houses, dancing ring dances, and making noise to protect against the evil winter/death powers.

Avebury's stone circle on the Wiltshire Downs in southwestern England is the largest yet found in that country. Originally it had 98 stones, some up to 5.5 m high, enclosing an area of 28½ acres. Two smaller circles stand within the outer one. The earthworks surrounding the horseshoe or circular space is bounded by a ditch with a bank beyond. Two serpentine stone avenues lead into the circle. They are one and a half miles long, 50 feet wide, and are defined by 100 pairs of stones set at intervals of 80 feet (Burl 1979).

In artist Dames' vision (Dames 1977) Avebury, together with Silbury Hill and the West Kenneth Long Barrow located nearby, was a religious center, perhaps the most important in Britain during the first half of the 3rd millennium B.C. The monuments were created to stage a religious drama that took place over a year's time. The seasonal rites reenacted the cycle of the life and death of nature. Each structure was regarded as a living character, as a superhuman body of the Goddess in spring, summer, fall, and winter. Dames visualizes that puberty rites were reenacted in early February in a wooden temple which once stood at the head of the river Kennet, the wedding of the Goddess with her male consort was celebrated on May 1 at the Avebury Henge, and the Pregnant Goddess was Silbury Hill who gave birth on the August Quarter Day (Lammas). Her delivery of the new crop was celebrated as First Fruits Festival (Big Sunday in Ireland) on a hilltop with dances and games. Finally, Summer's End or Winter's Eve (All Souls Day), the most perilous time, was marked by solemn festivals at the burial grounds. At this time the Tomb Lady took over from the Harvest Goddess inviting her people to follow her retreat into the underground, to West Kenneth Long Barrow, an enormous 340-foot-long earthen mound.

CONCLUSIONS

The Place and Function of the Goddess

The reason for the great number and variety of Old European images lies in the fact that this symbolism is lunar and chthonic, built around the understanding that life on earth is in eternal transformation, in constant and rhythmic change between creation and destruction, birth and death. The moon's three phases—new, waxing, and old—are repeated in trinities or triple-functional deities that recall these moon phases: maiden, nymph, and crone; life-giving, death-giving, and transformational; rising, dying, and self-renewing. Life-givers are also death-wielders. Immortality is secured through the innate forces of regeneration within Nature itself. The concept of regeneration and renewal is perhaps the most outstanding and dramatic theme that we perceive in this symbolism.

It seems more appropriate to view all of these Goddess images as aspects of the one Great Goddess with her core functions—life-giving, death-wielding, regeneration and renewal. The obvious analogy would be to Nature itself; through the multiplicity of phenomena and continuing cycles of which it is made, one recongizes the fundamental and underlying unity of Nature. The Goddess is immanent rather than transcendent and therefore physically manifest.

Let us note here that fertility is only one among the Goddess's many functions. It is inaccurate to call Paleolithic and Neolithic images "fertility goddesses," as is still done in archeological literature. Earth fertility became a prominent concern only in the food-producing era; hence it is not a primary function of the Goddess and has nothing to do with sexuality. The goddesses were mainly life creators, not Venuses or beauties, and most definitely not wives of male gods. The other prevalent general term for the prehistoric divinity is the "Mother Goddess," which is also a misconception. It is true that there are mother images and protectors of young life, and there was a Mother Earth and Mother of the Dead, but the rest of the female images cannot be generalized under the term Mother Goddess. The Bird and Snake Goddesses, for example, are not always mothers, nor are many other images of regeneration such as the Frog, Fish, or Hedgehog Goddess, who are incarnate of transformative powers. They impersonate Life, Death, and Regeneration; they are more than fertility and motherhood.

Eric Neumann, the eminent Jungian psychologist and author of the much-appreciated *The Great Mother* (1955), uses the term Great Mother in the sense of a psychic reality. According to him, the image of the Great Mother developed from the Archetypal Feminine, which ultimately is derived from the uroboros, symbol of the beginning, The Great Round, an unconscious and undifferentiated stage. The uroboric totality is also a symbol of the united primordial parents, from whom the figures of the Great Father and the Great Mother later separated out. The Great Mother eventually split into a Good and a Terrible Mother, according to the positive and negative elements of her character. Neumann also speaks of her transformative character, i.e., developing into the Lady of the Plants and the Lady of the Beasts. This psychological approach has opened new avenues in the interpretation of some aspects of the prehistoric Goddess. And yet I feel the term *mother* devalues her importance and does not allow appreciation of her total character. Further, much of Neumann's archet pe is based on post-Indo-European religious ideology, after the image of the Goddess had suffered a profound and largely debasing transformation. Hence, for the prehistoric period, I prefer the term "Great Goddess" as best describing her absolute rule, her creative, destructive, and regenerative powers.

My archeological research does not confirm the hypothetical existence of the primordial parents and their division into the Great Father and Great Mother figures or the further division of the Great Mother figure into a Good and a Terrible Mother. There is no trace of a father figure in any of the Paleolithic periods. The life-creating power seems to have been of the Great Goddess alone. A complete division into a "good" and a "terrible" Mother never occurred: the Life Giver and the Death Wielder are one deity. Her manifestations are manifold: she may be anthropomorphic or zoomorphic; she may appear in a triple aspect; she may be a waterfowl or a bird of prey, a harmless or a poisonous snake; but ultimately she is one indivisible Goddess. If "good" is life, birth, health, and increase of wealth, she can be called the good Fate. The term "Terrible Mother" needs explanation. The "vulture" or killer aspect of the Goddess is frightening indeed, but if we look at the symbols associated with the aspect of death it becomes clear that these symbols don't exist alone: they are interwoven with those promoting regeneration. The Vulture/Owl/Crow Goddess is both a foreboder of death and a Goddess with breasts and life-creating labyrinths in her abdomen, or she is a triangle (vulva) or an hourglass-shape (double triangle) with vulture's feet, or she is a bee or a butterfly. In her death aspect she is the same Fate who gives life, determines its length, and then takes it away when time comes. She does this because she controls the length of the life cycle. The Death Wielder does not punish men for evil doing or anything of the kind; she only fulfills her necessary duty. The regeneration starts at the moment of death. It begins within the body of the Goddess, in her moist uterus which is expressed in an animal form as a fish, frog, turtle, hedgehog, hare, or the head of the bull.

There was no division into the Lady of Plants and the Lady of Beasts; no deity ruled over the plants or animals separately. The power of the Life Creatrix and Regeneratrix was in animals, plants, water, mountains, and stones. The Goddess may be a bird, a deer, a bear, a vase, an upright stone, or a tree. The anthropomorphic Birth Giver was interchangeable with bear, deer, elk. The protectress of young life, the Nurse, or the Madonna, appeared both as human and as bird, snake, bear.

The unity with nature is particularly clear in the symbolism of the snake; its life energy ramifies into surrounding living creatures: the family members of the house which the snake guards, domestic animals, and trees. Of singular interest is the belief in the immortality of the snake because of its renewal through sloughing off the skin and because of its awakening in the spring after the hibernation period. Because the snake is immortal it is a link between the dead and the living; snakes embody the energy of the ancestors. So do the birds. Perhaps because of the snake-shaped neck of the swan, crane, stork, and goose and their periodic renewal each spring after they have spent the winter months in the south, the symbolism of the bird is interwoven with that of the snake. Both are incarnate of life energy and are the seats of the souls of the dead. The Snake and the Bird Goddesses are guardians (genii, penates) of the family, clan, and later in history, of the city (as Athena of Athens, whose symbols are bird and snake). They oversee the continuity of life energy, the well-being and health of the family, and the increase of the food supply.

The association of the giving and increasing Fate with waterfowl and the ram is that waterfowl was the main food supply from the Paleolithic, and sheep became the most important meat supply from the earliest Neolithic. Why the ram and not the ewe became the sacred animal of the Bird Goddess is difficult to know, but it can be surmised that because the ram's horns are coiled like a snake, it is more powerful as it is imbued with snake's vital energy.

The other functions of the Great Goddess concern fertility, multiplication, and renewal. The process of seasonal awakening, growing, fattening, and dying was seen as connecting humans, animals, and plants: the pregnancy of a woman, the fattening of a sow, the ripening of fruits and crops were interrelated, influencing each other. Again it can be noted that the rising and growing powers of earth dwell in all living things. The pregnancy or the fatness of a woman or an animal was considered to be as holy as the pregnancy of the earth before her flowering in the spring. Each protuberance in nature, be it a mound, a hill, on a menhir or on a female body—belly, buttocks, breasts, knees—was sacred.

The number two and doubleness—two seeds, fruits, buttocks—meant a blessed multiplication. Since it was more than one it had more strength and more influence on fertility. As was said before, fertility was not sexuality; it was multiplication, growing, flourishing. To this class of symbols belong the male deities of rising, flourishing, and dying vegetation: the young, strong, flourishing god and the old, sorrowful, dying god. Within the category of the Mother Earth, there is a division into the contrasting images of young and old, or into mother and daughter images, symbolic of seasonal rising and dying.

A summary of functions and images of the Neolithic Great Goddess and of the male Gods is given in the table on pages 328–329.

Continuity and Transformation of the Goddess in the Indo-European and Christian Eras

The outcome of the clash of Old European with alien Indo-European religious forms is visible in the dethronement of Old European goddesses, the disappearance of temples, cult paraphernalia, and sacred signs, and the drastic reduction of religious images in the visual arts. This impoverishment started in east-central Europe and gradually affected all of central Europe. The Aegean islands, Crete, and the central and western Mediterranean regions continued Old European traditions for several millennia more, but the core of the civilization was lost.

This transformation, however, was not a replacement of one culture by another but a gradual hybridization of two different symbolic systems. Because the androcentric ideology of the Indo-Europeans was that of the new ruling class, it has come down to us as the "official" belief system of ancient Europe. But the Old European sacred images and symbols were never totally uprooted; these most persistent features in human history were too deeply implanted in the psyche. They could have disappeared only with the total extermination of the female population.

The Goddess's religion went underground. Some of the old traditions, particularly those connected with birth, death, and earth fertility rituals, have continued to this day without much change in some regions; in others, they were assimilated into Indo-Euorpean ideology.

In ancient Greece, this created some strange, even absurd, images in the Indo-European pantheon of gods. Most strikingly visible is the conversion of Athena, the Old European Bird Goddess, into a militarized figure carrying a shield and wearing a helmet. The belief in her birth from the head of Zeus, the ruling god of the Indo-Europeans in Greece, shows how far the transformation went—from a parthenogenetic goddess to her birth from a male god! And yet this is not entirely surprising: Zeus was a bull (in Indo-European symbolism the Thunder God is a bull), and Athena's birth from the head of a bull was nothing else but a memory of birth from a bucranium, which was a simulacrum of the uterus in Old European symbolism.

The Death Wielder, the Goddess as a Bird of Prey, was militarized. Portrayals of the Owl Goddess on stone stelae acquired a sword or dagger during the Bronze Age in Sardinia, Corsica, Liguria, southern France, and Spain. The Greek Athena and Irish Morrígan and Badb are known to appear in battle scenes as vultures, crows, cranes, or ravens. The transformation of this Goddess into a mare also occurred during the Bronze Age.

Parthenogenetic goddesses creating from themselves without the help of male insemination gradually changed into brides, wives, and daughters and were eroticized, linked with the principle of sexual love, as a response to a patriarchal and patrilinear system. For example, Greek Hera became the wife of Zeus. Furthermore, Zeus had to "seduce" (with a nod toward historical accuracy, we might prefer the term "rape") hundreds of other goddesses and nymphs to establish himself. Everywhere in Europe, the Earth Mother lost her ability to give birth to plant life without intercourse with the Thunder God or god of the Shining Sky in his spring aspect.

In contrast, the Birth and Life Giver, the Fate or Three Fates, remained remarkably independent in the beliefs of many areas of Europe. Greek Artemis, Irish Brigit, and Baltic Laima, for instance, did not acquire any of the features of an Indo-European god, nor were they married to a god. The Baltic Laima appears in mythological songs together with Dievas, the Indo-European god of the light of the sky, to bless the fields and human life—not as his wife but as an equally powerful goddess.

A remnant in the historical era of the goddesses' ruling power is indicated by the usage of the term *queen* for those who were not married to Indo-European deities but who continued to be powerful in their own right. Herodotus wrote of "Queen Artemis" and Hesychius called Aphrodite "the queen." Diana, the Roman counterpart of the virgin Artemis, was invoked as *regina*.

The worship of the Goddess in Rome and Greece continued strong into the early centuries of our era. This is the time of the expansion of Christianity and of the Egyptian cults over the Roman world. The most inspired account in all ancient literature is contained in Lucius Apuleius' 2nd century A.D. *Golden Ass*, the earliest Latin novel, where Lucius invokes Isis from the depths of his misery. Then she appears and utters: "*I am she that is the natural mother of all things, mistress and governess of all the elements, the initial progeny of worlds, chief of the powers divine, queen of all* that are in Hell, the principal of them all that dwell in Heaven, manifested alone and under one form of all the gods and goddesses. At my will the planets of the sky, the wholesome winds of the seas, and the lamentable silences of hell be disposed; my name, my divinity is adored throughout the world, in divers manners, in variable customs, and by many names" (italics added by author). The text is an illumination with very precious details on the worship of the Goddess nearly 2,000 years ago.

Lucius' invocation is a testimony to the fact that goddesses meant more than gods to people in the first centuries of our era. In the Graeco-Roman world individuals obviously were not satisfied with what the official Indo-European religion offered. Secret cults—Mystery Religions (Dionysiac, Eleusinian), clearly continuous from Old Europe—were practiced. They provided a way to feel religious experiences in old ways.

In later Christian times, the Birth Giver and Earth Mother fused with the Virgin Mary. Thus it is not surprising that in Catholic countries the worship of the Virgin surpasses that of Jesus. She is still connected with life-water and miraculously healing springs, with trees, blossoms, and flowers, with fruits and harvests. She is pure, strong, and just. In folk sculptures of the Mother of God, she is huge and powerful, holding a tiny Christ on her lap.

Old European goddesses appear in European folktales, beliefs, and mythological songs. The Bird Goddess and anthropomorphic Life-giving Goddess continue as a Fate or Fairy and also as a luck- and wealth-bringing duck, swan, and ram. As a prophesier she is a cuckoo. As a Primeval Mother she is known as a supernatural deer (Irish mythology) or bear (Greek, Baltic, and Slavic).

Worship of the nonpoisonous snake as a symbol of life energy, cyclic renewal, and immortality continued until the twentieth century. The hibernating and awakening snake as a metaphor of dying and reawakening nature and as an essential symbol of the immortality of life energy was forgotten neither in Ireland nor in Lithuania of our century. The crown of a large snake (Queen) remains the symbol of wisdom.

The presence of the White Lady, "Death," who is also a bird of prey and a poisonous snake, was felt in many corners of Europe to this century. The shudder-inducing images—a tall slim woman dressed in white, an owl screeching, wailing like a bird of prey, crawling like a poisonous snake—are straight from the Neolithic. The White Lady was not transformed into an Indo-European black god of death. The use of bone and the colors white and yellow as symbols of death remained in European beliefs side by side with black as the color of death of the Indo-European and Christian religions.

The Killer-Regeneratrix, the overseer of cyclic life energy, the personification of winter, and Mother of the Dead, was turned into a witch of night and magic. In the period of the Great Inquisition, she was considered to be a disciple of Satan. The dethronement of this truly formidable goddess whose legacy was carried on by wise women, prophetesses, and healers who were the best and bravest minds of the time, is marked by blood and is the greatest shame of the Christian Church. The witch hunt of the 15th–18th centuries is a most satanic event in European history in the name of Christ. The murder of women accused as witches escalated to more than eight million. The burned or hanged victims were mostly simple country women who learned the lore and the secrets of the Goddess from their mothers or grandmothers. In 1484, Pope Innocent VIII in a Papal Bull denounced witchcraft as an organized conspiracy of the Devil's army against the Holy Christian Empire. In 1486, a handbook of the witch hunters, called *Malleus Maleficarum*, "Hammer of Witches," appeared and became an indispensable authority for terror and murder. The use of any means of physical and psychological torture to force confessions out of the accused was allowed. The period can boast of greatest creativity in the discovery of tools and methods of torture. This was the beginning of the dangerous convulsions of androcratic rule which 460 years later reached the peak in Stalin's East Europe with the torture and murder of fifty million women, children, and men.

In spite of the horrible war against women and their lore and the demonization of the Goddess, the memories of her live on in fairy tales, rituals, customs, and in language. Collections such as Grimm's German tales are rich in prehistoric motifs describing the functions of this Winter Goddess, Frau Holla (Holle, Hell, Holda, Perchta, etc.). She is the ugly Old Hag with a long nose, large teeth, and disheveled hair. Her strength lingers in her teeth and hair. She is a snow- and weather-making woman. At the same time she regenerates nature. She is a woman who brings out the sun. Once a year she appears as a dove, a blessing ensuring fertility. As a frog, Holla brings the red apple, symbol of life, back to earth from the well into which it fell at harvest. Her realm is the inner depth of mountains and caves (*Holla*, the name of the Goddess, and *Höhle*, the name for "cave" are certainly related. *Hell* in its present meaning is a doing of Christian missionaries). To Holla, as the Mother of the Dead, sacrifices were made in the form of baking a bread called *Hollenzopf*, "Holla's braid," at Christmas time. *Holler, Holunder*, "elder tree," was the sacred tree of the Goddess having healing powers. Under this tree lived the dead. The same goddess still plays a prominent role in beliefs of other Europeans as the Baltic Ragana, Russian Baba Yaga, Polish Jędza, Serbian Mora, Morava, Basque Mari, Irish Morrígan. This powerful goddess was not wiped out from the mythical world. Today she is an inspiration for the revival of herbology and other healing crafts and more than any other images of goddesses strengthens the confidence in women.

There is no question that Old European sacred images and symbols remain a vital part of the cultural heritage of Europe. Most of us were surrounded in childhood by the fairy world, which contained many images transmitted from Old Europe. In some nooks of Europe, as in my own motherland, Lithuania, there still flow sacred and miraculous rivers and springs, there flourish holy forests and groves, reservoirs of blossoming life, there grow gnarled trees brimming with vitality and holding the power to heal; along waters there still stand menhirs, called "Goddesses," full of mysterious power.

The Old European culture was the matrix of much later beliefs and practices. Memories of a long-lasting gynocentric past could not be erased, and it is not surprising that the feminine principle plays a formidable role in the subconscious dream and fantasy world. It remains (in Jungian terminology) "the repository of human experience" and a "depth structure." To an archeologist it is an extensively documented historical reality.

The World View of the Culture of the Goddess

Celebration of life is the leading motif in Old European ideology and art. There is no stagnation; life energy is constantly moving as a serpent, spiral, or whirl. Recall the richly painted vases of the Cucuteni, Dimini, Butmir, and Minoan cultures, and sense the moving, turning, rising, splitting, and growing energy they portray, the splendid combination of colors with ochre red, the color of life, predominating. Life columns, upward winding snakes, leafy trees, bees, and butterflies rising from tombs, caves, crevices, or the Goddess's powerful uterus. One form dissolves into another. The transformation of human to animal, snake to tree, uterus to fish, frog, hedgehog, and bucranium, bucranium to butterfly, was a perception of the reemergence of life energy in another form.

This is not to say that death was neglected. In art it is impressively manifested in the nakedness of bone, howling hounds, screeching owls, swooping vultures, and dangerous boars. The question of mortality was of profound concern but the deep perception of the periodicity of nature based on the cycles of the moon and the female body led to the creation of a strong belief in the immediate regeneration of life at the crisis of death. There was no simple death, only death *and* regeneration. And this was the key to the hymn of life reflected in this art.

Sacred images and symbols, goddesses and gods, their birds and animals, mysterious snakes, batrachians, and insects, were more real than actual daily events. They reveal to us the ultimate context in which Old Europeans lived. These symbols remain the only real access to this invigorating, earth-centered, life-reverencing worldview, since we are now far removed from the society that created this imagery. Freud would have denigrated such imagery as "primitive fantasies." Jung would probably have valued it as "the fruits of the inner life flowing out from the unconscious."

The Goddess in all her manifestations was a symbol of the unity of all life in Nature. Her power was in water and stone, in tomb and cave, in animals and birds, snakes and fish, hills, trees, and flowers. Hence the holistic and mythopoeic perception of the sacredness and mystery of all there is on Earth.

This culture took keen delight in the natural wonders of *this* world. Its people did not produce lethal weapons or build forts in inaccessible places, as their successors did, even when they were acquainted with metallurgy. Instead, they built magnificent tomb-shrines and temples, comfortable houses in moderately-sized villages, and created superb pottery and sculptures. This was a long-lasting period of remarkable creativity and stability, an age free of strife. Their culture was a culture of art.

The images and symbols in this volume assert that the parthenogenetic Goddess has been the most persistent feature in the archeological record of the ancient world. In Europe she ruled throughout the Paleolithic and Neolithic, and in Mediterranean Europe throughout most of the Bronze Age. The next stage, that of the pastoral and patriarchal warrior gods, who either supplanted or assimilated the matristic pantheon of goddesses and gods, represents an intermediary stage before Christianity and the spread of the philosophical rejection of this world. A prejudice against this worldliness developed and with it the rejection of the Goddess and all she stood for.

The Goddess gradually retreated into the depths of forests or onto mountaintops, where she remains to this day in beliefs and fairy stories. Human alienation from the vital roots of earthly life ensued, the results of which are clear in our contemporary society. But the cycles never stop turning, and now we find the Goddess reemerging from the forests and mountains, bringing us hope for the future, returning us to our most ancient human roots.

Glossary of Symbols

Antithetic snake heads or spirals
Energy symbols, starter of motion and torsion

Arcs, multiple
In vertical columns: rising life

Axe
Energy symbol, because of its roughly triangular form symbolically linked with the female triangle (vulva)

Batrachians (amphibians), toads, frogs, lizards
Epiphanies of the Goddess in her function of regeneration; symbols of the wandering uterus

Bear
Primeval birth-giver, pregnant woman, (bear-masked) mother

Bee
Symbol of regeneration and epiphany of the Goddess of Regeneration

Belly
(See *hill, oven, pregnant.*)

Bi-line
Pregnancy, doubleness, more than one

Bird
Main epiphany of the Goddess as Giver-of-all, including life and death, happiness, and wealth; *alias* Fate. Waterfowl (duck, goose, swan) bring happiness, wealth, nourishment; birds of prey (vulture, owl, raven, crow) are omens of death and epiphanies of the Death Wielder; prophetic birds (cuckoo, owl) prophesy spring, marriage, and death; birds of the soul (dove, cuckoo, and other small birds) are seats of the souls of the human dead.

Bird's feet
(See *feet.*)

Black
Color of fertility

Boar
Symbol of death and regeneration

Bone
Symbol of death. Phalange: epiphany of the Goddess of Death

Breasts
Pars pro toto of the Bird Goddess in her life- and nourishment- or wealth-giving functions. In megalithic tombs they represent the regenerative powers of the same Goddess.

Brush
Energy sign associated with the Goddess in her function of regeneration, often associated with vulva. Interchangeable with wings and ship. Apotropeic symbol in the shape of a comb.

Brautstein
German for "bridestone," a stone having the power to bestow fecundity on barren women. The polished surface of such stones is from the oft-repeated sliding of naked hindparts.

Bucranium
Bull head and horns, simulacrum of a woman's uterus; symbol of regeneration

Bull
Symbol of the source of life and regeneration. Epiphany of the Goddess of Regeneration. Appears with a head of a vulture on Minoan sarcophagi. Sacrificial animal in funeral rites.

Butterfly
Epiphany of the Goddess of Regeneration, emerging from a bucranium; in Minoan art, from between the horns of consecration. Related to hourglass and X.

Buttocks
Symbol of the strength of two, related to breasts, double fruit, double seed, and other doubles and considered to be life-creating and pregnant parts of the Goddess's body. In Bird Goddess representations, pronounced buttocks imitate a bird's body (if viewed from the profile).

Cairn
A heap or round mound of stones over graves, sometimes of white and shining quartz stones, symbolic either of the egg (regeneration) or of death (the color of bone)

Caterpillar
Symbol of becoming, related to the crescent moon and horn

Cave
The Goddess's regenerative womb

Centaur, bull-man
Stimulator of life energy

Checkerboard
Symbol of the sphere of water, life water. Alternates with net (see *net*).

Chevron, double or triple V
(See V.)

Circle, single or concentric
Engraved on rocks or on standing stones, a transmitter of the concentrated divine energy of the center (cupmark, well, menhir), related to the sacred ring dance

Comb
(See *brush.*)

Court tomb
A chamber tomb of anthropomorphic shape found in southwest Scotland and northern Ireland, hence the alternative name "Clyde-Carlingford tomb." Essential features include an elongated trapeze or triangular shaped cairn with an unroofed semicircular forecourt at one end. The court gives access to the burial chamber proper, which is either a gallery of two or more chambers or is outlined in an anthropomorphic (Goddess's) form. Dated to c. 3500–2200 B.C.

Crescent
Energy sign, symbol of becoming, denoting the beginning phase of the lunar cycle

Crow
Epiphany of the Goddess of Death and Regeneration. Interrelated with raven, owl, vulture. In Irish mythology, Badb is one of the names of the Celtic Triple Goddess Morrígan; in Baltic, of Ragana.

Cuckoo
The prophetic Goddess's (Fate's) bird, omen of spring and death. Epiphany of the Goddess in the spring season, turning into a hawk in the autumn and winter. Also a soul bird.

Cupmark
A depression in stone filled with the sacred water of the Goddess/Life giver. Source of life and health, related to the divine eye (see *eyes*) and well (see *well*).

Deer, doe
Primeval mother as supernatural deer-doe. Epiphany of the Birth-giving Goddess.

Dog
White (gray) hound, sacred to the Goddess of Death and her epiphany. Omen of death. On the other hand, stimulator and guardian of young life.

Dolmen
A round or rectangular chamber tomb ("large table") of early megalithic western Europe. The portal dolmen, a chamber tomb found mainly in Ireland, but also in Wales and Cornwall. The rectangular burial chamber usually becomes narrower and lower towards the rear; it is approached through two tall portal slabs which form a miniature porch or forecourt.

Double figures
Two fruits grown together, two seeds, caterpillars, snakes, phalli, or human figures and temples. Symbol of the strength of two, seasonal Earth Fertility Goddess, summer/winter, young/old duality.

Dove
Bird of spring and soul bird

Duck
Main epiphany of the Bird Goddess in her function as Apportioner and as deity bringing luck, wealth, and nourishment

Egg
Universal symbol of regeneration

Elk-doe or reindeer-doe
(See *deer.*)

Eyes
The generative source of the necrotic Owl Goddess, associated with aquatic symbolism (streams, cupmarks). Interchangeable with radiating suns, snake coils, and ram horns.

Feet, bird's
Pars pro toto of the Goddess of Death and Regeneration

Fish
Symbol of the uterus and regeneration, epiphany of the Goddess in her regenerative function

Fleece
The Bird Goddess's sign; appears on loom-weights and Bird Goddess figurines

Footprints
Symbolic of the Goddess's presence, a stimulating and healing force; if filled with water, related to cupmarks

Frog or toad
Symbol of the uterus or wandering uterus, epiphany of the Goddess of Death and Regeneration

Gallery grave
A corridor-like or vagina-shaped megalithic tomb, typical of Brittany. Dated to 3000–2500 B.C.

Goat, he-goat
Stimulator of awakening nature, guardian of young life, portrayed flanking the life tree. Participant in animal processions, symbols of cyclic time.

Gold, color of death
(See *bone, white.*)

Goose
One of the epiphanies of the Bird Goddess as Apportioner and as deity bringing wealth and nourishment

Gorgoneion, mask
Frightening face of the Snake and Bird Goddess in her death aspect

Hands, divine
Stimulating force, prophylactic against the powers of evil and death

Hare
Epiphany of the Goddess in her regenerative function

Hedgehog
Symbol of the uterus, epiphany of the Goddess of Death and Regeneration. Most likely derives from the form of the cow uterus.

Hill
Simulacrum of the pregnant belly of the Earth Mother (Pregnant Goddess)

Holed stone
Crawling through meant strengthening with the Goddess's energy stored in the stone; renewal, initiation, health.

Hook, crozier
Energy symbol, serpent force, related to horn and spiral

Horn
Energy sign, symbol of becoming, interchangeable with the crescent and hook

Hourglass (two triangles joined at tips)
Simplified anthropomorphic shape of the Goddess of Death and Regeneration in her guise as a bird of prey. Bird's claws reveal her identity.

Hypogeum
A subterranean tomb, most frequently egg-shaped, symbolic of regeneration. The grand tomb of Hal Saflieni in Malta was three stories high with many egg-shaped chambers.

Ithyphallic figure, male
Stimulator of rising life energy, interchangeable with phallus and snake

Knob
(See *omphalos.*)

Labyrinth
Regenerative womb associated with images of the Owl and Fish Goddess

Lens
(See *seed.*)

Life column
Symbol of life rising from water, cave, or womb in a variety of shapes, portrayed in tombs, temples, and on pottery; watery mass, multiple arcs, vertically winding snake, tree, snake and tree combined, fir tree or fern, phallus, stalagmites and stalactites in caves.

Lozenge
With a dot, sign of the pregnant Goddess, fertility symbol. Two triangles joined at bases, related to triangle symbolism, regeneration.

M
Sign for water, related to the Egyptian hieroglyph M, Greek *mu*, and emblem of the Goddess in her life-giving function

Meander
Water, angularized water snake; associated with waterbirds, especially ducks, and the Bird Goddess

Megalithic grave
A tomb built of large stones (*mega,* "large"; *lithos,* "stone"). (See *court tomb, dolmen, gallery grave, passage grave.*) Most megalithic structures served as ossuaries and shrines.

Menhir
A standing stone. Epiphany of the Bird Goddess, Giver of Life and Death (Fate)

Mound
Pregnant belly of the Earth Mother, akin to hill and oven

Mouth
As a round depression or open beak of the Bird Goddess: nurturing source of this Goddess. As a dash with three lines emanating: triple life source.

Mushroom
(See *phallus.*)

Net
Source, moisture, "water of life" or amniotic fluid, pubic hair, wool; associated with fish, lozenge, triangle, egg, and uterine signs and life-giving functions of the Goddess.

Octopus
Epiphany of the Goddess in her regenerative function, portrayed on Late Minoan sarcophagi

Oculi
(See *eyes.*)

Omphalos
Navel of the Earth Mother, concentrated life-producing power, stone or circular summit of a hill (pregnant belly of pregnant Earth Mother), knob or unevenness on a menhir, umbilical cord or snake on the Goddess's portrayals. Head of the abstract hill-shaped figure of the Goddess in megalithic art.

Oven, bread, shaped as a pregnant belly
Symbolic of the pregnant belly of the Earth Fertility Goddess; related to hill and mound

Owl
Prophetic bird, death messenger, epiphany of the Goddess as Death Wielder, but has regenerative qualities. Images appear on stelae and megalithic tombs of W Europe and as urns in SE Europe and W Anatolia.

Passage grave
The main category of megalithic or chamber tombs: a round mound covering the burial chamber, approached by a narrow entrance passage which is very distinct from the funerary chamber; symbolic of the regenerative Goddess's uterus and vagina. Found in Brittany, Scotland, Ireland, Wales, northwest Germany, and Sweden. Dated from the 5th to 3rd millennia B.C. Large passage graves with engravings (Gavrinis, Newgrange, Knowth) should be called "Tomb Shrines."

Phallus
Symbol of spontaneous life energy, interrelated with the life column, plant, and mushroom, closely linked with the Indian *lingam.* Fused in sculptures with the female body, the phallus enhances the life power of the Goddess Creatrix.

Pregnant, belly
Symbol of fertility. In the Neolithic, of the Earth or Grain Mother and Mother of the Dead

Pubic triangle
(See *triangle, vulva.*)

Ram
Magic, wealth-bringing animal, sacred to the Bird Goddess, associated with waterfowl and the snake. Ram horns interchange with snake coil and oculi motifs.

Raven
Epiphany of the Goddess of Death and Regeneration. In Germanic mythology of *Valkyrie,* in Celtic (Irish) of *Morrígan,* and in Celtic Gaul of *Nantotsuelta,* all interrelated goddesses. (See *crow, owl, vulture.*)

Red
The color of life

Seed
Birth and embryonic life symbol, homologue of the vulva

Serpent
(See *snake.*)

Serpentiform
A winding snake, often with 14–17 twinings denoting the waxing moon, or with 29–30 symbolizing the days of the moon cycle.

Ship
"Vehicle" to the afterlife and regeneration. In megalithic tomb-shrines, it appears in association with the serpent and the Goddess of Death and Regeneration. On Bronze Age rocks of southern Scandinavia, it is portrayed with serpent, life tree, sun, and cult scenes.

Snake
Life force; transfunctional symbol; coil, cosmic life source, with a meaning similar to the divine eye, sun energy, and full moon. Horizontally winding (see *serpentiform*), upward winding (see *life column*).

Sow
Sacred animal of the Pregnant Goddess (Earth Mother)

Spiral
Energy symbol, serpent force, symbolic abstraction of the dynamic snake

Stone
The Goddess's power. (See *brautstein, circle, holed stone, menhir, omphalos.*)

Stream
The Goddess's life- and health-giving water (see *well*) and rain water bringing abundance

Sun
Symbol of seasonal renewal associated with the Goddess of Death and Regeneration. Interchangeable with the Goddess's eyes, snake coil, and ram horn coils.

Swallow
Prophetic bird of spring

Swan
One of the epiphanies of the Bird Goddess, the diety bringing wealth, luck, happiness. Associated with music.

Toad
(See *frog.*)

Tomb
The Goddess's regenerative womb. (See *hypogeum, megalithic grave.*)

Triangle
Regenerative womb of the Goddess, the earliest of all known symbols (evidenced in the Paleolithic)

Tri-line, number three
Totality, abundance, triple source, triple spring; associated with birth/life-giving functions of the Goddess

Turtle
Symbol of regeneration, epiphany of the Goddess in her regenerative function, related to the frog and hedgehog

Umbilical cord or unevenness on stone projections (see *omphalos*)
Serpentine connection between the mother and new life. Appears on the Goddess's images in her aspect of death and regeneration, most frequently on the Owl Goddess.

Uterus
Symbol of regeneration as the Goddess's womb, womb-shaped tomb, and cave; in zoomorphic form as a fish, frog or toad, hedgehog, and bucranium

V
The Bird Goddess's emblem from Upper Paleolithic times, derived from a triangle (i.e., pubic triangle, vulva). A main sign in the sacred script of Old Europe.

Vulture
Epiphany of the Goddess of Death and Regeneration

Vulva
External female genitalia as the concentrated life-producing part of the Goddess in her birth-giving functions. Also a generic term for all vulvic shapes: oval, seed or lens, and triangle. *Pars pro toto* of the Goddess encountered on rocks from the Upper Paleolithic.

Waterbird
Main epiphany of the Bird Goddess in her life- and health-giving function

Wavy lines
Water, stream

Well
A source of life owned by the Life-giving Goddess (Fate). Concentrated life power under a stone (menhir), usually surrounded by a stone circle or ditch.

Whirl
Four-corner sign and cross. Energy signs, usually associated with the life column or rising Goddess of Regeneration, serving as stimulators.

White
The color of bone, symbolic of death. Relatives: yellow, gold, amber, marble, alabaster

Womb
(See *cave, tomb, uterus.*)

X
Four-corner sign and the emblem (cross-bands) of the Bird Goddess. On seals and figurines associated with the chevron. Framed: interchangeable with the hourglass and butterfly.

Types of Goddesses and Gods

The Old European evidence reveals clear-cut stereotypes of divinities, including anthropomorphic ones, and bird, snake, and other animal hybrids. They have been grouped into the following types:

The Bird Goddess

(figs. 2, 8–13, 15, 16, 39, 41, 42) She appears with a beak or pinched nose, long neck, hairdo or crown, female breasts, either wings or winglike projections, and protruding female buttocks outlined in the shape of a bird's body. She has no mouth, but sometimes a round depression in its place. Her posture is erect, but the upper part of her body is bent forward like a bird's. Meanders, V's, and chevrons are her symbols. She is associated with the number three as a triple source and with the ram, her sacred animal. Multiple chevrons, breasts, and a beak-and-eyes symbol are typical decorative designs on vases associated with her. She is worshipped in temples and house shrines from the Early Neolithic.

The Birth-Giving Anthropomorphic Goddess

(figs. 172–76) This aspect of the Goddess is portrayed in a naturalistic birth-giving pose. She is well evidenced in Paleolithic art and later in Old Europe. The vulva depicted alone may have served as *pars pro toto* of this Goddess. Her main epiphanies are deer/doe, elk/doe, and bear.

The Nurse or Mother Holding a Child

(fig. 184) She is portrayed in "hunchbacked" figurines or, in more articulate examples, as a bear-masked Madonna carrying a baby pouch. Mother or nurse images also appear in bird and snake form (fig. 211).

The Snake Goddess

(figs. 200–215) She has snakelike hands and feet, a long mouth, and round eyes; she wears a crown. The snake and its abstracted derivatives, the spiral and snake coil, are her emblems. The crown is the symbol of status, wisdom, and omniscience. As a guardian of life energy and its continuity, she is worshipped in house shrines.

The Bird of Prey Goddess

(figs. 285–302) Appears as Death or Death Messenger in the guise of a vulture, owl, or other birds of prey and carrion eaters; but she also embodies qualities of regeneration. In the megalithic tombs of western Europe she appears as an owl or other bird of prey in stone stelae, engravings, and paintings. In reduced form she is simply eyes, breasts, or vulva. Her supernatural eyes are interchangeable with snake coils, ram horns, and radiating suns. In the cremation graves of Danubian Europe and western Anatolia, the owl takes the shape of an urn. The Vulture and Owl Goddess is associated with the symbols of regeneration and energy: labyrinths, umbilical cords, spirals, serpents, concentric circles, concentric arcs, cupmarks, hooks, axes, and moon crescents and cycles.

The Goddess as Triangle and Hourglass

(figs. 373–82) She appears in caves, subterranean tombs, and megalithic graves as a regenerative womb. Painted on vases, this shape represents participants in ritual ring dances. The bird's claws attached to the hourglass shape identify it as another manifestation of the Bird of Prey Goddess.

The Stiff Nude as Death

(figs. 308–18, 320) She is portrayed with folded arms tightly pressed to her bosom and closed or tapering legs. She is masked. Her large, supernatural pubic triangle is the center of attention. A reduced image of her is a bone phalange, undecorated or with round (owl's) eyes (figs. 91, 92). Her images are made from materials the color of bone—marble, alabaster, light-colored stone or clay, and bone itself. She is evidenced from the Upper Paleolithic through Old Europe, with an extension into the mid-2nd millennium B.C. in the Aegean area and the Danube valley. Occasionally portrayed features of bird of prey and of a poisonous snake betray her identity with the Bird and Snake Goddess in her death-wielding aspect.

The Toad/Frog Goddess

(figs. 387–96) Appears in the Upper Paleolithic as an anthropomorphized batrakhian and continues throughout prehistory and history. During the Neolithic, images of the frog-shaped female body with a human head are found as reliefs on shrine walls and vases, carved out of marble, greenstone, blackstone, and other stone, or modeled in clay. The image is an epiphany of the Goddess of Regeneration. The toad/frog is a homologue of the regenerative uterus.

The Hedgehog Goddess

(figs. 379–404) Another epiphany of the Goddess in the function of regeneration. Appears in the shape of a hedgehog with a human head. The image most likely derives from the form of animal uterus. As a potent charm against sterility this symbol survived to the 20th century.

The Fish Goddess

(figs. 405–10) Hybrid of woman and fish marked with a labyrinthine design or net symbolic of generative power or uterine moisture. The fish must have been homologized with the Goddess's uterus from no later than the Upper Paleolithic and as such continues through prehistory and early history. Bird's feet shown on Fish Goddess sculptures identify her as Goddess of Death and Regeneration.

Bee and Butterfly Goddess

(figs. 420–32) An epiphany of the Goddess of Regeneration rising from a bucranium (i.e., uterus) or from caves and tombs. She is portrayed as an insect with human characteristics or as a woman with insect limbs and head. Prominent in Neolithic hypogea and in Minoan religion.

The Pregnant Goddess

(figs. 216–19) She is portrayed naturalistically as a nude with hands placed on her enlarged belly. Her fatness is emphasized and likened to field fertility. Her image is associated with lozenges, triangles, snakes, double-egg/double-fruit symbols, and two or four lines. Her sacred animal in Old Europe and later periods is the sow (figs. 225, 227). Although recorded in the Upper Paleolithic, this image probably becomes the Grain Mother not earlier than the Neolithic. She is the dominant image in the early phases of the Neolithic, usually found on oven platforms. Her belly is a bulging mound or oven.

Master of Animals: Male God Holding a Hook

He may be a forerunner, on the one hand, of the Silvanus, Faunus, and Pan, forest spirits and protectors of forest animals and hunters who also hold hooks; and on the other hand a descendent from Upper Paleolithic animal-robed figures.

Daimon of Fertility and Regeneration

In the form of an ithyphallic youthful man, phallic stand, phallus or snake, an attendant to the Goddess when she rises in the spring from the earth (fig. 278), he is a likely forerunner of Greek Hermes, god of luck and increase and protector of flocks, as well as Basque Aker-beltz and Sugaar, the Black He-Goat and Male Snake. Other representatives of the masculine principle, such as nude men with bird masks, probably are portrayals of participants in rituals or worshipers of the Goddess.

The God of Annual Renewal: Youthful and Sorrowful

(figs. 281, 282, 284) He is portrayed as a youthful or peaceful man sitting on a stool, hands either resting on his knees or supporting his chin. Since sorrowful figures are found together with seated pregnant figurines which probably represent harvest goddesses (old hags), it can be assumed that they portray a dying vegetation god. The goat-masked male sculptures may represent the youthful aspect, an early form of Dionysus.

Summary of Functions and Images of the Neolithic Great Goddess

A. LIFE-GIVING, DEATH-WIELDING, REGENERATION (lunar: rising, dying, self-renewing)		
I. "Giver of All": Giver of life and health, foreteller of spring, increaser (or decreaser) of material goods, and protectress of human and animal life and household	**II. Death Wielder**	**III. Regeneratrix**
1. Birth-Giver a. Anthropomorphic Giver of birth b. Primeval Mother in the shape of bear, deer-doe, or elk doe	1. Death Foreboder and Killer a. Vulture-woman, owl-woman, snake-woman b. Epiphanies: owl, raven, crow, other birds of prey; boar, white dog, poisonous snake	1. As Regnerative Vulva a. oval or seed-shaped b. triangle c. axe
2. Giver of Life Water and Health a. Standing stone (menhir) as epiphany of the Goddess, guardian of life water b. Vessel: anthropomorphic or bird-shaped. Aquatic images ("parallel line square Goddess" and others)	2. Death Goddess a. Bone (bone phalange with or without owl eyes) b. Anthropomorphic Stiff Nude "White Lady," sometimes with bird of prey or snake features c. Frightening mask (with features of a poisonous snake), antecedent of the Gorgon head	2. Anthropomorphized as a. triangle with breasts b. hourglass-shaped with vulture's/ owl's feet for hands
3. Spring and Future Foreteller a. Young (Artemis type) Goddess b. Spring birds: cuckoo, oriole, swallow, lark, dove		3. As Regenerative Uterus a. zoomorphic shape: bucranium, fish, frog, toad, hedgehog, turtle, lizard, hare b. anthropomorphized as fish-woman, frog-woman, hedgehog-woman
4. Increaser (or Decreaser) of Material Goods and Happiness a. Water-fowl/woman hybrid b. Epiphanies: duck, goose, crane, swan, stork, snake c. Sacred animal: ram		4. As Transformed Into a. bee, butterfly, or moth, usually portrayed rising from the head or between the horns of the bull b. anthropomorphic bee, butterfly, and other insects
5. Embodiment of Life Energy, Healer and Regenerator, Protector of Household a. Serpent-woman b. Crowned or horned snake c. Genii or penates of household, humans and animals in the shape of snakes or phallic men		5. As Life Column in the shape of aquatic column (wavy lines, concentric arches), vertically rising snake, phallus, or tree, associated with or flanked by symbols of becoming (uteri, horns, spirals, crescents, a moon cycle, dogs, he-goats, ithyphallic men)
6. Protectress of Young Life a. Nurse (carrying a pouch), hunchback figurines b. Madonna (holding baby), both anthro-pomorphic and zoomorphic (bird, snake, bear)		

B. FERTILITY, MULTIPLICATION, RENEWAL (chthonic: seasonal rising, growing, fattening, and dying)	
I. Giver of Seasonal Earth Fertility	**II. Mother of the Dead**
1. a. Anthropomorphic pregnant b. Sacred animal: sow. c. Metaphors of pregnant belly: hill, stone, oven, protuberance on stone or female body	1. Cave
2. Rising in the Spring a. Young with upraised arms b. Hill with an omphalos or snake	2. Grave in the shape of an egg, vagina and uterus, pregnant belly, or whole body of the Goddess; in this aspect inseparable from the Regeneratrix
3. Ripe pregnant, old pregnant, and androgynous	
4. Double Goddess: Mother/Daughter, summer/winter metaphor	

Functions and Images of Male Gods

I. Male Guardian/Owner of Wild Animals and Forests	II. Household Protector	III. Male God of Rising and Dying Vegetation
1. Anthropomorphic, bearded	1. Male snake/phallus	1. Anthropomorphic, young; epiphanies: bull, he-goat
2. Enthroned, holding a hook	2. Ithyphallic anthropomorphic	2. Old, sorrowful

Chronologies

CHRONOLOGY

How to put an accurate date on an archeological find of 8,000 to 5,000 years ago? Thanks to a variety of new techniques that tell time backwards, archeologists are incomparably more fortunate today than thirty or forty years ago. There are no written records, but there are two dating methods essential for the chronology of these millennia: the radiocarbon, or carbon 14; and dendrochronology, or tree-ring counting.

Carbon 14 is the best-known example of an atomic clock based upon radioactive decay. It changes its atomic structure by the processes of radioactivity at a fixed rate, specified in terms of its "half life." Half of a given amount decays in 5,730 years. The radiocarbon method can be applied to things that once were alive. Excavations normally yield organic material such as charcoal, grain seeds, twigs, bones. These do reveal traces of carbon 14, thereby helping date whatever inorganic objects were associated with them.

Some years later after the discovery of radiocabon dating in 1949 by W. F. Libby, by testing samples whose ages were already known, it was shown that carbon 14 dates are too young, in some periods even by 600 to 900 years. Thus the dates had to be double-checked by some other method. One of the approaches was to calibrate the radiocarbon dates with the tree-ring dates.

Tree-ring dating depends on the fact that some trees, especially conifers in the temperate zone, add a new growth layer around their trunks every year. The most ancient and useful tree for dendrochronology is the bristlecone pine found high in the White Mountains of east-central California, some as old as 4,600 years and possibly much more. The tree-ring calendar based on living and dead bristlecone pines was established by Arizona Laboratory of Tree-ring Research (started by E. Schulman and continued by C. W. Ferguson). By now this chronology goes back as far as 6700 B.C., and there is a good chance that the record will be soon carried back as far as 10,000 years before present.

For years the radiocarbon dates were compared with the tree-ring dates. Hundreds of samples were measured in several laboratories. By 1969 Hans Suess of University of California San Diego produced a graph, or "calibration curve," which shows by how much carbon 14 dates are too late, thus providing the means of correcting them. The calibration curve is enormously helpful for the establishment of the Neolithic and Copper Age chronology. The dates used in this volume are calibrated radiocarbon dates.

Most of the objects discussed and illustrated in this book are intentionally chosen from radiocarbon-dated contexts and then calibrated. In cases where they are not, if they are from early excavations or if their provenance is unknown, their chronology is based on typological and stylistic comparison with well-dated objects. Dates from the periods earlier than the 7th millennium B.C. are based on radiocarbon dates (their calibration is not possible).

Five chronological charts are given. 1. Upper Paleolithic; 2. Neolithic and Copper Age of east-central and southeast Europe; 3. Neolithic of western and central Europe; 4. Neolithic of northern and central Europe; and 5. Minoan Crete. Maps of the respective cultures and the distribution of sites mentioned in the text are provided on pages 337–353.

CHART 1
Upper Paleolithic chronology in western Europe
Classification of figurative styles from I to IV after Leroi-Gourhan 1967

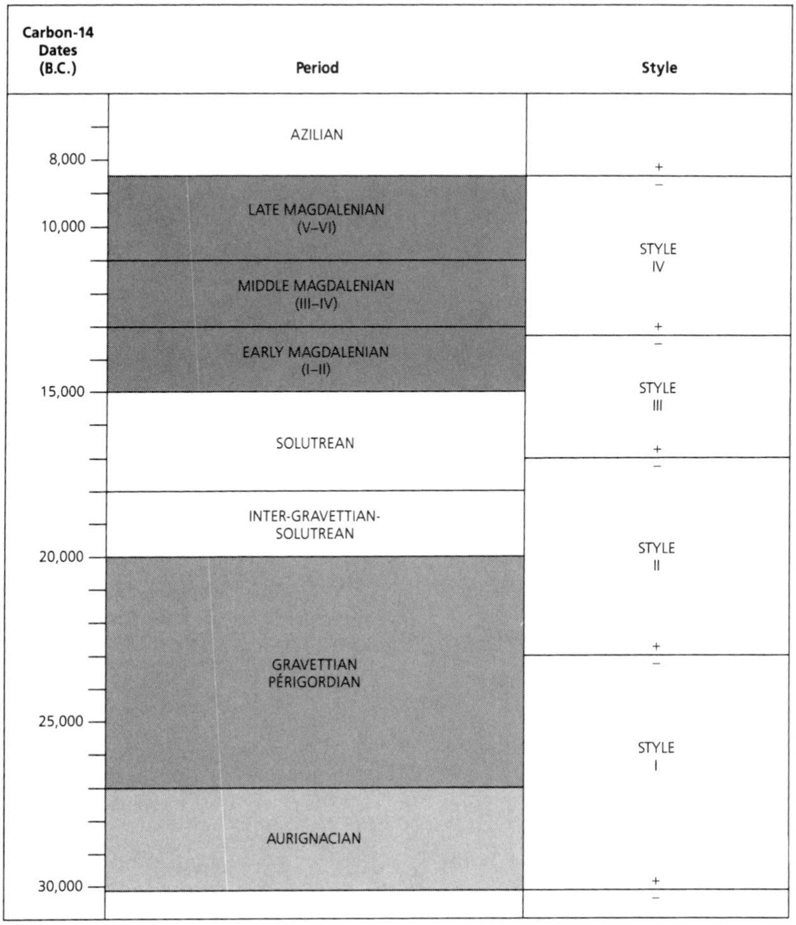
Carbon-14 Dates (B.C.)
Period
Style
8,000
10,000
15,000
20,000
25,000
30,000
AZILIAN
LATE MAGDALENIAN (V–VI)
MIDDLE MAGDALENIAN (III–IV)
EARLY MAGDALENIAN (I–II)
SOLUTREAN
INTER-GRAVETTIAN-SOLUTREAN
GRAVETTIAN PÉRIGORDIAN
AURIGNACIAN
STYLE IV
STYLE III
STYLE II
STYLE I

CHART 2
Chronological table of the Neolithic and Copper Age cultures in east-central and southeast Europe.
The 5th millennium in east-central Europe is Copper Age. The line at 3500 B.C. marks the beginning of the Circum-Pontic Early Bronze Age and the end of Old European Copper Age. Arrows indicate the continuity of culture. Dashed lines indicate the discontinuity of culture.

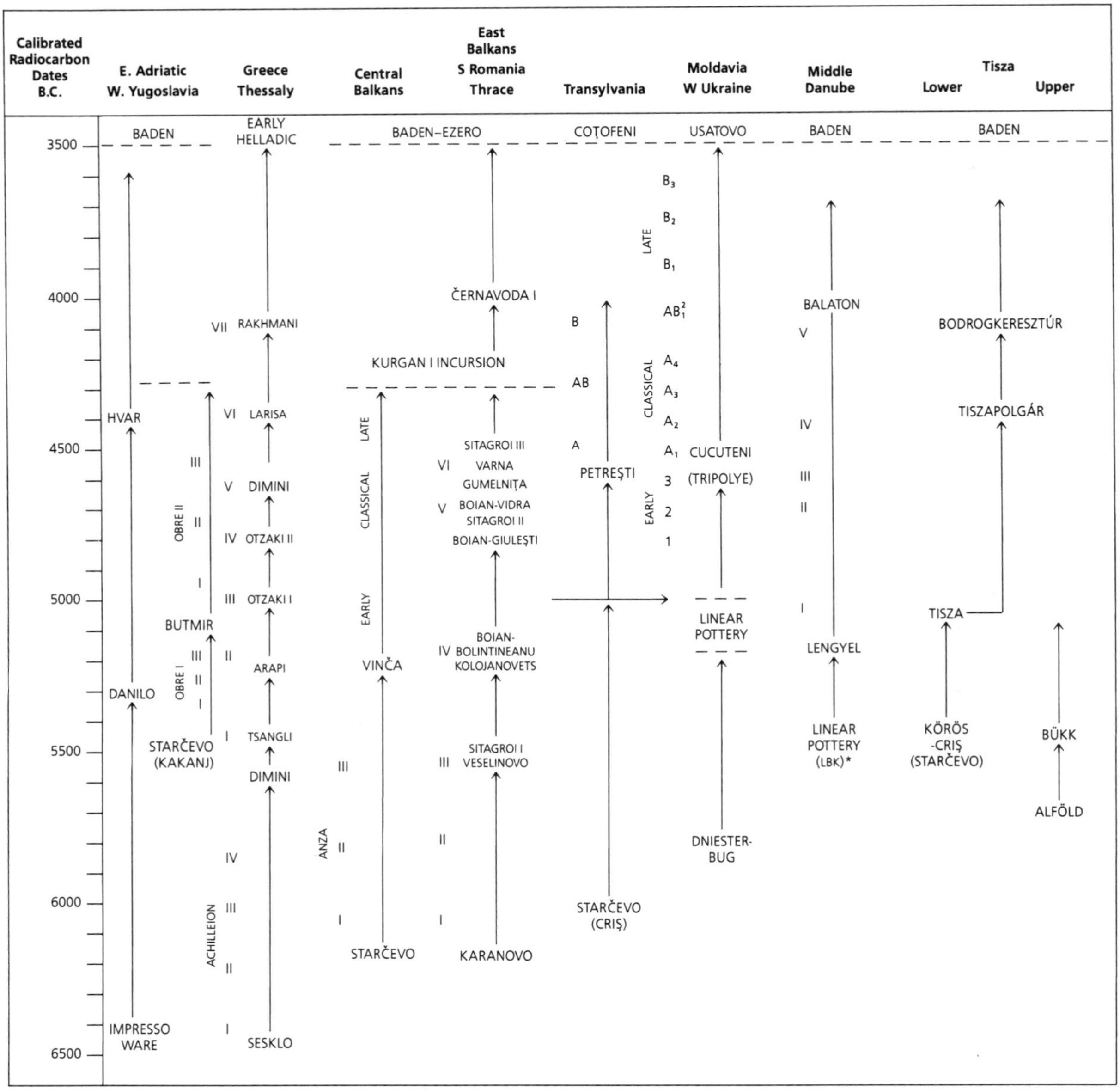

* LBK stands for Linearbandkeramik

CHART 3
General chronology of Neolithic cultures in western and central Mediterranean Europe.

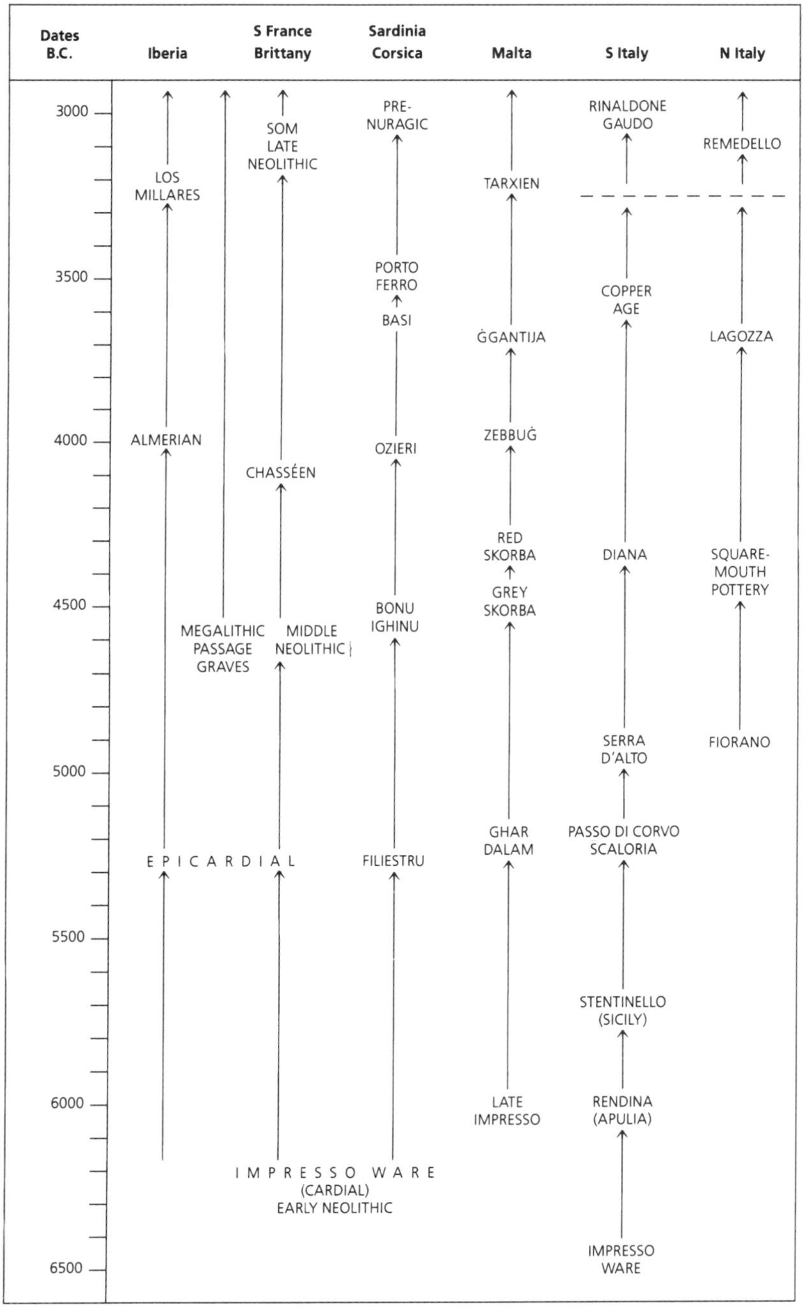

APPENDIX TO CHARTS 2 AND 3

Chronological Outline

B.C.	Major Events
7000–6500	Beginning stage of food production and settled village life in the coastal zones of the Aegean and Mediterranean Seas. Coastal and deep sea navigation. Trade in obsidian, flint, marble, and spondylus shells begins and continues for millennia.
6500–5500	Full-fledged Neolithic, with pottery, in the Aegean, Mediterranean, central and east Balkan, and Adriatic regions. Cultivation of wheat, barley, vetch, peas. All domesticated animals except the horse. Villages of closely grouped rectangular houses of mudbrick or timber with courtyards and first temples in the Aegean area and the Balkans.
5500–5000	Spread of the food-producing economy from east-central to central Europe: Moravia, Bohemia, southern Poland, Germany, and Holland (the Linear Pottery culture). Beginning of copper metallurgy in Yugoslavia, Romania, and Bulgaria. Increase in size of villages. Sacred script emerged for use in the religious cult. Rise of the Vinča, Tisza, Lengyel, Butmir, Danilo, Karanovo civilizations in east-central Europe, of Dimini in Greece.
5000–4500	Climax of culture in southeast and east-central Europe. Efflorescence of ceramic art and architecture including two-story temple buildings. Emergence in Moldavia and the western Ukraine of the Cucuteni (Tripolye) culture; in Transylvania, of Petreşti culture.
4500–4000	Continuous florescence of culture in southeast, south, and central Europe. Proliferating use of copper and gold in east-central Europe. Domesticated horse appears, brought by the Kurgan Wave No. 1 from the south Russian Volga steppe. In Greece, south Italy, Malta, Sardinia, and Corsica, Middle Neolithic culture of Old European tradition continues, typified by painted pottery, rock-cut tombs, shrines. In western Europe, evolves a Windmill Hill-Chasséen-Cortaillod-Michelsberg Middle Neolithic Culture, and in the coastal zone the megalithic Passage Grave culture.
4000–3500	Initial Kurganization (Indo-Europeanization) in east-central Europe: marked changes in habitation pattern (hilltop sites appear) and social structure (transformation from matrilineal to patriarchal system). Dwindling of Old European art; cessation of figurines, polychrome ceramics, and temple building (except in the Cucuteni culture). In all of Mediterranean and Western Europe culture continues. In the Baltic area, food production begins.
3500–3000	In east-central Europe strong influence from north of the Black Sea. Beginning of the Bronze Age. Formation of the Circum-Pontic metallurgical province with influences from the Caucasus and Transcaucasia. Disintegration of the Cucuteni civilization and amalgamation of Cucuteni with Kurgan. The Ezero complex in Bulgaria and the Baden culture in the mid-Danube region are formed from the crossing of the Old European substratum with eastern (Kurgan) elements. Emergence in north-central Europe of the Globular Amphora culture from the crossing with the Funnel-necked Beaker (TBK) culture. In Iberia, Brittany, Normandy, the British Isles, and southern Scandinavia the megalithic graves continued to be built. This is the period of large tomb-shrines in Brittany, Ireland, and Scotland and of remarkable temples and hypogea (subterranean tombs) of Malta and Sardinia.

CHART 4
General Neolithic chronology of northern and central Europe

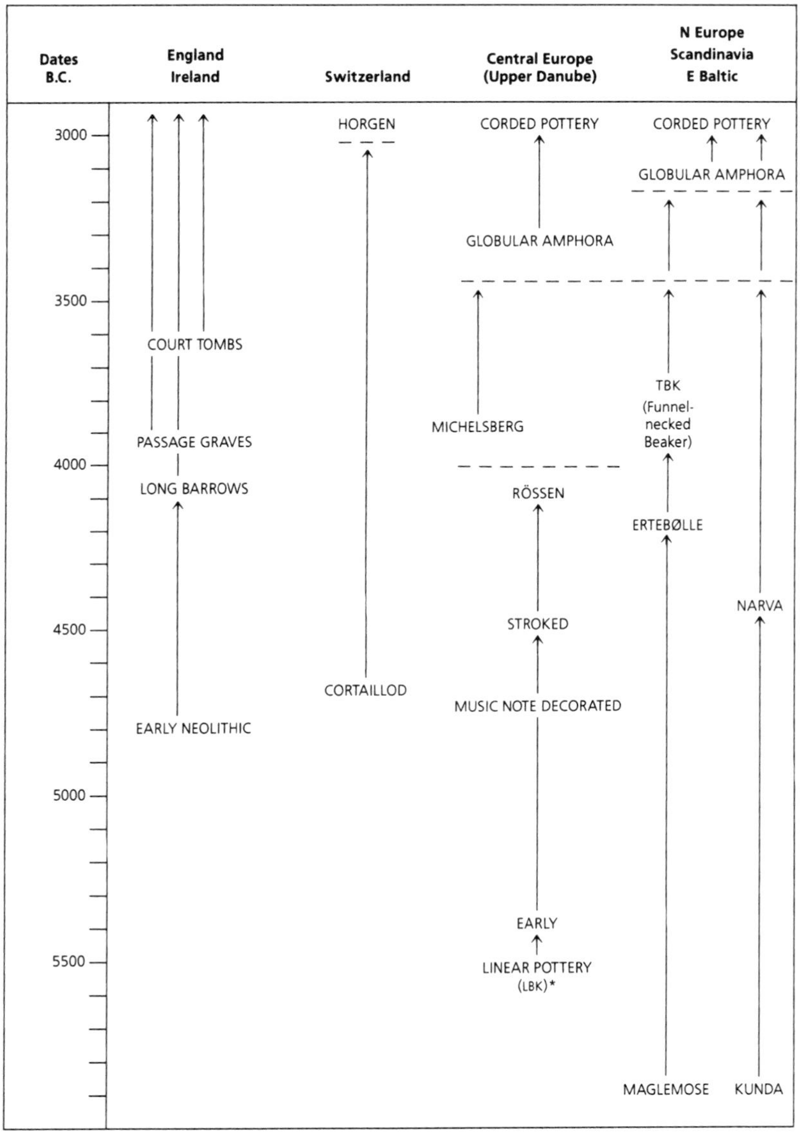

* LBK = Linearbandkeramik TBK = Trichterbecherkultur

CHART 5
Chronology of Minoan Culture, Crete

Dates B.C.	Period	Subdivision of Periods	Major Aspects
1100	SUBMINOAN		
1200			
		C	
1350		LATE MINOAN III B	
		A	
1400	LATE MINOAN (LATE BRONZE AGE)		Expansion of Mycenaean culture; fall of Knossos
1450		LATE MINOAN II	Destruction of Minoan sites
1500			
1550		B	Destruction of Thera (north of Crete)
		LATE MINOAN I	
1600		A	Second temple-palaces built, towns, villas
1700		MIDDLE MINOAN III	First temple-palaces destroyed by earthquake
1800	MIDDLE MINOAN (MIDDLE BRONZE AGE)	MIDDLE MINOAN II	
1930		B	First Cretan temple-palaces built
		MIDDLE MINOAN I	
		A	
2100			
2300		EARLY MINOAN III	
2600	EARLY MINOAN (EARLY BRONZE AGE)	EARLY MINOAN II	
		EARLY MINOAN I	
3000			

Maps Indicating Sites Mentioned in Texts

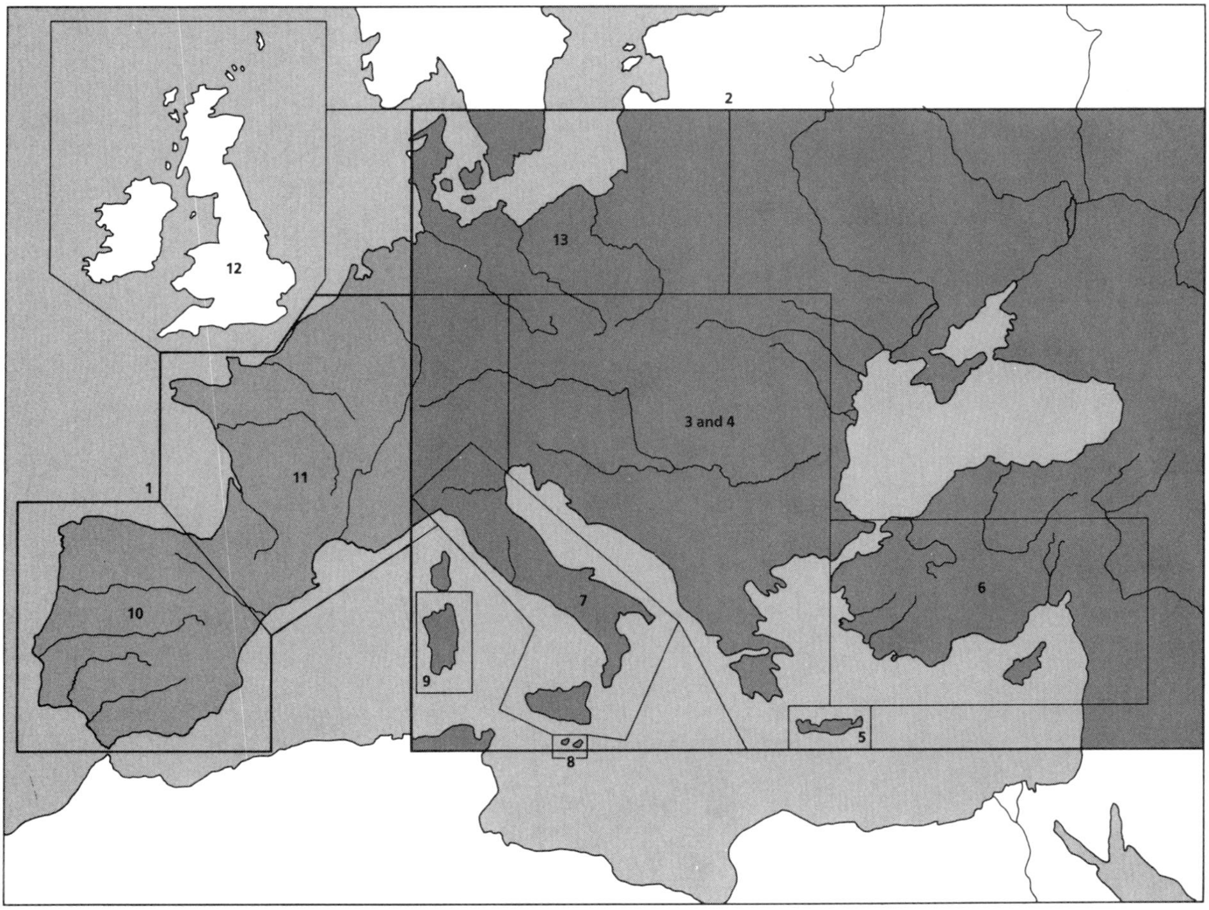

KEY MAP

MAP 1
Upper Paleolithic Sites in Spain and France

MAP 2
Upper Paleolithic sites in Italy, Switzerland, Germany, Czechoslovakia, Yugoslavia, Romania, Ukraine, and Russia

MAP 3
Neolithic Culture Groups and Sites in SE Europe, 6500–5300 B.C.

MAP 4
Late Neolithic, Chalcolithic, and Copper Age, East-Central Europe

MAP 5
Minoan Neolithic and Bronze Age

MAP 6
Anatolian/East Mediterranean Neolithic and Bronze Age

MAP 7
Italy, Sardinia, Malta: Neolithic, Chalcolithic, Copper and Early Bronze Age

MAP 8
Malta

MAP 9
Sardinia, Neolithic Sites

MAP 10
Spain and Portugal, Neolithic and Copper Age

MAP 11
France, Spain, and Portugal: Neolithic, Chalcolithic, Copper Age Sites (Chassée, Megalithic Brittany, SOM)

MAP 12
British Isles: Ireland and England

MAP 13
Central European Neolithic: Linear Pottery (Linearbandkeramik) Culture, Maglemose-Ertebølle in Denmark, East Baltic Narva Culture, and Funnel-necked Beaker Culture

MAP 1
Upper Paleolithic Sites in Spain and France.

1. Angles
2. La Marche
3. La Colombière
4. Les Eyzies
   Lascaux
   Le Gabillou
   Le Placard
   Teyfat
5. Bernifal
   Blanchard
   Castanet
   Font-de-Gaume
   La Ferrassie
   Lalinde, La Roche
   Laugerie-Basse
   Laugerie-Haut
   Laussel
   La Magdelaine
   Péchialet
   Sireuil
   Tursac
   Monpazier
6. Brassempouy
7. Isturitz
8. Lortet
   Labastide
   Gourdan
   Les Trois Frères
   La Vache
   Lespugue
   Niaux
   Le Portel
   Marsoulas
9. Tito Bustillo
10. Santian
    Altamira
    El Juyo
    La Pasiega
    El Castillo
    El Pendo
11. El Parpalló
12. La Pileta

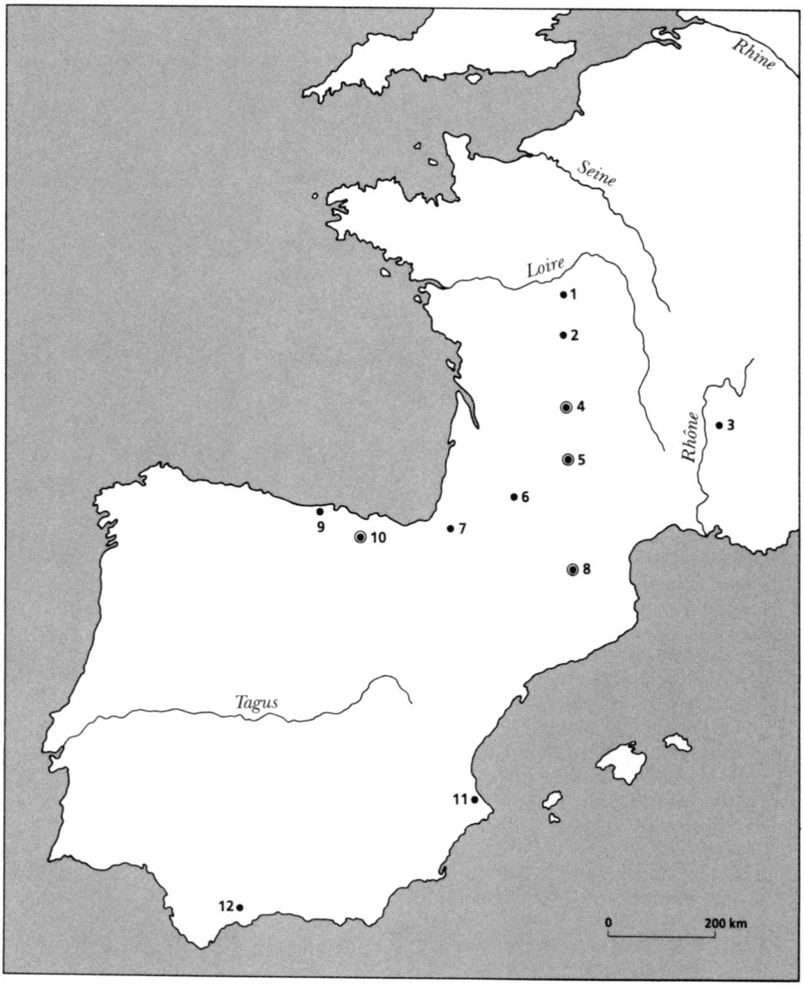

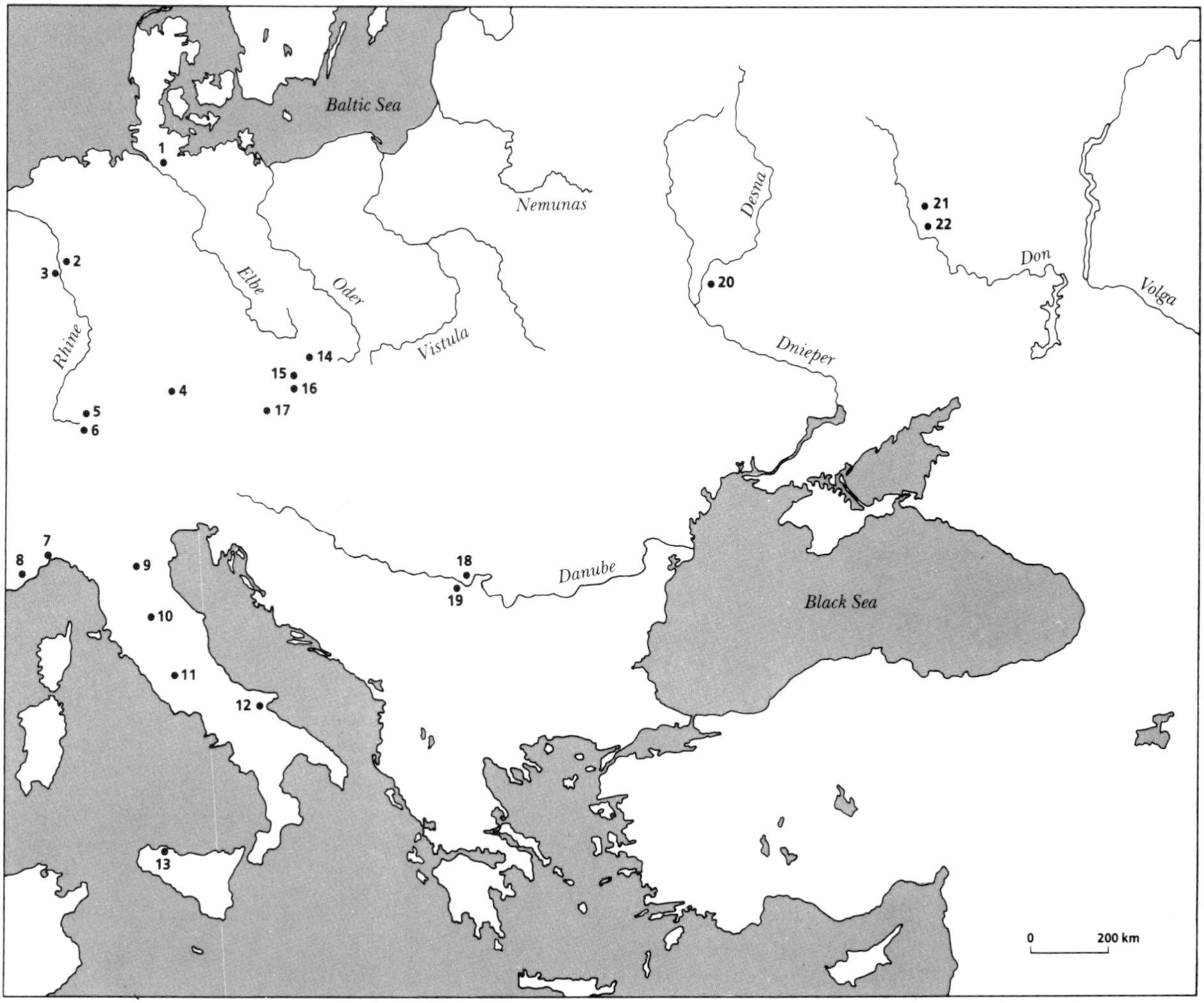

MAP 2
Upper Paleolithic Sites in Italy, Switzerland, Germany, Czechoslovakia, Yugoslavia, Romania, Ukraine, and Russia.

1. Ahrensburg
2. Oberkassel
3. Gönnersdorf
4. Weinberg
5. Petersfels
6. Schweizersbild
7. Arene Candide
8. Barma Grande
9. Savignano
10. Trasimeno
11. Polesini
12. Paglicci
13. Addaura
14. Předmosti
15. Pekarna
16. Dolní Vêstonice
17. Willendorf
18. Cuina Turcului
19. Vlasac
20. Mezin
21. Gagarino
22. Kostienki

MAP 3
Neolithic Culture Groups and Sites in SE Europe, 6500–5300 B.C.

I. Neolithic Greece: Sesklo culture in Thessaly and sites in S Greece
   1. Achilleion, Farsala, Thessaly; stratified settlement tell, Early and Middle Neolithic (Early and Classical Sesklo), from c. 6400 B.C. to 5600 B.C.
   2. Argisa (Argissa in Germ sp.), Larisa, Thessaly; stratified tell from Early Neolithic to Early Bronze Age
   3. Elateia, central Greece, Middle Neolithic
   4. Franchthi Cave, E Peloponnese; Mesolithic and Neolithic deposits
   5. Lerna, E Peloponnese; Neolithic settlement superimosed by Early Bronze Age deposits
   6. Lionakladi, C Greece; settlement tell
   7. Kyparisos, Thessaly; settlement tell
   8. Megali Vrisi, Tirnavos; settlement tell
   9. Narthakion, at Achilleion; Farsala, Thessaly, settlement of Late Sesklo date
   10. Nea Makri, Attica; settlement tell
   11. Nemea, Peloponnese; settlement
   12. Nea Nikomedeia, Macedonia, settlement with Early and Late Neolithic strata
   13. Pyrasos, Thessaly, near Volos; settlement tell
   14. Sesklo, Thessaly, W of Volos, settlement tell with a complete sequence, parallel to Achilleion
   15. Sofades, Karditsa, Thessaly; settlement tell
   16. Tsangli, C Thessaly; Classical Sesklo
   17. Tsani, C Thessaly; Classical Sesklo

II. Neolithic Bulgaria: Karanovo I–III Culture
   1. Azmak, Stara Zagora, C Bulgaria; stratified settlement tell
   2. Čevdar, east of Sofia; stratified settlement tell
   3. Karanovo, Nova Zagora, C Bulgaria; stratified settlement tell
   4. Muldava, Plovdiv, C Bulgaria; settlement

III. Neolithic Yugoslavia, W Bulgaria and Romania; Starčevo-Körös / (Criş) culture
   1. Anza I–III, C Macedonia, SE Yugoslavia; stratified settlement covered with Early Vinča stratum
   2. Endröd-Szujósketeszt, d. Békés, E Hungary; settlement, Körös group
   3. Gradešnica, Vraca, NW Bulgaria, settlement with Starčevo and Vinča deposits
   4. Kopancs, Körös group, SE Hungary; settlement
   5. Kotacpart-Vatatanya, Körös group, SE Hungary; settlement
   6. Lepenski Vir, Iron Gate, N Yugoslavia; sacred burial place and shrines
   7. Pernik, west of Sofia, W Bulgaria; settlement
   8. Porodin, Bitolj, W Macedonia, S Yugoslavia; settlement
   9. Röske-Lúdvár, Körös group, SE Hungary; settlement
   10. Slatina, Pernik, west of Sofia, W Bulgaria; settlement
   11. Szajol-Felsöföld, Körös, SE Hungary; settlement
   12. Tečić, R. Morava, C Yugoslavia; settlement
   13. Vršnik, Štip, C Macedonia, SE Yugoslavia; settlement
   14. Vlasac, Iron Gate, N Yugoslavia; sacred burial place and shrines. Mesolithic and Early Neolithic 3 km west of Lepenski Vir. See no. 6 above.

Warsaw
Kiev
Prague
Carpathian Mts.
Dnieper
Dniester
SZATMAR
DNIESTER BUG
Southern Bug
Danube
Tisza
Vienna
Budapest
Körös
Olt
Danube
Sava
Transylvanian Alps
Dinaric Alps
Beograd
Bucharest
STARČEVO
Danube
Black Sea
Nisăva
Morava
Balkan Mts.
IMPRESSO
Sofia
KARANOVO
Vardar
Adriatic Sea
IMPRESSO
Pindus Mts.
SESKLO
Athens
0
200 km

MAP 4
Late Neolithic, Chalcolithic, and Copper Age, East-Central Europe

I. Vinča Culture
1. Anza IV, C Macedonia; Early Vinča settlement
2. Banica at Belgrade, N Yugoslavia; stratified settlement
3. Beletinci, Novi Sad, N Yugoslavia; settlement
4. Crnokalačka Bara; settlement
5. Čuprija, Supska, C Yugoslavia; settlement
6. Drenovac, Svetozarevo, C Yugoslavia; settlement
7. Fafos, Kosovo Metohije, S Yugoslavia; settlement
8. Farcaşu de Sus, SW Romania; settlement
9. Gradac, C Yugoslavia; settlement
10. Gradešnica (II), Vraca, NW Bulgaria; stratified settlement
11. Gomolava, Sremska Mitrovica, N Yugoslavia; large tell site; Vinča deposits on the bottom
12. Hotărani, Olt, SW Romania; settlement
13. Jela, Odžaci, NW Yugoslavia; settlement
14. Krameniti Vinogradi, Aradac, Serbia, C Yugoslavia; settlement
15. Leskovica, SE Yugoslavia; destroyed settlement
16. Matejski Brod, Zrenjanin, N Yugoslavia; settlement
17. Medvednjak, Smederevska Palanka, C Yugoslavia; settlement
18. Parţa, R. Termeş, Timişoara, W Romania; settlement
19. Potporanj, Vršac, N Yugoslavia; settlement
20. Predionica, Priština, Kosovo-Metohije, S Yugoslavia; settlement
21. Radacje, Niš, SE Yugoslavia; settlement
22. Rast, Dolj, SW Romania; settlement
23. Rudna Glava, E Yugoslavia; copper mines
24. Slatino, Klustendil, W Bulgaria; settlement
25. Svetozarevo (see Drenovac)
26. Tartaria, Cluj, W Romania; settlement
27. Turdaş, Cluj, W Romania; settlement
28. Vădăstra, SW Romania; stratified settlement tell
29. Valač, Kosovska Mitrovica, S Yugoslavia; settlement
30. Verbicioara, Dolj, SW Romania; settlement
31. Vinča, 14 km east of Belgrade; stratified tell; complete sequence of Vinča culture; Starčevo deposits at the bottom

II. Karanovo IV–VI (Gumelniţa) Culture
1. Azmak, Stara Zagora, C Bulgaria; stratified tell
2. Bereketskaja Mogila, Stara Zagora, C Bulgaria; large tell settlement
3. Brailiţa, lower Siret, S Moldavia, Romania; settlement
   Căscioarele, lower Danube island, SE of Bucharest; island site: see no. 8.
4. Devetashka Cave, Plovdiv, C Bulgaria; cave sanctuary
5. Djadevo, Nova Zagora, C Bulgaria; large tell, numerous strata
6. Hotnica, lower Danube, N Bulgaria; sanctuary
7. Goljamo Delčevo, E Bulgaria; stratified settlement site
8. Gumelniţa, lower Danube, south of Bucharest, Romania; stratified settlement tell
9. Lovets, Stara Zagora, C Bulgaria; settlement
10. Kalojanovets, Nova Zagora, C Bulgaria; settlement
11. Karanovo IV–VI, Nova Zagora, C Bulgaria; stratified settlement tell
12. Ovčarovo, Trgovište, NE Bulgaria; stratified settlement tell
13. Pazardžik, Plovdiv, C Bulgaria; settlement
14. Radaşeni, S Moldavia, Romania; settlement
15. Ruse, lower Danube, N Bulgaria; settlement
16. Sitagroi I–III, Drama Plain, NE Greece; stratified settlement tell
17. Sulica, Stara Zagora, C Bulgaria; settlement
18. Sultana, lower Danube, S Romania; settlement
19. Tangiru, south of Bucharest, Romania; stratified settlement tell
20. Teiu, SE Romania; settlement tell
21. Varna, E Bulgaria; cemetery
22. Vidra at Bucharest, Romania; settlement tell
23. Yasatepe, C Bulgaria; settlement tell

III. Hamangia Culture
1. Baia, E Romania; cemetery
2. Cernavoda, E Romania; cemetery

IV. Petreşti Culture
1. Pianul de Jos, Transylvania; settlement
2. Petreşti, Transylvania; settlement

V. Cucuteni Culture
1. Bilcze Zlote, upper Dniester, W Ukraine; settlement
2. Brinzeni-Tsiganka, Moldavia; settlement
3. Buznea, Piatra Neamţ, Moldavia, NE Romania; settlement
4. Cucuteni near Tirgu-Frumoş, d. of Iaşi, NE Romania; stratified settlement
5. Draguşeni at Botoşani, upper Prut, Moldavia, NE Romania; settlement
6. Frumuşica at Piatra Neamţ, Moldavia, NE Romania; settlement
7. Ghělaeşti-Nedeia district of Peatra Neamţ, Moldavia, NE Romania; settlement and sanctuary
8. Habaşeşti near Tirgu-Frumoş, Moldavia, NE Romania, settlement
9. Izvoare, district of Bacău, Moldavia, NE Romania; stratified settlement
9a. Karbuna, lower Dniester, Soviet Moldavia; large deposit of copper artifacts in a vase
10. Koshilivtsi (Koszyłowce), upper Dniester, W Ukraine; settlement
11. Kriszczatek, Bukovina, upper Dniester; settlement
12. Krutoborodintsi W Ukraine; settlement
13. Luka Vrublevetskaya, upper Dniester, W Ukraine; settlement
14. Miorcani, Botoşani, Moldavia, NE Romania; settlement
15. Nezvisko, upper Dniester, W Ukraine; settlement (above Linear Pottery stratum)
16. Novye Ruseshty I, Kishenev, Soviet Moldavia; settlement
17. Petreni, M. Dniester, W Ukraine; settlement
18. Podei, Tirgu Ocna, NE Romania; settlement
19. Poduri Dealul Ghîndaru, Bacău, Moldavia, NE Romania; stratified settlement
20. Popudnya, near Uman', W Ukraine; settlement (temple model)
21. Sabatinivka, lower Bug, W Ukraine; temple
22. Şipenitsi (German: Schipenitz), upper Dniester, W Ukraine; settlement

(continued)

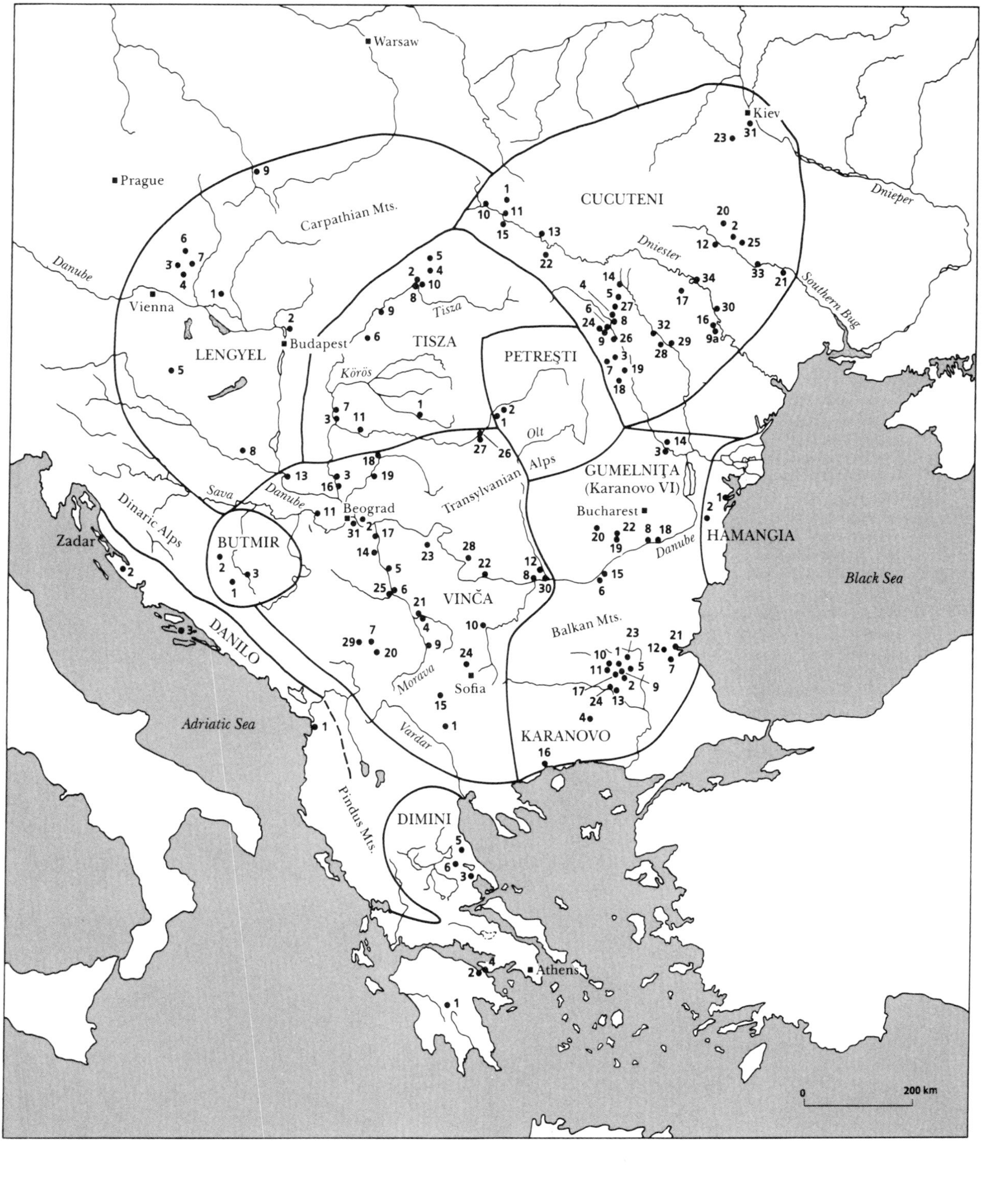
Warsaw
Prague
Kiev
Carpathian Mts.
CUCUTENI
Dnieper
Dniester
Southern Bug
Danube
Vienna
Budapest
LENGYEL
TISZA
Tisza
Körös
PETREŞTI
Olt
Transylvanian Alps
GUMELNIŢA
(Karanovo VI)
Bucharest
HAMANGIA
Black Sea
Sava
Danube
Dinaric Alps
Zadar
BUTMIR
Beograd
VINČA
DANILO
Balkan Mts.
Morava
Sofia
Vardar
KARANOVO
Adriatic Sea
Pindus Mts.
DIMINI
Athens
0
200 km

MAP 4 (continued)

23. Staraja Buda, SE of Kiev, Ukraine; settlement
24. Tirpeşti, district of Tg. Neamţ, upper Siret, Moldavia, NE Romania; settlement
25. Tomashevka, middle So Bug, W Ukraine; settlement
26. Traian-Dealul Fîntînilor, R. Siret, Moldavia, NE Romania; settlement; and Traian-Dealul Viei, settlement
27. Truşeşti at Botoşani, between Siret and Prut, Moldavia, NE Romania, settlement
28. Valea Lupului, M. Prut, district of Iaşi, Moldavia, NE Romania; settlement
29. Valeni, Moldavia, NE Romania; settlement
30. Varvarovka, district of Kishenev, Soviet Moldavia; settlement
31. Veremie, south of Kiev, W Ukraine; settlement
32. Vladeni, north of Iaşi, Moldavia, NE Romania; settlement
33. Vladimirivka (Vladimirovka), middle So Bug (Boh), W Ukraine; settlement
34. Vykhvatintsi, Rybnitsa, upper Dniester, W Ukraine; cemetery

VI. Lengyel Culture

1. Abraham, W Slovakia; settlement
2. Aszód, north of Budapest, settlement and cemetery
3. Hluboké Mašuvky, Znojmo, Moravia, Czechoslovakia; settlement
4. Křepice, Brno, Moravia, Czechoslovakia; settlement
5. Sé, Szombately, W Hungary; settlement
6. Střelice, Znojmo, Moravia, Czechoslovakia; settlement
7. Těšetice-Kyjovice, Brno, Moravia, Czechoslovakia; settlement
8. Zengövárkony, SW Hungary; settlement
9. Jordanów, Dzierżoniów, district of Wroclaw, Silesia

VII. Culture groups in the Tisza basin: lower Tisza (Tisza culture proper); upper Tisza (Meolithic Bükk, Copper Age Polgár, and Bodrogkeresztúr)

1. Battonya, Szakálhát group, Tisza culture district Békés; settlement
2. Bodrogkeresztúr; cemetery
3. Hódmesövásárhely, Tisza culture; settlement
4. Kenézlö, Borsod-Abaúj-Zemplén, Bükk culture, settlement
5. Sarazsadany-Templomdomb, district Borsod-Abaúj-Zemplén, Bükk culture; settlement
6. Polgár (see Tiszapolgár)
7. Szegvár-Tüzköves, Szentes, Tisza culture; settlement
8. Tiszadada at Kalvinháza, district of Szabolcs-Szatmár, Bükk culture; settlement
9. Tiszapolgár-Basatanya; cemetery
10. Tiszavasvári-Jozsefházá, district Szabolcs-Szatmár; Bükk culture; settlement
11. Vesztö-Mágor, Tisza culture, near Békés, E Hungary; stratified settlement tell

VIII. Butmir

1. Butmir at Sarajevo, W Yugoslavia; settlement
2. Nebo, NE of Sarajevo, W Yugoslavia; settlement
3. Obre II, northwest of Sarajevo, W Yugoslavia; stratified Butmir settlement

IX. Danilo-Hvar Culture

1. Malik, Albania; settlement
2. Smilčić, Zadar; stratified settlement
3. Hvar, cave site on the island of Hvar

X. Dimini Culture, Thessaly and Late Neolithic of S Greece

1. Asea, Peloponnese; settlement
2. Corinth, Peloponnese; settlement
3. Dimini at Volos, Thessaly; settlement
4. Gonia, east of Corinth; settlement
5. Rakhmani, Thessaly; settlement
6. Zarkou, Larisa, Thessaly; settlement

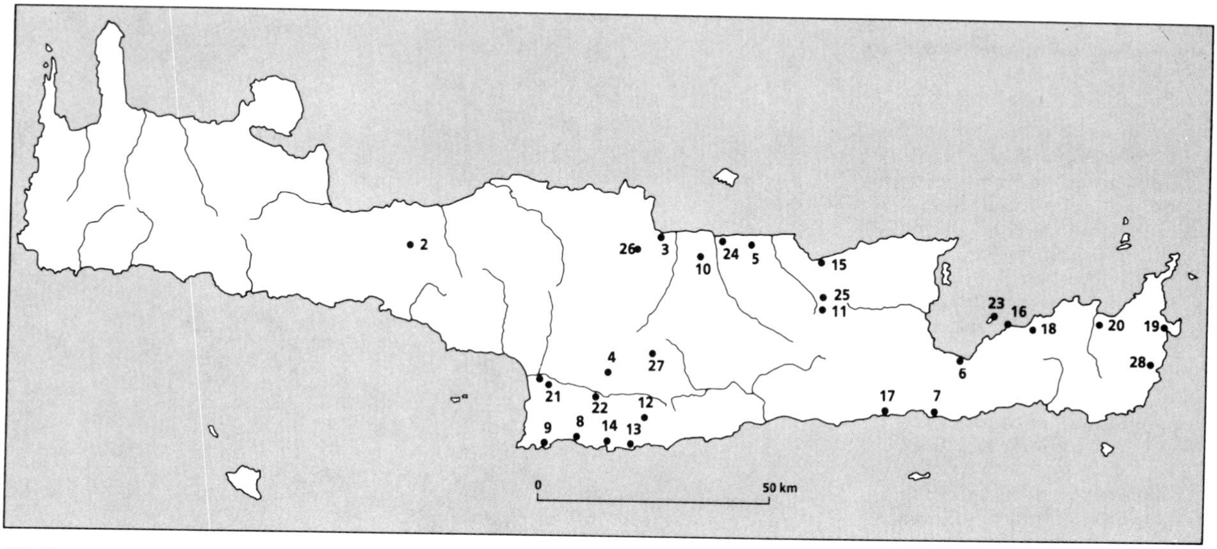

MAP 5
Minoan Neolithic and Bronze Age

I. Minoan

1. Aghia Triada; palace-temple
2. Armenoi, Rhetymno; cemetery (with sarcophagi)
3. Gazi; sanctuary
4. Gortyn; sanctuary
5. Gournes; cemetery
6. Gournia; town and cemetery
7. Ierapetra, Kato; Neolithic site
8. Kalantiana; tholos and settlement
9. Kali Limiones; graves

   Kato Ierapetra (see Ierapetra)
10. Knossos; palace-temple
11. Kophina; cave sanctuary
12. Koumasa; tholos tomb, settlement, and sanctuary
13. Landa; tholos tombs
14. Lebena; tholos tombs
15. Mallia; palace-temple
16. Mochlos; island; cemetery
17. Myrtos; EBA II settlement
18. Myrsini
19. Petsofa; hill sanctuary
20. Piskokephalo; hill sanctuary
21. Phaistos; palace-temple
22. Platanos; cemetery of tholos tombs
23. Pseira; island
24. Pyrgos; cave
25. Trapeza cave, Lasithi
26. Tylissos; town settlement
27. Vorou, cemetery
28. Zakros; palace-temple

MAP 6
Anatolian/East Mediterranean Neolithic and Bronze Age

I. Anatolia
1. Beycesultan near Çivril, W Turkey; settlement tell with Chalcolithic, Copper, and Bronze Age deposits
2. Çatal Hüyük, Konya Plain, C Turkey; stratified Neolithic settlement
3. Hacilar, Konya Plain, C Turkey; Neolithic stratified settlement tell
4. Can Hasan, Konya Plain, C Turkey; Neolithic settlement
5. Nudra, W Turkey, figurines
6. Troy near Çanakkale, at Hellespont, W Turkey; settlement tell with six Early Bronze Age periods
7. Yortan at Kirkağaç, Moesia; Early Bronze Age cemetery

II. Lebanon, Syria, and Israel
1. Byblos, prov. Beirut, Lebanon; stratified settlement
2. Mallaha, Proto-Neolithic settlement, Israel
3. Ras Shamra, Syria; Neolithic settlements and Canaanite city, 7th mill. to 12th cent. B.C.
4. Sha'ar Hagolan, Jordan Valley; Pottery Neolithic settlement

III. Cyprus
1. Kition (Larnaca), SE Cyprus; cemetery, Mycenaean III B.
2. Kouklia at Palaepaphos, SW Cyprus; Late Bronze Age cemetery
3. Lapithos at Karavas, district of Kyrenia, N Cyprus; necropolis of rock-cut tombs, Early and Middle Cypriot
4. Nikosia-Ayia Paraskevi MBA; idol of a bearded male
5. Sotira Arkolies, SW Cyprus; cemetery
6. Vounous at Bellapais, district of Kyrenia, N Cyprus, Early Cypriot I, II, III; necropolis of rock-cut tombs

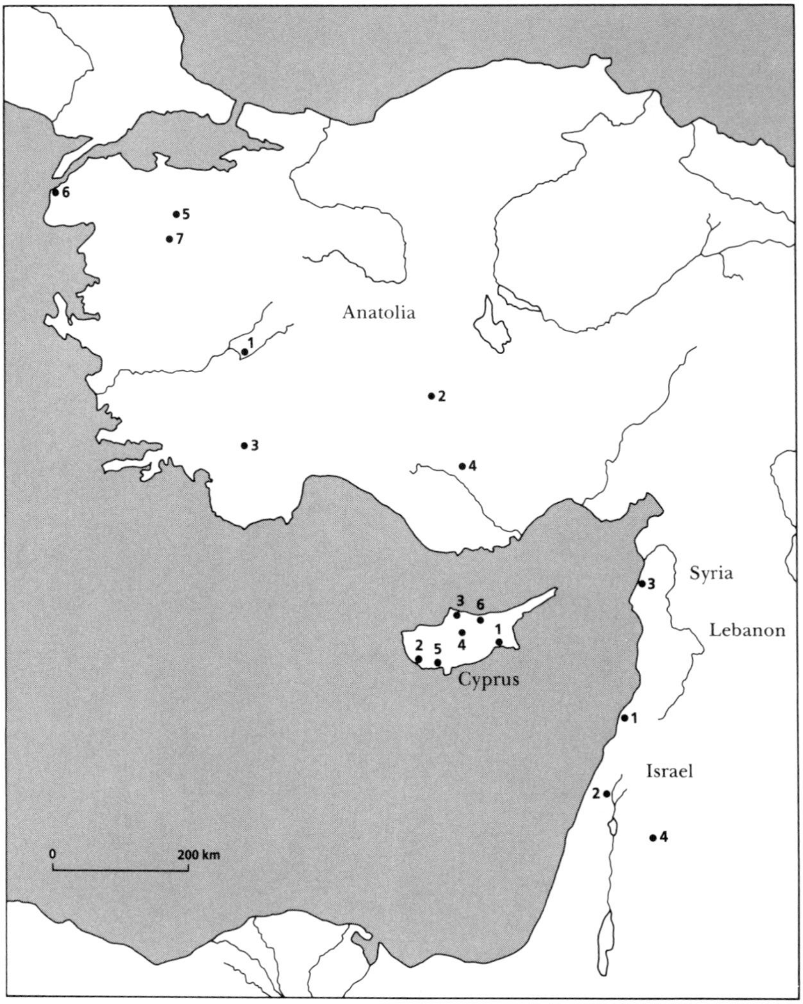

MAP 7
Italy, Sardinia, Malta: Neolithic, Chalcolithic, Copper, and Early Bronze Age

I. Italy Neolithic
1. Arene Candide, Liguria cave, with Epipaleolithic and Neolithic strata
2. Arnesano, Lecce, Apulia; rock-cut tomb
3. Castellucio dei Sauri, Foggia; stele
4. Castellucio, Noto, SE Sicily; Early Bronze Age rock-cut tombs and settlement
5. Chiusazza cave, Neolithic (Diana) and Chalcolithic (Conzo) strata, near Syracuse, Sicily
6. Cozzo Busoné, Agrigento; Neolithic cemetery
7. Gaban cave, Neolithic, near Trento, N Italy
8. Matera, a series of Neolithic settlements
9. Passo di Corvo; Neolithic settlement near Foggia
10. Rendina; Early Neolithic (Late Impresso) settlement near Melfi
11. Scaloria; cave at Manfredonia, Neolithic Scaloria culture
12. Serra d'Alto culture; Neolithic settlement near Matera

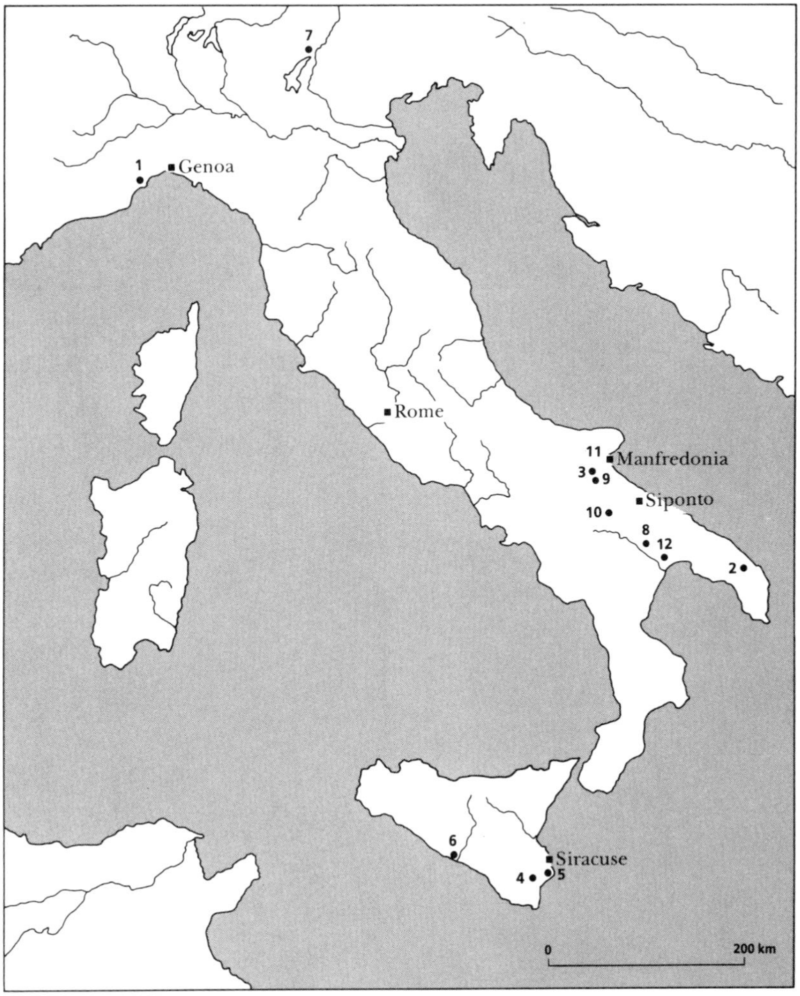

MAP 8
Malta

1. Ghar Dalam cave
2. Ggantija temple
3. Hal Saflieni, hypogeum
4. Haġar Qim temple
5. Mnajdra temple
6. Tarxien temple

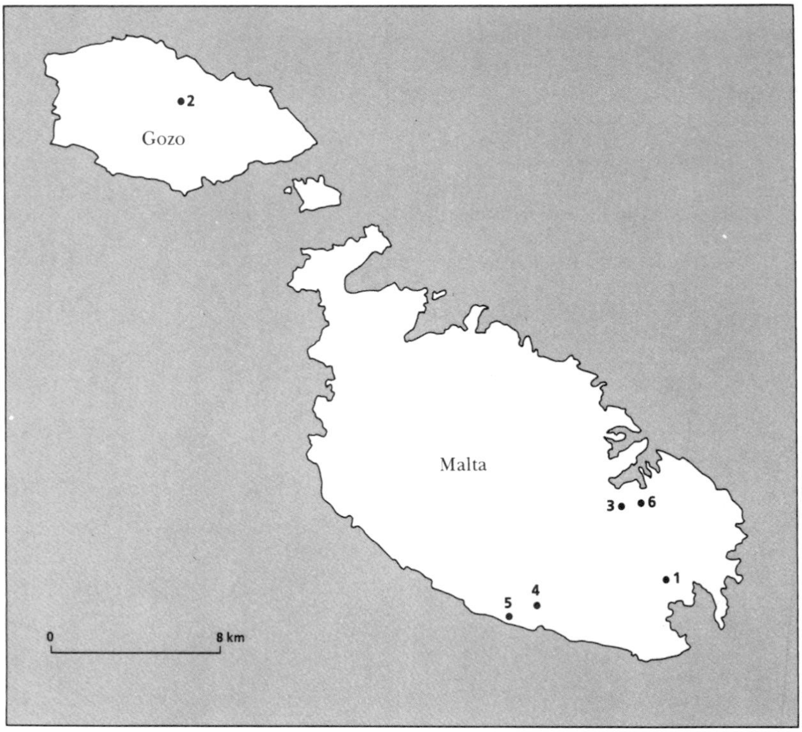

MAP 9
Sardinia, Neolithic Sites

1. Anghelu Ruju, Alghero; hypogeum
2. Bonu Ighinu; cave
3. Bue Marino, Cala Gonone, Dorgali; cave (Ozieri c.)
4. Cuccuru S'Arriu, Oristano; rock-cut tombs (Bonu Ighinu c.)
5. Filiestru, Mara; stratified cave
6. Mandra Antine, Thiesi; rock-cut tombs
7. Monte d'Accoddi, Sassari; sanctuary
8. Monte Miana cave, Santadi
9. Montessu, Villaperuccio, rock-cut tombs
10. Perfugas, Sassari; rock-cut tombs
11. Porto Ferro, Alghero; hypogeum
12. Puisteris, Mògoro; settlement
13. San Andrea Priu, Bonorva; hypogeum
14. Santa Mariedda, Olbia; settlement
15. Senorbi; settlement
16. Serra Is Araus, San Vero Milis; rock-cut tombs
17. Tintirriolu, Mara; stratified cave

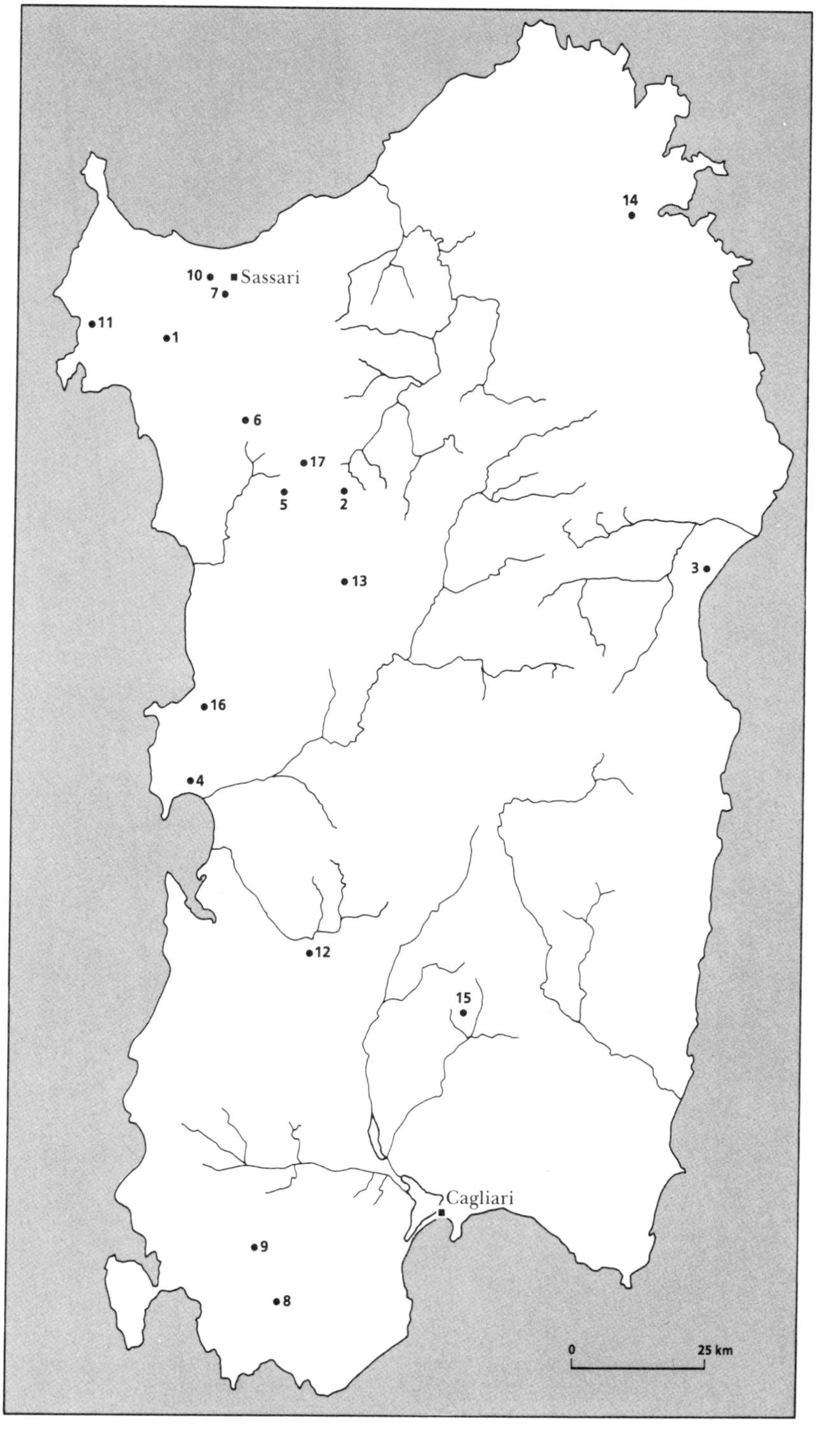

MAP 10
Spain and Portugal, Neolithic and Copper Age

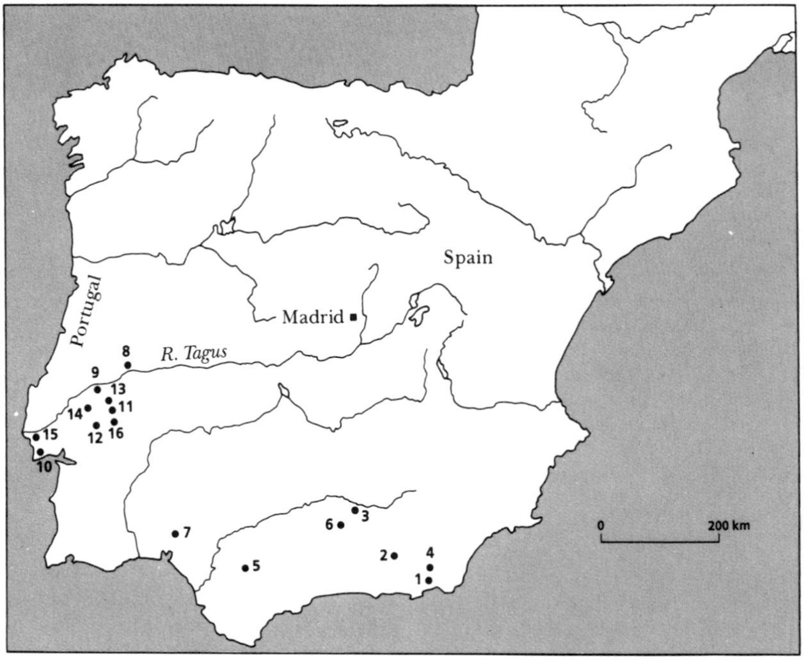

1. Almizaraque, Almeria, Spain; cemetery of megalithic tholos tombs and settlement
2. Asquerosa, Granada, Spain; statue menhir
3. Jaén, Prov. Jaén, Spain; grave, ivory statuette found in a pit
4. Los Millares, at Gádor, Almeria, Spain; megalithic passage graves with tholos and settlement
5. Morón de la Frontera, prov. Sevilla, Spain; megalithic tomb, menhirs
6. Torre del Campo, Prov. Jaén, Spain; cave, ivory statuette
7. Trigueroa, Prov. Huelva, Spain; megalithic tomb, relief of a deity
8. Vega del Guandancil, Prov. Cáceres, Spain; megalithic tomb (passage grave)
9. Arronches, E Portugal; statue menhir
10. Cabeço da Arruda, Frieira, Prov. Estremadura, Portugal; passage graves
11. Carajola, Monforte, Prov. Alentejo, Portugal; cemetery of megalithic passage graves
12. Crato, Portugal; statue menhir
13. Horta Velha do Reguengos, Barbacena, Prov. Alentejo; passage grave
14. "Marquesa," Marvão, Prov. Alentejo, Portugal; passage grave
15. S. Martinho de Sintra, Estremadura, Portugal; tholos tombs
16. Sobreira, Vila Fernando, Prov. Alentejo, Portugal; passage graves

MAP 11
France, Spain, and Portugal: Neolithic, Chalcolithic, Copper Age Sites (Chassée, Megalithic Brittany, SOM)

1. Aven Meunier I, St. Martin-d'Ardèche, Gard, S France; stele
2. Barnenez, Plouézoch, Brittany; passage graves
3. Braguassargues, Gard, S France; statue menhir
4. Capdenac-le-Bout, Lot, S France; settlement
5. Collorgues (Mas de l'Avengle), Gard, S France; statue menhir originally connected with a megalithic tomb
6. Gavrinis, Morbihan; S Brittany; passage grave
7. Ile Longue, Larmor-Baden, Morbihan; passage grave
8. Kermarquer, Morbihan, S Brittany; menhir with engravings of hooks
9. Kercado at Carnac, S Brittany; passage grave, c 4700 B.C. (one of the earliest radiocarbon dated)
10. La Gayette, Castelnau-Valence, Gard, S France; statue menhir
11. La Pierre Turquaise, Paris basin gallery grave
12. La Table des Marchands, Locmariaquer, Morbihan; passage grave
13. Lauris-Puyvert, Vaucluse, S France; stele probably from Chasséean cemetery
14. Les Pierres Plates, Locmariaquer, S Brittany; angled passage grave
15. Luffang, Crac'h, Morbihan, S Brittany; angular passage grave, engravings on three orthostats
16. Mané er H' Roek, Locmariaquer, Morbihan; Brittany megalithic tomb with a stele with engraving at the entrance
17. Mané Lud, Locmariaquer, Morbihan; passage grave with engraved orthostats
18. Orgon-Sénas, Bouches-du-Rhône, S France; stele
19. Petit Mont, Arzon, Morbihan, Brittany; passage grave with a rectangular chamber; eight orthostats with engravings
20. Razet, Coizard, Epernay, Dep. Marne; necropolis of rock-cut tombs
21. St. Théodorit, Gard, S France; stele

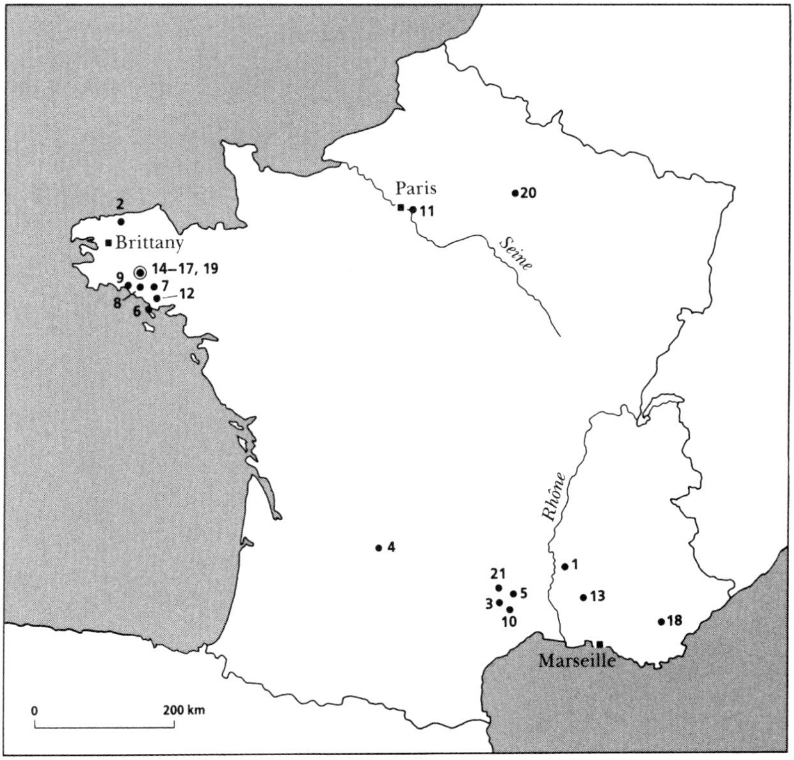

MAP 12
British Isles: Ireland and England

I. Ireland (megalithic tombs).
1. Ardmulchan, Meath; passage grave
2. Ballymarlagh, Antrim; passage grave
3. Ballyglass, Mays; court tomb
4. Carrowkeel, Sligo; passage grave
5. Creevykeel, Sligo; court tomb
6. Clady Holiday, Tyrone; passage grave
7. Dowth, Meath; passage grave, tomb-shrine
8. Fourknocks, Meath; passage grave, tomb shrine
9. Loughcrew, Ballinvalley, Meath; passage graves
10. Knowth, Meath; passage grave, tomb-shrine
11. Newgrange, Meath; passage grave, tomb-shrine
12. Sess Kilgreen, Tyrone; passage grave
13. Shanballyedmond, Tipperary; passage grave

II. England (megalithic tombs, rings, sanctuaries)
1. Avebury, Marlborough, Wiltshire; ring sanctuary
2. Baildon Moor, Yorkshire; passage grave
3. Calderstones, Lancashire; megalithic tomb
4. Câtel, Guernsey; stele
5. Isbister, Orkney, Scotland; passage grave
6. Maumbury Ring, Dorset
7. Norn's Tump, Gloucestershire; long barrow
8. Silbury, Marlborough, Wiltshire; hill sanctuary
9. South Yarrows, Caithness; passage grave
10. Windmill Tump, Gloucestershire; passage grave

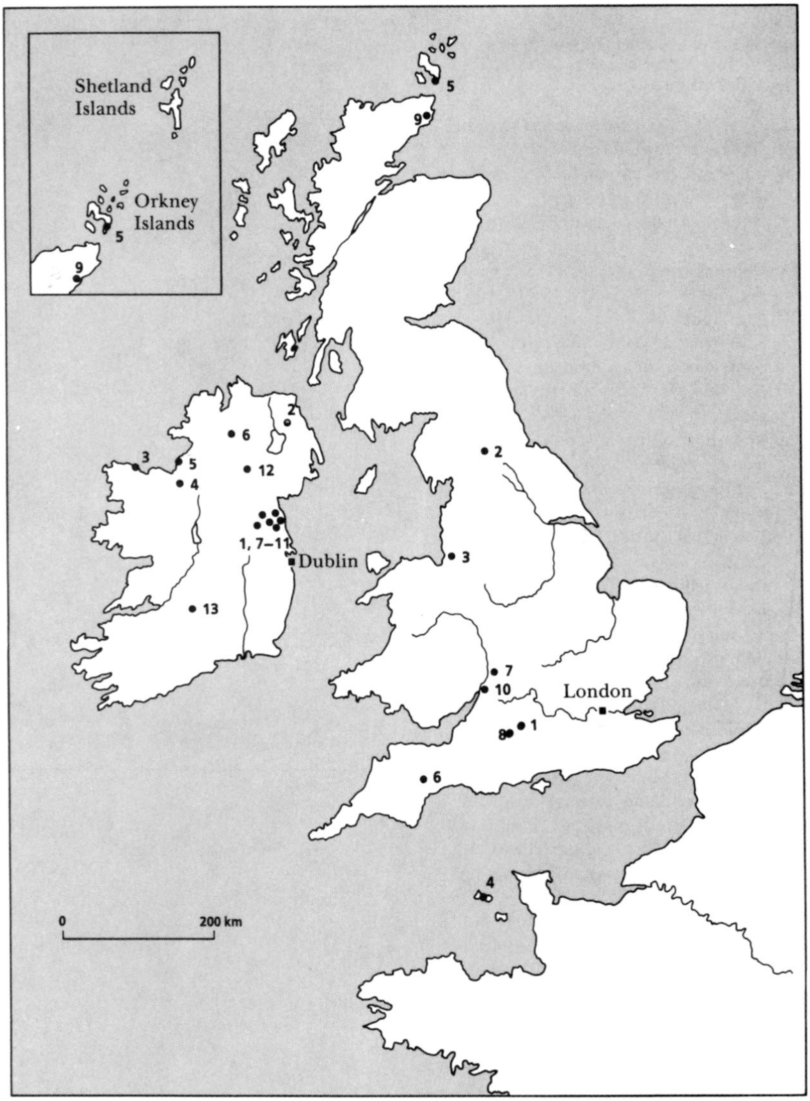

MAP 13
Central European Neolithic: Linear Pottery (Linearbandkeramik) Culture, Maglemose-Ertebølle in Denmark, East Baltic Narva Culture, and Funnel-necked Beaker Culture

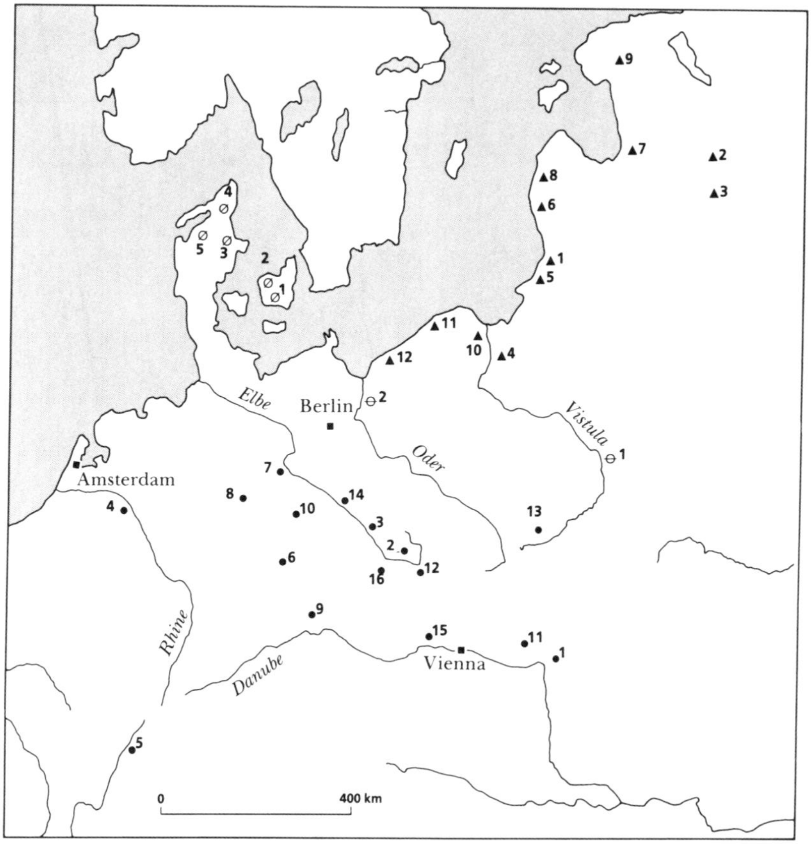

I. Linear Pottery
1. Békesmegyer, at Budapest, Želiezovce group, Hungary; settlement
2. Bylany; settlement, Bohemia
3. Dresden-Moritz, E Germany; settlement
4. Elsloo, Holland; settlement
5. Ensisheim, upper Rhine; cemetery
6. Gaukönigshofen, Würzburg, W Germany; settlement
7. Halle-Trotha, E Germany; settlement
8. Harth, C Germany; settlement
9. Hienheim, Bavaria; settlement
10. Lockwitz, E Germany; settlement
11. Nitra, Slovakia; cemetery
12. Nová Ves at Kolín, Bohemia; settlement
13. Olszanica, S Poland; settlement
14. Prohlis at Dresden, E Germany; settlement
15. Rybníki, Moravia; settlement
16. Statenice, Bohemia; settlement

II. Mesolithic Denmark (Maglemose and Ertebølle settlements)
1. Koge Sonakke, Zealand
2. Stensby, Zealand
3. Jordløse, Jutland
4. Resen; bog; amber bear
5. Ertebølle, Pottery Mesolithic

III. East Baltic Narva Culture
1. Juodkrantė, Kuršių nerija (Courish Lagoon), W Lithuania; amber figurines
2. Lubānas Meadows, peat-bog sites around Lake Lubānas, E Latvia
3. Nainiekste, E Latvia, north of Lake Lubānas; settlement
4. Neidenburg, N Poland (former East Prussia); amber female figurine
5. Nida, Kuršių nerija (Courish Lagoon), W Lithuania; amber figurines, pendants
6. Palanga, W Lithuania; amber collection
7. Sārnate, W Latvia, peat-bog site
8. Šventoji, W Lithuania; peat-bog site
9. Tamula, Eastonia; settlement; amber bear
10. Gdańsk; amber bear (isolated find)
11. Stolp, Pomerania; amber bear (isolated find)
12. Podejuch, Szczecin, S Baltic; Mesolithic

IV. Funnel-necked Beaker Culture
1. Ćmielów, Tarnobrzeg, S Poland; settlement
2. Mierzyń, W Poland; the Havel group of megalithic graves

● Linear Pottery (LBK)
⌀ Mesolithic Denmark
▲ East Baltic Narva
⊖ Funnel-necked Beaker

Bibliography and References

Abramova, Z. A.
1962 *Paleolitičheskoe iskusstvo na teritorii SSSR.* Moscow-Leningrad Arkheologija SSSR Svod arkheologicheskikh istochnikov, vyp. a4-3. English trans: "Palaeolithic Art in USSR." *Arctic Anthropology* 4 (1967): 1–179.
1970 "Paleoliticheskoe iskusstvo," *Kamennyj vek na territorii SSSR:* 78–89. Moscow (Nauka).

Acanfora, M. O.
1960 "Le stele antropomorfe di Castelluccio dei Sauri." *Rivista di Scienze Preistoriche* 25:95–123.

Afanas'ev, A. N.
1969 *Poeticheskie vozzrenija slavjan na prirodu* I–III. First published in Moscow, 1865–68; reprinted by Mouton, The Hague-Paris.

Albuquerque e Castro, L. de
1962 "L'art mégalithique au Portugal." *Atti del VI Congresso Internazionale delle Scienze Preistoriche e Protostoriche* 3:370–74.

Aldea, I. Al.
1972 "Santierul arheologic Ghirbom (Com. Berghin, Jud. Alba)." *Apulum* 10:3–18.
1975 "Santierul arheologic Ghirbom (Com. Berghin, Jud. Alba)," *Apulum* 13 (Alba Iulia): 25–33.

Alexiou, S.
1958 *I Minoiki thea meth' Upsomenon Kheiron* (Herakleion).
1968 *Guide to the Archaeological Museum of Heraclion.* Trans. by D. H. French. Athens: General Direction of Antiquities and Restoration.

Alexiou, S., N. Platon, and H. Guanella
1968 *Ancient Crete.* Trans. by D. J. S. Thomson. London: Thames and Hudson.

Alinei, M.
1987 "Rospo aruspice, rospo antenato." *Quaderni Di Semantica* 8, 2:265–96.

Almagro, M., and A. Arribas
1963 "Excavationes en el Poblado y necropolis de los Millares, Santa Fe de Mandujar (Almeria)." *Bibliotheca Praehistorica Hispana.* Madrid.

Almgren, O.
1934 *Nordische Felszeichnungen als religiöse Urkunden.* Frankfurt am Main: Diesterweg.

Anati, E.
1969 "The Magurata Cave, Bulgaria." *Archaeology* 22, no. 2: 92–100.
1976 *Evolution and Style in Camunian Art.* Archiv 6: Capodi Ponte, Centro Camuno di Studi Preistorici.
1981 *I testimoni dell'ultima rivoluzione culturale della preistoria. Le statue-stele della Lungiana.* Le Orne dell'Uomo. Milano: Jaca Book.

Angeli, W.
1972 "Goldamulette." *Idole, prähistorische Keramiken aus Ungarn.* Vienna: Naturhistorisches Museum N.F. 7, 27–30.

Angelov, N.
1959 "Zlatnoto sykrovishche ot Hotnica." *Arkheologiia* (Sofia) 1, 1–2: 38–46.

Anisimov, A. F.
1959 *Kosmologicheskie predstavlenija narodov Severa.* (Moscow, Leningrad).

Antonielle, U.
1926 "La statuetta feminile steatopigica di Savignano sul Panaro (Emilia)." *IPEK* 2:45–51.

Antonova, E. V.
1977 *Antropomorfnaja skul'ptura drevnikh zemledel'chev Perednej i Srednej Azii.* Moscow: AN, Institut vostokovedenija.

Armstrong, Edward A.
1958 *The Folklore of Birds.* London: Collins.

Arnal, J.
1976 *Les statues-menhirs, hommes et dieux.* Toulouse: Éditions des Hespérides.

Atkinson, B., et al
1904 *Excavations at Phylakopi in Melos. Journal of Hellenic Studies,* Supplement 4.

Atkinson, R. J. C.
1956 *Stonehenge.* Rev. ed. 1979. Harmonds-Worth: Penguin Books.

Atzeni, E.
1975 "Nuovi idoli della Sardegna Prenuragica." *Nota preliminare: Studi Sardi* 23 (1973–74): 24–43.
1978 "La dea-madre nelle culture prenuragiche." *Studi Sardi* 24 (1975–77): 3–18.
1980 "Menhirs antropomorfi e statue-menhirs della Sardegna." *Annali del Museo Civico della Spezia* 2 (1979–80): 9–64.
1981 "Aspetti e sviluppi culturali del neolitico e della prima età dei metalli in Sardegna." *Ichnussa: La Sardegna dalle origini all'età classica:* 1–51. Milan: Libri Scheiwiller.

Bachofen, J. J.
1967 *Myth, Religion and Mother Right: Selected Writings.* Trans. by R. Manheim. London: Routledge and Kegan Paul.

Badre, L.
1980 *Les figurines anthropomorphes en terre cuite à l'âge du Bronze en Syrie.* Bibliotheque archéologique et historique 103. Paris: Librairie Orientaliste Paul Geuthner.

Bahn, P. G.
1978 "Water mythology and the distribution of Palaeolithic parietal art." *Proceedings of the Prehistoric Society* 44:125–34.

Bailloud, G.
1964 *Le Néolithique dans le Bassin Parisien.* Paris: Centre National de la Recherche Scientifique.

Baltran Martinez, A.
1980 "Las pinturas de la cueva de Porto Badisco y el arte parietal 'Esquematico' Español." *Annali del Museo Civico della Spezia* 2 (1979–80): 65–79.

Balys, J.
1942 Reprinted in 1986: J. Balys *Lithuanian Agrarian Customs and Beliefs* (in Lithuanian with summary in English). A Treasury of Lithuanian Folklore, 10. Silver Spring, Md.: Lithuanian Folklore Publishers, 791–809.
1948 *Lietuvių tautosakos skaitymai.* Tübingen: Patria.

Bandi, Hans-Georg, and Johannes Maringer
1955 *Kunst der Eiszeit. Levantkunst. Arktische Kunst.* Basel: Holbein.

Banner, J.
1958 "Menschendarstellung auf einem Gefäss von Tószeg und die Frage der sogenannten Krötengefässe." *Prähistorische Zeitschrift* 37:244–54.
1959 "Anthropomorphe Gefässe der Theisskultur von der Siedlung Kökénydomb bei Hódmezővásárhely (Hungary)." *Germania* (Berlin): 14–35.

Barandiarán, J. M.
1947 "Las cavernas prehistorias en la mitologia vasca." Madrid: Cuodernos de historia primitiva.
1973 "Die baskische Mythologie." *Götter und Mythen in alten Europa.* Stuttgart: Ernst Klett.
1973 *Arte mueble del Paleolitico Cantabrico.* Monografias Arqueologicas 14. Zaragoza: Departamento de Prehistoria y Arqueologia.
1974 *Obras Completas* 1. Diccionario ilustrado de Mitologia Vasca y albunas de sus fuentes. Bilbao: La Gran Enciclopedia Vasca.

Barber, Elizabeth
1991 *Prehistoric Textiles.* Princeton, N.J.: Princeton University Press.

Baroja, Julio Caro
1975 *The World of the Witches.* Trans. from the Spanish by O. N. V. Glendinning. Chicago: University of Chicago Press.

Barrière, C.
1976 *L'art pariétal de la Grotte de Gargas: Palaeolithic Art in the Grotte de Gargas.* Trans. by W. A. Drapkin. BAR, Supplementary Series 14. Oxford.

Basanavičius, J.
1899 *Lietuviszkos pasakos* (Lithuanian Folktales). Shenandoah, Pa.: Dirva.

Batović, S.
1968 "Problem kulta phallosa u Danilskoj kulturi." Résumé in English: The Problem of the Phallus Cult in Danilo Culture. *Diadora* (Zadar) 4: 5–51.

Battaglia, R.
1927 "Le statue neolitiche di Malta e l'ingrassamento muliegre presso i Mediterranei." *IPEK* (Leipzig) 3: 131–57.

Bauer, P. V. C.
1902 *Eileithyia.* Columbia, Mo.: University of Missouri Studies 1, no. 4.

Bednarik, R. G.
1984 "Die Bedeutung der paläolithischen Fingerlinientradition." *Anthropologie* 22:73–79.

Beltrán, A.
1982 *Rock Art of the Spanish Levant.* Cambridge: Cambridge University Press.

Benac, A.
1973 "Obre II: A Neolithic Settlement of the Butmir Group at Gornje Polje." *Wissenschaftliche Mitteilungen des Bosnisch-Herzegowinischen Landesmuseums* (Sarajevo) 3. Heft A (Archaeology Series): 1–327.
"Obre I: A Neolithic Settlement of the Starčevo-Impresso and Kakanj Cultures at Raskaršče." Ibid: 327–430.

Berciu, D.
1956 "Cercetari şi Descoperiri Arheologice in Regiunea Bucureşti." *Materiale şi Cercetari Arheologice* 2: 493–562.
1959 "Sapaturile Arheologice de la Tangiru" (Summaries in Russian and French: "Les fouilles archéologiques de Tangiru"). *Materiale şi Cercetari Arheologice* 5: 143–54.
1961 *Contribuţii la problemele neoliticului in Rominia in lumina noilor cercetari.* Bucharest: Institute of Archaeology, Editura Academiei Republicii Populare Romîne.
1966 *Cultura Hamangia.* Bucharest: Editura Academiei Republicii Populare Romîne.
1966a "Manifestation d'art néolithique en Roumanie: Le 'couple' de Cernavoda." *IPEK* 21 (1964/65): 42–45.
1967 *Romania before Burebista.* London: Thames and Hudson.

Berezoviets, D. T.
1958 "Risunki na cheljusti byka." *Sovetskaja Arkheologija* 4:194–97.

Bernabó Brea, L.
1957 *Sicily before the Greeks. Ancient People and Places* 3. London: Thames and Hudson.

Betts, J. H., ed.
1980 *Die Schweizer Sammlungen* (Corpus der minoischen und mykenischen Siegel 10). Berlin: Gebr. Mann Verlag.

Bevau, E.
1986 Representations of Animals in Sanctuaries of Artemis and Other Olympian Deities. Oxford: BAR Series 315.

Bibikov, S. N.
1953 "Rannetripol'skoe poselenie Luka-Vrublevetskaja na Dnestre." *Materialy i Issledovanija po Arkheologii SSSR* 38: 1–408.
1975 "A Stone Age Orchestra. The Earliest Musical Instruments Were Made from the Bones of Mammoths." *The Unesco Courrier,* June 1975: 28–30.

Bierbaum, G.
1953 "Ein stichbandkeramischer Hausgrundriss von Dresden." *Prähistorische Zeitschrift* 34/35, 2 (1949/50): 125–35.

Biesantz, H.
1954 *Kretisch-mykenische Siegelbilder.* Marburg: N. G. Elwert.

Biezais, H.
1955 *Die Hauptgöttinnen der alten Letten.* Uppsala: Almquist and Wiksells.

Black, L.
1973 "The Nivkh (Gilyak) of Sakhalin and the Lower Amur." *Arctic Anthropology* 10:1.

Blegen, C. W.
1928 *Zygouries: A Prehistoric Settlement in the Valley of Cleonae.* Cambridge, Mass.: Harvard University Press.
1937 *Prosymna, the Helladic Settlement Predating the Argive Heraeum.* Cambridge: Cambridge University Press.

Boardman, J.
1967 *Pre-Classical: From Crete to Archaic Greece.* Harmondsworth: Penguin.

Bogaevskij, B. L.
1937 *Orudija proizvodstva i domashnie zhivotnye Tripol'ja.* Moscow and Leningrad.

Boghian, D., and C. Mihai
1987 "Le complexe de culte et le vase à décor ornithomorphe peint décourvert à Buznea (dép. de Iaşi)." *La Civilisation de Cucuteni en Contexte Européen*: 313–24. Session Scientifique Iaşi-Piatra Neamţ, Iaşi, Université "Al. I. Cuza.".

Bognár-Kutzián, I.
1944/1947 *The Körös Culture,* vols. 1–2. Dissertationes Pannonicae, ser. 2, no. 23: Budapest.
1963 *The Copper Age Cemetery of Tiszapolgár-Basatanya.* Budapest: Akademiai Kiádo.
1972 *The Early Copper Age Tiszapolgár Culture in the Carpathian Basin.* Budapest: Akademiai Kiádo.

Bökönyi, S.
1970 "Animal Remains from Lepenski Vir: The Vertebrate Fauna of this Early Center of Domestication Represent an Atypical Animal Husbandry." *Science* 167, no. 3926: 1702–4.

Bonev, A. G.
1976 "Glineni modeli na kultovi stylbove ot dve selishchni mogili v Tyrgovishchki okrug" (résumé in French: "Modèles en argile de piliers de culte de deux tells du dép. de Targovişte"). *Arkheologija* 1:24–25.

Bord, Janet and Colin
1982 *Earth Rites.* London: Granada.

Bosinski, G., and G. Fischer
1974 *Die Menschendarstellungen von Gönnersdorf der Ausgrabung von 1968.* Wiesbaden: Steiner.

Bosinski, G.
1981 *Die eiszeitliche Kunst in Deutschland und Schweiz.* Cologne: Rheinland Verlag; Bonn: Habelt.

Bossert, E. M.
1981 "Die gestempelten Verzierungen auf frühbronzezeitlichen Gefässen der Agäis." *Jahrbuch des deutschen archäologischen Instituts* 75:1–16.

Bossert, H. T.
1937 *The Art of Ancient Crete.* London: Zwemmer.

Bovio-Marconi, I.
1953 "Incisioni rupestri all'Addaura (Palermo)." *Bolletino di Paletnologia Italiana* (Rome) 8, pt.5: 5–20.

Bowen, E. G.
1973/74 "The Cult of St. Brigit." *Studia Celtica* 8–9:35–47.

Branigan, K.
1970 *The Foundations of Palatial Crete: A Survey of Crete in the Early Bronze Age.* States and Cities of Ancient Greece. London: Routledge and Kegan Paul.
1970 "Minoan Foot Amulets and Their Near Eastern Counterparts." *Studi Micenei* 11:7–23.

Bray, W.
1963 "The Ozieri Culture of Sardinia." *Rivista di Scienze Preistoriche* 18:155–90.

Brennan, M.
1983 *The Stars and the Stones: Ancient Art and Astronomy in Ireland.* London: Thames and Hudson.

Breton, L. le
1957 "The Early Period at Susa, Mesopotamian Relations." *Iraq* 19:79–124.

Breuil, H.
1908 "Petits instruments Magdaléniens à pointe bifide ou tridentiée de Bruniquel et quelques autres gisements." *L'Anthropologie* 19:183–90.
1933–35 *Les peintures rupestres schématiques de la Péninsule Ibérique,* I–IV (Paris).
1952 *Four Hundred Centuries of Cave Art.* New Edition. Trans. by M. E. Boyle. Montignac: Centre d'Études et de Documentation Préhistoriques.

Breuil, H., and R. de Saint-Perier
1927 *Les poissons, les batraciens et les reptiles dans l'art quaternaire.* Archives de l'Institut de Paléontologie Humaine, Mémoire 2. Paris: Masson et Cie.

Briffault, R.
1927 *The Mothers: A Study of the Origins of Sentiments and Institutions,* 3 vols. Abridged by Gordon Rattray Taylor; 1959, London: Allen and Unwin; 1977, New York: Atheneum. London and New York: Harper and Brothers.

Brøndsted, J.
1942 "A Frog as a Viking Age Burial Gift." *Acta Archaeologica* (Copenhagen) 13:315–18.
1957 *Danmarks Oldtid I Stenalderen.* København: Gyldendal.

Brukner, B.
1962 "Praistorisko naselje na potesu Beletintsi kod Obreža." Rad Vojvodjanskikh Muzeja 11:89–122.

Brunner-Traut, E.
1938 "Der Tanz im alten Ägypten nach bildlichen und inschriftlichen Zeugnissen." *Ägyptologische Forschungen* 6:1–90.

Buchholz, H.-G., and V. Karageorghis
1973 *Prehistoric Greece and Cyprus: an Archaeological Handbook.* Trans. by F. Garvie. London: Phaidon.

Buck, R. J.
1964 "Middle Helladic Matt-painted Pottery." *Hesperia* 33:231–313.

Bulle, H., and E. Kunze
1931 *Orchomenos,* vol. 2. Die neolithische Keramik. Munich: Abhandlungen der Bayerischen Akademie der Wissenschaften, Phil. Hist. Klasse, NF. 24.

Burl, A.
1976 *The Stone Circles of the British Isles.* New Haven: Yale University Press.
1979 *Prehistoric Avebury.* New Haven: Yale Univesity Press.
1980 *Rings of Stone.* New York: Ticknor and Fields.
1980a "Science or Symbolism: Problems of Archaeoastronomy." *Antiquity* 54:191–200.
1981 *Rites of the Gods.* London: Dent.

Butterworth, E. A. S.
1966 *Some Traces of the Pre-Olympian World in Greek Literature and Myth.* Berlin: de Gruyter.

Cameron, D. O.
1981 *Symbols of Birth and of Death in the Neolithic Era.* London: Kenyon-Deane.
1981a *The Ghassulian Wall Paintings.* London: Kenyon-Deane.

Campbell, J.
1975 *The Mythic Image.* Bollingen Series C. Princeton, N.J.: Princeton University Press.
1983 *The Way of the Animal Powers,* vol. 1. Historical Atlas of World Mythology. New York: Alfred van der Marck.

Carmichael, Alexander
1900 *Carmina Gadelica.* Edinburgh: Scottish Academic Press.

Cartailhac, E., and H. Breuil
1908 "Les peintures et gravures murales des cavernes pyrénéennes, III. Niaux (Ariège)." *L'Antropologie* 19:15–46.

Caskey, J. L.
1962 "Reports on Lerna." *Hesperia* 31:278–80.
1964 "Reports on Lerna." *Hesperia* 33:328–31.
1966 "Reports on Lerna." *Hesperia* 35:369–71.

Caskey, M. E.
1986 *Keos II. The Temple at Ayia Irini. Part I: The Statues.* Princeton, N.J.: American School of Classical Studies.

Castaldi, E.
1969 "Tombe di Giganti nel Sassarese." *Origini* 3:119–274.
1976 "Il culto del toro nella preistoria della Sardegna ed il problema delle tre cavità sull'alto dei prospetti delle tombe di giganti." *Archivo per l'Antropologia e la Etnologia* 106:439–58.
1978 "Una particolare rappresentazione zoomorfa in ipogei sardi." *Rivista di scienze preistoriche* (Florence) 33, fasc. 2: 393–98.

Castiglioni, O. C., and G. Calegari
1975 "I pendagli 'a busto ginemorfo' del paleolitico superiore centro-occidentale europeo, con un inventario ragionato dei reperti Italiani." *Museo Civico di Storia Naturale di Milano* 66, nos. 1–2: 25–52.

Cauvin, J.
1972 *Religions néolithiques de Syro-Palestine: Documenta.* Centre Rech. Écologie et Préhistoire Saint-André de Cruzières 1. Paris: J. Maisonneuve.

Chapouthier, F., and R. Joly
1936 "Fouilles executées à Mallia: Deuxième rapport." Études Crétoises 4. Paris: Paul Geuthner.

Chase, P. G., and H. L. Dibble
1987 "Middle Palaeolithic Symbolism: A Review of Current Evidence and Interpretations." *Journal of Anthropological Archaeology* 6:263–96.

Chernysh, E. K.
1962 "K istorii naselenija eneoliticheskogo vremeni v srednem Podnestrove." *Materialy i issledovanija po arkheologii SSR,* 102.

Chikalenko, L.
1930 "Die Bedeutung der schypenitzer Ansiedlung für das Verständnis der Entwicklung der ukrainischen bemalten Keramik." *Festschrift W. Demetrykiewicz,* Poznań: 123–34.
1953 "The Origin of the Paleolithic Meander." *The Annals of the Ukrainian Academy of Arts and Sciences in the U.S.* 3. 1. (7): 518–34.

Chollot-Varagnac, M.
1980 *Les origines du graphisme symbolique: Essai d'analyse des écritures primitives en préhistoire.* Paris: Fondation Singer-Polignac.

Christopoulos, G. A., ed. in chief
1974 *Prehistory and Protohistory: History of the Hellenic World.* University Park, Pa.: Pennsylvania State University Press.

Cipolloni Sampo, Mirella
1982 "Scavi nel villagio neolitico di Rendina (1970–76). Reprint from *Origini* XI, 1977–1982: 183–354.

Clark, G.
1975 *The Earlier Stone Age Settlement of Scandinavia.* Cambridge: Cambridge University Press.

Clark, R.
1963 *Grimes Grave.* London: Her Majesty's Stationery Office.

Clottes, J., and M. Carrière
1976 "La statue feminine de Capdenac-le-Haut (Lot)." *Congrès Préhistorique de France, 20ième session, 1974:* 145–50.

Coe, Paula Powers.
1986 "Fate, Fertility, Spinning, and Stones: A Comparative Study of Two European Goddesses." Unpublished term paper, UCLA.

Coldstream, J. N.
1973 *Knossos: The Sanctuary of Demeter.* London: Thames and Hudson.
1977 *Deities in Aegean Art: Before and After the Dark Age.* Inaugural lecture, Bedford College, London.
1977 *Geometric Greece.* London: E. Benn.

Coleman, J. E.
1985 "'Frying pans' of the Early Bronze Age Aegean." *American Journal of Archaeology* 89, 2: 191–219.

Comşa, E.
1959 "Sapaturile de la Dudeşti (reg. Bucureşti)." *Materiale şi Cercetari Arheologice* 5:91–98.
1974a "Die Bestattungssitten im rumänischen Neolithikum. *Jahresschrift für mitteldeutsche Vorgeschichte* (Halle/Saale) 58:113–56.
1974b *Istoria Comunitatilor Culturii Boian.* Biblioteca de Archeologie 23.
1979 "Les figurines en os appartenant à la phase moyenne de culture Gumelniţa." *Dacia* 23:69–78.

Conti, C.
1972 *Corpus delle incisioni rupestri di Monte Bego I.* Istituto Internazionale di Studi Liguri, Collezione de Monografie Preistoriche ed Archeologiche, VI. Bordighera.

Cook, A. B.
1914/1940 *Zeus: A Study in Ancient Religion.* Cambridge: Cambridge University Press.

Corpus
1966 *Corpus Vasorum Antiquorum, Deutschland* vol. 10. Universitat Heidelberg, vol. 3, ed. F. Canciani.
1969 *Corpus der minoischen und mykenischen Siegel* vol. 2. Iraklion Archaologisches Museum, pt. 1. Berlin: Gebr. Mann Verlag.
1969 *Corpus der minoischen und mykenischen Siegel* vol. 4. Iraklion Sammlung Metaxas. Berlin: Gebr. Mann Verlag.

Courtois, J.-C.
1969 "Splendeur d'Enkomi-Alasia, capitale de Chypre." *Archéologie vivante* 2, no. 3 (Mars-Mai): 93–112.

Crawford, O. G. S.
1957 *The Eye Goddess.* London: Phoenix House.

Crişmaru, A.
1977 *Draguşeni: Contribuţii la o monografie arheologica.* Botoşani: Comitetul Judetan de Cultura şi Educatie Socialista, Muzeul Judetean de Istorie Botoşanie.

Csalog, J.
1959 "Die anthropomorphen Gefässe und Idolplastiken von Szegvár-Tüzköves." *Acta Archaeologica* (Budapest) 10:7–38.
1960 "Das Krummschwert des Idols von Szegvár-Tüzköves." *Acta Archaeologica* 12:57–68.
1972 "Thronende Frauenidol von Szegvár-Tüzköves." *Idole, praehistorische Keramiken aus Ungarn: Ausstellung des Ungarischen Nationalmuseums Budapest im Naturhistorischen Museum, Wien.* Veröffentlichungen aus dem Naturhistorischen Museum, N.F. 7. Vienna: Verlag des Naturhistorischen Museums.

Cucoş, S.
1970 "Reprezentari de incaltaminte in plastica cucuteniana de la Ghelaieşti (Jud. Neamţ)." *Memoria Antiquitatis* 3:65–77.
1973 *Céramique néolithique du musée archéologique de Piatra Neamţ.* Acta Musei Petrodavensis, Bibliotheca Memoriae Antiquitatis 1: Piatra Neamţ.
1973a "Un complex ritual cucutenian descoperit la Ghelaeşti (Jud. Neamţ)." *Studii şi Cercetări de Istorie Veche* (Bucharest) 24.2:207–15.
1975 "Doua vase zoomorfe eneolitice." *Carpica* 7:7–14. Muzeul Judetean de Istorie şi Arta Bacău.
1978 "Decorul spiralic al ceramicii Cucuteni B." *Carpica* 10:55–88.
1981 "Sapaturile de la Valeni-Piatra Neamţ (1974–75)." *Memoria Antiquitatis* 6–8: 37–56.

Dales, G. F., Jr.
1960 *Mesopotamian and Related Female Figurines: Their Chronology, Diffusion, and Cultural Functions.* Unpublished Ph.d. dissertation, University of Pennsylvania.

Dames, M.
1976 *The Silbury Treasure: The Great Goddess Rediscovered.* London: Thames and Hudson.
1977 *The Avebury Cycle.* London: Thames and Hudson.

Dams, L.
1978 *L'art paléolithique de la caverne de la Pileta.* Graz, Austria: Akademisches Druck und Verlagsamsfelt.

Daniel, G. E.
1962 *The Megalith Builders of Western Europe.* Baltimore, Md.: Penguin Books.
1980 "Megalithic Monuments." *Scientific American* 242 (July): 78–90.

Daniel, G., and P. Kjaerum, eds.
1973 *Megalithic Graves and Ritual: Papers Presented at the 3rd Atlantic Colloquium, Moesgard, 1969.* København: Gyldendal.

Davison, J. M.
1961 *Attic Geometric Workshops.* Yale Classical Studies 16. New Haven: Yale University Press.

Dawkins, R. M.
1902 "Excavations at Palaikastro II. The Pottery." *Annual of the British School at Athens* 9:297–328.

Daunys, S.
1980 "Pirties tradicinės apeigos Adutiškio apylinkėje." *Kraštotyra* (Vilnius) 10: 61–64.

Della Santa, S. E.
1947 *Les figures humaines du paléolithique supérieur.* Anvers: De Sikkel.

Delporte, H.
1979 *L'image de la femme dans l'art préhistorique.* Paris: Picard.

Demargne, P.
1945 *Fouilles exécutées à Mallia: Exploration des nécropoles.* Études Crétoises 7. Paris: Paul Geuthner.
1947 *La Crète dédalique: Études sur les origines d'une renaissance.* Paris: E. de Boccard.
1964 *Aegean Art: The Origins of Greek Art.* Trans. by S. Gilbert and J. Emmons. London: Thames and Hudson.
1964a *Naissance de l'art grec.* Paris: Gallimard.

Demargne, P., and H. G. de Santerre
1953 *Fouilles executées à Mallia: Exploration des maisons et quartiers d'habitation* 1. Études Crétoises 9. Paris: Paul Geuthner.

Deonna, W.
1952 "La femme et la grenouille." *Gazette des beaux-arts* (ser. 6) 40: 229–40.

Dergachev, V. A.
1978 *Vykhvatinskij mogil'nik.* Kishinev: Izdatelstvo "Shtiintsa."
1986 *Moldavija i sosednie territorii v èpokhu bronzy.* Kishinev: Izdatelstvo "Shtiintsa."

Desborough, V. R. d'A.
1952 *Protogeometric Pottery.* Oxford Monographs on Classical Archaeology 2. Oxford: The Clarendon Press.

Des Gagniers, J., and V. Karageorghis
1976 *Vases et figurines de l'âge du bronze à Chypre: Céramique rouge et noire polie.* Quebec: Les Presses de l'Université Laval.

Deshayes, J., and D. Theocharis
1962 "Dikili Tach." *Bulletin de Correspondance Hellénique* 86, pt. 2: 912–33.

Detev, P.
1950 "Le tell Baniata près de Kapitan Dimitrievo." *Godishnik Narodne Muzej Plovdiv* 2:1–23.
1959 "Matériaux de la préhistoire de Plovdiv." *Annuaire de Musée National Archéologique* 3.3:15.
1960 "Vorgeschichtliche Gefässe mit menschen – und tierähnlichen Darstellungen in Bulgarien." *Archäologischer Anzeiger* fasc. 1: 1–15.
1965 "Modèles de decoration de l'enéolithique." *Archeologija* (Sofia) 7, no. 4: 65–73.
1968 "Praistoricheskoto selischte pri selo Muldava." *Godishnik, Plovdiv* 6:9–48.

De Valera, R.
1960 "The Court Cairns of Ireland." *Proceedings of the Royal Irish Academy* 60, sec. C, 2: 9–140.

Diamant, S., and J. Rutter
1969 "Horned Objects in Anatolia and the Near East." *Anatolian Studies* 19:147–77.

Dieterich, A.
1905 "Mutter Erde." *Archiv für Religionswissenschaft:* 37–125.

Dietrich, B. C.
1974 *The Origins of Greek Religion.* Berlin/New York: de Gruyter.
1982 "The Religious Prehistory of Demeter's Eleusinian Mysteries." *Études Préliminaires aux religions orientales dans l'empire romain.* Publ. by M. J. Vermaseren, vol. 92. La soteriologia dei culti orientali nell'impero romano: Collogio, Rome 1979: 445–71.

Dietz, S.
1974 "Two Painted Duck-Vases from Rhodes." *Acta Archaeologica* (Copenhagen) 45:133–43.

Dikaios, P.
1953 *Khirokitia.* Cyprus Dept. of Antiquities, Monograph 1. London: Oxford University Press.

Dimitrijević, S.
1968 *Sopotsko-Lendjelska kultura* [Résumé in German: 112–23]. Zagreb: Monographiae Archaeologicae 1.
1969 *Starčevačka kultura u Slavonsko-srijemskom prostoru i problem prijelaza ranog u srednji neolit u srpskom i hratskom podunavlju.* Vukovar: Gradski Muzej.

Dimitrov, M.
1962 "Kostena choveshka figurka ot s. Lovets, Starozagorsko." *Arkheologija* 4, 1:65–68.
1971 "Novi nakhodki ot neolitnata kultura Karanovo IV v Starozagorsko." *Izvestija na bulgarskite muzei* (Bulletin of Bulgarian Museums: Sofia) 1 (1969): 21–41 (with a résumé in French).

Dinu, M.
1957 "Santierul arheologic Valea Lupului." *Materiale şi Cercetari Arheologice* 3:161–78.

Doan, James E.
1980 "Five Breton Cantignes from Pardons." *Folklore* 91:27–40.
1981 "Cearbhall O Dalaigh as Archetypal Poet in Irish Folk Tradition. *Proceedings of the Harvard Celtic Colloquium* 1:95–123.
1987 "Women and Goddesses in Early Celtic History, Myth and Legend." *Irish Studies Program.* Working Paper 87-4/5. Boston: Northeastern University.

Dombay, J.
1960 "Die Siedlung und das Gräberfeld in Zengövárkony." *Archaelogia Hungarica* (Budapest) 37.

Dor, L., J. Jannoray, and H. and M. van Effenterre
1960 *Kirrha: Étude de préhistoire phocidienne.* Paris: E. de Bocard.

Doumas, C. G.
1968 *The N. P. Goulandris Collection of Early Cycladic Art.* Athens; dist. in the USA: Praeger.
1982 *Thera: Pompeii of the Ancient Aegean.* London: Thames and Hudson.
1983 *Cycladic Art. The N. P. Goulandris collection.* London: British Museum Publications Ltd.

Downing, Chr.
1981 *The Goddess: Mythological Images of the Feminine.* New York: Crossroad.

Dragomir, I. T.
1983 *Eneoliticul din sud-estul romaniei. Aspectul cultural Stoicani-Aldeni.* Bucharest: Editura Acad. RSR.
1987 "Un vase-support cucuténien: 'La ronde de Bereşti'." *La Civilisation de Cucuténi en Contexte Européen*: 289–99. Session Scientifique Iaşi-Piatra Neamţ 1984, Iaşi, Université "Al. I. Cuza."

Duerr, H. P.
1978 *Traumzeit: über die Grenze zwischen Wildnis und Zivilisation.* Frankfurt am Main: Syndikat.

Dumézil, G.
1947 "La tripartition indo-européenne." *Psyche* 2:1348–56.
1952 "Les dieux des Indo-Européens." In *Mythes et Religions.* Ed. P.-L. Couchoud, vol. 29. Paris: Presses Universitaires de France.
1969 *Idées Romaines.* Paris: Gallimard.
1970 *Archaic Roman Religion.* Trans. by P. Krapp. Chicago: University of Chicago Press.

Dumitrescu, H.
1952–1959 Results of the Excavations of the Site at Traian: *Studii şi Cercetări de Istorie Veche* 3 (1952): 121–40; 4 (1953): 45–68; 5 (1954): 35–68; 6 (1955): 459–86; and *Materiale şi Cercetări Arheologice* 3 (1957): 115–28; 5 (1959): 189–202.
1954 "O descoperire in legatura cu ritul de inmormintare in cuprinsul culturii ceramicii pictate Cucuteni-Tripolie." Summaries in Russian: 425–27, and French: "Une découverte ayant trait au rite d'enterrement dans l'aire de la culture de la céramique peinte Cucuteni-Tripolye: 427–29. *Studii şi Cercetări de Istorie Veche* 5, nos. 3–4: 399–429.
1958 "Deux tombes cucuténiennes à rite magique découvertes à Traian." *Dacia* 2:407–23.
1960 "Antropomorfnye izobrazhenija na sosudakh iz Traian." *Dacia* 4:31–52.
1961 "Connections Between the Cucuteni-Tripolie Cultural Complex and the Neighboring Eneolithic Cultures in the Light of the Utilization of Golden Pendants." *Dacia* 5:69–93.
1968 "Un modèle de sanctuaire découvert dans la station enéolithique de Cascioarele." *Dacia* 12:381–94.

Dumitrescu, H., and V. Dumitrescu
1959 "Sapaturile de la Traian-dealul Fintinilor." *Materiale şi Cercetari Arheologice* 6:157–78.

Dumitrescu, V.
1945 *La station préhistorique de Traian; fouilles de 1936, 1938, et 1940.* Reprinted from *Dacia* 9–10 (1941–44), Bucharest.
1954 *Habaşeşti, Monografie Arheologică,* in collaboration with H. Dumitrescu, M. Petrescu-Dimboviţa, and N. Gostar. Bucharest: Academiei RPR.
1965 "Cascioarele." *Archaeology* 18:34.
1966 "New Discoveries at Gumelnitza." *Archaeology* 19.3:162–72.
1968 *L'art néolithique en Romanie.* Bucharest: Meridiane.
1970 "Édifice destiné au culte découvert dans la couche Boian-Şpantov de la station-tell de Cascioarele." *Dacia* 15:5–24.
1974 *Arta Preistorica in Romania.* Bucharest: Meridiane.
1979 *Arta Culturii Cucuteni.* Bucharest: Meridiane.
1980 *The Neolithic Settlement at Rast.* Trans. by N. Hampartumian. BAR International Series 72. Oxford.

Efimenko, P. R.
1958 *Kostienki I.* Moscow: Academy of Sciences.

Eisler, Riane
1987 *The Chalice and the Blade: Our History Our Future.* San Francisco: Harper and Row.

Eisler, Robert
1951 "The Passion of the Flax." *Folk-lore* (London) 62:114–33.

Ekenvall, A.
1978 *Batrachians as Symbols of Life, Death, and Woman.* Trans. by B. and E. Frykman. Göteborg: University Library.

Eliade, M.
1958 *Birth and Rebirth: The Religious Meanings of Initiation in Human Culture.* Trans. by W. P. Trask. New York: Harper and Bros.

1958a *Patterns in Comparative Religion.* London: Sheed and Ward.

1959 "Structure et fonction du mythe cosmologique." *La naissance du monde.* Ed. by Esnoul et al: 469–95.

1960 *Myths, Dreams, and Mysteries: The Encounter Between Contemporary Faiths and Archaic Realities.* Trans. by P. Mairet. New York: Harper and Bros.

1974 *Death, Afterlife, and Eschatology.* Part 3 of *From Primitives to Zen.* New York: Harper and Row.

Ellis, L.
1984 *The Cucuteni-Tripolye Culture: A Study in Technology and the Origins of Complex Society.* BAR International Series 217.

Eogan, G.
1967 "The Knowth (co. Meath) Excavations." *Antiquity* 41:302–4.

1983 "A Flint Macehead at Knowth, Co. Meath." *Antiquity* 57:45–6.

1986 *Knowth and the Passage-tombs of Ireland.* London: Thames and Hudson.

Eogan, G. and H. Richardson
1982 "Two Maceheads From Knowth, Co. Meath." *Journal of the Royal Society of Antiquaries of Ireland* 112:123–38.

Erlenmeyer, M. L., and H. Erlenmeyer
1965 "Von den frühen Bildkunst der Kykladen." *Antike Kunst* 8.2.

Evans, A.
1902 "The Palace of Knossos." *Annual of the British School at Athens* 9:1–153.

1903 "The Palace of Minos." *Annual of the British School at Athens* 8 (1901–2).

1904 *Excavations at Phylakopi in Melos Conducted by the British School at Athens.* The Society for the Promotion of Hellenic Studies, Supplementary Paper 4: London.

1914 "The Tomb of the Double Axes and Associated Groups and the Pillar Room and Ritual Vessels of the 'Little Palace' at Knossos." *Archaeologia* 65:1–94.

1921–1935 *The Palace of Minos: A Comparative Account of the Successive Stages of the Early Cretan Civilization as Illustrated by the Discoveries at Knossos.* Vol. 1 (1921), vol. 2 (1928), vol. 3 (1930), vol. 4 (1935). London: Macmillan.

Evans, Estyn E.
1957 *Irish Folk Ways.* London: Routledge and Kegan Paul.

Evans, J. D.
1957–1960 ." *Annual of the British School at Athens* 59:132–240.

1959 *Malta.* Ancient Peoples and Places 11. New York: Praeger.

1964 "Excavations in the Neolithic Settlement of Knossos,

1971 *The Prehistoric Antiquities of the Maltese Islands.* London: The Athlone Press.

Fehrle, E.
1916–1919 "Das Sieb im Volksglauben." *Archiv für Religionswissenschaft* 19:547–51.

Ferguson, Ian F. G.
1986 "New Views on the Hypogeum and Tarxien." *Archaeology and Fertility Cult in the Ancient Mediterranean.* Amsterdam: B. R. Grüner Publishing Co.

Ferrier, J.
1971 *Pendeloques et amulettes d'Europe.* Anthologie et reflexions. Périqueux: Pierre Fanlac.

Feustel, R.
1970 "Statuettes feminines paléolithiques de la République Democratique Allemande." *Bulletin de la Société Préhistorique Française* 67:12–16.

1971 "Sexuologische Reflexionen über jungpaläolithische Objekte." *Alt-Thüringen* 11:7–16.

Feustel, R., ed.
1972 *Typentafeln zur Ur- und Frühgeschichte.* Weimar: Kulturbund der DDR.

Filip, J., ed.
1966 *Enzyklopädisches Handbuch zur Ur- und Frühgeschichte Europas.* Stuttgart/Berlin/Cologne/Mainz: W. Kohlhammer.

Fischer, U.
1951 "Zu den mitteldeutschen Trommeln." *Archeologia Geographica* (Hamburg) 2: 98–105.

Florescu, M.
1978 "Citera observaţii referitoare la ritul şi ritualurile practicate de purtatorii culturii Monteoru in lumina sapaturilor de la Cindeşti (Jud. Vrancea)." *Carpica* 10:97–136.

1979 "Contribuţii la cunoasterea conceptilor despre lume şi viata a comunitatilor tribale monteorene." *Carpica* 11:57–134.

Forman, W., and B. and J. Poulík
1956 *Prehistoric Art.* Trans. by R. Finlayson Samsour. London: Spring Books.

Formozov, A. A.
1976 "Neopublikovannye proizvedenija iskusstva paleoliticheskoj stojanki Mal'ta." *Sovetskaja arkheologija* 4:180–84.

Forsdyke, E. J.
1929 "Minoan Art." *Proceedings of the British Academy* 15:45–72.

Foster, J
1977 *Bronze Boar Figurines in Iron Age and Roman Britain.* BAR British Series 39.

Frank, R. M., and D. P. Metzger
1982 *The Mother Goddess in Basque Oral Traditions.* Ms. University of Iowa.

Frankfort, H.
1965 *Cylinder Seals: A Documentary Essay on the Art and Religion of the Ancient Near East.* Reprint of 1939 ed. London: Gregg Press.

Franz, M.-L. von
1972 *Problems of the Feminine in Fairytales.* Dallas: Spring Publications.

Freedman, M.
1968 "Geomancy." *Proceedings of the Royal Anthropological Institute of Great Britain and Ireland for 1968*: 5–16.

Freeman, Leslie G., Richard G. Klein, and Joaquin G. Echegaray
1983 "A Stone Age Sanctuary." *Natural History* 92, no. 8: 47–52.

French, D. H.
1961 "Late Chalcolithic Pottery in Northwest Turkey and the Aegean." *Anatolian Studies* 11:99–141.

1962 "Excavations at Can Hasan: First Preliminary Report, 1961." *Anatolian Studies* 12:27–40.

French, E.
1971 "The Development of Mycenaean Terracotta Figurines." *British School of Archaeology* 66:101–87.

Furness, A.
1953 "The Neolithic Pottery of Knossos." *Annual of the British School at Athens* 48:94–134.

1957 "Some Early Pottery of Samos, Kalimnos, and Chios." *Proceedings of the Prehistoristic Society* 22:173–212.

Furumark, A.
1972 "Mycenaean Pottery 1: Analysis and Classification." *Svenska Institutet i Athen* (1st ed. 1941) 4, 20: 1.

Gagniere, J., and J. Granier
1963 "Les Stèles Anthropomorphes du Musée Calvet d'Avignon." *Gallia Prehistoire* 6:31–62.

Galibin, A.
1916 *Bel'giiskie narodnye skazki.* St. Petersburg.

Gallay, A.
1977 *Le Néolithique moyen du Jura et des plaines de la Saône: Contribution à l'étude des relations Chassey-Cortaillod-Michelsberg.* Fanenfeld, Switzerland: Huber.

Gallis, K. J.
1983 "Evidence for Funerary Rituals at Cremation Burials Since Early Neolithic in Thessaly (Greece)." *Prehistoric Art & Religion Valcamonica Symposium '79.* Ed. by A. Beltran et al: 99–104. Capo di Ponte: Edizioni del Centro.

1985 "A Late Neolithic Foundation Offering From Thessaly." *Antiquity* 59:20–23.

Galović, R.
1959 *Predionica: Neolitsko Naselje Kod Prištine* (German translation, Predionica: Äneolithische Ansiedlung bei Priština). Priština: Archaeological Museum.
1966 "The Monumental Prehistoric Clay Figures of the Middle Balkans." *American Journal of Archaeology* 70.4:370–71.

1968 "Die Starčevo Kultur in Jugoslawien." *Die Anfänge des Neolithikums vom Orient bis Nordeuropa* 2:1–22.

Garašanin, D.
1954 *Starčevačka kultura.* Univ. of Ljubljana.

Gavela, B. et al.
1968 *Neolit centralnog Balkana.* Belgrade: National Museum.

Georgiev, G. I.
1958 "Za nyakoj orudija za proizvodstvo ot neolita i eneolita u Bulgarija." *Studia in honorem D. Dečev* (Sofia): 369–87.

1961 "Kulturgruppen der Jungsteinzeit und der Kupferzeit in der Ebene von Thrazien (Südbulgarien)." *L'Europe à la fin de l'âge de la pierre: Actes du Symposium consacré aux problèmes du Néolithique européen*: 45–100. Prague: Éditions de l'Académie Tchécoslovaque des Sciences.

1965 "The Azmak Mound in Southern Bulgaria." *Antiquity* 39:6–8.

1967 "Beiträge zur Erforschung des Neolithikums und der Bronzezeit in Südbulgarien." *Österreich: Arbeitsgemeinschaft für Ur- und Frühgeschichte*: 90–144.

Georgiev, G. I., and N. Angelov
1952–1957 "Razkopki na selishtnata mogila do Ruse prez 1948–1949 god." *Izvestija.* Bulgarska Akad. na Naukite, Archeol. Inst. 18 (1952): 119–94 and 31 (1957):

Georgiev, P.
1976 "Novi danni za kulta kam slantseto v balgarskite zemi prez IV hil.pr. n.e." *Vekove*: 74–76.

Georgiev, V.
1969 "Un sceau inscrit de l'époque chalcolithique trouvé en Thrace." *Studi Micenei ed Egeo-Anatolici*: 32–35.

Gerasimov, M. M.
1958 "Paleoliticheskaja stojanka Mal'ta." *Sovetskaja Etnografija* 3:35–51.

Gervasio, M.
1921 *Bronzi arcaici e ceramica geometrica nel Museo di Bari.* Bari: Commissione Provinciale di Archeologia e Storia Patria, Documenti e Monografia 16.

Gesell, G.
1972 *The Archaeological Evidence for the Minoan House Cult and its Survival in Iron Age Crete.* Ph.d. dissertation. Ann Arbor: University Microfilms.
1976 "The Minoan Snake Tube: A Survey and Catalogue." *American Journal of Archaeology* 80, no. 3: 247–60.

Giedion, S.
1957–1962 *The Eternal Present.* Vol. 1. The Beginnings of Art. The A. W. Mellon Lectures in the Fine Arts, 1957; Bollingen Series 35. New York: Pantheon.

Gimbutas, M.
1956 *The Prehistory of Eastern Europe: Mesolithic, Neolithic and Copper Age Cultures in Russia and the Baltic Area.* Harvard University, Peabody Museum, American School of Prehistoric Research, Bulletin 20.
1958 *Ancient Symbolism in Lithuanian Folk Art.* Memoirs of the American Folklore Society 49: Philadelphia.
1972 "Excavations at Anza, Macedonia." *Archaeology* 25.2: 112–23.
1974 *The Gods and Goddesses of Old Europe: 7000 to 3500 B.C.: Myths, Legends, and Cult Images.* London: Thames and Hudson; and Berkeley: University of California Press.
1976 "Figurines." *Neolithic Macedonia as Reflected by Excavation at Anza, Southeast Yugoslavia.* Ed. M. Gimbutas: 198–241. Monumenta Archaeologica 1; Los Angeles: Institute of Archaeology, University of California.
1976a "Ideograms and Symbolic Design on Ritual Objects of Old Europe (Neolithic and Chalcolithic Southeast Europe)." *To Illustrate the Monuments.* J. V. S. Megaw, ed.: 77–98. London: Thames and Hudson.
1977 "The First Wave of Eurasian Steppe Pastoralists into Copper Age Europe." *The Journal of Indo-European Studies* 5, no. 4: 277–339.
1977a "Gold Treasure at Varna." *Archaeology* 30, no. 1: 44–51.
1977b "Varna: A Sensationally Rich Cemetery of the Karanovo Civilization, about 4500 B.C." *Expedition* 19, no. 4: 39–46
1978 "Le fin de l'Europe ancienne." *La Recherche* (Paris) 87:227–35.
1979 "The Three Waves of the Steppe People into East Central Europe." *Actes Suisses d'Anthropologie* (Geneva) 43, no. 2: 227–35.
1980 "The Kurgan Wave #2, c. 3400–3200 B.C." *The Journal of Indo-European Studies* 8, 3–4: 273–317.
1980a "The Temples of Old Europe." *Archaeology* 33:41–50.
1981 "Vulvas, Breasts, and Buttocks of the Goddess Creatress." *The Shape of the Past: Studies in Honor of Franklin D. Murphy*: Ed. by Giorgio Buccellati and Charles Speroni; pp. 15–43. Los Angeles: Institute of Archaeology, University of California.
1981a "The 'Monstrous Venus' of Prehistory or Goddess Creatrix." *Comparative Civilizations Review* 7 (Fall): 1–26.
1982 *The Goddesses and Gods of Old Europe, 6500–3500 B.C.: Myths and Cult Images.* New and updated edition (first edition appeared as *The Gods and Goddesses of Old Europe*). London: Thames and Hudson.
1984 "Senosios Europos deivės ir dievai lietuvių mitologijoje." *Metmenys* (Chicago) 48:28–57.
1985 "Pre-Indo-European Goddesses in Baltic Mythology." *The Mankind Quarterly* 1:19–26.
1986 "Mythical Imagery of the Sitagroi Society." *Excavations at Sitagroi.* Ed. by C. A. Renfrew, M. Gimbutas, and E. Elster: 225–302, pls. 45–65. Monumenta Archaeologica 13. Los Angeles: Institute of Archaeology, University of California Los Angeles.
1989 *Achilleion: A Neolithic Settlement in Thessaly, Greece, 6400–5600 B.C.* (with Shan Winn, Daniel Shimabuku et al., contributors). Monymenta Archaeologica 14. Los Angeles: Institute of Archaeology, University of California.

Gimbutas, M., D. Shimabuku, Shan Winn, et al.
1988 *Achelleion: A Neolithic Settlement in Northern Greece, 6400–5600 B.C.* Los Angeles: Monumenta Archaeologica, University of California Los Angeles.

Giot, P. R., J. L'Helgouach, and J. L. Monnier
1979 *Préhistoire de la Bretagne.* Rennes: Ouest-France.
1981 "The Megaliths of France." *The Megalithic Monuments of Western Europe.* Ed. by Colin Renfrew: 18–29. London: Thames and Hudson.

Glišic, J.
1957 "Preistoriska naselje na Gladnicama kod Gračanice." *Glasnik Muzeja Kosova i Metohije* II.

Glob, P. V.
1970 *The Mound People: Danish Bronze-Age Man Preserved.* Trans. by J. Bulman. Ithaca: Cornell University Press.
1975 *The Bog People: Iron-Age Man Preserved.* Trans. by R. Bruce-Mitford. Ithaca: Cornell University Press.

Goldberg, N.
1983 *Changing of the Gods: Feminism and the End of Traditional Religions.* Boston: Beacon Press.

Goldman, B.
1931 *Excavations at Eutresis in Boeotia.* Cambridge, Mass.: Harvard University Press.

Goldman, G.
1987 "Gesichtsgefässe und andere Menschendarstellungen aus Battonya." *A Békés Megyei Múzeumok Közleményei* (Békés) 5: 13–60.

Golomshtok, E. A.
1938 *The Old Stone Age in European Russia.* Transactions of the American Philosophical Society 29: Philadelphia.

Graves, R.
1960 *The Greek Myths.* Vol. 1. Penguin Books.
1972 *The White Goddess.* New York: Farrar, Strauss and Giroux.

Graziosi, P.
1960 *Palaeolithic Art.* New York: McGraw-Hill.
1971 "Le pitture preisoriche delle Grotte di Porto Badisco e S. Cesarea." *Rendiconti della Classe di Scienze morali, storiche e filologiche.* Ser. 8. 26 1–2:1–8. Accademia Nazionale dei Lincei.
1973 "Nuove manifestazioni d'arte mesolitica e neolitica nel riparo Gaban presso Trento." *Rivista di Scienze Preistoriche* 30, nos. 1–2: 237–78.
1980 *Le pitture preistoriche della grotta di Porto Badisco: Origines studi i materiali publicati Istituto Italiano di Preistoria e Protoistoria.* Florence: Giunti Martello.

Grbić, M. et al.
1960 *Porodin, kasnoneolitsko naselje na Tumbi kod Bitolja* (résumé in German: Eine spätneolithische Anseidlung auf der Tumba bei Bitolj in Makadonien-Pelagonier). Bitola: Archaeological Museum.

Greger, Sonia
1986 "The Cretan Gorgona: Monster or Goddess?" *Cultural Attitudes to Animals Including Birds, Fish, and Invertebrates.* The World Archaeological Congress, September 1–7, 1986, Southampton.

Greimas, A. J.
1979 *Apie dievus ir žmones. Lietuvių mitologijos studijos.* Chicago: A and M Publications.

Griaule, M. and G. Dieterlen
1954 "The Dogon." *African Worlds: Studies in the Cosmological Ideas and Social Values of African Peoples*: 83–110. London: Oxford University Press.

Groenewegen-Frankfort, H. A.
1951 *Arrest and Movement: An Essay on Space and Time in the Representational Art of the Ancient Near East.* London: Faber and Faber.

Grundmann, K.
1932 "Aus neolithischen Siedlungen bei Larisa." *Athenische Mitteilungen* 57:102–23.
1937 "Magula Hadzimissiotiki: Eine steinzeitliche Siedlung im Karla-See." *Athenische Mitteilungen* 62:56–69.
1953 "Figürliche Darstellungen in der neolithischen Keramik Nord und Mittel-Griechenlands." *Jahrbuch des Deutschen Archäologischen Instituts* (Berlin) 68:1–37.

Gugitz, G.
1955 "Fest- und Brauchtumskalender für Österreich, Süddeutschland und die Schweiz." *Bücherreihe österreichische Heimat* 19 (Vienna).

Guilaine, J.
1976 *Premiers bergers et paysans de l'Occident méditerranéen.* Paris/The Hague: Mouton.

Gulder, A.
1960 "Die urnenfelderzeitliche 'Frauenkröte' von Maissau in Niederösterreich und ihr geistesgeschichtlicher Hintergrund." *Mitteilungen der prähistorischen Kommission der österreichischen Akademie der Wissenschaften* 10:1–157.

Gurba, J.
1956 "Miniaturowe gliniane modele toporków z miejsc. Grzegorzewice, pow. Opatów." *Wiadomości archeologiczne* (Warsaw) 23, 1: 114–15.

Gurina, N. N.
1956 *Oleneostrovskij mogil'nik.* Materialy i issledovanija po Arkheologii SSSR, 47, Moscow-Leningrad.

Hadaczek, K.
1914 *La colonie industrielle de Koszylowce* (Lviv).

Hadinham, E.
1974 *Ancient Carvings in Britain: A Mystery.* London: Garnstone Press.

Hall, N.
1980 *The Moon and the Virgin: Reflections on the Archetypal Feminine.* New York: Harper and Row.

Hallström, G.
1960 *Monumental Art of Northern Sweden from the Stone Age: Nämforsen and other Localities.* Stockholm: Almquist and Wiksell.

Hamp, Eric P.
1975 "Indo-European *āu̯ before consonant in British and Indo-European 'sun'." *The Bulletin of the Board of Celtic Studies* 26.2: 97–102.
1979–80 "Imbolc, óimelc." *Studia Celtica* 14–15: 106–13.

Hampe, R.
1936 *Frühe griechische Sagenbilder in Böotien.* Athens: Deutches Archäologisches Institut.

Hampe, R., and E. Simon
1981 *The Birth of Greek Art: From the Mycenaean to the Archaic Period.* New York: Oxford University Press.

Hančar, F.
1940 "Problem der Venusstatuetten im eurasiatischen Jungpaläolithikum." *Prähistorische Zeitschrift* 30–31.

Harrison, J. E.
1922 *Prolegomena to the Study of Greek Religion,* 3rd ed. Cambridge: Cambridge University Press.
1948 *Ancient Art and Ritual.* London/New York/Toronto: G. Cumberlege.
1962 *Themis: A Study of the Social Origins of Greek Religion.* First ed. 1912. Cleveland and New York: Meridian Books.

Hartuche, N. A., and F. Anastasiu
1968 *Brailița: Asezari și cimitire omenești datind din epoca neolitica pina in pragul orinduirii feudale* (Braila).

Haussig, H. W., ed.
1973 *Wörterbuch der Mythologie,* vol. 2. Götter und Mythen im alten Europa, with J. Balys, J. Miguel de Barandiarán, a.o. Stuttgart: Ernst Klett.

Hawkes, J.
1958 *Dawn of the Gods.* London: Chatto & Windus.

Hazzidakis, J.
1921 *Tylissos à l'époque minoenne: Étude de préhistoire crétoise.* Paris: Paul Geuthner.

Hedges, J. W.
1983 *Isbister: A Chambered Tomb in Orkney.* BAR British Series 115. Oxford.
1984 *Tomb of the Eagles.* London: John Muzzay.

Hegedüs, Katalin
1981 "Ojkokori lakotelep Czanytelek Hatarabol" (summary in English: "Excavations at the Neolithic Settlement of Czanytelek-Ujhalasto"). *Archaeologiai Értesitö* (Budapest) 108, 1: 3–12.

Heggie, Douglas C.
1981 *Megalithic Science. Ancient Mathematics and Astronomy in Northwest Europe.* London: Thames and Hudson.

Hein, W.
1900 "Die Opfer-Bärmutter als Stachelkugel." *Zeitschrift des Vereins für Volkskunde* (Berlin): 420–28.

Hencken, H. O'N.
1939 "A Long Cairn at Creevykeel, Co. Sligo." *Journal of the Royal Society of Antiquaries of Ireland* 69:53–98.

Hennessy, W. M.
1870–2 "The Ancient Irish Goddess of War." *Revue Celtique* I (Paris): 32–55.

Hensel, W.
1980 *Polska Starożytna,* 2nd ed. Wroclaw/Warsaw/Gdańsk: Ossolineum.

Hensel, W., and T. Wislański, eds.
1979 *Prahistoria ziem polskich* 2 (Neolit). Wroclaw/Warsaw/Cracow/Gdańsk: Polska Academia nauk.

Henshall, A. S.
1963 *The Chambered Tombs of Scotland,* vol. 1. Edinburgh: Edinburgh University Press.
1972 *The Chambered Tombs of Scotland,* vol. 2. Edinburgh: Edinburgh University Press.

Hentze, C.
1932 *Mythes et symboles lunaires.* Anvers: Editions "De Sikkel".

Herity, M.
1974 *Irish Passage Graves, Neolithic Tomb-Builders in Ireland and Britain 2500 BC.* New York: Barnes and Noble, and Dublin: Irish University Press.

Herscher, E.
1975 "New Light from Lapithos." *The Archaeology of Cyprus; Recent Developments.* Ed. by N. Robertson: 39–50. Park Ridge, N.J.: Noyes Press.

Higgins, R. A.
1967 *Greek Terracottas.* London: Methuen.
1973 *The Archaeology of Minoan Crete.* London: Bodley Head.

Höckman, O.
1965 "Menschliche Darstellungen in der bandkeramischen Kultur." *Jahrbuch Röm.-Germ. Zentral-Museums* 12: 1–34.

Holmberg, E. J.
1939 "Excavations at Asea in Arcadia, 1936–1938." *Göteborgs Högskolas Arsskrift* 45:1–23.
1964 "The Neolithic Pottery of Mainland Greece." *Göteborgs Kungl. Vetenskaps—och Vitterhets—sämhalles Handlingar.* Series A, VII, 2: 1–56.

Hood, S.
1978 *The Arts in Prehistoric Greece.* The Pelican History of Art. Harmondsworth: Penguin Books.

Hooijer, D. A.
1961 "The Fossil Vertebrates of Ksar'akil: A Palaeolithic Rock Shelter in the Lebanon." *Zoologische Verhandelingen* 49 (March 31, 1961). Leiden: E. J. Brill.

Hourmouziades, E. J.
1969 "Eiclesis ek Thessalias: Megali Vrisi." *Athens Annals. Archaeology:* 169–72.

Hourmouziades, G. Ch.
1972 *Megalo Pazaraki.* Archeion Tessalikon Meleton, Volos.

Hultkrantz, A.
1961 "The Owner of the Animals in the Religion of the North American Indians." *The Supernatural Owners of Nature*: 53–64. Stockholm: Almquist and Wiksell.

Ingersoll, E.
1923 *Birds in Legend, Fable, and Folklore.* New York: Longmans, Green, and Company.

Ivanov, I. S.
1978 "Les fouilles archéologiques de la nécropole chalcolithique à Varna (1972–1975)." *Studia Praehistorica* (Sofia) 1–2: 13–26.
1978 *Sakrovishchata na Varnenskija khalkoliten nekropol.* Sofia: Septemvri.

Ivinskis, Z.
1950 "Vatikano archyvas-aruodas lietuvių kultūros istorijai." *Aidai* (New York) March: 10–13.

Jacobsen, T.
1976 *The Treasures of Darkness: A History of Mesopotamian Religion.* New Haven: Yale University Press.

Jacopi, G.
1929 "Scavi nella necropoli di Jalisso, 1924–1928." *Clara Rhodos* 3.
1931 "Esplorazione archaeologica di Camiro I. Scavi nelle necropoli camiresi, 1929–1930." *Clara Rhodos* 4.

Jahn, U.
1977 Die deutchen Opfergebräuche bei Akerbau und Viehzucht. New York: Olms. First published in 1884.

James, E. O.
1959 *The Cult of the Mother-Goddess.* London: Thames and Hudson.
1961 *Seasonal Feasts and Festivals.* London: Thames and Hudson.

Janzon, Gunborg O.
1983 "Zoomorphic Figurines and Beads from Ire, Hangvar Parish, Gotland." *Fornvännen* 78:1–20.

Jensen, H.
1969 *Sign, Symbol, and Script: An Account of Man's Efforts to Write.* New York: G. P. Putnam.

Joffroy, R.
1979 *Vix et ses trésors.* Paris: Tallandier.

Johns, A. H., and Y. Johns
1972 *The Civilization of Prehistoric Cyprus.* Australia: Thomas Nelson.

Joussaume, R.
1987 *Dolmens for the Dead.* Batsford: Hachette.

Jovanović, B.
1964 "La céramique anthropomorphe de l'enéolithique des Balkans et du Bas-Danube." *Archaeologia Iugoslavica* 5:9–16.
1967 "La signification de certains éléments de culte du groupe de Starčevo." *Starinar* 18:11–20.
1978 "The Oldest Copper Metallurgy in the Balkans." *Expedition* 21.1:9–17.
1980 "The Origins of Copper Mining in Europe." *Scientific American* 245.5:152–67.
1982 Rudna Glava. Der älteste Kupferbau im Zentralbalkan. Belgrade: Bor.

Jovanović, B., and J. Glišic
1961 "Eneolitsko naselje na Kormadinu kod Jakova." Station enéolithique dans la localité de Kormadin près de Jakov. *Starinar* 1960:113–42.

Kaelas, L.
1981 "Megaliths of the Funnel Beaker Culture in Germany and Scandinavia." *The Megalithic Monuments of Western Europe.* Ed. by C. Renfrew: 77–91. London: Thames and Hudson.

Kaindl, R. Fr.
1908 "Neolithische Funde mit bemalter Keramik in Koszylowce (Ostgalizien)." *Jahrbuch für Altertumskunde* 2:144–50.

Kaiser, B.
1976 *Untersuchungen zum minoischen Relief.* Bonn: Habelt.

Kalicz, N.
1970 *Clay Gods: The Neolithic Period and Copper Age in Hungary.* Trans. by B. Balogh. Budapest: Corvina.
1970a *Dieux d'Argile l'âge de pierre et du cuivre en Hongrie.* Trans. by P. Komoly. Budapest: Corvina.

Kalicz, N., and J. Makkay
1972 "Gefässe mit Gesichtsdarstellungen der Linienbandkeramik in Ungarn." *Idole, prähistorische Keramiken aus Ungarn.* Naturhistorisches Museum (Vienna), N.F. 7:9–15, Taf. 11, 12.
1972a "Südliche Einflüsse im frühen und mittleren Neolithikum Transdanubiens." *Alba Regia* 12 (1971). Székésfehervar.

1977 *Die Linienbandkeramik in der grossen ungarischen Tiefebene.* Budapest: Akademiai Kiado.

Kalicz, N., and P. Raczky
1981 "The Precursors to the 'Horns of Consecration' in the Southeast European Neolithic." *Acta Archaeologica Academiae Scientiarum Hungaricae* 33, 1-4: 5-20.

Kalil, L.
1979 "La déesse Artémis: mythologie et iconographie." *Greece and Italy in the Classical World*; ed. by J. N. Coldstream: 73-87.

Kandyba, O.
1937 *Schipenitz: Kunst und Geräte eines neolitischen Dorfes.* Bücher zur Ur- und Frühgeschichte 5. Leipzig: A. Schroll and Co.

Karageorghis, J.
1977 *La grande déesse de Chypre et son culte à travers l'iconographie de l'époque néolithique au VIème s.a.C.* Lyons: Maison de l'Orient.

Karageorghis, V.
1962 *Treasures in the Cyprus Museum.* Cyprus Dept. of Antiquities, Picture Book 1: Nicosia.
1964 "Chronique des fouilles et découvertes archéologiques à Chypre en 1963." *Bulletin de Correspondance Hellénique* (École Française d'Athènes) 88. 1: 289-379.
1965 "Notes on some Centaurs from Crete." *Kritika Chronika*: 50-54.
1976 Kition: Mycenaean and Phoenician Discoveries. Proceedings of the British Academy 59. Mortimer Wheeler Lecture.

Karageorghis, V., and J. des Gagniers
1979 *La céramique Chypriote de style figuré: Âge du fer (1050-500 av. J.-C.).* Supplement. Consiglio Nazionale delle Ricerche, Istituto per gli Studi Micenei ed Egeo-Anatolici, Biblioteca de Antichità Cipriote 5. Rome: Edizioni dell'Ateneo e Bizzarri.

Karmanski, S.
1968 Žrtvenici, statuete i amuleti sa lokaliteta Donja Branjevina kod Deronja (Odžaci).
1977 *Katalog Antropomorfne i zoomorfne plastike iz okoline Odžaka* (Odžaci).

Katinčarov, R.
1973 "Otnosno datirovkata i interpretatsijata na mramornata figurka ot gr.Kazanlak." Summary in French: "Sur la datation et interpretation de la figurine en marbre de Kazanlak." *Archeologija* 15.3:22-30.

Keller, Josef
1955 "Das Fürstengrab von Reinheim (Kreis St. Ingbert, Saarland)." *Germania* 33, 1/2: 33-42.

Keller, O.
1963 *Die antike Tierwelt*, II. Hildesheim: Georg Olms Verlagsbuchhandlung.
1987 "Rana e rospo." *Quaderni Di Semantica* 8.2: 207-18.

Kendrick, T. D.
1928 *The Archaeology of the Channel Islands*, vol. 1. The Bailiwick of Guernesey. London: Methuen.

Kenna, V. E. G.
1960 *Cretan Seals, with a Catalogue of the Minoan Gems in the Ashmolean Museum.* Oxford: Clarendon Press.
1968 "Ancient Crete and the Use of the Cylinder Seal." *American Journal of Archaeology* 72. 4:321-36.

Kennedy, A. B.
1987 "Ecce Bufo: il rospo in natura e nell'iconografia degli Olmec." *Quaderni Di Semantica* 8.2:229-63.

Kenner, H.
1954 *Das Theater und der Realismus in der griechischen Kunst.* Vienna: A. Sexl.

Kerbelytė, B.
1973 *Lietuvių liaudies padavimų katalogas.* Vilnius, Lietuvių Kalbos ir Literatūros Institutas, Lietuvos TSR Akademija.

Kerényi, K.
1978 *Athene: Archetype of Virgin and Mother in Greek Religion.* Dallas: Spring Publications.

Kinsley, D.
1975 *The Sword and the Flute: Kali and Kršna.* Berkeley: University of California Press.

Klebs, R.
1882 *Der Bernsteinschmuck der Steinzeit von der Baggerei bei Schwarzort und anderen Lokalitäten Preussens.* Beiträge zur Naturkunde Preussens 5. Königsberg: W. Koch.

Klein, R. G.
1969 *Man and Culture in the Late Pleistocene.* San Francisco: Chandler Publishing.

König, M. E. P.
1973 *Am Anfang der Kultur: Die Zeichensprache des frühen Menschen.* Berlin: Gebr. Mann Verlag.

Korfman, M.
1979 "Eine weibliche Gottheit in der Frühbronzezeit Anatoliens." *Prähistorische Zeitschrift* 54: 187-200.

Korkuti, M.
1971 "Fouilles archéologiques 1967-69 en Albanie." *Studia Albanica* (Tirana) 8:130-32.

Korkuti, M., and A. Zhaneta
1972 "Fouilles 1969-70 dans l'agglomeration néolithique de Cakran (Fieri)." *Studia Albanica* (Tirana) 9.1:16-30.

Korošec, J.
1953 "Prehistorijska glinena plastika u Jugoslaviji." "Prehistoric Plastic Art in Yugoslavia." *Arheološki Radovi i Rosprave* (Ljubljana) 1:61-115.
1958 *Neolitska naseobina u Danilu Bitinju*, vol. 1. Zagreb: Academy of Arts and Sciences.

Kosmopoulos, L. W.
1948 *The Prehistoric Inhabitation of Corinth.* Munich: Müncher Verlag.

Kovács, T.
1973 "Askoi, Bird-shaped Vessels, Bird-shaped Rattles in Bronze Age Hungary." *Folia Archaeologica* 23:7-28.

Kriss, R.
1929 *Das Gebärmutter—motiv.* Augsburg.

Kübler, K.
1943 *Kerameikos* 4. Berlin: de Gruyter.

Kühn, H.
1956 *The Rock Pictures of Europe.* Fairlawn, N.J.: Essential Books.

Kunkel, O.
1955 "Die Jungfernhöhle bei Tiefenellern, eine neolithische Kultstätte bei Bamberg." *Münchner Beiträge* 5.

Kusurgasheva, A. P.
1970 "Antropomorfnaja plastika iz poselenija Novye Ruseshtv I." *Kratkie Soobshchenija Instituta Arkheologii*, AN SSR (Moscow), vyp. 123:69-77.

Kutzián, I.
See Bognár-Kutzián.

LTA
Lietuvių Tautosakos Archyvas (Lithuanian Folklore Archive). Vilnius: Lithuanian Academy of Sciences.

Laming-Emperaire, A.
1962 *La signification de l'art rupestre paléolithique.* Paris: Picard.

Larousse
1969 *New Larousse Encyclopedia of Mythology.* Intro. by Robert Graves. London: Larousse.

Laszló, A.
1972 "Vases néolithiques à face humaine, découvertes en Roumanie." *Alba Regia* 12:211-35.

Latkovski, L., Sr.
1978 *The Origin and Meaning of Jumis in Latvian Folklore.* Lecture presented at the 6th Conference of Baltic Studies, Toronto.

Laumonier, A.
1958 *Les cultes indigènes en Carie.* Bibliothèque des École Franc. d'Athènes et de Rome 188. Paris: E. de Boccard.

Lawler, L. B.
1964 *The Dance in Ancient Greece.* London: Adam and Charles Black.

Lawson, J. C.
1964 *Modern Greek Folklore and Ancient Greek Religion.* New York: University Books.

Legge, F.
1917 "The Most Ancient Goddess Cybele." *Royal Asiatic Society of Great Britain and Ireland* (London): 695-714.

Leisner, G. K., and V. Leisner
1956 *Die Megalithgräber der Iberischen Halbinsel: Der Westen*, vol. 1. Berlin: de Gruyter.
1959 Ibid., vol. 2

Leisner, V., and C. Cerdán Marquez
1952 *Los Sepulcros Megaliticos de Huelva.* Informes y Memorias 26. Madrid: Comisaría General de Excavations Arqueológicas.

Lèmozi, A.
1929 *La grotte-temple du Pech-Merle: Un nouveau sanctuaire préhistorique.* Paris: A. Picard.

Leroi-Gourhan, A.
1958 "La fonction des signes dans les sanctuaires paléolithiques." *Bulletin de la Société Préhistorique Française* 55:307-21.
1958a "Le symbolisme des grands signes dans l'art pariétal paléolithique." *Bulletin de la Société Préhistorique Française* 55:384-98.
1967 *Treasures of Prehistoric Art.* New York: Harry N. Abrams.

Leroi-Gourhan, A., and J. Allain, eds.
1979 *Lascaux Inconnu.* Gallia Préhistoire suppl. 13.

Le Roux, C.-T.
1982 "Nouvelles gravures à Gavrinis, Larmor-Baden (Morbihan)." *Bulletin de la Société Préhistorique Française* 79. 3:89-96.
1985 *Gavrinis et les îles du Morbihan. Les mégalithes du golfe.* Guides Archéologiques de la France. Impr. Nationale.

Letica, Z.
1973 *Antropomorfne figurine bronzanog doba u Jugoslaviji.* Dissertationes et Monographiae 16. Belgrade University.

Levi, D.
1952 "La necropoli di Anghelu Ruju e la civiltà eneolitica della Sardegna." *Studi Sardi* 10–11:3–20.
1956 "A Magnificent Crater and Rich Pottery from the Crete of 4000 Years Ago: New and Vivid Light on the Earliest Palace of Phaistos." *The Illustrated London News* 6 (Oct): 548–50.
1969 *Early Hellenic Pottery of Crete.* Reprint of the 1945 ed. Princeton Monographs in Art and Archaeology 23. Amsterdam: Adolf M. Hakkert.
1976 *Festòs e la civiltà minoica* 1. Incunabula Graeca 40. Rome: Edizioni dell'Ateneo.

Levy, R. G.
1963 *Religious Conceptions of the Stone Age and their Influence upon European Thought.* New York: Harper Torch Books.

L'Helgouach, J.
1957 "L'allée couverte de Prajou—Menhir en Trébeurden (Côtes-du-Nord). *Annales de Bretagne* 64:1–8.
1965 *Les sépultures mégalithiques en Armorique: Dolmens à couloir et allées couvertes.* Travaux du Laboratoire d'anthropologie préhistorique de la Faculté des Sciences. Rennes: Alençon, Impr. Alençonnaise.

Lichardus, J., and S. Šiška
1970 "Záchranny vyskum pohrebiska a sídliska lengyelskej kultúry vo svodíne roku 1965." *Slovenská archeológia* 18. 2:311–52.

Liègeois, J.
1976 "Les statues-menhirs de la Corse." *Actes di Congresso storico Liguria-Corsica May, Istituto internazionale di Studi Liguri,* Massa Si Canare.

Lies, H.
1963 "Eine neue Reliefplastik der Bandkeramik von Barleben, Kr. Wolmirstadt." *Ausgrabungen und Funde* 10:10–14.

Lilliu, G.
1957 "Religione della Sardegna prenuragica." *Bollettino di Paletnologia Italiana* 11.

Lilliu, G., and H. Schubart
1967 *Frühe Randkulturen des Mittelmeerraumes: Korsika-Sardinien-Balearen-Iberische Halbinsel.* Baden-Baden: Holle Verlag.

Lincoln, B.
1984 *Indo-European Myths of Creation, Destruction, and Society.* Ms., University of Minnesota.
1986 *Myth, Cosmos, and Society. Indo-European Themes of Creation and Destruction.* Cambridge, Mass. and London, England: Harvard University Press.

Littleton, C. Scott
1982 *The New Comparative Mythology. An Anthropological Assessment of the Theories of Georges Dumézil.* Third edition. Berkeley, Los Angeles, London: University of California Press.

Liungman, W.
1961 "Das Rå und der Herr der Tiere." *The Supernatural Owners of Nature.* Ed. by A. Hultkrautz, 72–100. Stockholm: Almquist and Wiksell.

Liversage, D.
1966 "Ornamented Mesolithic Artifacts from Denmark: Some New Finds." *Acta Archaeologica* (Copenhagen) 37:221–37.

Lloyd, S., and J. Mellaart
1962 *Beycesultan I.* Occasional Publications of the British Institute of Archaeology at Ankara 6, London.

Long, Ch. R.
1974 *The Ayia Triadha Sarcophagus. A Study of Late Minoan and Mycenaean Funerary Practices and Beliefs.* Studies in Mediterranean Archaeology, vol. 16. Göteborg.

Lo Schiavo, E., D. Pannedda, G. Tanda, et al.
1976 *Nuove testimonianze archeologiche della Sardegna centro settentrionale.* Dessisassari, Ministero per i Beni Culturali e Ambientali.

Lo Schiavo, F.
1978 "Figurazioni antropomorfe nella Grotta del Bue Marino-Cala Gronone (Dorgali)." *Sardegna Centro-Prientle dal Neolitico alla Fine del Mondo Antico:* 53–55.
1982 "La domus dell'Ariete (Perfugas, Sassari)." *Rivista di scienze preistoriche* 37, 1–2: 135–86.

Loze, I.
1969 "Novyj centr obrabotki jantarja neoliticheskoj épokhi v Vostochnoj Pribaltike." Résumé: "Un nouveau centre du travail de l'ambre à l'époque néolithique dans les pays Baltique est." *Sovetskaja arkheologija* 3:124–34.
1983 *Akmens laikmeta māksla Austrumbaltijā.* Riga: Zinatne.

Lumley, H. de., M.-E. Fonvielle, and J. Abelanet
1976 "Les gravures rupestres de l'âge du Bronze dans la région du Monte Bégo (Tende, Alpes-Maritimes)." *La préhistoire française* 2: 222–36. Paris: Éd. Centre National de la Recherche Scientifique.

Luquet, G. H.
1934 "Les Venus paléolithiques." *Journal de Psychologie* (Paris) 31: 429–60.

Lurker, M., ed.
1968 *Bibliographie zur Symbolik, Ikonographie und Mythologie.* Baden-Baden: Heitz.
1983 *The Gods and Symbols of Ancient Egypt.* London: Thames and Hudson.

MacCana, P.
1981–82 "Women in Early Irish Mythology." *Crane Baq* (Dublin): 4.

McNeill, F. Marian
1957–68 *The Silver Bough.* Glasgow: W. Macellan.

McPherson, J.
1929 *Primitive Beliefs in the North-east of Scotland.* London: Longmans.

Máchal, J.
1964 "Slavic Mythology." *The Mythology of all Races,* 1st ed. 1918. New York: Cooper Square.

McKay, J. G.
1932 "The Deer-Cult and the Deer-Goddess Cult of Ancient Caledonia." *Folklore* 43:144–74.

Mackenzie, D. A.
1917 *Myths of Crete and Pre-Hellenic Europe.* London: Greshan.

Mackie, E.
1977 *The Megalith Builders.* Oxford: Phaidon.

Maclean, C.
1964 "The Last Sheaf." *Scottish Studies* (Edinburgh) 8:193–207.

McMann, J.
1980 *Riddles of the Stone Age: Rock Carvings of Ancient Europe.* London: Thames and Hudson.

Maier, F. G.
1969 "Dans les nécropoles de Palaeopaphos." in "Chypre à L'aube de son histoire." *Archéologie vivante* 2, 3: 116–30.

Maier, K. A.
1961 "Neolithische Tierknochen-Idole und Tierknochen-Anhänger Europas." *Bericht Röm.-Germ. Komission:* 171–305.

Maier, R. A.
1957 "Zu einigen Fremdelementen der Cortaillod-kultur." *Germania* 35:6–10.

Makarenko, N. E.
1927 "Sculpture de la civilisation tripolienne en Ukraine." *IPEK*: 119–29.

Makarevich, M. L.
1960 "Issledovanija v rajone s. Stena na Srednem Dnestre." *Kratkie Soobshchenija Instituta Arkheologii* (Kiev) 10: 23–32
1906a "Ob ideologicheskikh predstavlenijakh u tripolskikh plemen." *Odesskoe arkheologicheskoe obshchestvo* (Odessa) 1, 34: 290–301.

Makkay, J.
1964 "Early Near Eastern and Southeast European Gods." *Acta Archaeologica* 16:3–64.
1965 "Die wichtigsten Fragen der Körös-Starčevo Periode." *Acta Antiqua et Archaeologica*: 3–18.
1969 "The Late Neolithic Tordos Group Signs." *Alba Regia* (Annales Musei Stephani Regis) 10:9–49.
1971 "A Chalcolithic Stamp Seal from Karanovo, Bulgaria." *Kadmos* 10:1–9.
1972 "Eingeritzte und plastische Menschendarstellungen der transdanubischen Linienbandkeramik." *Idole, Prähistorische Keramiken aus Ungarn.* Naturhistorisches Museum, N.F. 7:16–19, taf. 13–15, Vienna.
1978 "Excavations at Bicske, I. The Early Neolithic—the Earliest Linear Band Ceramic." *Alba Regia* (Székésfehervár) 16:9–60.
1983 "Foundation Sacrifices in Neolithic Houses of the Carpathian Basin." *Prehistoric Art & Religion Valcamonica Symposium '79.* Ed. by A. Beltran et al: 157–67. Capo di Ponte: Edizione del Centro.
1985 "Neuere Typen der Körös-Starčevo Plastik." *Journal of Mediterranean Archaeology* 3.

Mallowan, M. E. L.
1947 "Excavations at Brak and Chagar Bazar." *Iraq* 9, 2:89–259.

Malten, L.
1928 "Der Stier in Kult und mythischen Bild." *Jahrbuch des deutschen archaeologischen Instituts* 43:90–139.

Mannhardt, W.
1936 *Letto-preussische Götterlehre.* Riga: Lettisch-Literarische Gesellschaft 21.

Marazov, I.
1983 "Kultyt kym mechkata v drevna Trakija." *Izkustvo* (Sofia) 33, 4: 28–36.

Marinatos, Nanno
1984 *Art and Religion in Thera. Reconstructing a Bronze Age Society.* Athens: Dial. Mathioulakis.

Marinatos, S.
1968 *Excavations at Thera* 1–7. Bibliothèketesen Athenais Archaiologikes Hetaireias 64. Athens: Greek Archaeological Society.
1968 "Die Eulengöttin von Pylos." *Mitteilungen des Deutschen Archäologischen Instituts, Athenische Abteilung* (Berlin) 83: 167–74, pls.

Marinatos, S., and M. Hirmer
1960 *Crete and Mycenae.* Trans. by J. Boardman. London: Thames and Hudson.
1973 *Kreta, Thera und das mykenische Hellas,* 2nd. ed. Munich: Hirmer.

Marinescu-Bîlcu, S.
1961 "Doua vase zoomorfe din cultura Gumelniţa." *Studii şi Cercetări Istorie Veche* 12, 2:345-58.
1967 "Die Bedeutung einiger Gesten und Haltungen in der jungsteinzeitlichen Skulptur der ausserkarpatischen Gebiete Rumäniens." *Dacia* 11:47-58.
1971 "Aspects tardifs de la civilisation à céramique rubannée et sa contribution à la genèse de la civilisation Précucuteni I." *Praehistorische Zeitschrift* 46, 1:4-36.
1972 "A propos des influences de la culture Précucuteni sur la culture de Hamangia, à la lumière de quelques découvertes inédites de Dobrogea." *Dacia* 16:53-73.
1974 *Cultura Precucuteni pe teritoriul României.* Biblioteca de arheologie 22. Bucharest: Academy of R S Romania, Institute of Archaeology.
1974a "La plastica in terracotta della cultura precucuteniana." *Rivista di Scienze Preistoriche* 29, 2: 399-436.

Marinescu-Bîlcu, S., and B. Ionescu
1968 *Catalogul sculpturilor eneolitice din Muzeul raional Olteniţa.*

Markevich, V. I.
1965 "Issledovanija neolita na srednem Dnestre." *Kratkie soobshchenija Instituta Arkheologii,* 105:85-90. Moscow: Nauka.
1970 "Mnogoslojnoe poselenie Novye Ruseshty I." *Kratkie soobshchenija Instituta Arkheologii,* 123:56-68. Moscow: Nauka.
1981 *Pozdnetripol'skie plemena severnoj Moldavii.* Kishinev: Stiintsa.

Markotić, V.
1984 "The Great Greek Pan: An Early Hominid?" *The Sasquatch and Other Unknown Hominoids*: 251-64. Calgary: Western Publishers.

Marshack, A.
1970 "Polesini: A Reexamination of the Engraved Upper Palaeolithic Mobiliary Materials of Italy by a New Methodology." *Rivista di Scienze Preistoriche* (1969) 24:219-81.
1972 *The Roots of Civilization: The Cognitive Beginnings of Man's First Art, Symbol, and Notation.* New York: McGraw-Hill.
1974 "The Meander as a System: the Analysis and Recognition of Iconographic Units in Upper Palaeolithic Compositions." *Biennial Conference, Australian Institute of Aboriginal Studies,* 16. P. Ucko, ed.
1976 "Complexité des traditions symboliques du Paléolithique supérieur." *La Préhistoire Française, I. Les Civilisations Paléolithiques et Mésolithiques de la France.* Ed. by Henry de Lumley: 49-53. Paris: Editions du Centre National de la Recherche Scientifique.
1977 "The Meander as a System: the Analysis and Recognition of Iconographic Units in Upper Palaeolithic Compositions." *Form in Indigenous Art*: 286-317. Canberra: Australian Institute of Aboriginal Studies, and London: Duckworth.
1979 *Ice Age Art: The Exhibit.* An Exhibit of Ice Age Art and Symbol. Prepared by the American Museum of Natural History and Alexander Marshack, Curatorial Consultant, California Academy of Sciences.
1979a "Ukrainian Upper Palaeolithic Symbol Systems: A Cognitive and Comparative Analysis of Complex Ritual Marking." *Current Anthropology* 20:271-311.
1979b "Upper Paleolithic Symbol Systems of the Russian Plain: Cognitive and Comparative Analysis." *Current Anthropology* 20:271-311.
1981 *Epipaleolithic, Early Neolithic Iconography.* Paper delivered at Römisch-Germanisches Museum, Cologne, Feb. 18-25, 1981.
1983 "European Upper Paleolithic-Mesolithic Continuity: A Cognitive, Comparative Study of Ritual Marking." *Prehistoric Art and Religion: Valcamonica Symposium '79.* Ed. by A. Beltran et al: 111-19. Capo di Ponte: Edizioni del Centro.
1984 "Epipaleolithic, Early Neolithic Iconography: A Cognitive, Comparative Analysis of the Lepenski Vir/Vlasac Iconography and its Later Influence." *Journal of Mediterranean Anthropology and Archaeology* 2. Proceedings of the International Symposium "The Culture of Lepenski Vir and the Problems of the Formation of Neolithic Cultures in Southeastern and Central Europe."

Marshall, Dorothy N.
1979 "Carved stone balls." *Proceedings of the Society of Antiquaries of Scotland* 108 (1976-7): 40-72.

Masson, O.
1969 "Croyances et sanctuaires à l'époque préhistorique," in "Chypre à l'Aube de son Histoire." *Archéologie vivant* 2.3:53-72.

Masson, V. M.
1976 "Altin-tepe and the Bull Cult." *Antiquity* 50, 197:14-19.

Mataşa, C.
1946 *Frumuşica: Village préhistorique à céramique peinte dans la Moldavia du Nord.* Bucharest: Institute of Archaeology.
1964 "Asezarea eneolitica Cucuteni B de la Tirgu Ocna-Podei (raionul Tirgu Ocna, reg. Bacau)." *Archeologia Moldovei* 2-3:11-66.

Mateesco, C. N.
1965 "Contribution à l'étude de la civilisation de Vadastra: Phase Vadastra II." *Atti del VI Congresso Internationale delle Scienze Preistoriche e Protostoriche* (Rome) 2:258-63.
1970 "Sapaturi arheologice de Vădăstra." *Materiale şi Cercetări Arheologice* 9: 67-75. Bucharest: Institute of Archaeology.

Mateesco, C. N., and J. Voinescu
1982 "Representation of Pregnancy on Certain Neolithic Clay Figurines on Lower and Middle Danube." *Dacia* 26:1-2.

Mathieu, G.
1984 "Une figurine stylisée dans une tombe d'enfant de la nécropole rubanée d'Ensisheim." *Colloque Interrégional sur le Néolithique, 5-7 October 1984, Mulhouse.* Résumés des communications, Ministère de la Culture, Direction Régionale d'Alsace.

Matz, F.
1928 *Die frühkretischen Siegel: Eine Untersuchung über das Werden minoischen Stiles.* Berlin/Leipzig: W. de Gruyter.
1933 "Eine neue 'Pintadera' aus Thessalien." *Archaölogischer Anzeiger* 48:315-17.
1951 *Torsion: Eine formendkundliche Untersuchung zur ägäischen Vorgeschichte.* Akademie der Wissenschaften und der Literatur, Geistes- und Sozialwissenschaftliche Klasse, Abhandlungen 12; Mainz.
1958 *Göttererscheinung und Kultbild im minoischen Kreta.* Akademie der Wissenschaften und der Literatur, Geistes- und Sozialwissenschaftliche Klasse, 18: Mainz.
1962 *Crete and Early Greece: the Prelude to Greek Art.* Trans. by A. E. Keep. London: Methuen.

Matz, F., and I. Pini, eds.
1974 *Corpus der minoischen und mykenischen Siegel* 13. Nordamerika 2, Kleinere Sammlungen. Berlin: Gebr. Mann Verlag.

Matz, F. and H.G. Buchholz, eds.
Archaeologia Homerica
1967/87 Göttingen: Vandenhoeck and Ruprecht.

Maxim-Alaiba, R.
1987 "Le complexe de culte de la phase Cucuteni A_3 de Dumeşti (Vaslui)." *La Civilization de Cucuteni en Contexte Européen*: 269-86. Session Scientifique Iaşi-Piatra Neamţ, Iaşi, Université "Al. I. Cuza."

Mayer M.
1904 *Le stazioni preistoriche di Molfetta: Relazione sugli scave esequiti nel 1901.* Commissione Provinciale de Archeologia e Storia Patria, Documenti e Monografie 6. Bari: V. Vecchi.
1924 *Molfetta und Matera: Zur Prähistorie Süditaliens und Siciliens.* Leipzig: K. W. Hiersemann.

Megas, G.
1963 *Greek Calendar Customs.* Athens: Rhodis.

Meinardus, O. F. A.
1974 "Fertility and Healing Cult Survival in Athens, Haghia Marina." *Zeitschrift für Ethnologie* 99, 1-2: 270-76.

Meldgaard, J., P. Mortensen, and H. Thrane
1963 "Excavations at Tepe Guran, Luristan." *Acta Archaeologica* 34:97-133.

Mellaart, J. S.
1958 "Excavations at Hacilar: First Preliminary Report." *Anatolian Studies* 8:127-56.
1959 "Excavations at Hacilar: Second Preliminary Report, 1958." *Anatolian Studies* 9:51-65.
1960 "Anatolia and the Balkans." *Antiquity* 24:270-84.
1960a "Excavations at Hacilar: Third Preliminary Report, 1959." *Anatolian Studies* 10:83-104.
1961 "The Beginning of the Village and Urban Life." *The Dawn of Civilization.* Ed. by S. Piggott: 41-64. New York: McGraw-Hill.
1961a "Excavations at Hacilar: Fourth Preliminary Report, 1960." *Anatolian Studies* 11:39-75.
1961b "Hacilar: A Neolithic Village Site." *Scientific American* 205:86-97.
1962 "Excavations at Çatal Hüyük: First Preliminary Report, 1961." *Anatolian Studies* 12:41-65.

1963 "Excavations at Çatal Hüyük: Second Preliminary Report, 1962." *Anatolian Studies* 13:43–103.

1964 "Excavations at Çatal Hüyük, 1963. Third Preliminary Report." *Anatolian Studies* 14:39–119.

1964a "Earliest of Neolithic Cities: Delving Deep Into the Neolithic Religion of Anatolian Çatal Hüyük, part 2: Shrines of the Vultures and the Veiled Goddess." *Illustrated London News* 244:194–97.

1964b "Earliest of Neolithic Cities: The Origins of Pottery in Anatolian Çatal Hüyük, part 3: Wooden Vessels in Many Shapes." *Illustrated London News* 244:232–34.

1964c "Earliest of Neolithic Cities: Steps Toward the Personality and Nature of the People of Çatal Hüyük, part 4: Burial Customs and Grave Goods." *Illustrated London News* 244:272–75.

1964d "In the Dawn of Religion: A Reconstruction of a Funerary Rite Nearly 9000 Years Ago at Çatal Hüyük, in Anatolia." *Illustrated London News* 244: 728–29.

1964e "A Neolithic City in Turkey." *Scientific American* 210:94–104.

1965 *Earliest Civilizations of the Near East*. New York: McGraw-Hill.

1966 "Excavations at Çatal Hüyük, 1965: Fourth Preliminary Report." *Anatolian Studies* 16:165–91.

1967 *Çatal Hüyük: A Neolithic Town in Anatolia*. New York, McGraw-Hill.

1970 *Excavations at Hacilar, I, II.* Edinburgh: Edinburgh University Press.

1976 *The Neolithic of the Near East.* New York: Scribner.

Mellink, M. J.
1974 *Frühe Stufen der Kunst*. Berlin: Propyläen Verlag.

Merpert, N. Y., and R. M. Munchaev
1973 "Early Agricultural Settlements in the Sinjar Plain, Northern Iraq." *Iraq* 35, pt. 2:93–112.

Michaud, J.-P.
1972 "Chronique des fouilles et découvertes archéologiques en Grèce en 1971." *Bulletin de Correspondance Hellénique* 96. II. Chroniques et Rapports: 593–816.

Mihai, Constantin
1972–73 "Asezarile cucuteniene de la Giurgeşti şi Buznea in zona Tirgului Frumos." *Danubius* 6–7:11–13.

Mikov, V.
1934 "Idolnata plastika prez novokamennata epoha v Bulgaria." *Bulgarska Akademija na Naukite, Izvestija na Arkheologicheskija Institut VIII:* 183–214.

1970 "Materiali ot poslednija period na Bronsovata epokha ot severozapadha Bulgarija." *Arkheologiia* 3: 48–62.

Mikov, V., and N. Dzhambazov
1960 *Devetashkata peshehera*. French résumé: La grotte de Devetaki. Sofia: Akademie des Sciences du Bulgarie.

Milojčić, V.
1949 "Chronologie der jüngeren Steinzeit und Bronzezeit." *Germania* 37:65–84.

1950 "Die Askoskanne und einige andere ägäisch-balkanische Gefässformen." *Mitteilungen des deutschen archäologischen Instituts* 3:107–18.

1955 "Vorbericht über die Ausgrabungen auf den Magulen von Otzaki, Arapi, und Gremnos bei Larissa." *Archäologischer Anzeiger*: 182–231.

1959 "Ergebnisse der deutschen Ausgrabungen in Thessalien, 1953–1958." *Jahrbuch des Römisch-Germanischen Zentralmuseums* (Mainz) 6:1–56.

1960 "Hauptergebnisse der deutschen Ausgrabungen in Thessalien." *Jahrbuch des Römisch-Germanischen Zentralmuseums* (Mainz) 4.

Modderman, P. J. R.
1959 "Die bandkeramische Siedlung von Sittard." *Palaeohistoria* (Groningen) 6/7: 33–121.

1970 "Linearbandkeramik aus Elsloo und Stein." *Analecta Praehistorica Leidensia* 3 (3 vols, Gravenhage).

1971 "Neolithische und frühbronzezeitliche Siedlungsspuren aus Hienheim, Ldkr. Kelheim." *Analecta Praehistorica Leidensia* 4:1–25.

Monah, D.
1984 "Messages over Millennia." *Romanian Review* 9:17–31.

Monah, D., S. Cucoş, D. Popovici, and S. Antonescu
1982 "Sapaturile arheologice din tell-ul cucutenian dealul Ghindaru, Com. Poduri, Jud. Bacau." *Cercetari Arheologice* (Bucharest) 5:9–22.

Montelius, O.
1924 *La Grèce Préclassique*. Stockholm: I. Haeggström.

Morin, J.
1911 *Le dessin des animaux en Grèce d'après les vases peints*. Paris: Laurens.

Morris, R. W. B.
1977 *The Prehistoric Rock Art of Argyll*. Poole, Dorset: Dolphin Press.

Moszyński, K.
1934 *Kultura ludowa Słowian* 2. Warsaw: Książka i Wiedza.

Moure Romanillo, J. A.
1979 "Una plaqueta grabada del Magdaleniense superior de la grotte de Tito Bustillo." *Caesaraugusta* 49–50:43–53.

1985 "Escultura Magdaleniense descubierta en la Cueva de Tito Bustillo." *Ars Praehistorica* 2:3–11.

1986 "New Data on the Chronology and Context of Cantabrian Paleolithic Cave Art." *Current Anthropology* 27, 1:65.

Movsha, T. G.
1965 "Zobrazhennja ptakhiv na rozpisnomu posudi tripol'skoj kul'tury." *Arkheologija* (Kiev) 19:100–105.

1969 "Ob antropomorfnoj plastike tripol'skoj kul'tury." *Sovetskaja Arkheologija* 2:15–34.

1971 "Svjatilishcha tripol'skoj kul'tury." *Sovetskaja Arkheologija* 1:201–5.

1972 "Periodizatsija i khronologija serednjogo ta piznjogo Tripillja." *Arkheologija* (1972–75): 3–24.

1973 "Novi dani pro antropomorfnu realistichnu plastiku Tripillja." *Arheologija* 11: 3–21.

Müller, C. F., ed.
1980 *Kunst und Kultur Sardiniens vom Neolithikum bis zum Ende der Nuraghenzeit*. Karlsruhe: Müller.

Müller, V.
1929 *Frühe Plastik in Griechenland und Vorderasien: Ihre Typenbildung von der neolithischen bis in der griechisch-archaischen Zeit, 3000–600 v. Chr.* Augsburg: Felser.

Müller, S.
1897 *Nordische Altertumskunde* 1. Strassbourg: K. J. Trübner.

Müller-Karpe, H.
1966 *Handbuch der Vorgeschichte* 2. Jungsteinzeit. Munich: C. H. Beck.

1974 *Handbuch der Vorgeschichte* 3. Kupferzeit. Munich: C. H. Beck.

Mundkur, B.
1983 *The Cult of the Serpent: An Interdisciplinary Survey of Its Manifestations and Origins*. Albany: State University of New York Press.

Murray, A.
1934 "Female Fertility Figures." *Journal of the Royal Anthropological Institute of Great Britain and Ireland* 64:93–107.

Musch, J.
1986 *Paleolithic Sculptures from the Northwest European Plains*. Precirculated paper for the Southampton World Archaeology Congress, Sept. 1–7, 1986. Southampton.

Mylonas, G. E.
1929 *Excavations at Olynthus* 1. The Neolithic Settlement. Baltimore: Johns Hopkins Press.

1934 "Excavations at Haghios Kosmas." *American Journal of Archaeology* 38, 2: 258–79.

1940 "Macédoine Néolithique." In Greek. *Makedonika* 1:247–63.

1956 "Seated and Multiple Mycenean Figurines in the National Museum of Athens, Greece." *The Aegean and the Near East: Studies Presented to Hetty Goldman*: 110–22. New York: J. J. Augustin Press.

1961 *Eleusis and the Eleusinian Mysteries*. Princeton, N. J.: Princeton University Press.

1966 *Mycenae and the Mycenaean Age*. Princeton, N. J.: Princeton University Press.

Myres, J. L.
1902 "Excavations at Palaikastro. II: The Sanctuary-Site of Petsofa." *The British School at Athens* 9:356–87.

Nahodil, O.
1963 "Mutterkult in Sibirien." *Glaubenswelt und Folklore der sibirischen Völker* (Budapest): 491–511.

Nava, M. L.
1980 *Stele Daunie* 1. Studi e Materiali di Etruscologia e Antichità Italiche 18. Firenze: Sansoni.

1980a "Nuove stela antropomorfe da Castelluccio dei Sauri (Foggia). *Annali del Museo civico della Spezia* 2:115–49.

Neilmeyer, W.-D.
1982 *Kunst und Siedlung im geometrischen Griechenland*. Berlin: Gebr. Mann Verlag.

Neuland, L.
1977 "Jumis die Fruchtbarkeitsgottheit der alten Letten." *Studies in Comparative Religion*. Stockholm: Almquist and Wiksell International.

Neumann, E.
1955 *The Great Mother: An analysis of the Archetype*. Trans. by R. Manheim. Bollingen Series 47. New York: Pantheon.

Newall, V. ed.
1973 *The Witch Figure.* London: Routledge and Kegan Paul.

Newberry, P. E.
1928 "The Pig and the Cult-Animal of Set." *Journal of Egyptian Archaeology* 14:211–26.

Nica, M.
1976 "Circea, cea mai veche aşezare neolitica de la sud de Carpati." Résumé in French: "Circea, le plus ancien établissement néolithique au sud des Carpates." *Studii şi Cercetări de Istorie Veche şi Arheologie* 4. 27.

1980 "Reprezentarile antropomorfe in cultura Vădăstra, descoperite in aşezarile neolitice de la Hotarani şi Farcaşele, Judeţul Olt." *Oltenia, Studii şi communicari* 2:27–57.

Nica, M., and C. Cislaru
1981 Complexul cuptoarelor eneolitice de copt piine de la Curmatura, Judeţul Dolj." *Oltenia Studii şi communicari* 3:9–16.

Nica, M., and T. Niţa
1979 "Les établissements néolithiques de Leu et Padea, de la zone d'interférence des cultures Dudeşti et Vinča." *Dacia* 23:31–64.

Nicholls, R. V.
1970 "Greek Votive Statuettes and Religious Continuity, c. 1200–700 B.C." *Auckland Classical Essays Presented to E. M. Blaiklock.* Auckland: Auckland University Press, and Wellington: Oxford University Press.

Nikolov, Bogdan
1970 "Idolnata plastika ot s. Gradeshnica." Résumé in French: "La plastique des idoles du village Gradeshnica." *Archeologija* 12, 4:56–68.

1974 *Gradechnitza.* Photos by R. Staneva. Sofia: Nauka i Iskustvo.

1975 *Zaminets.* Photos by R. Staneva. Sofia: Nauka i Iskustvo.

Nikolov, V.
1979 "Unikalno skulpturno izobrazhenie." *Iskustvo* 1979 no. 4.

Nilsson, M.P.
1908 "Das Ei im Totenkult der Alten." *Archiv für Religionswissenschaft* 11:539.

1950 *The Minoan-Mycenaean Religion and its Survival in Greek Religion.* Lund: C. W. K. Gleerup.

1951 *Cults, Myths, Oracles, and Politics in Ancient Greece* (two appendices: The Ionian Phylae, The Phratries). Lund: C. W. K. Gleerup.

1957 *Griechische Feste von religiöser Bedeutung.* Reprint 1906, Leipzig edition. Stuttgart: Teubner.

1972 *Greek Folk Religion.* Philadelphia: Pennsylvania Paperbacks.

1975 *The Dionysiac Mysteries of the Hellenisic and Roman Age.* New York: Arno Press.

Niţu, A.
1968 "Reprezentari umane pe ceramica Criş şi liniara din Moldova." *Studii şi Cercetari Istorie Veche* 19, 3:387–95.

1968a "Tema plastica a Venerei Calipige pe ceramica neolitica Carpato-Balcanica." *Sesiunea stiencifica a Museelor* (Bucharest).

1969 "Ceramica Cucuteni B de la Miorcani (Botoşani)." *Memoria Antiquitatis* (Piatra Neamţ) 1: 279–298.

1972 "Reprezentările zoomorfe plastice pe ceramica neo-eneolitică Carpato-dunăreană." *Arheologia Moldovei* 7:9–96.

1975 "Decorul zoomorf pictat pe ceramica Cucuteni-Tripolie." *Arheologia Moldovei* 8:15–119.

1984 *Formarea şi clasificarea grupelor de stil AB şi B ale ceramicii pictate Cucuteni-Tripolie.* Anuarul Institului de Istorie şi Arheologie "A. D. Xenopol," Supliment 5: Iaşi.

Niţu, A. and M. Mantu
1987 "Thèmes plastiques anthropomorphes et zoomorphes de la céramique cucuténienne de style A de Poieneşti (dép. de Vaslui)." *La Civilisation de Cucuteni en Contexte Européen*: 301–07. Session Scientifique Iaşi-Piatra Neamţ, Iaşi, Université "Al. I. Cuza."

Niţu, A., S. Cucoş and D. Monah
1971 "Ghelaeşti (Piatra Neamţ) I. Sapaturile din 1969 in Aşezarea Cucuteniana Nedeia." *Memoria Antiquitatis* 3:11–64.

Novotný, B.
1958 *Počiatky vytvarneho prejavu na slovensku.* Die Anfänge der bildenden Kunst in der Slowakei. Bratislava: Slovenska Akadémia Vied.

1962 *Lužianska skupina a počiatky mal'ovanej keramiky na Slovensku.* Bratislava: Slovenska Akadémia Vied.

Nowottnick, G.
1935 *Deutsche Ernte in Sitte, Brauch, Sage und Volksdichtung.* Berlin: Weidmann.

Oates, Joan
1978 "Religion and Ritual in Sixth Millennium B.C. Mesopotamia." *World Archaeology* 10, 2: 117–24.

Obeyesekere, G.
1981 *Medusa's Hair.* Chicago: University of Chicago Press.

Olinas, F.
1964 "Russian *Golubec*, 'Grave marker, etc.' and some notions of the soul." *International Journal of Slavic Languages and Poetics* 8:77–86.

1978 Review of Lena Neuland. *Jumis: Die Fruchtbarkeitgottheit der alten Letten* 1977. *Slavic and East European Journal* 22, 4:557–59.

O'Kelly, C.
1973 "Passage-Grave Art in the Boyne Valley." *Proceedings of the Prehistorical Society* 39:354–82.

O'Kelly, M. J.
1982 *Newgrange: Archaeology, Art, and Legend.* London: Thames and Hudson.

Oldham, C.
1905 *The Sun and the Serpent: A Contribution to the History of Serpent Worship.* London: A. Constable and Co.

Oppenheim, M. von
1943 *Tel Halaf* 1. Berlin: Walter de Gruyter.

Orme, B.
1974 "Twentieth Century Prehistorians and the Idea of Ethnographic Parallels." *Man* 9:199–212.

Orthmann, W.
1966 "Keramik der Yortankultur in den Berliner Museen." *Istanbuler Mitteilungen* (Tübingen) 16:1–26.

Otto, W. F.
1954 *The Homeric Gods: The Spiritual Significance of Greek Religion.* Trans. of *Die Götter Griechenlands*, 1929. London: Thames and Hudson.

1965 *Dionysius: Myth and Cult.* Trans. and intro. by R. B. Palmer. Bloomington: Indiana University Press.

1975 *Aufsätze zur römischen Religionsgeschichte.* Beiträge zur Klass. Philologie 71. Meisenheim am Glen: Anton Hain.

Ovcharov, D.
1968 "Novi eneolitni choveshki figurki ot Tyrgovishchki okrug," *Arkheologija* (1968) 3:38–45.

Page, D. L.
1955 *The Homeric Odyssey.* Oxford: Clarendon Press.

Pales, L.
1972 "Les ci-devant Venus stéatopyges aurignaciennes." *Simposium International de Arte Rupestre* (Santander).

Papadopoulou, M. G.
1958 "Magoulitsa, établissement néolithique après de Karditsa." *Thessalika* 1:39–49.

Papathanassopoulos, G.
1983 *Neolithic and Cycladic Civilization.* Athens: National Archaeological Museum; "Melissa" Publishing House.

Passek, T. S.
1935 *La céramique tripolienne.* Leningrad/Moscow: Izvestia Gosudarstvennoj Akademii Istorii Material'noj Kul'tury.

1949 *Periodizatsija tripol'skikh poselenii.* Materialy i Issledovanija po Arkheologii SSSR 10: Moscow/Leningrad.

1951 "Tripol'skoe poselenie Polivanov-Jar." *Kratkie soobshchenija Instituta Arkheologii* 37: 41–64.

1954 "Itogi rabot v Moldavii v Oblasti pervobytnoj arkheologii." *Kratkie soobshchenija Akademii nauk SSSR* vyp. 5–6:76–97.

1965 "Kostjanye amulety iz Floresht." *Novoe v sovetskoj arkheologii*: 77–84.

Passek, T. S., and M. M. Gerasimov
1967 "Novaja statuetka iz Vulkaneshti." *Kratkie soobshchenija Instituta Material'noj Kul'tury* 111:38–41.

Passemard, L.
1938 *Les statuettes féminines paléolithiques dites stéatopyges.* Nimes: Teissiu.

Patai, R.
1978 *The Hebrew Goddess.* New York: Avon Books.

Patay, P.
1960 "Ornamente der Keramik der ungarländischen kupferzeitlichen Bodrogkeresztúrer Kultur." *Światowit* 23:363–88.

Paul, E.
1959 *Die böotischen Brettidole.* Repr. from *Wissenschaftliche Zeitschrift der Karl-Marx Universität, Leipzig* 8, 1958–59. Leipzig-journal.

Paul, I.
1965 "Un complex de cult descoperit in asezarea neolitica de la Pianul de Jos (Ein in der neolithischen Niederlassung von Pianul de Jos entdeckter Kultkomplex)." *Studii şi Comunicari* (Sibiu) 10–11:5–20.

1965 "Ein Kulttisch aus der jungsteinzeitlichen Siedlung von Deutschpein (Pianul de Jos)." *Forschungen zur Volks- und Landeskunde* (Bucharest): 8, 1:69–76.

Pausanias
1961 *Description of Greece.* 5 vols. Trans. by W. H. S. Jones. The Loeb Classical Library. London: Heinemann, and Cambridge, Mass.: Harvard University Press.

Pavlu, I.
1966 "Early 'Myths' Relating to the Neolithic Society." *Archeol. Rozhledy* 18:700–17, 719–21.

Pavuk, J.
1964 "Grab des Želiezovce-Typus in Dvory nad Žitavou." *Slovenská Archeológia* 12, 1:5–65.

1969 "Chronologie der Želiezovce-Gruppe." *Slovenská Archeológia* 17, 2:269–367.

1972 "Neolithisches Gräberfeld in Nitra." *Slovenská Archeológia* 20, 1:5–107.

Payne, H. et. al.
1940 *Perachora: The Sanctuaries of Hera Akraia and Limenia; Excavations of the British School at Athens 1930–33.* Oxford: Clarendon Press.

Pecorella, P. E., with S. Durante, N. F. Parise, and C. Saporetti
1977 *La Tombe dell'età dell Bronz - Tordo della necropli a mare di Ayia Irini.* Rome: Istituto per gli Studi Micenei ed Egeo-Anatolici.

Pendlebury, H. W., D. S. Pendlebury, and M. B. Money-Coutts
1936 "Excavations in the Plain of Lasithi, I: The Cave of Trapeza." *Annual of the British School of Archaeology at Athens* 36:5–131.

Pendlebury, J. D. S.
1939 *The Archaeology of Crete.* London: Methuen.

Pericot Garcia, L.
1942 *La cueva del Parpalló a Ganolia.* Madrid: Deputación Provincial de Valencia.

Pernicheva, L.
1978 "Glineni modeli na zhilishcha ot khalkolita v balgarskite zemi." *Arkheologija* 20, 2:1–13.

Perrot, J.
1970 "Le gisement Natoufien de Mallaha (Eynan), Israël." *Anthropologie* (Paris) 70, 5–6: 437–93.

Pesce, G.
1949 "La Venere di Macomer." *Rivista di Scienze Preistoriche* 4:123–33.

Peters, E.
1930 "Die Kunst der Magdalenien vom Petersfels." *Jahrbuch für Prähistorische und Ethnographische Kunst* 6.

Petkov, N.
1928–1929 "Predistoricheskaja bojadisana keramika ot Sofijskata kotlovina." *Godishnik na Muzeite v Plovdinski Okrug*: 185–98.

1959 "Neolitno selishte pri selo Slatina." *Arkheologija* 1, 1–2:100–105.

1961 "Novi danni za neolitnata kultura kraj Sofija." *Arkheologija* 3:64–72.

1962 "Risuvanijat ornament prez neolita v Sofijskoto pole i bliznite my okolnosti." *Arkheologija* 4, 3:43–48.

Petrescu-Dimboviţa, M.
1957 "Sondajul stratigrafic de la Perieni." *Materiali şi Cercetari Arheologice* 3:65–82.

1963 "Die wichtigsten Ergebnisse der archäologischen Ausgrabungen in der neolithischen Siedlung von Truşeşti (Moldau)." *Prähistorische Zeitschrift* 41:172–86.

1966 *Cucuteni: Monumentele Patriei Noastre.* (Bucharest).

1969 "Einige Probleme der Cucuteni-Kultur im Lichte der neuen archäologischen Grabungen." *Študijné Zvesti* 17:361–74.

Petrocheilou, A.
1984 *The Greek Caves.* Athens: Ekdotike Athenon S. A.

Pfannenschmid, H.
1878 *Germanische Erntefeste im heidnischen Cultus, mit besonderer Beziehung auf Niedersachsen.* Hannover: Hahn.

Picard, Ch.
1948 *Les Réligions préhelléniques.* Paris: Presses Universitaires de France.

Pidoplichko, I. G.
1976 *The Mezherich Mammoth Bone Houses.* In Russian with English summary and captions. Kiev: Institute of Zoology, UK. Nauk.

Pini, I.
1972 "Weitere Bemerkungen zu den minoischen Fussamuletten." *Studi Micenei* 15:179–87.

Platon, N.
1966 *Crete.* Trans. from Greek. Cleveland: The World Publishing Co.

1971 *Zakros: The Discovery of a Lost Palace of Ancient Crete.* New York: Scribners.

Polikarpovich, K. M.
1968 *The Paleolithic of the Upper Dniepr Region.* Minsk: Institute of History, Nauka i Tekhnika.

Polomé, E.
1954 "A propos de la déese Nerthus." *Latomus* 13:167–200.

Poor, H. V.
1958 *A Book of Pottery: From Mud to Immortality.* Englewood Cliffs, N.J.: Prentice Hall.

Popescu, D.
1956 "Cercetari arheologice in Transilvania." *Materiale şi Cercetari Arheologice* 2:43–250.

Popov, R.
1918 "Kodža-Dermenskata mogila pri gr. Šumen." *Izvestija na Bulgarskoto Arkheologičesko Družestvo* 6 (1916–18): 71–155.

Powell, Terence
1959 *The Celts.* London: Thames and Hudson.

Praetorius, M.
1871 *Deliciae Prussicae oder Preussische Schaubühne.* Berlin: A. Duncker.

Prendi, F.
1966 "La civilisation préhistorique de Maliq." *Studia Albanica* 1:255–80.

Raczky, P.
1980 "A Körös kultúra újabb figurális ábrázolásai a Középtiszavidékröl és törtenet: összefüggéseik." Summary in English: "New Figural Representations of the Körös Culture from the Middle Tisza Region and their Historical Connection." A Szolnok Megyei Múzeumok Évkönyve 1979–1980: 5–33.

Radimsky, V., and M. Hoernes
1895 *Die neolithische Station von Butmir* part 1; part 2., 1898. Prepared by Fr. Fiala and M. Hoernes (Vienna).

Raduncheva, A.
1971 "Za prednaznachenieto na njakoi glineni eneolitni zhivotinski figurki." ("Sur la signification de certaines figurines animales en argile de l'Enéolithique.") *Arkheologija* 2 (Sofia): 5, 8-66.

1976 *Prehistoric Art in Bulgaria from the Fifth to the Second Millenium B.C.* BAR International Series 13.

Ransome, H. M.
1937 *The Sacred Bee in Ancient Times and Folklore*, 58–62. New York: Houghton Mifflin.

Ray, B. C.
1987 "Stonehenge: A New Theory." *History of Religions*: 226–78.

Reitler, R.
1949 "A Theriomorphic Representation of Hekate-Artemis." *American Journal of Archaeology* 53:29–31.

Rellini, U.
1934 *La più antica ceramica dipinta in Italia.* Rome: Collezione meridionale editrice.

Rendić-Miocević, D.
1955 "Ilirske pretstave Silvana na kultnim slikama s podrucja Dalmata." Résumé in French: "Représentations illyriènnes de Sylvanus sur les monuments du culte dans le domaine Dalmate." *Glasnik Zemaljskog Muzeja u Sarajevu* ns. (Arheologija) 10: 5–40.

Renfrew, C.
1969 "The Development and Chronology of the Early Cycladic Figurines." *American Journal of Archaeology* 73:1–32.

1972 *The Emergence of Civilization: The Cyclades and the Aegean in the Third Millennium B.C.* London: Methuen.

1978 "The Mycenaean Sanctuary at Phylakopi." *Antiquity* 52:7–15.

Renfrew, C., ed.
1979 *Investigations in Orkney.* The Society of Antiquaries of London, distr. by Thames and Hudson.

Renfrew, C., and J. D. Evans
1966 "The Fat Lady of Saliagos." *Antiquity* 40, 159: 218–19.

Richards-Mantzoulinou, E.
1980 "Melissa Potnia." *Athens Annals of Archaeology* 12, 1:72–92.

Richter, G. M. A.
1949 *Archaic Greek Art.* New York: Oxford University Press.

1959 *A Handbook of Greek Art.* London: Phaidon Press.

Ridley, M.
1976 *The Megalithic Art of the Maltese Islands.* Poole, Eng.: Dolphin Press.

Rimantienė, R.
1979 *Šventoji.* Vilnius: Mokslas.

Ritchie, G.
1985 "Ritual Monuments." In C. Renfrew, ed., *The Prehistory of Orkney*: 118–31. Edinburgh: University Press.

Robbins, M.
1980 "The Assimilation of Pre-Indo-European Goddesses into Indo-European Society." *The Journal of Indo-European Studies* 8, 1–2:19–31.

Robertson, N., ed.
1975 *The Archaeology of Cyprus: Recent Developments.* Park Ridge, N.J.: Noyes Press.

Rodden, R. J. et al
1962 "Excavations at the Early Neolithic Site of Nea Nikomedeia, Greek Macedonia (1961 Season)." *Proceedings of the Prehistoric Society* n.s. 28:267–88.

Roman, P., and V. Boroneanţ
1974 "Locuirea neolitica din ostrovul Banalui de la Bura Vaii." *Drobeta*: 117–28. Bucharest: Muzeul Regiunii Portilor de Fier.

Rose, H. J.
1958 *A Handbook of Greek Mythology.* 6th ed. London: Methuen.

Rosetti, D.
1938 "Steinkupferzeitliche Plastik aus einem Wohnhügel bei Bukarest." *IPEK* 12:29–50.

Roska, M.
1941 *Die Sammlung Zsófia von Torma*. Kolozsvar.

Rouse, W. H. D.
1902 *Greek Votive Offerings: An Essay in the History of Greek Religion*. Cambridge: Cambridge University Press.

Rowland, B.
1978 *Birds with Human Souls: A Guide to Bird Symbolism*. Knoxville: University of Tennessee Press.

Ruckert, A.
1976 *Frühe Keramik Böotiens*. Beiheft zur Halbjahresschrift Antike Kunst 10. Bern: Franke Verlag.

Rudins'kij, M.
1931 *Industrie en os de la station paléolithique de Mezin*. Trans. by V. Vovk (Kiev): Akademija Nauk Ukrainskoj RSR.

Ruggles, C. L. N.
1984 *Megalithic Astronomy. A new archaeological and statistical study of 300 western Scottish sites*. BAR, British Series 123.

Ruggles, C. L. N.,
and A. W. R. Whittle, eds.
1981 *Astronomy and Society in Britain during the Period 4000–1500 B.C.* BAR, Oxford.

Ruju, A. A.
1980 "Appunti per una serazione evolutiva della Sardegna prenuragica." *Atti della XXII Riunione Scientifica dell'Istituto Italiano di Preistoria a Protostoria dalla Sardegna Centro-Settentrionale, 21–27 Ottobre 1978* (Firenze): 115–47.

Rutkowski, B.
1986 *The Cult Places of the Aegean*. New Haven and London: Yale University Press.

Rüttner-Cova, S.
1986 *Frau Holle. Die gestürzte Göttin. Märchen, Mythen, Matriarchat*. Basel: Sphinx Verlag.

Rybakov, B. A.
1965 "Cosmogony and Mythology of the Agriculturalists of the Eneolithic" 1966. *Soviet Anthropology and Archaeology* 4, 2: 16–36; 3: 33–51. Trans. from Russian; originally publ. in *Sovetskaja arkheologija* 1965, 1 and 2.
1981 *Jazychestvo drevnikh slavjan*. Moscow: "Nauka."

Rydh, H.
1929 "On Symbolism in Mortuary Ceramics." *Bulletin, Museum of Far Eastern Antiquities* (Stockholm) 1: 71–142.

Säflund, G.
1965 *Excavations at Berbati 1936–37*. Stockholm Studies in Classical Archaeology.

Sakellarakis, J. A.
1970 "Das Kuppelgrab A von Archanes und das kretsich-mykenische Tieropferritual." *Prähistorische Zeitschrift* 45:135–219.

Sakellariou-Xenaki, A.
1964 *Die minoischen und mykenischen Siegel des Nationalmuseums in Athen*. Corpus der minoischen und mykenischen Siegeln 1. Berlin: Gebr. Mann Verlag.

Salmony, A.
1949 "Some Palaeolithic Ivory Carvings." *Artibus Asiae* 12:107.

Sandars, N. K.
1968 *Prehistoric Art in Europe*. Pelican History of Art, Z 30. London: Penguin Books.

Santoni, V. di
1982 "Il mondo del sacro in età neolitica." *Scientific American* (edizione italiana) 29. 170 (October): 70–80.

Sartori, P.
1905 "Votive und Weihegaben des katholischen Volkes in Süddeutschland." *Globus* 87:93–96.

Sauter, M.-R., and A. Gallay
1970 "Les premières cultures d'origine méditerranéenne." *Ur- und Frühgeschichtliche Archäologie der Schweiz* 2 (Die jüngere Steinzeit): 47–66.

Sauvet, G. and S., and A. Wlodarczyk
1977 "Essai de sémiologie préhistorique: Pour une théorie des premiers signes graphiques de l'homme." *Bulletin de la Société Préhistorique Français* 74:545–58.

Savory, H. N.
1968 *Spain and Portugal: The Prehistory of the Iberian Peninsula*. London: Thames and Hudson.

Schachermeyr, F.
1955 *Die ältesten Kulturen Griechenlands*. Stuttgart: Kohlhammer.
1964 *Das ägäische Neolithikum*. Studies in Mediterranean Archaeology 6. Lund: C. Blom.
1976 *Die ägäische Frühzeit* I. Die vormykenischen Perioden des griechischen Festlandes und der Kykladen. Vienna: Österreichische Akademie der Wissenschaften.

Schaeffer, C. F. A.
1948 *Stratigraphie comparée et chronologie de l'Asie occidentale (III et II millénaires)*. London: Oxford University Press.

Schefold, K.
1959 *Griechische Kunst als religiöse Phänomen*. Hamburg: Rowohlt.
1964 *Frühgriechische Sagenbilder*. Munich: Hirmer.
1966 *Myth and Legend in Early Greek Art*. Trans. of Frühgriechische Sagenbilder by A. Hicks. London: Thames and Hudson.

Schliemann, H.
1976 *Ilios, the City and Country of the Trojans*. New York: Arno Press.

Schmidt, H.
1982 *Cucuteni in der oberen Moldau, Rumänien: Die befestigte Siedlung mit bemalter Keramik von der Stein-Kupferzeit bis in die vollentwickelte Bronzezeit*. Berlin: de Gruyter.

Schreiber, H.
1842 *Die Feen in Europa: Eine historisch-archäologische Monographie*. Freiburg im Breisgau: Groos.

Schweitzer, B.
1969 *Die geometrische Kunst Griechenlands: Frühe Formenwelt im Zeitalter Homers*. Cologne: dumont Schauberg.

Scully, V.
1962 *The Earth, The Temple and the Gods: Greek Sacred Architecture*. New Haven and London: Yale University Press.

Seager, R. B.
1910 *Excavations on the Island of Pseira, Crete*. Museum Anthropological Publications 3.1. Philadelphia: University of Pennsylvania, The University Museum.
1912 *Explorations in the Island of Mochlos*. Boston/New York: American School of Classical Studies at Athens.

Sébillot, P.
1902 "The Worship of Stones in France." *American Anthropologist* 4, 1:76–107.

Seger, H.
1928 "Der Widder von Jordansmühl." *IPEK*: 13–17.

Service, A., and J. Bradbery
1979 *Megaliths and Their Mysteries: The Standing Stones of Old Europe*. London: Weidenfeld and Nicolson.

Shapiro, M.
1983 "Baba-Jaga: A Search for Mythopoeic Origins and Affinities." *International Journal of Slavic Linguistics and Poetics* 27:109–35.

Shovkopljas, I. G.
1965 *Mezinskaja stojanka*. Kiev: Institute of Archaeology, Akademija Nauk URSR.

Sieveking, A.
1979 *The Cave Artist*. London: Thames and Hudson.

Simon, E.
1969 *Die Götter der Griechen*. Munich: Hirmer.

Sjöö, M., and B. Mor
1987 *The Great Cosmic Mother: Rediscovering the Religion of the Earth*. San Francisco: Harper & Row.

Sjoestedt-Jonval, Marie Louise
1949 *Gods and Heroes of the Celts*. Trans. by Myles Dillon. London: Methuen.

Skomal, S. N.
1983 *Wealth Distribution as a Measure of Prehistoric Change: Chalcolithic to Copper Age Cultures in Hungary*. Ann Arbor: University Microfilms International.

Skutil, J.
1940 "Die neolithischen Plastiken aus dem Kreise der mährischen bemalten Keramik." *IPEK* 13:36–56.

Slater, P. E.
1971 *The Glory of Hera: Greek Mythology and the Greek Family*. Boston: Beacon Press.

Smith, N. W.
1974 "The Ancient Background to Greek Psychology." *Psychological Record* 24: 309–24.

Sobrino-Buhigas, R.
1935 *Corpus Petroglyphorum Gallaeciae*. Santiago de Compostela: Gallaecia.

Solecki, R. L.
1981 *An Early Village Site at Zawi Chemi Shanidar*. Malibu: Undena Publications.

Soudsky, B.
1965 "Interprétation historique de l'ornement linéaire." *Památky Archeologicke* 58, 1:91–125.

Spiess, K. von
1914 "Die Kröte, ein Bild der Begärmutter." *Mitra*.
1940 "Die Krötenfrau." *Germanenen-Erbe* 7/8.

Spiteris, T.
1970 *The Art of Cyprus*. New York: Reynol & Co.

Spyropoulos, Th. G.
1970 "Excavation in the Mycenaean Cemetery of Tanagra in Boeotia." *Athens Annals of Archaeology* 3, 2:190–97.

Srejović, D.
1966 "Neolithic Anthropomorphic Figurines from Yugoslavia." *IPEK* (Berlin) 21 (1964–65): 28–41.
1969 *Lepenski Vir*. Beograd: Srpska Knijiževna zadruga.
1972 "Europe's First Monumental Sculpture: New Discoveries at Lepenski Vir." *New Aspects of Antiquity*. Ed. by M. Wheeler. London: Thames and Hudson.

Srejović, D., and L. Babović
1983 *Umetnost Lepenskog Vira* (Art of Lepenski Vir). Belgrade: Narodni Muzej.

Srejović, D., and Z. Letica
1978 *Vlasac: A Mesolithic Settlement in the Iron Gates* 1. In Serbo-Croatian with a summary in English. Serbian Academy of Sciences and Arts 12. Belgrade.

Stacul, G.
1963 *La grande madre: Introduzione all'arte neolitica in Europa*. Rome: De Luca.

Stančeva, M., and M. Gavrilova
1961 "Čoveski glineni figurki ot neolitnoto selishche v Sofija." *Archeologija* (Sofia) 3, 3:73–76.

Stekelis, M.
1972 *The Yarmukian Culture of the Neolithic Period*. Jerusalem: Magnes Press.

Stewart, J. R.
1962 "The Early Cypriote Bronze Age." *Swedish Cyprus Expedition* (Lund) 55, pt. 1a: 205–401.

Stipčević, A.
1981 *Kultni simboli kod Ilira*. Graota i prilozi sistematizaciji, Akad. Nauka i umjetnosti Bosne i Hercegovine, Knjiga Liv, Sarajevo.

Stoliar, A. D.
1977–78 "On the Genesis of Depictive Activity and its Role in the Formation of Consciousness." *Soviet Anthropology and Archaeology* 16, 3–4:3–42 and 17, 2:3–33.

Stone, M.
1978 *When God was a Woman*. New York/London: Harvest/Harcourt, Brace, Jovanovich.
1984 *Ancient Mirrors of Womanhood: A Treasury of Goddess and Heroine Lore from Around the World*. Boston: Beacon Press.

Straubergs, K.
1950 "Die letto-preussischen Getreidefeste.." *Arv* (Upsala) 5.

Swiny, H. and S.
1983 "An Anthropomorphic Figurine from the Sotira Area." *Report of the Department of Antiquities Cyprus* (Nicosia): 56–59.

Szénászky, J. G.
1978 "Der Vinča-Fund von Battonya." *A Békés Múzeumok Közleményei* 5:3–12.

Talalay, L. E.
1983 *Neolithic Figurines of Southern Greece: Their Form and Function*. Ph.D. dissertation, Indiana University.

Tálas, L., ed.
1987 *The Late Neolithic of the Tisza Region*. With contributions by N. Kalicz, P. Raczky, F. Horváth, J. Korek, and J. Makkay. Budapest: Szolnok.

Tanda, Giuseppa
1977 *Arte preistorica in Sardegna: Le figurazioni taurine scolpite dell'Algherese nel Quadro delle representazioni figurate degli ipogli Sardi a "domus de janus."* Quarterni 5: Sassari, Soprintendenza Archeologica, prov. Sassari e Nyoro.
1977a "Uno 'domus de janas' con motivi a spirali di Cargeghe-Muros (SS)." *Archivio Storico Sardo di Sassari* 3, 3:175–92.
1977b "Le incisioni della 'domus de janas' di Tisienari Bortigiadas." *Archivio Storico Sardo di Sassari* 3, 3:199–211.
1983 "Arte e religione in Sardegna. Rapporti tra i dati monumentali e gli elementi della cultura materiale." *Prehistoric Art and Religion. Valcamonica Symposium* 1979: 261–79. Capo di Ponte: Centro Camuno di Studi Preistorici.

Tasić, N.
1957 "Praistorisko naselje Kod Valača" (Prehistoric settlement at Valač). *Glasnik Muzeja Kosova i Metohije* 2, 4, 5: 45.
1973 *Neolitska plastika*. Belgrade: Gradskij Muzej.

Tasić, N., and E. Tomić
1969 *Crnokalačka Bara, Naselje Starčevačke i Vinčanske Kulture*. Dissertationes 8: Kruševac.

Tatton-Brown, V., ed.
1979 *Cyprus B.C. 7000 Years of History*. London: The Trustees of the British Museum.

Taylour, W.
1970 "New Light on Mycenaean Religion." *Antiquity* 44:270–79.

Theochares, D. R.
1956 "Nea Makri: Eine grosse neolitische Siedlung in der Nähe von Marathon." *Mitteilungen des Deutschen Archäologischen Instituts, Athenische Abteilung* 71, 1:1–29.
1958 "Thessalie précéramique: Esposé provisoire des fouilles." In Greek. *Thessalika* (Volos) 1: 70–86.
1959 "Pyrasos." *Thessalika* 3:29–67.
1962 "From Neolithic Thessaly (I)." In Greek with an English summary. *Thessalika* D: 63–83.
1967 *The Prehistory of Thessaly*. Tessalika Leletimata Volos.

Theocharis, D. R., ed.
1973 *Neolithic Greece*. Athens: National Bank of Greece.

Thimme, J.
1965 "Die religiöse Bedeutung der Kykladenidole." *Antike Kunst* 7:71–87.

Thimme, J., ed.
1977 *Art and Culture of the Cyclades: Handbook of an Ancient Civilization*. Trans. and English ed. by P. Getz-Preziosi. Karlsruhe: C. F. Müller.

Thom, A., A. S. Thom
1978 *Megalithic Remains in Britain and Brittany*. Oxford: Clarendon Press.

Thom, A., A. S. Thom, and A. Burl
1980 *Megalithic Rings*. BAR British Series 80.

Thomas, L.-V.
1975 *Anthropologie de la mort*. Paris, Payot.

Thompson, W. I.
1981 *The Time Falling Bodies Take to Light: Mythology, Sexuality and Origins of Culture*. New York: St. Martin's Press.

Thomson, G.
1962 "The Arkoudiotissa." *Kretika Chronika* 15–16, pt. 3:93–96.
1978 *The Prehistoric Aegean: Studies in Ancient Greek Society*. London: Lawrence and Wishart.

Tichý, R.
1962 "Osidleni s volutovou keramikou na Morave." *Pregled Archeologicky* 53:245–91.
1970 "Zu einigen neolithischen Kultgegenständen aus Mohelnice." *Sbornik československé spolecnosti archeologické pri ČSAV* 4:7–19.

Tiné, S.
1965 "Gli scavi nella Grotta Chiusazza." *Bollettino di Paleontologia Italiana* n.s.16, 74: 123–286.
1972 "Un culto neolitico nelle acque nella grotta Scaloria." *Symposium sulla religioni della Preistorica* (Valcamonica).
1983 *Passo di Corvo e la civiltà neolitica del Tavoliere*. Genoa: Sagep Editrice.

Todorova, H.
1973 "Novaja kul'tura srednego neolita v severovostochnoj Bolgarii." *Sovetskaja Arkheologija* 4:16-31.
1973a "Novo nakhodishe ot prekhoda mezhdu neolita i eneolita v severnoj Bolgarii." *Arkheologija* (Sofia) 1:59–64.
1974 "Kultszene und Hausmodell aus Ovčarovo, Bez. Targovişte." *Thracia* 3:39–46.
1976 "Die äneolithische Siedlung und Wohnung in Nordostbulgarien." *Istrazhivanija* (Novi Sad) 5:155–60.
1976a *Ovcharovo*. Sofia: Septemvri.
1978 *The Eneolithic Period in Bulgaria in the Fifth Millenium B.C.* BAR International Series 49: Oxford.

Todorova, H., V. Vasilev, S. Ivanov, M. Hopf, H. Quitta, and G. Kohl
1975 *Selishchnata mogila pri Goljamo Delchevo*. Sofia: Bulgarian Academy of Sciences.

Todorović, J., and A. Cermanović
1961 *Banjica, naselje vinčanske kulture*. Belgrade: Belgrade City Museum.

Tompa, F.
1929 "Die Bandkeramik in Ungarn: Die Bükker- und die Theiss Kultur." *Archaeologia Hungarica* (Budapest) 5–6.

Torbrügge, W.
1968 *Prehistoric European Art*. New York: Harry N. Abrams.

Trogmayer, O.
1972 "Frühneolithische anthropomorphe Gefässe." *Idole, prähistorische Keramiken aus Ungarn*: 7–8, taf. 1–4, Naturhistorisches Museum, N.F. 7 (Vienna).

Trump, D. H.
1972 *Malta: An Archaeological Guide*. London: Faber and Faber.
1980 *The Prehistory of the Mediterranean*. New Haven/New York: Yale University Press.
1981 "Megalithic Architecture in Malta." *The Megalithic Monuments of Western Europe*. Ed. by C. Renfrew: 64–76. London: Thames and Hudson.
1983 *La Grotta di Filestru a Bonu Ighinu, Mara (SS)*. Quaderni della Soprintendenze ai Beni Archeologici per le provincie di Sassari e Nuoro, 13: Dessi, Sassari.

Tsedakis, J.
1971 "Cemetery at Armenoi Rethymni." *Athens Annals of Archaeology* 4, no. 2:216–22.

Tsountas, Ch.
1908 *Hai proistorikai akropoleis Diminiou kai Sesklou*. Athens: P. D. Sakellariou.

Tsvek, O. V.
1964 "Tripil'ska posudina z antropomorfnimi zobrazhennjami." *Arheologija* (Kiev) 16: 79.

Tulane, E.
1944 "A Repertoire of the Samarran Painted Pottery." *Journal of Near Eastern Studies* 3:57–65.

Tulok, M.
1971 "A Late Neolithic Idol of Conical Type," *Acta Archaeologica Academiae Scientiarum Hungaricae* (Budapest) 23: 3–17.

Turner, A.
1973 *Vultures*. New York: D. McKay.

Twohig, E. S.
1981 *The Megalithic Art of Western Europe*. Oxford: Clarendon Press.

Ucko, P. J.
1968 *Anthropomorphic Figurines of Predynastic Egypt and Neolithic Crete, with Comparative Material from the Prehistoric Near East and Mainland Greece*. London: A Szmidla.

Ucko, P. J., and A. Rosenfeld
1967 *Palaeolithic Cave Art*. London: Weidenfeld and Nicholson.

Ujváry, Z.
1968 "Anthropomorphe mythische Wesen in der agrarischen Volksüberlieferung Ungarns und Europas." *Acta Ethnologica Academiae Scientiarum Hungaricae* (Budapest) 17.

Uspenskij, B. A.
1982 *Filologischeskie razyskanija v oblasti slavjanskikh drevnostej.* Moscow: Academy of Sciences.

Vagnetti, L.
1974 "Preliminary Remarks on Cypriote Chalcolithic Figurines." *Report of the Department of Antiquities, Cyprus* (Nicosia): 24–34.

Valla, F. R.
1975 *Le Natoufien, une culture préhistorique en Palestine.* Cahiers de la Revue Biblique 15. Paris: J. Gabalda.

Vankina, L. V.
1970 *Torfjaniikovaja stojanka Sarnate.* Riga: Izd. Zinatre.

Varela Gomes, M.
1983 "Aspects of Megalithic Religion According to the Portuguese Menhirs." *Prehistoric Art & Religion: Valcamonica Symposium '79.* Ed. by A. Beltran et al: 385–401. Capo di Ponte: Edizione del Centro.

Vasić, M.
1932–1936 *Praistorijska Vinča* 1 (1932); 2–4 (1936). Belgrade: Izdanje Drvavne Štamparje.

Vasil'ev, A.
1948 "Medvezhii prazdnik." *Sovetskaja etnografija* 4: 78–104.

Vencl, S.
1961 "Studie o Sáreckém Typu." *Sborník Narodního Muzeá v Praze* 15, 3: 93–140.

Vermeule, E.
1964 *Greece in the Bronze Age.* Chicago: University of Chicago Press.
1979 *Aspects of Death in Early Greek Art and Poetry.* Berkeley: University of California Press.

Vermeule, E., and V. Karageorghis
1982 *Mycenaean Pictorial Vase Painting.* Cambridge, Mass.: Harvard University Press.

Vidossi, G.
1987 "Il Rospo-utero nel folklore." *Quaderni Di Semantica* 8.2: 219–21.

Vildomec, F.
1940 "Ein jungsteinzeitliches Gefäss mit eingestochenen Menschengestalten und Tier-plastiken Strzelitz (Südmähren)." *Wiener prähistorische Zeitschrift* 27:1–6.

Vlassa, N.
1963 "Chronology of the Neolithic in Transylvania in the Light of the Tartaria Settlement's Stratigraphy." *Dacia* 7:1–10.

Voinesco, J., and C. Mateesco
1980 "Figurine anthropomorphe en argile de Vadastra en rapport avec un rituel d'accouchement du Néolithique Moyen au Bas-Danube." *L'Anthropologie* (Paris) 84:183–97.

Vries, J. de
1961 *Keltische Religion.* Stuttgart: Kohlhammer.

Vulpe, R.
1938 "Figurine thériomorphe de la civilisation Cucuteni B." *IPEK* 12:57–65.
1957 *Izvoare: Sapaturile din 1936–1943.* Summaries in Russian and French: "Izvoare: Les Fouilles de 1936–1943." Biblioteca de Arheologie 1: Bucharest.

Vycichl, W.
1973 "Die Mythologie der Berber." *Götter und Mythen im alten Europa.* Stuttgart: Ernst Klett.

Wace, A.
1949 "Prehistoric Stone Figurines from the Mainland." *Hesperia* supplement 8:423–507.

Wace, A. J. B., and M. S. Thompson
1912 *Prehistoric Thessaly.* Cambridge: Cambridge University Press.

Wainwright, G.
1968 "Durrington Walls: A Ceremonial Enclosure of the 2nd Millennium B.C." *Antiquity* 42:20–26.
1970 "Woodhenge." *Scientific American* 233:30–38.

Walberg, G.
1976 "Kamares: A Study of the Character of Palatial Middle Minoan Pottery." Acta Universitatis Upsaliensis, Borees 8: 203. Stockholm: Almquist and Wiksell.

Waldstein, C.
1902–1905 *The Argive Heraeum.* 2 vols. Boston/New York: Houghton Mifflin.

Walker, B.
1983 *The Woman's Encyclopedia of Myths and Secrets.* San Francisco: Harper and Row.

Walker-Kosmopoulos, L.
1948 *The Prehistoric Inhabitation of Corinth.* Munich: Münchner Verlag.

Warner, M.
1976 *Alone of Her Sex: The Myth and Cult of the Virgin Mary.* New York: Alfred Knopf.

Warren, P.
1970 "The Primary Dating Evidence for Early Minoan Seals." *Kadmos* 9:29–37.
1972 *Myrtos: An Early Bronze Age Settlement in Crete.* London: Thames and Hudson.
1975 *The Aegean Civilizations.* Oxford: Elsevier-Phaidon.

Wasson, R. G., C. Ruck, and A. Hoffmann
1978 *The Road to Eleusis: Unveiling the Secret of the Mysteries.* New York: Harcourt, Brace, Jovanovich.

Watkins, T.
1969 "A la découverte des premières agglomérations villageoises." *Archéologie vivante* 2, 3 (Mars-Mai): 29–52.

Webster, T. B. L.
1959 "Die mykenische Vorgeschichte des griechischen Dramas." *Antike und Abendland* 8:7–14.

Weinberg, S. S.
1937 "Remains from Prehistoric Corinth." *Hesperia* 6:487–525.
1951 "Neolithic Figurines and Aegean Interrelations." *American Journal of Archaeology* 55, 2: 121–33.
1962 "Excavations at Prehistoric Elateia, 1959." *Hesperia* 31:158–209.

Weinberg, S. S., and H. S. Robinson
1960 "Excavations at Corinth, 1958." *Hesperia* 29:225–54.

Wernick, R.
1973 *The Monument Builders.* The Emergence of Man Series. New York: Time-Life Books.

Wilamowitz-Moellendorff, U. von
1959 *Der Glaube der Hellenen.* 2 vols. 3rd. ed. Basel: B. Schwabe.

Wilde, Lady
1902 *Ancient Legends, Mystic Charms and Superstitions of Ireland: With Sketches of the Irish Fast.* London: Chatto and Windus.

Willetts, R. F.
1962 *Cretan Cults and Festivals.* New York: Barnes and Noble.
1978 *The Civilization of Ancient Crete.* Berkeley/Los Angeles: University of California Press.

Winn, S. M. M.
1981 *Pre-Writing in Southeastern Europe: The Sign System of the Vinča Culture ca. 4000 B.C.* Calgary: Western Publishers.

Wiślański, T.
1979 "Plemiona kultury pucharów lejkowatych." *Prahistoria Ziem Polskich* 2. [Neolit] Ed. by W. Hensel and T. Wiślański: 165–260. Warsaw: Polska Akademia Nauk, Ossolineum.

Wölfel, D.
1961 *Die Religionen des vorindogermanischen Europa.* Christus und die Religionen der Erde. Vienna: Herder.

Wood-Martin, W. G.
1902 *Traces of the Elder Faiths of Ireland, a Folklore Sketch: A Handbook of Irish Pre-Christian Traditions.* 2 vols. London: Longmans, Green and Co.

Wrede, H.
1968–1969 "Ägyptische Lichtbräuche bei Geburten: Zur Deutung der Froschlampen." *Jahrbuch für Antike und Christentum* 11/12: 83–93.

Wreschner, E. E.
1976 "The Potential Significance of the Pebbles with Incisions and Cupmarks from the Yarmukian of Sha'ar Hagolan, Israël." *Bulletin Soc. Roy. Belge Anthrop. Préhist.* 87:157–65.

Wünsch, R.
1902 *Das Frühlingsfest der Insel Malta.* Leipzig: B. G. Teubner.

Yakar, J.
1985 *The Later Prehistory of Anatolia,* parts 1 and 2. BAR International Series 268.

Yavis, C. G.
1949 *Greek Altars: Origins and Typology, Including the Minoan-Mycenaean Offertory Apparatus* (St. Louis).

Yeivin, E., and I. Mozel
1977 "A 'Fossil directeur' Figurine of the Pottery Neolithic A." *Tel Aviv* (Journal of the Tel Aviv University Institute of Archaeology) 4, 3–4:194–200.

Yule, P. von
1981 *Early Cretan Seals: A Study of Chronology.* Marburger Studien zur Vor- und Frühgeschichte 4. Mainz/Rhein: Philipp von Zabern.

Zaèts, I. I.
1973 "Klishchiv- nove poselennja tripil's'koj kul'turi na Pivdennomu Buzi." *Arheologija* (Kiev): 48–50.

Zammit, T.
1924 "Neolithic Representations of the Human Form from the Islands of Malta and Gozo." *Journal of the Royal Anthropological Institute of Great Britain and Ireland* 54:67–100, and plates 5–20.

Zervos, C.
1935 *L'art de la Mésopotamie de la fin du 4e. millénaire au 15e. siècle avant notre ère: Elam, Sumer, Akkad.* Paris: Editions "Cahiers d'Art".
1954 *La civilisation de la Sardaigne du début de l'énéolithique à la fin de la période nouragique.* Paris: Editions "Cahiers d'Art."
1956 *L'art de la Crète, Néolithique et Minoenne.* Paris: Editions "Cahiers d'Art."
1957 *L'Art des Cyclades du début à la fin de l'âge du bronze, 2500–1100 avant notre ère.* Paris: Editions "Cahiers d'Art."
1959 *L'art de l'époque du Renne en France.* Paris: Editions "Cahiers d'Art."
1962 *Naissance de la civilisation en Grèce.* Paris: Editions "Cahiers d'Art."

Zois, A.
1968 *Der Kamares-Stil: Werden und Wesen.* Tübingen: Fotodruck Präzis.

Sources of Illustrations

See *Bibliography and References* for full titles of publications.

Abbreviations of names of draftspersons: *LW* Linda Williams; *JB* James Bennett; *PR* Patricia Reis; *ST* Samir Twair; *EB* Elena Bechis; *JV* Janis Velissariou; *JM* J. v.d. Marel; *MH* M. H. Heemskerk.

COLOR PLATES

1 After *Preistoria Daciei*, Radu Florescu, ed., photography by Ion Miclea. Bucharest: Meridiane, 1980.

2 Photo Miodrag Djordjević. Publ. in M. Gimbutas, *Gods and Goddeses of Old Europe*, London: Thames and Hudson, 1974. First publ. in *Glasnik Muzeja Kosovo i Mitohije*, 7–8:3.

3 Author's photo, 1969. First publ. in M. Grbić et al., *Porodin*, Bitolj Archaeological Museum, 1960.

4 Author's photo. Courtesy Archaeological Museum, Syracuse. Publ. in black and white in L. Bernabó Brea, *Sicily*, London: Thames and Hudson, 1957.

5 After Alexander Marshack, *Ice Age Art*, an exhibition catalogue 1979; prepared by American Museum of Natural History and Alexander Marshack, California Academy of Sciences.

6 Courtesy J. Paul Getty Museum, Malibu, California.

7 Postcard, National Museum Athens, Editions "Hannibal."

8 Author's photo. Publ. in Ilze Loze, *Akmens laikmeta māksla Austrumbaltijā*, Riga: Zinātne, 1983.

9 After *Romania Today*, June 1984, No. 6. Piatra Neamţ Museum.

10 Author's excavation 1973. Photo L. Tloupas.

11 Courtesy Archaeological Museum Štip, SE Yugoslavia. Publ. (in black and white) in M. Gimbutas, *The Gods and Goddesses of Old Europe*, London: Thames and Hudson, 1974. Photo Miodrag Djordjević, 1968.

12 Courtesy Koszta József Museum in Szentes, SE Hungary. Photo K. Kónya. First publ. in J. Czalog "Die anthropomorphen Gefässe und Idolplastiken von Szegvár-Tűzköves," *Acta Archaeologica*, 1959. Appears in black and white in author's *The Gods and Goddesses*, 1974.

13 Photo by Marie-Thérèse Kantor. Publ. (in black and white) in Jean Arnal, *Les statues-menhirs, hommes et dieux*, Paris, Editions des Hespérides, 1976. Also in A. d'Anna, *Les statues-menhirs et stèles anthropomorphes du midi mediterranéen*, Paris: Editions du Centre National de la Recherche Scientifique, 1977.

14 After G. Papathanassopoulos, *Neolithic and Cycladic Civilization*, Athens: National Archaeological Museum, "Melissa" Publishing House.

15 Courtesy Cagliari Achaeological Museum, Sardinia (excavation by V. Santoni 1978–79).

16 After *Kunst und Kultur Sardiniens vom Neolithikum bis zum Ende der Nuraghenzeit*, C. F. Müller, ed. Karlsruhe: Catalogue of the exhibition.

17 Author's photo, 1978. Courtesy Varna Archaeological Museum.

18 Author's photo, 1978. Courtesy Nova Zagora Museum, Bulgaria.

19 After Dragoslav Srejović and Ljubinka Babolvić, *Umetnost Lepenskog Vira*, Belgrade: Publishing House Jugoslavija, 1983.

20 Author's photo, 1982. Courtesy Khania Museum, Crete.

21–23 Courtesy Vladimir Dumitrescu. Publ. in V. Dumitrescu, *Arta culturii Cucuteni*, Bucharest: Editura Meridiane, 1979.

24 Photo Karlene Jones Bley, 1987.

FIGURES

1 (1) Leroi-Gourhan, 1967; (2–5) Müller-Karpe 1968; (6–8) Abramova 1970. *LW*

2 (1) Rudinskij 1931 (also Shorkovplias 1965); (2) Golomshtok 1938. *LW*

3 (1,2) Chollot-Varagnac; (3) Dumitrescu 1974. *LW*; (4) Boroneamţ, 1969. *JB*

4 (1) Theocharis 1956; (2) Wace and Thompson 1912. *JV*

5 Zervos 1956. *LW*

6 Tsountas 1908. *JV*

7 Institute of Archaeology, Bucharest (Courtesy Roman). *LW*

8 Author's excavation 1970. *LW*

9 (1) Mellaart 1970; (2) *Pregled Výzkumu* 1971; (3) Schmidt 1945.

10 Courtesy Svetozarevo Museum, Yugoslavia. *PR*

11 Evans 1971. *LW*

12 (1) Courtesy Herakleion Museum (J. Hazzidakis exc.), *JB*; (2) Matz and Biesantz 1964. *LW*

13 Florescu 1979. *JB*

14 (1) Schweitzer 1969; (2) Morin-Jean 1911.

15 Korfman 1979. *LW*

16 (1) Roska 1941; (2) Vasić 1936. *LW*

17 Various publications and museums of Yogoslavia and W Romania. *LW*

18 Courtesy Naroden Muzej Vršac. *LW*

19 (1,4) Rodden 1962; (2,3) Gimbutas 1974; (5) Kutzian 1944; (6) Petkov 1961. *LW*

20 (1) Tsountas 1908; (2) courtesy Iaşi Museum, Romania; (3) Gimbutas 1974. *LW*

21 Gimbutas 1974. Courtesy Smederevska Palanka Museum, Yugoslavia. *LW*

22 (1) Prähistorische Staatssammlung, Würzburg; (2) Montelius 1924.

23 Courtesy Naroden Muzej Štip, SE Yugoslavia. *LW*

24 (1–4) Marshack 1972; (5,6) Leroi-Gourhan 1967. *JB*

25 *Mainzer Zeitschrift* 1935.

26 (1) Breuil & De Saint Perrier 1927; (2) Clark 1975; (4) Bierbaum 1953; (5) H. Dumitrescu 1954, *JB*; (6) Herakleion Museum; (7) Foggia Archaeological Museum.

27 Raczký 1980. *LW*

28 (1,2) courtesy Stara Zagora Archaeological Museum, Bulgaria; (3) Atzeni 1981, pl. 8; (4) S. Nosek, *Swiatowit* 18 (1947): 145.

29 Marshack 1976, American Scientist 64, 2.

30 (1) Pericot 1942; (2,3) Passek 1954. *ST*

31 (1) Modderman 1970; (2) Szénászky 1979; (3) Weinberg 1937; (4) Thevenot & Carre 1976. *LW*

32 (1) Kalicz and Makkay 1972; (2) Courtesy Sofia Archaeological Museum. *LW*

33 (1) Kalicz and Makkay 1972; (2) Vasić 1936. *LW*

34 Goldman 1979. *LW*

35 Kalicz and Makkay 1972. *LW*

36 Tinè 1972. *PR*

37 Golomshtok 1938. *JB*

38 Golomshtok 1938. *JB*

39 Vasić 1936. *LW*

40 Galović 1959. *JB*

41 Mateescu 1970.

42 Czalog 1959. *LW*

43 (1) Kutzián 1947; (2) Blegen 1937; (3) courtesy Piatra Neamţ Museum. *LW*

44 Nica 1976. *JB*

45 Lémozi 1929; also Delporte 1979, fig. 42.

46 Marshack 1972. *LW*

47 Castiglioni and Calegari 1975. *LW*

48 Marshack 1972 (originally publ. by Křiž 1903).

49 Efimenko 1958. *PR*

50 Clottes and Carrière 1976. *PR*

51 Dumitrescu 1974. *LW*

52 Courtesy Archaeological Museum, Bitolj. Photo K. Kónya 1971.

53 Courtesy Volos Museum. Photo K. Kónya 1971. Publ. Hourmouziadis 1969.

54 Excavation of Kalicz and Karólyi 1978. Courtesy N. Kalicz, Institute of Archaeology, Budapest.

55 (1) Vasić 1936; (2) courtesy Šabac Museum, N Yugoslavia; (3) Dumitrescu 1980. *LW*

56 Atzeni 1981. *LW*

57 (1) Gimbutas 1981a; (2) Mellaart 1967; (3) Radimský 1896. *LW*

58 Courtesy National Museum, Belgrade. Photo M. Djordjević 1968.

59 Kalicz 1972. *PR*

60 (1) Alexiou 1958, *LW*; (2) *Journal of Hellenic Studies XXII* 1902, *PR*.

61 Excavation of Kalicz and Karólyi 1978. Courtesy N. Kalicz, Institute of Archaeology, Budapest.

62 Exposition Catalog, Niš Museum 1971. *LW*

63 A. Evans 1921. *PR*

64 Nikolov 1974. *PR*

65 Kalicz and Makkay 1977. *JB*

66 Kalicz 1963.

67 (1) Schliemann 1976, *LW*; (2) Courtesy Athens National Museum.

68 Author's photograph 1980. Foggia Archaeological Museum, Italy. Published Acanfora 1960.

69 Kendrick 1928, republished by Müller-Karpe 1974. *PR*

70 Author's photo. *JB*

71 Photograph and collection, D. Tloupas, Larisa, Greece.

72 Marshack 1980.

73 Bosinski and Fischer 1974.

74 (1) Wace and Thompson 1912; (2) Holmberg 1964. *LW*

75 Vasić 1936. *JM*

76 Passek 1935. *JB*

77 Schliemann 1976. *LW*

78 (1) Dumitrescu 1980; (2) Kalicz 1969. *JB*

79 Drawing from a photo by M. Djordjevic, courtesy Naroden Muzej, Belgrade. *EB*

80 Reprinted from Catalog Museum Niš 1971. *LW*

81 (1) Tasić 1973; (2) Repertoriul 1985. *JB*

82 (1,2) Roska 1941; (3) Orthmann 1966. *LW*

83 Object in private collection, Munich. Photo courtesy *Prähistorische Sammlung*, Munich.

84 (1) Atzeni 1981; (2) Hensel 1980. *PR*.

85 (1) Marinescu-Bîlcu 1974; (2) Winn 1981; (3) Nilsson 1950. *LW*

86 Forman and Poulík 1956.

87 Wreschner 1976.

88 Vasić 1936. *JB*

89 Vasić 1936.

90 Gimbutas 1974. *LW*.

91 Leisner 1943. *JB*

92 (2) Mathieu 1984. *JB*

93 Leisner 1943. *JB*

94 (1,2) Almagro and Arribas 1963, *PR*; (3) Herity 1974, *JB*; (4) Brennan 1983.

95 (1) Schmidt 1932, *LW*; (2) Cucoş 1978, *JB*; (3) Mylonas, *LW*.

96 Bernabó Brea 1957. *EB*, *LW*

97 (1,2) McMann 1980 1980; (3) Courtesy National Parks and Monuments, Dublin.

98 McMann 1980.

99 (1–3) Wreschner 1976; (4) Yeivin and Mozel 1977. *JB*

100 Radimský and Hoernes 1895. *JB*

101 (1) Todorova 1975; (2) Mikov 1934. *LW*

102 Courtesy National Parks and Monuments, Dublin (G. Eogan's excavation).

103 (1) Florescu 1980 (cover jacket).

104 (1) Gimbutas 1976, *EB*; (2–4) Roska 1941, *LW*.

105 Tsountas 1908. *EB*

106 (1) Popescu 1956, (2) Goldman 1979, *JB*; (3) Dumitrescu 1974, *LW*.

107 Courtesy of Pernik Archaeological Museum, Bulgaria (Chodžaev excavation 1976). *LW*

108 Courtesy Stara Zagora Museum, Bulgaria. *JB*

109 (1) Römisch-Germanisches Museum, Mainz; (2) Courtesy Varna Archaeological Museum, Bulgaria (drawing from author's photo). *JB*

110 Jovanović 1978. *JB*, *ST*

111 Graziosi 1975. *JB*

112 Todorova 1974. *JB*

113 Fischer 1951.

114 Courtesy British Museum (copy Römisch—Germanisches Museum).

115 Courtesy Ethnographic Museum, Belgrade. *JB*

116 Mellaart 1970. *LW*

117 (1,2) Vasić 1936; (3) courtesy Regional Museum Priština (from author's photo). *JM*

118 Nikolov 1974. *LW*

119 Dumitrescu 1966. *LW*

120 (1) Tsountas 1908; (2) Grundmann 1953. *LW*

121 Detev 1965. *JM*

122 Kosmopoulos 1948. *JM*

123 Seger 1928. *JB*

124 Nica 1980. *JB*

125 Lo Schiavo 1982; photo courtesy Sassari Archaeological Museum.

126 Hensel 1980. *PR*

127 Courtesy Herakleion Museum, Crete. *PR*

128 (1) Kalicz 1980, (2) Katinčarov 1973, *LW*; (3) Nikolov 1974, *JB*

129 (1) Garašanin 1954; (2) Stančeva and Gavrilova 1961. *LW*

130 Chollot-Varagnac 1980. *JB*, *ST*

131 (1,2) Marshall 1979; (3,4) Pendlebury 1939. *LW*

132 (1) Galović 1968; (2) Weinberg 1962. *JM*

133 (1) Courtesy National Museum of Athens, 6745; (2) courtesy Nauplion Museum, Peloponnese. Drawings after author's photos. *LW*

134 (1) Hartuche and Anastasiu 1968; (2) Montelius 1924. *LW*

135 Dumitrescu 1966. *JM*

136 Montelius 1924. *LW*

137 Courtesy National Museum, Athens (drawn from author's photo). *LW*

138 (1) Müller-Karpe 1974; (2) Mellaart 1962.

139 Graziosi 1975. *LW*

140 Warren 1972. *LW*

141 Courtesy National Museum, Athens (drawing from a postcard). *LW*

142 Courtesy Musée du Louvre, Paris (drawing from author's photo). *JB*

143 (1) Courtesy Regional Museum, Kosovska Mitrovica (drawing from author's photo), *JM*; (2) Masson 1969.

144 Detail of vase (from author's photo), Cyprus exhibition in National Museum, Athens. *LW*

145 Mylonas 1963. *JM*

146 (1) Marshack 1972, *PR*; (2) Abramova 1970, *EB*.

147 (1) Wace and Thompson 1912; (2) author's excavation 1973–74; (3) Gimbutas 1976 (author's excavation 1969–70). *LW*

148 (1) Thimme 1977 and Korfmann 1979; (2) Schliemann 1976. *LW*

149 Gallis 1985. *EB*

150 Tichý 1962. (1) *LW*

151 Schliemann 1976. *LW*

152 Kandyba 1937. *JB*

153 Kandyba 1937. *JB*

154 (1,2) Paul 1969; (3) Cucoş 1981. *LW*

155 (1) Kandyba 1937, *ST*; (2) Georgiev and Angelov 1957, *LW*.

156 (1) Wace and Thompson 1912; (2) Betts 1979, *Corpus MM*, 2. *LW*

157 (1) Tompa 1929; (2) Roska 1941. *LW*

158 (1) Courtesy Nauplion Museum, Greece (drawing from author's photo), *LW*; (2) *Archéologie Vivante*, II, 3, 1969, *JB*.

159 Courtesy Parks and Monuments, Dublin.

160 Delporte 1979. *PR*

161 Golomshtok 1939. *PR*

162 Skutil 1940. *PR*

163 (1,2) Perrot 1970; (3) Mellaart; (4) Leroi-Gourhan 1967. *PR*

164 Srejović 1969. *JB*

165 (1,2) Movsha 1971. *LW*

166 Bossert 1937. *JB*

167 (1) Mellaart 1967; (2) Betts 1979, *Corpus*, 2. *JB*

168 (1) Leroi-Gourhan 1968, *JB*; (2) Winn 1981, *LW*; (3) Graziosi 1973.

169 (1) Delporte 1979; (2) Kalicz 1979–80. *PR*

170 Courtesy Paul Getty Museum, Malibu.

171 Courtesy Svetozarevo Museum, Yugoslavia (drawing from Linda Williams's photo). *LW*

172 Delporte 1979. *PR*

173 (1,2) Delporte 1979, *PR*; (3) Gaussen 1964.

174 Author's excavation 1973–74, publ. in Gimbutas 1989. *PR*, *EB*

175 Dumitrescu 1974. *EB*

176 Courtesy Archaeological Museum, Valetta, Malta (drawing from a cast in British Museum). *EB*

177 Mellaart 1963 (excavation 1962).

178 Nica 1980. *JB*

179 Alexiou 1958. *LW*

180 Mellaart 1970. *JB*

181 Detev 1968. *JB*

182 Kübler 1943. *ST*

183 Rimantienė 1979. *JB*

184 (1) Courtesy Kosovska Mitrovica Museum; author's photo; (2) Courtesy Naroden Muzej, Belgrade; photo K. Kónya 1971.

185 Marshack 1972.

186 Courtesy Archaeological Museum, Zadar. Photo K. Konya 1971.

187 (1) Novotný 1962, *LW*; (2) Kandyba 1937, *JB*

188 Courtesy National Museum, Athens.

189 Marshack 1972.
190 Author's excavation 1973. (1), *EB*; (2), *LW*.
191 Courtesy Archaeological Museum, Bitolj, S Yugoslavia. Photo K. Kónya 1971. (1) *JB*.
192 Courtesy Matera Archaeological Museum, Italy. *JB*
193 (1) Mellaart 1964, *JB*; (2,3) courtesy Peatra Neamţ Museum, *LW*; (4) Graziosi 1973, *JB*; (5) Betts 1979, *LW*.
194 (1) Petkov 1959; (2) Kutzián 1944; (3) Srejović 1969. *LW*
195 Georgiev and Angelov 1948–49. *LW*
196 (1) Kalicz and Makkay 1977, *ST*; (2) Hadaczek 1914.
197 Marshall 1979.
198 Tsountas 1908.
199 (1) Kalicz and Makkay 1977, *JB*; (2) d'Anna 1977, *ST*.
200 Weinberg 1951. *JB*
201 Ucko 1968. *LW*
202 (1) Author's excavation 1973 (publ. 1989); (2) Dumitrescu 1963, *JB*; (3) Rodden 1962, *LW*.
203 Thimme 1965. *LW*
204 (1–4) Graziosi 1971; (5) Lumley, Fonvielle and Abelanet 1976; (2–4) *PR*.
205 Mellaart 1970. *LW*
206 (1) Bruckner 1962; (2) Arthur Evans 1921. *LW*
207 (1) Gimbutas 1986 (C.A. Renfrew's and author's excavation 1968); (2) Dales 1960. *LW*
208 (1) Bossert 1937; (2) Arthur Evans 1903. *LW*
209 Courtesy Herakleion Museum, Crete. *LW*
210 Arthur Evans 1903. *JB*
211 (1) Tsountas 1908; (2) Mylonas 1956. *LW*
212 Waldstein 1905. *PR*
213 Courtesy National Museum, Athens. *JB*
214 Keller 1955.
215 Makarevich 1960; reproduced from Gimbutas 1974. *LW*
216 (1) Leroi-Gourhan 1967; (2,3) Abramova 1962; (4) Delporte 1979. *JB*
217 Author's excavation 1973 (publ. 1989). *PR*
218 Author's excavation 1973 (publ. 1989). Photo D. Tloupas.
219 Tloupas Collection, Larisa, Thessaly, Greece.
220 Author's surface collection, 1973, Larisa Archaeological Museum. *PR*
221 Courtesy Peatra Neamţ Museum. *JB*
222 Mellaart 1964. *JB*
223 Paul 1965. *LW*
224 (1) Crîşmaru 1977; (2) Markevich 1960. *JB*
225 Gimbutas 1974. Photo M. Djordjević.
226 Dumitrescu 1981. *JB*
227 *Praistorijska nalašista*, Novi Sad 1971. *LW*
228 Courtesy Hódmezövásárhely Museum, Hungary; photo Römisch-Germanisches Museum, Mainz.
229 Catalogue of the exhibition, Les premiers agriculteurs, Saint Germain-en-Laye 1979. *JB*
230 (A) Dames 1976; (B) Burl 1979.
231 Twohig 1981. *JB*
232 Alexiou 1969. *EB*
233 Nica and Cişlaru 1981. *JB*
234 Atzeni 1981. *ST*
235 Bernabó Brea 1957. *JB*
236 Herity 1974. *JB*
237 Evans 1971. *JB*
238 Wiślański 1979.
239 (1–3) De Valera 1960; (4) Photo courtesy National Parks and Monuments, Dublin. *ST*
240 (1) O'Kelly 1983; (2,3) De Valera 1960.
241 Müller-Karpe 1974 (after Henshall 1963). *ST*
242–44 Srejović and Babović 1983. *JB*
245 Müller-Karpe 1974.
246 Harrison 1962.
247 (1,2) Niţu 1975. *LW*
248 Passek 1935. *LW*
249 (1) Kusurgasheva 1970; (2) Markevich 1970. *LW*
250 (1) Matz 1928; (2) Branigan 1970. *LW*
251 J.D. Evans 1959. *ST*
252 Marshack 1972. *LW*
253 Dumitrescu 1974. *LW*
254 (1) Kalicz & Makkay 1974; (2) Raczky 1980; (3) Marinescu Bîlcu 1974. *PR*, *JB*
255 J.D. Evans 1971. *PR*
256 (1) Dimitrov 1969; (2) Kusurgasheva 1970; (3) Passek 1949. *LW*
257 Nikolov 1974. *PR*
258 (1) Sauvet and Wlodarczyk 1977, *JB*; (2) Twohig 1981; (3) Schmidt 1932, *JB*; (4) *JB*, *EB*.
259 Dumitrescu 1974. *LW*, *JB*
260 Petrescu-Dîmboviţa 1966. *LW*
261 Betts 1979, vol. 4. *JB*
262 Grbić *et al.*, 1960. *LW*
263 (1) Theocharis 1973; (2) Kandyba 1937. *LW*
264 Delporte 1979.
265 (1) Marshack 1979a, *ST*; (2) Leroi-Gourhan 1967.
266 (1) Gimbutas 1976 (author's excavation 1969–70), *JB*; (2) Winn 1981; (3) Marinescu-Bîlcu 1974.
267 (1) V. Nikolov 1979, *JB*; (2) Passek 1949, *LW*.
268 D'Anna 1977. *PR*
269 Dumitrescu 1974. *LW*
270 Thimme 1977. *LW*
271 (1) Dumitrescu 1980; (2) Thimme 1977. *LW*
272 After Delaporte 1979.
273 Cucoş 1973. *LW*
274 Cucoş 1973. *LW*
275 (1) Marshack 1972; (2–5) Dams 1978; (6,7) Leroi-Gourhan 1967; (8) Bandi-Maringer 1955. (1–6) *ST*
276 Kusurgasheva 1970. *ST*
277 Bovio-Marconi 1953. *ST*
278 Johansen 1958, also Schweitzer 1969. *ST*
279 Tasić 1957.
280 Courtesy Kosovska Mitrovica Museum; photo Djordjević 1968.
281–82 Courtesy Volos Archaeological Museum, Greece; photos K. Kónya 1971. Publ. Theocharis 1973 and Gimbutas 1974.
283 Photo and collection D. Tloupas, Larisa, Greece.
284 Courtesy National Museum, Bucharest. Photo Kónya 1971.
285–86 Mellaart 1966. *JB*
287 Dams 1978. *ST*
288 Leroi-Gourhan 1967. *ST*
289 Rimantienė 1979. *JB*
290 Klebs 1882. *JB*
291 Courtesy Nemzeti Museum, Budapest.
292 Schliemann 1976. *PR*
293 Florescu 1978. *PR*
294 D'Anna 1977. *PR*
295 Bailloud 1964 (after J. de Baye 1874). *JB*, *PR*
296 Granier, *Gallia Préhistorique* 6 (1963). *PR*
297 Leisner 1959. *PR*
298 Twohig 1981. *JB*
299 Herity 1974. *PR*
300 Nikolov 1974. *PR*
301 D'Anna 1977. *PR*
302 Almagro Gorbea 1965. *JB*
303 Graziosi 1975. *JB*
304 (1) Courtesy Kishenev, Institute of History, *LW*; (2) publ. Gimbutas 1956; (3) Loze 1983, *JB*.
305 Yule 1981. *ST*
306 Petkov 1957 (publ. Gimbutas 1974: 118). *LW*
307 Delporte 1979. *JB*
308 Berciu 1966. *JB*
309 Courtesy Stara Zagora Museum, Bulgaria. Photo Kónya 1971.
310 Dimitrov 1962. Photo Kónya.
311 (1) Gimbutas 1956, *JB*; (2) Georgiev and Angelov 1957, *LW*.
312 Passek 1954.
313 Graziosi 1973. *PR*
314–15 Courtesy Museo Archaeologico Nazionale, Cagliari, Sardinia. Publ. Atzeni 1981.
316 Santoni 1982. *JB*
317 Courtesy Museo Archaeologico Nazionale, Cagliari, Sardinia.
318 Graziosi 1973. *JB*
319 Zervos 1954 (also Atzeni 1981). *PR*
320 Zervos 1957 (also Doumas 1983). Goulamdris Collection, Athens. *PR*
321 Thimme 1977. *JB*
322 Müller-Karpe 1974.
323 Letica 1973. *ST*
324 Author's photo, Varna 1978.
325 Radunčeva 1974 (b) *JB*
326 (1) Ivanov 1978; (2) *L'art de premiers agriculteurs*, Saint Germain-en-Laye Museum, 1979 (catalogue). *JB*
327 Dumitrescu 1974.
328 A. Evans 1904. *LW*
329 Cartailhac and Breuil 1908. *ST*
330 (1) Müller-Karpe 1968; (2) Gimbutas 1972; (3) Leisner 1959. *ST*
331 (1) Dietz; (2) Evans 1903.
332 Vulpe 1957. Photo Kónya 1971, Peatra Neamţ Archaeological Museum, Romania.
333 Marinescu-Bîlcu 1974. *LW*
334 J. D. Evans 1971. *LW*
335 Buchholz and Karageorghis 1969. (a) *LW*
336 (1) Schmidt 1932, *LW*; (2) Kandyba 1937.
337 Kandyba 1937.
338 Angelov 1959.
339 Kandyba 1937. *JB*
340 Milojčić 1949. *LW*

341 (1) Kaindl 1908, *LW, JB*; (2) Montelius 1924.
342 Matz 1928. *LW*
343 Twohig 1981. *JB*
344 Twohig 1981.
345 Herity 1974 and Brennan 1983.
346 Alexiou 1958 and Tsedakis 1971. *JB*
347 Alexiou 1958. *JB*
348 Author's photo 1984. H. Nikolaios Museum, Crete.
349 Mellaart 1963. *JB*
350–51 Dumitrescu 1970. *JB*
352 Courtesy Zemaljski Muzej, Sarajevo. Photo Kónya 1971.
353 Bossert 1937.
354 Courtesy Nauplion Museum. *LW*
355 Tsountas 1908. *PR*
356 (1) Delporte 1979 (originally publ. in Antonielli 1926); (2) Courtesy Prähistorische Staatssammlung, Munich. *PR*
357 Marshack 1972. *EB*
358 Makkay 1985.
359 Swiny 1983.
360 Alexiou 1958. *LW*
361 Niţu 1975. *LW*
362 Dinu 1957. *LW*
363 Kandyba 1977. *LW*
364 Vlassa 1963. *JB*
365 Desborough 1952. *LW*
366 Matz 1928 and Yule 1981. *JB*
367 Schliemann, reproduced from Alexiou 1969. *JB*
368 *Clara Rhodos*, IV, 359. *LW*
369 Musch 1986. Found by Ger Zijlstra, now in private collection of Herman van der Made, the Hague.
370 M. O'Kelly 1982.
371 Müller-Karpe 1974. *EB*
372 (1) V. Dumistrescu 1974; (2, 3) Evans 1959.
373 H. Dumitrescu 1960. (2) *JB*
374 Courtesy Nemzeti Museum, Budapest (author's photo; drawing from a slide), *PR*; (2) Theocharis 1973.
375 Tanda 1977. *JB*
376 (1) Müller-Karpe 1974, *ST, EB*; (2) Bertran 1985, *JB*.
377 Atzeni 1981. *JB*
378 (1–4) Mason and Merpert 1981; (5) Anati 1969; (6) Spyropoulos 1970 and Long 1974. *JB*
379 Bernabó Brea 1957.
380 (A) Müller-Karpe 1966; (B) Mellaart 1970. *LW*
381 Wislański 1979, *JB*
382 Alexiou 1958. *LW*
383 Gimbutas 1963. *JB, ST*
384 Kühn 1956; Müller-Karpe 1974; Almgren 1934. *JB*
385 Coleman 1984.
386 Almgren 1934. *JB*
387 Breuil and Saint Perrier 1927.
388 Author's excavation, Achilleion 1973–74; publ. 1989.
389 Vasić 1936, III.
390 Mellaart 1963 and 1970. *LW*
391 Zervos 1956. *LW*
392 Karageorghis 1967. *ST*
393 Gulder 1962. (1) *PR*
394 (1) Gimbutas 1958; (2) Tsountas 1908. *PR*
395 (1) Cipolloni Sampò 1982; (1) courtesy Herakleion Museum (drawing from author's photo); (3) courtesy Aghios Nikolaios Museum. *ST*
396 (1) Gulder 1962; (2–4) Müller-Karpe 1968. *ST*
397 Andree 1904. *JB*
398 Dams 1978. *ST*
399 Dumitrescu 1968. *LW*
400 (1) Courtesy Institute of Archaeology, Bucharest; photo Kónya 1971; (2) courtesy Peatra Neamţ Museum; photo Kónya 1971.
401 (1) Courtesy National Museum, Belgrade (R. Galović); (2) courtesy Institute of Archaeology, Bucharest (Dumitrescu 1968). Photo Kónya 1971.
402 (1) Hampe and Simmon 1981; (2, 3) Furumark 1941. *ST*
403 Courtesy Louvre Museum (publ. *Ugaritica*, 2, pl. 37, 2).
404 *Clara Rhodos*, IV. *ST*
405 Ruckert 1976. (1) *LW, JB*
406 Breuil & Saint Perrier, 1927. *JB*
407 Courtesy Prähistorische Staatssammlung, Munich. Belgrade University Museum.
408 Srejović and Babović 1983. *JB, ST*
409 Courtesy Herakleion Museum, Crete (publ. Marinatos and Hirmer 1960). *ST*
410 Courtesy Khania Museum. Author's photograph.
411 Cameron 1981. *JB*
412 Thimme 1977. *JB*
413 Gimbutas 1986. *LW*
414 (1) Marinescu Bîlcu 1961; (2) Modderman 1971. *LW*
415 Courtesy Piatra Neamţ Museum, Romania. Photo Kónya 1971 (first publ. by Matasa 1964). (b) *LW*
416–17 Tanda 1977b. *JB*
418 Furumark 1972. *ST*
419 Maier 1969. *JB*
420 Courtesy Archaeological Museum, Cracow (drawing from a photograph by Kónya 1971). *LW*
421 Schachermeyr 1955. *LW*
422 (1) Mellaart 1970; (2) Rosetti 1938. *LW*
423 Lo Schiavo 1978. *JB*
424 Atzeni 1981. *ST*
425 Yule 1981. *ST*
426–27 Zervos 1956. *LW*
428 Courtesy Herakleion Museum (drawing after author's photo) *LW*
429–30 Herakleion Museum (drawing after author's photo). *JB*
431 Courtesy Khania Archaeological Museum (drawing after author's photo). *JB*
432 (1) Courtesy National Museum, Athens (drawing after author's photo), *JB*; (2) Furmark 1941.
433–34 Dams 1978. *ST*
435 Giedion 1962. *ST*
436 Courtesy Brno Archaeological Museum. Photo Kónya 1971.
437 Wace and Thompson 1912. *JV*
438 Courtesy Zemaljski Muzej, Sarajevo. Photo Kónya 1971.
439 (1) Passek 1935; (2, 3) Kandyba 1937.
440 Berciu 1961. (1) *LW*, (2) *EB*
441 (1) Courtesy Stara Zagora Museum; (2) Wace and Thompson 1912, *ST*; (3) Tasić 1973.
442 Author's photograph 1980.
443 (1) Dumitrescu 1954; (2) Berciu 1961. *LW*
444 (1) Berciu 1961, *ST*; (2) Dumitrescu 1954, *LW*.
445 Chernysh 1961. *ST*
446 Twohig 1981. *JB*
447 Liliu and Schubart 1967. *ST*
448 Tsountas 1908. *JB, MH*
449 Brennan 1983.
450 Brennan 1983. *JB*
451 Brøndsted 1957. *JB*
452 Berciu 1961. (1) *ST*; (2) *EB*
453 (1) Kalicz and Makkay 1977. *ST*
454 Pericot 1942. *ST*
455–56 Twohig 1981. *JB*
457 (1) Müller-Karpe 1974; (2) Dumitrescu 1974; (3) Briard 1976. *JB*
458 (1, 3) Twohig 1981, *JB*; (2) Le Roux 1985.
459 Anati 1969. *JB*
460 Niţu 1972. *LW*
461 Schmidt 1932. *MH*
462 Courtesy Peatra Neamţ Museum. Photo Kónya 1971.
463 (1) Courtesy Archaeological Museum, Iaşi. Photo Kónya 1971.
464 (1–3) Kandyba 1937; (4,5) Passek 1935. *JB*
465 Dumitrescu 1974. *LW*
466 (1) Dimitrov 1971, *JB*; (2) Prendi 1966, *LW*.
467 (1) Popov 1916–18; (2) author's photo; Varna 1976. *ST*
468 Dombay 1960. *ST*
469 (1) Niţu 1975; (2) Dinu 1957. *LW*
470 Mikov and Džambazov 1960. (1) *JB*, (2) *EB*
471 (1) Graziosi 1973, *JB*; (2) Theocharis 1973, *ST*; (3) Passek 1935, *LW*.
472 Mihai 1972–73. *JB*
473 Ionescu 1974. *JB*
474 Breuil and Saint Perrier 1927. *JB*
475 (1) Winn 1981; (2) Markevich 1970. *LW*
476 (1,2) Banner 1958; (3,4) Kühn 1956.
477 Matz 1928. *JM*
478 Passek 1935. *JM*
479 Brøndsted 1957. *JB*
480 Saint Germain-en-Laye Museum, France. *JB*
481 Courtesy Cracow Archaeological Museum. Photo Kónya 1971.
482 Niţu 1975, originally Bogaevski 1937. *LW*
483 Author's photo 1980, Malta.
484 Dams 1978. *ST*
485 Mellaart 1963. *ST*
486 Mellaart 1963.
487 Twohig 1981. *JB*
488 (1) Theocharis 1967; (2) Dumitrescu 1974; (3) courtesy Nova Zagora Museum.
489–90 Foreman and Poulík 1956.
491 Courtesy National Parks and Monuments Dublin.
492 Courtesy Piatra Neamţ Museum, Romania.

Index